C000008659

William Langland, Walter W. Skeat

The Vision of William concerning Piers the Plowman

Vol. IV

William Langland, Walter W. Skeat

The Vision of William concerning Piers the Plowman
Vol. IV

ISBN/EAN: 9783348014809

Printed in Europe, USA, Canada, Australia, Japan

Cover: Foto ©ninafisch / pixelio.de

More available books at **www.hansebooks.com**

NOTES TO "PIERS THE PLOWMAN."

N.B. The reader is requested to observe that the C-TEXT is made the *basis* of these notes; and, whenever a reference is given, it is to the C-text, unless the letter 'A' or 'B' be expressly prefixed. In such a case, 'B. 1. 6' (*or* 'B. i. 6') would mean Text B, Passus 1, line 6.

At the beginning of each note the references to the other texts are supplied. Thus '3. (b. pr. 3; a. pr. 3.)' is to be understood to mean that the lines corresponding to line 3 (of Passus I of the C-text) are B-text, prologue, l. 3, and A-text, prologue, l. 3. When there is *no* corresponding line in the A-text, the statement '*not in a*' is expressly added; so likewise for the B-text. Whenever the letter *a* appears by itself within a square bracket, thus—[a], it is to be considered as an abbreviation for 'A-text'; so with the letters *b*, *c*.

Sometimes a note is given upon a passage in [a] or [b], when there is no corresponding line in [c]. In such a case, a line is prefixed to the reference. Thus the reference to the 7th line of the prologue of the B-text appears as '—(b. pr. 7; a. pr. 7).'

If, in using [a] or [b], there be a difficulty in finding the place in the Notes, see the Scheme of the arrangement of lines, prefixed to each Passus. *Transposed* passages are marked in the Scheme by (*a*), (*b*), &c., and occur twice in the Scheme. If not found in one place, look in the other; generally, in the one marked with square brackets. Thus, the note to B. prol. 210 follows the note to B. prol. 143.

SCHEME OF THE CONTENTS OF C. PASSUS I,

AS COMPARED WITH B. PROLOGUE AND A. PROLOGUE.

N.B. The straight stroke (—) denotes that the passage is wanting in that text in which it appears. The word '*like*' signifies that the passages have merely a general resemblance, more or less close; in other passages the language is nearly identical, with the exception of minor variations. The passages marked (*a*), (*b*), &c., are *transposed*, appearing in different positions in different texts.

C. PASSUS 1.	B. PROLOGUE.	A. PROLOGUE.
1—4	1—4	1—4
5	——	——
6—18	*like* 5—16	5—16
19—35	17—33	17—33
36	——	
——	34, 35	34, 35
37—50	36—49	36—49
——	50—52	——
51—84	53—86	50—83
85, 86	87, 88	——
87, 88	*like* 89, 90	——

PLOWMAN.   1

44322

C. Passus 1.	B. Prologue.	A. Prologue.
89—92	91—94	——
93, 94	*like* 95, 96	——
95—124	——	——
125—133	97—105	——
——	106	——
134—137	107—110	——
138	*unlike* 111	——
139—141	112—114	——
——	115	——
142—147	*like* 116—124	——
148—150	125—127	——
151	*like* 128—131	——
152—156	132—136	——
——	137	——
157	138	——
158		——
——	139—145	——
(a) 159—164	(a) [210—215]	(a) [84—89]
165—170	146—151	——
——	152	——
171—176	153—158	——
——	159	——
177—179	160—162	——
——	163, 164	——
180—194	165—179	——
——	180	——
195—205	181—191	——
——	192—196	——
(b) [212—215]	(b) 197—200	——
206—211	201—206	——
(b) 212—215	(b) [197—200]	——
——	207	——
216, 217	208, 209	——
(a) [159—164]	(a) 210—215	(a) 84—89
218		——
——	——	90—95 *
219—223	216—220	96—100
——	221	101
——	222	——
224—231	223—230	102—109

NOTES TO C. PASSUS I. (B. Prologue ; A. Prologue.)

Passus signifies a portion or 'fytte' of a poem. In an entertainment given to Queen Elizabeth at Kenilworth, a minstrel, after singing a portion of a song, was instructed to make "a pauz and a curtezy, for *primus passus*," i. e. to signify that the first part was over. See Ritson's Metrical Romancëes, vol. i. p. ccxxii. Compare—"Thus passed is the *first pas* · of this pris tale;" William of Palerne, l. 161.

* Apparently the original sketch whence were derived B. prol. 87—94, and C. 1. 85—92.

C. 1. 1. [B. prol. 1; A. prol. 1.]   *softe*, mild, warm.   Cf. "as *soft* as air;" Ant. and Cleop., v. 2. 314.

2. (b. pr. 2; a. pr. 2.) *I shop me into shrobbis*, I betook me to the shrubs, i. e. to such shelter as shrubs afford; in other words, to an out-of-door life, independent of the shelter of a roof. The B-text has—*I shope me in shroudes*, i. e. I put myself into rough clothes, I put on rough clothes. The A-text has—*into a schroud*, i.e. into a rough outer garment. Cf. *shopen hem heremites*, arrayed themselves as hermits; B. prol. 57; A. prol. 54. *Shop*, lit. shaped; the phrase *I shope me* generally means *I got myself ready*, as in *he 'shop hym to walke*, he got ready to set off walking; Pass. xiv. l. 247. *As y a shepherde were*, as if I were a shepherd; referring (according to the context) either to the out-of-door life of the shepherd, or to his rough outer garments. Since *shepherd* is the reading of nearly all the MSS. of the C-text, it is probable that the word *shepe* (B-text), or *scheep* (A-text), has the same signification, viz. that of shepherd. I believe that I have seen examples of this use of the word, but can only give one instance in which it (probably) occurs. John *Schep* was the assumed name of John Balle (Walsingham, ed. Riley, ii. 33); and in a rude hexameter, which gives the names of the leaders in Wat Tyler's rebellion, we have

"Jak *Chep*, Trouche, Jon Wrau, Thom Myllere, Tyler, Jak Strawe;"
where another reading for *Chep* is *Schep*. See Political Poems, ed. Wright, vol. i. p. 230. Let it be remembered that Chaucer has *hunte* for *hunter*, Kn. Ta. 1160; that *prisune* means *a prisoner*, Genesis and Exodus, ed. Morris, l. 2044; that *message* means *a messenger*, Chaucer's Man of Lawes Tale, l. 333, &c.; and observe the double use of *kerd*, which does duty both for the A.S. *heord*, a flock, and A.S. *hyrde*, a guardian. The poet expressly tells us what his dress was like further on, where he describes himself as being "thus robed in russett," Pass. xi. l. 1. See note to that line.

3. (b. pr. 3; a. pr. 3.) *In abit as an ermite*. The simple shepherd's dress resembled that of a hermit. *Vnholy of werkes*. This Dr Whitaker paraphrases by—"not like an anchorite who keeps his cell, but like one of those unholy hermits who wander about the world to hear and see wonders." Or it may simply be supposed to be inserted parenthetically, and to express the author's opinion of hermits in general; an opinion which he elsewhere repeats more than once. See particularly Pass. x. l. 203; and cf. note to l. 51 below.

5. (*not in* b *or* a.) "And saw many cells, and various strange things." The *cells* are the cells of the various religious houses which he visited; cf. Chaucer's Prol. l. 172, and see Cutts, Scenes and Characters of the Middle Ages, p. 123. That the word should be spelt *selles* or *sellys* in some MSS. need not surprise us, since Dr Morris prints *selle* in the very line of Chaucer to which I refer. I wish to add here, once for all, that it is unnecessary to refute, or even to mention, all the oddities of explanation that appear in Dr Whitaker's notes. Here, for instance, he tells us that *cellis* ought to be *sellis*, inasmuch as it is "pure Saxon, from *sellic*, wonderful;" but he omits to tell us how this compound adjective (*sél-líc*) could possibly produce the plural substantive *selles*. *Selcouthe* is from the A.S. *seld-cúð*,

seldom known, strange, rare. It occurs again in Pass. xiv. ll. 175, 178. But I must beg leave to refer the reader, for the meanings of particular words, to the Glossary to this work, or to Dr Stratmann's Old English Dictionary. It is needless to cite such references as may easily be found there; though, in the present instance, I will give them by way of example. *Selcouth* occurs (he tells us) in Layamon, l. 280; Genesis and Exodus, ed. Morris, l. 3972; Ancren Riwle, p. 8; Ormulum, l. 19217; King Alisaunder, ed. Weber, l. 154; William of Palerne, l. 2329; Prick of Conscience, l. 1518.

6. (b. pr. 5; a. pr. 5.) *Ac* is rightly translated by the *Bote* (= but) of the A-text. *May morwenyng;* the familiar expression *on a May morning* is almost equivalent to *once upon a time.* All readers of our early poets will remember the fondness which they exhibit for the month of May, especially when writing an exordium. Cf. Pass. xvii. l. 10.

Maluerne hulles, the Malvern hills in Worcestershire, on the border of Herefordshire. The poet mentions them thrice, viz. here, in l. 163 of this Passus, and in Pass. x. 205. It may be that the first sketch of the poem was composed in that locality, but we must not be misled into supposing that the poem has much to do with Worcestershire. It is clear both from very numerous allusions and from the whole tone of the poem, that the place which the poet knew best and most delighted to describe was the city of London. It cannot be too strongly impressed upon the reader (especially as the point has often been overlooked) that one great merit of the poem consists in its exhibition of *London* life and *London* opinions; and that to remember the *London* origin of, at any rate, the larger portion of the poem is the true key to the right understanding of it. Though William is supposed to be bodily present on the Malvern hills, he is soon *fast asleep* there; and it is of the London world that he dreams.

7. (b. pr. 6; a. pr. 6.) *A ferly* [a, b, *not* c] means a wonder. Cf. "And I will show you *ferlies* three;" Sir W. Scott: Ballad of Thomas the Rhymer. *Of fairy,* [a, b, *not* c] due to fairy contrivance. In William of Palerne (ed. Skeat), l. 230, we have the same expression *of feyrye* used to signify that a child is *of fairy origin.* On the word *fairy,* see Tyrwhitt's note to l. 6441 of the Canterbury Tales; and especially Keightley's Fairy Mythology, i. 12; ii. 239, 285. It is evident that the word is ultimately from the Latin *fatum;* whence Ital. *fatare,* to enchant; *fata* (probably short for *fatata*) a woman possessing supernatural power, a fay (Fr. *fée*). Cf. Span. *hada* or *hadada,* a fairy, witch; *hadado,* lucky; *hadador,* a sorcerer. It is worth remembering that the word *fuerie* in Middle-English has three senses, none of them being equivalent to the modern *fairy.* Thus it means (1) enchantment, as in the present passage; cf. Ch. Squ. Tale, l. 201; (2) fairyland; cf. Ch. Squ. Tale, l. 96; and note the expression "the contree of Fairye" in the Tale of Sir Thopas; (3) the people of fairyland, as in l. 3 of the Wyf of Bathes Tale. It is used in the modern sense in Antony and Cleopatra, iv. 8. 12.

Me þouȝte, [a, b, *not* c] it seemed to me; A.S. *me þúhte* (from *þincan*), which is distinct from *þóhte,* the past tense of *þencan.*

——(b. pr. 7; a. pr. 7.) *Forwandred*, tired-out by wandering; the A-text simply reads *of wandringe*. *Went me*, turned me, went; to *wend* originally meant to *turn*. Mr Hales suggests that the word *me* is here used merely as an 'ethic' dative, i. e. in the manner so common in our Elizabethan dramatists, and well illustrated in Abbott's Shakespearian Grammar, 3rd ed. sect. 220. But I feel compelled to say that this explanation is both out of place and unnecessary in the present instance, on account of the known use and power of the verb *to wend*. A few examples will make this clearer. We find the phrase "*wend* þe from wynne," turn thyself from joy; Cædmon, ed. Thorpe, p. 56, l. 28. "A! *wend te* awei!" ah! turn thyself away; Ancren Riwle, ed. Morton, p. 52. "þus nou ssel eurich . . . . *him-zelue wende*," thus now must every one turn himself; Ayenbite of Inwyt, ed. Morris, p. 269, last line. And at p. 180 of the last-mentioned work is a still clearer example— "ase þe wedercoc þet is ope þe steple, þet *him went* mid eche wynde," as the weathercock that is upon the steeple, that turns itself with each wind. Many more examples might be adduced, but those who will make themselves familiar with the language of the present poem will not require them. We have already had *shop me* (= betook myself) in the very second line.

——(b. pr. 10; a. pr. 10.) *Sweyued so merye*, sounded so pleasantly.

14. (b. pr. 13; a. pr. 13.) "I looked eastward, according to the position of the sun, i. e. towards the sun;" or [*as in* a, b] "on high, towards the sun." The poet, in his vision, finds himself in a wilderness, that is, in the wide universe, with power to survey a large part of it. On the East side he beholds a tower which is the abode of Truth; i. e. of God the Father, as is more particularly explained in Pass. ii. 12; cf. viii. 232—279. To the West is a deep dale, the residence of Death and of wicked spirits, containing [a, b, *not in* c] a dungeon, which is elsewhere explained as being the castle of Care, and the abode of Falsehood or Lucifer; Pass. ii. 57. In the central space between these is the 'fair field' of this world (Matt. xiii. 38). Thus the poet beholds heaven before him, and the world beneath him, whilst hell lies behind him.

It is most interesting to observe that this magnificent conception was probably suggested to the poet by what he may have beheld on the occasion of seeing some Morality performed. There are several passages, especially in Passus xxi., which shew that he was quite familiar with the pageants which were then so popular. In a Dissertation on Pageants, by T. Sharp, there is an old drawing (an engraving of which is placed opposite to p. 23) which excellently illustrates the present passage. We learn from it that, in representing the Morality of the "Castell of Perseueraunce," five scaffolds were erected for the purpose around an enclosed central space. On the South, was 'caro skaffold,' the scaffold representing the Fleshly nature of man; on the West was 'mundus skaffold,' or the scaffold representing the World; on the North was 'Belyal skaffold,' in allusion to the supposed abode of Lucifer in the North (see note to Pass. ii. 113); on the North-east, 'Coveytyse skaffold,' or the abode of Avarice; and on the East 'deus skaffold,' or the abode of God.   A careful examination of Mr Sharp's work will render the whole matter sufficiently clear.

It is worth while, however, to add a very apposite quotation from the Chester Plays, ed. Wright, p. 10; where the Creator is represented as saying—

> " The worlde, that is bouth voyde and vayne,
>   I forme in the formacion,
> With a *dongion of darckenes,*
>   Which never shall have endinge."

21. (b. pr. 19; a. pr. 18.) *As the worlde asketh,* as the way of the world requires. In many other places, *aske* answers to our modern *require*. Cf. "as matrymony askyth;" Myroure of our Lady, ed. Blunt, 1873, p. 192; and see Pass. ii. 34.

23. (b. pr. 21; a. pr. 21.) *Settyng,* planting [c, b]; *Eringe,* ploughing [a]. *Swonken,* laboured. *Ful,* very; used like the German *viel,* though etymologically related to *voll.*

24. (b. pr. 22; a. pr. 22.) *That,* that which; "and won that which these wasteful men expend in gluttony."

26. (b. pr. 24; a. pr. 24.) *Contenaunce,* outward appearance. *Disgised* [b] *degyset* [a], decked out in strange guise. See a curious passage in Chaucer's Persones Tale (*de superbia*) about the "strangeness and *disgisines*" of precious clothing. Cf. Knight de la Tour, ed. Wright, p. 64.

27. (b. pr. 25; a. pr. 25.) The A-text has *To* instead of *In;* the sense is the same.

28. (b. pr. 26; a. pr. 26.) *Ful harde,* very hardly, i. e. lived a very hard life. The B-text has *ful streyte,* very strictly. Observe that *-e* is a common adverbial ending.

29. (b. pr. 27; a. pr. 27.) *Heueneryche,* of the kingdom of heaven. This is an instance of a neuter noun forming the genitive case in *-e.* This genitive in *-e* is not common, except in the case of *feminine* nouns.

30. (b. pr. 28; a. pr. 28.) *Ancres,* anchorites. The *Ancren Riwle,* i. e. the Rule of Anchoresses, is the name of a prose work written in the early part of the thirteenth century; it has been edited by Mr Morton for the Camden Society. The word *ancre* is both masculine and feminine.

31. (b. pr. 29; a. pr. 29.) *Carien,* wander, go up and down. The reader will observe that, as shewn by the footnotes to all three texts, the MSS. use *carien* and *cairen* as equivalent forms. The better form of the word is *cairen;* perhaps from A.S. *cerran,* to turn about, rather than (as Dr Stratmann suggests) from Icel. *keyra,* to drive. See examples of the use of A.S. *cerran* in Bosworth's larger A.S. Dict.; and, to the examples given by Stratmann s. v. *cairen,* add the following:—

> " I am come hither a venterous Knight,
>   And *kayred* thorrow countrye farr;"
>   Percy Folio MS. ed. Hales and Furnivall, ii. 62. 116.
> "Then I *kered* to a knight;"—*Id.; ib.* 61. 118.

See also *keere, keered, kere,* and *kyreth* in the Glossary to the same work.

32. (b. pr. 30; a. pr. 30.) *For no*, &c., for (the sake of) any luxurious living, to please their body.   Double negatives, like the *no* here following *noght*, are very common.

35. (b. pr. 33; a. pr. 33.) William here speaks [a, b, *not in* c] of the guiltless or honest minstrels, who played instruments merely to gain a livelihood; but this class of men had a bad name, and he proceeds to satirize the unscrupulous jesters and slanderers, whom *alone* he mentions in the C-text. The subject of *minstrels* is very fully treated of in Ritson's Ancient Romances, vol. i, in Warton's History of English Poetry, Percy's Reliques, &c.   See also Chambers' Book of Days, i. 430.   Ritson tells us that the instruments they used were the harp, fiddle, bagpipe, pipe, tabour, cittern, hurdy-gurdy, bladder (or canister) and string, and, possibly, the Jew's-harp.   The minstrels of King Edward III.'s household played the trumpet, cytole, pipe, tabret, clarion, and fiddle.   When men or women were conveyed to the pillory, it was common to hire minstrels to accompany them, no doubt to call people's attention to them, and to heighten their disgrace.   Much is to be learnt about them from William's poem, as he mentions them frequently, and in Pass. xvi. 194, seqq. there is a long description of a minstrel who also gained a livelihood by selling cakes.   Another name for them is *gleemen*. *Jangelers, Jesters, Japers, Disours* (story-tellers), *Jougleors* or *Jugglers* (*joculatores*), all belong to the same fraternity. .Cf. Pass. iii. 99.   See also Tyrwhitt's note on Chaucer, Cant. Tales, 11453.

——(b. pr. 35; a. pr. 35.) *Iapers*, jesters; *Iangelers*, idle talkers, chatterers, babblers.   Cotgrave gives—"*Iangler*, to jangle, prattle, tattle saucily or scurvily;" and—"*Jangleur*, m. a jangler, saucy pratler, scurvy tatler, scurrile jeaster."   See note to Pass. iii. 99.   The phrase "Judas's children" is equivalent to "children of Satan," the reference being to Judas Iscariot. See note to l. 56 below; and cf. Pass. xix. 175, 176.

37. (b. pr. 36; a. pr. 36.) "Invent foul fancies for themselves, and make fools of themselves, and (yet) have their wit at their will, (able) to work if they wished."   The sentence is elliptical, and incomplete; we must mentally connect with the next line by saying—"*as for such fellows*, that which Paul preaches about them, I might (but will not) prove it (*or* adduce it) here; (else might I be blameworthy myself, since) he who speaks slander is Lucifer's servant."   The text of S. Paul which William does *not* quote is *Qui non laborat, non manducet* (2 Thess. iii. 10), which is written in the margin of the Oriel MS.   The quotation *Qui*, &c., is *not* from S. Paul, nor does William say that it is; yet it has some resemblance to Eph. v. 4, Col. iii. 8.

41. (b. pr. 40; a. pr. 40.) *Yoden*, went.   In a long note in Warton's Hist. Eng. Poetry, vol. ii. p. 73 (ed. 1840), it is argued that *yede* corresponds to the A.S. *eode*, went, and not to *ge-eode*, which is transitive, and signifies *entered*.   That is, the *y* does not *here* answer to the A.S. prefix *ge-*, but is the effect of phonetic spelling, in the same way as we so often find *yale, yerthe*, for *ale, earth*.   A very familiar instance is the A.S. pronoun *eow*, with its

possessive *eower*, now spelt *you, your*. Accordingly, the A-text has *eoden* here, at least in the Vernon MS.

42. (b. pr. 41; a. pr. 41.) *Hure*, their. The bag or wallet was the beggar's inseparable companion, and was used for receiving the broken pieces of meat and bread bestowed upon him as alms. Cf. Pass. x. 154. He also always carried a *bourdon*, or *staff*.

> 'That maketh beggares go with *bordon* and *bagges*.'

Song of the Husbandman; see Polit. Songs (Camd. Soc. 1839), p. 150. *Ycrammyd*, crammed, the *y-* being the A.S. prefix *ge-*.

43. (b. pr. 42; a. pr. 42.) *Atten*, at the. It is also written *at the, at then*, or *atte*; and very frequently *atten ale* is written *atte nale*. In Chaucer's Cant. Tales, ed. Tyrwhitt, 6931, we find *at the nale*; where most of the MSS. printed in the Six-text edition (Group D, l. 1349) have *atte nale*. So also *at the nende* for *at then end*. *Then* or *ten* is the dative of the article; hence this corruption is generally found after a preposition. Another similar corruption is *the tone, the tother*, from *that one, that other*; where the *t* is the sign of the neuter gender, as in *tha-t, i-t*; compare the Latin *d* in *i-d, quo-d, illu-d*. *Ale* here means an *ale-house*, and such is the best interpretation of it in Launce's speech in Two Gent. of Verona, ii. 5. 61—"Thou hast not so much charity in thee as to go *to the ale* with a Christian;" for only just above Launce says again—"If thou wilt, go with me *to the ale-house*." See Staunton's Shakesp. vol. i. p. 43. Respecting *ale*, see Babees Book, ed. Furnivall, p. 208; Chambers' Book of Days, i. 637; Our English Home, p. 88.

44. (b. pr. 43; a. pr. 43.) The B-text has *hij* for *þey*; and [a] has *heo*. *Hij* is written for *hy*, a variation of *hi*, much as *ij* is written for *ii* or *y* in Dutch.

45. (b. pr. 44; a. pr. 44.) Compare

> "And ryght as *Robertes men* · raken [*wander*] aboute,
> At feires & at ful ales · & fyllen the cuppe."

Pierce the Ploughmans Crede, l. 72. "Robartes men, or Robertsmen, were a set of lawless vagabonds, notorious for their outrages when Piers Plowman was written. The statute of Edw. III. (an. reg. 5, c. xiv.) specifies 'divers manslaughters, felonies, and robberies, done by people that be called *Roberdesmen, Wastours*, and *drawlacches*.' And the statute of Richard II. (an. reg. 7, c. v.) ordains, that the statute of King Edward concerning *Roberdesmen* and *drawlacches* should be rigorously observed. Sir Edward Coke (Instit. iii. 197) supposes them to have been originally the followers of *Robin Hood* in the reign of Richard I. See Blacktone's Comm. bk. iv. ch. 17."—Warton's Hist. Eng. Poetry, vol. ii. p. 95, ed. 1840. William of Nassyngton says that they tried the latches of people's doors, contrived to get into houses, and then extorted money either by telling some lying tale or playing the bully. See Pass. viii. 11, and the confession of *Roberd the robber* in the B-text, Pass. v. 469. See also the description of the *wastour*, Pass. ix. 149; and of the *brytonere*, id. 152.

48. (b. pr. 47; a. pr. 47.) *Seint Iame*, i. e. Saint James or Santiago. His

shrine at Compostella, in Galicia, was a famous place of pilgrimage; see Southey's poem of The Pilgrim to Compostella. Cf. Pass. v. 122. See a good popular account of him in Chambers' Book of Days, ii. 120 (July 25). A book called The Stacyons of Rome and The Pilgrims' Sea-voyage (ed. Furnivall, 1867, for the Early English Text Society) well illustrates this passage. Rome abounded with shrines at which several thousands of years of remission from purgatory could be obtained. The Sea-voyage is a satire upon the inconveniences of the pilgrimage to Compostella. For a note on *Palmer*, see Pass. viii. 162. One of the questions put to Lord Cobham at his trial was this—"Holy chirche hath determyned that it is needeful to a crystyn man to go a pylgrimage to holy placeys, and there specyally to worschype holy relyques of seyntes, apostlys, martires, confessourys, and alle seyntes approved be the chirche of Rome. How fele ȝe thys artycle?"—Fasciculus Zizaniorum, p. 442. For a good popular article on the Pilgrims of the Middle Ages, see pp. 157—194 of Scenes and Characters of the Middle Ages, by the Rev. E. L. Cutts. Out of the numerous allusions to Saint James in early writers, I select the few following.

> "At Rome sche had been, and at Boloyne,
> In Galice at seynt Iame, and at Coloyne;"
>
> Chaucer's Prol. 465.

"The idolaters come thither [i. e. to the tomb of Sagamoni Borcan] on pilgrimages from very long distances and with great devotion, just as Christians go to the shrine of Messer Saint James in Gallicia;" Marco Polo, ed. Yule, ii. 259.

> "And she was full of tales
> Of tydynges in Wales,
> And of sainct James in Gales;"
>
> Skelton, ed. Dyce, i. 106; cf. ii. 170.

"The Italians, yea, those that dwell neare Rome, will mocke and scoffe at our English (and other) pilgrims that go to Rome to see the Pope's holinesse, and St Peter's chaire, and yet they themselves will runne to see the reliques of St James of Compostella in the kingdom of Galicia in Spaine, which is above 1200 English miles;" Weever's Funeral Monuments, p. 172. See also Wordsworth's Eccl. Biog. 4th ed. i. 175.

49. (b. pr. 48; a. pr. 48.) It is remarkable that the author should have changed the ironical expression *wyse tales* of the A-text and B-text into the more prosaic *un-wyse tales* of the C-text. He seems to have wished to guard against all possibility of a mistake as to his real opinion.

50. (b. pr. 49; a. pr. 49.) That pilgrims were privileged to exaggerate pretty freely seems to have been very generally understood. Thus in Trevisa's translation of Higden's Polychronicon, i. 225, we find a passing allusion to "pilgrims and palmers, þat faste con liȝe." Again, in Foxe's Acts and Monuments, W. Thorpe tells Archbishop Arundel, that "if these men and women be a moneth out in their pilgrimage, many of them shall be an halfe yeare after great janglers, tale-tellers, and liars." See Wordsworth's Eccl. Biog. 4th ed. i. 312.

51. (b. pr. 53; a. pr. 50.)   See the chapter on Hermits in Cutts's Scenes and Characters of the Middle Ages, pp. 93—151. He rightly observes that the popular notion of a hermit viz. that he lived altogether in retirement, is quite wrong as far as concerns England in the fourteenth century. A man could only become a hermit by consent of the bishop of the diocese, and he was admitted as hermit in a formal religious service. Mr Cutts gives a summary of the service for habiting and blessing a hermit, from the Pontifical of Bishop Lacy of Exeter, of the fourteenth century; another account may be found in Lewis's Life of Bishop Pecock, ed. 1744; p. 94. Mr Cutts observes that the hermit "dressed in a robe very much like the robes of other religious orders; lived in a comfortable little house of stone or timber; often had estates, or a pension, for his maintenance, besides what charitable people were pleased to leave him in their wills, or to offer in their lifetime; he lived on bread and meat, and beer and wine, and had a chaplain to say daily prayers for him, and a servant or two to wait upon him; his hermitage was not always up in the lonely hills, or deep-buried in the shady forests—very often it was by the great high roads, and sometimes in the heart of great towns and cities." The last assertion, strange as it may seem, is abundantly evident from a very extraordinary passage which appears in Piers the Plowman (in the C-text *only*), viz. at Pass. x. 140—218. There was even a hermitage upon London wall; Riley's Memorials of London, p. 117. See also the passage in the same work (p. 584) which tells us how, in A.D. 1412, a pretended hermit suffered the punishment of the pillory "for that, whereas he was able to work for his food and raiment, he, the said William Blakeney, went about there [in London] barefooted and with long hair, under the guise of sanctity, and pretended to be a hermit, saying that he was such, and that he had made pilgrimage to Jerusalem, Rome, Venice, and the city of Seville in Spain;" all of which he admitted to be untrue. Compare also the description of 'an heap of hermits;' Pass. ix. 183; and the passage about hermits in Pass. xviii. 6—36.

52. (b. pr. 54; a. pr. 51.)   Our Lady of Walsingham's shrine was much resorted to; its celebrity almost surpassed that of St Thomas's shrine at Canterbury. In Blomefield's Norfolk we read that King Henry VIII. walked barefoot from Barsham to this shrine [no very great distance] and presented Our Lady with a necklace of great value. He also tells us that the common people had an idea that the Milky Way pointed towards Walsingham, and they called it *Walsingham-way* accordingly. It is remarkable that the Milky Way is, in Spain, called *the road to Santiago*; see Quart. Review, Oct. 1873; p. 464. The reason is obvious, viz. that the roads leading to such places of pilgrimage were as crowded with pilgrims as the Milky Way is with stars. It is impossible to cite all the numerous references to Walsingham. The best account is that given by Erasmus, in his Colloquy entitled Peregrinatio Religionis Ergo; an abstract of which will be found in Cutts's Scenes and Characters of the Middle Ages, p. 180. Quotations from the original will be found in the Percy Folio MS. iii. 465—471, in the essay

prefixed to the ballad beginning—"As yee came ffrom the holy land Of
walsingham;" to which the reader is particularly referred. See also Weever's
Funeral Monuments, pp. 111, 131. There is an interesting allusion in the
Paston Letters, ed. Gairdner, i. 48, where Margaret Paston writes to her
husband saying—"My moder be-hestyd a-nodyr ymmage of wax, of the
weytte [*weight*] of yow, to oyer [*our*] Lady of Walsyngham, and sche sent
iiij. nobelys to the iiij. orderys of Frerys at Norweche to pray for yow, and I
have be-hestyd to gon on pylgreymmays to Walsingham, and to Sent
Levenardys [*St Leonard's priory, Norwich*] for yow." In a footnote in
Milman's Latin Christianity, vi. 134, he tells us that, "when the Lollards,
by preaching against pilgrimages, endangered the interests of our Lady of
Walsingham, Bishop Spencer swore that, if any of Wyclif's preachers came
into his diocese, he would burn or behead him;" a threat which was
effectual. The significance of the word *wenches* will best appear from the
notice of the 'wenches' whom the Sompnour had 'at his retenue,' as described not far from the beginning of Chaucer's *Freres Tale*; or from the
Examination of William Thorpe, in Foxe's Acts and Monuments, who told
Archbishop Arundel—"I know well that when divers men and women will
goe thus, after their owne wils and finding out, on pilgrimage, they will
ordaine with them before, to have with them both men and women, that can
well sing wanton songs." Wyclif was very outspoken in his attacks upon
the abuses to which pilgrimages occasionally gave rise, as has been said
above. The following quotation may suffice. Speaking of the journey to
Jerusalem made by Joseph and Mary, he says—"Among Jewis was this
religioun kept, that men shulden go bi hemsilf, and wymen bi hemsilf; for
thei kepten hem fro lecherie in siché pilgrimage; but now pilgrimage is
mene for to do lecherie;" Wyclif's Works, ed. Arnold, i. 83. Ruins of the
convent, with two wells called the 'wishing-wells,' are still to be seen at
Old Walsingham, Norfolk. The monastery was founded for Augustinian or
Black Canons. See Chambers' Book of Days, i. 795, ii. 8, 174.

53. (b. pr. 55; a. pr. 52.) *Lobies*, loobies or lubbars; *longe*, tall. Compare the following curious example. "Dauid with a mighty stroke of a
stone out of a slyng hyt Goly on the heed; and leyd hym streyght alonge on
the grounde, as *longe a lobour* as he was." Horman's Vulgaria, leaf 269.

54. (b. pr. 56; a. pr. 53.) In Chaucer's Monkes Prologue, the *cope* is the
mark of a *monk*; in Pierce the Ploughman's Crede, it is that of a *mendicant
friar*. In Chaucer's Prologue, the Frere has a semi-cope. See also l. 59
below, and Pass. x. 210.

55. (b. pr. 57; a. pr. 54.) *And made hem-selue* is a sort of translation of
the older phrase of the B-text, which has *And shopen hem*, i. e. and arrayed
themselves as; see note to l. 2.

56. (b. pr. 58; a. pr. 55.) The four Orders of mendicant friars are
severely satirized in The Ploughman's Crede; see notes in my edition on ll.
29, 486. They were the Carmelites (white friars), Augustines (Austin
friars), Jacobins or Dominicans (black friars), and Minorites (gray friars).

They are easily remembered by Wycliffe's jest upon them. He takes the initial letters C, A, I, M, to form the word *Caim* (which was the usual spelling of *Cain* at that date), and declares them to be *of Cain's kin*. To be *of Cain's kin*, or *of Judas' kin* (see l. 35 above, in the B-text) was a proverbial expression equivalent to being *children of Satan*.

58. (b. pr. 60; a. pr. 57.) To *glose* is to comment upon. The comment-aries often strayed from and superseded the text. See Chaucer, Sompnoures Tale, l. 80. *As hem good lykede,* as it pleased them well. *Lykede* is very frequently thus employed as an impersonal verb. *Hem* is the dative case. *Good* is an adjective, but is used here with an adverbial force.

60. (b. pr. 62; a. pr. 59.) The B-text has *maistres Freris*, master-friars; where the two nominatives plural are in apposition. *At lykyng* [b, a, *not* c], at their liking, as they like.

62. (b. pr. 64; a. pr. 61.) "Since Love has turned pedlar." This alludes to the money received by friars for hearing confessions. Besides this, the friars literally resembled pedlars when they carried about with them knives and pins to give away to women. See the description of the *Frere* in Chaucer's Prologue.

64. (b. pr. 66; a. pr. 63.) The three texts differ here, using different expressions for the same thought. The sense of the B-text is—"Except Holy Church and they [the friars] hold better together, the greatest mischief on earth will be increasing very fast." The regular friars and secular clergy were so far from 'holding together,' that they quarrelled fiercely as to the right of hearing confessions. See Pass. vii. 120.

66. (b. pr. 68; a. pr. 65.) See Chaucer's description of a *Pardonere*, in his Prologue; and Massingberd's English Reformation, p. 127. For a passage on papal bulls, see Wyclif's Works, iii. 308.

69. (b. pr. 71; a. pr. 68.) *Of falsnesse of fastinges*, of breaking their vows of fasting. The first *of* belongs to *asoilie* or *assoilen*.

70. (b. pr. 72; a. pr. 69.) *Lewede*, unlearned; it exactly answers to the modern adj. *lay*. *Lyuede hym wel*, believed him entirely.

72. (b. pr. 74; a. pr. 71.) The B-text and A-text have *He bonched*, &c.; lit. he banged them with his brevet, and bleared their eyes. We should now say, he thrust his brevet in their faces. The word is *bouched* in Mr Wright's edition, but my collation of MSS. shews this to be an error; and, indeed, no such word as *bouch* exists. On the other hand, we find "Bunchon, *tundo, trudo*," in the Prompt. Parvulorum; Palsgrave gives—"To bounche or pushhe one; he buncheth me and beateth me, *il me pousse*." Lydgate also, as quoted in Halliwell's Dictionary, s. v. Bonchen, has—"They bonchen theire brestis with fistes wondre soore;" MS. Ashmole 39, fol. 47; Skelton has—"With that he gaue her a *bounce;*" ed. Dyce, i. 158; and in Horman's Vulgaria, leaf 135, back, I find—"He came home with a face all to-bounced, Domum reuersus est facie contusa."

To *blear one's eye* is a common phrase for to blind, delude, cajole. See Chaucer, C. T. 3863, 4047, 17201.

" Wyth fantasme, and fayrye,
'Thus sche *blerede hys yye.*"
Ly Beaus Disconus, l. 1432 ; Ritson's Met. Rom. vol. ii.

73. (b. pr. 75 ; a. pr. 72.) *Rageman ;* properly a catalogue or roll of
names ; here applied to the charter or bull with numerous bishops' seals.
Mr Wright has a long note upon the word *Ragman-roll* at p. 81 of his Anec-
dota Literaria, 1844. He prints, at p. 83, a poem with the title of 'Ragman-
roll,' from MS. Fairfax 16. There was even a game with this name, which
is described in Wright's Homes of Other Days, p. 247. In imitation, probably, of the bull with many seals hanging from it, a parchment-roll was
provided, on which were written verses descriptive of persons' characters ; and
against each verse was fastened a string. The parchment was rolled up, with
the ends of the strings hanging out. The player chose one of the strings,
and thus learnt his character. Gower alludes to this game in the lines—

" Venus, which stant withoute lawe,
In non certeine, but as men drawe
Of *Rageman, upon the chaunce,*
She leyeth no peys [*weight*] in the balaunce.''
                    Conf. Amant. ed. Pauli ; iii. 355.

The Scottish nobles gave the name of *ragman-rolls* to the collection of deeds
by which they were constrained to subscribe allegiance to Edward I., A. D.
1296 ; see Jamieson's Scottish Dictionary. In the Towneley Mysteries, at
p. 311, a demon is introduced who produces a long catalogue of sins, saying—

" Here a *rolle of ragman* of the rownde tabille
Of breffes in my bag, man, of synnes dampnabille,
Unethes may I wag, man, for-wery in your stabille," &c.

See also Skelton, Garlande of Laurell, l. 1490, and Dyce's note ; P. Pl. Crede,
l. 180 ; Cowel's Law Dictionary ; and Todd's Johnson, s. v. *rigmarole.*

Rings and *brooches* are often thus mentioned together. Near the end of
the Pardoner's Tale, Chaucer makes the Pardoner ask the people to offer
' broches, spones, ringes.'

76. (b. pr. 78 ; a. pr. 75.) " Were the bishop a truly holy man, or worth
(i. e. fit to have) both his ears, his seal would not be sent (to the pardoner,
for him) to deceive the people with." The expression *blessid* is used by the
poet to mean ' truly righteous' or ' truly holy,' as we learn from his use of it
in Pass. x. 13, q. v. The phrase 'worth both his ears' is a satirical expression, signifying that the person spoken of is one to whom his ears are of some
use, not one who turns a deaf ear to the complaints of the poor.

78. (b. pr. 80 ; a. pr. 77.) " Yet it is not against the bishop that the
young fellow preaches ; for (often) the parish-priest and he (agree to) divide
the money, which the poor people would else get." Sometimes, instead of
quarrelling (as described in Pass. vii. 120), the priest and pardoner compounded matters, and divided the spoil. Chaucer, however, in his Prologue,
l. 704, makes the pardoner more than a match for the parson, and represents
him as cheating both the parish-priest and his flock too. The phrase *noʒt by
þe bysshop* might also be translated to mean ' not by the bishop's leave,' but

the two preceding lines shew that the pardoner could easily obtain such leave; as is, moreover, made abundantly clear in a note in Wordsworth's Eccl. Biog. i. 284 (4th edition).   Hence we must consider it as spoken ironically, meaning—"But you may be sure it is never against the bishop that he preaches." The use of *by* in the sense of *against*, or *with reference to*, is common in Middle English.   See 1 Cor. iv. 4, and the examples in Trench's Select Glossary and Eastwood and Wright's Bible Word-book.

Yf þei ne were, if they did not exist; we should now say, if it were not for them.   It is a common Middle-English idiom.

82. (b. pr. 84; a. pr. 81.) *Pestelence tyme.* There were three great pestilences which were long remembered; we may even count a fourth.   For the dates of the two first, see note to Pass. vi. 115; the third lasted from July 2 to Sept. 29, 1369.   The first was also called the *great* pestilence, and is probably here meant.   In Pass. vi. 115, William speaks of *these pestilences*, with obvious reference to the *first and second* ones.

83. (b. pr. 85; a. pr. 82.) *To haue,* i. e. and petitioned the bishop that they might have.   Cf. Chaucer, Prologue, where he says of the good parish priest,

> "He sette not his benefice to huyre . . . .
> And ran to *Londone*, unto seynte Poules,
> *To seeken him a chaunterie for soules.*"

84. (b. pr. 86; a. pr. 83.) These chantry-priests, who 'sang for simony,' were sometimes called *annueleres;* see Chaucer, Chan. Yeom. Tale, l. 1.   The little side-chapels, in which they sang their *annuels*, or anniversary masses for the dead, were called *chantries*, a name which still survives.   See a curious note on the arrangements at St Paul's Cathedral, in Dean Milman's History of Latin Christianity, vol. vi. p. 373, note *h.*

85. (b. pr. 87; *not in* a.) The whole of the passage in ll. 85—217 (b. pr. 87—209) is peculiar to the later texts of the poem, and is not found in the A-text, or earliest draught, with the exception of six lines, found in A. pr. 84—89.   It is of much interest and importance, and refers entirely to *London;* it was probably inserted here, because London has just been mentioned.

86. (b. pr. 88; *not in* a.) *Crownynge,* i. e. the tonsure, which was a token of their clerical calling.   Wyclif has the same expression, where he says, "First, whanne men speken of holy Chirche, thei undirstonden anoon prelatis and prestis, monkis and chanouns and freris, *and alle men that han crownes;*" Wyclif's Works, ed. Arnold, iii. 447.   On the tonsure, see Mrs Jameson, Legends of Monastic Orders, p. xxxii.   Mr Peacock, in his notes to Myrc, p. 69, gives the following long list of references.   "For illustrations of the history of the clerical tonsure, consult Bingham, Antiq. Christ. Church, b. vi. c. iv; Rock, Church of our Fathers, i. 185; Lyndwood, Provinciale, lib. i. tit. 14, p. 69; Beda, Eccl. Hist. lib. v. cap. xxi; Beyerlinck, Magnum Theatrum Vitæ Humanæ, sub voc. *Tonsura;* Martene, De Antiq. Eccl. Rit. (Venetiis, 1783), vol. ii. p. 14; vol. iii. pp. 284, 293, 300, 335; vol. iv. pp. 113, 174, 238, 274."

89. (b. pr. 91; *not in* a.) "Lie (i. e. lodge, dwell) in London during Lent, and at other times."

90. (b. pr. 92; *not in* a.) *Tellen*, count. Formerly, the three principal courts of law, the King's Bench, the Common Pleas, and the Exchequer, had a separate jurisdiction. The Exchequer decided only such cases as related to the collection of the revenue, and hence the ecclesiastics who held office in it are said here to *challenge*, i. e. to *claim* the King's debts from the various *wards* or divisions of the city. The *wardmote* is the court, or *meeting*, held in each ward; see it fully described in the Liber Albus, p. 33. They also claimed for the King all *waifs* and *strays*, i. e. property without an owner and strayed cattle (as Mr Wright explains it); but see *streyues* in the Glossary.

"Summe beth in ofice wid the king, and gaderen tresor to hepe,
And the fraunchise of holi cherche hii laten ligge slepe."
Political Songs (Camd. Soc. 1839), p. 325.

We read also in the Complaint of the Ploughman (Polit. Poems, i. 325), the following account of the ' canons seculer : '—

"They have great prebendes and dere,
Some two or three, and some mo;
A personage to ben a playing fere,
And yet they *serve the King also*,
And let to ferme all that fare
To whom that woll most give therefore;" &c.

The following passage from Wyclif's Works (iii. 215) is to the point here. He says—"For nowe prelatis and grete religious possessioners ben so occupied aboute worldly lordischipis and plea and bysinesse in herte, that thei may not be in devocion of preiynge and thought of hevenely thingis, and of here owene synnys and othere mennys, and studie and prechynge of the gospel, and visitynge and confortynge of pore men in here diocisis and lordischipis. And tho goodis that ben overe here owene sustenaunce and necessaries, that schulde be departid among pore men most nedi, ben now wastid in festis of lordis and riche men, in festis and robis and yiftis of men of lawe, in alle countries where here lordischipis ben, and in riche clerkis of the Chauncerie, of the Comyn Benche and Kyngis Benche, and in the Checher [*Exchequer*]; and of justicis and schereves and stiwardis and bailifis, that litil or nought cometh to hem, or here chirchis and coventis, but name of the world, and thought and bisynesse and care and sorowe. . . . And yit thei don not the office of curatis, neither in techynge ne prechynge, ne yevynge of sacramentis, ne resceyvynge of pore men in the parische; but setten there an ydiot for viker or parische prest, that kan not and may not do the office of a good curat, and yit the pore parische fyndith hym. . . . And thus thei han worldly lordischipis, and reulen not the peple, ne meyntene the lond as lordis." See also pp. 277, 335 of the same.

93. (b. pr. 95; *not in* a.) Wyclif complains in the same strain—"But our Priests ben so busie about wordlie [*worldly*] occupation, that they seemen better Baylifs or Reues, than ghostlie Priests of Jesu Christ. For what man is so busie about marchandise, and other worldly doings, as bene

Preists that showld bee light of heauenlie life to al men about them."—Two Treatises against Friars, ed. James, p. 16. See also Wyclif's Works, ed. Arnold, iii. 277, 335. On the duties of a Treasurer; see the Babees Book, p. 318. In Pecock's Repressor, ii. 324, 336, is an answer to the charge brought by the Wycliffites, that some bishops and abbots held courts and decided causes.

95—124. (*not in* b, a.) This curious passage is peculiar to the C-text. The foot-note on p. 7 gives a part of what must have been the true form of lines 107—123, where the lack of alliteration shews that some corruption has crept into the text.

96. (*not in* b, a.) The term *idolatry*, as applied to the worship of images, may be found in Wyclif. "Also bischopis and freris putten to pore Cristen men that thei seyne, that ymagis of Cristis crosse, of the crucifixe, of the blessid vergyne Marye, and of other seintus, in no maner bene worthi to be worschipid, but that alle men worschipynge in ony manere thoo ymagis or any payntyngus, synnen ande done *ydolatry*, and that God dose not ony myracle by hem, and that alle men doynge pilgrimage to hem, or ony manere hem worschipynge, *or putting lighttis or ony devocions bifore thoo ymagis*, bene cursid."—Works, ed. Arnold, iii. 462. On the next page we find—"hit semes that this offrynge to ymagis is a sotile caste of Anticriste and his clerkis, for to drawe almes fro pore men, and cumber worldly prestis with muck, that thai nouther know God ne hemselfe," &c.; see also p. 293. The sense of ll. 96—102 is—"Ye suffer idolatry in many different places, and boxes, bound with iron, are set forth, to receive the toll paid through such untrue sacrifice. In remembrance of miracles, much wax hangs there (at the shrine); all the world knows well that the stories told cannot be true. But ye prelates suffer laymen to live and die in such misbelief, because it is profitable to you to purseward."

Compare also the following passage from the Ploughman's Tale :—

"Yet they mote have some stocke or stone,
  Gaily painted, and proudly dight,
To maken men leven upon,
  And saie that it is full of might;"

Polit. Poems, ed. Wright, i. 331.

It is right to add that there is probably a special force in the epithet "bound with iron" as regards the boxes mentioned in l. 97. It seems that such boxes were known to be meant for the reception of alms. This appears from a passage in Riley's Memorials of London, p. 586, where it is recorded how a certain William Derman was punished with the pillory because he "pretended to be, and called himself, a domestic and serjeant of the House or Hospital [of Bedlem] aforesaid, for collecting alms and other works of charity for the said hospital. And so, under false colour, he walked about the city *with a box bound with iron*, . . . and collected many alms therein."

There is another allusion to these alms-boxes in B. xv. 208.

103. (*not in* b, a.) *Ich lyue wel*, I verily believe.

106. (*not in* b, a.) *Ful*, fell. Observe the various readings *fil* and *fel*.

109. (*not in* b, a.) *syngen*, sin. This curious form of the verb occurs frequently in the C-text (MS. P). It is found also in Myrc's Instructions for Parish Priests, ed. Peacock, 1. 1073; and in Genesis and Exodus, ed. Morris, l. 172. See other examples in Stratmann, s. v. *sunegen*; and cf. A.S. *syngian*. The story of Hophni and Phinehas, alluded to in the B-text, x. 280—282, is, in the C-text, placed here, in the Prologue.

110. (*not in* b, a.) *Maumettes*, idols. Thus, in the Persones Tale (De Avaritia), Chaucer says—"an idolastre peraventure ne hath not but o *maumet* or two, and the avaricious man hath many; for certes, every florein in his coffre is his *maumet*." The Old French *mahommet*, an idol, shews that the word is borrowed from the name of Mahomet. The false notion that the Mahometans were idolaters was very prevalent in the middle ages. Colonel Yule, in his edition of Marco Polo, vol. i. p. 174, quotes from Weber's Metrical Romances (vol. ii. p. 228) the following lines :—

> " Kyrkes they made of crystene lawe,
> And here *maumettes* lete downe drawe."

He adds—"So Correa calls a golden idol, which was taken by Da Gama in a ship of Calicut 'an image of Mahomed.' Don Quixote too, who ought to have known better, cites with admiration the feat of Rinaldo in carrying off, in spite of forty Moors, a golden image of Mahomed." Selden also, in his Table Talk, art. *Popery*, says—"We charge the prelatical clergy with popery, to make them odious, though we know they are guilty of no such thing; just as heretofore they called images mammets, and the adoration of images mammetry, that is, Mahomets and Mahometry; odious names, when all the world knows that Turks are forbidden images by their religion." The word is not to be confused with *mammet*, a doll or puppet, as is often done. See *Mammet* and *Mawmet* in Wedgwood's Etymological Dictionary.

125. (b. pr. 97; *not in* a.) *Houres*, i. e. canonical hours, prayers made at stated times in the day; see *Hours* in Hook's Church Dictionary, and the full account in the Ancren Riwle, p. 21. Cf. Pass. ii. 180.

126. (b. pr. 98; *not in* a.) *Drede ys*, there is a fear; it is to be feared.

127. (b. pr. 99; *not in* a.) *Constorie*, also spelt *Consistorie*, which is the fuller and more correct form; a church council or assembly of prelates. It is here used of the Last Great Assembly held by Christ at the Day of Judgment. "*Consistory*, a word used to denote the Court Christian, or Spiritual Court. Every bishop has his consistory court, held before his chancellor or commissary, in his cathedral church, or other convenient place of his diocese, for ecclesiastical causes;" Hook's Church Dictionary. Cf. Pass. iv. 179, 476; also B. ii. 177. See Courts (Consistory) in the Index to the Parker Society's publications.

131. (b. pr. 102; *not in* a.) I.e. Peter deputed the power of the Keys to the four cardinal virtues, viz. to Prudence, Temperance, Fortitude, and Justice; see Pass. xxii. 274—310. The old English names are Sleight, Temperance, Strength, and Doom; see Ayenbit of Inwyt, p. 124, where we read further that—"Thise uour uirtues byeth y-cleped cardinals, uor thet hi byeth be*gh*est

amang the uirtues, huer-of the ycalde [*old*] filosofes speke. Vor be thise uour uirtues the man gouerneth himzelue ine thise wordle, as the apostles gouerneth holy cherche be his cardinals." In MS. Q. Γ. 29, in Jesus College, Cambridge, printed in Reliquiæ Antiquæ, ed. Halliwell and Wright, p. 154, is the passage—"*Prudentia* habet in dextro latere astutiam et versutiam; in sinistro autem hebitudinem mentis. *Justitia*. namque habet in dextro latere pleonesiam, hoc est, plus justo; in sinistro vero meonesyam, hoc est, minus justo. *Fortitudo* itaque habet in dextro.latere audaciam, in sinistro ignaviam. *Temperantia* igitur habet in dextro latere castitatem et continentiam; in sinistram vero l x x x r k b m et l k b k d k n f m;" (i. e. luxuriam et libidinem; the vowels being denoted by the letters that follow them alphabetically; so that *a, e, i, o, u* are denoted by *b, f, k, p, x*). In Pass. xxii. 409—425, Conscience reproves evildoers by telling them that without the cardinal virtues they will be lost; whereupon a shameless vicar replies that if so, many a man will be lost, and that he never knew a 'cardinal' but such as came from 'the pope. The same play upon the word occurs here. So in Shakespeare, Henry VIII. iii. 3. 103—

> "Upon my soul, two reverend *cardinal virtues!*
> But *cardinal sins* and hollow hearts I fear ye."

In the works published by the Parker Society, we have the following allusions. The cardinals are so called from *cardine*, Bullinger's Works, iv. 117; they are *cardines mundi*, Jewel's Works, ii. 1020; they have always been pernicious to England; Cranmer's Works, ii. 184; Latimer's Works, i. 119.

132. (b. pr. 104; *not in* a.) *Closynde ʒates*, closing gates. This is a sort of translation of the Latin *cardinalis*, which is derived from *cardo*, a hinge. The power of the keys is, as it were, made for the moment into a power of the hinges.

133. (b. pr. 105; *not in* a.) *Ther*, where. This sense of *there* should be carefully observed. Cf. l. 204 (b. pr. 190).

To closye with heuene, to close heaven with. The reader of Middle English must note, once for all, that the preposition *with* is commonly so placed as to follow its verb immediately. Thus, in the B-text, ii. 31, *to marye with myself* means "to marry myself with;" and in the same, ii. 116, *to wratthe with treuthe* means "whereby to make Truth angry;" both of those passages were altered in the C-text, as if to avoid the apparent ambiguity. So in Chaucer's Squire's Tale, l. 471, *to helen with your hurtes* means "to heal your hurts with;" and in l. 641, *to helen with this hauk* means "to heal this hawk with." See also Pierce the Ploughman's Crede, l. 116, &c.

We may also note the occasional use of the infinitives in.-*ye* or -*ie*; thus *to closye* is to close; so *asoilie*, in l. 68, and *rebukie* in l. 110 above; *cracchy*, B. prol. 186. It occurs also in the present tense, as in *louye*, i. e. may love, in l. 149 below.

134. (b. pr. 107; *not in* a.) *At court*, at the court of Rome. The B-text has *atte courte*, i. e. at the court. *Cauʒt han*, have caught; B-text, *cauʒt of*,

i. e. received.   The author revised his work in the minutest particulars, as is evident throughout.   It is impossible to point out the extremely numerous variations, which the reader can only discover by a careful comparison of the texts.

——(b. pr. 111; *not in* c, a.) I *can* speak more, for I have much I could say about them; yet I *cannot* speak more, out of reverence, for the power of electing a pope is a high and holy thing.   Such seems to be William's meaning.   Observe that the C-text has an entirely different and less ambiguous line, viz. l. 138.

139. (b. pr. 112; *not in* a.) Tyrwhitt supposed that this part of the poem was written after the death of the Black Prince, when his son Richard was heir-apparent.   But more close investigation shews that the *king* is really Richard II., and that the date of composition of this portion (as it appears in the B-text) was rather 1377 than 1376.   Line 140 is very significant; and, in many MSS., is under-scored as worthy of attention.   In the Political Songs of England, ed. Wright (Camden Soc.), p. 363, Mr Wright collects some "expressions of the popular doctrine concerning the kingly character held by our forefathers."   His quotations are from MS. Cotton, Nero A. 1. foll. 71, 72; from the Proverbs of Alfred, since printed in An Old English Miscellany, ed. Morris, p. 106; from the Political Songs, p. 117; from the present passage of Piers the Plowman; and from Richard the Redeles, Pass. i.   See also Pass. xxii. 467—481.

141. (b. pr. 114; *not in* a.) *Kynde witte* (a very common phrase in our author) is what we now call *common sense.*

143. (b. pr. 117; *not in* a.) "Contrived that the commons should provide their provisions" [c]; *or,* "Contrived that the commons should provide for themselves" [b]; where *themselves* appears to be equivalent to *all of them.*

144. (b. pr. 118; *not in* a.) *Alle craftes,* all handicrafts; the B-text has *Of kynde witte craftes,* handicrafts that could be pursued by help of common intelligence.   Besides the king, knights, clergy, and commons, there was a fifth class, of ploughmen, &c., mere tillers of the soil, who were looked upon as inferior to the rest.   The B-text is here more explicit.

——(b. pr. 123; *not in* c, a.) I have no doubt that the *lunatic* is *William himself.*   He is here expressing his favourite loyal hope that the king may so govern as to be beloved by all loyal subjects.   For the use of *lunatic* there are three reasons: (1) it conveys a touch of satire, as though it were a mad thing to hope for; (2) a *lunatic* is privileged to say strange things; and (3) he expressly declares, at the beginning of Pass. xv. (B-text), that people considered him a *fool,* and that he *raved.*   This opinion he bitterly adopts.   He makes the lunatic, however, speak *clergealy,* i. e. like a scholar.

The word *thing* does not necessarily imply contempt; it merely signifies a creature, a person.   Cf. "For he was a ful dughti *thing;*" Cursor Mundi (Text C), l. 8182; ed. Morris.   There is a most curious illustration of this passage in Walsingham, shewing what liberties were sometimes taken in addressing royalty.   It is remarkable that Walsingham enters the circumstance which he narrates under the year 1387, so that our poet, writing ten years earlier, cannot be supposed to refer to the same event. The historian says— "Interea venit quidam miles exercitatus, sed *sensu vacuus*, Dominus Hugo de Lynne, qui eo quod stultus erat et sensum perdiderat, eleemosyna dominorum plurium sustentabatur. Ab isto igitur Rex jocando quæsivit, quid acturus esset contra proceres, qui congregati dicebantur in prædicta sylva. Cui mox Hugo, cum summa melancholia, respondit :—' Exeas,' inquit, ' et aggrediamur eos, et cujuslibet matris filios perimamus.; et per oculos Dei, hoc completo, peremisti omnes fideles amicos· quos habes in regno.' Quod responsum, etsi stulte prolatum, sapientes quam maxime ponderant."—Th. Walsingham; Hist. Anglic. ed Riley, ii. 164.

149. (b. pr. 126; *not in* a.) *Leue*, grant. No two words have been more hopelessly confused than *leue* and *lene*. See *Leue* in the Glossary. The line means—"And grant thee to govern thy land, so that loyalty (i. e. thy lieges) may love thee."

151. (b. pr. 128; *not in* a.) Conscience [*B-text*, the angel] condescends to speak, but only in Latin, since common people ought not to be told how to justify themselves; all who could not understand Latin or French had best suffer and serve. The angel's reproof to the king is in Leonine or riming verses, of which the first is a hexameter, and is put into the mouth of the king himself. The remaining six [six in the B-text, but the C-text omits the last but one of them] are alternate hexameters and pentameters, and contain the angel's charge to the king. The verses may have been composed by William himself, and may be thus translated :—

(You say) "I am a king, I am a prince," (but you will be) neither perhaps hereafter.
O thou who dost administer the special laws of Christ the King,
That thou mayst do this the better, as you are just, be merciful!
Naked justice requires to be clothed by thee with mercy ;
Whatever crops thou wouldst reap, such be sure to sow.
If justice is stripped bare, let it be meted to thee of naked justice;
If mercy is sown, mayest thou reap of mercy !

It may be added, that long pieces of advice to kings are common at this period of English. Thus, in Gower's Confessio Amantis, lib. vii., is a long disquisition on politics. Again, there is Occleve's poem, entitled De Regimine Principum. Both these, and many like them, are founded on a spurious treatise ascribed to Aristotle, and entitled Secretum Secretorum. Gower, like William, addresses his advice to Richard II., and with much freedom. See Warton; Hist. E. P. ii. 230; ed. 1840.

——(b. pr. 139; *not in* c, a.) *Goliardeys*. "Un goliardois, Fr.; *Goliardus*, or *Goliardensis*, Lat. This jovial sect seems to have been so called from Golias, the real or assumed name of a man of wit, toward the end of the thirteenth century, who wrote the Apocalypsis Goliæ, and other pieces in burlesque Latin rimes, some of which have been falsely attributed to Walter Map . . . In several authors of the thirteenth century, quoted by Du Cange, the *Goliardi* are classed with the *joculatores et buffones*."—Tyrwhitt; note on

l. 562 of Chaucer's Cant. Tales.   But it would appear that *Golias* is the sole
invention of Walter Map, and that the original 'Golias' poems are really
his.   He named his imaginary Bishop Golias after the Philistine slain by
David; not without some reference, perhaps, to the O. Fr. *goule*, Lat. *gula*,
gluttony.   Soon after, *Goliardus* meant a clerical buffoon; later still, it meant
any *jougleur*, or any teller of ribald stories; in which sense it is used by
Chaucer; Prologue, l. 560.   See Morley's English Writers, vol. i. p. 586.
William's *Goliardeys* is "a glutton of words," one full of long pieces which he
could recite; cf. the Latin phrase *helluo librorum*. He is here made to quote,
in an altered form, two lines which are also found as under :—

> "O rex, si rex es, rege te, vel eris sine re, rex;
>   Nomen habes sine re, nisi te recteque regas, rex."
>
>   Political Poems, ed. Wright, i. 278.

Compare also—

> "Legem quoque dicimus regis dignitatem
>   Regere; nam credimus esse legem lucem,
>   Sine qua concludimus deviare ducem."
>
>   Political Songs (Camd. Soc.), p. 115.

And again—

> "Non a regnando rex est, sed iure regendo."
>
>   Political Poems, i. 57.

——(b. pr. 143; *not in* c, a.)   The commons are not supposed to have
understood the angel's advice given in Latin, but they just knew as much as
was good for them to know; they could just say—

> "Precepta regis sunt nobis vincula legis."

☞ Observe the break here in the B-text; for notes to B. prol.
146, &c. see l. 165 below, &c.

159. (b. pr. 210; a. pr. 84.)   Lines 159—164 (b. pr. 210—215, a. pr.
84—89) will be found in Text A, as well as in the later ones; but it will be
observed that this passage comes very much earlier in the C-text than in the
B-text, having been transposed from its former place. The law-sergeants are
here spoken of.   "Lawyers were originally priests and of course wore the
tonsure; but when the clergy were forbidden to intermeddle with secular
affairs, the lay lawyers continued the practice of shaving the head, and wore
the coif for distinction's sake.   It was at first made of linen, and afterwards
of *white silk :*" British Costume, p. 126.   It was a sort of skullcap; Strutt,
Manners and Customs, iii. 76.   Dugdale, in his Originales Judiciales, p.
112, says : "In token or signe that all justices are thus graduate (i. e.
serjeants-at-law), every of them always, whilst he sitteth in the king's court,
weareth a *white coif of silk*, which is the principal and chief insignment of
habit, wherewith serjeants-at-law in their creation are decked; and neither
the justice, nor yet the serjeant, shall ever put off the quoif, no, not in the
king's presence, though he be in talk with his majesties highness;" Brand,
Pop. Antiq. ed. Ellis, iii. 117, note.   The white silk hoods are again alluded
to in Pass. iv. l. 451.

161. (b. pr. 212; a. pr. 86.) *To plede*, to plead; the B-text has *plededen*, pleaded. This verb is derived from the O. Fr. *plet*, a plea, which is corrupted from the Lat. *placitum*, an opinion. Hence *plead* and *please* are from the same root. By the Statute of 36 Edw. III., c. 15 (A.D. 1362), it was enacted that pleadings should henceforward be conducted in English, but recorded in Latin. They were not *recorded* in English till the fourth year of George II.

The *penny* was an important coin in the time of Edward III.; but it should be observed that *any* coin, such as a florin, could be sometimes called a *penny*, in which case a *half-penny* would mean the half-florin, and a *farthing* (*fourth-ing*) the fourth part of the florin. See note to Pass. iii. 157. There is a satirical poem in praise of 'Sir Peny,' who was much sought after by all men, including lawyers.

> " Sir Peny mai ful mekil availe
> To tham that has nede of cownsail,
>   Als sene is in assise."
> Hazlitt; Early Popular Poetry, i. 165.

162. (b. pr. 213; a. pr. 87.) *Vnlose*, unclose, i. e. open; indeed, the Cotton MS. reads *open*, as noted in the footnote (C-text). The A-text likewise has *vnloseþ*, the present tense; but the B-text has *vnlese*, which is properly the past tense, signifying unclosed, and is fitly joined with the past form *plededen* in the preceding line of that text.

163. (b. pr. 214; a. pr. 88.) "Thou mightest better measure the mist on Malvern hills than get a *mum* out of their mouth, until money be exhibited to them." A *mum* is anything approaching to a word, a *mumble;* as may be well illustrated from the Towneley Mysteries, p. 194, where we find the line—

> "Though thi lyppus be stokyn [*tightly closed*], yit myght thou say *mom!*"

In the Merry Wives of Windsor, v. 2. 6, Slender says—"I come to her in white, and cry *mum!*" The whole of this passage is imitated by Lydgate;

> " Unto the common place [*pleas*] I yode thoo, .
>   Where sat one with a *sylken hoode:*
> I dyd hym reverence, for I ought to do so,
>   And told my case as well as I coode,
>   How my goods were defrauded me by falshood.
> I *gat not a mum of his mouth* for my meed,
>   And for *lack of mony*, I myght not spede."
> Lydgate's London Lyckpeny; Specimens of English,
> 1394—1579, ed. Skeat, p. 24.

☞ **Observe the break here in the B-text; the transposed passage (a) ends here.**

165. (b. pr. 146; *not in* a.) This well-known fable, of the rats and mice trying to hang a bell round the cat's neck, is nowhere so well told as here. Mr Wright says—"The fable is found in the old collection, in French verse of the fourteenth century, entitled Ysopet; and M. Roþert has also printed a Latin metrical version of the story from a MS. of the same century. La Fontaine has given it among his fables." It is a well-known story in Scottish history, that this fable was narrated by Lord Gray to the conspirators against

the favourites of King James III., when Archibald, Earl of Angus, exclaimed, "I am he who will bell the cat;" from which circumstance he obtained the name of Archibald Bell-the-Cat. In the present instance, the rats are the burgesses and more influential men among the commons; the mice, those of less importance. The cat can be no other than John of Gaunt, Duke of Lancaster, concerning whom rumours were spread that he aspired to the royal dignity; this greatly offended the people, who were fond of Richard for the sake of his father, their beloved Black Prince. The speech made by the Duke, Oct. 13, 1377, indignantly repelling all such accusations, is entered on the Parliamentary Rolls, and may be read in Lingard's History of England, 8vo., 1825; vol. iv. p. 224. Still more clearly is this shewn by the curious resolution adopted by the insurgents under Wat Tyler, who "swore to admit of no king of the name of *John*," in order to express their detestation of the Duke; see Lingard's History of England, vol. iv. p. 240. But the indignation against him does not seem to have lasted long; see Milman, Hist. of Latin Christianity, vi. 113. I may also cite a Petition printed in Wyclif's Works, ed. Arnold, iii. 508, which begins with the words—"Plese it to oure most noble and most worthi King Richard, kyng bothe of Englond and of Fraunce, and to the noble *Duk of Lancastre*, and to othere grete men of the rewme," &c.

There is an allusion to this fable of belling the cat in a Poem on the Times (printed in Political Poems, ed. Wright, i. 274), which Mr Wright refers to the year 1388. The author may accordingly have merely followed our poet. The lines are:—

> " He and he seyd wel, *et sermo placere uidetur*,
> The cattys nec to belle *hic et hic ligare ueretur*."

Certainly Skelton had carefully read Piers the Plowman; and he too alludes to the fable in his Colin Clout, ll. 162-5 (ed. Dyce, i. 317).

The word *ruton* is not uncommon; it is often called *rotten*, as in the line —" Here a *rotten*, here a mousse;" Chester Plays, ed. Wright, p. 51.

——(b. pr. 152; *not in* c, a.) *Doute* in Old English almost always means *fear*, as here. *Loke*, look about us; cf. l. 187 (b. pr. 172).

173. (b. pr. 155; *not in* a.) *Ous lotheth*, it loathes us, i. e. we loathe.

176. (b. pr. 158; *not in* a.) The reading *resonable* of the C-text makes it obvious that the form *renable* of the B-text is a mere contraction of the same word; cf. the various readings in the footnotes. Chaucer has the same contracted form in the Freres Tale, l. 211—"And speke as *renably*, and faire, and wel." Again, in Myrc's Duties of a Parish Priest (ed. Peacock, 1868), the Cotton MS. has 'renabulle tonge' where the Douce MS. has 'resonable.' But it was often regarded as if formed from the verb *renne*, to run; hence it is still used in Norfolk in the form *runnable*; i. e. glib, loquacious. In the following it has, apparently, the older meaning:

> " Hir maners might no man amend;
> *Of tong* she was *trew and renable*,
> And of hir semblant soft and stabile."

Ywaine and Gawaine, l. 208; in Ritson's Met. Rom., vol. i. p. 10.

——(b. pr. 159; *not in* c, a.) "Said, for a sovereign remedy for himself;" i. e. as far as himself was concerned. So again, in l. 206, the mouse says—"I sigge it for me," I say it, as *far* as I am concerned. This line was omitted in the revision, viz. in the C-text.

178. (b. pr. 161; *not in* a.) *Byȝes*, necklaces. *Colers of crafty werke*, collars of skilful workmanship; alluding to the gold chains, such as are still worn by sheriffs, &c.

——(b. pr. 164; *not in* a.) "And at other times they are elsewhere," viz. away from London, living in retirement.

195. (b. pr: 181; *not in* a.) *Leten*, considered, esteemed; cf. B. iv. 160.

201. (b. pr. 187; *not in* a.) *Lete the cat worthe*, to let the cat be, to let it alone. Cf. Pass. iii. 49. *Worthe* is the A.S. *weorðan*, to be. When Alexander tamed Bucephalus, we read that

> " Soone hee leapes on-loft · and *lete hym worthe*
> To fare as hym lyst faine · in feelde or in towne."
>   William of Palerne, &c.; ed. Skeat, 1867; p. 216.

203. (b. pr. 189; *not in* a.) [*Is*] *seuen ȝer passed*, [it is] seven years past, seven years ago. N.B. This line, in the C-text, is marked '204,' by a misprint; the lines are not, however, misnumbered.

204. (b. pr. 190; *not in* a.) The expressive word *elynge, elenge*, or *ellinge*, still common in Kent, includes the meanings *sad* and *solitary*. Henry VIII., in a letter to Anne Bullen, speaks of "his *ellengness* since her departure;" Hearne's edition of Avesbury, p. 360. The word occurs again, Pass. xxiii. 2; and B. x. 94; and is used both by Chaucer and Occleve. See also the various readings of l. 3075 of Cursor Mundi, ed. Morris.

205. (b. pr. 191; *not in* a.) " Uæ tibi, terra, cuius rex puer est, et cuius principes mane comedunt;" Ecclesiastes x. 16. In MS. Digby 53 is a note to this effect—

> " Þar þe child is kinge and þe cuerl [*churl*] is alderman, and þe wale [*stranger*] biscop, wa þene lede [*wo to the people*]; unde versus,
> " Ue populo cuius puer est rex, censor agrestis,
> Exterus antistes; hii mala multa mouent."

A similar saying is attributed to Beda in An Old English Miscellany, ed. Morris, p. 184; cf. Robert of Brunne, Handlyng Synne, l. 10976. When Robert Crowley reprinted *Piers Plowman*, in the time of *Edward VI.*, he added, for obvious reasons, this sidenote: "Omnium doctissimorum suffragio, dicuntur hec de lassiuis, fatuis, aut ineptis principibus, non de etate tenellis. Quasi dicat, ubi rex puerilis est." In this and other quotations, I follow the peculiar spellings of the originals. The use of *e* for *æ* in Latin words is very common.

☞ **A break in the B-text here; for note to B. prol. 192, see note to l. 212.**

207. (b. pr. 202; *not in* a.) Observe how *the cat* (John of Gaunt) is here distinguished from *the kitten* (Richard II.).

208. (b. pr. 203; *not in* a.) *Ne carpen of*, nor shall men talk about.

Supply *shal* from the line above. *Costide me neuere*, would never have cost *me* anything; for I would not have subscribed to it.

209. (b. pr. 204; *not in* a.) "And, even if I *had* subscribed, I would not own it, but would submit and say nothing."

211. (*not in* b, a.) "Till misfortune, that chastens many men, teaches them better." The corresponding line (in position) in [b] is l. 206, expressed in totally different language.

☞ **End of the break in the B-text.**

212—215. (b. pr. 192—200; *not in* a.) The wise mouse here suggests that the rats want keeping in order themselves, and even mice have been known to help themselves to people's malt. And (in the B-text, which is here fuller than the later one) he adds that the cat may sometimes be expected to go out catching rabbits, and meanwhile he will let the rats and mice alone. "Better a little loss than a long sorrow; (for there would, if the duke died, be) confusion amongst us all, though we be rid of a tyrant." William uses *the mase* (b. pr. 196) to mean *confusion, bewilderment;* and the whole line is explanatory of the 'long sorrow' mentioned above.

The lines—"We mice (the lower order of commons) would eat up many men's malt, and ye rats (the burgesses) would wake men from their rest," &c. —are almost prophetical. The rising of the peasantry under Wat Tyler took place but a short time after they were first written, viz. in June, 1381. No doubt our poet disapproved of the violence of that movement; as is shewn by his curtailment of the passage in the C-text.

☞ **A break in the B-text here; for notes to B. prol. 202—204, see notes to ll. 207—209.**

217. (b. pr. 209; *not in* a.) *Diuine ȝe*, guess ye the meaning; I dare not.

☞ **A break in the B-text here; for notes to B. prol. 210—214, see notes to ll. 159—163.**

219. (b. pr. 216; a. pr. 96.) From this point to the end of the Passus (or Prologue) the contents of the three Texts are much the same.

221. (b. pr. 218; a. pr. 98.) "The trade of brewing was confined almost wholly to females, and was reckoned among the callings of low repute."— Note to Liber Albus, ed. H. T. Riley; p. 307. At p. 312 of the same we read, "If any *brewer* or *brewster*," &c. This accounts for the feminine termination in the form *brewesteres* [b]. So too we find *bakers* [c, a], but *baxteres* [b], because baking also was to some extent in female hands. The retail-dealers or 'regratresses' of bread were almost always females; see Riley's Liber Albus, pp. 232, 309; and sometimes they baked their bread themselves; Riley's Memorials of London, p. 324, note 1. See, however, the note to the next line here following

222. (b. pr. 219; a. pr. 99.) *Wollewebsteres* [b], female weavers of woollen. But the distinction between *webbe*, a male weaver, and *webstere*, a female weaver, is not always made. Thus, in Pass. vii. 221 we find—

"My wif was a *webbe* · and wollen cloth made."

And it may be admitted that the termination *-ster* (properly a feminine one, as in the modern *spinster*) does not seem to have been very carefully used at this period. On this point I beg leave to refer the reader to a passage, too long for quotation, in Marsh's Lectures on the English Language, ed. Smith, pp. 207, 208, 217. See also the remarks in Trench's English Past and Present, pp. 153—157; J. Grimm, Deutsche Grammatik, vol. ii. p. 134; vol. iii. p. 339; Koch, Engl. Gram. iii. 47. In Wright's Vocabularies, vol. i. p. 214, the words *baxter* and *brewster* are treated as masculine nouns, whilst, at p. 216 of the same, they are feminine. An excellent example of the old feminine use of this termination is afforded by *witegystre*, a prophetess, in the A.S. version of S. Luke ii. 36, as distinguished from *witega*, a prophet, used in other passages.

——(b. pr. 222; *not in c, a.*) "Of labourers of every kind there leapt forth some." For *alkin* we sometimes find *alle kyn, alle kynne, alles kinnes,* and even the odd form *alle skinnes.* The full form is *alles kynnes,* of every kind. It is in the genitive case. The word *labourers* in the Statutes of Edward III. is comprehensive, including masons, bricklayers, tilers, carpenters, ditchers, diggers, &c.

223. (b. pr. 220; a. pr. 100.) This line varies; we find—"tailors and tanners, and tillers of earth" [c]; "tailors and tinkers, and toll-takers in markets" [b]; "tailors, tanners, and tuckers also" [a]. A *tucker,* now chiefly used as a proper name, is the same as a fuller of cloth; and a *tucking-mill* means a fulling-mill for the thickening of cloth. A description of the process of fulling or felting may be seen in the English Cyclopædia, 1861, Arts and Sciences, vol. viii. col. 1000.

225. (b. pr. 224; a. pr. 103.) *Deux saue dame Emme!* God save dame Emma! or *Dieu vous saue, dame Emme* [b, a]. Evidently the refrain of some low popular song. In B. xiii. 340, the poet speaks of "dame Emme of Shoreditch," which was a low locality.

227. (b. pr. 226; a. pr. 105.) "Good geese and pigs! let's go and dine!" It was the practice thus to tout for custom, standing outside the shop-door. In the same way the taverners kept crying out, "White wine! Red wine! A taste for nothing!" &c. Here again Lydgate copies from William:—

> " *Cokes* to me they toke good entent,
>   Called me nere, for to dyne;
> And profered me good brede, ale, and wyne . . .
> Then I hied me into Est Chepe;
>   One cries *ribes of befe, and many a pie;*
> Pewtar potts they clatteryd on a heape;
>   Ther was harpe, pipe, and sawtry," &c.

London Lyckpeny; MS. Harl. 542.

The quotation just cited (being taken from another MS.) differs somewhat from the passage as printed in Specimens of English, 1394—1579, ed. Skeat, pp. 25, 26.

The phrase '*goo we to dyner*' occurs in the Paston Letters, ed. Gairdner, i. 317.

229. (b. pr. 228 ; a. pr. 107.) White and red wines, chiefly imported from France, were common. Though *Osey* is said to come from Portugal in the first volume of Hackluyt's Voyages, p. 188, yet the name is certainly a corruption of *Alsace*. Thus *Ausoy* is written for Alsace frequently in the Romance of Partenay, and Roquefort explains the O.Fr. *Aussay* to mean *Alsatia*. It seems to have been a sweet, straw-coloured wine ; and there were, in fact, several kinds of it, a list of which is given in Zedler's Universal Lexicon, vol. xliii. col. 261. The wines of Gascony, of the Rhine, and of Rochelle, need no explanation. But I am unable to tell what is meant by the reading of the C-text in l. 230, where, instead of a mention of the Rhine, as in the former versions, we find the readings *ruele, rule, ruel*, or *rewle*. The only place which I can find with a name resembling this is Roulx (also-spelt Roeux, Roeles, or Roelles), about three miles from Mons, in Hainault. It can hardly be the same as the word *ruel* in Pass. x. l. 79.

The roste to defye, to digest the roast meat. This is well illustrated by the following oft-quoted passage :—

> " Ye shall have rumney and malmesyne,
> Both ypocrasse, and vernage wyne,
> Mount rose and wyne of Greke,
> Both algrade, and respice eke,
> Antioche, and bastarde,
> Pyment also, and garnarde,
> Wyne of Greke, and muscadell,
> Both clarè, pyment, and *Rochell*
> The reed your stomake *to defye*,
> And pottes of *Osey* set you by."
> Squyr of Lowe Degre ; Ritson's Met. Rom. iii. 176.

Again, in a MS. Glossary printed in Reliquiæ Antiquæ, i. 6, we find the expression—" *digere paulisper vinum quo mades*, defye the wyn of the wheche thou art dronken and wexist sobre." See also Wyclif's Works, i. 89.

For a long note upon wines, see the Babees Boke, ed. Furnivall, pp. 202 —207 ; cf. Henderson's History of Ancient and Modern Wines, 1824 ; Liber Albus, p. 618 ; Tyrwhitt's note to Chaucer, C. T. 12497.

SCHEME OF THE CONTENTS OF PASSUS II.

(B. Pass. I ; A. Pass. I.)   Ed. Wright, pp. 15—27 ; ll. 460—879.

C-TEXT.	B-TEXT.	A-TEXT.
ii. 1—23	i. 1—23	i. 1—23
——	24	24
24	25	25
——	26	26
25	27	27
26—28	*like* 28—30	28—30
(a) 29	(a) [33]	——

C-TEXT.	B-TEXT.	A-TEXT.
ii. 30	i. 31	i. 31
31	32	——
(a) [29]	(a) 33	
32—45	34—47	32—45
——	48	46
46	49	47
——	50	48
47—66	51—70	49—68
67	——	——
68—78	71—81	69—79
——	82	80
79—93	83—97	81—95
(b) [102, 103]	(b) [102, 103]	(b) 96, 97
(c) [97]	(c) 98	(c) 98
(d) 94	(d) [100]	(d) [100]
95		
96		
(c) 97	(c) [98]	(c) [98]
——	99	99
(e) 98	(e) [104]	(e) [102]
(d) [94]	(d) 100	(d) 100
99, 100	——	——
101	101	101
(b) 102, 103	(b) 102, 103	(b) [96, 97]
(e) [98]	(e) 104	(e) 102
104	——	——
105, 106	105, 106	103, 104
——	107—110	105—108
107—109	like 111—115	like 109—111
110, 111	like 116, 117	——
——	118—121	——
112—125		——
126	122	112
——	——	113
127—132	123—128	114—119
——	129	120
133, 134	130, 131	121, 122
——	132, 133	123, 124
135—139	134—138	125—129
140, 141	139 (and Latin)	——
142—146	140—144	130—134
——	145	135
147	146	——
148	like 147—149	like 136
149	150	137
——		138
150, 151	151, 152	——
152, 153	like 154, 153	——
154—161	155—162	——
162—187	163—188	139—164
188	——	——
189—191	189—191	165—167

C-TEXT.	B-TEXT.	A-TEXT.
	i. 192, 193	i. 168, 169
ii. 192—197	194—199	170—175
		176, 177
198—203	200—205	178—183
204, 205	like 206, 207	184, 185

NOTES TO PASSUS II. (B. Passus I; A. Passus I.)

C. 2. 3. [B. 1. 3. A. 1. 3.] *A loueliche lady of lere,* i. e. *A lady, loue-liche of lere,* A lady, lovely of countenance.

5. (b. 1. 5; a. 1. 5.) Here, for *sone* [b, a], the C-text has *Wille,* the poet's own name. For *slepest þou, syxt þow,* the B-text has *slepestow, sestow,* by a common habit. So in A.S., we find *sceallu* for *scealt þu,* i. e. shalt thou.

6. (b. 1. 6; a. 1. 6.) *Muse,* confused medley of people.

8. (b. 1. 8; a. 1. 8.) *Haue thei worship,* if they have honour.

9. (b. 1. 9; a. 1. 9.) *Thei holden no tale,* they keep no account, they regard not.

11. (b. 1. 11; a. 1. 11.) *What may thys be to mene,* what is the meaning of this? *To mene* takes the place of the A.S. *gerund,* where *to* is a preposition governing the dative case, and *mene* is for *mænanne,* a dative formed from the infinitive *mænan,* to mean. Thus *to mænanne* is, literally, *for a meaning.*

12. (b. 1. 12; a. 1. 12.) The tower is that mentioned in Pass. i. 15. *Truth* is here synonymous with the *Father of Faith,* i. e. God the Father and Creator.

15. (b. 1. 15; a. 1. 15.) *Fyue wittis,* five senses, viz. of hearing, sight, taste, smell, and touch. They are enumerated, for example, in Ælfric's Homilies, ed. Thorpe, vol. i. p. 138, where the A.S. names are "gesihþ, and hlyst, and swæc, and stenc, and hrepung." In Ratis Raving, ed. Lumby, pp. 29—32, we find their names, in Lowland Scottish, to be "sycht, heringe, smelinge, taist, and tuechinge." In the English translation of Grosteste's Castle of Love, ed. Weymouth, p. 57, 'speche' is substituted for *taste,* probably by mistake. In Pass. xvi. 256 is the passage—

"Bi so thow be sobre · of syght and of tounge bothe,
    In ondyng, in handlyng · in alle thy *fyue wittes.*"

Compare Tennyson's Song of the Owl:—

"Alone and warming his *five wits,*
    The white owl in the belfry sits."

20. (b. 1. 20; a. 1. 20.) *In comune thre thynges,* three things in common; viz. clothing, meat, and drink. "The chief thing for life is water, and bread, and clothing, and an house to cover shame." Ecclus. xxix. 21; cf. xxxix. 26. Hence, in Spenser, F. Q. i. x. 37—39, the first three of the seven beadmen, who perform works of mercy, are represented as supplying lodging, meat and drink, and clothing.

— (b. 1. 24; a. 1. 24.) *For myseise,* as a remedy against disease or discomfort. This curious use of *for* is worth notice. It is sufficiently common.

— (b. 1. 26; a. 1. 26.) *That thow worth,* so that thou become the worse
for it. Cf. note to l. 185 below.

25. (b. 1. 27; a. 1. 27.) Chaucer also cites this example of Lot, in the
23rd line of the Pardoner's Tale. See also the curious note by Tyrwhitt to
the Canterbury Tales, L 16993. And cf. B. Pass. xiv. 74—80.

. *For note to* b. 1. 31, *see note to* L 30.

29. (b. 1. 33; *not in* a.) The word *gerles* here refers to Lot's two sons,
Moab and Ammon. There are several examples of the application of the
word to the male sex. Thus, in the Coventry Mysteries, ed. Halliwell, p.
181, one of the Roman knights engaged in the Slaughter of the Innocents
says—"Here *knave* gerlys I xal steke," i. e. their knave-girls I shall pierce;
and again, at p. 182, he says—"Upon my spere A *gerle* I bere;" whilst, at
p. 186, we have the expression—"whan the *boys* sprawlyd at my sperys
ende." In Chaucer's Prologue, l. 664, the word *gurles* means young people;
there is nothing to shew of which sex they were. "It fared in earliest
English not otherwise with *wench.* This, in its diminutive form *wenchel,* is
applied in the Ormulum, l. 3356, to the newly born Babe in the manger;"
Trench, Select Glossary, s. v. *Girl.*

30. (b. 1. 31; *quotation not in* a.) The quotations from the Bible are, in
general, sufficiently close to the text of the Vulgate version. It is unnecessary to point out where they occur when (as here) the reference is sufficiently
indicated in the marginal note.

. *For note to* b. 1. 33, *see note to* l. 29.

33. (b. 1. 35; a. 1. 33.) "Moderation is a remedy, though thou mayst
desire much;" or, "mayst yearn for much [a, b]." This line reappears in
Richard the Redeles, ii. 139, q. v. "Mesure is a mery mene" is quoted as
a proverb both by Skelton and Heywood. See the lines upon it in Heywood's
Third Century of Epigrams (epigram 28), quoted in a note to Warton's
History of English Poetry, vol. iii. p. 90, ed. 1840. Another form of the
proverb is "Measure is treasure;" Dyce's Skelton, ii. 238, 241. In the
Ancren Riwle, p. 286, it takes the form—"Best is euer imete," moderation
is always best.

34. (b. 1. 36; a. 1. 34.) This means—"Not all which the body desires is
good for the soul, nor is all that is dear to the soul a source of life to the
body. Believe not the body, for a lying teacher instructs it, viz. this miserable world, which would fain betray thee."

38. (b. 1. 40; a. 1. 38.) This passage bears an entirely different sense
in the latest text from that which it has in the former ones. The C-text
means—"For the fiend and thy flesh follow (i. e. persecute thee) together,
whereas that protector (viz. Moderation) looks after thy soul, and whispers
to thy heart, and instructs thee to beware, and (warns thee of) what would
deceive thee." The B-text means—"For the fiend and thy flesh follow thee
together, and both *this* (i. e. the fiend) and *that* (i. e. thy flesh) pursue thy
soul, and suggest evil to thy heart," &c. The A-text means—"For the fiend
and thy flesh follow together, and put thy soul to shame; behold it (i. e. an
inclination to evil) in thine heart." In no text is the sense very clear.

40. (b. l. 42; a. l. 40.) For *ware*, *wary*, the B-text has *ywar*. This is an instance of the prefix *y-*, the A.S. *ge-*, being prefixed to an adjective. It is the A.S. *gewær*, wary, cautious, from which the modern form *aware* seems to have been corrupted, though its form would correspond better with the less common A.S. *on wáre*, in caution, on guard. *I wisse*, I teach, is to be distinguished from the adverb *I-wis*, certainly, which is only too often confounded with it; and both again are different from *I wot*, I know, and *I wist*, I knew, which are from the verb *to wit*.

45. (b. l. 47; a. l. 45.) *Aposed hym of*, questioned him concerning; for *of*, Texts A and B have *with*. For *appose* in the sense of to question, to examine, see the quotations in Richardson.

48. (b. l. 52; a. l. 50.) "Et ait illis Iesus: Cuius est imago hæc, et superscriptio? Dicunt ei, Cæsaris. Tunc ait illis: Reddite ergo quæ sunt Cæsaris, Cæsari; et quæ sunt Dei, Deo." Matt. xxii. 20, 21 (Vulgate).

52. (b. l. 56; a. l. 54.) "And (Common Sense should be) preserver of your treasure, and should bestow it on you in your need." The reading *tour* (= tower) of the A-text is probably due to an error of the scribes; the footnote shews that several A-text MSS. have the form *tutour*. If we retain *tour*, it must mean a safe place of custody. For the meaning of *take*, see note to Pass. iv. 47.

53. (b. l. 57; a. l. 55.) Here both C-text and A-text have *he*, referring to 'wit' (see footnote, A-text), i. e. to Common Sense. But the B-text has *hij*, i. e. they, referring to both Common Sense and Reason. *Husbandry* means economy, as in Shakespeare, Macbeth ii. 1. 4, "There's *husbandry* in heaven," because no stars were out. The phrase *to hold* (i. e. keep) *together* has occurred before; B. prol. 66.

54. (b. l. 58; a. l. 56.) *For hym*, for the sake of Him who made her.

55. (b. l. 59; a. l. 57.) Here the poet asks the meaning of the "deep dale," with reference to that described in Pass. i. 17. In [b] and [a] he enquires about the "dungeon in the dale," on account of the difference of the wording of the original description. See B. pr. 15; A. pr. 15. The word *dungeon* does not appear in Pass. i. of the C-text, and is consequently omitted in the present passage.

60. (b. l. 64; a. l. 62.) *Fond hit*, found, or discovered it [c]; *founded it*, originated it [b, a]. Here *it* refers to *falsehood*, not to the *castle of care*; for, with our author, to *found* is to *originate*, not *to lay foundations*.

62. (b. l. 66; a. l. 64.) *Cayme*, Caim. See note to Pass. i. 56.

63. (b. l. 67; a. l. 65.) *Iuwene*, of Jews. The gen. pl. ending is *-en* or *-ene*; see B. l. 105.

64. (b. l. 68; a. l. 66.) The idea that Judas hanged himself upon an *elder* occurs in Shakespeare, Love's Labour's Lost, v. 2. 610; and in Ben Jonson—"He shall be your *Judas*, and you shall be his *elder-tree* to hang on;" Every Man out of Hum. iv. 4. See Nares. On the other hand, we read that "the *Arbor Judæ* is thought to be that whereon Judas hanged himself, and not upon the *elder-tree*, as it is vulgarly said;" Gerrard's Herbal, ed. Johnson, p. 1428; quoted by Brand, Pop. Ant. iii. 283. Mr

Wright points out a passage in Sir John Maundeville, who says that the very elder-tree was still in existence when he visited Jerusalem; see p. 93 of Halliwell's edition of Maundeville's Travels.

65. (b. 1. 69; a. 1. 67.) *Lettare*, preventer, hinderer, destroyer. *Lyeth hem* [b, a], lieth to them, deceives them.

66. (b. 1. 70; a. 1. 68.) *That*, those that.

71. (b. 1. 74; a. 1. 72.) *Wissede*, instructed. See note to l. 40 above.

73. (b. 1. 76; a. 1. 74.) *Ich vnderfeng þe*, I received thee, viz. at baptism. Hence the allusion to *borwes*, i. e. pledges, sureties, in the next line.

——(b. 1. 82; a. 1. 80.) *Wroughte me to man*, shaped me so that I became a man. There are other instances of this phrase. Cf. B. 1. 62.

79. (b. 1. 83; a. 1. 81.) *Teche me to*, direct me to. *Teach* is here used in its original sense, to indicate, point out by a *token* or sign; the A.S. *tæcan* being cognate with the Greek δεικνυναι. *Thys ilke*, this same, this very thing. The word *tresour* alludes to l. 43; the dreamer now alters his question.

82. (b. 1. 86; a. 1. 84.) *Ich do hit on Deus caritas*, I appeal to the text *God is love* (1 John iv. 8) as my authority. Cf. *I do it on the kinge*, i. e. I appeal to the king; B. iii. 187.

84. (b. 1. 88; a. 1. 86.) The phrase *none other* [b] means—not otherwise (than the truth); and answers to *not elles* [a].

86. (b. 1. 90; a. 1. 88.) *By the gospel*, by what the gospel says. In the next line we are referred to St Luke, that is, to the parable of the unjust steward, where those to whom are to be committed the 'true riches' are taught to be faithful in that which is least; Luke xvi. 10—13. See also Luke viii. 21.

89. (b. 1. 93; a. 1. 91.) "Christians and heathens alike claim to learn the truth."

92. (b. 1. 96; a. 1. 94.) *Trangressores* [b] is marked in the MSS. as a Latin word. Latin words are strongly underlined, frequently with a *red* stroke.

93. (b. 1. 97; a. 1. 95.) This line, with a slight variation, reappears in Richard the Redeles, ii, 97.

₊ For *notes* to b. 1. 98, 99, *and* a. 1. 98, 99, *see note to* l. 97, *and the note next below it.*

94. (b. 1. 100; a. 1. 100.) *With hym and with hure*, with him and her, i. e. with every man and woman. Chaucer has the same expression— "Flemer of feendes out of him and here;" Man of Lawes Tale, l. 460.

97. (b. 1. 98; a. 1. 98.) *Apendeth to* [c, a], or *Appendeth for* [b] signifies pertains to, belongs to.

——(b. 1. 99; a. 1. 99.) *A Fryday*, one single Friday. *A Friday* generally means *on Friday*, but not here. Another reading is *o*, i. e. one.

₊ For *note to* b. 1. 102, a. 1. 96, *see note to* l. 102.

98. (b. 1. 104; a. 1. 102.) An *apostata* was one who quitted his order *after* he had completed the year of his noviciate. This is very clearly shewn by the following statement of a novice,—

" Out of the ordre thof I be gone,
 Apostata ne am I none,
Of *twelue* monethes me wanted *one*,
 And odde days nyen or ten."
        Monumenta Franciscana, p. 606.

The writer of this was one who had been a novice in the order of St Francis, but left it to become a Wicliffite. See my preface to Pierce the Ploughman's Crede, p. xiii. Compare—" And also [ye say], that a freer that leveth his hubit . . may not be assoiled till he take it againe, but is *apostata*, as ye saine, and cursed of God and man both ? "—Jack Upland, in Political Songs, ed. Wright, ii. 32. The form *apostata* occurs several times in Massinger; similarly, Shakespeare has *statua* for *statue*. The plural form *apostataas* is used by Wyclif; see Wyclif's Works, ed. Arnold, iii. 368, 430, 476.

99. *(not in* b, a.) *Forbere sherte*, to go without a shirt. This was a form of penance. See note on *wolwarde* in B. xviii. 1 (C. xxi. 1).

102. (b. 1. 102; a. 1. 96. *David, &c.* This may refer to 1 Sam. xxii. 2, to 1 Chron. xi. 1—3, or, still more probably, to 1 Chron. xii. 17, 18. When King Horn was dubbed a knight, as told in the romance of that name, he was girt with a sword, his spurs were fastened on him, and he was set upon a white steed. A few lines lower, at l. 105, we find Christ described as knighting the angels. *By hus daies,* i. e. in his time.

⁎⁎ *For note* to b. 1. 104, a. 1. 102, *see note to* l. 98.

105. (b. 1. 105; a. 1. 103.) *Kyngene kynge* [b, a], king of kings. The genitive plural in *-ene* is from the A.S. ending *-ena*, as in *Witena gemote*, meeting of wits (wise men). In like manner, we have *lordene,* i. e. of lords, in l. 95 above; and *Iewene,* of Jews, in l. 63. Wyclif says, in speaking of true religion, that—" Jesu Christ and his Apostles bene chiefe *knights* thereof, and after them holy Martirs and Confessours ; " Two Treatises against Friers, ed. James, p. 19; reprinted in Wyclif's Works, ed. Arnold, iii. 367. Observe Chaucer's use of the phrase " Christ's knights," with reference to Rom. xiii. 12, in the Second Nonnes Tale (C. T. 15851). It is well to remember that the original sense of *knight* was *servant*. In the A.S. version of the Gospels, the disciples are called " learning-cnihtas." Cf. Pass. ix. 47.

Ten ; so in all the MSS., otherwise we might have expected *nine ;* for the angels were generally distributed into three hierarchies of three orders each ; first, seraphim, cherubim, and thrones ; second, dominions, virtues, and powers ; third, principalities, archangels, and angels. William here enumerates the seraphim and cherubim, *seven such orders more*, and *one other*. But the *one other* is the order over which Lucifer presided, as implied by l. 107. This makes up the *ten* orders, as having been the *original* number. And that this is the true explanation is rendered certain by a passage in Early English Homilies, ed. Morris, 1868, p. 219, where the preacher enumerates the nine orders, and adds that the *tenth* order revolted and became evil ; that the elder of the tenth order was called ' *leoht berinde,*' i. e. light-bearing or Lucifer, who was beautifully formed, but who grew moody and said that he would sit in the *north part* of heaven, and be equal to the Almighty.   For this sin he was driven out of heaven with his host.   It must be added, that this *tenth* order was, in *one* instance, purposely reckoned as *above*, not *below*, the other nine; for the Franciscan Friars used to call themselves the Seraphic Order, having installed their founder, St Francis, "*above* the Seraphim, *upon tho throne from which Lucifer fell*."—See Southey's Book of the Church, ed. 1848, p. 182. A similar explanation is given in the Towneley Mysteries, p. 7:

> "*Ten orders* in heven were,
> Of angels, that had offyce sere;
> Of ich order, in thare degre,
> The ten parte felle downe with me [*i. e. with Lucifer*];
> For they held with me that tyde . . .
> God has maide man with his bend [*hands*]
> To have that blis withouten end,
> The *nine ordre* to fulfille
> That after us left, sich is his wille."

Here the last two lines mean—"to make up a tenth order in addition to the nine that remained behind after us; such is His will."   And in this case, the *tenth order* is mankind, and is reckoned as *below* the other nine; Ps. viii. 5.   In Ælfric's Homilies, ed. Thorpe, i. 343, is a passage which Mr Thorpe thus translates: "The Lord said yet another parable concerning ten shillings, and of which one was lost and was found.   That parable again betokens the nine hosts of angels.   Instead of the tenth host mankind was created; for the tenth had been found guilty of pride, and thrust from heavenly bliss to hell torments.   There are now nine companies, named *angeli, archangeli, virtutes, potestates, principatus, dominationes, throni, cherubim, seraphim*.   The tenth perished.   Then was mankind created to supply the place of the lost company."   In the Cursor Mundi, ed. Morris, p. 32, are the lines—

> "Of angels wald he serued be
> That suld of ordres haf thris thre;
> He ches till him, that lauerd hend,
> The men suld mak the ordre tend."

The arrangement in nine orders was drawn up by St Thomas Aquinas from the conceptions furnished by the pseudo-Dionysius.   Cf. Spenser, F. Q. i. 12. 39; Dante, Paradiso, c. 28; Tasso, Gier. Lib. 18. 96; Milton, P. L. 5. 748; Peacock's edition of Myrc's Instructions to Parish Priests, l. 766, and note; Warton's Hist. of Eng. Poetry, ed. Hazlitt, iii. 233, note 4; &c. Speaking of the Chester Mystery of the Fall of Lucifer, Dean Milman says,— "This drama, performed by the guilds in a provincial city in England, solves the insoluble problem of the origin of evil through the intense pride of Lucifer. God Himself is present on the scene; *the nine Orders* remonstrate against the overweening haughtiness of Lucifer, who, with the devils, is cast down into the dark dungeon prepared for them;"—Hist. of Lat. Christ. vi. 409; cf. Chester Plays, ed. Wright, p. 25.   See also the Ormulum, i. 34; and Chambers' Book of Days, i. 635.   Allusions to this fall of Lucifer are very common; see Wycliffe's Two Treatises, p. 35; Ayenbite of Inwyt, ed. Morris,

1868, pp. 16, 182; Genesis and Exodus, ed. Morris, 1865, p. 3; Cædmon, ed. Thorpe, p. 18, &c. Chaucer's Monkes Tale begins with the Fall of Lucifer. See a long note by myself in Notes and Queries, 3rd S. xii. 110; and cf. next note.

111. (b. 1. 117; *not in* a.) *Ponam pedem,* &c. An inexact quotation from Isaiah xiv. 13, 14: "In cœlum conscendam, super astra Dei exaltabo solium meum, sedebo in monte testamenti, in lateribus aquilonis. Ascendam super altitudinem nubium; similis ero Altissimo." It is curious that wherever the fall of Lucifer is mentioned, as in most of the places cited in the note above, there is often mention made also of Lucifer's sitting in the *north.* We find it even in Milton, P. L. v. 755—760:

> " At length into the limits of the *north*
>   They came; and Satan to his royal *seat,*
>   . . . .
>   The palace of great *Lucifer,*" &c.

So in Skelton's Colin Clout:

> " Some say ye sit in trones [thrones]
>   Like princes *aquilonis.*"

So in the Anglo-Saxon Version of the Hexameron of St Basil, ed. Norman, 1849, p. 16, which agrees closely with Isaiah; see Mr Kitchen's note (upon that text) to Spenser, F. Q. i. 4. 12. And, in Chaucer's Freres Tale, l. 115, the fiend lives "in the north contre." In our C-text, ll. 112—118, William inquires *why* Lucifer chose the *north* side, but fears he shall offend *Northern men* if he says much about it. Yet he hints that the north is the place for cold and discomfort, and suitable enough for the fallen angel. A still more explicit explanation will be found in the Myrour of Our Lady, ed. Blunt, p. 189, where the writer is explaining the sense of the Latin hymn commencing—Cœlestis erat curia. "Fyrste ye shall vnderstande that the northe wynde is colde and bytyng, and makyth fayre flowres som tyme to fade. And therfore by the northe ys vnderstonded the fende lucyfer, that by coldenesse of hys malyse caused other aungels that are lykened to fayre flowres to falle from blysse. The holy goste also ys vnderstonde by the sowthe," &c. And again, "The courte of heuen was fylled wyth fayre flowres, wherof the *nynte parte* faded, by the wodnesse [*madness*] of the northe." And, in the Icelandic Gylfaginning we find—"niðr ok norðr liggr Helvegr," i. e. downwards and *northwards* lieth the way to hell.

The author of the Gest Hystoriale of The Destruction of Troy (E. E. T. S. ed. Panton and Donaldson) had probably read Piers the Plowman, as appears from ll. 9247, 9320, and 9794, as compared with P. Pl. iii. 168, i. 167, and B. iii. 25 respectively. Hence it is probable that the passage in the Destruction of Troy, ll. 4395—4418, was really suggested by the present passage of our author.

112. (*not in* b, a.) Here *wolde . . . þan* = chose . . . rather than; see footnote to l. 114.

114. (*not in* b, a.) *Ther the day roweth,* where the day beams. The very uncommon verb *rowen* means to beam, lit. to make or shew *rows* or streaks;

it occurs again in Pass. xxi. 128. *Cf. day-rawe*, a day-streak, i. e. daybreak; see *Dayrawe* in Gloss. to Allit. Poems, ed. Morris (E. E. T. S.); also *dáyerewe* in Stratmann, p. 119; and cf. "rowes rede," i. e. red streaks, in Proem to Chaucer's Complaint of Mars, l. 2. The explanation "grows red" in note 4 to Pref. III, p. lxxxv, is therefore wrong. By the expression *sonne side* is meant the *south;* see ll. 117, 122.

116. (*not in* b, a.) *Lacke no lyf*, blame no man. See *Lyf* in the Glossary.

118. (*not in* b, a.) *No man leue other*, let no one believe otherwise.

124. (*not in* b, a.) *Hewes*, labourers. See Critical Note, C-text, p. 451.

——(b. l. 119; *not in* c, a.) *Nyne dayes.* So Milton—"Nine days they fell;" P. L. vi. 871; and so Hesiod (Theogony, 722) of the fall of the Titans.

127. (b. l. 123; a. l. 114.) Mr Wright says—"In the Master of Oxford's Catechism, written early in the fifteenth century, and printed in Reliquiæ Antiquæ, vol. i. p. 231, we have the following question and answer—*C.* Where be the anjelles that God put out of heven, and bycam devilles? *M.* Som into hell, and som reyned in the skye, and som in the erth, and som in waters and in wodys." This was an easy way of accounting for all classes of fairies, some of whom were supposed to be not malignant; for the fallen spirits were supposed to be not all equally wicked. The Rosicrusians, in like manner, placed the sylphs in the air, the gnomes in the earth, the salamanders in the fire, the nymphs in the water; and, as Pope says, in his Introduction to the Rape of the Lock—"The gnomes, or demons of the earth, delight in mischief; but the sylphs, whose habitation is the air, are the best-conditioned creatures imaginable." We find the same idea in the Cursor Mundi, ed. Morris, ll. 491—496; and in the Short French-verse copy of the Graal, in the History of the Holy Grayl, ed. Furnivall (Roxburghe Club, 1861), ll. 2101, &c., in vol. i. Appendix, p. 25. In Salomon and Saturn, ed. Kemble, p. 186, is a passage which Mr Kemble thus translates: "Tell me, whither departed the angels that apostatised from God in heaven? I tell thee, God divided them into three portions; one portion He placed in the drift of the sky; the second portion in the drift of the water; the third portion in the abyss of hell." The difference between fiery spirits, aërial spirits, water devils, and terrestrial devils is explained in Burton's Anatomy of Melancholy, pt. 1, sec. 2, mem. 1, subsec. 2. Some divided the air into three parts, as described in the Myrour of Our Lady, ed. Blunt, p. 303, where we are told that in the second part of the air "dwelle fendes vnto the day of doume; and there are gendered tempastes of weder, and hayle, and snowe, and thunder, and lyghtnynge and suche other. And therfore, in nyghtes tyme, when the lower parte of the ayre ys darke by absence of the sonne, and in tempastes of weder, the fendes come downe to the erthe more homly then in other tymes." This explains the first 'stage-direction' in Longfellow's Golden Legend—"Night and Storm. Lucifer, with the Powers of the Air, trying to tear down the Cross on the Spire of Strasburg Cathedral."

129. (b. l. 125; a. l. 116.) *Hym pokede* [c], urged him on; *he pult out* [b] is the same as *he put out* [a]; i. e. he put forth, exhibited.

131. (b. 1. 127; a. 1. 118.) *Ther wrong ys*, where Wrong is, i. e. where Lucifer is [c]; *with that shrewe*, with that wicked one [b, a]. *Shrew* was used for wicked people of either sex; see Trench, Select Gloss.; and Myrc, ed. Peacock, p. 69.

133. (b. 1. 130; a. 1. 121.) The expression *eastward* [*not in* a, b] refers to the idea already expressed in Pass. i. 14, that the tower of Truth, or abode of the Trinity, is situated in the East.

——(b. 1. 132; a. 1. 123.) The texts referred to are those cited above, viz. Reddite Cæsari, &c. (1. 48), and Deus caritas (1. 82). This line (omitted here in the C-text) occurs again below; see 1. 202 (b. 1. 204; a. 1. 182).

135. (b. 1. 134; a. 1. 125.) *Lere it þus lewede men* [c], teach it thus to unlearned men; or, *Lereth it this lewde men* [b, a], teach it to these unlearned men. To *lere* is to teach, *lerne* is to learn. *Lerne* sometimes also means *to teach*, as in provincial English; and sometimes even *lere* is *to learn*, as in Chaucer. In German, the words *lehren* and *lernen* are pretty well distinguished. *This* and *thise* are both used as plurals of *this*. A *lewd* man means a lay-man, as distinguished from a *clerk* or scholar.

137. (b. 1. 136; a. 1. 127.) *Kynde knowing*, natural understanding; but in 1. 142, the 'kynde knowyng' is identified with conscience.

138. (b. 1. 137; a. 1. 128.) "In what manner it grows, and whither (i. e. in what way) it is out of my intelligence," i. e. beyond my scope [c]; *or else*, "By what contrivance (*or* power) it commences to exist in my body, or where it begins" [b, a].

139. (b. 1. 139; *not in* a.) I have not yet traced the original of this Latin rimed (or Leonine) hexameter. Probably William composed it for the occasion. It recurs in Pass. viii. 1. 55.

144. (b. 1. 142; a. 1. 132.) The Latin quotation is in [c] only. There is something like it in Pope Innocent's treatise De Contemptu Mundi, i. 24; "Melius est ergo mori uitae quam uiuere morti." But if we turn to Pass. xviii. 40, we see that the reference is really to the story of Tobit, who preferred death to reproach; "expedit enim mihi mori magis quam uiuere;" Tobit iii. 6.

147. (b. 1. 146; *not in* a.) *Tryacle*, a sovereign remedy. "*Theriaca*, from which *treacle* is a corruption, is the name of a nostrum invented by Andromachus, who was physician to Nero;" Bacon's Advancement of Learning, ed. Wright; note at p. 296. Cf. "we kill the viper, and make a *treacle* of him;" Jeremy Taylor, vol. vi. p. 254. Again—

> "If poison chance to infest my soul in fight,
> Thou art the *treacle* that must make me sound."
> Quarles's Emblems; Bk. v. Embl. 11.

Pliny has—"Fiant ex uipera pastilli, qui *theriaci* uocantur a Græcis;" Nat. Hist. lib. xxix. c. iv; and, in lib. xx. c. xxiv, he gives a recipe for making a *theriacum*. See Southey's Common-Place Book, vol. ii. p. 599; Trench, English Past and Present; Trench, Select Glossary; &c. A full account of the history of this word is given by Professor Morley, at p. 21 of his Library of English Literature, with reference to the use of the word *triacle* in the old poem of The Land of Cokaygne, l. 84. The chief point to be observed is that it was considered to be an antidote against poisons, because it contained the flesh of vipers. Hence arose the saying that "venom expels venom," quoted by our author in Pass. xxi. 156, and further-illustrated by him with reference to the scorpion. Professor Morley observes that— "since *triacle* was an electuary made with honey and tinged with saffron, the uncrystallisable syrup that drains from the sugar-refiner's mould had some resemblance to it, and inherited its name." Cf. Rich. Redeles, ii. 151.

——(b. l. 147; *not in* a.) *That spise*, that species, that kind of remedy for sin; referring to Love or Charity.

——(b. l. 149; *not in* a.) *Lered it Moises*, taught it Moses; viz. in Deut. vi. 5, x. 12, &c.

149. (b. l. 150; a. l. 137.) *Plonte*, plant. By comparing the various footnotes, it is clear that the right reading is *plonte, plante*, or *plaunte;* and not *plente = plenty* [b], or *playnt = plaint* [a]. See Critical Note, B-text, p. 390; and cf. Isaiah liii. 2. *Prechet* [a] is put for *preche hit*, i. e. preach it, proclaim it.

——(a. l. 138; *not in* c, b.) "Where thou art merry at thy meat, when men bid you play and sing." This alludes to the very common custom of introducing music and singing at feasts. The guests not unfrequently took the harp as it was passed round, and displayed their skill. Thus, in Gower's Confessio Amantis, Appolinus, when a guest in the hall of king Pentapolin, takes the harp in his turn, and proves himself a proficient in the musical art. See Cutts, Scenes and Characters of the Middle Ages, p. 280.

Observe the use of the word *me* here; it is used as an impersonal pronoun, like the French *on*, and takes a verb in the singular number. The word ȝedde is the A.S. *giddian*, which occurs so frequently in Alfred's translation of Boëthius. Cf. *yeddinges* in Ch. Prol. 237.

150. (b. l. 151; *not in* a.) *Hit*, sc. love; here used of the love of Christ, which heaven could not contain, till it had "poured itself out upon the earth" [c], or till it had "eaten its fill of the earth" [b], i. e. participated in the human nature by Incarnation. When it had taken flesh and blood, it became light as a linden-leaf, and piercing as a needle.

152. (b. l. 154; *not in* a.) "As light as linden" was an old proverb, of which several examples may be found. It occurs, e. g. in the Towneley Mysteries, p. 80; Joseph of Arimathie, ed. Skeat, l. 585; Skelton, Bowge of Courte, l. 231; and probably has reference to the lightness of the wood of the linden or lime-tree, which caused it to be much used for making shields. Thus the A.S. *lind* is frequently used in the sense of shield. In the present case, the proverb takes the form "as light as a leaf upon a linden," with reference to the ease with which the breeze stirs the leaves of that tree; and Chaucer has the very expression in the Envoy to his Clerkes Tale—"Be ay of chere as lyght as leef on lynde."

159. (b. l. 160; *not in* a.) *The mercement he taxeth*, he imposes the fine. Blount, in his Law Dict., says—"There is a difference between *amerciaments*

and *fines:* these [i. e. the latter], as they are taken for punishments, are punishments certain, which grow expressly from some statute; but amerciaments are arbitrarily imposed by affeerors." See the whole of his article on *Amerciaments.* Cf.—"Of those who are at the mercy of his lordship the king, and have not been *amerced* in any sum;" Liber Albus, p. 69. "I soppose they wyl distreyn for the *mersymentes;*" Paston Letters, ed. Gairdner, i. 109. See Pass. ix. 37.

160. (b. 1. 161; *not in* a.) *To knowe it kyndely,* to understand it by natural reason; cf. ll. 137, 142. In Pass. xi. ll. 127—174, there is a description of the castle of *Caro* (man's body), which is guarded by the constable *Inwit* (conscience); and it is said of Inwit and of the five senses that—

"In the herte is hir home · and hir moste reste;" B. ix. 55.

163. (b. 1. 164; a. 1. 140.) *That falleth,* &c. That belongs to the Father; i. e. it is God the Father who implanted Conscience in man's heart.

166. (b. 1. 167; a. 1. 143.) *He,* sc. God the Son.

169. (b. 1. 170; a. 1. 146.) *One,* alone; dat. case of *on,* one, A.S. *án.*

175. (b. 1. 176; a. 1. 150.) *Eadem,* &c. Matthew vii. 2; Luke vi. 38. *Remecietur* is no misprint. Some Latin words are not always spelt alike in old MSS. Thus *scintilla* is frequently spelt *sintilla,* as in Pass. vii. 338, and *commodat* is spelt *comodat,* as in B. v. 246.

177. (b. 1. 178; a. 1. 154.) *That nother chit,* that neither chides. The expression *that in cherche wepeth* [b, a] probably refers to a child that is being baptized; baptism being often accompanied by tears on the part of the infant. The word *chast* here means innocent; and the application of the epithet to a child just baptized would be peculiarly appropriate.

178. (b. 1. 179; a. 1. 155.) *Bote yf,* unless. *Lene the poure* [c, b], lend to the poor; *loue the pore* [a], love the poor.

180. (b. 1. 181; a. 1. 157.) "Ye have no more merit in the saying of mass or of the 'hours,'" &c. The *hours* were the services said at stated times, viz. matins, prime, tierce, sext, nones, vespers, and compline.

181. (b. 1. 182; a. 1. 158.) The context shews that *Malkyn* is here equivalent to a wanton, but ugly slattern. "There's more maids than Maukins" is quoted as a proverb in Camden's Remaines, ed. 1657, p. 304; see Hazlitt's Proverbs, p. 392. The nearest parallel passage in Chaucer is at the 30th line of the Man of Lawes Prologue; but the name *Malkin* is probably also used with some significance in the Miller's Tale; C. T. 1. 4234, ed. Tyrwhitt. The word itself was probably originally regarded rather as the diminutive of the once common name Matilda than of Mary. Hence we find, in the Prompt. Parv.—"Malkyne, or Mawt, propyr name, Molt, Mawde. *Matildis, Matilda.*" In provincial English *mawkin* denotes various things that are put to a servile purpose, as, e. g. a cloth used to sweep out an oven (Prompt. Parv.), or a scarecrow. In Scotland, it means a hare. See *Malkin, Mawkin* in Halliwell's Dictionary, and Bardsley's English Surnames, p. 64.

184. (b. 1. 185; a. 1. 161.) "As dead as a door-nail" is still a common proverb; but there is an earlier instance of its use than in the present pas-

sage. It occurs twice in William of Palerne (ed. Skeat, ll. 628, 3396), which was written about A.D. 1350. Mr Timbs, in his 'Things not generally known,' says that the door-nail meant in this proverb is the nail upon which, in old doors, the knocker strikes; and which may accordingly, I suppose, be considered as particularly dead owing to the number of blows which it receives; and the same explanation is given by Webster. We find the proverb in Shakespeare.

> "*Falstaff.*   What, is the old king dead?
> *Pistol.*   As nail in door."—2 K. Hen. IV. v. 3. 125.

It is certain, however, that the term *doornail* was also used more generally, viz. of the nails with which doors in the olden times were so plentifully studded; for they were sold by the thousand, as we learn from Riley's Memorials of London, p. 262; and Burton speaks of the milky way as "that *via lactea*, or confused light of small stars, like so many nails in a door;" Anat. Mel. pt. 2. sec. 2. mem. 3. The B-text has *dore-tre*, i. e. door-post; *tree* being used here, as not unfrequently in our older authors, in the sense of timber or dead wood; cf. *rood-tree, axle-tree, boot-tree,* &c.; and see 'Specimens of English,' ed. Morris and Skeat, p. 239, l. 117.

The text referred to is—"Sicut enim corpus sine spiritu mortuum est, ita et fides sine operibus mortua est;" S. Jacob. ii. 26.

185. (b. l. 186, 192; a. l. 168.) *Worth,* shall be; lit. becomes. The word *worth* is here used as the sign of the future tense, as is so commonly the case with the cognate German form *wird.* Cf. *worst,* i. e. thou shalt be; Pass. viii. 265.

186. (b. l. 187; a. l. 163.) Dan Michel, in his Ayenbite of Inwyt (ed. Morris, p. 233) says that virginity with love is as a lamp without oil, and refers to the Parable of the foolish virgins. No doubt William was likewise thinking of that parable in writing the present passage.

191. (b. l. 191; a. l. 167.) "They chew up their charity (i. e. they eat up what they should give away), and then cry out for more." This striking expression was copied by William's imitator, the author of Pierce the Ploughman's Crede; see the *Crede,* ed. Skeat, l. 663.

192. (b. l. 194; a. l. 170.) *And encombred,* i. e. and, nevertheless, they are encumbered. For *encombred,* cf. Chaucer, Prol. 508.

195. (b. l. 197; a. l. 173.) "And it is a bad example, believe me, to the laity" [c]; or, "And it is a lesson to the laity, to be all the later in giving alms," i. e. to put off the giving away of alms [b, a]. We have *dele* in the same sense below (l. 197) in the phrase "for I dele yow alle," i. e. for it is I who distribute gifts to you all. For the use of *lewede,* cf. l. 135.

197. (b. l. 199; a. l. 175.) These words, '*date,* &c.,' begin the verse which has already been partially quoted above, at l. 175. See Luke vi. 38. There should probably be *no stop* at the end of this line in the A-text; but we should take the two unique lines of the Harleian MS. in immediate connection with it. The sense then is:—"for I distribute to you all your grace and your good luck, to help you win your livelihood; and do ye therefore,

by alms-doing, acknowledge me by means of that which I send you, in a natural manner."

198. (b. 1. 200; a. 1. 178.) The general sense is :—"and such alms-doing is like the lock (or, as we should now say, the *key*) of divine love, and lets out divine grace, to comfort the afflicted that are oppressed with sin."

200. (b. 1. 202; a. 1. 180.) "Thus love is the physician of life, and relief of all pain, and the graft (engrafting) of grace, and the most direct way to heaven" [c]; *or,* "Love is the physician of life, and next our Lord himself, and also the direct way that leads to heaven" [b]; *or,* "Love is the dearest thing that our Lord requires (i. e. that which He most expects of us), and eke," &c. [a].

201. (b. 1. 203; a. 1. 181.) The expression *graith gate,* meaning *direct way,* occurs in the History of Wallace, by Blind Harry, v. 135—
    "For thair sloith-hund the *graith gate* till him yeid;"
i. e. for their sleuth-hound went straight towards him.

202. (b. 1. 204; a. 1. 182.) Repeated from above; see l. 81.

205. (b. 1. 207; a. 1. 185.) The Texts end the Passus differently; the sense is either—"Love it, quoth that lady, for I may not stay longer to teach thee what love is; and therewith she took leave of me" [c]; or else, "I may no longer stay with thee; now may the Lord preserve thee" [b, a].

SCHEME OF THE CONTENTS OF C-TEXT, PASSUS III;

AS COMPARED WITH B. PASS. II AND A. PASS. II.

(Wright's edition, pp. 28—42; ll. 880—1355.)

C-TEXT.	B-TEXT.	A-TEXT.
iii. 1—6	ii. 1—6	ii. 1—6
7		
8—13	7—12	7—12
	13, 14	
14—18	*like* 15—19	*like* 13—15
19—21	20—22	*like* 16, 17
22		
23—27	23—27	*like* 18—20
28, 29		
0	28	21
31—35	*like* 29—33	
36—44	*like* 34—42	
45—48	*like* 43—46	*like* 22—29
		30—33
49—52	47—50	
53—57	51—55	*like* 34—36
		37—44
	56	

C-TEXT	B-TEXT	A-TEXT
iii. 58—73	ii. 57—72	like ii. 45—58
74—78	like 73	59
79—100	74—95	like 60—69
101—104	• like 96—100	—
105—108	like 101—103	like 70, 71
—	104—106	72—74
109—112	107—110	75—78
—	—	79
113—120	111—118	80—87
121—124		
125, 126	119, 120	88, 89
	121, 122	90, 91
—	—	
127—136		
137—150	like 123—136	like 92—106
151—161	137—147	107—117
—		118
162—174	148—160	119—131
175—180	like 161—164	132—135
—		136—139
—	165	• 140
—		141—143
—	166, 167	144, 145
181—189	like 168—178	like 146—153
190—198	179—187	154—162
199	—	—
200—213	188—201	163—176
(a) 214	(a) [204]	(a) 177
—		178, 179
215, 216	202, 203	180, 181
(a) [214]	(a) 204	(a) [177]
—		182
217	205	183
	206, 207	
—	208, 209	—
218, 219	208, 209	184, 185
220—242	210—232	186—208
243—248	—	—
249—252	233—236	209—212

NOTES TO C. PASSUS III. (B. Pass. II; A. Pass. II.)

2. (b. 2. 2; a. 2. 2.) *For marye loue, of heuene,* for the love of Mary of heaven. In exactly the same way we have *of the lordes folke of heuene* = of the people of the Lord of heaven, B. i. 157; and *for the lordes loue of heuene,* B. vi. 19; in both of which places the C-text has *in heuene,* probably as being a clearer expression; see C. ii. 156; ix. 16. Again we find *for crystes loue of heuene,* i. e. for the loue of Christ of (or in) heaven, B. vi. 223, where the C-text substitutes another phrase altogether.

5, 6. (b. 2. 5, 6; a. 2. 5, 6.) "Look upon thy left hand; and see where • he [Falsehood] stands; and not he only, but Favel [Flattery] also," &c.

The word *favel* here, signifying flattery (from Lat. *fabula*), must be carefully distinguished from the same word (cognate with German *fahl*) as used to denote the colour (or the name) of a horse. Occleve, in his De Regimine Principum, ed. Wright, pp. 106, 111, fully describes *favelle* or flattery, and says—"In wrong preisyng is all his craft and arte." So in Wiat's 2nd Satire, l. 67, we are told that it is base to

> "Affirme that *fauell* hath a goodly grace
> In eloquence," &c.

Skelton has the word also:—

> "The fyrste was *Fauell*, full of flatery,
> Wyth fables false that well coude fayne a tale;"
> > Bowge of Courte, l. 134.

See Dyce's Skelton, i. 35; ii. 107, 264. Douce, in his Illustrations to Shakespeare, i. 475, rightly distinguishes between the two words, and correctly remarks that the phrase 'to curry favour,' originally 'to curry favel,' is not connected with the word here used, but has reference to *favel* as denoting a yellow-coloured horse. The similarity of the words naturally drew them together, so that *to curry favel* easily took the sense of to flatter or cajole. See quotations for the phrase in Richardson and Nares, to which I can add the following:—

> "Sche was a schrewe, as have y hele,
> There sche *currayed favell* well."
> > How a Merchant did his Wyfe betray, l. 203;
> > in Ritson's Ancient Popular Poetry.

And again—"Curryfauell, a flatterer, *estrille;*" Palsgrave.

9. (b. 2. 8; a. 2. 8.) *A woman.* Here William carefully describes the Lady Meed, who represents both Reward in general, and Bribery in particular; the various senses of *Meed* are explained in Pass. iv. 292—342. Female dress at this date was very extravagant, and we may compare with the text the following remarks in Lingard's History. "Her head was encircled with a turban or covered with a species of mitre of enormous height, from the summit of which ribbons floated in the air like the streamers from the head of a mast. Her tunic was half of one colour, and half of another: a zone deeply embroidered, and richly ornamented with gold, confined her waist, and from it were suspended in front two daggers in their respective pouches;" vol. iv. p. 91. The present passage appears in the early text of 1362, otherwise William's description of Meed would have served admirably for Alice Perrers, who obtained a grant of Queen Philippa's jewels, and "employed her influence to impede the due administration of justice in favour of those who had purchased her protection;" and against whom the following ordinance was made in 1376: "Whereas complaint has been brought before the king, that some women have pursued causes and actions in the king's courts by way of maintenance, and for *hire and reward*, which thing displeases the king, the king forbids that any woman do it hereafter; and in particular Alice Perrers," &c. See Lingard, iv. 142. Indeed it is very likely that William perceived this likeness in first revising his poem; for the description

of Meed's clothing was amplified in the B-text, and he *added* the *very* significant line,

> "I had wondre *what she was* · and *whas wyf she were.*"

How Alice treated King Edward in his last illness is well known. Whitaker
suggests that the Lady Meed is the original of Spenser's *Lady Munera*; see
Spenser, F. Q. bk. v. c. ii. st. 9. Skelton, who borrowed several things from
our author, did not forget to introduce 'mayden Meed' into his Ware the Hauke,
l. 149. The following curious passage has a singular resemblance to the
description given in the text. It is printed in Reliquiæ Antiquæ, vol. ii. p.
19, from a fragment in MS. E. D. N. no. 27, in the College of Arms, and Sir
F. Madden supposed the writing, which is not easily legible, to be of the
time of Edward II. If so, our poet must (one would think) have met with
it; but may it not be an imitation of the A-text, which was written as early
as 1362? The passage in question runs thus :—

> "As I stod on a day · me-self under a tre,
> I met in a morueninge · a may [*maid*] in a medwe;
> A semlier to min sithe · saw I ner non:
> Of a blak bornet (?) · al was hir wede
> *Purfiled with pellour* · down to the teon [*toes*];
> A red hod on hir heved · shragid al of shridis,
> *With a riche riban* · *gold begon*" [i. e. encircled with gold].

10. (b. 2. 9; a. 2. 9.) *Purfild with peloure*, having her robe edged with
fur. See Chaucer's Prologue, l. 193, and Morris's note. Compare—"The
purful of the garment is to narowe'; *Segmentum* vestimenti est iusto angus-
tius;" Hormanni Vulgaria, leaf 110 b. See also the Book of the Knight
of la Tour-Landry, ed. Wright, p. 30. The laws about the kinds of furs to
be worn by different ranks were very minute in their particulars; see
Memorials of London, ed. Riley, pp. 20, 153. Furred hoods, in particular,
were much in fashion. Cf. Pass. vi. 129, 134.

— (b. 2. 14; *not in* a.) *Enuenymes to destroye.* It was a common belief
that precious stones could cure diseases, and that they were as antidotes
against poisons. Thus "Richard Preston, citizen and grocer, gave to the
shrine of St Erkenwald his *best sapphire stone*, for *curing of infirmities of
the eyes*," &c.; note in Milman's Lat. Christ. vi. 375; where Milman quotes
from Dugdale, p. 21. Burton praises the virtues of the "beryl, chalcidonye,
carbuncle, coral, emerald, saphyre," and other stones; and says of the
sapphire that it is "the fairest of all precious stones, of skye-colour, and
a great enemy to black choler, frees the mind, mends manners," &c.; Anat.
of Melancholy, pt. 2, sec. 4, mem. 1, subsec. 4. See also the alliterative
Morte Arthure, ed. Brock, ll. 212—215, and the Ancren Riwle, pp. 134—
136.

14. (b. 2. 15; a. 2. 13.) The word *engreyned* [b] means dyed in grain, i. e.
dyed of a fast colour. The verb *engreynen*, to dye of a fast colour, occurs in
B. xiv. 20; q. v. In Pierce the Ploughman's Crede, l. 230, a friar's kirtle
is described as being of such fine texture (*ground*) that it would bear being
dyed in grain. See the excellent note by Mr Marsh, in his Lectures on the

English Language (p. 55, ed. Smith), upon the signification of to *dye in grain;* and see *Greyn* in the Glossary to the Babees Book.

17. (b. 2. 19; a. 2. 15.) The force of *"What* is this womman" [b, a] is best given by the modern phrase *"what sort of a* woman is this?" A similar use of *what* occurs in Layamon, l. 13844, where Hengist, before describing himself and his companions, says—"Ich the wullen cuðen *what* cnihtes we beoð," i. e. I will inform thee *what sort of knights* we are.

19. (b. 2. 20; a. 2. 16.) *Mede* is here used in the worse of the two senses above indicated, viz. in the sense of Bribery. We find a good example of this use in the Chronicle of London [ed. Nicolas], p. 13, where we are told that, in the twelfth year of Henry III., a common seal was granted to the city of London, and it was ordered that any one who shewed reasonable cause should be permitted to use it, "and that no *mede* schulde be take no [*nor*] payed of eny man in no manner wyse for the said seall."

So again in A Song on the Times (about A.D. 1308)—

"Thos kingis ministris beth i-schend
　　To riȝt and law that ssold tak hede,
And, al the lond for tamend,
　　Of thos thevis hi taketh *mede*."
Political Songs, ed. Wright, p. 197.

"Many one for *mede* doþ ful euyl;
Me sey [*people say*] ofte—'*mede* ys þe deuyl;'"
Rob. of Brunne, Handlyng Synne, l. 8330.

Indeed, complaints of this character were, unfortunately, extremely common, and shew a disgraceful laxity of principle amongst advocates and judges at this period. In l. 23, Bribery is said to be intimately known even in the Pope's palace, just as is so explicitly declared in A Poem on the Times of Edward II.—

"Voiz of clerk is sielde [*seldom*] i-herd at the court of Rome,
Ne were he nevere swich a clerk, silverles if he come."
Political Songs, ed. Wright, p. 324.

20. (b. 2. 21; a. 2. 17.) *Leaute,* Loyalty. William arrays Love, Loyalty, Soothness, Reason, Conscience, Wisdom, and Wit on the one side, and Meed (daughter of Favel or False), Wrong, Favel or Flattery, Simony, Civil, Liar, and Guile upon the other. Wisdom and Wit waver in their allegiance, but are won back again. The texts partially differ.

27. (b. 2. 27; *not in* a.) *As men of kynde karpen,* as men say concerning kinship. The B-text has—*as kynde axeth,* as nature requires or provides; cf. Rich. Redeles, ii. 191. For *bona* some MSS. have *bonus,* for the sake of euphony, much as in French we have *mon* for *ma* before nouns beginning with a vowel.

30. (b. 2. 28; a. 2. 21.) *Herre,* higher; see the various readings. With this form compare *ferre,* farther; Chaucer's Prol. 48; *derre,* dearer, Ch. Kn. Tale, 590; *nerre,* nearer, in the proverb—"Nere is my kyrtyl, but *nerre* is my smok;" Paston Letters, ed. Gairdner, i. 542.

——(b. 2. 31; *not in* a.) *To marye with myself;* we should now arrange the words, *to marry myself with. With* in Early English is always near its verb, a puzzling arrangement to a learner. So in P. Pl. Crede, "to coueren with our bones," l. 116. So again, in l. 116 [b] below, *to wratthe with treuthe* means to anger Truth with. Mercy is here the dowry which Holy Church brings to the man who espouses her.

39. (b. 2. 38; *not in* a.) See Ps. xv. 1 (called Ps. xiv. in the Vulgate).

41. (b. 2. 39; *not in* a.) *Mansed*, cursed. The word *maused* in Mr Wright's text is a misprint, as he explains in a note on p. 537, and in his Glossary. See Pass. xxiii. 221, and Rich. Redeles, iii. 105.

49. (b. 2. 47; *not in* a.) *Lete hem worthe*, &c.; let them be, till Loyalty be a justice or judge. Cf. note to Pass. i. 201.

51. (b. 2. 49; *not in* a.) *Ich bykenne the crist*, I commend thee to Christ; *crist* is here in the dative case.

55. (b. 2. 53; a. 2. 35.) *Retynaunce*, retinue, suite of retainers; for various spellings see footnotes to [b] and [a]. The word is rare, but is used by Gower (qu. in Halliwell), and in Wyclif's Works, ed. Arnold, iii. 478, where we have the plural *retenauncis;* (printed *retenauntis*, as it may have been written, owing to the confusion between *c* and *t*; though there are some misprints in this edition which cannot be laid upon the scribes.) Though the word is not easily to be found in the French Dictionaries, it presents no difficulty, being formed from *retenir*, just as *maintenance* is from *maintenir*.

56. (b. 2. 54; a. 2. 36.) *Brudale*, bride-ale or bridal. An *ale* means a feast merely. There were leet-ales, scot-ales, church-ales, clerk-ales, bid-ales, and bride-ales. At the *bride-ale*, moreover, the bride herself often brewed ale for her wedding-day, which her friends purchased at a high price, by way of assisting her and amusing themselves at the same time. This led to abuses, and we find in the court-roll of Hales Owen, in the 15th year of Elizabeth, an order "that persons brewing wedding-ale to sell, should not brew above 12 strike of malt at most." See Brand's Popular Antiquities, ed. Ellis, ii. 144.

——a. 2. 43 (*not in* c; b). *A proud*, a proud one; a good illustration of *a fayr* as used by Chaucer, Prol. 165.

60. (b. 2. 59; *not in* a.) *Brokours*. In the reign of Edward I., a law was passed that "no one shall be *broker*, but those who are admitted and sworn before the Mayor;" Liber Albus, ed. Riley, p. 505. The duties of the *bedel* are to be found in the same work, at p. 272. See note to l. 111.

63. (b. 2. 62; *not in* a.) In Passus xxiii., the church is described as assailed by numerous enemies. One is *Simony*, who causes good faith to flee away, and falseness to abide (xxiii. 131), and who boldly vanquishes much of the wit and wisdom of Westminster Hall by the use of many a bright noble. He is also there described as contriving divorces. Skelton introduces the 'dame Simonia' in his Why Come ye Nat to Courte, l. 212. Simony is introduced again, as a person, in Sir Peny, printed in Ancient Scottish Poems, 1770, p. 154:—

> "So wily can syr Peter wink,
> And als sir Symony his servand,
> That now is gydar of the kyrk."

And again, in an ancient Scottish poem, ibid. p. 253, many disorderly persons are invited to a feast, amongst whom are "Schir Ochir and Schir Simony;" i. e. Sir Usury and Sir Simony. See Warton's Hist. of Eng. Poetry, ed. Hazlitt, iii. 287, note 5.

The exact signification of *sisour* does not seem quite certain, and perhaps it has not always the same meaning. The Low-Latin name was *assissores* or *assissiarii*, interpreted by Ducange to mean—"qui a principe vel a domino feudi delegati *assisias* tenent;" whence Halliwell's explanation of *sisour* as a person deputed to hold assizes. Compare—

> "Þys fals men, þat beyn *sysours*,
> Þat for hate a trewman wyl endyte,
> And a þefe for syluer quyte;"
>
> Robert of Brunne, Hand. Synne, 1335.

Mr Furnivall's note says—"*Sysour*, an inquest-man at assizes. The *sisour* was really a juror, though differing greatly in functions and in position from what jurymen subsequently became; see Forsyth's Hist. of Trial by Jury." In the tale of Gamelyn, however, it is pretty clear that "the xii *sisoures* þat weren on þe quest" (l. 871) were simply the twelve gentlemen of the jury, who were hired to give false judgment (l. 786). By *Cyuile* is meant a practitioner in the civil law.

66. (b. 2. 65; *not in* a.) *Brocour* is here used in the general sense of a contriver of bargains, a match-maker.

67. (b. 2. 66; *not in* a.) *Here boþeres wil* [c], or *here beire wille* [b], means "the will of them both."

79. (b. 2. 74; a. 2. 60.) The form of this mock charter may be compared with that of the charter whereby the Black Prince was invested, in 1362 (the very year in which William wrote the first version of his poem) with the principality of Aquitaine. It is given at length in Barnes's Life of Edward III. Compare the curious Charter of John, constable of Chester, quoted by Ritson, in his Metrical Romances, vol. i. p. clxxxv; and cf. p. ccxxii of the same volume.

81. (b. 2. 76; *not in* a.) *Hye kynde*, loftiness of nature, or perhaps simply high rank [c]; *free kynde*, liberal nature, liberality, generosity [b]. Cf. *fredom* = liberality, in Chaucer, Prol. 46; and the phrase "be *fre* of thy dispence" in the Envoy to the Clerkes Tale.

83. (b. 2. 78; a. 2. 61.) *Feffed*, has granted; or, as in [b], *Feffeth*, grants to them; lit. *enfeoffs*, i. e. invests them with a fief or fee. In l. 160, *feffe* means simply *to fee.* See also l. 137. An instance of the use of it will be found in the Glossary to the Babees Book; and the Promptorium Parvulorum has— "Feffyd, *feofatus, feofactus*." In Blount's Law Dictionary we find—"*Feoffment* signifies *donationem feudi*, any gift or grant of any honours, castles, manors, messuages, lands, or other corporeal or immoveable things of like nature, to another in fee; that is, to him and his heirs for ever;" &c.

85. (b. 2. 80; *not in* a.) *To bakbyten*, to backbite or defame. See the quotations in Richardson, to which I may add—*Bacbitares* þe biteð oðre men bihinden;" Ancren Riwle, p. 86; and the following:

"What sey ye of þys *bakbyters*,
Þat wykkcde wurdes aboute bers?"

Rob. of Brunne, Hand. Synne, l. 1514.

"Euere behynde a mannys bak
Wyþ euyl þey fynde hym to lak;"

Rob. of Brunne, Hand. Synne, l. 3538.

"A nedder and a *bakbytere;*"—ibid. l. 4173.

See also note to B. v. 89.

91. (b. 2. 85; a. 2. 65.) The expression *alle the costes about* [b] means—all the borders of it, all the neighbouring country; cf. Matt. viii. 34. The expression *I crovne hem togedere* [a] means—I invest them with conjointly, giving them a crown as the symbol of investiture.

92. (b. 2. 87; *not in* a.) In a note in his glossary, s. v. *brocage*, Mr Wright explains the term to mean a treaty by a broker or agent, and adds—"It is particularly applied to treaties of marriage, brought about in this way. In the Romaunt of the Rose, l. 6971, Fals Semblant says—

'I entremcte me of *brocages*,
I make péce and mariages.'

So in the Miller's Tale (C. T. 3375) it is said of Absolon—

'He woweth hire by menes and *brocage*,
And swor he wolde ben hire owen page;'

that is, he wooed her by the agency of another person, whom he employed to persuade her to agree to his wishes."

The borghe of thuflhe, the borough of Theft.

94. (b. 2. 89; *not in* a.) *Waitynges of eyes*, watchings with the eyes, i. e. wanton looks, amorous glances. Cf. *after mede wayten*, i. e. look wistfully for some bribe, in l. 78 above.

96. (b. 2. 91; *not in* a.) "Where the will is ready, but power fails." Cf. Pass. vii. 184, 193.

99. (b. 2. 94; *not in* a.) *Iangle*, to gossip, to chatter idly. *Iape*, to mock, to gibe. See note to B. prol. 35, and compare the following.

"*Jangelyng* is whan a man spekith to moche biforn folk, and clappith as a mille, and taketh no keep [*heed*] what he saith;" Chaucer, Persones Tale, De Superbia. "A philosophre saide, whan men askid him how men schulde plese the poeple, and he answerde, 'do many goode werkes, and spek fewe *jangeles.*' After this cometh the synne of *japers*, that ben the develes apes, for thay maken folk to laughen at her *japes* or *japerie*, as folk doon at the gaudes [*tricks*] of an ape; suʒh *japes* defendith [*forbids*] seint Poule;" ibid., De Ira. "Ye are fulle of *iangelyng*, and haue an euelle tonge, and canne not holde youre pees;" Knight de la Tour, ed. Wright, p. 39. "He is but a tromper [*deceiver*] and a *japer*;" ibid., p. 33. See Chaucer for several other examples of both words. In Robert of Brunne's Handlyng Synne, ll. 9263, seqq., is a tale of some women who *jangled* in church. In Horman's Vulgaria, leaf 76 b, we find—"He is a great iangler; *Impendio loquax.*" Many examples might be added. Cf. B. x. 31.

100. (b. 2. 95; *not in* a.) *Frete*, to eat, viz. before the proper time for eating arrived. See Pass. vii. 434.

104. (b. 2. 100; *not in* a.) It is necessary to remember that *he* and *hus* in this line are used vaguely and indefinitely, so that *he* is merely put for *such a one.* In the B-text, the apparent change from the plural to the singular, in *his* (l. 98) following upon *hem* (l. 97) is to be explained in a similar manner. There are many other similar examples in our author.

105. (*not in* b, a.) "During this life to follow Falseness, and the folk that believe on him."

106. (b. 2. 102; *not in* a.) Before *a dwelling*, i. e. a habitation, an abode, we must supply *he geueth hem*, from l. 97. In the B-text, it follows as an accusative case after the verbs *to have and to hold* in the preceding line.

——(b. 2. 104; a. 2. 72.) ȝeldyng, giving up in return; cf. Pass. vii. 343. Compare the phrase—"to yield a crop;" Cymbeline, iv. 2. 180.

110. (b. 2. 108; a. 2. 76.) *Of paulynes queste* apparently means, belonging to the inquest or jury of Paulines; but in [b], the phrase is *of paulynes doctrine*, of the doctrine (or order) of the Paulines; and in [a] it is *Paulynes doctor*, a doctor of the Paulines. *Literæ Paulinæ* is explained by Ducange to mean letters of excommunication, and, as William expressly lets us know that the Paulines were busy in the consistory courts, they may have been principally concerned with such matters. The name is not common, but I have observed the following uses of it. "In the same yere [1310] began the ordre of *Paulyns*, that is to say, Crowched Freres."—A Chronicle of London (edited in 1827, and published by Longmans), p. 43. But Matthew Paris says that the order of Crutched Friars came into England A.D. 1244. In a poem called the Image of Ypocrisie, written about A.D. 1533, a list is given of orders of *monks*, which includes the *Paulines*, the Antonines, Bernardines, Celestines, &c. The word *Paulynes* occurs again below, b. 2. 177; a. 2. 152 (*not in* c).

111. (b. 2. 109; a. 2. 77.) *Budele.* "The duties of the beadle, in ancient times, lay more on the farm than in the law-court. . . . In many places, the bedelry and the haywardship were held together by one person," &c. See Nooks and Corners of English Life, by Timbs; p. 233. The oath of the Bedels is given at p. 272 of the Liber Albus. They were to suffer no persons of ill repute to dwell in the ward of which they were bedels, to return good men upon inquests, not to be regrators themselves, nor to suffer things to be sold secretly. And at p. 289 of the same we find—"Item, that the *bedel* have a good horn, and loudly sounding." It is remarkable that, in [c], William changed *Bokyngham-shire* (which was celebrated for thieves, see Hazlitt's Proverbs, p. 94) into '*Banbury soken.*' This may have been an intentional fling at the beadle of Banbury, with whom he may have quarrelled; for it is to be noted that Banbury is at no great distance from Shipton-under-Wychwood, where William's father is said to have farmed land. It is somewhat remarkable, also, that Latimer uses the term "Banbury glosses" to signify corruptions of the truth; Latimer's Works (Parker Soc.), ii. 299.

The word *soken*, or *soke*, as in *Hamsoken*, *Portsoken*, is sufficiently well-known as a law-term. It means (1) a privilege; and (2) the district within which such a privilege or power is exercised. Chaucer (Reves Tale, C. T. 3985) uses *soken* of a miller's privilege of grinding corn within a particular district.

113. (b. 2. 111; a. 2. 80.) *Munde the miller* is mentioned again in B. x. 44, where the term denotes an ignorant fellow. Here it doubtless means a thief; cf. Chaucer, Prol. 562.

114. (b. 2. 112; a. 2. 81.) Skelton also has the remarkable expression "in the deuylles date"; Bowge of Courte, ll. 375, 455; Magnyfycence, ll. 954, 2198. But he may have copied it from William.

130. (*not in* b, a.) The word *lexita* in Low-Latin merely means *deacon;* see Ducange. There were several saints named Lawrence, but *the deacon* is the one most famous and best known. His day is August 10, and a good account of him will be found in Chambers' Book of Days under that date; vol. ii. p. 196. He suffered martyrdom at Rome about A.D. 257 or 259, by being broiled on a gridiron over a slow fire. In Ælfric's Homilies, ed. Thorpe, i. 416, will be found a long account of his martyrdom. Among the words which he is represented as saying during his last torture is a passage bearing some resemblance to the text, which Mr Thorpe thus translates :—" I will offer myself to the Almighty God . . . for the afflicted spirit is an acceptable sacrifice to God"; p. 431. And again, at p. 427, he is represented as saying—" Saviour Christ, God of God, have mercy on thy servant; for, accused, I denied thee not; questioned, I acknowledged thee." The expression "open heaven's gates" clearly refers to the story on the same page, to the effect that the saint prayed "that these standing about may know that thou comfortest thy servants;" whereupon a soldier named Romanus beheld an angel standing before St Lawrence with a handcloth, wiping his sweating limbs. The fine east window of the church of St Lawrence at Ludlow contains numerous representations of various passages in the saint's life.

142. (b. 2. 128; a. 2. 98.) The phrase *but if* [b, a] is practically *one* word, with the meaning *except, unless.* Chaucer has it also; Cant. Tales, Group B, 2001, 3688; Group F, 687; &c.

143. (b. 2. 129; a. 2. 99.) The word *fikel* [b] is equivalent to *faithles* [c], or to *a faylere* [a]. The sense of *fikel* in Middle Eng. is not *changeable*, but *treucherous;* see Pass. iv. 158. A good example of the word in the same sense occurs in Havelok, l. 1210.

151. (b. 2. 137; a. 2. 107.) *Wytty is treuthe*, wise is Truth. It must be remembered that Truth means God the Father, as in Pass. ii. 12.

154. (b. 2. 140; a. 2. 110.) *Bisitte* [b, a], or *sitte* [c], means—sit close to, press upon, oppress. *Ful soure* [c, b], very bitterly; *sore* [a], sorely. In my edition of Chaucer's Prioresses Tale, &c. is a note to C. T. Group B, 2012, which I here reprint. 'Chaucer has here *Abyen it ful soure*, very bitterly shalt thou pay for it. There is a confusion between A.S. *súr*, sour, and A.S. *sár*, sore, in this and in similar phrases; both were once used, but we should now use *sorely*, not *sourly*. In Laȝamon, l. 8158, we find "þou salt it sore abugge," thou shalt sorely pay for it; on the other hand we find in P. Plowm. B. 2. 140—

"It shal bisitte ʒowre soules·· ful *soure* atte laste."
So also in the C-text, though the A-text has *sore*. Note that, in another
passage, P. Plowm. C. xxi. 448 (B. xviii. 401), the phrase is—" Thow shalt
abygge *bitere*," thou shalt bitterly pay for it.'

.157. (b. 2. 143; a. 2. 113.) *Floreynes*, florins; the name of which is derived from the city of Florence; indeed, we find the spelling *florences* three
times in the Percy Folio MS., ed. Hales and Furnivall. We read in Fabyan
(ed. Ellis, p. 455) under the year 1343—"In this yere also, kynge Edwarde
made a coyne of fyne golde, and named it the *floryne*, that is to say, the
peny of the value of vis. viii*d*., the halfe peny of the value of iiis. iiii*d*., and
the farthynge of the value of xx*d*., which coyne was ordeyned for his warris
in Fraunce; for the golde thereof was not so fyne as was the noble, whiche
he before in his xiiii. yere of his reygne had causyd to be coyned." So in
Thomas Walsingham, vol. i. p. 262, ed. Riley. The value of a *noble* was
also 6*s*. 8*d*. See note to Pass. iv. 47.

174. (b. 2. 160; a. 2. 131.) *Westemynstre*. William seems to have been
very familiar with the courts of law at Westminster, as appears from the
present and two following Passus. In Pass. xxiii. 284, we again find him
speaking of the 'false folk' who repair 'to Westmynstre.' The number of
statutes enacted there in the reign of Edward III. is considerable. See Liber
Albus, p. 470.

175. (b. 2. 161; a. 2. 132.) Those who had horses could anticipate
others at the court, by performing the journey more quickly, and they could
thus obtain a first audience and administer a bribe. In a poem on The Evil
Times of Edward II. we have—

"Coveytise *upon his hors* he wole *be sone there*,
And bringe the bishop silver, and rounen in his ere."
                                        Polit. Songs (Camd. Soc.), p. 326.

William, however, represents Meed as riding on the back of a sheriff, and
makes False and Favel ride upon reeves, &c.; or, as in the B-text, which is
differently expressed, he supposes sheriffs and sisours to serve for horses, puts
saddles on the sompnours, and turns provisors into palfreys.

178. (*not in* b, a.) The curious word *saumbury* does not occur elsewhere,
to my knowledge, in English literature. But it is easy to see what it means,
and whence it was derived. The reading *I-sadeled* is a gloss upon *in saumbury*, so that the sense is that Meed was to be carried about very gently in
a comfortable saddle, or rather, as we shall see presently, in a sort of litter.
A *saumbury* means, I suppose, a comfortable litter for a lady to ride upon,
and is evidently closely connected with the old word *saumbue*, a saddle-cloth,
which occurs in MS. Harl. 2252, fol. 115, as quoted in Halliwell's Dict. s. v.
Sambus.

Turning to Roquefort's Glossaire, we find the following :—
"*Sambue*, housse d'une selle de cheval, harnois.
          Un palefrois bien enselez
          D'une moult riche *sambue*.—Roman de Merlin, MSS."
"*Sambue*, sorte de char principalement à l'usage des dames, litière ;" &c.

Burguy gives it only in the former sense, and gives the Old High-German form as *samboh* or *sambuh.* Ducange has—"*Sambuca*, sella equestris ad mulicrum usum." Wackernagel gives the High-German forms thus:— "*Sambüch, sambuoch, sombóch,* Art verhängter Frauen- und Kriegs-Wagen, ml. *sambuca.*" It also appears in Low-Latin in the form *sabuta;* since Ducange has—"*Sabuta*, currus quo nobiles feminœ uehebantur species: item currus uel equi ornatus." The latter is clearly a more corrupt form, due to the loss of *m* before *b*; indeed, Ducange cites the form *sambuta* also. The sense is clear; and we may suspect that the word was of Teutonic origin.

Fram syse to syse, from one assize to another.

182. (b. 2. 170; a. 2. 148.) *Provisor* sometimes means a purveyor; but here has the usual sense in which it is employed in our statutes, viz. one that sued to the Court of Rome for a *provision.* A *provision* meant the providing of a bishop or any other person with an ecclesiastical living by the pope, before the death of the actual incumbent. The great abuses occasioned by this practice led to the enactment of the statutes of *Provisors* (25 Edw. III. c. vi., 27 Edw. III. c. i. § 1, and 38 Edw. III. c. i. § 4, and c. ii. § 1—4), wherein it was enacted that the bishop of Rome shall not present or collate to any bishopric or ecclesiastical benefice in England; and that whoever disturbs any patron in the presentation to a living, by virtue of a papal provision, such provisor shall pay fine and ransom to the king at his will; and be imprisoned till he renounces such provision. And the same punishment was enacted against such as cite the king, or any of his subjects, to answer in the court of Rome. See Blount's Law Dict., Wordsworth's Eccl. Biog. p. 145, and Blackstone's Comment. bk. iv. c. 8.

187. (b. 2. 172; a. 2. 150.) The curious form *southdenes* (*suddenes*, b; *sodenes*, a) is only a variation of *sub-deans;* cf. the spelling *subdeanes* in MS. C [b]. In Robert of Brunne's Handlyng Synne, l. 1680, we have "*Suddekene*, or dekene hy," where his French original has—"*Sodekene*, deakene, et presbiter." Similarly, in a Poem on the Evil Times of Edward II., ed. Hardwick (Percy Society), stanza 66, the word *sub-bailiffs* takes the strange form *southbailys.* Respecting such forms as *supersedeas*, Pegge, in his Anecdotes of the English Language, p. 141, remarks—"Writs in law processes for the most part take their names from the cardinal *verb* on which their force turns, and which, from the tenor of them, is generally in the subjunctive mood, as being grammatically required by the context. . . . These being formerly in Latin, and issuing in the king's name, the proper officer was called upon in the second person of the singular number, after a short preamble," &c. Hence *habeas, capias, supersedeas, fieri-facias,* and the like; and amongst them is *summoneas*, which has been corrupted into *summons*, and is, accordingly, in the singular number. A writ of *supersedeas* is, most often, a writ or command to suspend the powers of an officer in certain cases, or to stay proceedings.

——(b. 2. 173—175; *not in* c, a.) "As for archdeacons, &c., cause men to saddle them with silver, in order that they may permit our sin, whether it be adultery or divorces, or secret usury."

——(b. 2. 177; a. 2. 152.) *Paulynes prynes.* It may be that *prynes* is here the plural adjective, agreeing with *Paulynes,* as *French* adjectives not unfrequently ·take *s* in the plural. If so, the phrase means "the confidential Paulines." Otherwise, it must mean "the confidential men of the Paulines' fraternity;" which comes to much the same thing. The MSS. of the A-class read *Paulines peple,* i. e. the people of the Paulines. Cf. note to l. 110, above.

191. (b. 2. 180; a. 2. 155.) This means—"And provide food for ourselves from (or at the expense of) adulterers." The whole passage refers to the practice of prosecuting or fining such victims as would prove most profitable. A parallel passage may be found in Chaucer's Prologue, ll. 649—665.

196. (b. 2. 185; a. 2. 160.) *Tome,* leisure. The adjective *toom* means empty. *Toom tabard* (empty tabard) was a nickname given to the king of Scotland, John Baliol, on account of his little wit. It occurs in Burns' Halloween: "Because he gat the *toom* dish thrice," &c. In William of Palerne, l. 3778, the bodies of the slain in battle are collected and borne

"til the tentis, til thei might haue · *tom* hem to berie."

See also Cursor Mundi, ed. Morris, 1206, 2128. This word is not to be confused with *time.*

204. (b. 2. 192; a. 2. 167.) *And,* if [c, b]; *ʒif* [a]. *And* is often written for *an,* if; and conversely, *an* is often written for the copulative conjunction *and,* as in B. ii. 207.

208. (b. 2. 196; a. 2. 171.) *Maynpryse,* furnish bail, be security for. A person arrested for debt or any other personal action might find *mainprise* or bail, before the sheriffs or their clerks thereunto deputed. The person finding bail was called a *mainpernour,* lit. a taker by the hand, by metathesis from *mainpreneur.* See Liber Albus, p. 177; and cf. Pass. v. ll. 84 and 107. The word is well illustrated by the following passage. "My seyd Lord hayth putte a bille to the Kynge, and desyryd meche thÿnge, qwych is meche after the Comouns desyre, and all is up-on justice, and to putte all thos that ben indyted under arest with-owte suerte or *maynpryce,* and to be tryed be lawe as lawe wyll." It is evident that the finding of mainprise was used for screening rich offenders, and defeating the ends of justice.

212. (b. 2. 200; a. 2. 175.) *Eny kynnes yiftes,* gifts of any kind. *Eny kynnes* is the genitive singular, and is also spelt *enys kynnes,* or even assumes the odd form *any skynes;* as in MS. T [a].

216. (b. 2. 203; a. 2. 181.) *For eny preier,* in spite of any prayer. Cf. note to l. 240.

217. (b. 2. 205; a. 2. 183.) *Dene,* din, noise [c]; *dome,* sentence, decision [b, a], as in Chaucer, Prol. 323. Though the word *din* is not in Stratmann, it is not uncommon; it occurs in Old Eng. Hom. 2nd Ser. p. 117, on which Dr Morris has the note—"See An Old Eng. Miscell. (ed. Morris), 25, 782; Gen. and Ex. 3467; Allit. Poems, B. 862; Troy Book. 1197. O.E. *dýne, gedýne,* thunder, din."

221. (b. 2. 211; a. 2. 187.) *Dud hym to gon,* prepared himself to depart.

The compassion shewn to Guile by merchants, and to Liar by pardoners, grocers, minstrels, and friars, is a brilliant touch of satire. See Pref. I (A), p. ix.

223. (b. 2. 213; a. 2. 189.) For pictures of London *shops*, see Chambers' Book of Days, i. 350.

226. (b. 2. 216; a. 2. 192.) "Lurking through lanes, pulled about by many." The word *lug* is especially used of pulling by the *lugs* or ears. "*Lugg*, to pull by the ears. 'I'll *lugg* thee, if thou do'st so;' *North;*" Pegge's Supplement to Grose's Prov. Dict. See Rich. Redeles, iii. 336.

228. (b. 2. 218; a. 2. 194.) "Everywhere hooted (or hunted) away, and bidden to pack off." *Ouer-al* is here just the German *überall*. Some MSS. favour the reading *hooted*, others *hunted;* it makes but little difference. See Rich. Redeles, iii. 228.

240. (b. 2. 230; a. 2. 206.) *For knowynge of comers*, to prevent recognition by visitors or strangers.

249. (b. 2. 233; a. 2. 209.) *Flowen into hefnes*, fled away (or escaped) into corners or hiding-places. A good example of *flowe* in the sense of *fled* will be found in Merlin, qu. by Ellis in his Met. Rom. (ed. Halliwell), p. 109.

> "Did so that alle the other *flowe*,
> And this kinges *flowen* also."

252. (b. 2. 236; a. 2. 212.) *Atachèd*, taken prisoner. "Persons attached on suspicion were in general allowed to go at large, in the interval before trial, upon surety or bail;" note to Liber Albus, p. 73; cf. pp. 77, 78, 88, 183, 349. See Pass. iv. 18, 19.

SCHEME OF THE CONTENTS OF PASSUS IV.

(B. Passus III; A. Passus III.)

Cf. Wright's edition; pp. 43—64; ll. 1356—2078.

C-TEXT.	B-TEXT.	A-TEXT.
iv. 1—10	iii. 1—10	iii. 1—10
11	—	—
12—18	11—17	11—17
19	18	—
20	19	18
—		19, 20
21—31	20—30	21—31
32, 33	—	
34—39	31—36	32—37
—	37	38
40—43	38—41	39—42
(a) [49]	(a) 42	(a) 43
44	—	
45—48	43—46	44—47

C-TEXT.	B-TEXT.	A-TEXT.
iv. (a) 49	iii. (a) [42]	iii. (a) [43]
50—52	47—40	48—50
. 53—55	like 50, 51	like 51, 52
56—64	52—60	——
65 ·	like 61	like 53
66	62	
67, 68	63, 64	54, 55
69—72	65—68	
73	69	(2) { 61
——	70—72	{ 62—64
74		(1) { 56, 57
75, 76	73, 74	{ 58—60
——		{ 65, 66
——	75	——
77, 78	like 76, 77	like 67, 68
79, 80	78, 79	69, 70
81	like 80—82	like 71—73
82--85	83—86	74—77
86—114	——	——
115—126	87—98	78—89
	99	90
——		91—94
127, 128	100, 101	95, 96
	102	97
——	——	98
129—132	like 103, 104	like 99, 100
133	105	101
(b) [137]	(b) 106	(b) 102
134	107	103
. 135, 136	——	——
(b) 137	(b) [106]	(b) [102]
	108	104
138—145	——	——
146—169	109—132	105—128
170	——	——
171—189	133—151	129—147
190	——	——
191, 192	152, 153	148, 149
(c) [201]	(c) [162]	(c) 150
193—196	154—157	151—154
197	158	——
198—200	159—161	155—157
(c) 201	(c) 162	(c) [150]
202	163	——
203—210		
211	like 164	like 158
212	——	——
213	like 165	like 159
	166	160
214—233	167—186	161—180
——	187—199	181—193

C-TEXT.	B-TEXT.	A-TEXT.
iv. 234—258	—	—
259—265	iii. 200—206	iii. 194—200
	207	201
266—277	208—219	202—213
	220	214
278—282	221—225	215—219
283, 284	*like* 226	*like* 220
285—287	227—229	221—223
	230—233	224—227
		228—230
	234—244	
	245—249	*like* 231—236
288—312		
313, 314	*like* 250—252	*like* 237—239
	253, 254	240, 241
315, 316	255, 256	242, 243
317—411		
412—419	*like* 257—261	*like* 244—248
		249
420—428	*like* 262—270	*like* 250—256
429—437	*like* 271—279	*like* 257—265
438, 439	280, 281	
(d) [442—445]	(d) [284—287]	(d) 266—269
440, 441	282, 283	270, 271
(d) 442—445	(d) 284—287	(d) [266—269]
446, 447	288, 289	272, 273
448	290	
449—452	291—294	274—277
453, 454	*like* 295, 296	*like* 278, 279
		280
455, 456	297, 298	281, 282
457—496	*nearly* 299—339	
	340—343	
497—501	*like* 344—349	

NOTES TO C. PASSUS IV. (B. PASS. III; A. PASS. III.)

13. (b. 3. 12; a. 3. 12.) *That,* i. e. they that, they who; cf. *they that* [b], *heo that* [a]. Many of the minor difficulties of construction can be at once solved by simple comparison of the three texts. It is therefore unnecessary to point them out in every case.

14. (b. 3. 13; a. 3. 13.) *Somme* (which is the reading of nearly all the MSS. of the B- and C-types) is simply the modern word *some*, but must be considered as partitive, and hence equivalent to *some of them.* This is certainly the right explanation. I thought at one time that we might take it to mean *together;* cf. A.S. *samen, sqmod,* together; indeed, the word *samen* actually occurs just below, in l. 27. But the A.S. *gesome* can hardly bear this sense of together; it means rather at peace, reconciled; see Cædmon, ed. Thorpe, p. 6, l. 1; *some* = reconciled, in Layamon, l. 9883; *gsome* (possibly meaning *at peace*) in Robert of Gloucester, ed. Hearne, p. 40, l. 10; all of which point away from the word here employed. The A-text simply has *soone* or *sone*, i. e. soon.

20. (b. 3. 19; a. 3. 18.) *Conscience's cast and craft*, Conscience's contrivance and art. In [b], the reading is *conscience*, which is merely another form of the genitive case. "In O.E. of the 15th century, if the noun ended in a sibilant or was followed by a word beginning with a sibilant, the possessive sign was dropped; as, a *goose* egg, the *river* side;" Morris, Hist. Outlines of Eng. Accidence, p. 102. Hence the phrase "for *conscience* sake," Rom. xiii. 5; and the like.

23. (b. 3. 22; a. 3. 23.) The MSS. carefully distinguish between the spellings of the words *coupes* and *cuppes* here; and for *cuppes* we have, in [a], the reading *peces*. The words must, therefore, not be confused, if we can avoid it; and I think it possible that our author intended to make a distinction in sense between the French *coupe* and the A.S. *cuppa*, both borrowed, probably, from the same Latin word, viz. *cuppa*. *Coupe* may perhaps denote a vessel of large size, or a bowl. Thus, in Layamon, l. 24612, where the earlier text says that Sir Bedivere went foremost with a golden bowl (mid guldene bolle), the later text has the words 'mid gildene *coupe*;' yet, unluckily for the purpose of distinction, we find *bolle* equated, in another passage, to *coppe*; viz. in l. 14996. We find also '*coupes* of golde' in the Ayenbite of Inwyt, ed. Morris, p. 35, but the context does not help us. The form *coppe* or *cuppe* seems to have been chiefly used for a smaller drinking-vessel, containing enough for one person only; cf. Chaucer, Prol. 134, and note the following quotation. "Some do vse to set before euerye man a lofe of bread, and *his* cup, and some vse the contrary;" Babees Book, p. 67. That this, smaller cup was also called a *pece*, appears from the Promptorium Parvulorum, p. 388, where Mr Way quotes the following:—"A pece of siluer or of metalle, *crater, cratera*."—"*Crater, vas vinarium*, a pycce or wyne cuppe."—"*Pece*, to drink in, *tasse*. Pece, a cuppe, *tasse, hanap*." It was called *pece* to distinguish it from the *pot* or large flagon.

> "A capone rosted broght she sone,
> A clene klath, and brede tharone,
> And a *pot* with riche wine,
> And a *pece* to fil it yne."
>
> Ywaine and Gawin, l. 757 (Ritson's Met. Rom. i. 33).

The phrase 'peces of siluer' occurs again below, in B. 3. 89.

25. (b. 3. 24; a. 3. 25.) *Moton.* "Ye shall vnderstande that a *moton* is a coyne vsed in Fraunce and Brytaygne, and is of value, after the rate of sterlynge money, upon vs., or thereabout."—Fabyan's Chronicles, ed. Ellis, p. 468. It was so called from its bearing an impression of a *lamb* (or *mutton*); on the other side was a figure of St John the Baptist. In Cotgrave's French Dictionary, we find—"*Mouton à la grande laine*, a sheep wellwoolled, or of great burthen; also, a coine of gold stamped on the one side with a sheep, on the other with a cross *fleury*, having at each angle a flowerde-luce; John duke of Berry first caused it to be made about the year 1371." Cotgrave, however, must refer here to a different coinage. They were really

in use at an earlier period; as, at p. 297 of Memorials of London, ed. Riley, there is mention made (under date A.D. 1357) of a Teutonic knight, from whom some unknown thieves stole 400 golden shield-florins and *moutons d'or*, of the coinage of Philip and John, kings of France. Hence there is nothing strange in the use of the word in the A-text, written in 1362. The word is explained by Ducange, under its Low-Latin form *multo*.

26. (b. 3. 25; a. 3. 26.) *Had lauht here leue at*, had taken their leave of. *To lacche leue*, to take leave, is a common phrase. The author of the Alliterative 'Troy-Book,' ed. Panton and Donaldson, has a line almost identical with this one, as it stands in [b] and [a]. "Than laght thai hor leue, tho lordes, in fere;" l. 9794.

The taking of bribes seems to have been a common failing with justices at this time. Compare—

"Hoc facit pecunia Quam omnis fere curia jam duxit in uxorem; Sunt justiciarii Quos favor et denarii alliciunt a jure."

Polit. Songs (Camd. Soc.), p. 225.

In particular, ladies seem to have had great influence:

"Sed si quædam nobilis Pulcra, vel amabilis, cum capite cornuto, auro circumvoluto, Accedat ad judicium, Hæc expedit negotium, ore suo muto.'

See also note above, Pass. iii. 9.   *Ibid.* p. 226.

34. (b. 3. 31; a. 3. 32.) *Do calle*, cause to be called over. When the verb *do* is followed by an *active* verb in the infinitive mood, the latter is commonly best interpreted by giving it a *passive* signification. Numerous examples of this are given in my Glossary to William of Palerne, s. v. *Done*. Thus, in l. 66 below, we may consider *do peynten and portreyn* as equivalent to "cause it to be painted and pourtrayed." So also *dón saue* = cause to be saved, Pass. x. 328.

35. (b. 3. 32; a. 3. 33.) *Shal no lewednesse lette*, no ignorance shall hinder.

37. (b. 3. 34; a. 3. 35.) "Where really skilful clerks shall limp along behind in the rear." See *Clokke* in Glossary.

38. (b. 3. 35; a. 3. 36.) *Frere*. Great sinners went to confession to a *friar* rather than to a parish-priest. Wycliffe complains of this, saying— "For commonlie if there be anie cursed Jurour [swearer], extortioner, or avoutrer [adulterer], he will not be shriuen at his owne Curate, but go to a flattering Friar, that wil assoile him falsly, for a little mony by yeare, though he be not in wil to make restitution, and leaue his cursed sinne." Two treatises against Friars, ed. James, 1608; p. 53; or Wyclif's Works, ed. Arnold, iii. 394; cf. pp. 377, 387. See Chaucer, Prol. 223.

47. (b. 3. 45; a. 3. 46.) *Took hym a noble*. Tyrwhitt remarks (note to Cant. Tales, 13852), that—"*to take*, in our old language, is also used for *to take to, to give*, as in l. 13334,

He *tok* me certain gold, I wot it wel."

Pecock, in his Repressor, i. 285, distinguishes between *take* = to lend, and *ʒeue* = to give, in the following sentence. "Oon scoler seith to an other

scoler thus: Y *take* this book to thee, that thou leerne in it . . . neither the scoler seith to his felow thus, Y ʒeue to thee this book, that thou leerne in it."
• Whether the *noble* or *florin* was first coined, and what was the exact value of them, seem somewhat doubtful, unless we can depend upon the statement of Fabyan quoted above, Pass. iii. 157, and upon the following statement of the same, under the year 1339,—"In this yere also the kynge chaungyd his coyne, and made the noble & the half noble of the value of vi *s.* viii *d.*, which at·this day is worthe viii *s.* ix *d.* or x *d.*, & the halfe noble after the rate, if they kepe the trewe weyght," &c.   There is a similar statement in A Chronicle of London, p. 57, under the 14th year of Edward III., which seems, as in Fabyan, to signify 1339 rather than 1340:—"also the kyng made the coyne of goold: that is for to seyne, the *noble*, the half noble, and the ferthyng."   Walsingham gives the date 1343 for the coinage of *florins ;* but some consider the true date to be 1344,   In the English Cyclopædia, under the heading *Coin*, we are told that—"it is from Edward III. that the series of English gold coins really commences, for no more occurs till 1344, when that prince struck florins.   The half and quarter-florin were struck at the same time.   The florin was then to go for *six shillings*, though now it would be intrinsically worth nineteen.   This coin being inconvenient, as forming no aliquot part of larger ideal denominations, seems to have been withdrawn.   None have yet been found, but a few quarter-florins are preserved in cabinets, and one half-florin is known.   In consequence, in the same year, the noble was published, of 6 *s.* 8 *d.* value, forming half a mark, then the most general ideal form of money.   The obverse represents the king standing on a vessel, asserting the dominion of the sea.   The noble was also attended by its half and quarter.   This coin, sometimes called the *rose noble*, together with its divisions, continued the only gold coin, till the angels of Edward IV., 1465, and the angelets or half-angels, were substituted in their place.   Henry V. is said to have diminished the noble, still making it go for its former value.   Henry VI. restored it to its size, and caused it to pass for 10 *s.*, under the new name of ryal," &c.   William clearly intimates that *florins* were by no means scarce, and this seems at first sight to contradict that which has been said above.   But the fact is simply, that most of the florins were coined abroad, chiefly at Florence; and it was ordered that florins de escu, and florins of Florence, should be current along with the sterlings, according to their value.   Compare note to l. 25, where mention is made of the knight who lost 400 shield-florins (florins de escu) and moutons d'or.   And see Ruding's Annals of the Coinage.

51. (b. 3. 48; a. 3. 49.) "We have a window in working (i. e. being made), that will stand us very high," i. e. that will cost us a large sum.   For *stonden*, [b] has *sitten*, but the sense is the same.   A list of people who glazed windows for a new church of the Friars Minors is given in Monumenta Franciscana, p. 515.   One of the names of subscribers to the expense is that of Isabella, mother of Edward III.   The practice of glazing windows is satirized also by William's imitator in the *Crede*, ll. 123—128.   It was usual to introduce

portraits or names of the benefactors in stained glass. In his notes to Myrc's Instructions for Parish Priests, at p. 76, Mr Peacock remarks that "the following inscription, wrought in stained glass, once decorated a window in the church of Blyton, co. Lincoln. 'Priez for ye gild of Corpus Xpi [i. e. *Christi*] quhilk yis window garte mak.'—Harl. MS. 6829, f. 193." See ll. 64—74 below.

62. (b. 3. 58; *not in* a.) Lechery was one of the seven deadly sins. See Pass. vii. 170; and note to Pass. vii. 3.

67. (b. 3. 63; a. 3. 54.) The word *sustre* (sister) has a direct allusion to the letters of fraternity, by means of which any wealthy person could belong to a religious order of the mendicant friars. "Another marvellous way," says the Rev. F. C. Massingberd, "by which the rich were brought to share in all the graces of poverty, without practising its privations, was by *conventual letters*, or charters of fraternization; by which the person presented with them was entitled to all the benefit of the prayers, masses, and meritorious deeds of the order;" English Reformation, p. 118. Cf. Pass. x. 342, 343; and xxiii. 367.

71. (b. 3. 67; a. 3. 59.) *Thy kynde wille*, *(and) thi cost;* "thy natural disposition, and thy expenses; as also their covetousness, and who really possessed the money" [c, b]; or, "God knoweth who is courteous, or kind, or covetous, or otherwise" [a].

——(b. 3. 73; a. 3. 71.) *Or to greden after goddis men,* or to cry out for God's men, i. e. to send for the friars.

——(b. 3. 75; *not in* c, a.) "For thus the Gospel bids good men give their alms." *Bit* is for *biddeth;* so also *rat* = readeth, Pass. iv. 410; *rit* = rideth, B. iv. 13; *halt* = holdeth, B. iii. 241; &c.

77. (b. 3. 76; a. 3. 67.) The passage contained in C. iv. 77—85 (B. iii. 76—86; A. iii. 77—87) was the one printed in Parallel Extracts from twenty-nine MSS. of Piers Plowman, edited by myself for the E. E. T. S. in 1866, by way of preparation for the present edition. Since that date, many additional MSS. have been brought to light, so as to make it worth while to reprint this passage from all the MSS. that are accessible; and this, accordingly, I propose to do. See the remarks on the dialect of this passage in Pref. II. p. xliii (B-text).

79. (b. 3. 78; a. 3. 69.) *Pillories.* Under the xvth year of Edward IV., Fabyan tells us that—"this yere this mayer [Robert Basset, salter] dyd sharpe correccion vpon bakers for makynge of lyght brede, in so muche that he sette dyuerse vpon the pyllory, ... and a woman named Agnes Deyntie was also there puuysshed for sellyng of false myngyd [mixed] butter." Lydgate has a ballad about Fraudulent Millers and Bakers, whose true heritage is the pillory (MS. Harl. 2255); it is printed in the Appendix to A Chronicle of London. In Riley's Memorials of London, there is frequent mention of the punishment of the pillory for various offences, chiefly for fraudulent practices. Thus, in A.D. 1316, two bakers were so punished for making bread "of false, putrid, and rotten materials; through which,

persons who bought such bread were deceived, and might be killed, p. 121. In A.D. 1387, a baker's servant was put on the pillory for inserting a piece of iron into a loaf, in order to make it seem of full weight; p. 498. Others were so punished for enhancing the price of wheat, pp. 314, 317; for selling putrid meat or carrion, pp. 240, 266, 271, 328, &c.; for selling sacks of charcoal of short measure, p. 446; &c. Sometimes fraudulent bakers were drawn upon a hurdle; ibid. pp. 119, 120, 122, 423. A particular kind of pillory for women was called the thewe; ibid. pp. 319, 367, 368, 486, 525. Compare the following passage:—

> "Bakares and breowares for alle men heo gabbe;
> Lowe heo holdeþ heore galun, mid beorme heo hine fulleþ,
> And euer of þe purse þat seoluer heo tulleþ;
> Boþe heo makeþ feble heore bred and heore ale,
> Habbe heo þat seoluer, ne telleþ heo neuer tale."
>
> An Old English Miscellany, ed. Morris, p. 189.

See also Mr Peacock's excellent note upon this subject in his edition of Myrc's Instructions for Parish Priests, p. 80. Myrc gives a form for excommunication, which includes under the ban "alle þat falsen or vse false measures, busshelles, galones & potelles, quartes; or false wightes, poundes, or poundrelles; or false ellen yerdes, wetyngly, oþer þan þe lawe of þe lond woll;" ibid. p. 22. See also Strutt, Manners and Customs, ii. 73; and a long note to Hudibras, ed. Bell, vol. i. p. 231. Cf. note to Pass. v. 122.

Pynyng-stoles, stools of punishment, also called *cucking-stools*. The *cucking-stool* was a seat of ignominy; see Chambers' Book of Days, i. 211.—"In Scotland, an ale-wife who exhibited bad drink to the public was put upon the *Cock-stule*, and the ale, like such relics of John Girder's feast as were totally uneatable (see Bride of Lammermoor) was given to the poor folk." It was different from the *ducking-stool*, which was a punishment for scolds. See Brand; Popular Antiquities, iii. 102 (note), and 103. Brand seems to confound the two. Cf. note to Pass. v. 122.

——(b. 3. 80; a. 3. 71.) This line recurs in Rich. Redeles, iii. 216.

——(b. 3. 81; a. 3. 72.) *Parcel-mele*, by small parcels, i. e. retail.

82. (b. 3. 83; a. 3. 74.) *Regratrye*, selling by retail. The wholesale dealer was called an *Engrosser* (whence our *grocer*), because he sold in the *gross* or *great* piece. The retail dealer was called a *Regrater* or *Regrateress*; cf. ll. 113, 118, and Pass. vii. 232. Cotgrave has—"*Regrater*, to dresse, mend, scowre, furbish, trim, or trick up, an old thing for sale."—"*Regrateur*, m. An huckster; mender, dresser, scowrer, trimmer up of old things for sale."—"*Regratiere*, f. An hucksteresse; also, a Regrateresse." See Memorials of London, ed. Riley, where regrators of ale are forbidden to sell ale on London bridge, A.D. 1320. And again, in Riley's translation of the Liber Albus, p. 232, we read—"No baker shall give unto the *regratresses* the six-pence on Monday morning by way of hansel-money, or the three-pence on Friday for curtesy-money; but, after the ancient manner, let him give thirteen articles of bread for twelve." It is worth while to add, that this last passage explains clearly the meaning of the common expression, *a baker's dozen*—meaning *thirteen*.

The bakers did not sell the bread to the public, but to the regratresses, or women who took the bread round to each customer's door.   The regratress's profit came from the fact that, according to "the ancient manner," she received 13 *loaves at the price of* 12 from the baker, and sold them *separately* to various customers afterwards at a price which was duly regulated and might not be exceeded.   Such restriction of prices was strictly enforced in the various markets; see the numerous regulations of this kind in the Liber Albus and the Memorials of London.   But if, on the one hand, we are wiser than our ancestors in permitting free competition in trade, we are sometimes unwisely lax, on the other hand, in repression of fraud and adulteration.   The frauds and adulterations of the *regraters* were a constant source of annoyance, and were frequently complained of.   Compare—

> "Si status conspicimus, nullus excusatur:
> Quod in shopis venditur, male mensuratur;
> Quilibet perjurio vel fraude lucratur, &c."
> > Monumenta Franciscana, ed. Brewer, p. 593.

84. (b. 3. 85; a. 3. 70.) "For, if they had made their profits honestly, they would not have built (houses for themselves) so loftily; nor could they have bought for themselves such tenements; be ye full sure of it."

Wyclif has the following remarks upon this subject.   "Also it semeth that marchauntis, groceries, and vitileris rennen in the same curs fully.   For thei conspiren wickidly togidre that noon of hem schal bie over a certeyn pris, though the thing that thei bien be moche more worthi, and thei knowen wel this; and that non of hem schal sille betere chepe [*sell cheaper*] than another, though he may wel forth it so, and it be not so moche worth as another mannis chaffer; thus he schal be ponysched sore yif he do trewe and good conscience.   Certis all this peple conspirith cursedly ayenst treuthe, charite, and comyn profit;" Works, ed. Arnold, iii. 334.

87. (*not in* b, a.) "Though they deliver to them a dishonest quantity, they consider it as no fraud; and, though they do not fill up to the top the measure that has been scaled according to law, they grasp as much money for it as they would do for the full true measure."   The allusion is to the scaling or marking of measures, to insure their being true.   Thus it was ordered, "that no brewster or taverner shall sell from henceforth by any measure but the gallon, pottle, and quart; and that these shall be scaled with the seal of the Alderman; and that the tun of the brewster shall be of 150 gallons, and be sealed with such seal of the Alderman;" &c. &c.   Liber Albus, ed. Riley, p. 233.

93. (*not in* b, a.) Compare a similar passage in Pass. xx. 268—271.

106. (*not in* b, a.) In 1276, a fire occurred in the city because a man left a candle burning and fell asleep; Riley's Mem. of London, p. 8.   In 1302, Thomas Bat bound himself to keep the city indemnified from peril of fire that might arise from the circumstance that his houses were covered with thatch; ibid., p. 46.

108. (*not in* b, a.) In a Charter of Edward the Second, we find it ordered

"that an inhabitant [of the city of London], and especially an Englishman by birth, a trader of a certain mistery or craft, shall not be admitted to the freedom of the city aforesaid except upon the security of six reputable men, of such certain mistery or craft," &c.; Liber Albus, ed. Riley, p. 127; see also pp. 388, 425. It is clear, from William's complaint, that men who had enriched themselves contrived to obtain the freedom of the city without too close enquiry as to the manner in which their wealth had been acquired.

117. (b. 3. 89; a. 3. 80.) *Presentes.* Presents made, not in money, but in silver cups, &c. See note to l. 23.

——(b. 3. 90; a. 3. 81.) To *maintain* was to aid and abet others in wrong-doing, by supplying them with money or exerting influence in their behalf. It was a recognized law term; and Blount observes that—"there lies a writ against a man for this offence, called a Writ of Maintenance. See Coke on Littleton, fol. 368 b." Cf. Paston Letters, ed. Gairdner, i. 145, 151; Wyclif's Works, ed. Arnold, iii. 322; and see ll. 231, 288, below.

123. (b. 3. 95; a. 3. 86.) The quotation is not from Solomon, but from Job xv. 34:—"fire shall consume the tabernacles of bribery." Mr Kemble justly points out that this is one of the numerous instances in which wise sayings were commonly attributed to Solomon, whether they were his or not. See Salomon and Saturn, ed. Kemble, p. 108.

125. (b. 3. 97; a. 3. 88.) The sense of *blewe* in this passage is no doubt livid, dull gray; cf. Icel. *blár*, livid. So in the Towneley Mysteries, p. 224, we have "as *blo* as led," as livid as lead. Compare our phrase—"to beat black and *blue*." Palsgrave has—"*Blo*, blewe and grene coloured, as ones body is after a drie stroke, *iaunastre:*" see Dyce's Skelton, ii. 103.

——(b. 3. 99; a. 3. 90.) *Yeresyyues,* lit. year-gifts. "*Yeresgive* is a toll or fine taken by the king's officers on a person's entering an office; or rather, a sum of money or bribe, given to them to connive at extortion or other offences in him that gives it; see Chart. Hen. II.; fourth Chart. Hen. III.; and ninth Chart. Hen. III.;" Privilegia Londini, by W. Bohun, of the Middle Temple, 1723; quoted in Notes and Queries, 4th Ser. iv. 560. This definition perfectly suits the present passage, but we may fairly assume, from the form of the word, that it once meant an *annual* donation (like the modern Christmas box), generally given, it would appear, upon New Year's day. It came to be so troublesome that we find special exemptions from it, as in the following:—"Also, that the city of London shall be quit of Brudtol, and Childewite, and *Yeresgive,* and Scot-ale;" Liber Albus, ed. Riley, pp. 117, 138.

Palsgrave has—"Newe-yeres gifte, *estrayne;*" and Cotgrave—"*Estreine,* f. a New-years Gift, or Present; also, a Handsell."

127. (b. 3. 100; a. 3. 95.) *The kynge.* Richard II. had just ascended the throne when the first revision of the poem was made, but the description was originally intended for Edward III., for whom it is much more suitable. See notes to ll. 163 and 233.

129. (b. 3. 103; a. 3. 99.) *As hus kynde wolde,* as his nature disposed him. See Pass. ix. 161, and Rich. Redeles, ii. 142.

138. (b. 3. 107; a. 3. 103.) The C-text varies here somewhat. The sense (of that text) is—"Yet I forgive thee this offence; it is God's forbidding (i. e. may God forbid) that thou vex me and Truth any more; if thou mayst be taken (in such an offence), I shall cause thee to be enclosed in Corfe castle, as if you were an anchorite there, or in some much worse abode;" &c. Corfe Castle (*not mentioned in* b, a) is well described in Timbs's Abbeys, Castles, and Ancient Halls of England, vol. ii. pp. 371—376. The allusion is doubtless significant. It was in Corfe Castle that Edward II. was confined in 1327, before his removal thence to Bristol, and finally to Berkeley. Again, the use of the word anchorite may refer to the curious story of the hermit Peter, who prophesied evil to king John, for which he was "committed to prison within the castle of Corf; [and,] when the day by him prefixed came without any other notable damage unto king John, he was by the kings commandement drawne from the said castell into the towne of Warham, and there hanged, togither with his sonne;" Holinshed's Chronicle, sub anno 1213. See Shakespeare's King John, iv. 2. 147, and Mr Staunton's note upon the passage. There is, too, a grim humour in the words "oþer in a wel wors wone;" for Mr Timbs quotes from Dr Maton's Observations, vol. i. p. 12, the following remarks upon Corfe Castle. "We could not view without horror the dungeons which remain in some of the towers; they recalled to our memory the truly diabolical cruelty of king John, by whose order 22 prisoners, confined in them, were starved to death."

163. (b. 3. 126; a. 3. 122.) In the expression *your father*, the person really referred to (in the original draft of the poem) was Edward II., the father of Edward III., who was upon the throne at the time when the A-text was composed. It is true that the reading of the Vernon MS., adopted as the *basis* of the A-text, is—"Vr fader Adam heo falde," i. e. she overthrew (lit. felled) our father Adam; but the various readings in the footnotes shew that such a reading is a mere mistake on the part of the scribe of that MS., and does not appear in any other MS. whatever. (The word "Adam" was retained in the sidenote to the B-text only by an oversight, and should be struck out.) The matter is put beyond doubt by the words in Meed's reply, where she says (A. iii. 180, 181) that "she never did kill any king, nor gave counsel to that effect; that she never did what Conscience accused her of, and that she appealed to the king himself as witness." The really remarkable point is that the poet, after revising his work twice, should have allowed this expression to stand; but we may note that the latter part of the line is altered in [c], and the new line is not inapplicable to the Black Prince, whose troubles arose from the failure of Don Pedro to supply him with the money which he had promised. There are, however, several such apparent inconsistencies, shewing that, much as the poet altered his work in revision, there were some passages which—probably because they were too well known to his readers—he did not feel wholly at liberty to interfere with. In such cases we must consult the earlier texts, if we would avoid being misled. See the remarks upon this subject in Pref. II. (B-text), pp. v, vi.

164. (b. 3. 127; a. 3. 123.) "She (i. e. Meed or Bribery) hath poisoned popes, and she impairs holy church." The reader need not suppose that the allusion here is any actual poisoning of any special pope; it is probably only a brief mode of reference to the famous saying attributed to an angel—"This day is *poison* shed abroad upon the church." Still, it is not a little remarkable that Lord Cobham, in his Examination, after quoting the same saying, went on to remark, with reference to the popes—"But indeede, since that same time, one hath put down an other, one hath *poisoned* an other, one hath cursed an other, and one hath slaine an other;" Wordsworth's Eccl. Biog. i. 380. Pope Benedict XI., who died in 1304, is said to have been poisoned. See note to Pass. xviii. 220 for further information.

167. (b. 3. 130; a. 3. 126.) *Talewys*, full of tales, loquacious, addicted to talebearing, slanderous. As Dr Stratmann gives no instance of the use of this word except by our poet, I add a few by way of illustration.

> "And sone, thy tong thou kepe also,
> And be not *tale-wyse* be no way;"
> How the Wise Man taught his Son, l. 33;
> in Ritson's Anc. Pop. Poetry.

> "[Be not] to toilose, ne to *talewijs*, for temperaunce is best;"
> Babees Book, p. 12.

See Mr Furnivall's Glossary to the Babees Book for other examples. The A.S. *tálu* means *censure*, and *wís*, a common suffix, means *knowing*; hence the compound *tal-wis* means *censorious*. The word *tale*, in Middle English, commonly has a bad sense, and signifies a lie, or something near it; see l. 47 above; and cf. Pass. i. 49.

171. (b. 3. 133; a. 3. 129.) *Sysours*; see note to Pass. iii. 63; to which may be added the following illustration:—

> "And this *assisours*, that comen to shire and to hundred,
> Damneth men for silver, and that nis no wonder.
> For whan the riche justise wol do wrong for mede,
> Thanne thinketh hem thei muwen the bet, for thei han more nede
>   To winne:
> Ac so is al this world ablent, that no man douteth sinne."
> Polit. Songs, ed. Wright, p. 344.

A *sompnour, somner*, or *summoner* was an officer who summoned delinquents to appear in an ecclesiastical court. See the description of the Sompnour in Chaucer's Prol.; and in the Prologue to the Freres Tale. And Wyclif says—"Also somenors, bailies, and servauntis [*serjeants*], and othere men of lawe, kitten [*cut*] perelously mennis purses; for thei somenen and aresten men wrongfully to gete the money out of his purse, and sumtyme suffren hem to meyntene hem in wrongis for money, to robbe othere men bi false mesures and weighttis;" Works, ed. Arnold, iii. 320.

174. (b. 3. 136; a. 3. 132.) Compare the following passage:—

> "For if there be in countre an horeling, a shrewe,
> Lat him come to the court, hise nedes for to shewe,
> And bringe wid him silver and non other wed,
> Be he nevere so muchel a wrecche, hise nedes sholen be sped
>   Full stille;

For Coveytise and Simonie han the world to wille."
Polit. Songs, ed. Wright, p. 324.

175. (b. 3. 137; a. 3. 133.) *Grotes*, lit. great coins, because, until they were coined, there was no silver coin larger than the penny. Cf. Du. *groet*, Fr. *gros*. "In this yere [1349] the kynge caused to be coyned grotes and halfe grotes, the whiche lacked of the weyghte of his former coyne, ii *s.* vi *d.* in a *li.* [*libra*, pound] Troy."—Fabyan, p. 461. The *groat* should have been equal to four silver pennies, but was only equal to about three and a half. A drawing of one may be seen in Knight's Pictorial Hist. England, i. 837.

177. (b. 3. 139; a. 3. 135.) "And she seizes true men [the true man; *a*, *b*] by the top," i.e. by the head. See Halliwell, who quotes—"Thou take hym by the toppe and I by the tayle;" Chester Plays, ii. 176.

183. (b. 3. 145; a. 3. 141.) Compare the following extract from Wyclif's Works, ed. Arnold, iii. 307. "And whanne many londis schulde falle into the kyngis hondis, bi eschet or othere juste menes, thes worldly clerkis and veyn religious *meden* gretly the kyngis officeris and men of lawe, to forbarre the kyngis right, and maken hemself lordis wrongfully. And thus bi the kyngis goodis thei maken his officeris and lege men to forswere hem [*themselves*], and defraude here lege lord. . . . Also many worldly peyntid clerkis geten the *kyngis seel*, hym out-wittynge, and senden to Rome for beneficis moche gold; and whanne the king sendith his *privcy seel* for to avaunce goode clerkis, and able bothe of good lif and gret cunnyng to reule, thei bryngen forth hereby many worldly wrecchis, unable to reule o soule for defaute of kunnyng and good lyvyng, and thus *vsen the kyngis seel* ayenst Goddis honour and the kyngis, and profit of Cristene peple, where the kyng undirstondith [*supposes*] to do wel bi here suggestion."

184. (b. 3. 146; a. 3. 142.) *Provisors.* A writ summoning one to appear for contempt of the sovereign was called *præmunire*, from its first word. "Numerous statutes have defined what shall be such a contempt as amounts to a præmunire. Most of the earlier are directed against *provisors*, as they were called, or persons who purchased from Rome provisions for holding abbeys or priories, &c., before those benefices were vacant (25 Edw. III., Stat. 5, c. 22. Stat. 6), or for exemption from obedience to their proper ordinary (2 Hen. IV. c. 3), or bulls for exemption from tithes," &c.—English Cyclopædia, s. v. Præmunire. William seems to allude to the purchase of sees in particular, as he speaks of 'these bishops,' l. 186.

"That which tended most of all to the ruin of the parochial clergy was the system of *provisors;* by which persons who had been presented to livings by the patrons were ejected by others, who during the life of a former incumbent had obtained what was called a *provision* from the pope to succeed on the next vacancy;" Massingberd's Engl. Ref. p. 238.

Complaints of bribery at the court of Rome were common. A Poem on the Evil Times of Edward II. says:—

"Voiz of clerk is sielde [*seldom*] i-herd at the court of Rome,
Ne were he nevere swich a clerk, *silverles if he come;*"
Polit. Songs, ed. Wright, p. 324.

185. (b. 3. 147; a. 3. 143.) See the passages upon Simony in Wyclif's Works, ed. Arnold, iii. 226, 278—287, and 488. Wyclif's definition of it is —"For whoevere cometh to presthod or benefice by yifte of money-worth, bi preiere or servyce, cometh in by *symonye*, as Seynt Gregoir and the lawe techeth."

188. (b. 3. 150; ·a. 3. 146.) The word *loteby*, meaning paramour or concubine, was used of both sexes. See Halliwell's Dictionary; Robert of Brunne, Handl. Synne, l. 1732; and cf. the following :—

> "Now am I younge, stoute, and bolde, . . .
> Now frere menour, now jacobin,
> And with me folwith my *loteby*
> To don me solace and company ;" Rom. Rose, 6339—

where, in the French original, we find the word to be *compaigne*.

> "She stal awai, mididone,
> And wente to here *lotebi* ;" Seven Sages, ed. Weber, l. 1443.

194. (b. 3. 155; a. 3. 152.) "She lieth against the law, and hindereth it (in its) way." *Gate* = way, as in B. i. 203.

195. (b. 3. 156; a. 3. 153.) "So that the truth cannot find its way out," i. e. cannot appear. Here *forth* = means of egress, way out.

196. (b. 3. 157; a. 3. 154.) *Louedayes.* Days on which extra services were rendered to the lord in seed-time or harvest were sometimes called boon-days or love-days; "but it more commonly meant a law-day, a day set apart for a leet or manorial court, a day of final *concord* and *reconciliation:* [as we read in the Coventry Mysteries :]—

> 'Now is the *love-day* mad of us foure fynially,
> Now may we leve in pes as we were wonte.'

"Hock-day was usually set apart for a love-day, law-day, or court-leet."— Timbs' Nooks and Corners of English Life, pp. 224, 228. [Hock-day was the second Tuesday after Easter.] William uses the term again, B. v. 427, and it occurs in Chaucer, Prol., l. 258. It was so called because the object was the amicable settlement of differences; but it is clear, from our author, that on such occasions much injustice was frequently done to the poor. This is remarkably confirmed by a passage in Riley's Memorials of London, p. 173, where it was ordered (A.D. 1329)—"that no one of the City . . shall go out of this city, to maintain [i. e. unjustly abet] parties, such as taking seisins, or holding *days of love*, or making other congregations within the city or without, in disturbance of the peace of our Lord the king, or in affray of the people, and to the scandal of the city." See also p. 158, where a day of love was appointed at St Paul's church, to settle a trade dispute by arbitration. Cf. Tyrwhitt's note to Chaucer, Prol. 260; Wyclif's Works, ed. Arnold, iii. 322; Paston Letters, ed. Gairdner, i. 496; and Titus Andronicus, i. 1. 491.

198. (b. 3. 159; a. 3. 155.) *The mase, &c.* "It is bewilderment for a poor man, though he plead (here) ever." Some MSS. have *plede* instead of *mote;* and both [a] and [c] omit *hir*, which is also spelt *here*, *heer*, as recorded in the footnotes to [b]. The word *mote* is not common as a *verb*, but we find it in Robert of Brunne's Handlyng Synne, l. 9803, with the

gloss *plete* written above it; a clear proof that *plead* was the sense intended by it.

——(b. 3. 164.) *Clergye* most frequently means *learning*, as opposed to *lewdness*, ignorance. It probably means so here, as bribery makes clever men covetous.

203. (*not in* b, a.) See the remarks on this passage in Pref. III (C-text), p. xvi. And compare Richard the Redeles, Pass. i.

221. (b. 3. 174; a. 3. 168.) It is a mark of respect for Meed to address the king in the plural number, and a mark of familiarity or contempt to address Conscience in the singular. This distinction is very carefully observed by our author, by Chaucer, and by the author of William of Palerne. See Abbott, Shakesp. Grammar, 3rd edit. art. 231.

227. (b. 3. 180; a. 3. 174.) The reading is either—*hanged on myn hals*, hung upon my neck [c]; or *hanged on myne half* [b], i. e. hung upon my side, clung to my party. The word is *never* here written *hals* [neck] in MSS. of the B-class, although curiously enough, the Vernon MS. has *nekke*.

230. (b. 3. 183; a. 3. 177.) *Yut Ich may*, &c. "Yet I may perhaps, as far as I might have the power, honour thee with gifts." In Cursor Mundi, ed. Morris, l. 109, two MSS. have the word *menske* where the other two have *worschipe*.

233. (b. 3. 186; a. 3. 180.) Meed here repudiates the charge made against her, and appeals to the king himself. It is singular that this passage, which originally referred to Edward II., should have been retained in the C-text; but, upon this point, consult the note to l. 163 above. Observe also that the next note refers to a passage in the B-text, which must be similarly referred back to its original form in the A-text, before we see that the king who was "not annoyed in Normandy" was Edward III., and not Richard II., whose reign was (in A.D. 1377) only just begun.

——(b. 3. 188; a. 3. 182.) This alludes to Edward's wars in Normandy, and, in particular, to the treaty sealed at Bretigny, near Chartres, on the 8th of May, 1360. Edward renounced his claim to the crown of France, and his claim to Normandy, Anjou, Touraine, and Maine, and restored all his conquests except Calais and Guisnes; but reserved Poitou, Guienne, and the county of Ponthieu. The dauphin agreed to pay for the ransom of his father King John, the sum of 3,000,000 scutes (*escus*) or crowns of gold. See Lingard, iv. 118; Thomas Walsingham, i. 290; Fabyan, p. 471. The sufferings of the English in their previous retreat from Paris to Bretagne were very great, and they encountered a most dreadful tempest near Chartres, with violent wind and heavy hail. Hence the allusions in the text to the cold, to the lengthening out of winter till May, to the dim cloud, and to the famine from which the army suffered. "It is to be noted," says Stow, "that the 14 day of April, and the morrow after Easter Day (1360), King Edward with his host lay before the city of Paris; which day was full dark of mist and hail, and so bitter cold, that many men died on their horsebacks with the cold; wherefore unto this day it hath been called the *Black Monday*."

Meed suggests that, instead of exacting money, Edward should have foregone it, or even have paid some, to secure to himself the kingdom of France. The articles agreed to at Bretigny were never fulfilled; Lingard, iv. 130. In the C-text, this passage is much altered.

——(b. 3. 190; a. 3. 184.) *For colde*, i. e. to keep off the cold.   See note to Pass. ix. 59.

245. (*not in* b, a.)   See note 1, p. lxxi, of Pref. III (C-text).   I may add that Walsingham (ed. Riley, ii. 170) also says that, in the year 1387, a French messenger was caught, on whom was found a compact, by which the king of France was to buy Calais and the adjacent country from Richard.

248. (*not in* b, a.)   This is well illustrated by the Crowned King, ll. 94—100, printed at the end of the C-text; p. 528.   And cf. Pass. xxii. 32.

259. (b. 3. 200; a. 3.-194.) *Mareschal.*   "When the king summoned his military tenants, the earl constable and earl mareschal held the principal command under the sovereign; but in armies raised by contract, he appointed two or more mareschals, whose duty it was to array the forces and to direct their movements."—Lingard, iv. 190.   The word occurs in the Crowned King, l. 102, printed at the end of the C-text, p. 528.

263. (b. 3. 204; a. 3. 198.) The sense of *brol* is a brat; the reading in [a] is *barn*.   We find—"a beggers *brol*," P. Pl. Crede, 745 ; "Al bot the wrech *brol* that is of Adamis blode;" Reliq. Antiq. ii. 177; "Belial *brolles*," i. e. children of Belial; Wyclif, iii. 238.

.——(b. 3. 220; a. 3. 214.) The two earlier versions here differ remarkably; and, in the last revision, the line was cut out. In [a], we have—"the king pays or rewards his men, to keep peace in the land;" but in [b] it runs—"the king receives a fine from his men, to keep peace," &c.   The discrepancy is best explained by rejecting the reading of the Vernon MS. (taken as the basis of the A-text), and substituting for it the reading of U (the MS. in University College, Oxford), which agrees with the B-text exactly; see the footnotes in [a].   The reference is to a great abuse then prevalent; the king sometimes accepted a fine from a delinquent who should have been brought to justice, but who thus obtained the 'king's peace.'   Compare Pass. v. 78.

281. (b. 3. 224; a. 3. 218.) *Alle kyne crafty men*, skilled workers (craftsmen) of every kind.   *Alle kyne* is here a corrupter form of *alle kynes* or *al-kynnes*, a genitive case; see the B-text; and cf. note to Pass. xi. 128.

290. (cf. b. 3. 247; a. 3. 234.) "They that live in an unlawful manner have liberal hands for giving bribes."   The Latin original is quoted in [b]. *Large* in Middle-English often means *liberal;* cf. the sb. *largesse*, and see l. 454 below.

292. (cf. b. 3. 230; a. 3. 224.) In the two first texts, Conscience here distinguishes between the two meanings of Meed, viz. (1) divine reward, shewn by God towards well-doers, and (2) corruption or bribery.   In the C-text, Conscience enters into a new and elaborate distinction between Meed (or reward, or prepayment, or bribe), and Mercede (or wages due for work

actually done). The whole passage is very curious, but the long illustration from grammar in ll. 335—409 is barely intelligible, and very dull reading, in fact the dullest passage which our author ever wrote; yet it may very well have given great satisfaction to some of his readers, who delighted in such subtilties. A similarly elaborated passage occurs in Pass. xx. 111—122.

301. (*not in* b, a.) The phrase *præ manu* in Latin sometimes means in hand, in readiness. By *præ manibus* the poet evidently means payment in advance, prepayment before the work is done; see the four lines following, and cf. Pass. x. 45, where the phrase recurs.

309. (*not in* b, a.) "According to the Bible, that bids that no one shall withhold the hire of his servant over the evening till the next morning;" cf. Levit. xix. 13. Robert of Brunne oddly refers us to the 'gospel' for this text, where he says—

"For þe gospel commaundeþ ryȝte,
Holde nat hys seruyse ouer nyghte."—Handlyng Synne, 2441.

yet the French text which he is translating is quite correct :—

"Car deus comande en la ley,
Qe le luer de ouerer od tey
Ne demeorge iesqes le matin;"

i. e. "For God commands, in the Law, that the hire of the workman may not remain with thee till the morning."

——(b. 3. 236; *not in* c, a.) *Assoileth it*, solves the question.

——(b. 3. 237; *not in* c, a.) *Of o colour*, of one colour, pure, spotless.

——(b. 3. 240; a. 3. 227.) The quotation ends—*innocentem non accepit*.

330. (*not in* b, a.) This belief, that Solomon is still left in hell, is repeated at Pass. xii. 220. See note to that line.

331. (*not in* b, a.) This singular line means, as it stands—"So that God giveth nothing (to any man), but sin is a comment upon it;" which may be explained as signifying that God gives things to men with a clause of revocation; and the comment or explanation of the text is given by the word *sin;* i. e. sin against Him revokes the promise. But when we remember that the 'glose,' or comment on a text, was commonly in Latin, it is clear that the true reading is not the *English* word 'synne,' as in the MSS., but the *Latin* word 'sin;' a theory which is sufficiently proved by the fact that the excellent Ilchester MS. has the reading 'si,' as recorded in the footnote, and the same reading is found in MS. Digby 102; see Pref. to C-text, p. xlvii, l. 4, and the footnote. We thus get the very simple sense—"So that God giveth nothing without an *if;*" which is unquestionably what is intended. The use of *sin* may be illustrated by the parable of the unfruitful tree:—"et siquidem fecerit fructum; *sin* autem, in futurum succides eam;" Luc. xiii. 9.

337. (*not in* b, a.) "In a settled and secure (or regular) manner, agreeing with themselves (according to rule)." The reader must puzzle out this passage for himself, by help of the sidenotes, if he cares to read it. Some lines are very curious; e. g. ll. 369, 370; 381—385.

358. (*not in* b, a.) Quoted from John i. 14.

368. (*not in* b, a.) "In which are good and bad; and to grant the will of neither of them."

369. (*not in* b, a.) This is interesting evidence, that it was then beginning to be considered right for a son to bear the same surname as his father.

372. (*not in* b, a.) It is well to remember that *taylende* does not mean *tail-end* (as in MS. F), but *tallying*, reckoning, enumeration or computation of property. Blount, in his Law Dictionary, explains that *tail* is a term used of fee (or property) that is not fee simple, being not in the owner's free power to dispose of. In Sir J. Cullum's Hist. of Hawsted, an old 'bill' is quoted in which a certain Robert Eland claimed "that the seid maner of Hausted shuld be *tailled* to his wyfe;" 2nd ed. p. 121. Cf. notes to Pass. viii. 4, and Pass. xi. 80.

410, 416. (b. 3. 257; a. 3. 244.) *Rat*, reads; contracted from *redeth;* it occurs again in Pass. xiv. 5; cf. Pref. III (C-text), p. lxxiii. l. 25. It occurs also in Polit. Songs, ed. Wright, p. 327, l. 88; and (in the form *ret*) in Old Eng. Homilies, ed. Morris, 1 Ser. 125. *Regum*, the book *of Kings;* i. e. the first two books, generally called the books of Samuel. See 2 Sam. xviii.; 1 Sam. xv.

——(b. 3. 258; a. 3. 245.) There is no apparent alliteration, but Langland considers *v* and *f* to answer to one another, as in Pass. iii. 61, so that *veniaunce* rimes to *fel;* whilst in the second half of the verse *Saul* rimes to *children* (*shildren*).

418. (b. 3. 261; a. 3. 248.) See Exod. xvii. 8 [misprinted xviii. 8 in the marginal note] for the sin of Amalek.

420. (b. 3. 262; a. 3. 250.) *Hoteth be boxome*, bids (thee) be obedient.

425. (b. 3. 267; *not in* a.) The word *mebles*, i. e. moveables, meant not only corn, cattle, and merchandise, but money, fuel, furniture, and wearing apparel; Lingard, Hist. Eng. iv. 174. "*Movable good*, as cuppe, or chalice, mytir, bacul [staff]; or *unmovable good*, as hous, feeld, wode;" Pecock's Repressor, ii. 386.

437. (b. 3. 279; a. 3. 265.) "In case it should annoy me [men *in* b], I make *no* ending," i. e. draw no conclusion; but the A-text has—"I will make an end," i. e. say no more.

442. (b. 3. 284; a. 3. 266.) *Somme*, to some whom I will not specify; dat. plural, used indefinitely. See note to l. 14 of this Passus.

450. (b. 3. 292; a. 3. 275.) "Loyalty, and no one else, shall execute the law upon him" [b, c]; *or*, "Loyalty shall execute the law upon him, or else he shall lose his life" [a]. See *Lyf* or *Lif* in the Glossary.

——(b. 3. 295; a. 2. 278.) "Meed, from amongst misdoers, makes many lords, and rules the realms so as to supersede the lord's laws" [b]; *or*, "Meed, from amongst misdoers; makes men so rich, that (corrupt) Law is become lord, and Loyalty is poor" [a]. (N.B. In the sidenote to B. iii. 297, for "Common Sense," read "Natural Affection;" so also in the sidenote to C. iv. 455.)

451. (b. 3. 203; a. 3. 276.) *selk houe,* (white) silk hood. Cf. note to
Pass. i. 159.

456. (b. 3. 298; a. 3. 282.) With this line Pass. iii., in the A-text, ab-
ruptly terminates. The admirable addition here made was suggested, I feel
confident, by the recent proclamation of a *jubilee,* in the last year of Edward
III. (Feb. 1377), proclaimed because the king had attained the *fiftieth* year
of his reign; Lingard, iv. 146. Taking his cue from this, the poet hopes
that the new reign of Richard II., then just begun, may usher in a new era
of perfect peace; but, in ll. 481—5, he suddenly prophesies that certain
rather unlikely events will first happen, thus revealing his fear that no such
good time was really at hand.

The above suggestion is fully confirmed by a passage in John of Bridlington's pretended prophecies, bk. iii. c. viii., where the jubilee of Edward
III. is described in the lines—

"Pacis erunt dies, belli terrore remoto," &c. ;

and the writer, in his commentary, takes great care to explain that the
jubilee means the 50th year of Edward's *reign,* not of his *life.*

461. (b. 3. 303; *not in* a.) *Baselardes.* "Temp. Rich. II., civilians wore
swords called *baselards* or *badelaires.* Example; monument of a civilian,
King's Sombourne Church, Hants, 1380.—Godwin's Handbook of English
Archæology, p. 261. "The *baselard* was of two kinds, straight and curved
... By Statute 12 Rich. II., c. vi., it was provided that—'null servant de
husbandrie ou laborer ne servant de artificer ne de vitailler porte desore
enavant *baslard,* dagger, nespee [*nor sword*] sur forfaiture dicelle.' · Priests
were strictly inhibited from wearing this instrument of war, but the rule was
constantly broken."—Note by Peacock to Myrc's Instructions for Parish
Priests (Early English Text Society); p. 67. In Wright's Essays, ii. 269,
will be found a Ballad on the Baselard, printed from a Sloane MS. It shews
that the weapon had a red sheath, a twisted haft, a silver chape or plate at the
end of it, &c. The frequent enactments against the wearing of weapons by
civilians, &c., in the reigns of Edward III. and Richard II., shew how often
this law was disregarded. See Liber Albus, pp. 335, 554, 555. See also
note to l. 467, below.

464. (b. 3. 306; *not in* a.) See Isaiah ii. 4, quoted in note to l. 480
below.

465. (b. 3. 307; *not in* a.) The Old French *picois,* signifying a mat-
tock or pick-axe, has given rise to the tautological form *pick-axe* which
we now employ; the modern form is a mere clever corruption, due to
the foreign form of the old termination, and is not to be found in our older
authors. In the Prompt. Parv. we have "Pykeys, mattokke;" in Riley's
Memorials of London, p. 284, there is mention of '5 pikeyses;' in the
Paston Letters, ed. Gairdner, i. 106, 'pikoys' is used as a plural; and
Robert of Brunne, in his Handlyng Synne, ll. 940-1, remarks :—

"Mattok is a pykeys,
Or a pyke, as sum men seys."

467. (b. 3. 309; *not in* a.) To hunt (not with hounds, but) with *placebo* [b] means to be diligent in singing *placebo*, i.e. in saying the Office for the Dead. In B. xv. 122, we find the author speaking of ploughing with *placebo* :—

> "Sire Johan and sire Geffray · hath a gerdel of syluer,
> A *basellarde* or a ballok-knyf · with botones ouer-gylte,
> Ac a portous that shulde be his plow · *placebo* to segge,
> Hadde he neure scruyse to saue syluer therto · seith it with yvel wille."

Another spelling of *portous* is *porthors;* it means a breviary. The *placebo* was an antiphon in the Office for the Dead at Vespers, which began—"*Placebo* domino in regione uiuentium" (Ps. cxvi. 9, or cxiv. 9 in the Vulgate). Our word *dirge* is a contraction of *dirige*, as here used. This word begins the antiphon "Dirige, Dominus meus, in conspectu tuo uitam meam" (cf. Ps. v. 8), used in the first nocturn at mattins, in the Office for the Dead. For further illustration, see Mr Way's note to *Dyryge* in the Promptorium; Mr Arnold's note to Wyclif's Works, iii. 374; and Dr Rock's Church of our Fathers, iii. 123.

"Efter euesong anonriht siggeth ower [your] *Placebo* eueriche niht, hwon ge beoth eise; bute gif hit beo holiniht vor the feste of nie [nine] lescuns thet cumeth amorwen, biuore Cumplie [compline] other efter Uhtsong [nocturns], siggeth *Dirige*, mit threo psalmes, and mit threo lescuns eueriche niht sunderliche;" Ancren Riwle, p. 22. To sing *placebo* came to be used in a humorous sense, viz. to flatter. "Flattereres ben the deueles chapeleyns, that singen ay *Placebo;*" Chaucer, Pers. Tale, De Ira. Hence the name *Placebo* for a flattering character in the Merchauntes Tale. Cf. Ayenbyte of Inwyt, ed. Morris, p. 60; Dyce's Skelton, ii. 121.

468. (*not in* b, a.) "And pray, saying their Psalter and Seven Psalms, for all sinful people." The Seven Psalms are the seven penitential psalms, viz. Pss. 6, 32, 38, 51, 102, 130, 143; all of which are read on Ash Wednesday.

——(b. 3. 310; *not in* c, a.) To "ding upon David" means to practise singing the Psalms repeatedly. In some verses in MS. Arundel 292, fol. 71 verso, printed in Reliq. Antiq. i. 292, we have the very expression:—

> "I donke vpon David til my tonge talmes;"

i. e. till my tongue fails me; cf. Du. *talmen*, to loiter, be idle.

474. (b. 3. 316; *not in* a.) *After the dede*, according to the deed; cf. "neither reward us *after* our iniquities" in the Litany.

480. (b. 3. 322; *not in* a.) Isaiah ii. 4: "Et iudicabit gentes, et arguet populos multos : et conflabunt gladios suos in uomeres, et lanceas suas in falces : non leuabit gens contra gentem gladium, nec exercebuntur ultra ad prælium."

481. (b. 3. 323; *not in* a.) Fanciful prophecies were then in vogue; see those of John of Bridlington, in Political Poems, ed. Wright, vol. i. William has another similar one at the end of Pass. ix. This present one merely vaguely hints at a final time when Jews and Mahometans shall be converted. Line 483 is sufficiently clear. The 'middle of a moon' (cf. B. xiii. 155)

means the full moon, and, in particular, the Paschal full moon; whilst 'to torne' means 'to be converted.' The sense is, accordingly, that "the Paschal full moon (with the events of the crucifixion) shall cause the Jews to be converted to Christianity; and next, at the sight of their conversion, Saracens also shall declare their belief in the Holy Ghost; for both Mohammed and Meed shall then meet with ill-success." Compare Pass. xviii. ll. 317—322.

The mention of "six suns" in l. 482 is no doubt an allusion to the portents supposed to have been seen in the sky on various occasions. In the Complaint of Scotland, ed. Murray, p. 58, we find the following. "The historigraphours rehersis, that there vas three sonnis sene at one tyme in the lyft, befoir the ciuil veyris [wars] that occurrit betuix anthonius and agustus cesar; and alse ther vas thre munis sene in the lyft, quhen domitius caius and flauius lucius var consulis of rome." In the third part of Henry VI., Act ii. sc. 1, l. 25, we have—

"Dazzle mine eyes, or do I see *three suns?*" &c.

We might fancifully interpret the "ship" and the "half sheaf of arrows" to refer to a portent signifying invasion by an enemy (cf. Pass. ix. 351, 352); but the reader may be pleased to see some other sense in it, and the point is obviously one that cannot be settled; nor is it of any importance.

486. (b. 3. 328; *not in* a.) 'As wrath as the wind,' i.e. as angry as a boisterous wind, is evidently a proverbial expression. Our author has it again in Rich. Redeles, iii. 153.

487. (b. 3. 330; *not in* a.) The quotation is not from the book of Wisdom, but from Prov. xxii. 9. Meed quotes only *half* of it, for which Conscience reproves her, and quotes the rest, l. 499. The full verse is— "Uictoriam et honorem acquiret qui dat munera; animam autem aufert accipientium." Occleve quotes the same text in his De Regimine Principum, ed. Wright, p. 167,—

"Victorie and honour he shalle hym purchace,
That is of yiftes free."

492. (b. 3. 335; *not in* a.) The lady read but *half* the text. It is— "Omnia autem probate, quod bonum est tenete," 1 Thess. v. 21.

——(b. 3. 342.) *Were gode*, would be good.

498. (b. 3. 344.) "So he that refers to Wisdom" or rather to Proverbs [c]; *or*, "And if ye refer again to Wisdom" [b].

500. (cf. b. 3. 348.) "He wins worship, who is willing to give a reward, but he that receives or accepts it is a receiver of guile" [c]; *or*, "But though, by giving a reward, we win worship and obtain a victory, yet the soul that receives the present, is to that extent under an obligation" [b]. Both of these are translations of the text in the note to l. 487. *Sonde* (lit. a thing sent) means a present. Mr Donaldson, in a note to l. 3330 of the alliterative Troy Book, says that a present is [in Scotland, I suppose] sometimes called a *send*.

SCHEME OF THE CONTENTS OF PASSUS V.

(B. Passus IV ; A. Passus IV.)

Cf. Wright's edition ; pp. 65—76 ; ll. 2079—2472.

C-TEXT.	B-TEXT.	A-TEXT.
1—9	1—9	1—9
10	——	10
11—17	10—16	11—17
18, 19	17, 18	——
20, 21	19, 20	18, 19
22, 23	*like* 21, 22	20, 21
24, 25	23, 24	22, 23
26	25	
27—31	*like* 26—30	*like* 24—28
32—34	*like* 31, 32	——
——	33	
35—39	*like* 34—39	——
——	40, 41	
40, 41	*like* 42, 43	*like* 29, 30
42—50	*like* 44—52	31—39
51—55		——
56—64	53—61	40—48
65	62	——
66	63	49
	64	50
——		
(a) 67, 68	(a) [74, 75]	(a) *like* [60, 61]
69, 70	65, 66	51, 52
——	67—73	53—59
(a) [67, 68]	(a) 74, 75	(a) *like* 60, 61
71	——	——
72—76	76—80	62—66
		67
——	——	
77—96	81—100	68—87
——	101	88
97, 98	103, 102	90, 89
99—109	104—114	91—101
(b) 110	(b) 115	(b) [106]
111—113	116—118	102—104
114	119	*like* 105
(b) [110]	(b) [115]	(b) 106
115		
116, 117	120, 121	——
118—122	*like* 122—126	*like* 107—109
123	——	
124—147	127—150	110—133
	151	——
148	152	——
——	153—156	——
149, 150	——	——

C-TEXT.	B-TEXT.	A-TEXT.
v. 151—155	*like* iv. 157—160	*like* iv. 134—136
156—159	161—164	137—140
———	———	141—143
160—163	165—168	———
———	169, 170	
164, 165	———	———
166	171	*like* 144
———	172	145
167—174	173—180	———
175, 176	*like* 181, 182	———
177—180	183—186	146—149
———	187—189	150—152
181—183	———	———
184—187	*like* 190—192	*like* 153—155
———	193—195	156—158
188—196	———	———

NOTES TO PASSUS V. (B. PASSUS IV.; A. PASSUS IV.)

2. (b. 4. 2; a. 4. 2.) *Sauhtne*, be reconciled. I would call attention to the letter *n* in this word. In Mœso-Gothic, verbs in -*nan* have a passive signification; thus *fulljan* means *to fill*, but *fullnan* means *to become full*. According to this analogy, we find the A.S. *sehtian* or *sahtlian* = to make peace, to reconcile others; but *sahtnan* (if such a form were to occur, and it no doubt once existed) would mean to become at peace, to be reconciled. The word is therefore correctly spelt here, and has the sense of to become at peace, be reconciled. See *sauhten, sahtlien, sahtnien* in Stratmann; and add to the examples there given, the references—Gamelyn, l. 150; Cursor Mundi, l. 16; Pricke of Conscience, l. 1470.

17. (b. 4. 16; a. 4. 17.) *Caton his knaue*, Cato his servant. The servant of Reason is no doubt here called Cato out of respect for Dionysius Cato, whom our author often quotes; see note to Pass. ix. 338. In the next line we may have mention of Tom True-tongue, an imaginary name which has occurred before, iv. 478; and elsewhere we have mention of an opposite character, viz. Tom Two-tongued, xxiii. 162. Here, however, the name is lengthened out into a whole sentence. For similar long names, not unlike those of Puritan times, see l. 20 below; ix. 80, 81, 82, 83.

19. (b. 4. 18; *not in* a.) *Lesynges*, leasings, lies, idle tales to laugh at. Compare—

"Trofels [*trifles*] sal i yow nane tell,
Ne *lesinges* forto ger [*make*] yow lagh."
Ywaine and Gawaine, l. 150 (Ritson's Met. Rom.).

20. (b. 4. 19; a. 4. 18.) Here Reason tells his servant Cato to put a saddle upon Patience or Sufferance (represented here as a horse), and further to restrain it with the girth called Advise-thee-beforehand [c], *or* Witty-word [b], because it is the habit of Will (the horse's temper) to wince and kick, and to shew signs of impatience. The word *warroke* is very rare, but

appears again in Mr Wright's Volume of Vocabularies, 1st Series, p. 154.
To *make wehe* (b. 4. 22) is to make a neighing sound, to neigh; *wehe* being,
like the Welsh *wihi*, an imitation of that sound. Chaucer uses the word in
his Reves Tale (C. T. l. 4064) to express the same sound. At p. 148 of a
life of Wyclif by Le Bas, a passage is quoted from that author in which the
body is compared to a horse, which is restrained by the bridle of abstinence.
In the Ayenbite of Inwyt also (ed. Morris, 1868, p. 204) is a similar passage.
"Thanne the bodiliche wyttes byeth ase thet hors thet yernth wyth-oute
bridle zuo thet hit deth falle his lhord. Ac the herte chaste ham of-halt mid
the bridle of skele;" i. e. then the bodily wits are as the horse that runneth
without bridle, so that it causes its lord to fall. But the chaste heart restrains them with the bridle of reason. Cf. James i. 26; iii. 2, 3. In the
Trial of Treasure (in Dodsley's Old Plays, ed. Hazlitt, iii. 297), we have the
very same idea. The character named Inclination is led in "in his bridle,
shackled," and begins a speech with "*We-he! he! he! he!* ware the horse-
heels, I say; I would the rein were loose, that I might run away."

26. (b. 4. 25; *not in* a.)* *Which*, what sort of, what kind of; a common
meaning of *which*, especially before *a*. Cf. note to Pass. iii. 17.

27. (b. 4. 26; a. 4. 24.) *Waryn*, also spelt Guarin, or Guerine, was once
a common and popular Christian name; whence Fitz-warren, and other surnames. See Bardsley's English Surnames, p. 24.

43. (b. 4. 45; a. 4. 32.) *His sone*, Edward the Black Prince, a great
favourite with the people. He did not leave England to take possession of
Acquitaine till Feb. 2, 1363. William having once inserted this in the earliest
version of his poem, does not seem to have thought it worth while to alter it,
as he retains the expression *his sone* even in [c]. Cf. note to l. 171.

45. (b. 4. 47; a. 4. 34.) *Putte vp a bylle* [c, a]; *Put forth a bille* [b];
The former is the more usual expression, as in Fabyan's Chronicles [1410-
11] :—"The commons of this lande *put vp a bylle* vnto the kyng," &c. The
sense is—brought forward a petition. Compare—"And my mayster coun-
ceyll [*counsels*] yow that ȝe shuld meve the Meyer and all the Aldermen with
all her Comoners to ryde ayens [i. e. *to meet*] my Lord, and that ther ben
made *byllez*, and *putte them up* to my Lord," &c.; Paston Letters, i. 151.
"Sir, I cende yow a copy of the *bylle* that my Lord of Yorke *putte un-to* the
kynge;" ibid. i. 153.

With respect to this appeal of Peace to the king, see the scene in Sir F.
Palgrave's Merchant and Friar, p. 242, where a maiden appeals to the king,
saying—"from our Lord the King, he who wears the English-Saxon crown,
and who hath sworn to observe the good laws of the Confessor, do I now
demand that even justice which hath been refused to me at home." At p.
238 of the same work, it is explained that the appeal was made, in the first
instance, to the Triers or Auditors of petitions, who were appointed at the
opening of every new Parliament.

46. (b. 4. 48; a. 4. 35.) *Wrong* is a representative of the oppressive
tribe known as *the king's purveyors*. The peasantry often complained of them

bitterly, accusing them of taking things by violence; see the next note. In the poem of King Edward and the Shepherd (printed by Hartshorne in his Ancient Metrical Tales) is the following :—

> "I hade catell, now have I non;
> Thay take my bestis, and don thaim slon,
>   And payen but a *stick of tre* . . . .
> Thai take geese, capons, and henne,
> And alle that ever thei may with renne,
>   And reves us our catell . . . .
> Thei toke my hennes and my geese,
> And my schepe with all the fleese,
>   And ladde them forth away."

So in Political Songs (Camd. Soc. 1839), p. 186—

> "Est vitii signum pro victu solvere *lignum*."

So in God spede the Plough, printed at the end of Pierce the Ploughman's Crede, ed. Skeat, 1867, p. 70 :—

> "The kyngis puruiours also they come,
>   To haue whete and otys at the kyngis nede;
> And over that befe and Mutton,
>   And butter and pulleyn [*poultry*], so God me spede!
> And to the kyngis court we moste it lede,
> And our payment shalbe a *styk of A bough;*
>   And yet we moste speke faire for drede—
> I praye to God, spede wele the plough!"

A long complaint against these purveyors will be found in the Towneley Mysteries, at p. 90. A very similar complaint appears in Robert of Brunne's Handlyng Synne, ll. 7420-3 :—

> "Also do þese lordynges,
> þey trespas moche yn twey þynges,
> þey rauys a mayden aȝens here wyl,
> And mennys wyuys þey lede awey þertyl."

To add to the troubles of the peasantry, they were liable to be imposed upon by *false* purveyors, mere impostors who wished to practise extortion; see Riley's Memorials of London, p. 645.

The reader may compare the petition of John Paston, A.D. 1450, (Paston Letters, i. 106), couched in similar terms, and describing the violent conduct of Lord Molyns. The occasion was different, but the spirit of lawless violence very much the same. See note to l. 61.

51. (*not in* b, a.) St Giles's down is near Winchester; see note to Pass. vii. 211.

58. (b. 4. 55; a. 4. 42.) To *maintain* was the technical term for to aid and abet in wrongdoing; cf. iii. 207, iv. 187, &c. See note to B. iii. 90. *Hewes*, domestics; A.S. *hiwan*, domestics, servants. The A-text has *owne*, i.e. own people, but some MSS. have *hynen*, i.e. hinds. Whitaker took it to mean *ewes!*

69. (b. 4. 56; a. 4. 43.) "He forestalls (my sales) at fairs." To *forestall* was to buy up goods before they had been exposed in the market. It was strictly discouraged; see Liber Albus, ed. Riley, p. 172; and Memorials

of London, ed. Riley, pp. 83, 387. "Byers of great [i. e. engrossers], regraters, and *forestallers of the markette* bye good chepe, and selle dere.
Sectores minoris res emunt, et pluris vendunt;" Hormanni Vulgaria, leaf
235, back. .

61. (b. 4. 58; a. 4. 45.) *And taketh me*, &c.; and gives me a tally (and
nothing else) for ten or twelve quarters (of oats). The statements in the
note to l. 46 were often true in *two* senses; the peasants were paid (1) by
a wooden tally, and (2) by a beating, as William says in the following line,
as it stands in [b] and [a]. An exchequer tally was an account of a sum
lent to the Government. The tally itself was a rod of hazel, (one of a pair
that *tallied*) with notches on it to indicate the sum lent. It was not easy to
realize this sum afterwards. Cf. Chaucer, Prol. 570—

> "For whether that he payde, or *took by taille.*"

And Jack Cade says to Lord Say (2 Hen. VI. iv. 7. 38) that "our forefathers
had no other books but the score and the tally." The tally is still used to
some extent, not only in England, but in China. See Marco Polo, ed. Yule,
ii. 60. Palgrave has—" A payre of *taylles*, suche as folke vse to score vpon for
rekennyng;" ed. 1530, fol. xiii.

——(b. 4. 72, *and* 73; a. 4. 58, *and* 59; *not in* c.) See notes below, following that to l. 68.

68. (b. 4. 75; a. 4. 61.) It is clear that *handy-dandy* in this passage
means a covert bribe or present, as, for instance, a bag conveyed to the
judge's hand which he was to open at leisure, when he would find the contents satisfactory. The explanation in Halliwell's Dictionary is as follows:
—" *Handydandy*. A game thus played by two children. One puts something secretly, as a small pebble, into one hand, and with clenched fists he
whirls his hands round each other, crying, 'Handy-spandy, Jack-a-dandy,
which good hand will you have?' The other guesses or touches one; if right,
he wins its contents; if wrong, he loses an equivalent." For a somewhat
fuller notice, see Halliwell's Popular Rhymes and Nursery Tales, 1849, p. 116.
The explanation in Brand (Pop. Antiq. ed. Ellis, ii. 420) is rather confused.
Douce, in his Illustrations of Shakespeare, ii. 167, quotes from a tract—"as
men play with little children at *handye-dandye, which hand will you have,*
when they are disposed to keep any thinge from them;" but it should be
added that the game is then almost sure to end in the child's receiving a
present. Florio, in his Ital. Dictionary, 1598, has:—" Bazzicchiare, to
shake betweene two hands; to play *handy-dandy.*" In King Lear, iv. 6. 157,
the word seems to mean simply—guess which you please. Shakespeare says
—" See how yond justice rails upon yond simple thief! Hark in thine ear:
change places, and, *handy-dandy*, which is the justice, which is the thief?"

The taking of bribes by justices has been already commented on, in notes
to Pass. iv. ll. 26, 174. I add a line from Gower—

> "Jus sine jure datur si nummus in aure loquatur."
> Polit. Poems, ed. Wright, i. 358.

——(b. 4. 72; a. 4. 58; *not in* c.) *But if Mede, &c.;* "unless Meed cause it to be otherwise, thy misfortune is aloft." William often uses *make it* in the sense of to bring it about, to cause it to be so; cf. C. ix. 212. But when the words *it make* are preceded by *but*, they mean 'cause it to be otherwise;' cf. viii. 28. *Myschief* commonly signifies mishap or ill-luck in Middle-English; cf. ix. 212, 233. *Vppe* is here an adverb, signifying on high, aloft, in the ascendant.

——(b. 4. 73; a. 4. 59; *not in* c.) *Lyth in his grace.* Offenders convicted of great crimes were put *in the king's grace,* who could hang them and confiscate their property, unless he were pleased to show mercy. Sometimes he was satisfied with exacting a heavy fine; cf. ll. 84, 85.

78. (b. 4. 82; a. 4. 69.) "In the royal court, the usual penalty on conviction was placing the culprit 'at the king's mercy;' that his goods and chattels were forfeited, unless—which, indeed, often happened—the monarch graciously condescended to accept a fine by way of compromise;" Europe in the Middle Ages, p. 106.

82. (b. 4. 86; a. 4. 73.) *Seuen yere,* seven years; put for a long, but indefinite period. So again in Pass. vii. 214, xi. 73. And in Gammer Gurton's Needle (in Dodsley's Old Plays, ed. Hazlitt, iii. 249), Diccon says—"What if I have? Five hundred such [i. e. such lies] have I seen within these *seuen years.*" See note to Pass. vii. 214.

85. (b. 4. 89; a. 4. 76.) "And (let the meinpernour) be pledge for his misfortune, and buy a remedy for him." See note to Pass. iii. 208, and cf. l. 173 below. This is one of the numerous passages in which *bale* and *boot* (woe and advantage) are opposed to each other. Compare the common old proverb, "when the bale is hext, the bote is next," i. e. when the tribulation is greatest, the remedy is nearest; which occurs among the Proverbs of Hending. See ll. 88, 89, below.

104. (b. 4. 109; a. 4. 96.) Note the three different endings of the line. *For his luther werkes,* for his evil deeds [c]; *but lowenesse hym borwe,* unless Humility (or Submission) go bail for him [b]; *bote more loue hit make,* unless a greater degree of love cause it to be otherwise [a]; where *make* is used, as in b. 4. 72; c. viii. 28.

107. (b. 4. 112; a. 4. 99.) *Menepernour,* i. e. *mainpreneur,* taker by the hand, a surety; see note to iii. 208. There is a good example of the word in Occleve's De Regim. Principum, ed. Wright, p. 86—

> "And to prison he goth, he get [*getteth*] no bettir,
> Till his *maynpernour* his areste unfettir," &c.

110. (b. 4. 115; *not in* a.) *Harlotrie,* ribaldry, buffoonery, jester's tales. Cf. Chaucer, Prol. l. 561. See note to l. 113.

111. (b. 4. 116; a. 4. 102.) *Purnele* or *Peronelle* (from Petronilla) was a proverbial name for a gaily dressed bold-faced woman; it would be long before she put away her finery in a box. This line is almost repeated in Pass. vi. 129; see also Rich. Redeles, iii. 156. May 31 was dedicated to S. Petronilla the Virgin. She was supposed to be able to cure the quartan ague; Chambers' Book of Days, ii. 389. The name, once common, now scarcely

survives except as a surname, in the form Parnell;. see Bardsley's English
Surnames, p. 56. A *hutch* was the usual name for a clothes-box, such as
was often placed at the foot of a bed; see Our English Home, p. 101. Pictures of *hutches* are given in Wright's Homes of Other Days, at pp. 274, 275,
276, 279. It also signified boxes of another kind; thus Palsgrave has—
"Byn, to kepe breed or corne, *huche.*" In Joseph of Arimathie, ed. Skeat,
.it occurs in the forms *whucche*, ll. 39, 237, and *wȝucche*, ll. 267, 281; in the
sense of a large ark or wooden box. "Hutche or whyche, *Cista, archa ;*"
Prompt. Parv.; see Way's note. A.S. *hwæcca.*

112. (b. 4. 117; a. 4. 103.) *And children*, &c.; and the cherishing of
children be chastised with rods [c, a]; *or*, and the cherishing of children be,
that they be chastised with rods [b]. *To cherish* is to cocker, spoil. *Children*
is the genitive plural, like *klerken* in l. 114.

113. (b. 4. 118; a. 4. 104.) *Harlotes*, ribalds, jesters, buffoons; it is applied to both sexes, but much more commonly to *males* in Middle English.
In a note to the Canterbury Tales, l. 649, Tyrwhitt remarks that, in l. 6068
of the Romaunt of the Rose, the expression "king of harlotes" is a translation
of the French *roy de ribaulx.* Mr Wright, in speaking of the same passage,
viz. the description of the Sompnour in Chaucer's Prologue, says—"this
passage gives us a remarkable trait of the character of the ribald, or harlot,
who formed a peculiar class of Middle-age society. Among some old glosses
in the Reliquiæ Antiquæ, vol. i. p. 7, we find '*scurra*, a harlotte.' In the
Coventry Mystery of the Woman taken in Adultery, it is the young man
who is caught with the woman, and not the woman herself, who is stigmatised
as a harlot." In Riley's Memorials of London, p. 474, a man is said to have
spoken against the lord mayor, and to have "asserted the said mayor to be
a false scoundrel or *harlot.*" See also Mr Wright's remarks on the word
ribald in his Political Songs, p. 369. The sense is—"And till the holiness
of harlots be (observed as) a high holiday." *Ferye* is the Latin *feria ;* and
an is the indefinite article. All doubt about the meaning is removed by the
fortunate circumstance that the expression 'an heigh ferye' occurs again in
B. xiii. 415, where the sense is obvious. The odd explanation by Whitaker
has already been commented on; C-text, Critical Notes, p. 454. The reading of [b] and [a] is to the same result, but very differently expressed.
There, the sense is—"And till the holiness of harlots be considered as of
small value, i. e. as of common occurrence;" the *literal* sense being—"be
considered as worth a hind." The value of a hind or farm-labourer (*hyne*)
was not considered as very great; indeed, the Rawlinson MS. (R) writes
nauȝte in place of the 'an hyne' of other B-text MSS.

116. (b. 4. 120; *not in* a.) "And till religious men, fond of riding about,
be shut up in their cloisters" [c]; *or*, "And till religious men, fond of roam-
ing, say *recordare* in their cloisters." The word *religious* means one of a
religious order, a monk or a friar. The words *outrider* [c] and *roamer* [b] refer to the use of horses by such men, and to their fondness for pilgrimages;
see B. x. 306—313. *Recordare* is the first word of a mass for avoiding

sudden death, appointed by Pope Clement at Avignon, the recital of which secured to the bearers 260 days' indulgence.· This is best shewn by the following rubric from the Sarum Missal, 1532; fol. lij. "Missa pro mortalitate evitanda, quam dominus papa clemens fecit et constituit in collegio, cum omnibus cardinalibus; et concessit omnibus penitentibus vere contritis et confessis sequentem missam audientibus .cclx. dies indulgentie. Et omnes audientes sequentem missam debent portare in manu vnam candelam ardentem dum missam audiunt per quinque dies sequentes; et tenere eam in manu per totam missam genibus flexis: et eis mors subitanea nocere non poterit; et hoc est certum et approbatum in auinione et in partibus circumuicinis." Then follows—"*Officium.* Recordare, domine, testamenti tui, et dic angelo percutienti, cesset iam manus tua: vt non desoletur terra: ·et ne perdas omnem animam viuam :" &c.

By Clement must be meant Clement V., who removed the papal see to Avignon in 1309, and died in 1314. It was he who first made public sale of indulgences in 1313, and whose decretals and constitutions, known as the *Clementines*, were collected and published shortly after his death.

117. (b. 4. 121; *not in* a.) Saint Benedict, founder of the Benedictine order of monks, was born about A.D. 480, and died about A.D. 542. Saint Dominic (A.D. 1170—1221) founded the order of Dominican or Black Friars. Saint Bernard, of Cistercium or Citeaux, near Chalons, better known as S. Bernard of Clairvaux, founded the order of Cistercians or Bernardines; he was born A.D. 1091, died 1153. St Francis of Assisi, founder of the Franciscan order of friars or Friars Minorites, was born 1182, died 1226.

120. (b. 4. 124; *not in* a.) "Till bishops be as bakers, brewers, and tailors," i. e. till bishops provide bread, ale, and clothing for the needy [c], *or*, as in [b], "Till bishops' horses be turned into beggars' chambers;" i. e. till the money spent by bishops on horses go to furnish rooms for beggars. *Bayard* [b] was a common name for a horse; originally, for a horse of a bay colour. 'As bold as blind Bayard' was an old proverb, which occurs in Chaucer, near the end of the Chan. Yem. Tale; in Lydgate's Warres of Troy, Book V; and in Skelton, ed. Dyce, i. 123, l. 101.

122. (b. 4. 126; a. 4. 109.) The reading in [b] and [a] is—*There I shal assigne*, where I (Reason) shall ordain. There is no need to go to Gallicia. Compare—

"But, bi *seint Jame of Galice*, that many man hath souht,
The pilory and the cucking-stol beth i-mad for nouht."
                              Political Songs (Camden Soc.), p. 345.

In the C-text, Reason. *does* assign places to find S. James in; viz. *prisons, poor cottages*, and *sick-rooms*. By '*for* pilgrymages' in l. 123 we must understand '*instead of* pilgrimages.'

125. (b. 4. 128; a. 4. 111.) *Rome-renners*, runners to Rome. "And (until) all Rome-runners bear no silver over sea that bears the image of the king, for the sake of enriching robbers that dwell in France [c]; *or*, beyond sea" [b, a]. Part of the procurator's oath to the English king was—"that he would not

send money out of the kingdom without the royal license."—Lingard, iv. 205. In 1376, the commons presented a petition to the king, stating that the taxes paid yearly by them to the pope amounted to five times the royal revenue. " In the reign of Henry III., the Italians, who were beneficed here, drew from England more than thrice the amount of the king's revenues, fleecing, by means of priests, who were aliens also, the flock which they never fed."— Southey; Book of the Church, p. 187 (6th ed., 1848). "The Parliament were determined and obstinate in their resistance to the burthens imposed on the kingdom and on the clergy by the papal court; and they were strong, as representing the will of the nation, and sure that their resistance was not disapproved by the king. It was not, perhaps, the taxation of the clergy to which they were so resolutely opposed, so much as the continual drain of specie, which was considered as the impoverishment of the realm, and was as yet but imperfectly prevented by the bills of exchange, brought into use chiefly by the Lombard and Italian bankers;" Milman, Hist. of Latin Christianity, vi. 111. Perhaps it is proper to add that by the words *in France* our poet refers to the papal residence at Avignon; cf. Pass. xxii. 424. Fabyan says that in 1365, Peter's pence were commanded to be no more gathered, but he adds—"neuerthelesse at this present tyme [Henry VII.] they be gaderyd in sondry shyres of Englande;" p. 477.

128. (b. 4. 131; a. 4. 114.) "On penalty of forfeiting that property, in case any one finds him ready to cross over" [c]; *or*, "finds him (*or it*) at Dover" [b, a]. *Ho so* = whoso, whosoever; i. e. in case any one. *Ouerwarde* = in the direction of (crossing) over. *At Dover* refers to the then existing law—"that no pilgrim should pass out of the realm, to parts beyond the seas, but only *at Dover*, on pain of a year's imprisonment;" Ruding's Annals of the Coinage, 3rd ed. 1840, vol. i. p. 211.

140. (b. 4. 143; a. 4. 126.) "For the man named *nullum malum* met with one called *inpunitum*," &c. This is merely a way of introducing the words in italics. The quotation is repeated in Pass. xxi., at l. 435. It is taken from the following :—"Ipse est iudex iustus . . . qui nullum malum praeterit impunitum, nullum bonum irremuneratum;" Pope Innocent; De Contemptu Mundi, lib. iii. cap. 15. Innocent may have been thinking of some passage in Boethius, who has similar expressions in more places than one. Compare— "Manet etiam spectator desuper cunctorum praescius Deus, . . . bonis praemia, malis supplicia dispensans;" de Consol. Philosoph. lib. v. prosa 6. And again—"nec sine poena unquam esse uitia, nec sine praemio uirtutes;" Boethius, de Consol. Philosoph. lib. iv. prosa 1. We find a similar quotation in An Old Eng. Miscellany, ed. Morris, p. 60, l. 60; and in Old Eng. Homilies, ed. Morris, 1st Ser. p. 41, l. 1.

——(b. 4. 156; *not in* c, a.) *I falle in*, I fall amongst, I meet with. Warin Wisdom used to meet with a florin (of course by mere accident), and suddenly find himself unable to plead.

169. (b. 4. 175; *not in* a.) See the passage from Wyclif's Works, iii. 307, quoted in the note to Pass. iv. 183.

171. (b. 4. 177; *not in* a.) The remark 'yf iche regne eny whyle' was obviously intended, when first introduced, as a direct allusion to the very recent accession of Richard II., as is also the story of belling the cat in the Prologue. The B-text seems to have been written in 1377, whereas the A-text (which omits the phrase *if I reign any while*) has always (rightly) been assigned to the year 1362, when Edward was already in the thirty-sixth year of his long reign. But this allusion loses its original force when retained in the C-text, since Richard had then been on the throne for many years. It was, however, retained with some reason, with a new significance; since, in 1389, Richard had, for the first time, begun his reign on his own account, by taking the management of affairs into his own hands. The latter part of this Passus has been already commented upon at some length in the C-text (Preface iii.), pp. xvi and xvii, and in the Critical Note, B-text, p. 397.

176. (b. 4. 182; *not in* a.) *Withoute the comune help*, unless the commons help me [c]; *but the comune wil assent*, unless the commons will assent [b].

——(b. 4. 189; a. 4. 152.) *Be my conseille comen*, when my council is come. The Trinity MS. (printed by Mr Wright) has *By my counseil commune*, by my common council; which is certainly a corrupt reading.

189. (*not in* b, a.) *Vnsittynge suffraunce*, unbecoming tolerance; i. e. fraudulent connivance. See the phrase again in Pass. iv. 208.

190. (*not in* b, a.) See note to Pass. iii. 187.

194. (*not in* b, a.) *Lukes*, Lucca; see note to Pass. ix. 109. See this passage discussed in Pref. III (C-text), p. xvii.

SCHEME OF THE CONTENTS OF C. PASSUS VI.

(B. Pass. V. 1—60; A. Pass. V. 1—42; WITH AN INSERTION OF A PASSAGE FROM B. Pass. X. 292—329; A. Pass. XI. 201—210.

Cf. Wright's edition; pp. 77—80; and pp. 191—193.

C-TEXT.	B-TEXT.	A-TEXT.
vi. 1—108	——	——
——	v. 1—8	v. 1—8
109—113	*like* 9—12	*like* 9—11
114	——	——
——		12
115, 116	*like* 13	*like* 13
117—125	14—22	14—22
126—128	*like* 23—25	*like* 23—25
129—134	26—3	26—31
135, 136	32, 33	——
137, 138	34, 35	32, 33
——	36—40	——

C-TEXT.	B-TEXT.	A-TEXT.
vi. 139	v. 41	——
140	——	——
141, 142	42, 43	v. 34, 35
——	44	——
143—146	45—48	36—39

(*Here comes in the passage from* B. X. 292—329; A. XI. 201—210.)

147, 148	x. 292, 293	xi. 201, 202
——	x. 294	xi. 203
149—152	*like* x. 295—299	*like* xi. 204—207
153—156	*like* x. 300—305	
157—160	*like* x. 306—308	*like* xi. 208—210
161—174	*like* x. 309—323	——
175, 176	——	——
——	x. 324, 325	——
177, 178	x. 326, 327	——
——	x. 328	——
179, 180	*like* 329	——

(*Here the insertion from* B. X. *ends.*)

181, 182	v. 49, 50	——
183—191	——	——
192, 193	*like* v. 51, 52	——
194—197	——	——
——	v. 53—56	——
198—200	v. 57—59	v. 40—42
201	v. 60	——

NOTES TO PASSUS VI.

1. (*not in* b, a.) Lines 1—108 are peculiar to the C-text, and are of great interest, being to some extent autobiographical. Here William tells us of his life in Cornhill, where he lived, clothed like a loller, with his wife Kit and his daughter Calote (mentioned in Pass. xxi. 473), yet not much liked by the lollers and hermits around him. He then describes his own laziness in amusing terms. See the remarks upon this passage in the C-text, Pref. iii. p. lxix.

Perhaps I ought to remark here that there is no particular difficulty about his statement that he was married. See Milman, Hist. of Lat. Christianity, ed. 1855, v. 72; vi. 101.

2. (*not in* b, a.) *Lollere.* Though much has been written on this important word, the history of it has not been very well made out; chiefly, I think, because the passages concerning it in Piers the Plowman have not been sufficiently observed. The standard passage upon it will be found in Pass. x. 98—254, every word of which requires careful reading. The word occurs there several times; see ll. 103, 107, 137, 140, 158, 192, 213; cf. also ll. 215, 218. See also l. 31 of the present Passus. It occurs also in Chaucer, at the eleventh line after the conclusion of the Man of Lawes Tale (Group B, l. 1173, in the Six-text Edition), and I quote here, for the reader's convenience, my note upon that line at p. 141 of the Prioresses and other Tales, Oxford, 1874.

"The reader will not clearly understand this word till he distinguishes between the Latin *lollardus* and the English *loller*, two words of different origin which were *purposely* confounded in the time of Wyclif. The Latin *Lollardus* had been in use before Wyclif. Ducange quotes from Johannes Hocsemius, who says, under the date 1309—'Eodem anno quidam hypocritae gyrovagi, qui *Lollardi,* sive Deum laudantes, vocabantur, per Hannoniam et Brabantiam quasdam mulieres nobiles deceperunt.' He adds that Trithemius says in his Chronicle, under the year 1315—'ita appellatos a Gualtero Lolhard, Germano quodam.' Kilian, in his Dictionary of Old Dutch, says—'Lollaerd, mussitator, mussitabundus;' i. e. a mumbler of prayers. This gives two etymologies for *Lollardus.* Being thus already in use as a term of reproach, it was applied to the followers of Wyclif, as we learn from Thomas Walsingham, who says, under the year 1377—'Hi uocabantur a uulgo *Lollardi,* incedentes nudis pedibus;' and again, 'Lollardi sequaces Joannis Wyclif.' But the Old English *loller* (from the verb *to loll*) meant simply a lounger, an idle vagabond, as is abundantly clear from a notable passage in Piers the Plowman, C-text (ed. Skeat), x. 188—218; where William tells us plainly—

> ' Now kyndeliche, by crist · beþ suche callyd *lolleres,*
> As by englisch of oure eldres · of old menne techynge.
> He that *lolleþ* is lame · oþer his leg out of ioynte,' etc.

This will explain how it was that when the Wycliffites were called lollers, they sometimes turned round, and said their opponents were the *true* lollers, the *true* idle fellows. [Here was inserted a wrong reference; but I believe the foregoing statement to be correct.]

"Here were already two (if not three) words confused, but this was not all. By a bad pun, the Latin *lolium,* tares, was connected with *Lollard,* so that we find in Political Poems, i. 232, the following—

> ' Lollardi sunt zizania,
> Spinae, uepres, ac *lollia,*
> Quae uastant hortum uineae.'

This obviously led to allusions to the Parable of the Tares, and fully accounts for the punning allusion to cockle, i. e. tares, in [Chaucer, Group B.] l. 1183. Mr Bell observes that *lolium* is used in the Vulgate Version, Matt. xiii. 25; but this is a mistake, as the word there used is *zizania.* Gower, Prol. to Conf. Amant., speaks of—

> ' This newe secte of *lollardie,*
> And also many an heresie.'

Also in book V.—

> ' Be war that thou be nought oppressed
> With anticristes *lollardie,*' etc.

The reader should observe that William elsewhere uses the phrase *to be lolled up* (lit. to be made to dangle about) as a euphemism for *to be hung;* Pass. xv. 131. Also, in P. Pl. Crede, l. 532, to *loll* means to accuse of heresy; see my note to that line. See also Knyghton, ed. Twysden, col. 2706; Hardwick's Glos. to Elmham, Hist. Monast. Cant.; Pecock's Repressor, pp. 128, 654; Pict. Hist. of England, ii. 140; Prompt. Parv., p. 311, note 3; Mosheim, Eccl. Hist. iii. 355.

Speaking of "the itinerant priests," Prof. Rogers says—"These men, privileged by their order, wandered about the country preaching, and subsisting partly on the alms of their hearers, partly on their gains as scribes. The accounts of which I have been able to make so large a use are regularly engrossed by clerks, who received what in these times would have been considered handsome payment for the service, in the customary fee of half a mark. That this work was performed by migratory writers, I think clear from the facts that the character of the medieval writing is so singularly uniform, although accounts may be taken from very distant places, and also that any change in the form of the letters is as sudden as it is universal." Hist. Agric. in Eng., by J. E. Thorold Rogers, i. 95.

3. (*not in* b, a.) *Lytel y-lete by*, lightly esteemed. Cf. note to Rich. Redeles, iii. 284.

5. (*not in* b, a.) "For I composed verses about those men, as Reason taught me." To *make* is to write verses, to compose, and a poet was called a *maker*. See fuller remarks upon these words in the note to B. xii. 16.

6. (*not in* b, a.) "For, as I passed by Conscience, I met with Reason." The allusion is to his vision of Conscience in the last Passus; still, he is here in a waking dream only, and represents himself as again beholding this creature of his imagination; passing by him indeed, but only to meet another phantom, with whom he converses. The dialogue is really carried on between William's carnal and spiritual natures, between his flesh and. his spirit.

10. (*not in* b, a.) "Being in health (of body), and in soundness or unity (of mind), a certain being thus cross-examined me."

13. (*not in* b, a.) *Coke* = (1) to cook; (2) to put hay into cocks. A *coker* sometimes means a reaper (Halliwell), but the explanation that it formerly meant a charcoal-burner is not quite satisfactory. Richardson quotes the following. "Bee it also prouided, that this act, nor anything therein contained doe in any wise extende to any *cockers* of haruest folkes that trauaile into anie countrie of this realme for haruest worke, either corne haruest, or hay haruest, if they doe worke and labour accordingly;" Rastall, Statutes; Vagabonds, &c., p. 474. The context shows that the sense is— "Or put hay into cocks for my harvestmen."

14. (*not in* b, a.) The first *mowe* signifies to mow hay; the second (also spelt *mouwen, muwe, mywen*) means to put into a mow, to stack.

16. (*not in* b, a.) *Haywarde.* See Mr Way's note to this word in the Promptorium Parvulorum. "The *heyward*," he says, "was the keeper of cattle in a common field, who prevented trespass on the cultivated ground." In fact, the word signifies a *hedge-warden*, one whose duty it was to see that the cattle were kept within their proper boundaries. In the Romance of Alexander, ed. Weber, l. 5754, we have—

> " In tyme of heruest mery it is ynough,
> Peres and apples hongeth on bough;
> The hayward bloweth mery his horne,
> In eueryche felde ripe is corne."

Mr Timbs, in his Nooks and Corners of English Life, p. 224, remarks that " in the illustrations of an old Saxon calendar, in the Cotton Library, the hayward is shown standing on a hillock, cheering the reapers with his horn." I have seen a similar illustration in an illustrated sheet in the Bodleian Library. See also Bardsley's English Surnames, p. 198; Wyclif's Works, i. 104; and see further remarks in the note to Pass. xiv. 45. Cf. Pass. xxii. 334. ·

20, 21. (*not in* b, a.) "Or a craft of any other kind, such as is necessary for the community, in order to provide sustenance for them that are bedridden." This recognises the duty of the young to provide for the aged and infirm.

24. (*not in* b, a.) *To long,* i. e. too long in the back or legs, too tall. Occleve says the very same of himself; De Regim. Principum, ed. Wright, p. 36—

> " With ploughe kan I not medle, ne with harwe,
> Ne wote nat what lond goode is for what corne;
> And for to lade a carte or fille a barwe,
> To whiche I never used was a-forne.
> My bak unbuxom bathe suche thynge forsworne," &c.

By *unbuxom* is meant here unbending, stiff, not lissome. Our author alludes, doubtless, to the nickname of 'Long Will' which had been bestowed upon him by his neighbours; see B. xv. 148. We have already had *long* in the sense of *tall;* see Pass. i. 53.

33. (*not in* b, a.) *Broke* means having broken bones, or some permanent injury; cf. ix. 143; x. 99; 169—172.

36. (*not in* b, a.) "My father and my friends found means to send me to school." To *find* is to *provide for.* Cf. Chaucer's Prol. 301, 302.

39. (*not in* b, a.) *By so,* provided that I will continue in well-doing.

41. (*not in* b, a.) *Longe clothes.* This refers to the dress which he wore as being one of the secular clergy. On this subject, see Cutts's Scenes and Characters of the Middle Ages, pp. 241—244. For example, we there learn that John Stratford, Archbishop of Canterbury, A.D. 1342, tried to restrain the clergy from appearing " publicly in an outer garment short, or notably scant," &c.

44. (*not in* b, a.) " I live *in* London, and *upon* London," i. e. upon the work which London affords. He was one of the " great crowd of priests who gained a livelihood by taking temporary engagements to say masses for the souls of the departed." See Cutts's Scenes and Characters of the Middle Ages, p. 207; also pp. 201, 202.

46. (*not in* b, a.) *Primer;* a book of elementary religious instruction. See Dr Burton's preface to his edition of King Henry the Eighth's Three Primers, where he shews that the word was in use at least as early as 1527,

when a Primer of the Salisbury use was printed.   The word occurs in the fifth stanza of Chaucer's Prioresses Tale, and in the Promptorium Parvulorum, A.D. 1440.   "The Creed, Pater Noster, and Ave Maria always held a prominent place in the Primer;" Hook's Church Dictionary.   "My *primer* clothed with purpill damaske" occurs in a will dated 1493; Cullum's Hist. of Hawsted, 2nd ed. p. 137.   Sir John Cullum's note says—"The primer contained a collection of prayers, psalms, hymns, &c., in Latin and English; retained with alteration, after the Reformation.   Brit. Top. vol. ii. p. 323."

We are told that souls may be helped out of purgatory "as to lernyd men, as bi masses singyng, saing of sawters, *placebo*, and *dirige*, commendacions, .vij. psalmes, and the .xv. psalmes, with the letenye, bi almesdede and bi pilgrimage: and also bi lewid men with the paternoster, the ave Maria, and the crede, almesdede, fastyng, and pilgrimage, and bi many other good dedis;" Vision of Wm. Staunton, 1409; MS. Reg. 17 B. 43; quoted in St Patrick's Purgatory, by T. Wright, p. 149.   For *placebo* and *dirige*, see note to Pass. iv. 467.

47. (*not in* b, a.) *Sauter*, psalter.   *Seven psalmes;* i. e. the seven penitential Psalms, in very frequent use; viz. Psalms vi. xxxii. xxxviii. li. cii. cxxx. cxliii.; all of which are still read on Ash-Wednesday.

52. (*not in* b, a.)   "I have no bag (for victuals), nor bottle (for drink), but only my belly (wherein to bestow food)."   This accurate description of his mode of obtaining a livelihood is very interesting.

56. (*not in* b, a.)   *Crouned*, crowned (with the tonsure).   See note to Pass. i. 86.   The opposite expression, 'uncrowned,' occurs in l. 62 below.

59. (*not in* b, a.)   *It ben aires*, they are heirs.   This is the usual idiom of the period.   Cf. "hit are bote fewe folke;" Pass. xvi. 288; "than aren hit pure poure thynges;" Pass. xvi. 309; also "hit am I;" Chaucer, C. T. 3764.

70. (*not in* b, a.)   For a comparison between this passage and P. Pl. Crede, ll. 744—760, see Pref. to C-text, p. xviii.

79. (*not in* b, a.)   "And choose Simon's son to keep the sanctuary."   The phrase 'Simon's son' means the son of Simon Magus, i. e. one who has been guilty of Simony, or one whose wealth was his only recommendation.   See Pass. x. 257; and note to Rich. Redeles, iv. 55.   It is an expression resembling that of 'Judas' children'; B. prol. 35.

88. (*not in* b, a.)   *Fynt ous alle þynges*, provides us with all things; cf. B. vii. 121—129; and B. xiv. 48.

89. (*not in* b, a.)   "I can not see that this applies."   The word *lyeth* here means *applies, is to the point*.   Conscience tells him that his remarks are not quite to the point; and, in the next line, uses the word 'parfytnesse' with reference to the word 'parfyt' in l. 84.

101, 102. (*not in* b, a.)   "And to enter upon a period that will turn all the periods of my life to profit."

——(b. 5. 6; a. 5. 6.)   This line somewhat resembles Rich. Redeles, iv. 65.

——(b. 5..8; a. 5. 8.) "Babbling" in prayer is spoken of and censured in Becon's Works, i. 134, 135, 169; and in Bullinger, iv. 204 (Parker Society).

109. (b. 5. 9; a. 5. 9.) Here begins the Second Vision, which may be called the Vision of the Seven Deadly Sins and of Piers the Plowman; the subject of the First Vision having been the Field Full of Folk, Holy Church, and the Lady Meed. This second Vision begins with the same scene as the First, viz. the scene of the Field Full of Folk (see l. 111), only that now Reason and Conscience appear in the king's presence, and Reason preaches a sermon before the assembled multitude. (N.B. In [a], it is *Conscience* who is the preacher.)

115. (b. 5. 13; a. 5. 13.) *Thuse pestilences*. There were three (some reckon four) terrible pestilences at this period, which were long remembered, and proved such scourges that the land was left partly untilled, causing severe famines to ensue. They took place in 1348 and 1349, 1361 and 1362, and 1369; a fourth was in 1375 and 1376. The *two first* are really the ones alluded to, the A-text having been written before the third took place. The first of them is computed to have begun at varying dates. Mr Wright gives an extract from a register of the Abbey of Gloucester (MS. Cotton, Domit. A. viii., fol. 124) to this effect—"Anno Domini m°. ccc°. xlviij°., anno vero regni regis Edwardi III post conquestum xxxij°., incepit magna pestilentia in Anglia, ita quod *vix tertia pars* hominum remansit;" and he adds—"This pestilence, known as the *black plague* [or *black death*] ravaged most parts of Europe, and is said to have carried off in general about two-thirds of the people. It was the pestilence which gave rise to the Decamerone of Boccaccio. For an interesting account of it, see Michelet's Hist. de France, iii. 342—349." See also the marvellous description of it by Boccaccio himself. Lingard says that it reached Dorchester in August, and London in September, 1348. Fabyan says it began in August, 1348. Sir H. Nicolas, in The Chronology of History, p. 345, says it began May 31, 1349, which is surely the wrong year. A fuller account is given in Prof. Thorold Rogers' Hist. of Agricult. and Prices in England, i. 294, who says—"The Black Death appeared at Avignon in Jan. 1348, visited Florence by the middle of April, and had thoroughly penetrated France and Germany by August. It entered Poland in 1349, reached Sweden in the winter of that year, and Norway, by infection from England, at about the same time." . . . "On the 1st Aug. 1348, the disease appeared in the seaport towns of Dorsetshire, and travelled slowly westwards and northwards . . to Bristol. . . . The plague continued to Oxford, and . . reached London by the 1st of November. It appeared in Norwich on the 1st of January [1349], and then spread northwards." It terminated on the 29th September, 1349. The *second* pestilence is the one to which William more immediately alludes. It lasted from August 15, 1361, to May 3, 1362; see Sir H. Nicolas, as above. Some records are dated from the times of these plagues. Allusions to them as God's punishments for sin are common in the writers of the period. See the next note.

117. (b. 5. 14; a. 5. 14.) *Southwest wynd.* Tyrwhitt first pointed out that this is an allusion to the violent tempest of wind on Jan. 15, 1362, which was a *Saturday.* He refers to the mention of it by Thorn, Decem Script. col. 2122; by Walsingham (see Riley's edition, vol. i. p. 296); and by the Continuator of Adam Murimuth, p. 115. The last notice is the most exact. "A.D. m.ccc.lxii, xv die Januarii, *circa horam uesperarum*, uentus uehemens *notus Australis Africus* tantâ rabie erupit," &c. Walsingham calls it *nothus Auster Africus.* It is alluded to by many other chroniclers also. Fabyan says, p. 475—"In this xxxvii yere, vpon the daye of seynt Maurycc, or the xv daye of Januarii, blewe so excedynge a wynde that the lyke therof was nat seen many years passed. This began *about euynsong tyme* in the *South*," &c. He says it lasted for five days. We find the same notice again in A Chronicle of London, p. 65, where it is said to have taken place, in the year 1361, on "seynt Maurys day." This means the same year (viz. 1361-2), which was called 1361 during the months of January and February, and 1362 afterwards; according to the old reckoning. Fabyan wrongly calls it the day of St Maurice; the 15th of Jan. is the day of St *Maur*, a disciple of St Bennet. It is noticed again in Hardyng's Chronicles, ed. Ellis, 1812, p. 330; in Riley's Memorials of London, p. 308; and in the Eulogium Historiarum, ed. Haydon, iii. 229. Blomefield tells us that it blew down the spire of Norwich Cathedral. It will be observed that the second great pestilence was prevailing at the time. In the prophecies of John of Bridlington, printed in Wright's Political Poems, there is a similar mention of the first two pestilences and of the tempest. The first pestilence is spoken of in lib. iii. cap. 10; the second, in lib. iii. cap. 11. And, in the latter passage, we find the line—
"Est Notus infestus Saturni cum ruet aestus"—
with the commentary—"tunc erit Notus infestus, i. ventus inter Austrum et Orientem qui Notus dicitur; erit contrarius et destructivus ex infectione constellacionis Saturni."

118. (b. 5. 15; a. 5. 15.) These judgments (as they seemed to be) were looked upon as due to *Pride,* because it was the chief and most pernicious of the seven deadly sins; see Pass. vii. 3. The very same thought occurs in the following quotation from Political Songs, ed. Wright, p. 344—
"Pride priketh aboute, wid nithe [*malice*] and wid onde [*envy*];
Pes and love and charite hien hem out of londe
So faste,
That God wole for-don the world; we muwe be sore agaste."
127. (b. 5. 24; a. 5. 24.) Compare Pass. i. 24; ix. 139—176.
129. (b. 5. 26; a. 5. 26.) Compare note to Pass. v. 111; and see vii. 3.
131. (b. 5. 28; a. 5. 28.) *Thomme Stowe,* &c. A difficult passage. Whitaker has *Stone* and *wynen,* and explains it—"He taught Thom. Stone to take two sticks, and fetch home Felice, his spouse, from drinking wine." This does not explain *pyne.* The MSS. have *Stowue, stouue, Stowe; of stowe;* in the Trinity MS. (R. 3. 14) the other word is clearly *wynene;* whilst MS. Laud 656 has the unmistakeable form *wyfen;* and Whitaker himself notes

that MS. Phillipps 8252 has the form *wycyn*. Like *kyngene*, *clerken*, it is a genitive plural, and as *pyne* invariably means punishment, *wynen pyne* is only one more allusion to the *women's punishment*, the *cucking-stool*. I suppose the sentence to mean that *Tom Stowe*, who had neglected his wife and let her get into bad ways, or who had allowed her to be punished as a scold, had much better fetch her home than leave her exposed to public derision. Such an errand would require a strong arm, and two staves would be very useful in dispersing the crowd. I do not think it is meant that he is to beat *her*, for then *one* would have sufficed; nor would Reason give such bad advice.*

133. (b. 5. 30; a. 5. 30.) *Watte*, the contraction of *Water*, which was another form of *Walter*, and by no means uncommon. Thus in P. Pl. Crede, l. 657, one copy has *Wat*, whilst two other copies have *Water*. Cf. "nout Willam (*sic*) ne *Water*;" Ancren Riwle, p. 340; and cf. Shak., 2 Hen. VI. iv. 1. 35.

134. (b. 5. 31; a. 5. 31.) Nothing so invited satire as the head-dresses of the females. Chaucer makes the wife of Bath's to have weighed *ten pounds!* The hair was generally enveloped in a caul of net-work of gold, which fitted close to both sides of the face. Thus, in the *Crede*, we read of "great-headed queans, *with gold by the eyes*," l. 84.

Even as early as in the reign of Edw. I., we find that only ladies of the upper class were permitted to wear furred hoods; Liber Albus, p. 584.

135. (b. 5. 32; *not in* a.) *Bette* was a male name, and has already been applied to a beadle; Pass. iii. 111. It was probably a mere variation of *Bat*, a shortened form of Bartholomew; see Bardsley's English Surnames, p. 72. Of course *bad* means 'commanded'; Mr Bardsley seems to have taken it to be an adjective!

136. (b. 5. 33; *not in* a.) *Beton* was a female name, as shewn by the context, and by Pass. vii. 353. It was a pet name for Beatrice; see Bardsley's English Surnames, p. 58 and Index. Beton was probably Bette's daughter.

138. (b. 5. 35; a. 5. 33.) *Wynnynge* means success in business, gain by trading. *Forwene* means to spoil by over-indulgence (lit. to *for-wean*, i. e. to wean amiss), and is well illustrated by the following quotation. "De unwise man & *forwened* child habbeð boðe on lage; for þat hie habben willeð boðe here wil;" i. e. the unwise man and the spoilt child have both one law (custom); for they both desire to have their will; Old Eng. Homilies (2nd Series), ed. Morris, p. 41. Cf. A.S. *forwened*, proud, i. e. spoilt, over-indulged; and see Rich. Redeles, i. 27, where William says of King Richard's courtiers that they "walwed in her willis · *forweyned* in here youthe." The advice is addressed to the chapmen or traders, and means—"let no success in your business induce you to spoil your children in their infancy." In the A-text, the line means—"let them lack no awe, whilst they are young." In the next line (of the B-text only) the advice is continued thus:—"nor (allow yourselves) to please them unreasonably, on account of any virulence (lit. power) of a pestilence." It is worth observing that ll. 36—41 of the B-text do not appear in [a]; and consequently, by the time they were added, both

the third and fourth pestilences, viz. of 1369 and 1375, had taken place. Hence there was additional reason to fear that the anxiety to rear children would lead to excessive indulgence to them.

——(b. 5. 38; *not in a.*) *The leuere childe*, &c.; "to the dearer child, the more teaching is necessary." This was a common proverb, as pointed out by Mr Wright, and is found in the proverbs of Hendyng, written about 1300 —"*Luef child lore byhoueth*, Quoth Hendyng." See Specimens of Early English, ed. Morris and Skeat, p. 36; or Reliq. Antiq. i. p. 110. So in the poem called How the Goodwife Taught her Daughter—

> "And ȝif thou loue thin childryn, loke thou holde hem lowe;
> ȝif any of hem do amys, curse hem nought ne blowe,
> But take a smerte rodde, and bete hem alle by rowe,
> Till thei crye mercye, and be here gylte aknowe."
> Hazlitt's Early Pop. Poetry, vol. i. p. 191.

The original source is Prov. xiii. 24—"Qui parcit uirgæ, odit filium suum; qui autem diligit illum, instanter erudit."

142. (b. 5. 43; a. 5. 35.) *That hij preche*, that which they preach. Cf. B. iv. 122.

144. (b. 5. 46; a. 5. 37.) *Religion*, religious orders, as in Pass. x. 36. *Religious* is used in the same sense four lines below. *Religiuns* is used in the sense of 'religious communities;' Aucren Riwle, p. 24.

146. (b. 5. 48; a. 5. 39.) This idea is enlarged upon in ll. 147—178 below; and this is doubtless the reason why the latter passage, which in the B-text was in a different place (viz. in the tenth Passus) was shifted so as to occupy its present position.

☞ Note the sudden leap here, from B. 5. 48 (A. 5. 39) to B. 10. 292 (A. 11. 201).

147. (b. 10. 292; a. 11. 201.) The passage contained in ll. 147—180 answers to B. x. 292—329, and a part of it answers also to A. xi. 201—210. It is, in fact, the first of the *inserted* passages which have been discussed in the C-text, Pref. pp. lxxviii and lxxix; where I have already remarked that it is "now made to form a part of Reason's sermon, instead of part of Scripture's discourse. It shortens the latter, and comes in much more naturally as a part of the former. The change is a considerable improvement, and skilfully managed."

Lines 291—303 of the B-text are found in one MS. only. See Critical Note to B. x. 291, at p. 406 of that text.

By 'Gregory the great clerk' is meant pope Gregory I., surnamed the Great, born about A.D. 544, died A.D. 604. But it would be no easy task to find the passage referred to. Tyrwhitt, in a note to l. 179 of the Prologue to the Canterbury Tales, says, "the text alluded to is attributed by Gratian, *Decret.* P. ii. Cau. xvi. Q. 1. c. viii, to a Pope Eugenius—'Sicut piscis sine aqua caret uita, ita sine monasterio monachus.'" William quotes it from his 'morales' [b], i.e. from the 'Moralium Libri xxxiv,' one of the most important of Gregory's works. The phrase 'Gregori the grete clerk' occurs

again in Pass. xxii. 270; q. v.   In Kingsley's The Hermits, p. 74, a quotation is given from the life of St Antony by Athanasius, published by
Heschelius in 1611, in which monks who stay away from their retreats are
likened to fishes upon dry land.

151. (b. 10. 297; a. 11. 206.) *Roteþ and sterueth*, becomes· rotten and
dies.   In [a] and [b] we find *roileth*, the meaning of which, in this passage,
is (probably)—wanders about, ranges about restlessly.   It is clear that there
are at least two distinct words which assume the form *roil*.   Mr Wedgwood
rightly points out the distinction between the verb to *roil* or *rile* in the sense
of to disturb, trouble, vex, and the same verb in the sense of to range about
restlessly.   Mr Atkinson, in his Cleveland Glossary, gives "*Roil*, v. n. to
romp or play boisterously, to make a petty disturbance by riotous play," and
connects this with Icel. *rugl* or *ruglan*, disturbance, and *rugla*, to disturb;
after which he cites the present passage of Piers the Plowman.   This is, I
suspect, a mistake; since the Cleveland verb is evidently *roil*, to disturb, and
is connected with *rollick*.   We should rather take notice of the following
passages, as being more to the point.

   In Chaucer's Wife of Bath's Prologue, Six-text, D. l. 653, we have—
         "Man shal not suffre his wyf go roule aboute—"
where, for *roule*, the Lansdowne MS. has *roile*.

   Roile is used in the sense of to wander about in Holinshed's Chronicles,
vol. ii. p. 21, col. 2.   We find in the Prompt. Parv. p. 436—"Roytyn, or
gon ydel a-bowte, roytyn or *roylyn*, or gone ydyl abowte, *vagor, discurro*."
In Levins' Manipulus Vocabulorum, we have "to *Royle* abroad, *diuagari*;"
ed. Wheatley, p. 214, l. 43. ˙ In Harman's Caveat (ed. Furnivall, p. 31) we
read of rascals that 'wyll wander,' of whom he says again—"These vnrewly
rascales, in their *roylynge*, disperse themselues into seuerall companyes," &c.
Compare also—"he will not wander nor *royle* so farre aboute;" Turberville,
Book of Venerie, ed. 1575, p. 141.   And again—"*royling* aboute in ydle-
nes;" Sir T. More, Dialogue concerning Heresies, ed. 1557, p. 194, col. 2.

   It is remarkable that there is also a pair of substantives which take the
same form, and are respectively connected ·with the pair of verbs already
mentioned.   Thus *roil*, in the sense of a romp, a hoyden, a big ungainly
woman, may be referred to the verb *roil*, to disturb, to romp; whilst, in connection with the verb *roil*, to wander loosely about, we find the substantive
roil applied to a staggering, stumbling, and tired horse.   I give two examples
of the latter.
         "But sure that horse which tyreth like a *roile*," &c.;
               Gascoigne's Complaint of Phylomene (qu. by Richardson).
"For it hath ben often tymes sene that by the good swimming of horse
many men haue ben saued; and, contrary wise, by a timorouse *royle*, where
the water hath vneth come to his bely, his legges hath foltred [*faltered, given
way*]: wherby many a good and propre man hath perisshed;" Sir T. Elyot:
The Governour, Book I. ch. 17; ed. 1531.   See also a passage from Heywood quoted in Dyce's Skelton, ii. 379.

I conclude, then, that the sense of *roileth* in this passage is 'plays the vagabond;' in allusion to the habits of the mendicant friars.

157—161. (b. 10. 306—309; a. 11. 208—210.) Warton, in his Hist. Eng. Poetry, ed. 1840, vol. ii. p. 57, has the following note upon the present passage. "Walter de Suffield, bishop of Norwich, bequeathes by will his pack of hounds to the king, in 1256; Blomefield's Norfolk, ii. 347. See Chaucer's Monke in the Prologue, l. 165. This was a common topic of satire. It occurs again, fol. xxvii. a [of Crowley's edition of Piers Plowman; i. e. in Pass. iv. 469]. See the Testament of Love, ed. Urry, p. 492, col. 2. The Archdeacon of Richmond, on his visitation, comes to the priory of Bridlington in Yorkshire, in 1216, with ninety-seven horses, twenty-one dogs, and three hawks; Dugdale's Monasticon, ii. 65." It would be easy to give many further examples. "The bishops and abbots of the middle ages hunted with great state, having a large train of retainers and servants; and some of them are recorded for their skill in this fashionable pursuit. Walter, bp. of Rochester, who lived in the 13th century, was an excellent hunter, and so fond of the sport, that at the age of fourscore he made hunting his sole employment, to the total neglect of the duties of his office. (P. Blensensis, Epist. lvi. p. 81.) In the succeeding century an abbot of Leicester surpassed all the sportsmen of the time in the art of hare-hunting (Knyghton, apud Decem Scriptores, p. 263); and, even when these dignitaries were travelling from place to place, upon affairs of business, they usually had both hounds and hawks in their train. Fitzstephen assures us, that Th. à Becket, being sent as ambassador from Henry the Second to the court of France, assumed a state of a secular potentate; and took with him dogs and hawks of various sorts, such as were used by kings and princes (Stephanid. vit. S. Thom.);" Strutt's Sports and Pastimes, ed. Hone, p. 11.

The following account of the doings of a 'parsoun' is to the same effect.

"And when he hath i-gadered markes and poundes,
He priketh out of toune wid haukes and wid houndes
Into a straunge contre, and halt a wenche in cracche;
And wel is hire that first may swich a parsoun kacche."

Political Songs, ed. Wright, p. 327.

."And thise abbotes and priours don aȝein here rihtes;
Hii riden wid hauk and hound, and contreseten knihtes;
Hii sholde leve swich pride, and ben religious," &c.

Ibid. p. 329.

"ȝyf þou delyte þe often stoundes
Yn horsys, haukys, or yn boundes,
ȝyf þou clerk auaunsede be,
Swyche game ys nat grauntede to þe."

Robert of Brunne; Hand. Synne, 3086-9.

Wyclif too speaks of "a worldly preest . . . wiþ fatte hors, and jolye and gaye sadeles, and bridelis ryngynge be þe weye, and himself in cost[l]y cloþes and pelure;" Works, ed. Arnold, iii. 520.

See also The Ploughman's Tale, in Wright's Political Poems, i. 307, 334, especially noting the lines where the author says it is not right

> "That a man should a monke 'lord' call
>   Ne serve on knees, as a king"—

which hints at the same practice as is mentioned in our text, l. 162.

159. (b. 10. 307; a. 11. 209.) For note on *lovedays*, see note to Pass. iv. 196.

160. (b. 10. 308; a. 11. 210.) The verb to *prike*, meaning to ride about, is the verb usually employed by the poets and ballad-writers.

> "The tanner seyde—'what manner man are ye?'
> 'A *preker abowt*,' seyd the kyng, 'in manye a contre.'"

The King and the Barker; in Hazlitt's Early Pop. Poetry, i. 5. The word *poperith* [a] is of extremely rare occurrence; I know of no other instance of its use.

164. (b. 10. 312; *not in* a.) 'Little had lords to do;' i. e. lords might have found something better to do. The form *a-do* is doubtless short for *at do*, as proved by the instances in Mätzner's Engl. Gramm. vol. iii. p. 58; the word *at* being (as in Icelandic) the usual sign of an infinitive of purpose. Hence, for *a-do* [c], we find *to done* in [b].

165. (b. 10. 313; *not in* a.) The sense is—'to men belonging to religious orders, who do not care though the rain falls on their altars;' i. e. who do not even attempt to repair the roofs of their churches, though the rain falls on the altar itself. This passage is cleared up by the following words of Wyclif. "Also freris bylden mony grete chirchis and costily waste housis, and cloystris as hit were castels . . . where-thorw parische chirchis . . . ben payred [*impaired*], and in mony placis undone . . , For, by þis new housinge of freris, þof hit rayne on þo auter of þo parische churche, þo blynde puple is so disseyved þat þei wil raþer gif to waste housis of freris þen to parische chirchis," &c.; Works, ed. Arnold, iii. 380. Cf. l. 176 below.

In the Vision of Wm. Staunton (A.D. 1409), in MS. Reg. 17 B. xliii, quoted by Mr T. Wright at p. 149 of his St Patrick's Purgatory, we are told that "those who had let their churches fall into decay, so that rain and hail fell into the chancel and on the very altars" are punished in hell "by showers of terrible rain and hail."

166. (b. 10. 314; *not in* a.) "That is, where they have vicars of their own body, residing on their appropriated benefices;" Whitaker.

169. (b. 10. 317; *not in* a.) This famous prediction, so curiously fulfilled in the time of Henry the Eighth, was certainly written before the event, as Warton remarks, being found in MSS. written before A.D. 1400. It was merely due to the prevalent views as to the supreme power of the king; see Gower's Confessio Amantis, ed. Pauli, iii. 381; and cf. Pass. i. 148—157; iii. 245—248; iv. 381—385; v. 166—175; &c. Wyclif was of the like opinion. "For siþ clerkis ben lege men to kingis in whos landis þei ben inne, kyngis han power of God to punische hem in Goddis cause, boþe in bodi and in catel;" Works, ed. Arnold, ii. 88.

170. (b. 10. 318; *not in* a.) The use of the word *bete* (beat) renders it extremely probable that our author is referring to the very same passage of the Bible as was taken by Wyclif for the text of the sermon whence the

passage at the end of the last note is quoted, viz. John ii. 15; "And when he had made a scourge of small cords, he drove them all out of the temple." Or the reference may be to Jeremiah xxiii. 5, 11, 12; or Isaiah xxxii. 1.

171. (b. 10. 319; *not in* a.) Ducange gives *monialis* with sense of 'a nun;' and *moniale*, 'a nunnery.' For an explanation of *canon*, see the word in Hook's Church Dictionary. "Regular canons were such as lived under a rule, that is, a code of laws published by the founder of that order. They were a less strict sort of religious than the monks, but lived together under one roof, had a common dormitory and refectory, and were obliged to observe the statutes of their order;" &c., &c. See Wyclif's Works, i. 216; iii. 345; Wright's Political Songs, notes on p. 372.

172. (b. 10. 320; *not in* a.) I do not know whence the Latin phrase is taken. The nearest Biblical passage is in Levit. xxv. 10:—"Reuertetur homo ad possessionem suam, et unusquisque rediet ad familiam pristinam;" which has reference to the year of jubilee. This may be the passage intended; cf. Pass. iv. 455—480, and the note to iv. 456. Cf. Jerem. vi. 16.

——(b. 10. 321; *not in* a.) *Beatus vir* means the first Psalm, so called from the first two words. The 'teaching' is that of the 6th verse—"the way of the ungodly shall perish."

173. (b. 10. 322; *not in* a.) The Latin version has—"Hi in curribus, et hi in equis: nos autem in nomine Domini Dei nostri inuocabimus. Ipsi obligati sunt, et ceciderunt: nos autem surreximus et erecti sumus." Cf. Psalm xx. 7, 8, in the A. V. The allusion is to the use of *horses* by the monks; see note to l. 157.

174—176. (b. 10. 323—325; *not in* a.) The two texts vary very much here. The sense is—"Friars shall, in that day, find bread in their refectory without having to beg for it, sufficient for them to live upon for ever after; and Constantine shall be their cook, and the coverer (*or* recoverer) of their church" [c]; *or*—"And then shall friars find in their refectory a key of Constantine's coffers, wherein is the property that Gregory's spiritual children have spent so ill" [b]. The word *freitour*, corrupted to *fratery* or *fratry*, is used by Tyndal to signify a refectory (Tyndal's works, Parker Society, ii. 98); and described in a note to Grindal (Works, Park. Soc. 272, *note*). Mr Cutts says—"it would answer to the great chamber of mediæval houses, and in some respects to the Combination-room of modern colleges;" Scenes and Characters of the Middle Ages, p. 80. It was not necessarily the common hall, but might be a separate room; and it would appear probable, from some quotations given in Fosbroke's Antiquities, that the monks dined in the *freitour* on *feast-days*, which is probably the reason for the use of the word in this place. Cf. Pierce the Ploughman's Crede, ll. 203, 212, 220, 284, 701; Bale's Kynge Johan, p. 27; Wright's Polit. Songs, p. 331; St Brandan, p. 13; Wyclif's Works, i. 292. Halliwell refers also to Davies' Ancient Rites, 1672, pp. 7, 124, 126. "*Freytowre*, refectorium;" Prompt. Parv. "A *frayter* or place to eate meate in, refectorium;" Withal's Dict., ed. 1608, p. 250. The original form was the O.Fr. *refretoir* (Roquefort).

The allusion to Constantine is explained in the note to xviii. 220, q. v.

The word *couerer* may either mean 'one who covers;' i. e. one who provides or mends a roof, in allusion to l. 165; or it may mean 'one who recovers or restores,' since *keuere* or *couere* is sometimes thus used; Will. of Palerne, 1521.   By 'Gregory's god-children' is meant the monks of England, because the monastic state was introduced into England by St Augustine, who was sent hither by pope Gregory the Great, A.D. 596.

Our author seems to be looking forward to a time when the friars should be supported by some kind of regular endowment, under state control. This was a strange remedy to suggest, but he seems to have thought any plan better than their subsistence upon alms.

177. (b. 10. 326; *not in* a.)   The 'abbot of England' [c] is a less happy phrase than the 'abbot of Abingdon' [b].   Mr Wright says—" There was a very ancient and famous abbey at Abingdon in Berkshire.   Geoffrey of Monmouth was abbot there.   It was the house into which the monks, strictly so called, were first introduced in England, and is, therefore, very properly introduced as the representative of English monachism."   An excellent account of the Abbey of Abingdon will be found in Timbs's Abbeys and Castles of England, ii. 197—199, where he reminds us that " The *Chronicle of Abingdon* gives us a trustworthy record of this great Benedictine establishment during a period of 500 years."   See also Monumenta Franciscana, p. 633.

With respect to the abbots of Abingdon at the time of our author's work, we find that on July 24, 1362, the royal assent was given to the election of Peter de Hanneye, and the temporalities were restored to the abbey on the 2nd of August.   Willis and Steevens mention a Vincent as his successor, and there is a memorandum among the excerpts from the Patent Rolls in MS. Harl. 6950, which in some degree indicates a vacancy :—"An. 39 Edw. iii. [1365] Abb. Abendon vacat."   But if so, Peter de Hanneye was probably restored, since "Petrus abbas" occurs in Rymer's Fœdera in 1397, and Richard de Salforde is expressly stated to have been elected to the abbacy, on the death of Peter de Hanneye, on the 6th of March, 1399, the temporalities being restored on March 13.   Salforde is said to have died in 1415. See Dugdale, Monasticon, i. 509.

178. (b. 10. 327; *not in* a.)   *On here crounes,* on their shaven crowns; alluding to the tonsure, as usual.   This is a poor and unlucky alteration, since the B-text has *of a kynge.*   However, the C-text has the word *kyng* in the line following.

☞ Note the sudden leap here, from B. 10. 329 (A. 11. 210) back to B. 5. 49 (A. 5. 40).

181—197.   Much altered from B. v. 49—56, and not found in [a].   The advice to the king and nobles to cherish the commons is lengthened, and made more emphatic, ll. 183—191 being new.   Four lines are added in the advice to the pope; ll. 194—197.   But the advice to the lawyers is omitted.

185, 186. (*not in* b, a.)   "Let not counsel of any kind, nor any avarice

part you; so that one understanding and one will may keep all that you
have the charge of."

198. (b. 5. 57; a. 5. 40.) Here all three texts once more come together.
The poet advises those who had been wont to go on pilgrimage to Compostella or to Rome to try and find out the way to *Saint Truth*. This subject, of performing a pilgrimage to the shrine of Truth, is taken up again at
Pass. viii. 155—181; see especially viii. 157, 177. By *Saint Truth* is here
meant the Truth of the Divine Nature, formerly spoken of as being God the
Father (ii. 12), but here identified with the Holy Ghost, as appears by the
next line.

200. (b. 5. 59; a. 5. 42.) A usual ending of a homily was—"Qui cum
patre et spiritu sancto uiuit et regnat per omnia secula seculorum. Amen;"
Old Eng. Homilies, ed. Morris, ii. 115. In the present case, we have to
substitute *filio* for *spiritu sancto*. Compare—

> "And whan this frere had sayd al his entent,
> With *qui cum patre* forth his way he went."
>
> Chaucer, Somp. Tale, 25.

SCHEME OF THE CONTENTS OF C. PASSUS VII.

(B. Pass. V. 61—391; A. Pass. V. 43—221; WITH INSERTIONS FROM
B. Pass. XIII. 278—409; ALSO FROM B. Pass. V. 463—484;
A. Pass. V. 236—259.)

Cf. Wright's edition; pp. 81—100; 263—270; and 104—106.

N.B.   See also the Scheme of C. Passus XVI.

C-TEXT.	B-TEXT.	A-TEXT.
vii. 1—11	v. 61—71	v. 43—53
12—29	——	——
30—37	*like* xiii. 278—284	——
38—40	——	——
——	xiii. 285—291	——
41—60	*like* xiii. 292—313	——
61, 62	——	——
(*a*) [170—174]	(*a*) v. 72—75	(*a*) 54—58
63, 64	76, 77	59, 60
65—67	——	——
——	78—86	61—69
——	87	——
——	——	70—73
68	88	——
——	89—93	——
——	94	74
——	——	75, 76

C-TEXT.	B-TEXT.	A-TEXT.
—	v. 95—105	v. 77—87
—	106	—
—	107—114	88—95
—	115	—
—	116—119	96—99
—	xiii. 314—324	—
vii. 69—85	like xiii. 325—342	—
86, 87	v. 120, 121	(see 72)
88—94	122—128	100—106
95—98	like 129—132	—
99—101	—	—
102·	like 133	—
103, 104	134, 135	—
105—123	—	—
—	136—146	—
124—138	like 147—163	—
139—150	—	—
—	164—168	—
151—169	169—187	—
(a) 170—174	(a) [72—75]	(a) [54—58]
175	—	—
176, 177	like xiii. 343, 344	—
178—185	xiii. 345—352	—
—	xiii. 353, 354	—
186—195	—	—
—	xiii. 355—361	—
196—199	v. 188—192	107—110
200—202	193—195	—
203	196	111
—	197	—
204—233	198—227	112—141
—	228—231	142—145
234—238	232—236	—
—	237—239	—
239—243	240—244	—
244	—	—
—	245—249	—
245, 246	250, 251	—
247	—	—
—	252	—
248—251	253—256	—
252	—	—
—	257—262	—
253—255	like 263—267	—
256—259	—	—
260—266	xiii. 362—368	—
—	xiii. 369, 370	—
267—271	xiii. 371—375	—
—	xiii. 376—383	—
272—277	xiii. 384—389	—
—	xiii. 390, 391	—
278—285	xiii. 392—399	—

C-TEXT.	B-TEXT.	A-TEXT.
vii. 286		
287, 288	v. 268, 269	
———	270, 271	
289, 290	*like* 272	
291—293	———	
———	273	
294—297	274—277	
———	278, 279	
298—303	*like* 280—283	
304—308	———	
———	284—289	
309		

Note the transposition here ; the two earlier texts go to ll. 334 and 350 [c].

C-TEXT.	B-TEXT.	A-TEXT.
310—313	[463—466]	[236—239]
314, 315		
———	[467, 468]	[240, 241]
316—321	[469—474]	[242—247]
———		[248, 249]
322—329	[475—482]	[250—257]
———	[483]	[258]
330	[484]	[259]
331—333		
334—336	*like* 290, 291	———
337—339		———
340, 341	292, 293	
———	294	———
342—348	295—301	———
———	302	
349	.303	———
350, 351	304, 305	146, 147
352		———
353—358	306—311	148—153
		154
359—366	312—319	155—162
(b) [369]	(b) 320	(b) [164]
367	321	163
368		
(b) 369	(b) [320]	(b) 164
370		
371—380	322—331	165—174
381, 382	*like* 332	*like* 175
383, 384	333, 334	176, 177
385	———	*like* 178
386—388	335—337	179—181
———	338	*like* 182
389—394	339—344	183—188
395		189
396, 397	345, 346	190, 191
398	347	———
399—421	348—370	192—214
422	———	*like* 215
423, 424	———	

C-TEXT.	B-TEXT.	A-TEXT.
——	v. 371—373	——
vii. 425—429	374—378	——
——	xiii. 400—403	——
430	xiii. 404	——
——	xiii. 405—409	——
431	——	——
——	v. 379	——
432	*like* 380	——
433	——	——
434, 435	*see* 381—384	——
——	385	——
436	——	——
——	386	v. 216
437—441	387—391	217—221

NOTES TO PASSUS VII.

1. (b. 5. 61; a. 5. 43.) "Then ran Repentance, and repeated his (i. e. Reason's) theme, and made Will weep water with his eyes." *Will* means the author himself, who elsewhere calls himself Will in the same off-hand manner. Cf. Pass. ii. 5; xi. 71; also B. 8. 124; 15. 148; and A. 12. 51, 84, 94. Cf. also—"wepte water with his eyghen;" B. 14. 324.

3. (b. 5. 63; a. 5. 45.) Here begins the Confession of the Seven Deadly Sins. Few subjects are more common in our old authors than this one, of the Seven Deadly Sins. See, for instance, Chaucer's Persones Tale, *passim ;* Ælfric's Homilies, ed. Thorpe, ii. 219; Wyclif's Works, iii. 225; the Ancren Riwle, ed. Morton, pp. 198—204; Religious Pieces (ed. Perry, E. E. T. S.), pp. 11, 22; Dan Michel's Ayenbite of Inwyt, ed. Morris, p. 16; the Calendar of Shepherds, chapter viii., as described in Warton's Hist. Eng. Poetry, ed. 1840, ii. 387; Political, Religious, and Love Poems, ed. Furnivall, p. 215; Hymns to the Virgin and Christ, ed. Furnivall, p. 62; Spenser's Faerie Queene, bk. i. c. 4; &c., &c. In the Ancren Riwle each of these sins is represented by some animal; so that we have (1) the Lion of Pride; (2) the Nedder (or Adder) of Envy; (3) the Unicorn of Wrath; (4) the Scorpion of Lechery; (5) the Fox of Avarice; (6) the Sow of Gluttony; and (7) the Bear of Sloth. Our author was probably aware of these symbols, for he says of a *proud* man that he was "as a *lyon* on to loke," B. 13. 302; of *Envy*, that he had an *adder's* tongue, B. 5. 87; and, in describing *Gluttony*, he speaks of "two greedy *sows*," vii. 398.

From the two books above-mentioned as edited by Mr Furnivall we obtain the names of the seven virtues which were considered as remedies against the seven sins; and a similar list may be found in the Ancren Riwle, pp. 276—288, and in the Ayenbite of Inwyt, p. 159. The following is a list of the sins, with their Latin and Middle-English names, in the order in which they occur in the C-text of Piers the Plowman. (N.B. By 'A. R.' is meant the Ancren Riwle; and by 'A. I.' the Ayenbite of Inwyt.)

1. *Superbia* (Pride); prude, A. R.; prede, A. I.

2. *Inuidia* (Envy); onde, A. R.; enuie, A. I.

3. *Ira* (Anger); wreðde, A. R.; felhede, *or* hate, A. I.

4. *Luxuria* (Lechery); lecherie, A. R. and A. I.

5. *Auaritia* (Covetousness); coueitise, P. Pl.; giscunge, A. R.; auarice, *or* couaytyse, *or* scarsnesse, A. I.

6. *Gula* (Gluttony); giuernesse, A. R.; glotounye, A. I.

7. *Accidia* (Sloth); slouhðe, A. R.; onlosthede, *or* slacnesse, A. I.

The following is a list of their opposites or remedies:

1. *Humilitas* (Humility); edmoduesse, A. R.; boȝsamuesse, A. I.

2. *Caritas* (Charity, Love); luue, A. R.; loue, A. I.

3. *Patientia* (Patience); þolemodnesse, A. R.; mildnesse, A. I.

4. *Castitas* (Chastity); chastete, A. I.

5. *Eleemosyna* (Bounty); largesse, A. I.

6. *Abstinentia* (Abstinence); sobrete, A. I.

7. *Uigilantia* (Business); gostlich gledscipe, A. R.; prouesse, A. I. ·

All of these remedies are mentioned in Pass. viii. 272—275, with the exception that 'pees' is put in the place of Business or Watchfulness.

We have the expression "seven sinꝰ" in Pass. xvii. 44, with a discussion of some of them in the context. See also Pass. xxiii. 70, 114, 121, 159, 215, 273, 373.

Of all the seven sins, Pride is considered as the chief, and the root and spring of all the rest. It is expressed in Shakespeare by *ambition:*—

"Cromwell, I charge thee, fling away *ambition;*
By that sin fell the angels."—Henry VIII. iii. 2. 441.

Cf. note to Pass. ii. 105. It is singular that it is the only vice which William personifies by a female. He doubtless does so with particular reference to extravagance in dress, to repress which a special Statute was passed in 1363; see Lingard, iv. 91 (*note*). In the C-text, however, is a long additional passage (ll. 14—60), in which the confession of Pernel Proud-heart is supplemented by that of a male example of Pride. In Pass. xxii. 337, Pride is made leader of the Vices, who attack the Church of Unity; and in Pass. xxiii. 70, Pride is Antichrist's standard-bearer. See Chaucer's Persones Tale, De Superbia.

6. (b. 5. 66; a. 5. 48.) *An heire*, i. e. a hair-shirt. It is said of a good widow, that "she made greate abstynence, and wered the *hayre* vpon the wednesday and vpon the fryday;" Knight de la Tour, ed. Wright, p. 193. The same is said of Saint Cecilia in Chaucer, Cant. Ta. 15601; and of Sir Thomas More, in Roper's life of him, ed. Singer, 1822, p. 91. Bp. Fisher tells us that the Lady Margaret "had her shertes and gyrdels of heere, which, when she was in helthe, everi weke she fayled not certayn days to weare;" Memoir of Margaret, Countess of Richmond and Derby, by C. H. Cooper, p. 76. Chaucer speaks of "wering of *here*, or of stamin, or of habergeons on hir naked flesh for Cristes sake;" Pers. Tale, near the end.

14. (*not in* b, a.) In revising his work for the last time, William made one considerable alteration in the plan of his work, which has already been fully explained in the Preface to the C-text, p. lxxx.; but I repeat here the

most essential part of the remarks. The fact is that, in his B-text, the poet did, to some extent, enlarge upon the favourite and common subject of the Seven Deadly Sins *twice over*; once in the proper place (B. Pass. V.), and a second time, in describing the character of Haukyn, the active man (B. Pass. XIII.). But, on revising his work, he saw how much could be gained by combining the two sets of descriptions in one, and at the same time making a few alterations and additions. Accordingly, the description of Haukyn's *pride* (B. 13. 278—313) was so placed as to form a part of the allegorical character of Pride (C. vii. 30—60). The result is that the poet now gives us *two* examples of Pride; one, Pernel Proud-heart, a *female* character, ll. 3—13; and a second, named simply Pride, a *male* character, ll. 14—60.

16. (*not in* b, a.) *Vnboxome*, disobedient. The right word, because *bux-omnesse*, i. e. obedience or humility, was considered as the opposite virtue to pride; see note to l. 3. Cf. l. 19. "*Inobedient* is he that disobeieth for despyt to the commaundementz of God, and to his sovereigns, and to his gostly fader;" Ch. Pers. Ta. De Superbia.

20. (*not in* b, a.) *Demed*, i. e. I judged others; the nominative *I* must be supplied. So also before *scorned* in l. 22.

27. (*not in* b, a.) "Seeming to be a sovereign (*or* principal) one, where-soever it befell me (*or* fell to my lot) to tell any tale, I believed myself wiser in speaking or in counselling than any one else, whether clerk or layman."

30. (b. 13. 278; *not in* a.) Here begins the supplementary passage, introduced into this place from what was the description of Haukyn in [b].

31. (b. 13. 279; *not in* a.) *Ich haue*, I possess. His apparel was more costly than his property warranted.

32. (b. 13. 280; *not in* a.) *Me wilnynge*, myself desiring; *hym willynge* [b], himself desiring. This is a remnant of the A.S. idiom, according to which two ablatives or datives could be used together like the Latin ablative absolute; see Vernon's A.S. Grammar, p. 75. *Aueyr* = Fr. *avoir*, i. e. pro-perty. See *Avere, Avoir* in Halliwell. This line is partly repeated at l. 41.

35. (cf. b. 13. 282; *not in* a.) *For eny vndernymynge*, in spite of any reproof. This use of *for* is not uncommon; cf. Mätzner, Engl. Gramm. vol. ii. pt. i. p. 444. *Vndernymynge*, reproof; see note to B. 5. 115, at p. 108.

37. (b. 13. 284; *not in* a.) *Pope-holy*, lit. holy as the pope; but used to mean hypocritical. This odd word is fully illustrated in Dyce's Skelton, ii. 230. Roquefort, in his Glossaire de la Langue Romaine, has—"*Papelardie, papelardise* : hypocrisie, tromperie, subtilité, mauvaise foi; en bas Lat. *papelardia*," after which he quotes a passage from the Roman de la Rose—

> "Une autre imaige estoit escripte,
> Que bien sembloit estre ypocrite,
> *Papelardie* est appellée," &c.

This appears in the English version, l. 413, thus:—

> "Another thing was down there writ,
> That seemed like an ipocrite,
> And it was cleped *pope-holy*," &c.

See the whole passage.

Roquefort also gives "*Papclard, papelart*, hypocrite, faux dévot, flatteur, trompeur;" cf. "*Popelot*, a deceiver," in Halliwell. It looks as if the English *pope-holy* was an ingenious modification of the Old French *papelard*, in like manner as *crayfish* has resulted from *écrévisse*. The word occurs four times in Skelton, i. 209, l. 24; 216, l. 247; 240, l. 472; 386, l. 612. In the last passage we have "*Pope-holy* ypocrytis." Barclay, in his Ship of Fooles, fol. 57, ed. 1570 (*or* ed. Jamieson, i. 154), has :—

"Ouer sad or proude, disceitfull and *pope-holy*."

It occurs also in Lydgate and in the Interlude of the Four Elements; see the quotations in Dyce. And again we have—"Ye *poopeholy* prestis, fulle of presomcioun;" Polit. Poems, ed. Wright, ii. 251.

——(b. 13. 291; *not in* c, a.) "And especially to intermeddle, where he has nothing to do with the matter."

42. (b. 13. 293; *not in* a.) See Critical Note to the B-text, at p. 411.

46. (cf. b. 13. 298; *not in* a.) *And for ich songe shulle*, and because I sang shrilly. *Shill* or *shull* for *shrill* is not uncommon; cf. Eng. *speak* from A.S. *sprécan*; and observe the various readings.

——(b. 13. 299; *not in* c, a.) That is, he was in the habit of boasting that he was liberal in lending money, though he knew he should lose it.

58. (b. 13. 311; *not in* a.) "And what I knew and was capable of, and of what kin I came." The words *couthe* and *knewe* are transposed in [b].

59. (cf. b. 13. 312; *not in* a.) *When hit to pruyde sounede*, when it tended to my pride, when it contributed to make me proud. This use of *sounen* is common; see, e. g. Chaucer's Prologue, l. 307; Cant. Tales, Group B. 3157, 3348; F. 517.

62. (cf. b. 13. 314; *not in* a.) In the account of the Confession of the Seven Deadly Sins, the confessor is supposed to be Repentance; in that of the Confession of Haukyn (B. xiii), the confessor is Conscience. In the revised account (C. vii), only the name of Repentance is retained.

☞ For notes to B. v. 72—75 (A. v. 54—58), see l. 170 below.

63. (b. 5. 76; a. 5. 59.) The reader should compare William's descriptions of Envy, &c., with the descriptions in Dunbar's Dance of the Seven Deadly Sins, and in Spenser's Faerie Queene, bk. i. canto iv. Skelton probably copied hence some of his traits of Envy in his Philip the Sparowe, ll. 905—948. It is pretty clear that Skelton had access to a MS. of the B-type in particular; he died several years before Crowley's printed edition was published. But the famous description of Envy is in Ovid; Metam. ii. 775.

"Pallor in ore sedet; macies in corpore toto :
nusquam recta acies; liuent rubigine dentes :
pectora felle uirent; lingua est suffusa ueneno.
Risus abest, nisi quem uisi fecere dolores.
Nec fruitur somno, uigilantibus excita curis :
sed uidet ingratos, intabescitque uidendo,
successus hominum; carpitque et carpitur una :
suppliciumque suum est."

See also Chaucer's Persones Tale ; and, in particular, consult Burton's Anatomy of Melancholy, pt. 1, sec. 2. mem. 3. subsec. 7. I may note a slight misprint here ; in B. 5. 76, for *scrifte* read *schrifte*, as in B. 5. 124.

64. (b. 5. 77 ; a. 5. 60.) *Mea culpa.* The form of confession contained the words—"Peccaui nimis cogitatione, locutione, et opere : *mea culpa.*" See Proctor on the Common Prayer, p. 193.

———(b. 5. 78 ; a. 5. 61.) A *pelet* was a pellet or ball used as a war-missile ; see Chaucer, House of Fame, iii. 553. As these were commonly made of stone, the comparison 'pale as a pellet' is perfectly natural and intelligible. See Mr Way's note, in the Prompt. Parv., upon the word "*Pelot*, rownde stone of erthe or other mater ;" and the mention of *gun-stones* in Strutt, Customs and Manners of the English, ii. 32.

———(b. 5. 79 ; a. 5. 62.) *Caurimaury*, evidently the name of some coarse rough material ; see the Glossary. Whether it is connected with *kersey*, I cannot say. It is worth observing that in Prof. Rogers's Hist. of Agriculture and Prices in England, vol. ii. p. 536, there is a mention of the buying of a material called *Taursmaurs* (together with Persetum and Camelot, i. e. perse and camlet) in the year 1287. I much suspect that this is a misprint for *Caursmaurs*, as the letters *c* and *t* are often written alike in old MSS.

———(b. 5. 80 ; a. 5. 63.) *Kirtel*, a kind of under-jacket, worn beneath the jacket or *kourteby*. The very various explanations given are due to the fact that the word was loosely used. A *full kirtle* was a jacket and petticoat ; a *half kirtle* was either one or the other ; and the term *kirtle* alone could signify any one of the three. The context must always be considered. See Gifford's note to Cynthia's Revels (Jonson's Works, ii. 260), quoted in Dyce's Skelton, ii. 149 ; my note to P. Pl. Crede, l. 229 ; Strutt, Dress and Habits, p. 349.

———(b. 5. 87 ; *not in* c, a.) Possibly an allusion, as already hinted, to the adder as the emblem of Envy. Skelton has the same idea in his description of Envy :—

"His serpentes tonge
That many one hath stonge ;" Philip Sparowe, 920.

Cf. Ps. cxl. 3 ; Rom. iii. 13.

——— ———(a. 5. 70.) The odd reading *vernisch* (varnish) is inferior to that of *verious* (T) or *vergeous* (U). In former times, *verjuice* was used as a sauce with boiled capon, crab, goose, &c. See *Verjuice* in the Index to the Babees Book. "Verjuice, or green juice, which, with vinegar, formed the essential basis of sauces, and is now extracted from a species of green grape, which never ripens, was originally the juice of sorrel ; another sort was extracted by pounding the green blades of wheat ;" Lacroix : Manners, Customs, and Dress during the Middle Ages, p. 167. It was also made from crab-apples ; see Rogers's Hist. of Agriculture and Prices in England, i. 18.

——— ———(a. 5. 71). *Walleth*, creates nausea. Cf. "*Walsh*, insipid" in Atkinson's Cleveland Glossary ; "*Wallowish*, nauseous" in Halliwell. Note the various readings *walewith*, *walweth*, which shew that *is* not the more usual verb *wallen*, to boil, here, though the sense is much the same. See also *Wamble* in Halliwell.

——(b. 5. 89; *not in* c, a.) The word *back-biting* is rather old. We find it in the Ancren Riwle, p. 82; and, at p. 86, is a mention of "*Bacbitares*, þe biteð oðre men bihinden, beoð of two maneres;" and it is explained that there are two kinds of them, those who openly speak evil of others, and those who pretend to be friendly. In An Old Eng. Miscellany, ed. Morris, p. 187, we read "Alle *bacbytares* heo wendeþ to helle." Mr Jesse, in his Anecdotes of the British Dog, v. 2. p. 94, says that in the Rolls of Parliament, at the opening of the parliament of 2 Richard II., in the year 1378, we find the phrase—"Qi sont appellez *bacbyters* sont auxi come chiens qi mangeont les chars crues," &c. Chaucer, in his description of Envy (Persones Tale), describes five kinds of 'backbytyng.'

——(b. 5. 91; *not in* c, a.) *Gybbe*, Gib; short for Gilbert, whence Gibbs, Gibson, Gibbons, Gipps, &c. A *Gib-cat* means a male-cat; we now say a Tom-cat. We have "Gibbe our cat" in the Rom. of the Rose, l. 6208. See *Gib-cat* in Nares, and Bardsley's Eng. Surnames, p. 38.

——(b. 5. 93; *not in* c, a.) Palsgrave has "Wey of chese, *maige*." There is a peculiar force in the mention of *Essex*, because the Essex 'wey' was of unusual weight. Webster says that a *wey* is generally equivalent to 32 cloves of 7 pounds; i.e. to 2 cwt. In Arnold's Chronicle, however, ed. 1811, p. 263, is the following note. "The weyght of Essex chese is in England .ccc. weyght; fyue score xij li. for the C. The weyght of Suffolke chese is xij score and xvi. li.;" i.e. the Suffolk wey is 2 cwt. 32 lbs.; but the Essex wey is 3 cwt.

——(b. 5. 94; a. 5. 74.) *Ennuyed*, annoyed; various readings *anoyed*, *ennyed*, *enuyed*. The alliteration shews that the word is really *ennuyed*, annoyed, not *enuyed*, envied. The same appears from Chaucer's description of Envy, where he says—"Thanne cometh accusing, as whan a man seketh occasioun to *annoyen his neighebor*," &c.

——(b. 5. 95; a. 5. 77.) "And lied against him to lords, to make him lose his money." Cf. Rom. Rose, 6940.

——(b. 5. 101; a. 5. 83.) *Hailse hym hendeliche*, greet him courteously; cf. Pass. x. 309. Tyrwhitt (note to C. T. 13575) is wrong in not distinguishing between *hailsen*, to salute, greet (Icel. *heilsa*, to say *hail* to one, to greet), and *halsen*, to embrace, and sometimes to beseech (A.S. *healsian*, to take round the neck). But Palsgrave makes the distinction correctly, giving "I *haylse* or greete, *Ie salue*," and "I *halse* one, I take hym aboute the necke, *Iaccole*;" p. 577. See *halch* in Gloss. to Percy Folio MS.; *hailsen* in Gloss. to The Destruction of Troy, ed. Panton and Donaldson; and *halsynge* in l. 187 below.

——(b. 5. 107; a. 5. 88.) "Christ give them sorrow;" a form of cursing; repeated in Pass. xx. 307. The 'bowl' and the 'broken (i. e. torn or ragged) sheet' were things of small value, yet Envy could not refrain from cursing the thief. The bowl was probably a wooden one, used to contain scraps of broken victuals. It was sometimes large enough to contain a baby. "And at the londes ende lay · a litell *crom-bolle*,

> And thereon lay a litell childe · lapped in cloutes."—Crede, l. 437.

It was also used for washing out-of-doors, and was thus easily lost.

> "In washing by hand, *have an eye to thy boll*,
> For launders and millers are quick of their toll."

Tusser; Points of Huswifery; Washing.

The word *bolle* also meant a large drinking-cup; see note to l. 420.

The expression '*broken* sheet' sounds odd, but it is a provincial expression. Grose, in his Provincial Glossary, ed. 1790, has—"*Break*, to break, to tear. *Hamp*. In this county *break* is used for *tear*, and *tear* for *break*; as 'I have *a-torn* my best decanter or china dish;' 'I have *a-broke* my fine cambrick apron.'" So also we find mention of a "*broken* surplice, with manye an hole;" Test. of Love, pt. ii, in Chaucer's Works, &c., ed. 1561, fol. ccxcvi, col. 2.

——(b. 5. 110; a. 5. 91.) In [b] it is *Eleyne* (Ellen), a female, who has the new coat; in [a] it is *Heyne*, a male. The coat was an article of female as well as of male attire, but the word is much more often used in the latter sense, to which it is now restricted. See Solomon's Song, v. 3.

——(b. 5. 111; a. 5. 92.) *And al þe webbe-after*, and (I wish that) the whole piece of cloth (from which the coat was cut) was mine too.

——(b. 5. 112; a. 5. 93.) *Of*, at. *Liketh*, pleases. Compare a poem on the Seven Sins printed in Reliquiæ Antiquæ, i. 136, where Invidia says—

> "I am ful sory in my hert
> Off other mens welefare and whert;
> I ban and bakbyte wykkedly,
> And hynder alle that I may sikerly."

Robert of Brunne (Handl. Synne, 3992), says of the envious—

> "Gladnes here haue they none
> But whan here negheburs haue mysgone."

And Chaucer says of envy that it is "sorwe of other mennes prosperite; and, after the word of seint Austyn, it is sorwe of other mennes wele, and joye of other mennes harm."

——(b. 5. 114; a. 5. 95.) "And I judge that they do ill, where I do much worse."

——(b. 5. 115; *not in* c, a.) "Whoever reproves me for it." Mr Wright misinterprets *vndernymeth* in his Glossary. Pecock, in his Repressor, uses the word often. He begins that work with "*Vndirnyme* thou," &c. as a translation of the Lat. "argue" in 2 Tim. iv. 2. It is very common in Wyclif's Bible, with the sense of "to reprove, to blame." So also in Jack Upland, sect. 15—"Why *vnderneme* ye not your brethren for their trespasse after the law of the gospel, sith that *vnderneming* is the best that may be?" See l. 35 above.

——(b. 5. 119; a. 5. 99.) *Bitter*, bitternesse. "Thanne cometh eek *bitternes* of herte, through which *bitternesse* every good deede of his neighebore seemeth to him *bitter* and unsavery;" Chaucer; Persónes Tale, De Inuidia. "Hir stomacke swellyth by bytter gall and vyle;" Barclay's Ship of Fools, ed. Jamieson, ii. 6.

☞ **Here there is a sudden leap, from B. 5: 119 to B. 13. 325.**

69. (b. 13. 325; *not in* a.) Here, again, the description of Haukyn's envy [b] is shifted so as to form part of the Confession of Envy; see note to l. 14 above, and cf. Preface to C-text, p. lxxx.

70. (b. 13. 326; *not in* a.) *By*, concerning, with reference to.

74. (b. 13. 330; *not in* a.) It has already been noted, in the footnotes, that the right reading is not *brend*, but *fret*, of which *vrede, vride, wreþed*, are variations or corruptions. *Fret* is the past tense, as in xxi. 202, being often used as a strong verb in Middle-English; see examples in Stratmann, who gives the forms *freet, frat, fret*. The comparison is excellent. Envy fretted himself internally, just as the inner edges of a tailor's pair of shears grate against each other when used.

75. (b. 13. 331; *not in* a.) A *shappester* or *shepster* was a female cutter-out or *shaper* of garments, and not a female sheep-shearer, as suggested by Mr Wright, and asserted by Mr Timbs, in his Nooks and Corners of Old England, p. 229. "*Shepster* is *shapester*, one who *shapes*, forms, or cuts out linen garments, as appears from Palsgrave, v. *Schepstarre*, and Nares, v. *Shepster;*" Student's Manual of the English Language, by G. P. Marsh, ed. Smith, p. 217. The word is not in the original edition of Nares, but in the later edition by Wright and Halliwell, where two good illustrations are given. "A sempster or *shepster*, sutrix;" Withal's Dict. ed. 1608, p. 146; and—"Mabyll the *shepster* chevissheth her [*performs her work*] right well; she maketh surplys, shertes, breeches, keverchiffs, and all that may be wrought of lynnen cloth;" Caxton's Boke for Travellers. Elyot also renders *sarcinatrix* by "a *shepster*, a seamester." See Notes and Queries, 1 S. i. 356. The curious may see pictures of these shears in use in Lacroix; Manners, Customs, &c., in the Middle Ages, pp. 276, 277; figs. 208, 214, 215.

——(b. 13. 332; *not in* a.) *Lyf* probably means here a living person, a man, as so often elsewhere in our author.

78. (b. 13. 335; *not in* a.) *Crompe*, cramp; see xxiii. 82. For this afflic-tion the common remedy was the charm called a cramp-ring, i. e. a ring blessed by the king upon Good Friday, and worn by the sufferer; see Chambers, Book of Days, i. 418; Ridley's Works (Parker Society), p. 501. For *cardiacle*, see note to Pass. xxiii. 82.

81. (b. 13. 338; *not in* a.) The word *witch* was formerly used of both sexes. See the quotations in Trench's Select Glossary; Riley's Memorials of London, pp. 471, 475; and cf. Pass. xxi. 46 (b. 18. 46).

83. (b. 13. 340; *not in* a.) Nothing more is known of the cobbler of Southwark, or dame Emma of Shoreditch, who were probably famous in their own day. They were evidently dealers in sorcery and charms for diseases. Cf. note to Pass. i. 225.

☞ **Here ends the second insertion from B. Pass. xiii.**

86. Agrees with B. 5. 120 and A. 5. 72. At l. 88, the agreement is with B. 5. 122 and A. 5. 100.

87. (b. 5. 119; *not in* a.) "Envy and ill-will are difficult things to digest." There are other examples of the use of the singular verb with a pair of nominatives; see B. 5. 99.

88. (b. 5. 122; a. 5. 100.) This question is addressed by Envy to his confessor, Repentance. "Cannot any sugar or sweet thing (be found to) assuage my swellings, nor any valuable medicine (*or* expectorant, *b, a*) drive it out of my heart, nor any shame or confession (relieve me), except one were (actually) to scrape my maw?" A forcible way of expressing the question—"can none but the most violent measures relieve my moral sickness?" *Diapenidion* answers almost exactly to the modern barley-sugar, being a kind of sweet stuff twisted into a thread, and used to relieve coughs, &c. The prefix *dia* is explained by Cotgrave as "a tearme set before medicinall confections or electuaries, that were devised by the Greeks." Hence Life is said to "drive away death with *dias* and drugs;" xxiii. 174. The termination *penidion* means a little twist (of thread, originally), being a diminutive of the Greek πήνη, a thread. This *penidion* became *pénide* in French, and *pennet* in English, according to Cotgrave's explanation, who says—" *Penide*, f. a pennet; the little wreath of sugar taken in a cold." We find too—" *Pénide* (du grec *péné*, fil de tisserand, corde) sucre tors, cuit à la plume avec une décoction d'orge, coulé chaud sur un marbre huilé, malaxé ensuite entre les mains enduites d'huile d'amandes douces, enfin allongé et tortillé comme une *corde*. Les pénides different du sucre d'orge en ce que celui-ci est coloré par quelques gouttes de safran et qu'on le laisse refroider sans le remuer pour qu'il conserve sa transparence. On les donne dans les rhumes comme pectorales," &c.; Dict. Universel des Sciences; Paris, 3rd ed. 1857; par M.-N. Bouillet. Another receipt for making diapenidion is given in Notes and Queries, 4 S. vi. 202. This puzzling word is thus completely explained; it only remains for me to add that I am indebted for the explanation of it to Professor Morley.

For further examples of *dias*, see note to Pass. xxiii. 174.

Compare—"certes, than is loue the medicyn that casteth out the venym of envye fro mannes hert;" Chaucer's Pers. Tale; Rem. cont. Invidiam.

"So youth, brought up in lewdness and in sin
    Shall skant it *shrape* so clean out of his mynde
    But that styll after some spot wyll byde within."
        Barclay's Ship of Fools, ed. Jamieson, i. 47.

93. (b. 5. 127; a. 5. 105.) "I *am* sorry; I am but seldom otherwise." Surely a clever rejoinder.

96. (b. 5. 129; *not in* a.) *Nameliche*, especially. Note the mention of London, and that this passage is not in [a]. There is but little mention of London in [a]; probably because the author was not much acquainted with it in 1362. The C-text (l. 95) has—"I am a broker of back-biting;" but the B-text (l. 130) means—"I caused detraction to be made by means of a broker,

to find fault with other men's ware." That is, he employed brokers to depreciate his neighbour's goods; *be* = by. The oath of the brokers, given at p. 273 of the Liber Albus, obliged them not to be themselves dealers in the merchandise of which they were brokers, nor to make any bargain unless they could bring buyer and seller together, and could lawfully witness the sale. On *backbiting*, see note to B. 5. 89 above, at p. 107.

103. (b. 5. 134; *not in* a.) *Ira.* Curiously enough, William entirely omitted this vice in his earliest version. Seeing his mistake, he elaborated the character with great care. He makes Wrath to have been a *friar*, the nephew of an abbess; he was first employed as gardener to the convent, and afterwards as cook in the kitchen; but, in [c], the mention of gardening is omitted. William doubtless refers to the terrible wrath then displayed by the secular clergy against the friars, and by the friars against them, and even by one order of friars against another. Compare the description of *Ire* in Chaucer, Somp. Tale, 299; Seneca, de Irâ, Burton's Anat. of Melancholy, pt. 1. sec. 2. mem. 3. subsec. 9; &c.

113. (*not in* b, a.) "Unless I had weather to suit me, I blamed God as the cause of it." Compare l. 111 with Rich. Redeles, prol. 35.

Lines B. 5. 134—152 are printed at length from the Oriel MS. in B. pref. p. xviii.

114. (*not in* b, a.) *Angres*, afflictions, troubles, crosses; see B. 15. 254, 266; and note to Pass. xiii. 207.

118. (*not in* b, a.) *Vore*, a southern form of *fore*, may have either of two meanings. We find (1) *fore*, a furrow; Prompt. Parv.; and (2) *fore*, a course, march, expedition; see Stratmann. The latter makes the better sense, viz. "Friars follow my course (or track)." Cf. "heo nomen heore *vore*," they took their course, Layamon, l. 13667; "so forleost þe hund his *fore*," so the dog loses his track; Owl and Nightingale, l. 815 (or 817).

119. (*not in* b, a.) "And prove the prelates to be imperfect." Cf. B. 5. 145.

120. (*not in* b, a.) "And prelates complain of them, because they (the friars) shrive their parishioners." Cf. B. 5. 142. "For comynly, if þer be any cursid iurour, extorsioner, or avoutrer [*adulterer*], he wil not be schryven at his owne curat, bot go to a flatryng frere, þat wil asoyle him falsely for a litel money by ȝeere, þof he be not in wille to make restitucioun and leeve his cursid synne;" Wyclif's Works, ed. Arnold, iii. 394.

> "But if we schryve not the pore, whi ben persons so wrothe,
> And paroche-prestes also, for schryvynge of her parischens?"
>   Reply of Friar Daw; Polit. Poems, ed. Wright, ii. 87.

See also Milman, Hist. Latin Christianity, vi. 104; Crede, l. 468; Chaucer, Prol. 218, &c.; Massingberd, Eng. Reformation, p. 112. And see below, Pass. xxiii. 323—367.

——(b. 5. 138—150; *not in* c, a.) A slightly difficult, but important passage. It means—'I (continually) grafted lying tales upon *limitors* and *lectors*, till they bare leaves of servile speech, to flatter lords with, and afterwards they blossomed abroad in (my lady's) bower, to hear confessions. And now there is fallen therefrom a fruit, that folk would much rather shew their schrifts to *them*, than shrive themselves to their own parsons. And now that the parsons have found out that friars share (the profits of confession) with them, these *possessioners* preach (to the people) and calumniate the friars; and the friars (on the other hand) find *them* to be in fault, as people bear witness, (and say) that when they preach to the people, in many places around (it will be found) that I, i. e. Wrath, go with them, and teach them out of my books. Thus both parties talk about spiritual power, so that each despises the other, till either they are both beggars, and live by the spiritual authority which I give them, or else they are all rich, and ride about (like rich people). I Wrath never rest from following about this wicked folk—for such is my grace." Cf. C. 5. 124—127. Wrath here insinuates that the quarrel generally terminates in one of two ways; either the secular clergy turn beggars like the friars, or the friars obtain wealth enough to buy horses like the secular clergy. The quarrel was, as to which should hear confessions; see note to l. 120 above, at p. 111.

——(b. 5. 138; *not in c, a.*) *Limitours* were members of a convent to whom a certain limited district was assigned to beg in, in order that, each mendicant having a certain round to make, no family might be left unsolicited. Bread, bacon, cheese, logs of wood, &c., were often ready for the limitour when he called. "Why heire [hire] you to ferme your *limitors*, giving therefore each yeare a certain rent, and will not suffer one in another's *limitation*, right as yee were your-selves lords of countries?" Jack Upland, in Polit. Poems, ed. Wright, ii. 21. See also Massingberd's Eng. Reformation, p. 110; and Chaucer, Prol., l. 209; and Somp. Tale, l. 3.

Listres are *lectors*. This is ascertained by the following entry in the Promptorium Parvulorum, A.D. 1440. "*Lyyslerre* [*various readings* lystyr, lystore, listyr] *Lector*." The editor, Mr Way, says this is "the *reader*, who occupied the second place in the holy orders of the Church." By *second* place is meant second in ascending order. The seven orders, excluding the bishop, were the ostiary (door-keeper), lector, exorcist, acolyth, sub-deacon, deacon, and presbyter. Some MSS. have *legistres*, but this would mean *lawyers* or *justices*, and would be out of place; cf. B. 7. 14. Mr Wright guessed *listres* to mean deceivers, from A.S. *list*, deceit; and Lye translates the A.S. *lyster* by the Latin *fautor*, one who favours or flatters; but this can have little to do with the present passage. *Lister* as a proper name is also quite a different word, being corrupted from *litster*, a dyer. Lastly, in Cutts's Scenes and Characters of the Middle Ages, p. 38, it is suggested that, as a *limitor* was one who had a certain district assigned to him, so a *lister* was one who went where he *listed*. Surely this is wrong, for a *pleaser* cannot mean *one who goes where he pleases*; I can only suppose it to be a mere guess. The word *limitor* was differently formed, being derived, not from the verb *to limit*, but from *limit* as a substantive; which makes all the difference. See *Limiters* and *Lectors* in the Index to the Parker Soc. publications.

——(b. 5. 143; *not in c, a.*) I may repeat here (from the Critical Notes) that the reading in the text is supported by Lord Ashburnham's MS.; see the quotations from it in B. pref. p. xvi.

——(b. 5. 144; *not in* c, a.) *Possessioneres;* see Chaucer's Sompnoures Tale, l. 14. Tyrwhitt says—"An invidious name for such religious communities as were endowed with lands. The Mendicant orders professed to live entirely upon alms." Mr Wright says—"the regular orders of monks, who possessed landed property and enjoyed rich revenues," &c. But it is clear that, in the present passage, a *possessioner* means one of the *beneficed clergy,* as the word *persones* is used as an equivalent. And it is worth remarking, that this same explanation will suit the context in Chaucer's Sompnoures Tale much better than if we suppose *monks* to be intended. Observe, for instance, l. 19:—

"Nought for to holde a *prest* jolif and gay;"

and, farther on, the friar says,—

"These curates ben ful negligent and slowe;"

"This every lewed *vicary* or *persoun*
Can say, how ire engendreth homicyde," &c.

Nothing can give us so clear an idea of a friar as the commencement of this tale of Chaucer's.

In other passages, *possessioners* is used more generally, and it could be applied either to the *monks,* who possessed property in common, or to the *parochial clergy,* who possessed it as laymen did; as pointed out in the note to Bell's Chaucer, iii. 104. It is probably applied to the monks by Wyclif (Works, ed. Arnold, iii. 359):—"Aftirward men þenken þat al þes newe sectis or ordris, boþe *possessioneres* and beggeris, shulden ceese by Cristis lawe." See also pp. 433, 513 of the same volume; P. Pl. Crede, 681 (note).

125. (b. 5. 149; *not in* a.) It is clear that *spirituallte* here means spiritual power, authority, or rank. In Barclay's Ship of Fools, ed. Jamieson, i. 159, ii. 57, it is used to signify men in orders, men who undertook spiritual work. The word *religion* has a similar double meaning.

129. (b. 5. 154; *not in* a.) *Hem* (or *hir*) *were leuere,* it were liefer to them (or to her); i. e. they (or she) had rather swoon or die. See Chaucer, Prol. 293.

133. (b. 5. 158; *not in* a.) "And made them broths of various scandals." Compare—"then serue potage, as wortes, *Iowtes,* or browes, with befe, motton, or vele;" Babees Book, p. 274. Mr Furnivall says (ib. p. 287)—"These are broths of beef or fish boiled with chopped herbs and bread; Household Ordinances, p. 461. Others are made 'with swete almond mylke,' ib. See 'Joutus de Almonde,' p. 15, *Liber Cure;* also pp. 47, 48." See "*Jowtys,* potage," in Prompt. Parv.; Mandeville's Travels, ed. Halliwell, p. 58; Gower, ed. Pauli, iii. 161, 162.

Chaucer likewise reproves 'jangling' near the end of his 'De Ira' in the Persones Tale; cf. note to B. prol. 35.

135. (b. 5. 160; *not in* a.) *A prestes file,* a priest's concubine, as Mr Wright suggests in his Glossary, such being a meaning of the French *fille.*

So in MS. Harl. 1701, fol. 30, we find—"For to rage with ilka *fyle.*" See *File* and *Fyllok* in Halliwell's Dictionary. Of course it might mean simply 'a priest's daughter,' but this does not so well suit the context. Still, I may remind the reader that the miller's wife, in Chaucer's Reves Tale, l. 23, was 'a parson's daughter;' and in the tale of the 'sacrilegious carollers' in Robert of Brunne, Handling Synne, l. 9017, one of the offenders is "þe prestys doghetyr of þe toune."

136. (b. 5. 161; *not in* a.) *In the chapon-cote,* in the hen-house [c]; *in chiritime,* at cherry-time [b]. "In some counties cherry-fairs are frequently held in the cherry-orchards. They are the resort of the gay and thoughtless, and as such frequently metaphorically alluded to by the early writers. Thus Occleve, MS. Soc. Antiq. 134, fol. 257 [or Occleve, De Regim. Princ. ed. Wright, p. 47]—'This lyf, my sone, is but a *chery-feyre;*'" Brand, Pop. Antiq., ed. Ellis, ii. 457. See the full illustrations of *Cherry-fair* in Halliwell's Dictionary; Babees Book, ed. Furnivall, p. 52, l. 144; Skelton, ed. Dyce, ii. 85; Wright, Homes of Other Days, p. 310.

——(b. 5. 162; *not in* a.) *I-made* (written *made* in WCB) is the first person of the past tense, which is sometimes found with the prefix *I-* (A.S. *ge-*). The sense is—I, Wrath, fed them with wicked words; lit. I prepared their vegetables with wicked words. There is clearly a pun here, in the contrast of *words* with *worts.*

138. (b. 5. 163.) *Thow lixt,* thou liest. Cf. Crede, 542; Chaucer, Six-text, D. 1618.

——(b. 5. 165.) *Her eyther,* each of them. *Other,* the other.

——(b. 5. 166.) *Seynt Gregorie.* "It appears that some Abbesses did at one time attempt to hear the confessions of their Nuns, and to exercise some other smaller parts of the clerical function; but this practice, I apprehend, was soon stopped by Gregory IX., who has forbidden it in the strongest terms.—Decretal. l. v. tit. 38. c. x.;" Tyrwhitt, Introd. Discourse to Cant. Tales, note 7. Tyrwhitt gives the Latin text of the Decretal.

——(b. 5. 167.) *Were prest,* should be a priest, i. e. should hear confessions. For *ordeigned,* Crowley reads *prouided.*

——(b. 5. 168.) *Infamis;* so in the MSS. It is put for the nom. plural. Cf. Pass. xxii. 162. See Critical Note, B-text, p. 398.

144. (*not in* b, a.) 'Imparked in pews;' i. e. fenced in by the pew as a park is fenced in by palings; see xviii. 13. This is said to be the earliest passage in which the word *pew* occurs. It also supports the supposition that pews were originally for women only. See note to Peacock's edition of Myrc, p. 74; and see *Pews* in Index to Parker Soc. publications.

145. (*not in* b, a.) 'How little I love Letice at-the-Style.' Letice is Lat. Lætitia. From 'at-the-style' comes the name Styles; see Bardsley's Eng. Surnames, pp. 85, 90. 'Sim at-the-style' is mentioned below, l. 207.

146. (*not in* b, a.) 'Because she received the holy bread before me, my heart began to change (towards her).' On the difference between 'holy-

bread' and the eucharistic wafer, see Peacock's edition of Myrc, p. 89 ; and cf. note to Pass. xvi. 210.

149. (*not in* b, *but cf.* 5. 164; *nor in* a.) 'Till each called the other a whore, and (it was) off with their clothes;' i. e. with their outer garments, and hoods, which they tore off each other's backs and heads.   Note the various readings—'they cast off their hoods,' F; '(it was) on with their claws,' I.   The last expression is indeed graphic.

154. (b. 5. 172; *not in* a.) *Thei laken hem togeders,* they take counsel together; viz. as to what punishment they shall assign to me.   On the additional lines in MS. F., see Crit. Note, C-text, p. 455.

156. (b. 5. 174; *not in* a.) *Chapitele-house,* chapter-house.   See the chapter-house described in Cutts's Scenes and Characters of the Middle Ages, p. 79.   "If any had a complaint to make against any brother, it was here made and adjudged.   Convent business was also here transacted."

157. (b. 5. 175; *not in* a.) *Baleysed,* punished with a *baleis* or rod; see Pass. xii. 124.   The Prompt. Parv. has—'Baleys, *virga.*'   Mr Way's note is—"Hereafter occurs in the Promptorium 'ȝerde, baleys, *virga.*'   *Virga* is rendered 'a ȝerde or a rodde,' Med. and Ort. Voc.; and such the *baleys* seems to have been, and not a besom, *balai,* in the present sense of the word.   Matthew Paris (ed. Wats, p. 848) relates that in 1252 a person came to perform penance at St Albans, 'ferens in manu virgam quam vulgariter *baleis* appellamus,' with which he was disciplined by each of the brethren. Wats, in the Glossary, observes, 'Ita Norfolcienses mei vocant virgam majorem, et ex pluribus longioribus viminibus; qualibus utuntur pædagogi severiores in scholis.' . . . . Forby does not notice it; but the verb to *balase* occurs amongst the provincialisms of Shropshire; see Hartshorne's Salopia Antiqua."   The quotation from Matthew Paris is given at length in Warton, Hist. Eng. Poetry, ed. 1840, ii. 82, note 53, from which we further learn that the culprit was 'vestibus spoliatus,' and that the discipline was administered *in the chapter-house.*

159. (b. 5. 177; *not in* a.) *Feble,* weak, thin, poor, watery.   Compare—
     "I have sytten metelesse,
     All this daye kepynge youre beestes.
     My dyner *feble* it was."
The Frere and the Boye, l. 151; in Ritson's Anc. Pop. Poetry. So in Havelok, l. 323, the expression "*feble* wede" means poor or miserable clothing.   In the Praier and Complaynte of the Ploweman (Harl. Misc. vi. 112), the poor man is said to have "*feble* mete, and *feble* drink, and *feble* clothinge."

168, 169. (b. 5. 186, 187.) The words *me* and *my* in [b] are evident blunders, but are found in most of the MSS. of that type; perhaps in all. Yet Crowley has *hym* and *his,* and probably followed his copy.   In the C-text, the author has altered them to *hym* and *hus* (= his).   By *he,* is meant Repentance; by *hym,* Wrath.   "Esto sobrius" probably refers to the text "Sobrii estote," 1 Pet. v. 8.

☞ **In the earlier texts, the description of Luxuria comes sooner; at B. 5. 72 (A. 5. 54). For note to B. 5. 188 (A. 5. 107) see p. 117.**

170. (b. 5. 72; a. 5. 54.) In the two earlier texts, the confession of Luxury is very short. The poet's chief warning is there directed against getting drunk upon a Saturday, when work was over sooner than on other days, as it was the eve of Sunday. The votive mass of the Virgin Mary was said upon Saturday, and hence, in her honour, "there arose a custom, amid all ranks, of vowing to keep, for a certain length of time, a rigid fast each Saturday;" Rock, Church of our Fathers, iii. 281. For further allusions to Luxury, see Pass. xvii. 91, xxiii. 114.

174. (b. 5. 75; a. 5. 58.) To 'drink with the duck' is to drink water, as a duck does.

☞ **Here comes in a passage from B. 13. 343—361.**

176, 177. (b. 13. 343, 344; *not in* a.) The former of these lines in the B-text (13. 343) is really dropped in the C-text, but may most conveniently be commented on here. The word *wisloker*, i. e. more wisely, more carefully, is worth notice. The ending *-loker* (for *-liker*) answers to the modern ending *-lier*. Examples are common. The very word *wysloker* occurs in Polit. Songs, ed. Wright, p. 194. So also *louelokeste*, loveliest, Pass. vii. 192 (just below); *lyghtloker*, more lightly, Pass. viii. 216; *slilokeste*, most slily, xii. 266; *wilfulloker*, more wilfully, P. Pl. Crede, l. 648; *semloker*, more seemly, Gaw. and Grene Knight, ed. Morris, l. 83; *wrothcloker*, more angrily, Allit. Poems, ed. Morris, C. 132; *worthloker*, more worthy, id. C. 464.

The latter line in the B-text (13. 344) is expanded into two in the C-text (7. 176, 177).

——(13. 356; *not in* c, a.) *Colmy*, smutty, dirty, grimy. The word is scarce, but occurs in King Horn, ed. Lumby, l. 1082, where Horn, disguised as a beggar, is described as having "a *colmie* snute," a smutty nose. And again, in l. 1064, Horn is described as in the act of disguising himself, for which purpose he "al *bicolmede* his swere," i. e. entirely blackened his neck. Mätzner, in his edition of King Horn, alters these forms to *colwie* and *bicolwede;* but quite unnecessarily, as our text proves. The sense is determined by l. 1203 of the same poem, which runs—"He wipede that *blake* of his swere." Compare—"*Culme* of a smeke [smoke], *fuligo;*" Prompt. Parv.; also—"*Colwyd*, carbonatus" in the same, and see Way's note. *Collow, Collar*, or *Colley*, is used in various dialects to signify soot, or smut in wheat; see Halliwell, who quotes "All his *collow* and his soot" from Cotton's Works, ed. 1734, p. 190. Hence Shakespeare's "*collied* night;" Mid.-Nt. Dream, i. l. 145. Cf. *collier*, and A.S. *col*, coal.

The Trin. MS. (W) has the inferior spelling *colomy*, which is left unexplained in Mr Wright's Glossary.

——(13. 360; *not in* a.) This resembles C. vii. 243, which see; and see the note to that line below.

☞ **End of the third insertion from B. Pass. xiii.**

196. (b. 5. 188; a. 5. 107.) See the *facsimile* of ll. 196—240, given with the C-text, from MS. Laud 656 ; a reading of it is given at p. xxviii of the Preface to that text.   The vice of Avarice is discussed in Burton, Anat. of Melancholy, pt. 1. sec. 2. mem. 3. subsec. 12.   He refers to the character of a covetous man in Theophrastus; &c.   Cf. Pass. xvii. 80; xxiii. 121.

197. (b. 5. 189; a. 5. 108.) *Heruy*, Harvey.   Skelton has the same name for a covetous man.

> "And *Harny* Hafter, that well coude picke a male."
> Skelton, ed. Dyce, i. 35.

198. (b. 5. 189, 190; a. 5. 109.) *Bytelbrowed*, having beetling or prominent brows.   This rather scarce word occurs in The Destruction of Troy, ed. Panton and Donaldson, l. 3824, and in A Balade Pleasaunte, stanza 3 (Chaucers Works, ed. 1561, fol. 344).   "The *beetled browes* signifieth malice, cruelty, letchery, and envy;" Shepherdes Kalender, sig. P 2. See also Rom. and Juliet, i. 4. 32.

199. (b. 5. 192; a. 5. 110.) 'And like a leathern purse his cheeks flapped about; (they were) even longer than (i. e. hung down lower than) his chin, and they trembled with age.'

201. (b. 5. 194; *not in* a.) 'His beard was shaven like bondmen's bacon' [c]; i. e. cut off in rather a ragged manner: or, 'His beard was beslobbered, as a bondman's is with bacon' [b].   Warton notes numerous examples of *menne* as the form of the genitive plural, e. g. Pass. iv. 102, v. 115, vi. 29, vii. 293, ix. 29, x. 214, &c.; the very word *bondmenne* occurs again, vi. 70. The form *mennes* also occurs, as in viii. 220.

203. (b. 5. 196; a. 5. 111.) In Chaucer's Prologue, l. 541, the *tabard* is the dress of the ploughman.   In a poem printed in Reliq. Antiq. i. 62, it is used of a poor man's upper garment.   In the Coventry Mysteries, p. 244, Annas is represented as a bishop, in a scarlet gown, over which is "a blew *tabbard* furryd with whyte."   In Sharp's Dissertation on Pageants, p. 28, a similar garment, used for a bishop in a mistery, is called a "*taberd* of scarlet." See also Dyce's Skelton, ii. 283; Ducange, s. v. *Tabartum;* Strutt's Dress and Habits, ii. 301; Riley, Mem. of London, p. 5, note 6; &c.   Dresses of a *tawny* colour (see B-text) were used by minstrels.   Thus, we have "nine ells of *tawny* cloth for three minstrels;" and again, "a noise of musicians [i. e. a company of them] in *townie* coats;" and again, a minstrel who acted before Queen Elizabeth at Kenilworth had "poynets [*points?*] of tawny chamlet." See Cutts, Scenes and Characters of the Middle Ages, p. 305.   Jews also used to wear orange-tawny bonnets, and hence Avarice is rightly fitted with 'a tawny tabard;' for "usurers should have orange-tawney bonnets, because they do Judaize;" Bacon's Essays, 41.

——(b. 5. 197; *not in* c, a.) Compare Chaucer's Chan. Yem. Prol. l. 82— "It is al baudy and to-tore also."   *Baudy* means dirty.

204. (b. 5. 198; a. 5. 112.) Hazlitt, in his Book of Proverbs, p. 216, has— "If a louse miss its footing on his coat, 'twill be sure to break its neck."

And Palsgrave has—"He hath made my gowne so bare that a lowse can get no holde on it;" ed. 1852, p. 620.

205. (b. 5. 199; a. 5. 113.) The word *welch* is plainly written in most of the MSS. of [c] and [b]. In MS. L [b] it may be read either *welche* or *welthe*, and I thought at one time that the reading *welþe* of MS. W. decided the question in the latter direction. However, MS. R [b] has the spelling *welsch*, which is equally good evidence on the other side. MS. T [a] has *walsshe scarlet*, i. e. Welch (or foreign) scarlet, but this is an evasion of the difficulty. The Vernon MS. has *walk*, and this gives the most likely solution of the word. It is probable that *welche* is a mere variation of *walk*, i. e. walking-place. Chaucer says of Emily that she was "in hire *walk;*" Kn. Tale, 211. The change of vowel from *a* to *e* is common, as in *wallen* = *wellen*; to boil; *walken* = welkin, &c.; and the change of *k* to *ch* is one of the commonest changes in Middle English. The other solution is that the reading is *welthe*, where *welthe* is for *welt*, a border; thus Cotgrave has—"Bordure, f. A border, *welt*, hem, or gard of a garment;" and Holland speaks of "apparell with a plaine white *welt* or guard" [i. e. border]; see Bacon's Adv. of Learning, ed. W. A. Wright, p. 280. But I can find no evidence for the spelling *welthe*, and the change of *t* into *th* presents (to me at least) greater difficulties than even the double change in *welche* for *walk*. It must be remembered, too, that *welk* is the old past tense of *to walk* (see Halliwell) which renders the suggested vowel-change more likely.

207. (b. 5. 201; a. 5. 115.) *Symme atte the Style* [c, b]; *Simme atte noke*, i. e. Sim at the oak [a]. On these and similar names, see Bardsley's English Surnames, pp. 85—90, already referred to in the note to l. 145 above, q. v. In the Coventry Mysteries, ed. Halliwell, p. 131, we find "Jak at the style," "Whatt [Wat] at the welle," and "Bette the bakere," the last being similar to "Bette the bouchere" in l. 379 of this Passus. The form "atte noke" is for "atten oke," i. e. *at then oke*, where *then* is a later form of *tham* (A.S. *þæm*), the old dative sing. of the def. article, as explained in the note to Pass. i. 43. In the name Atterbury, it is interesting to notice that the *feminine* form of the article is preserved. If we had to write "at the town" in Anglo-Saxon, we should put *at thære byrig*, because the sb. *burh* (our *borough*) becomes *byrig* (our *bury*) in the dative case; and, as it is a feminine noun, it takes the feminine dative article, viz. *thære*. The form Attenborough is later, and due to a change of gender of the substantive. Besides *atte noke*, we even find *atte norcharde* (i. e. *at then orcharde*), whence the name *Norchard;* so also *Nash* from *ash*, *Nalder* from *alder*, *Nelmes* from *elms*, *Noveno* from *oven;* Bardsley's Eng. Surnames, p. 86.

209. (b. 5. 203; a. 5. 117.) We have here three different equivalent expressions, viz. 'a leasing (i. e. a lie) or two' [c]; 'a leaf or two' [b]; 'a lesson or two' [a]. The expression 'a leaf or two' is to be explained by observing that, in the next line, Avarice talks of his *lesson*, and of learning his *Donet* or primer in l. 215. In like manner, still keeping up the allusion to reading, he learns to lie just a leaf or two, i. e. as much as would fill a couple

of leaves. All ambiguity is removed by the parallel passage in Richard the Redeles, Prol. 37—

. . "ȝif him list to loke · *a leef other tweyne.*"

Note also " a lesson other tweyne ; " id. i. 9.

.211. (b. 5. 205 ; a. 5. 119.) *Wy* is Weyhill, near Andover in Hampshire. Weyhill fair is a famous one to this day, and lasts eight days. The fair for horses and sheep is on Oct. 10 ; that for cheese, hops, and general wares, on Oct. 11, and the six days following. " The tolls derived from the sheep-fair form part of the stipend of the rector of Weyhill ; " *Standard* newspaper, Oct. 11, 1870. Warton has a long note upon fairs, which should be consulted ; see Hist. Eng. Poetry, ed. 1840, ii. 55 ; ed. 1871, ii. 259. " One of the chief of them," he says, " seems to have been that of St Giles's hill or down near Winchester, to which our poet here refers. It was instituted, and given as a kind of revenue to the bishop of Winchester, by William the Conqueror, who by his charter permitted it to continue for three days. . . . In the fair, several streets were formed, assigned to the sale of different commodities ; and called the Drapery, the Pottery, the Spicery, &c." Fairs long continued to be the principal marts for purchasing necessaries in large quantities. Winchester fair is mentioned in the Liber Albus, p. 201. Compare the description of Stourbridge fair (near Cambridge) in Prof. Rogers's Hist. of Agriculture and Prices in England, i. 141.

213. (b. 5. 207 ; a. 5. 121.) ' The grace (or favour) of guile ' is a satirical expression. We speak rather of ' the grace of God.'

214. (b. 5. 208 ; a. 5. 122.) *Thys seuen yer,* these seven years ; see note to Pass. v. 82. Add the illustrations—" That is the best dance without a pipe That I saw *this seven year ; "* The Four Elements, in Old Plays, ed. Hazlitt, i. 47 ; also Much Ado about Nothing, iii. 3. 134, &c. And see Pass. i. 203, xi. 73.

215. (b. 5. 209 ; a. 5. 123.) *Donet,* primer. " Properly a Grammar, from *Ælius Donatus,* the Grammarian. . . . Among the books written by bishop Pecock, there is the *Donat* into Christian religion, and the Folower to the Donat."—Warton's Hist. Eng. Poet. ii. 56, ed. 1840. See also the note in Dyce's Skelton, ii. 343 ; *Donet* in Gloss. to Pecocke's Repressor, ed. Babington, and in Tyrwhitt's Gloss. to Chaucer ; *Donat* in Cotgrave ; and see Prompt. Parv. p. 126, note 3.

216. (b. 5. 210 ; a, 5. 124.) In 1353, statutes were passed regulating the length and breadth of cloth.—Thom. Walsingham, ed. Riley, i. 277.

217. (b. 5. 211 ; a. 5. 125.) *Rayes,* striped cloths. *Ray* means properly a *ray, streak, stripe ;* but it was commonly used in the above sense. It was enacted—" that cloths of *ray* shall be 28 ells in length, measured by the *list* [edge], and 5 quarters in width."—Liber Albus, p. 631. " A long gown of *raye*" occurs in Lydgate's London Lyckpeny ; see Specimens of English, 1394—1579, ed. Skeat, p. 25. Cf. " And a robe of *ray ; "* Sir Launfal, pt. ii. l. 42, in Hazlitt's Fairy Tales, &c. p. 65. See also Barclay's Ship of Fools, ed. Jamieson, i. 35, l. 16. The Latin name for striped cloth was

radiatus; see Prof. Rogers's Hist. of Agriculture and Prices in England, i. 577.

218. (b. 5. 212; a. 5. 126.) *To brochen,* &c. ;—'To pierce them with a packing-needle, and I fastened them together; and then I put them in a press, and penned them fast in it,' &c.

221. (b. 5. 215; a. 5. 139.) *Webbe* (A.S. *webba*) is a male weaver in Chaucer, Prol. 362; the fem. is both *webbe* (A.S. *webbe* in Beowulf, ed. Grein, l. 1942) and *webster.* Observe *spynnesters,* i. e. female spinners, in the next line; and cf. note to Pass. i. 222.

223. (b. 5. 217; a. 5. 131.) *The ponnde,* &c. She paid the people whom she employed by the pound, and used too heavy a weight; thus cheating them of their dues.

224. (b. 5. 218; a. 5. 132.) *Auncel,* a steelyard. From the descriptions by Cowell (in Halliwell) and Phillips, it is clearly that kind of steelyard known as the 'Danish steelyard,' which has a fixed weight and a moveable fulcrum. The fulcrum was obtained by simply poising the machine upon the forefinger, a very uncertain method. Hence Blount tells us, in his Law-Dictionary, that, "because there was wont to be great deceit [in its use], it was forbidden, 23 Edw. 3, Stat. 5. cap. 9; 34 ejusdem, cap. 5; and 8 Hen. 6, cap. 5. . . . By a Constitution made by Henry Chicheley, Archbishop of Canterbury, Anno 1430—Pro abolitione ponderis vocati *le auncel-weight,* seu *scheft* [shift], seu *pounder,* &c., doloso quodam stateræ genere; qui utitur, excommunicandus." In A.D. 1356, we find "one balance, called an *auncere,*" valued at 12*d.*; and "2 balances, called *aunceres,*" valued at 6*s.*; see Riley's Memorials of London, p. 283. We also find mention of "Thomas le Aunseremaker" in Riley's Memorials of London, pref. p. xxii; cf. Bardsley's Eng. Surnames, p. 359. A weighing-machine named a *peson* is mentioned in the Paston Letters, ed. Gairdner, i. 474.

226. (b. 5. 220; a. 5. 134.) *Peny-ale* is common ale, thin ale, as is certain from its being spoken of as a most meagre drink, suitable for strict-living friars, in B. 15. 310. *Podyng-ale* (*puddyng-ale* in Trin. MS.) was probably named from its being thick like *pudding.* Thus in Pass. xxii. 402, a fraudulent brewer boasts of drawing *thick ale* and *thin ale* out of one hole in a cask. The penny-ale was sold at *a penny a gallon,* but the best ale at 4*d.* See l. 230; and cf. Liber Albus, pp. 274, 311; Strutt, Manners and Customs, ii. 81; Stowe's Chron. p. 218; Babees Book, ed. Furnivall, p. 208.

227. (b. 5. 221; a. 5. 135.) In [a], the reading *linen be hemseluen* of course means "live by themselves." But in [b] the reading is *lay by hymselue,* where *hymselue* probably refers to the *ale;* see the next line, and note the common use of *hym* for *it.* Indeed, Crowley has the reading *it-selfe.* In [c], however, the reading returns to *hemselue,* and the sense is the same as in [a].

231. (b. 5. 225; a. 5. 139.) *In coppemel,* by cups at a time. She knew better than to measure it in a gallon measure. Concerning ale-measures, see Liber Albus, p. 233.

233. (b. 5. 227; a. 5. 141.) *Hockerye*, i. e. the retail trade. A *huckster* was one who retailed ale, &c. from door to door. "Item, that no *brewer* or *brewster* sell any manner of *ale* unto any *huckster*," &c.—Liber Albus, p. 312. And again—"that no *hucstere* shall sell ale;" Riley's Memorials of London, p. 347. Mr Riley observes that the term *huckster* is generally applied, in the City books, to females only.

——(b. 5. 228; a. 5. 142.) *So the ik*, so may I thrive [b]; see Tyrwhitt, note to Cant. Tales, l. 3862; *sothely*, soothly, verily [a].

——(b. 5. 230; a. 5. 144.) *Walsyngham*. See note to Pass. i. 52.

——(b. 5. 231; a. 5. 145.) *Rode of Bromeholme*, cross of Bromholm in Norfolk. In A Chronicle of London, p. 10, we find, anno 1224 [rather 1223 or 1222] "the emperour Baldewyn, which whanne he wente to bataile to fyghte with Godes enemyes, he hadde a croos boren before hym, whiche crosse seynt Eleyne made of the crosse that Cryst deyde upon; and there was an Englyssh prest that tyme with hym that was called Sir Hughe, and he was borne in Norfolke, the whiche prest broughte the same crosse to Bromholm in Norfolke." Mr Wright refers to Matthew Paris (p. 268); and adds—"In the MS. Chronicle of Barthol. de Cotton, it is recorded at the date 1223—Eo tempore Peregrinatio de Bromholm incepit." Hence Avarice could visit Our Lady of Walsingham, and the piece of the true cross at Bromholm in one journey, and pray to be brought out of debt by having his cheating tricks forgiven him. It is interesting to remember that Bromholm priory was within a mile of Paston hall, the residence of the Paston family. See Paston Letters, ed. Gairdner, pref. p. xxv. Mr Gairdner remarks that "many of the pilgrims to Walsingham turned aside on their way homeward to visit the Rood of Bromholm." The story of the finding of the True Cross by Helen, mother of Constantine, is well known. See Legends of the Holy Rood, ed. Morris. Cf. Chaucer, Reves Tale, 366; Pardoneres Tale, 489.

*** 234—309. (b. 5. 232—289.) *Not found in the* A-text.

——(b. 5. 238.) He pretends that he thought *restitution* was the French for *robbery*. *Rifle* was used in a stronger sense then that it is now. Cf. "he had called him a malefactor, and common *rifler*;" Riley's Memorials of London, p. 208. Norfolk is evidently considered as one of the least refined parts of the island, being in an out-of-the-way corner; and we are to infer that French was almost unknown there. The common proverb—'Jack would be a gentleman if he could speak French'—shews that the common people had much difficulty in learning it. Trevisa fixes the date 1355 as the year, *just before* which children began to learn to translate Latin into *English* instead of *French*, as formerly. See Warton, Hist. Eng. Poetry, ed. 1840, i. 5; Dyce's Skelton, ii. 93.

239. (b. 5. 240.) *Tserie*, usury. "All usury was prohibited as a sin by the Canon Law;" Southey; Book of the Church, p. 187. See Bacon's 41st Essay; Barclay's Ship of Fools, ed. Jamieson, ii. 168, 169.

241. (b. 5. 212.) *Lumbardes and Jewes*. "A set of *Lombards* established themselves here, in connexion with the legates, to advance money upon all

sums due to the Pope, for which they exacted the most exorbitant usury,"
&c.—Southey, *as above.* Cf. Pass. v. 194; Chaucer, Schipm. Tale, l. 367;
Polit. Poems, ed. Wright, ii. 184; and see *Lumber* in Trench's Select
Glossary. The Jews were constantly accused of being the offenders, whenever clipped coin was found, which was very often. Thus in the 7th year of
Edward I., "the viii day of seynt Martyn, alle the Jewes of Engelond were
taken for clippyng of money;" A Chron. of London, p. 28. See the chapter
on 'Jews in England' in Annals of England, p. 162; and the chapter on
'Jews' in Lacroix; Manners, Customs, &c. during the Middle Ages, p. 434.

243. (b. 5. 244.) 'And lent (the light coin) for love of the pledge, which
I set more store by and considered more valuable than the money or the men
to whom I lent it.' The B-text is more awkward, because it involves a
change in the subject of the sentence. However, it certainly means—'and
lend it for love of the cross, (for the borrower) to give me a pledge and lose it,'
where the latter 'it' refers to the pledge; cf. B. 13. 360. The key to the
passage is to remember that borrowers often gave pledges of much value.
Owing to a positive want of money, "Christians did not feel any scruple in
parting with their most valued treasures, and giving them as pledges to the
Jews for a loan of money when they were in need of it. This plan of lending on pledge, or usury, belonged specially to the Jews in Europe during the
Middle Ages;" P. Lacroix: Manners, Customs, and Dress during the
Middle Ages, p. 451. Sir John Maundeville says that a King of France
bought the crown of thorns, spear, and one of the nails used at the Crucifixion, from the Jews, "to whom the Emperour had *leyde hem to wedde,* for
a gret summe of sylvre." *For love of the cross* is a clever pun, as *cross* refers
frequently to the cross on the back of old coins, and was a slang name for a
coin, as in Shakespeare; 2 Hen. IV. i. 2. 253; see note to Pass. xviii. 200.
Cross-and-pile is the old name for *heads and tails.* It is clear enough what
Avarice did: he first clipped coins and then lent them, taking a pledge which
he hoped would not be redeemed.

——(b. 5. 246.) Compare—"Iucundus homo qui *miseretur et commodat,*
disponet sermones suos in iudicio." Ps. cxii. 5 (cxi. 5, Vulgate). Avarice
obtained more manors through his customers being in arrears of payment,
than he could have obtained by practising liberality. *Maneres* is spelt
manoirs in the Trinity MS. printed by Mr Wright.

——(b. 5. 249.) In an ordinance against usurers (38 Edw. III.) we find
that certain persons exerted themselves to maintain usury—"which kind of
contract, the more subtly to deceive the people, they call *exchange* or *chevi-
sance,* whereas it might more truly be called *mescheaunce* (wickedness);"
Liber Albus, p. 319, and see p. 344. Cotgrave has—"*Chevissance,* f: an
agreement or composition made; an end or order set down, between a
creditor and debtour." Cf. Chaucer, Prol. 282. On *usury,* see note (on l.
372) in Peacock's edition of Mirk, p. 77, and note to l. 239 above.

250. (b. 5. 254.) Avarice, in his dealings with knights, used to buy silk
and cloth from them at a sufficiently cheap rate; and he now ironically calls

his customers mercers and drapers, who never paid anything for their apprenticeship.

——(b. 5. 261.) 'As courteous as a dog in a kitchen.' This alludes to an old ironical proverb, which appears in French in the form—"Chen en cosyn [*cuisine*] compaignie ne desire;" in Latin in the form—"Dum canis os rodit, sociari pluribus odit;" and in Middle English—"Wil the hund gnaʒh bon, i-fere neld he non;" i. e. while the hound gnaws a bone, companion would he none. See Wright's Essays, i. 149.

——(b. 5. 263.) The third word in the line may be either *leue* or *lene*. The distinction is, that *leue* means grant or permit, followed by a clause; but *lene* means grant or give (lit. lend), followed by an accusative case. By this test, we should read *lene* (and not *leue*, as printed), because the phrase is *lene þe grace*, i. e. give thee grace. In the present case, however, it looks as if the poet may have begun the sentence with *god leue* (a common expression), and afterwards finished the sentence another way; i. e. he may have meant—"God grant never, unless thou the sooner repent, for thee (to have) grace upon this earth to employ thy property well."

253. The arrangement here is rather hard to follow. Line 253 really answers to B. 5. 263; l. 254 to B. 5. 266; l. 255 to B. 5. 265. Next, ll. 256 —259 are new, but include a Latin quotation following after B. 5. 279. Then comes the passage in ll. 260—285, borrowed from B. 13. 362—399; whilst, at l. 287, the author returns to B. 5. 268. See the Scheme at the beginning of the Passus; at pp. 100, 101.

257. (cf. b. 5. 279.) In Peter Cantor, cap. 153 (ed. Migne) is the expression "Nec dimittitur peccatum, nisi restituatur ablatum." To this Migne adds the reference—"Reg. 4. jur. in 6, ex Aug."—which I do not understand. However, the following is, I suspect, the original source. "Si enim res aliena, propter quam peccatum est, cum reddi possit, non redditur, non agitur pænitentia, sed fingitur; si autem ueraciter agitur, non remittetur peccatum, nisi restituatur ablatum; sed, ut dixi, cum restitui potest;" S. Augustini Epist. cliii., sect. 20; Opera, ed. Migne, ii. 662.

☞ Here comes in a passage from B. 13. 362—399. For notes to B. 5. 268, &c., see p. 124, &c.

260. (b. 13. 362.) "I mixed my wares, and made a good shew; the worst (of them) lay hidden within; I considered it a fine trick."

267. (b. 13. 371.) *Half-acre* was a colloquial term for a small lot of ground; cf. Pass. ix. 2, 3.

270. (b. 13. 374.) "And if I reaped, I would over-reach (i. e. reach over into my neighbour's ground), or gave counsel to them that reaped," &c. *Rope* should rather be *rope*; see various readings; cf. the double form ʒede, ʒode. Mr Wright reminds us that, in olden times, "the corn-lands were not so universally hedged as at present, and that the portions belonging to different persons were separated only by a narrow furrow, as is still the case in some of the uninclosed lands in Cambridgeshire." We find a similar allusion in Robert of Brunne, Handlyng Synne, ll. 2445-8 —

" What sey men of þes fals husbandys,
þat ere aweye falsly mennys landys,
Of a lande, þurghe and þurghe,
Takyn and eryn awey a furghe ? "

——(b. 13. 376.) "And whoever borrowed from me, bought off the time
(i. e. paid for extension of time) by presents which he made privately, or
else he paid some (part of it) for certain." Here *somme* = some; *certeyne*
= assuredly, as in Chaucer. Otherwise, *somme certeyne* = a fixed amount.
The borrower would, at the appointed day, either make Avarice a present,
or pay a sum down, on the understanding that the rest would be paid
another time. This line much resembles C. 7. 247.

278. (b. 13. 392.) "Bruges was the great mart of continental commerce
during the 13th, 14th, and 15th centuries."—Wright. In Letter-book I
(A.D. 1399—1422) in the Records of the City of London, fol. 205, is a Letter
of the Burgomaster, Echevins, and Councillors of the Vill of Bruges, sent
unto the King (Henry IV); Liber Albus, p. 532. See an account "Of the
commoditees of Braban and Selande, and Henaulde" (Hainault), in Polit.
Poems, ed. Wright, ii. 180.

279. (b. 13. 393.) *Prus*, Prussia. As early as in the reign of Henry III.
we find that the import-due "for one hundred stockfish imported from Pruz"
was "one farthing;" Liber Albus, p. 209. See the account "Of the commoditees of Pruse" in Polit. Poems, ed. Wright, ii. 169. Some of these
were—" bere, bacon, osmonde [a kind of iron], coppre, bowestaves [see the
quotation in Halliwell], stele, wex, peltreware [furs], grey, pyche, tarre,
borde, fflex, Coleyne [Cologne] threde, ffustiane, canvas, carde, bokeranie,
sylver-plate, wegges [wedges] of silvere and metall." Mr Wright remarks
that "Prussia was then the farthest country in the interior of Europe
with which a regular trade was carried on by the English merchants." The
present passage implies that it was carried on at some risk.

☞ **Here ends the fourth insertion from B. Pass. xiii.**

287. This line corresponds to B. 5. 268.

290. (*not in* b.) The Latin quotation has occurred before; see note to
Pass. ii. 144. And it occurs again; see note to Pass. xviii. 40.

294. (b. 5. 274.) "Thou art the slave of another, when thou seekest
after dainty dishes; feed rather upon bread of thine own, and thou wilt be a
free man." I have not succeeded in tracing the source of this quotation.

297. (*cf*. b. 5. 277.) *By þy myght*, according to thine ability. After this
line two lines of the B-text (ll. 278, 279) have been dropped, but the Latin
quotation following them has been preserved at an earlier place. See note
to l. 257 above.

301. (*not in* b.) *Parte with þe*, share with thee; according to the principle of the proverb, that the receiver is as bad as the thief. See the parallel
passage in Pass. xviii. 41—50.

303. (b. 5. 282.) By the 'sauter-glose' is meant the gloss or commentary
upon the Psalter. The Glosa Ordinaria upon the verse here referred to con-

tains a remark fróm Augustine—"Sic misericordias dat, vt scruet ueritatem; vt nec peccata sint impuuita eius cui ignoscit." This is probably what the poet had in mind. Ps. li. (l. in the Vulgate) is called *Miserere mei Deus* from the three first words in it. In verse 6 (8 in the Vulgate) we find—"Ecce enim ueritatem dilexisti: incerta et occulta sapientiae tuae manifestasti mihi." St Augustine's own comment on the text is—"Impunita peccata etiam eorum quibus ignoscis non reliquisti. *Ueritatem dilexisti:* id est, sic misericordiam prærogasti, vt scruares et ueritatem;" Opera, ed. Migne, iv. 592.

——(b. 5. 285.) Ps. xviii. 25 (xvii. 26 in the Vulgate) has—"Cum sancto sanctus eris, et cum uiro innocente innocens eris."

——(b. 5. 289.) The Latin quotation is omitted in some MSS. It is not quite exact. "Suauis Dominus uniuersis: et miserationes eius super omnia opera eius." Ps. cxliv. 9, Vulgate.

☞ **Here comes in a passage which will be found in B. 5. 463—484; A. 5. 236—259. For note to B. 5. 291, see p. 127.**

309. (*cf.* b. 5. 463; a. 5. 236.) The first line of this passage has been curiously altered. We find in [a] and [b]—"And yet I will pay back again, if I have so much (as will suffice for it), all that I have wrongfully acquired ever since I had knowledge (of things);"—and this forms part of the Confession of Sloth. But in [c] we are introduced to a new penitent, a companion of Avarice, who was a Welshman, and bore the singular name of Evan Pay-again-if-I-have-enough-all-that-I-wrongfully-acquired-since-I-had-knowledge, &c., &c. The name 'yevan' (see various readings) is clearly the Welsh Evan, i. e. John. His long surname is similar to others that our author uses elsewhere; see Pass. v. 18, ix. 80—83.

——(b. 5. 467; a. 5. 240.) *The rode of chestre,* the cross or rood at Chester. Mr Wright quotes from Pennant's Tour in Wales (edit. 1778, p. 191), to shew that a famous cross once stood in a spot formerly known as the *Rood-eye,* i. e. Rood-island, but now known only by the corrupted name of *Roodee,* and used as a race-course. (See, on this corruption, my note in Notes and Queries, 4 S. iii. 228.) There was also at Chester a college of the Holy Cross. See Chambers, Book of Days, i. 428. The "rode of chester" is again mentioned in Rich. Redeles, prol. 56.

316. (b. 5. 469; a. 5. 242.) *Ryfeler* in [c] is equivalent to *robbere* in [b] and [a]. We have already had the verb *rifle* in the sense of to rob; l. 236 above. *Rifler* was sometimes used as a term of reproach; thus we read of one man calling another "a malefactor and common *rifler;*" Riley, Memorials of London, p. 203. As for *robber,* the similarity of the word to *Robert* early gave rise to a pun, whereby *Robert* came to be used as an equivalent for *thief.* Thus in Political Songs, ed. Wright, p. 49, occurs the expression—"per *Robert, robber* designatur." Even as early as the 12th century, the name *Robert* was explained to mean *robber;* see Polit. Poems, ed. Wright, p. 354, l. 4 from bottom. John Ball, in his proclamation to the

commons of Essex, used the expression—"biddeth Peres Plou3man go to his
werke, and chastise well *Hobbe the robber*," &c.   T. Walsingham, Hist.
Anglicana, ed. Riley, ii. 33.   See also the note to Pass. i. 45.

Reddite; i.e. the text—"Reddite ergo omnibus debita;" Rom. xiii. 7.
Compare the definition of Robbery in Reliq. Antiq. ii. 38—

> "For whan his soule is hethen flemed [*hence banished*],
> Thorou Gods law he shal be demed,
> And parchaunce to endles payne,
> *But he 3elde it here agayne.*"

317. (b. 5. 470; a. 5. 243.) "And, because there was nothing wherewith (to make restitution), he wept very sorely." *Wher-of* [b] = *wher-
with* [c, a].

320. (b. 5. 473; a. 5. 246.) In the apocryphal gospel of Nicodemus,
the name of the penitent thief is *Dismas* or *Dimas*, and that of the other
thief, *Gestas*.   See Cowper's Apocryphal Gospels, pp. 246, 364, 426; Cov.
Myst. p. 316.   Other names for them are Titus and Dumachus; compare—

> "Then on my right and my left side
> These thieves shall both be crucified,
> And *Titus* thenceforth shall abide
> In Paradise with me."—Longfellow's Golden Legend.

321. (b. 5. 474; a. 5. 247.) The allusion is to the words of the thief—
"Domine, *memento* me, cum ueneris in regnum tuum;" Luke xxiii. 42.
It is well worth notice that the penitent thief is spoken of, in [b], under
the heading "Accidia;" but, in [c], under "Confessio Auaricie."   The
former is the right place.   It was a stock example of an argument against
Wanhope, as the possible result of Sloth.   See Chaucer, Pers. Tale, *de
Accidia;* so also Robert of Brunne, in his remarks upon Sloth, in Hand.
Synne, l. 5205—5210.

322. (b. 5. 475; a. 5. 250.) *Reddere ne haue*, have no means wherewith
to make restitution [c, b]; *no red haue*, have no guidance [a].   *Red* is for
rede, i.e. counsel, guidance, good advice from others.

323. (b. 5. 476; a. 5. 251.) "Nor ever expect to earn enough, by any
craft that I know" [c]; *or*, "on account of any craft that I know" [a]; *or*,
"by help of any handicraft, the amount that I owe" [b].   *Craft* is here used
in a good sense, viz. that of skill in trade, as we use *handicraft*.   The word
owe [b] has two senses in Middle-English; (1) to possess, and (2) to owe in
the modern sense.   To obviate confusion, the scribe of MS. Laud 581 [b]
has written *debeo* above the word, as printed.

329. (b. 5. 482; a. 5. 257.) "That he would polish anew his pike-staff,
called Penance (or Penitence [b, a]);" to which [a] and [b] add—"and by
help of it leap over the land (i.e. be a pilgrim) all his life-time."   A pilgrim
always carried a staff, generally with a spike at the end, whence it was called
a pike-staff.   It was also called a *bordoun*, as in viii. 162.   A *land-leper* or
land-loper was a vulgar name for a pilgrim, the word *leap* meaning to *run*,
like the German *laufen*.   Thus Cotgrave has—"*Villotier*, m.: A vagabond,
land-loper, earth-planet, continuall gadder from towne to towne."   The

word *hym* (b. 5. 483; a. 5. 258) has reference to the pike-staff. Cf.
viii. 180.

330. (b. 5. 484; a. 5. 259.) "Because he had associated with *Latro*,
who was Lucifer's aunt" [c, b]; *or* 'Lucifer's brother' [a]. The word *latro*
· is doubtless used with reference to the expression in Luke xxiii. 39—
"Unus autem de his qui pendebant *latronibus*."

☞ **End of the transposed portion of B and A: return to B. 5.
290, and (at l. 350) to A. 5. 146.**

338. (b. 5. 291.) There is a parallel passage in Hampole's Pricke of Conscience, l. 6311.—6319 :—

> "For the mercy of God es swa mykel here,
> And reches over alle, bathe far and nere,
> That alle the syn that a man may do,
> It myght sleken, and mare thar-to.
> And thar-for says *Saynt Austyn* thus,
> A gude worde that may comfort us:
> *Sicut scintilla ignis in medio maris,*
> *ita omnis impietas viri ad misericordiam Dei.*
> 'Als a litel spark of fire,' says he,
> 'In mydward the mykel se,
> Right swa alle a mans wykkednes
> Un-to the mercy of God es.'"—(Ed. Morris, p. 171.)

And again, in a poem printed in Reliq. Antiq. ii. 229, from MS. Phillipps
8336, we find—

> "Also the lanterne in the wynd that sone is aqueynt,
> Ase sparkle in the se that sone is adreynt."

And again—"yf they hadde done ony venyall synne, it was put anone
aweye by the love of charyte, lyke a drope of water in a fornays;" The
Golden Legende (1527), fol. cccix.

A similar quotation from Seint Augustine, with a list of venial sins, will
be found in Chaucer, Pers. Tale, near the end of *pars secunda penitentiæ.*

The nearest passage to this which I have yet found is the following :—
"Tanquam unda misericordiæ peccati ignis exstinguitur."—S. August. in
Ps. cxliii. 2 (Vulgate).

341. (b. 5. 293.) *To bygge the with a wastell*, to buy thee a cake with. See
note to B. ii. 31.

349. (b. 5. 303.) *Lerede yow to lyue with*, taught you to live upon [c];
Lent yow of owre lordes good, lent (i. e. gave) you, of our Lord's *wealth ;*
i. e. spiritual strength [b].

359. (b. 5. 312; a. 5. 155.) *Pionys*, seeds of the pæony. They were
used as a medicine, but sometimes also as a spice, as here. See note in
Liber Albus, p. 197. Speaking of remedies against the falling sickness, we
find, in Batman vpon Bartholome (lib. 7. c. 10)—"Also he [Plato] sayth,
that *piany* borne and drouken helpeth much; and this confirmeth Galen,
Constantine, and Dioscorides."

360. (b. 5. 313 ; a. 5. 156.) *Fastinge-daies.* We learn from l. 352 that the

circumstances here described took place on a *Friday*, a fitting day for Glutton to go to church and confess. Cf. also ll. 434, 439. The scene here described with such vivid dramatic power took place, it is evident, in some large ale-house in London, not very far from Cock Lane, Smithfield (l. 366), from Cheapside (b. 5. 322), and from Garlickhithe (b. 5. 324). It was also very near a *church* (ll. 355, 366). At one time I supposed that the 'Boar's Head,' in Eastcheap, immortalized by Shakespeare, might have been the very tavern here meant. The Boar's Head is mentioned in a will of the date of Richard II; it boasted to be "the chief tavern in London," and (which is very curious) its back-windows looked out on to the burial-ground of St Michael's, a church which is now pulled down, but has given its name to St Michael's Lane. The will above mentioned further shews that "the tenement called the Boar's Head" was given to a college of priests, founded by Sir William Walworth in St Michael's Church; which might account for the name of 'the church' not being given; see Larwood's History of Signboards, pp. 378—380. But it was said by Mr French (Athenæum, July 18, 1868) that the Boar's Head is not mentioned as being a tavern till 1537; and the localities mentioned point rather to Cheapside, with its famous Bow church, the bell of which was rung every evening at 9 o'clock; Chambers, Book of Days, i. 301. Moreover, William lived at one time in *Cornhill*, which is close by. See Pass. vi. 1, and cf. note to l. 377 below. In any case, Glutton may be considered as the Sir John Falstaff of the scene.

By way of comment, note the advice given by Robert of Brunne, in his Handlyng Synne, l. 1020—

> "Holy chyrche wyl þe werne [*warn, i. e. forbid*]
> þe halyday to go to þe tauerne."

Respecting fennel, Lydgate says, in his Prologue to the Siege of Thebes,

> "But toward night, eate some fenell rede,
> Annis, comin, or coriander sede."

362. (b. 5. 315; a. 5. 158.) Here we find the forms *sywestere* (sewster, needlewoman) in [c], and *souteresse* (female shoemaker) in [b], where [a] has *souters wyf*. *Sesse* or *Cesse* is *Cis*, the short for Cicely, i. e. Cecilia; see Bardsley's Eng. Surnames, p. 59. In a song in Ritson's Ancient Songs, i. 139, where some 'gossips' meet together at a tavern, the name of one of them is *Scyscely*. See the paraphrase in Pref. to A-text, p. vi.

365. (b. 5. 318; a. 5. 161.) A hackney-man was one who let out horses on hire; the term occurs A.D. 1308, in Riley's Memorials of London, p. 63.

366. (b. 5. 319; a. 5. 162.) Women of ill repute might be put in the pillory; and if so, they were afterwards to be led "through Chepe and Newgate, to *Cokkeslane*, there to take up their abode."—Liber Albus, p. 395. Cock Lane, West Smithfield, has been lately rebuilt. See also note to l. 367. The church may have been Bow church; see note to l. 360. Or again, it may have been St Peter's in Cornhill (cf. note to l. 377), since that church was emphatically *the* church, and its rector had precedence of all others; see Memorials of London, ed. Riley, p. 653.

367. (b. 5. 321; a. 5. 163.) *Syre Peeres,* Sir Piers. Observing Chaucer's line in the Prol. to the Non. Pr. Tale—

"Wherfor, *sir* monk, or dan *Piers* by your name"—

and remembering that *Sir* was, at that date, the usual title of a monk or priest, we may feel sure that the same is intended here. The word *prydie* occurs nowhere else, and may be a mere name; but I strongly suspect that (like most things in our author) it has some definite meaning. I would therefore suggest that it is put for *prie-dieu,* which means a sort of fald-stool; and is, accordingly, a hint at the proper duties of Sir Piers. But here, by a severe stroke of satire, this ecclesiastic, who should be praying to God, is found on a tavern-bench, beside Pernel of Flanders, about the significance of whose name there is no doubt whatever. The reader who will turn to Riley's Memorials of London, p. 535, will find, in the Regulation as to street-walkers by night, who were especially "Flemish women," that they were forbidden "to ledge in the city, or in the suburbs thereof, by night or by day; but they are to keep themselves to the places thereunto assigned, that is to say, to the stews on the other side of Thames, and *Cokkeslane.;* on pain of losing and forfeiting the upper garment that she shall be wearing, together with the hood, every time that any one of them shall be found doing to the contrary of this proclamation." This explains, at the same time, the allusion to Cock Lane in the line above, and agrees with the following list of the characteristics of London, as given in MS. Trin. Coll. O. 9. 38, printed in Reliq. Antiq. ii. 178.

"Haec sunt Londonis, pira, pomaque, regia thronus,
Chepp-stupha, *coklana,* dolum, leo, verbaque vana."

The name *Purnel* or *Pernel* has been commented on above, in the note to Pass. v. 111; see also note to Pass. xviii. 71.

368. (*not in* b, a.) *Tyborne,* Tyburn. Executions were formerly very frequent. See Knight's Pop. Hist. Eng. VII. chap. vi.; Butler's Hudibras, I. ii. 532; Dr Johnson's poem of London, l. 238, with the note on it in Hales's Longer English Poems, 1872, p. 313. Tyburn was afterwards called Westbourn; its site varied (see Hales), but one position of it is still marked, at the junction of Edgeware Road and Oxford Street. There seems to have been another place of execution, in the parish of St Thomas-a-Waterings, in Southwark, called, by way of distinction, Tyburn *of Kent;* see Pegge's Kenticisms, ed. Skeat, Proverb 11.

369. (b. 5. 320; a. 5. 164.) *Dauwe* is for *Davie* or *David.* Cf. "When *Dauie Diker* diggs and dallies not;" Gascoigne's Steel Glas, 1078; in Specimens of English, 1394—1579, ed. Skeat, p. 322. Hence the names Dawson, Dawkes, Dawkins, Dakin (for Dawkin), Dawes, &c. For *diker,* i.e. ditcher, the Vernon MS. has *disschere,* i. e. a maker of metal dishes; but some other MSS. of the A-text (as T and U) have the reading *dykere,* which is certainly correct. The word *disschere* comes in more fitly a few lines further down, viz. in l. 372 (b. 5. 323; a. 5. 166). Mr Bardsley, in his English Surnames, p. 349, remarks that the 'disher' all but invariably

worked in pewter, and quotes the names of John le Discher, Robert le Dis-shere, and Margaret la Disheress.

371. (b. 5. 322; a. 5. 165.) *Rakere,* or *Rakyer of Chepe,* a scavenger of West Cheap, or Cheapside. The word *rakyer,* evidently meaning a raker or street-sweeper, occurs in a Proclamation made in the 31st year of Edw. III. See Riley's Memorials of London, pp. 67, 299, 522, and Liber Albus, p. 289. The explanation "a vagrant chapman," in Pref. to A-text, p. vi., note 6, is wholly wrong.

372. (b. 5. 323; a. 5. 166.) A *roper* means a ropemaker; the phrase "corder or roper" occurs A.D. 1310, in Riley's Memorials of London; where mention is also made of a "roperie" or rope-walk, situate in the parish of Allhallows' the Great, Thames Street. Palsgrave has "Ropar, a ropemaker, *cordier,*" and Levins has "Roper, *restio.*" There is a story about a "ropers wiff" in the Knight de la Tour, ed. Wright, p. 79.

373. (b. 5. 324; a. 5. 167.) *Garlekhithe* [b] is near Vintry Ward. Stow says—"There is the parish church of St James, called at Garlick-hithe, or Garlick-hive; for that of old time, on the bank of the river Thames, near to this church, garlick was usually sold;" Survey of London, ed. 1842, p. 93. The next landing-place, westward, is Queen Hithe. See Smith's English Gilds, p. 1.

It has been suggested that *Griffin* is an allusion to the Griffin (Griffin to the vulgar eye, though Cockatrice in the Heralds' office), which was em-blazoned on the ancient shield of the principality of Wales.—Notes and Queries, 3rd S. xii. 513. The Harleian MS. 875 (A-text) has *Gruffith,* i. e. Griffith, a common Welsh name.

375. (b. 5. 326; a. 5. 169.) *To hansele,* as a bribe, i. e. to propitiate him. On this word, see the article in Halliwell's Dictionary, and cf. Brand's Pop. Antiq. ed. Ellis, iii. 262. It occurs again in Rich. the Redeles, iv. 91.

377. (b. 5. 328; a. 5. 171.) *To þe newe fayre,* or *Atte new faire,* at the new fair. I am told there is a reference here to an old game called handi-capping. It seems that Hikke chose Bette to be his deputy. Then Bette and one appointed by Clement tried to make a bargain, but could not settle it till Robyn was called in as umpire, by whose decision Clement and Hikke had to abide. But it is clear, from Riley's Memorials of London, that 'The neue Feyre' was another name for what was afterwards called an 'Evechep-yuge.' In 1297, a sort of mart called 'The neue Feyre' was held in Soper Lane, now Queen Street, Cheapside. Later, there were two 'Evechepynges,' one in Cheapside, the other and principal one in Cornhill; and they were held at hostelries or taverns. The passages relating to them are too long for quotation. See Riley's Memorials of London, pp. 33, 35, 75, 339, 532; and Liber Albus, p. 624. In fact, "to chaffer at the new fair" became a pro-verbial phrase for to exchange, as is clear from a passage in Wyclif's Works, iii. 167. Compare Rob. of Brunne, Hand. Synne, ll. 5977—5980—

"For men þat loue to do gylerye,
At þe alehous make þey marchaundye,

> To loke ȝyf þey kunne com wyþynne,
> Here negheburs þyng falsly to wynne."

383. (b. 5. 333; a. 5. 176.) *Rapliche* [c, a], quickly; *in rape* [b], in haste. To the examples in Stratmann add—"He ros vp *raply ;*" Arthur, ed. Furnivall, (E. E. T. S.) 1864, l. 87; and Rich. Redeles, pr. 13.

394. (b. 5. 344; a. 5. 188.) In a tavern-song in Ritson's Ancient Songs, i. 138, we find—

> "And lette the cuppe goo route,
> Good gosyp."

Compare Gower's Conf. Amant. ed. Pauli, vol. iii., where we find at p. 13—

> "Some laugh and some loure;"

and at p. 3—

> "With drie mouth he sterte him up,
> And saith—'now *baillez ça* the cuppe.'"

So in Polit. Poems, ed. Wright, i. 277—

> "Thei cry, 'Fyl the bowles, *bonus est liquor, hic maneamus.*'"

And the beginning of an old catch is—

> "Trole, trole the bowl to me,
> And I will trole the same again to thee;"

note in Hazlitt's Old Plays to the song in Act ii. of Gammer Gurton's Needle. And see "Fill the cup, fill" in Hazlitt's Proverbs, p. 131.

397. (b. 5. 346; a. 5. 191.) *Yglobbed*, gulped down, swallowed. In Smith's Eng. Gilds, p. 59, we find that an alderman of the Gild of St John the Baptist, in Lynn, was allowed the extraordinary quantity of *two* gallons of ale, and every brother *or sister* that was sick "in tyme of drynkyn" was to have "a potel." A *pottle* (see l. 399) is two quarts, or half a gallon; a *gill* is a quarter of a pint, or the thirty-second part of a gallon. We find mention of "gallons, potells, and quarts" in Riley's Memorials of London, p. 78; and see Chester Plays, ed. Wright, pp. 53 and 142.

398. (b. 5. 347; *not in* a.) To *godely, gotheli,* or *yothelen,* is to rumble. The word is very rare, but may be found three times at p. 135 of Popular Treatises on Science, ed. Wright, where it is used of the rumbling sound of thunder. It is probably much the same word as that used at p. 66 of the Ayenbite of Inwyt, where it is said of slanderers or railers that "þe on godeleþ þanne oþrene," i. e. the one rails at the other. Cf. Icel. *gutla,* to gurgle. It occurs again in Pass. xvi. 97.

402. (b. 5. 351; a. 5. 195.) *Wexed* [c, b], waxed, or stopped up; *I-wipet* [a], wiped. The word 'waxed' is here used merely in jest; to *wax* meant to stop tight, to stop up "as tight as wax," because it was sometimes used for that purpose. Thus, in the Romans of Partenay, ed. Skeat, at l. 2817, when Raymond wanted to stop up a hole in a door through which he had been peeping, we read—

> "But to ende the hole were stopped and faste made,
> A litell cloute cute he without delay,
> *With wax melled*, stopped the hole alway."

Wips is an old spelling of *wisp*, like *crips* for *crisp*, or *waps* for *wasp*. Cf. "Wyspe, *torques, torquillus;*" Prompt. Parv. It means a little twist of straw, as fully explained in Brand's Popular Antiq., ed. Ellis, iii. 396.

404. (b. 5. 353; a. 5. 197.) Gleemen were sometimes blind in former times, as now, and were led, in like manner, by a dog who consulted only his own ideas as to the course to be taken. See Ritson, Met. Rom. i. ccxiv.

405. (b. 5. 354; a. 5. 198.) We find in the Tale of Beryn—

"Sometyme thou wilt avaunte [*go in front*], and sometyme arere."

406. (b. 5. 355; a. 5. 199.) "Like one who lays nets, to catch birds with."

408. (b. 5. 357; a. 5. 201.) *Thrumbled* [c] or *thrompelde* [a] obviously has the sense of *stumbled* [b]. This rare word may be related to *thrumde* in Layamon's Brut, l. 54, which means compacted, compiled, or pressed together, and to A.S. *þrym*, a throng, crowd, heap. Perhaps it comes near to what is implied when we say that a man falls "all in a heap," or that he is "doubled up;" but examples are wanting to shew its precise force. Shakespeare (3 Hen. VI. iv. 7. 11) has—

"For many men that stumble at the threshold
Are well foretold that danger lurks within"—

on which Douce (Illustrations of Shak. ii. 30) remarks—"To understand this phrase rightly, it must be remembered that some of the old thresholds or steps under the door were, like the hearths, raised a little, so that a person might stumble over them unless proper care were taken." In fact, *threshold* is a corruption of the older *threshwold*, meaning that piece of wood (*wold*) which received the tread of feet, and was, as it were, subject to continual *threshing* or beating. The spelling *threschefolde* occurs in Chaucer's tr. of Boethius, ed. Morris, p. 7, the form *-folde* being intermediate in form between *-wolde* and *-olde*.

420. (b. 5. 369; a. 5. 213.) *Ho halt* [c], who holds? i.e. who detains? *Bolle* signified not only a bowl, but a capacious cup; hence the reading *cuppe* [a]. Cf. "Twelve hanaps of gold, called *bolles;*" Riley's Mem. of Lond. p. 429. Hence the term *boller* for a deep drinker, as in Pass. x. 194.

421. (b. 5. 370; a. 5. 214.) "His wife and his conscience reproved him for his sin" [c]. Some MSS. of [b] have *wit*, i. e. his common sense; others have *wif*, as in [a].

424. (*not in* b, a.) "Thou, O Lord, who art aloft, and didst shape (or create) all creatures." *Lyf*, in the sense of creature, occurs again elsewhere; see the Glossary.

427. (b. 5. 376; *not in* a.) Hard swearing was extremely common; see Chaucer, Pard. Tale, C. T. 12565; also the discussion in the Shipm. Prol.; and Pers. Tale, *De Ira.*

429. (b. 5. 378; *not in* a.) *Nones.* See note to Pass. ix. 146, and see l. 434 below.

☞ **Here is a very short digression to B. 13. 400—409.**

——(b. 13. 400.) The passage in ll. 400—409, preserved only in the

Rawlinson MS., was afterwards made the groundwork of the extended description of Gluttony in the C-text.   See this explained in Crit. Note to B-text, xiii. 293; pp. 411, 412.

Garnement, garment; for the spelling, see B. xiv. 24.

——(b. 13. 401.) *Beflobered it*, muddied it, made it dirty.   Compare— "*Flop*, a mass of thin mud;" Barnes, Dorsetshire Glossary.   See *flober* in B. xiv. 15.

——(b. 13. 404.) "And ate more meat, and drank more, than his natural powers could well digest."   Compare this line and the next with C. vii. 430, 431.

——(b. 13. 407.) "So that he falls (lit. becomes) into despair, and expected not to be saved."   Perhaps a better reading would be *warth*, the past tense; this makes better sense, and is nearer to the form *wrathe* in the MS.; see footnote.   For a note on *wanhope*, see note to Pass. viii. 59.

End of the digression.

430. (cf. b. 13. 404; *not in* a.) Here our author takes a few expressions from the Confession of Haukyn in B. 13. 404, 405.   The line means— "More than my natural constitution could well digest" [c]; *or*, "And ate more meat and drank more than his natural constitution could digest" [b].   See note to Pass. i, 229.

431. (cf. b. 13. 405; *not in* a.) "And, like a dog that eats grass, I began to vomit."   *Et* is for *eteth*, 3 p. s. pr. tense.   From *brake* comes *parbreak*, used by Spenser, F. Q. i. 1. 20.

☞ **Here is the return to B. 5. 380.**

432. (b. 5. 380; *not in* a.) "And wasted that which I might have spared (or saved);" the B-text being the more explicit.   The word *spele*, to spare, is rare; but see Pass. xiv. 77, and the three other examples in Stratmann. It also occurs in Morris's edition of the Old Eng. Homilies, 2nd Series, p. 31, l. 4, where it is mistranslated 'spillest,' but the error is corrected in a Note at p. 235.

434. (cf. b. 5. 381; *not in* a.) "In other manner ben distinct the spices [*kinds*] of glotonie, after Seint Gregorie. The first is, for to ete before time. The second is, whan a man geteth him to delicat mete or drinke;" &c. Chaucer, Pers. Tale, *De Gulá*.

SCHEME OF C. PASSUS VIII.

(B. Pass. V. 392—VI. 2; A. Pass. V. 222—VII. 2; with an
insertion from B. Pass. XIII. 410—457.)

Cf. Wright's edition; pp. 100—105; 270—272; and 106—117.

N.B. See also the Scheme of C. Passus XVI.

C-TEXT. VIII.	B-TEXT. V.	A-TEXT. V.
viii. 1—27	v. 392—418	——
——	419	——
28—32	420—424	——
——	425, 426	——
33, 34	*like* 427, 428	——
35—49	429—443	——
50	——	
51—55	444—448	——
56—69	449—462	v. 222—235

The passage in B. 5. 463—484 (A. 5. 236—259) *corresponds to* C. vii.
10—330; *see notes to* Pass. vii. p. 125, *and the Scheme on* p. 101.

70—74	xiii. 410—414	——
——	xiii. 415	——
75, 76	*like* xiii. 416	——
77—117	xiii. 417—457	——

The passage inserted from B. 13. 410—457 *ends here.*

118, 119	——	——
120—129	v. 485—494	——

(*The Latin quotation varies.*)

130, 131	*like* 495, 496	——
——	497, 498	——
132—144	499—511	——
145—149	——	——
150—154	512—516	——
155	517	260
——	——	261
156, 157	518, 519	262, 263
——		vi. 1, 2
158, 159	520, 521	vi. 3, 4
——		vi. 5
160—174	522—536	vi. 6—20
175, 176	538, 537	vi. 22, 21
177—186	539—548	vi. 23—32
(a) 187	(a) [551]	(a) [vi. 37]
188	549	vi. 33
189—191	——	——
——	550	vi. 34
		vi. 35
(a) [187]	(a) 551	(a) vi. 37
	552	vi. 36
——	553—555	
——		vi. 38

C-TEXT.	B-TEXT.	A-TEXT.
viii. 192—199	v. 556—563	vi. 39—46
—	564	—
200, 201	565, 566	vi. 47, 48
202	—	—
203	567	vi. 49
204, 205	*like* 568, 569	*like* vi. 50
206—208	570—572	vi. 51—53
209, 210	—	—
211—238	573—600	vi. 54—81
239	—	—
—	—	vi. 82—84
240—242	601—603	—
243—245	604—606	vi. 85—87
246, 247	608, 607	vi. 89, 88
	609	vi. 90
248—250	*like* 610—612	*like* vi. 91—93
251	—	—
252	613	vi. 94
253	—	—
254, 255	614, 615	vi. 95, 96
		vi. 97
256—260	—	—
—	616, 617	—
261—275	618—632	vi. 98—112
—	633	—
276, 277	—	—
278—291	634—647	vi. 113—126
	648—651	—
292—306	—	—
307, 308	vi. 1, 2	vii. 1, 2

NOTES TO C. PASSUS VIII.

(B. PASS. V. 392—VI. 2; A. PASS. V. 222—VII. 2; WITH AN INSERTION FROM B. XIII. 410—457.)

N.B. Lines 392—425 (B-text) are quoted in a note to Drayton's Polyolbion; Song xi.

4. (b. 5. 395; *not in* a.) "If I am once in bed, no ringing (of the church-bell) shall make me get up till I am ready for dinner, unless some call of nature renders it necessary." In this passage 'tail-end' is simply used for 'tail;' there are other passages in which *tailende* means talliage, income, or revenue, from the verb *tailen;* see, e.g. B. 8. 82 (A. 9. 74); and cf. *ytayled* in l. 35 below (C-text). *Hit made =* should cause it; so in l. 28 below, we have 'bote syknesse hit make.'

Chaucer, in the Pers. Tale, *de Accidiá*, has—"Than cometh sompnolence, that is, sluggy slumbring, which maketh a man hevy, and dull in body and in soule, and this sinne cometh of slouthe: and certes, the time that, by way of reson, man shuld not slepe, is by the morwe [*early in the morning*], but if

ther were cause resonable." Mr Wright (Homes of Other Days, p. 105)
remarks that "in Huon of Bordeaux (p. 270) one of the chief heroes is
accused of laziness, because he was in bed after the cock had crowed."

Compare also the following :—

> "In slewthe then thai syn, Goddes workes thai not wyrke,
> To belke thai begyn, and spew that is irke,
> His hede must be holdyn ther in the myrke,
> Then deffes hym with dyn the belles of the kyrke
>   When thai clatter;
> He wishys the clerke hanged
> For that he rang it;" &c.—Towneley Myst. p. 314.

7. (b. 5. 398; *not in* a.) *Rascled* [c]; *roxed* [b], stretched himself. *Rox*
is much the same as the Lowland Scotch *rax*, to stretch, which is, indeed,
only a form of *reach*. *Rasclen* is a secondary verb, derived from *rax*, and
perhaps influenced in form by the A.S. *wraxlian*, to wrestle. We find in
Layamon's Brut, ed. Madden, l. 25991—

> "And seoððen he gon ramien · and raxlede swiðe,
> & adun lai bi þan fure · & his leomen strahte;"

which Sir F. Madden interprets by—"and afterwards he gan to roar, and
vociferated much, and down lay by the fire, and stretched his limbs." But
surely *raxlede* means 'stretched himself' in this passage also. The explanation
is found in Levins's Manipulus Vocabulum, ed. Wheatley, which has—
"Raskle, *pandiculari*," col. 35; and again—"Ruskle, *pandiculari*," col. 194.
So also *I raxled* = I stretched myself, roused myself; Allit. Poems, ed.
Morris, A. 1174.

Remed [c], *rored* [b], roared. Observe that this word occurs in the
passage from Layamon just quoted. Compare the description of Sloth given
by Robert of Brunne, Handlyng Synne, ll. 4258-60, 4280-2—

> "Whan he beryþ a bel ryng, ·
> To holy cherche men kallyng,
> þan may he nat hys bedde lete . . . .
> þan cumþ one aboute pryme,
> 'Rys up,' he seyþ, 'now ys tyme.'
> þan begynneþ he to klawe and to *raske*."

10. (b. 5. 401; *not in* a.) Here we may again compare Robert of Brunne's
description of Sloth, ll. 4244-6—

> "Moche ys a man for to blame,
> þat kan nat wurschep goddys name
> Wyþ paternoster ne wyþ crede," &c.

11. (b. 5. 402; *not in* a.) This seems to be the earliest mention of Robin
Hood. The next earliest is in Wyntoun's Chronicle, written about A.D.
1420, where Little John is also mentioned. But Mr Wright thinks that one
of the extant Robin-Hood ballads is really of the date of Edward II. See
his Essays on England in the Middle Ages, ii. 174. *Randolf, erl of chestre*,
might be the Randulph or Randle, Earl of Chester, who lived in Stephen's
time, and was earl from A.D. 1128 to 1153; but I have no hesitation in de-
ciding that the reference is really, as Ritson supposed, to his grandson of

the same name, who married no less exalted a personage than Constance, .
widow of Geoffrey Plantagenet, and mother of Prince Arthur; and who was
earl from 1181 to 1231 or 1232. Both were celebrated men, but the latter
is the more likely to be meant, as being better known and later in date;
besides which, there is a story on record, that, when this Randle was
besieged by the Welsh in Rhuddlan castle, he was released by a *rabble
of minstrels*, led by Roger Lacy (see Ritson's Ancient Songs, vol. i. pp.
vii. and xlvi.; Percy's Essay on the Ancient Minstrels; and Dugdale's
Baronage); and, since some privileges were conferred on the minstrels in
consequence of this exploit, the least they could do in return would be to
make 'rymes' concerning him. There were really *three* Randulphs, father,
son, and grandson, but not much is known of Randulph II. The exploits
of Randulph III. are told in the Percy Folio MS.; and also in the legend of
Fulke Fitzwarine, printed in Coggleshall's Chronicon Anglicanum, ed. Jos.
Stevenson (Rolls Series) 1875. The lives of the Earls of Chester are detailed in an exhaustive manner by Mr Hales, in the edition of the Percy
Folio MS. 1867; vol. i. p. 258. Concerning Robin Hood, see also Chambers,
Book of Days, ii. 606, and i. 580. The 'Robin-Hood games' were held on
May 1.

The expression 'a ryme (*or* geste, *or* tale) of Robin Hood' came to mean,
proverbially, any idle story. See two examples of this in Barclay, Ship of
Fools, ed. Jamieson, ii. 155, 331; see *Hood* (*Robin*) in the Index to the
Parker Soc. publications; and the note to l. 19, below.

14. (b. 5. 405; *not in* a.) In like manner Chaucer says—"Now cometh
slouthe, that wol not suffre no hardnes ne no penaunce;" Pers. Tale, *de
Accidiâ.*

19. (b. 5. 410; *not in* a.) *Atte nale*, at the ale-house; see notes to Pass.
i. 43. We here read that Sloth, who was a priest (see l. 30) used to resort
to the ale-house, like the 'Sir Piers' mentioned in Pass. vii. 367; and even
ventured to talk scandal in the church itself. Barclay is explicit in his
denunciation of the latter practice, which was carried to a shameless extent.

> "And in the mornynge whan they come to the quere,
> The one begynneth a fable or a hystory,
> The other lenyth theyr erys it to here,
> Takynge it in stede of the Inuytory;
> Some other maketh respons, antym, and memory,
> And all of fables and Iestis of Robyn hode,
> Or other tryfyls that skantly ar so gode."
>   Barclay's Ship of Fools; ed. Jamieson, ii. 155.

22. (b. 5. 413; *not in* a.) *Harlotrie*, a scurrilous tale. In a MS. Glossary
printed in Reliq. Antiq. i. 7, we find—"*Scurra*, a harlotte;" and "*Scurrilitas*,
a harlotrye." See also B. 13. 416; and l. 76 below. -

Somer game of souteres, a summer game played by shoemakers. A
summer game is probably the same as *summering*, a rural sport at Midsummer.
See Nares, who refers to Brand's Pop. Antiq., i. 240 (4to ed.); Strutt's
Sports and Pastimes, p. xxvi.; and Mr Markland's Essay on the Chester

Mysteries, in the 3rd vol. of Malone's Shakespeare, p. 525, ed. Boswell. Nares also quotes an extract about "May-games, wakes, *summerings*, and rush-bearings." The great day was on St John the Baptist's eve, i. e. June 23, or Midsummer eve. The games themselves answered to what we now call 'athletic sports;' and it was usual to conclude them with large bonfires. They were not confined to England, as may be illustrated by a passage in Keightley's Fairy Mythology, vol. i. p. 288, where, in the course of a story relating to the island of Rügen in the Baltic, we are told that—"St John's day, when the days are longest and the nights shortest, was now come. Old and young kept the holiday, had all sorts of plays, and told all kinds of stories." I add a few illustrative quotations, some of which shew that these games were not always very respectably conducted.

> "Another Romayn told he me by name,
> That, for his wyf was at a *someres game*,
> Without his witing, he forsook hire eke."
>
> Chaucer; Wyf of Bathes Prologue.

> "Daunces, karols, *somour-games*,
> Of many swych come many shames."
>
> Rob. of Brunne, Haud. Synne, l. 4684.

"In the Pleasant and Stately Morall of the Three Lordes and Three Ladies of London, printed by Ihones, 1590, is the following passage descriptive of the popular amusements and customs of the period in the metropolis, and alluding to the Midsummer Watch very pointedly—

> 'Let nothing that's magnifical,
> Or that may tend to London's graceful state,
> Be unperform'd, as showes and solemne feastes,
> Watches in armour, triumphes, cresset-lights,
> Bonefires, belles, and peals of ordinaunce
> And pleasure. See that plaies be published,
> Mai-games, and maskes, with mirth and minstrelsie,
> Pageants and school-feastes, beares and puppet-plaies.'"
>
> T. Sharp; Diss. on Pageants, p. 177.

"On the Vigil of St John the Baptist, commonly called Midsummer Eve, it was usual in most country places, and also in towns and cities, for the inhabitants, both old and young, and of both sexes, to meet together, and make merry by the side of a large fire made in the middle of the street, or in some open and convenient place, over which the young men frequently leaped by way of frolic, and also amused themselves with various sports and pastimes, more especially with running, wrestling, and dancing."—Strutt; Sports and Pastimes, p. 317. He refers to Bourne's Antiq., vol. ix. c. 27; and to verses on Midsummer Eve by Barnaby Googe.

"'Why,' quoth I, 'could they caste the barre and sledge well?' 'I wyll tell you, syr,' quoth hee, 'you knowe there hath bene *manye games this sommer*. I think verely, that if some of these lubbars had bene there, and practysed amongest others, I beleue they woulde have carryed awaye the beste games. For they were so strong and sturdye, that I was not able to stande in their handes.'"—Harman's Caveat, ed. Furnivall, p. 47. See also the descriptions of the settings of the watch and the processions ˙on Midsummer's Eve and St Peter's Eve given by Stowe in his Survey of London (folio, 1633), pp. 84, 85, and the description of the Cotswold games at Whitsuntide in Chambers, Book of Days, i. 714.

There is a parallel passage to this in King Alisaunder, ed. Weber, ll. 21, 22—

> "That hadde levere a ribaudye
> Than to here of God, other of seynte Marie."

25. (b. 5. 416; *not in* a.) *Late I passe* [b], I let pass, I pay no heed to. Cf. Chaucer, Prol. 175.

27. (b. 5. 418; *not in* a.) Cf. Shakesp. Hen. VIII. iii. 2. 294—

> "I'll startle you
> Worse than the sacring-bell, when the brown wench
> Lay kissing in your arms, lord cardinal."

The latter·part of the line in [c] seems to mean—"then I have mention made of me at the friars' convent," i. e. by the friars. The word *memorie* is a little obscure, but Cotgrave gives one sense of *memorie* as "thought had, or mention made, of things absent or past." It must here mean that Sloth was mentioned by name by the friars in their prayers, because he had bought from them a letter of fraternity. See Wyclif's Treatise "Of Lettris of Fraternite," where we read—"þei graunten letters of bretherhed under her comyne secle, þat her breþer schal have part of alle her gode dedes, bothe *in lif* and in deth, and rekkenen mony werkes;" Works, ed. Arnold, iii. 420. I suppose the word *memorie* more often bears the signification of commemoration or service for the dead. Cf. the quotation in note to l. 19 above; also—

> "Their pennie Masses, and their Complynes meete,
> Their Diriges, their Trentals, and their shrifts,
> Their *memories*, their singings, and their gifts."
>> Spenser; Moth. Hub. Tale, 452.

——(b. 5. 419; *not in* a.) *Ite, missa est;*·the concluding words of the service of the mass. From this form of words, the words *Missa* and *Missal* are said to be derived.

28. (b. 5. 420; *not in* a.) *Bote syknesse hit make*, unless sickness causes it (to be so); i. e. unless an attack of illness frightens me into confession. See this expression repeated in l. 65 below; and cf. note to l. 4 above.

29. (b. 5. 421; *not in* a.) "Yet I tell not the half (of my sins)" [c]; "and then I shrive myself by guess" [b], i. e. I mention sins at random when I cannot call them to mind.   Compare—

> "And some alle þe ȝere wyllyn abyde
> Of shryfte tyl þe lentyn tyde . . .
> And sum men, yn alle here lyue,
> Clenly ne wyle þey hem schryue."
>> Rob. of Brunne; Hand. Synne, 4786.

31. (b. 5. 423; *not in* a.) *Solfye*, i. e. *sol-fa*. To *sol-fa* is to practise singing the scale of notes. See a poem on Learning to Sing, pr. in Reliq. Antiq. i. 292—"I *solfe* and singge after," &c.; and see *solfa* in the Index to Dyce's edition of Skelton.

——(b. 5. 425; *not in* a.) *Beatus vir*, Ps. i. or cxii. *Beati omnes*, Ps. cxxviii. Wyclif speaks of "unable curatis, þat kunnen not the ten comaundements, ne rede her sauter;" Works, iii. 277. We must remember that it was not uncommon for a man to know the whole Psalter by heart; Rock, Church of Our Fathers, iii. 5.

34. (*not in* b, a; *but cf.* b. 5. 428.) *Catoun*, Cato; see note to Pass. ix. 338.

——(b. 5. 428; *not in* c, a; *but cf.* c. 8. 34.) *Canoun*, the canon-law; see *Canoun* in the Glossary. *Decretales*, Decretals; a collection of popes' edicts and decrees of councils, forming a part of the canon-law. Five books of them were collected by Gregory IX., in 1227; and a sixth by Boniface VIII., in 1297. See *Decretals* in Haydn's Dict. of Dates.

35. (b. 5. 429; *not in* a.) "If I buy and give a pledge for anything, then, unless it be marked on a tally," &c. The B-text means—"If I buy (anything) and give a pledge for it (without paying down the money), then," &c.; the general sense being the same.

36. (b. 5. 430; *not in* a.) The alliteration shews that the true reading is 3*if* [b], not *yf* [c].

45. (b. 5. 439; *not in* a.) I. e. unless something eatable is held in the hand. We may compare the proverbial phrase used by Chaucer (C. T. 4132)—
"With empty hand men may na haukes tulle;"
and again (C. T. 5997)—
"With empty hand men may no haukes lure."

52. (b. 5. 445; *not in* a.) *Forsleuthed*, wasted by idle carelessness. *And sette hous a fuyre*, and set the house on fire (by my carelessness).

55. (b. 5. 448; *not in* a.) A Leonine hexameter; I do not know from whom it is quoted.

57. (b. 5. 450; a. 5. 223.) *Vigilate* refers to Mk. xiii. 37—"Quod autem uobis dico, omnibus dico: Vigilate." *Veille*, probably 'watcher;' observe the reading *wakere* in MS. H. [a].

59. (b. 5. 452; a. 5. 225.) *War fro wanhope*, beware of despair. This is an allusion to the usual supposed result of Sloth; see l. 81 below, and observe how Chaucer, in his Persones Tale (*de Accidiâ*), describes the result of Sloth in the words—"Now cometh wanhope, that is, despair of the mercy of God," &c. So also in Rob. of Brunne, Hand. Synne, l. 5171—
"Sloghenes, hyt wyl þe grope
To brynge þe yn-to whanhope."

So also in the Ayenbite of Inwyt, ed. Morris, p. 34; q. v., and Chaucer, Pers. Tale, very near the end. On the word *Wanhope*, see Trench, Eng. Past and Present. Cf. B. 13. 407.

Wolde [b], who would, *or* which would; the relative being omitted.

61. (b. 5. 454; a. 5. 227.) In Hampole's Prick of Conscience, ed. Morris, ll. 3398—3411, the ten things that destroy venial sins are holy water, almsdeeds, fasting, the sacrament, the Pater Noster, shrift, the

bishop's blessing, the priest's blessing, *knocking upon the breast as practised by a meek man*, and extreme unction. *Bidde god of grace*, pray to God for His grace; cf. l. 121 below.

65. (b. 5. 458; a. 5. 231.) *Bote sycknesse hit make* [c, a], unless sickness cause it (to be otherwise), unless sickness be the cause; *but sykenesse it lette* [b], unless sickness prevent it.

☞ **Observe the break here, owing to the insertion from B. 13. 410—457. For notes to B. 5. 463—484 (A. 5. 236—259) see pp. 125, 126.**

70. (b. 13. 410; *not in* a.) *Braunches*, branches; the usual theological term for the subdivisions of a subject. In the Ayenbite of Inwyt (p. 31, l. 6, and p. 33), the 'boughs' of Sloth are lukewarmness, timidity of heart, &c.; and the six 'points' that bring a man to 'wanhope' are disobedience, impatience of control, murmuring, weariness of life, desire of death, and actual despair. See also Chaucer's Persones Tale; De Septem Peccatis Mortalibus.

In the English translation of Calendrier des Bergers (Shepherd's Calendar), ed. 1656, sig. D 6, and sig. E 6, we find—"The first great branch of the tree of vicis is pride, and he hath xvii branches growin[g] out of him," &c. And again—"Here endeth the branches and small spraies of the sinne of Wrath, and hereafter followeth the xvii. [*read* xvi.] branches of Sloth, as, Evill thought, Annoy of wealth, readinesse to evill Pusillanimity, Evill will, breaking vowes, Impenitence, Infidelity, Ignorance, Vain Sorrow, slowly (*sic*), evill hope, Curiosity, Idlenesse, Evagation, letting to do good, Desolation."

——(b. 13. 415; *not in* c, a.) *Heigh ferye*, high holiday; see note to Pass. v. 113. Barclay, Ship of Fools, ed. Jamieson, ii. 270, says—

> "The folys disgysed moste set their intent
> On *hyest dayes*, and most solemne also
> In suche disfygured maner for to go."

He mentions "Christis feste," Christmas-day, Easter, and "Witsontyde" as being such days.

83. (b. 13. 423; *not in* a.) *Fool sages*, foolish wise men; alluding to the jesters, who were professed fools, yet often made sensible remarks. See l. 104 below.

87. (b. 13. 427; *not in* a.) The Latin is perhaps not so much a quotation as a maxim of law. Richardson (s. v. *Consense*) quotes—"But whosoeuer was the manqueller of this holy man, it shall appere, that both the murtherer and the *consenter* had condigne and not vndeserved punishment, for their bloudye stroke and butcherly act."—Hall, Edw. iv. an. 10.

90. (b. 13. 430; *not in* a.) So Chaucer, Pers. Tale, *De Ira*, says—"Flaterers ben the deuils nourices, that nourish his children with milke of losengerie. ... Flaterers ben the deuils enchauntours, for they maken a man to wenen himself be like that he is not like."

97. (b. 13. 437; *not in* a.) Strutt, in his Sports and Pastimes, p. 177, gives several examples of the amounts of money paid to minstrels, such as

the following, for example. "At the marriage of Elizabeth, daughter of Edward I., to John, Earl of Holland, every *king's minstrel* received 40 shillings." Compare Froissart's account of the rewards given to minstrels by Gaston de Foix; vol. iv. cap. 41.

107. (b. 13. 447; *not in* a.) "And fiddle for thee the story of Good Friday;" i. e. and, instead of having a fiddler to play to you, let a learned man recite the events of the crucifixion. See Crit. Note to B. 13. 437—454; B-text, p. 412.

109. (b. 13. 449; *not in* a.) "To cry before our Lord for a *largesse*, in order to shew your excellent praise." To "cry largesse" is to ask for a bounty, and is a common phrase. I give an example of its contemporary use. "The king held a great court and gave a sumptuous feast, and at supper the heralds received large gifts from the lords and ladies, and *cried largesse*," &c.; French Chronicle of the Betrayal of Richard II., translated by B. Williams, p. 140. The term is still used in some parts by gleaners, who cry 'largesse!' when they see a stranger passing by. I heard it thus near Hunstanton, in Norfolk, in 1873. The use of the word obviously originated in a desire to propitiate the Norman nobles by addressing them in French.

112. (b. 13. 452; *not in* a.) *By hus lyue*, during his lifetime. *Litheth hem*, listens to them [c]; *lythed hem*, listened to them [b].

117. (b. 13. 457; *not in* a.) "With their evil-speaking, which is a song of sorrow, and the very fiddle of Lucifer;" meaning that evil-speaking, such as was indulged in by flatterers and jesters, leads men to destruction. Cf. Pass. i. 40. For *lay*, Mr Wright prints *lady*, which is the reading of his MS.; but it is a mere error of the scribe, since the other MSS. and Crowley have *lay* or *laye*.

☞ **Here ends the inserted passage from B. Pass. xiii.**

119. (*not in* b, a.) Here *þat* is put for *them that*. "For he listens to and loves them that despise God's law." The Latin quotation much resembles that quoted at B. 15. 336; see note to that line.

120. (b. 5. 485; *not in* a.) Here Repentance is personified, as in Pass. vii. 1, 12, 62, 331, 423; he is the priest to whom the various penitents make their confession. "Then was Repentance ready, and advised them all to kneel, and said—'I shall beseech, on the part of all sinners, that our Saviour will shew them His grace.'" To *beseech of* is to *beseech for*, to beg to obtain. Cf. to *bidde god of grace*, i. e. to pray to God for His grace, in l. 61 above.

126. (b. 5. 491; *not in* a.) *Ade*, written for *Adæ*, i. e. of Adam. Professor Stubbs has kindly pointed out to me that this is taken from a passage in the Sarum Missal, viz. from the Canticle 'Exultet' sung upon Holy Saturday (Easter Eve) at the blessing of the Paschal candle :—"O certe necessarium Ade peccatum et nostrum; quod Christi morte deletum est. O felix culpa, que talem ac tantum meruit habere redemptorem." Wyclif alludes to the same passage; see Wyclif's Works, ed. Arnold, i. 321.

129. (b. 5. 494; *not in* a.) "And madest Thyself, together with Thy Son, like unto our soul and body" [c]; *or*, "and us sinful men alike" [b]. The sense is clearer than the construction.   Cf. b. 5. 495.

130. (b. 5. 495; *not in* a.) *Thi self sone* [b], Thy Son Himself.   *In oure secte* [c]; *in owre sute* [b].   It makes no difference, since *secta* (from Lat. *sequi*) meant, in mediæval Latin, either the right of prosecuting an action at law or the *suit* or action itself; where *suit* is from the Fr. *suivre*, the equivalent of *sequi*.   And again, *secta* meant a *suit* of clothes, and such is the meaning here.   We should now say—"in our *flesh*."   Cf. ll. 137, 141. "There were also at least two *qualities of cloth*, the *secta generosorum*, and the *secta valettorum*, the distinction being so marked that I have felt myself able to draw up a table which shall contain both qualities;" Hist. Agric. in England, by J. E. T. Rogers, i. 578.   See 'Sect' in Wedgwood's Etymological Dictionary, which makes it clear that *sect* is from *sequi*, not *secare*.   *Secta* even means a *suite* or set of people; cf. "and thereupon he produced his *suit*."—Liber Albus, p. 342; where the Latin has *sectam*, i. e. his set of witnesses.

———(b. 5. 498; *not in* a.)   *It ladde*, led it (i. e. the sorrow) captive.   See Eph. iv. 8, Ps. lxviii. 18.

131. (b. 5. 500; *not in* a.)   *Meel-tyme of seyntes*, meal-time of saints.   This expression seems to be a figurative one, having reference to the time of the crucifixion, when Christ's blood was shed upon the cross.   It can hardly refer directly to the sacrifice of the mass, because that was more usually celebrated at an earlier hour of the day; see Rock, Church of Our Fathers, iii. pt. 2. 43.   It has also been suggested that there is reference here to Canticles i. 7, q. v.   I prefer to take it in connection with the succeeding context, and to suppose that the poet is speaking of the crucifixion as having been a time of refreshment to our forefathers who sat in darkness; the force of which reference can only be understood by readers who are familiar with the apocryphal gospel of Nicodemus.

The quotation from Isaiah ix. 2 is explained in the apocryphal Gospel of Nicodemus with reference to the "Harrowing of Hell," i. e. the descent of Christ into hell to fetch out the souls of the patriarchs.   Isaiah is there introduced as explaining to the other saints that the moment of fulfilment of his prophecy has arrived.   See the whole account, as there narrated; and cf. Pass. xxi. 369.

135. (b. 5. 502; *not in* a.)   Compare this with the account given of the Harrowing of Hell in Pass. xxi.   This line, e. g., nearly agrees with Pass. xxi. 371; and the expression *blewe* (b. 5. 503) is explained by *þat breþ* in Pass. xxi. 367.

137. (b. 5. 504; *not in* a.)   *In oure secte*, in our *suit*, i. e. in a human body; see note to l. 130.   The reference is to the Resurrection.

140. (b. 5. 507; *not in* a.)   *Ymad*, composed, narrated.   To *make* is to compose, especially in verse; but here it is applied to prose writings.

141. (b. 5. 508; *not in* a.)   *In owre armes* [b], in our armour, or in arms

marked with our device: a phrase taken from the terms of a tournament. See Pass. xxi. 21.

149. (*not in* b, a.) "And because of that great mercy, and for the love of Mary thy mother." The construction is explained in the note to Pass. xvi. 131.

150. (b. 5. 512; *not in* a.) *Rybaudes*, ribalds. See a long note in Political Songs, ed. Wright, 1839, p. 369. It was chiefly applied to the lowest class of retainers, who could be relied on to do the lord's dirty work. "In the household of the King of France there was a *Rex ribaldorum*, whose office was to judge disputes, &c., which might arise among retainers of his class." The same statement is made by Thynne, in his Animadversions on Speght's Chaucer, with citations of authorities; he quotes from the second book of De Rebus Gallicis by Johannes Tyllius the words—"iam tum homines perditi *Ribaldi*, et *Ribaldæ* mulieres puellæque perditæ vocantur." See also Ducange, s. v. *ribaldus* and *goliardiæ*. Cf. Pass. ix. 75.

152. (b. 5. 514; *not in* a.) *Hente*, seized. In Ps. lxxi. 20, we find "thou shalt quicken me again," but the Vulgate has the past tense instead of the future—"conversus vivificasti me."

153. (b. 5. 515; *not in* a.) Ps. xxxii. (xxxi. in the Vulgate) begins with—"Beati quorum remissæ sunt iniquitates, et quorum tecta sunt peccata."

☞ **Here begins A. Passus vi.**

155. (b. 5. 520; a. 6. 3.) Here the three texts agree once more. It is probable that the first two lines of A. Passus VI. (found in H only) are spurious. Yet they are useful for connecting the sense with the lines preceding.

157. (b. 5. 519; a. 5. 263.) *God leyue that thei mote*, God grant that they might do so [c, *also* a]; *treuthe to seke*, to seek Truth [b]. The A-text is misprinted; for *lene*, read *leue;* see note to B. 5. 263, on p. 123.

161. (b. 5. 523; a. 6. 7.) *Paynym*, pagan, Saracen (because of his foreign appearance) is the reading of [c] and [b]; but [a] has *Palmere.* This excellent description of a Palmer should be noted. Mr Wright aptly draws attention to a similar description in Sir Walter Scott's Marmion, canto i. st. 23, 27. Instead of quoting these familiar lines, I give Sir Walter Scott's note—"A *Palmer*, opposed to a *pilgrim*, was one who made it his sole business to visit different holy shrines; travelling incessantly, and subsisting by charity: whereas the Pilgrim retired to his usual home and occupations when he had paid his devotions at the particular spot which was the object of his pilgrimage." In the notes to Bell's edition of Chaucer, this statement is challenged, and it is asserted that a *palmer* meant a pilgrim to the Holy Land *only*, but many passages shew that it was often used in a much wider signification, and I see no good reason for altering Sir Walter's definition, which seems to have been copied from Speght. Mr Cutts, in his Scenes and Characters of the Middle Ages, which the reader should consult, says (at p. 167)—"When the pilgrim reached the Holy Land, and had visited the

usual round of the holy places, he became entitled to wear the palm in token of his accomplishment of that great pilgrimage; and from that badge he derived the name of Palmer." And this, no doubt, is the true explanation, viz. that a palmer was one who made it his business to go on pilgrimages, and that he earned his standing as a professional pilgrim by going to the Holy Land. This is well illustrated by the speech of the Palmer in Heywood's Interlude of *The Four P's*, where he enumerates the various shrines which he has visited. See also the romance of Sir Isumbras, who went about as a palmer; and cf. Chaucer, Prol. 13; King Horn, ed. Lumby, l. 1027; Spenser, F. Q. ii. 1. 52, with Kitchen's note in Clar. Press ed., p. 182; Ancren Riwle, p. 350; Rock, Church of Our Fathers, iii. 432; and Staunton's note to All's Well That Ends Well, Act iii. sc. 5.

162. (b. 5. 524; a. 6. 8.) *Bordon*, a staff; not a burden, as erroneously explained by Fosbrooke. The list may have been wound round it for use in case of accident. It would, at any rate, have been more useful than a bagpipe (!), which was recommended by Archbishop Arundel as a solace for a pilgrim who "striketh his toe upon a stone, and hurteth him sore, and maketh him to bleed;" see the Examination of William Thorpe as recorded by Foxe, and reprinted in Wordsworth's Ecclesiastical Biography, i. 312 (4th edition). Cf. Cutts, Scenes and Characters of the Middle Ages, p. 174. King Horn, when disguised as a palmer, carried a 'burdon' and a 'scrippe;' K. Horn, ed. Lumby, l. 1061.

163. (b. 5. 525; a. 6. 9.) "Wound round and round it, after the manner of a climbing plant." The *withiewind* was a name for the wild convolvulus. Cotgrave has—"*Liseron*, m. Withiwind, Bindweed, Ropeweed, Hedge-bells." And Minsheu says—"Woodbinde, binde-weede, or *withiewinde*, because it windes about other plantes." Cf. A.S. *wiðwinde*, convolvulus or bindweed.

164. (b. 5. 526; a. 6. 10.) The *bowl* and *bag* were invariably carried, the former to drink out of, the latter to hold scraps of meat and bread. See Cutts, Scenes and Characters of the Middle Ages, p. 174.

165. (b. 5. 527; a. 6. 11.) The *ampullæ* were little phials, containing holy water or oil. They were generally made of lead or pewter, nearly flat, and stamped with a device denoting the shrine whence they were brought. "The chief sign of the Canterbury pilgrimage was an ampul (*ampulla*, a flask); we are told all about its origin and meaning by Abbot Benedict, who wrote a book on the Miracles of St Thomas;" Cutts, as above, p. 170. A drawing of one is given on the next page.

Dr Rock (Church of Our Fathers, iii. 423—442) has some remarks on this passage which should be consulted; but I unhesitatingly reject his clumsy punctuation of this line, which raises more difficulties than it solves. The 'hundred' of ampuls is simply a poetic exaggeration which can mislead no one. In the story of The Pardonere and the Tapstere, it is said of the Canterbury pilgrims, that—"they set their signys upon their hedes, and som oppon their cappe."

166. (b. 5. 528; a. 6. 12.) On pilgrims' *signs*, see Chambers, Book of

Days, i. 338. "Besides the ordinary insignia of pilgrimage, every pilgrimage
had its special *sigus*, which the pilgrim on his return wore conspicuously
upon his hat or his scrip, or hanging round his neck, in token that he
had accomplished that particular pilgrimage;" Cutts, Scenes and Characters of the Middle Ages, p. 167; which see. Thus the *ampullæ* were
the special signs of the Canterbury pilgrimage; the scallop-shell was the
sign of the pilgrimage to Compostella; whilst the signs of the Roman
pilgrimage were a badge with the effigies of St Peter and St Paul, the cross-
keys or 'keyes of rome' (l. 167), and the vernicle (l. 168). The proper sign
of the pilgrimage to the Holy Land was the cross or 'crouche' (l. 167); this
"was formed of two strips of coloured cloth sewn upon the shoulder of the
robe; the English pilgrim wore the cross of white, the French of red, the
Flemish of green;" Cutts, as above, p. 167. And see Marsh, Lectures on
the Eng. Language, 2nd Ser. 1862, p. 313. Edmund Crouchback, brother
of Edward I., was so named from his having taken the cross.

Syse [c] certainly means Assisi, in Umbria, the place of birth and death
of the celebrated St Francis, founder of the Franciscan order of friars.
Plenary indulgence was granted to all pilgrims who visited the church of St
Mary of Angels at Assisi on a particular day of the year. See the life of St
Francis in Sir Jas. Stephens' Essays in Eccl. Biog. (4th ed.), p. 85. The B-
text and A-text have the reading *Sinai;* with reference to the convent of St
Katharine there. *Shilles of galys*, shells of Gallicia. See the legend of the
scallop-shell of St James of Compostella in Cutts, as above, p. 169. Cf.
Pass. i. 48; v. 124; and see A. Borde's Introduction of Knowledge, ed.
Furnivall, ch. xxxii., with the quotation from Hall's Chronicle, ed. 1809, p.
518, in the note.

168. (b. 5. 530; a. 6. 14.) The *vernicle*, as worn by pilgrims, was a copy
of the handkerchief of St Veronica, which was miraculously impressed with
the features of our Lord. "Inter has feminas una fuit Bernice, sive Veronice,
vulgo Veronica, qui sudarium Christo exhibens, ut faciem sudore et sanguine madentem abstergeret, ab eo illud recepit, cum impressa in illo
eiusdem Christi effigie, ut habet Christiana traditio;" Cornelius a Lapide,
in S. Matt. xxvii. 32. This is one of the numerous cases in which a legend
has been invented to explain a name. Bernice, Berenice, or Veronica, was
the traditional name of the woman who was cured of an issue of blood,
the name having been suggested by the actual mention of a Bernice in
the Acts of the Apostles. Ere long, it was popularly explained as being
equivalent to the words *vera icon*, i.e. true likeness, inscribed under the
celebrated portrait of Christ impressed upon a handkerchief, and preserved in St Peter's Church at Rome. Copies of this portrait were called
Veronicæ or *Veroniculæ*, whence the English name *vernicles*. See the introduction to the Anglo-Saxon Legends of St Andrew and St Veronica, ed.
C. W. Goodwin, published by The Cambridge Antiquarian Society in 1851;
The Legends of the Holy Rood, ed. Morris, pp. 170, 171 (where two old
drawings of the vernicle are reproduced); Mrs Jameson's Sacred and

Legendary Art, ii. 269—271; The Coventry Mysteries, ed. Halliwell. p. 318; The Stacyons of Rome, ed. Furnivall, ll. 37 and 59; the word *Vernacle* in the Index to the Parker Soc. publications: Dante, Paradiso, xxxi. 104, with Cary's note; Chambers, Book of Days, i. 100; Cowper, Apoc. Gospels, lxxxiv. 218, 223, 277, &c.; Chaucer, Prol. 685.

171. (b. 5. 533; a. 6. 17.) Pilgrims to *Sinai* used to visit the convent of St Catharine, with its various relics; see Maundeville's Travels, ed. Halliwell, p. 59. Also, at p. 74 of the same, we read that "whan men comen to Jerusalem, here first pilgrymage is to the chirche of the *Holy Sepulcre*, where oure Lord was buryed." See Maundeville's description of it.

172. (b. 5. 534; n. 6. 18.) The numerous sights at *Bethlehem* are described by Maundeville, ed. Halliwell, pp. 70—72. Concerning *Babylon*, see the same work, pp. 56, 57.

173. (b. 5. 535; a. 6. 19.) *Ermanie*, Armenia. *Alisaundre*, Alexandria. *Damascle* (better spelt *Damaske*), Damascus. The curious form *Assye* in the A-text (Vernon MS.) is probably only another spelling of *Assisi*; see note to l. 166 above.

By going to *Armenia*, the pilgrim could see Noah's ark, as asserted in Heywood's *Four P's;* see Hazlitt's Old Plays, p. 334, note 5. *Alexandria* was much used as a port of arrival for pilgrims; besides which, they could see there a certain head of a monster "with two hornes," kept there "for a marveyle," as related by Sir John Maundeville, ed. Halliwell, p. 47. Moreover, "in that cytee was seynte Kateryne beheded, and there was seynt Mark the evangelist martyred and buryed . . . And ȝit there is at Alizandre a faire chirche," &c.; id., p. 55. *Damascus* was considered as having been the scene of the Creation of Adam; see Chaucer's Monkes Tale.

177. (b. 5. 539; a. 6. 23.) *Corseynt* is for O. French *cors seint*, i. e. *corps saint*, holy body; and hence, a saint or sainted person. The word occurs at p. 44 of Langtoft's Chronicle, ed. Hearne; and Hearne remarks that the French text has *le cors seint* or holy body. See Halliwell's Dictionary; and to the examples there given add—

"And hys ymage ful feyre depeynte,
  Ryȝt as he were a *cors seynt*;" Rob. of Brunne, Hand. Synne, 8739.

182. (b. 5. 544; a. 6. 23.) *Peter!* i. e. by St Peter. This is a very common exclamation, of which there are several instances. See e. g. Chaucer's House of Fame, ii. 526, in Morris's edition; where Tyrwhitt's edition has *Parde*. It occurs again in The Schipmannes Tale, where Tyrwhitt gives the correct reading; C. T. 13144; also in the Prologue of the Wyf of Bath, and in the Freres Tale; C. T. 6028, 6916. Compare also Pass. ix. 1. It possibly originated with the popes, as Innocent III. used to swear by St Peter; see Southey's Book of the Church, p. 156.

As to the duties of a ploughman, here described in ll. 186—192 (b. 5. 548—556), we should compare the poem of How the Plowman lerned his Paternoster, printed in Hazlitt's Early Popular Poetry, vol. i., and in Reliq. Antiq. i. 43. We there read—

> " He coude eke sowe and holde a plowe,
>   Bothe dyke, hedge, and mylke a cowe ;
>   Thresshe, fane, and gelde a swyne
>   In every season and in tyme.
>   To mowe and repe both grasse and corne
>   A better labourer was never borne.
>   He coude go to plowe with ox and hors,
>   With whiche it were, he dyde not fors ;
>   Of shepe the wolle of for to shere
>   His better was founde no-where ;
>   Strype hempe he coude to cloute his shone,
>   And set gese abrode in season of the mone ;
>   Fell wode, and make it as it sholde be ;
>   Of fruytte he graffed many a tre.
>   He coude theche a hous, and daube a wall,
>   With all thing that to hosbandry dyde fall.
>   By these to ryches he was brought,
>   That golde ne sylver he lacked nought.
>   His hall-rofe was full of bakon-flytches ;
>   The chamber charged was with wyches [i. e. *filled with
>   hutches or boxes*],
>   Full of egges, butter, and chese,
>   Men that were hungry for to ease.
>   To make good ale, malte had he plentye,
>   And Martylmas-befe to hym was not deyntye,
>   Onyons and garleke had he inowe,
>   And good creme, and mylke of the cowe."

See also Chambers, Book of Days, i. 96.

The character of PIERS THE PLOWMAN is here introduced for the first time.   When all the penitents and searchers after Truth are at fault, when even a palmer declares he never heard of any saint of that name, the homely ploughman steps forward, declaring that he knows Truth well.   It was his own conscience and his native common sense that led him to this knowledge. We may *here* take Piers as the type of Honesty, not without remembering that the poet *afterwards* identifies him with the truest of all Teachers of men, our Lord Christ Jesus ; see Pass. xxi. 19—24.

192. (b. 5. 556 ; a. 6. 39.) Cf. also l. 189. *To paye*, lit. to pleasure, i. e. to His satisfaction.   By Truth is meant God the Father.   *Paye* is not here equivalent to *pay* in the modern sense, notwithstanding the occurrence of *hyre* (hire) in the next line.

195. (b. 5. 559 ; a. 6. 42.) " He does not withhold wages from any servant beyond the evening," i. e. till next day.   See Pass. iv. 310.

201. (b. 5. 566 ; a. 6. 48.) *For seynt Thomas shryne*, for all the wealth on St Thomas' shrine at Canterbury.   No shrine could boast more wealth than this of Beket, the object of the journey of Chaucer's Canterbury pilgrims. Mr Wright remarks—" It may not perhaps be generally known that an interesting description of this shrine, when in its glory, is given by Erasmus, Colloq. *Peregrinatio Religionis ergo*."

204. (b. 5. 568 ; a. 6. 50.) Piers here directs the pilgrims how to reach

Paradise. There are several points of resemblance between the rest of this Passus and a French poem by Rutebuef, and we may fairly infer, both from this and other passages, that William was acquainted with Rutebuef's writings. The particular poem here, to some extent, followed is 'La Voie de Paradis, ou, ci commence La Voie d'umilitei,' printed in Œuvres de Rutebuef, ed. Jubinal, ii. 24—55. See also another poem 'La Voie de Paradis,' in the same volume, p. 227. Rutebuef, in his turn, imitated a similar poem by his predecessor Raoul de Houdaing, a poet of the 13th century.

208. (b. 5. 572; a. 6. 53.) The way to Truth lies through the love of God and of our neighbour, i. e. through the ten commandments, most of which are named below, viz., the fifth in l. 214, the third in l. 217, the tenth in l. 220, the eighth and sixth in l. 224, the fourth in l. 226, and the ninth in l. 227.

217. (b. 5. 579; a. 6. 60.) *Swery-nat*, &c.; swear not unless it be necessary, and, in particular, (swear not) idly by the name of God Almighty. The whole phrase forms, in William's allegorical language, the name of a place.

226. (b. 5. 588; a. 6. 69.) Robert of Brunne, in his Handlyng Synne, l. 801, says—

> "The þryd commaundement yn owre lay
> Ys—holde weyl þyn halyday."

He explains that this means that we are to keep holy the Sunday, but he further proceeds to argue in favour of the Saturday half-holiday, ll. 845, seqq.—

> "Sum tyme hyt was wnt [*wont*] to be dowun [*done*],
> To halewe þe saterday at þe noun [*noon*],
> Namelyche [*especially*] yn Inglonde,
> And nawer so moche, y vndyrstonde.
> When þat custome was wnt to be,
> þan was grace and grete plente;
> And þere men hauntede [*observed*] þat custome lest [*least*]
> Falleþ oft tyme grete tempest."

He adds that it was ordained in honour of Our Lady, because she alone had firm faith in the Resurrection. Cf. note to Pass. vii. 170.

227. (b. 5. 589; a. 6. 70.) *Blenche*, turn aside. So, in the Tale of Beryn—

> "And when thou approchist and art the castell nygh,
> *Blench* fro the brode gate, and enter thow nat there."

Bergh, a hill; corrupted in several MSS. to *borgh*, a borough. In [a] we find the reading *brok*, a brook, with alternative readings *bourne* or *bak* (beck, stream), and *berwe*, another form of *bergh*.

228. (b. 5. 590; a. 6. 71.) *Frithed in*, enclosed by a wood, wooded thickly round. A *frith* is a wood, as in—"Both by *frith* and fell;" Sir Peny, l. 75; in Ritson's Anc. Pop. Poetry. See further examples in Stratmann. It occurs also in Political, Religious, and Love Poems, ed. Furnivall, p. 56, l. 124, in the phrase "in *frith* or foreste." See Bardsley's English Surnames, p. 91. Dr Murray translates the phrase "*frythe* or felle" in Thomas of Erceldoune, l. 319, by "enclosed field or open hill." The line means—"It (i. e. the hill of Bear-no-false-witness) is hedged round by florins

and many other fees;" i. e. by the bribes which tempt man to break the ninth commandment..

232. (b. 5. 594; a. 6. 75.) This description of Truth's abode may have been partly imitated from the French poem Le Chastel d'Amour, by Bishop Grosteste, translated under the title of the Castle of Love. Cf. Cursor Mundi, pp. 568—580; and the prose treatise known as the "Abbaye of Saynte Spirite," or the Abbey of the Holy Ghost, in Religious Pieces in Prose and Verse, ed. Perry, 1867 (E. E. T S.). William's originality is most surprising; this is one of the few places where there are traces of his borrowing from others; cf. note to l. 204 above. See "Castel off Loue," ed. Weymouth, p. 31; whence I quote the following lines :—

> "On trusti roche heo [i. e. the castle] stondeþ fasto,
> And wiþ depe diches beþ bi-caste.
> And þe carnels so stondeþ vp-riht,
> Wel i-planed and feir i-diht.
> Seue barbicans þer beoþ i-wrouht;
> With gret ginne al bi-þouht,
> And euerichon haþ ȝat and tour;
> þer neuer me fayleþ socour."

See also note to l. 270.

235. (b. 5. 597; a. 6. 78.) *Kernels*, battlements; spelt *kirnels* in Cursor Mundi, 9901, and *carnels* in the Castle of Love; see note to l. 232. In a long note upon the word, Mr Weymouth shews that the French *créneau* (Old Fr. *crenel* or *kernel*) had two senses, viz. (1) a battlement; and (2) a loop-hole. But it comes to much the same thing, as the battlements have embrasures between them. Cf. Lat. *crena*, a notch, Fr. *cran*, whence Lat. *crenellus*, O.Fr. *crenel* ; cf. Eng. *cranny*. We often find that, in olden times, the barons obtained leave to *crenellate*, or fortify, their castles. In the Ancren Riwle, p. 62, we have—"þe *kerneaus* of þe castel beoð hire huses þurles;" i. e. the loopholes of the castle are the windows of their houses.

236. (b. 5. 598; a. 6. 79.) *Boteraced*, buttressed. In MS. B (Bodley 841) of the B-text, we have *bretaskid*; in MS. Vernon (A-text) we have *brutaget*, and in MS. U (Univ. Coll. Oxford, A-text, note) we have *brtleschid*. These words signify 'provided with a *bretage* or *bretische*,' i. e. with a parapet. See *Brattice* in Wedgwood. Colonel Yule, in his edition of Marco Polo, i. 302, says—"*Bretesche, Bertisca* (whence O.E. *brattice*, and *bartizan*) was a term applied to any boarded structure of defence or attack, but especially to the timber parapets and roofs often placed on the top of the flanking-towers in mediæval fortifications; and their use quite explains the sort of structure here intended;" viz. in Marco Polo's Travels, bk. ii. cap. iv.

249. (b. 5. 611; a. 6. 92.) "To open and undo" [c]; "to lift up the wicket" [b, a]. The reading *wynne vp* [a] presents no difficulty; it means to get up or lift up by force; compare the Lowland Scotch use of the verb *win*. But the word in [b] may be read either as *wayne* or as *wayue*, and there is authority for either form. With *wayue* compare—"*wafte* he vpon

his wyndowe" (he waved open his window), Allit. Poems, ed. Morris, B.
453; and cf. Icel. *veifa*, to wave. And, on the other hand, compare the expression *to win up*, and see the numerous examples of the use of the verb
wayne in the Destruction of Troy, ed. Panton and Donaldson (E. E. T. S.).
I incline to the reading *wayne*. See the footnotes for the various readings.

250. (b. 5. 612; *cf.* a. 6. 93.) Note the various readings—"shut against
us all" [c]; "ate unroasted apples" [b]; "ate their bane" [a]. Mr
Wright quotes a singular burlesque passage in the Reliq. Antiq. i. 83—
"Peter askud Adam a full greyt dowtfull question, and seyd—'Adam, Adam,
why ete thu the appell unpard?' 'Forsothe,' quod he, 'for y had no wardens
[*pears*] fryde.'" The Latin quotation is thus Englished in MS. Harl.
7322, fol. 143 :—

> "þe ȝates of parais · þoruth eue weren iloken,
> And þoruth oure swete ladi · Aȝein hui beoþ nouþe open."
>
> Political, Rel., and Love Poems, ed. Furnivall, p. 230.

Compare also the following :—

> "Paradise yettis all opin be throu the"—

where *the* = *thee*, the person addressed being the Virgin Mary; see Morris's
edition of Chaucer, vol. vi. p. 310.

> "All þis world was for-lore · *eua peccatrice*,
> Till our lord was y-bore · *de te genitrice;*
> With *aue* it went a-way;" &c.
>
> An Old English Miscellany, ed. Morris, p. 194.

Here is the usual punning allusion to *Eoa*, or Eve, by whom the world was
lost, and whose name, when reversed, becomes *Aoe*, which was the first word
of Gabriel's greeting to Mary, and therefore the beginning of the world's
salvation; see Coventry Myst. ed. Halliwell, p. 112.

> "Heuene gate was keiyed clos
> Til lambe of love now he deyede," &c.
>
> Legends of the Holy Rood, ed. Morris, p. 205.

Here *keiyed* (keyed, fastened) is printed *keiþed* in Dr Morris's edition, but
the correction is easy, as in another version, at p. 140, the corresponding
line is—"Heuene ȝates weore *closed* clos." Our poet uses the very word—
y-keyed—in l. 266 below. In the Coventry Mysteries, p. 31, it is said of
paradise that—"The ȝatys be schet with Godys keye." In the Anglo-Saxon
version of Ælfric's Homily on the Assumption of the Virgin, ed. Thorpe, i.
446, we have a passage which the editor translates by—"Through our old
mother Eve the gate of heaven's kingdom was closed against us, and again,
through Mary it is opened to us, by which she herself has this day gloriously
entered." This homily is imitated from Jerome's epistle to Paula and Eusto-
chium, but the only passages which I can find there which contain the idea
are the following :—"Ac per hoc, quicquid maledictionis infusa est per Euam,
totum abstulit benedictio Mariæ;" and again—"Quapropter gaudete, gaudete,
inquam, quia uobis uia patefacta est cœlorum ;" Opera S. Hieronymi, ed.
Migne, vol. 11, col. 127 and col. 141. But I suspect that these are the
original passages whence were derived, not only the sentence quoted by our

author, but most of the other allusions. Hence also came probably the expressions in some of the Latin hymns. The hymn *Aue maris stella* begins thus :—

> " Aue, maris stella, Dei mater alma,
> Atque semper uirgo, Felix cæli porta.
> Sumens illud Aue Gabrielis ore,
> Funda uos in pace Mutans Euæ nomen."

The hymn *O gloriosa Virginum* contains the passage :—

> " Quod Eua tristis abstulit Tu reddis almo germine,
> Intrent ut astra flebiles Cæli recludis cardines.
> Tu Regis alti ianua Et aula lucis fulgida," &c.

The latter passage is paraphrased in A Myrour of Our Lady, ed. Blunt, p. 258. Both hymns may be found in the Breviary, and were sung on the day of the Assumption of the Virgin.

251. (*not in* b, a.) *Vnleek hure*, unlocked it; (*hure* = her, i. e. the gate); see the footnote. *Of grace*, out of her grace, as a favour.

265. (b. 5. 622; a. 6. 102.) *Worst þow*, thou shalt be; also written *worstow* [b], and *worþestou* [a]. *Dryuen out as deuh*, driven forth and dispersed like dew. "Therefore they [the wicked] shall be as the morning cloud, and as the early dew that passeth away, as the chaff that is driven with the whirlwind out of the floor, and as the smoke out of the chimney;" Hosea xiii. 3.

268. (b. 5. 625; a. 6. 105.) *To lete wel by thiselue*, to think much of thyself; cf. l. 263.

270. (b. 5. 627; a. 6. 107.) *Seuene sustres*, seven sisters. To counteract the seven deadly sins, seven Christian virtues were enumerated by early theologians. Thus, in the Ayenbite of Inwyt (ed. Morris, p. 159) we find this list. " Boȝsamnesse, a-ye [*against*] Prede. Loue, a-ye Enuye. Mildenesse, a-ye Felhede. Prouesse, a-ye Slacnesse. Largesse, a-ye Scarsnesse. Chastete, a-ye Lecherie. Sobrete, a-ye Glotounye." See note to Pass. vii. 3, where all the ' seven sisters ' are mentioned except ' Peace,' who takes the place of Business. These seven virtues are mentioned also in the Castle of Love, ed. Weymouth, p. 39; cf. note to l. 232. The passage runs thus :—

> " þe seue barbicans abouten
> þat with gret gin beon i-wrouȝt with-outen,
> And witeþ [*guard*] þis castel so wel
> Wiþ [*against*] arwe and wiþ quarel [*cross-bow bolt*],
> þat beþ þe seuen vertues with winne,
> To ouercome þe seuen dedly sinne."

They are then enumerated; and are—Boxumnesse, Trewe loue, Abstinence, Chastite, Largesse, Mekenesse, and Gostliche gladynge. This list agrees with the one in the text, if we remember that Boxumnesse (obedience) answers to Patience, Trewe loue to Charity, Mekenesse to Humility, and Gostliche gladynge (spiritual joy) to Peace. Cf. Cursor Mundi, p. 577. Sometimes the number of the seven guardians was made up in another way, viz. by adding the three chief spiritual virtues, Faith, Hope, and Charity, to the four cardinal ones, viz. Prudence, Temperance, Justice, and Fortitude.

It is probable that the idea of this passage is a very old one. There is something very like it in Hermas, Pastor, bk. iii. similitude ix. v. 140 (ed. Hone), in Hone's Apocryphal Gospels. "Hear the names of those virgins which . . . stand at the corners of the gate . . . The first is called Faith; the second, Continence; the third, Power; the fourth, Patience; the rest which stand beneath these are Simplicity, Innocence, Chastity, Cheerfulness, Truth, Understanding, Concord, Charity." Or see the translation of The Shepherd of Hermas by C. H. Hoole, p. 145.

277. (*not in* b, a; *but* cf. b. 5. 633.) "For she pays for (i. e. ransoms) prisoners in places and in pains." See *Prison* in the Glossary.

282. (b. 5. 638; a. 6. 117.) *Bote grace be the more,* unless mercy be extended.

283. (b. 5. 639; a. 6. 118.) *Kitte-pors,* thief. On cut-purses, see Chambers, Book of Days, ii. 669.

285. (b. 5. 641; a. 6. 120.) *Wyte God,* God defend (us); an old oath, from the verb *witen* in the sense of defend, guard. It occurs in the French Romance of King Horn, MS. Harl. 527, fol. 72 b, col. 2—"Ben iurez *Wite God* kant auerez ben tant," i. e. you freely swear 'God defend us,' when you shall have drunk so much. Observe that this is quite different from the more common expression "God wot," i. e. God knows. See *Wite* in Gloss. to Havelok, in Gloss. to Specimens of English, 1298—1393, and in Stratmann.

Wafrestre, a female seller of wafers; see note to Pass. xvi. 199.

288. (b. 5. 644; a. 6. 123.) *Mercy* is identified here with the Virgin Mary; see the quotation at l. 250. Cf. Cursor Mundi, l. 10062.

——(b. 5. 651; *not in* c, a.) "Thou shalt say I am thy sister; I know not where they have gone to;" or, "what has become of them." *Bicome* is the past tense pl., and the phrase *where þei bicome,* is like the modern— "where they can have got to;" or, "what has become (*or* come) of them." The best illustration of this is from the romance of Joseph of Arimathie, ed. Skeat, l. 607, where the white knight is described as vanishing from sight, in consequence of which the spectators wonder "wher þe white kniht *bi-com,*" i. e. where he had gone to, or what had become of him. Other good instances of the use of the word are in Rich. Redeles, i. 49; and in the Life of St Cristopher, l. 111, printed in Mätzner's Altenglische Sprachproben, i. 197; see Mätzner's note.

292. (*not in* b, a.) *Villam emi,* I have bought a farm; St Luke xiv. 18. So below, we have mention of one who had bought five yoke of oxen (Luke xiv. 19), and of another who had just married a wife (Luke xiv. 20).

299. (*not in* b, a.) "Then was there one named Active, he seemed to be a husband." Here *husband* may mean husbandman, as is not unusual; or, more likely, it is to be taken literally in this passage. It is necessary to remark that the character of Active is described hereafter at some length; see Pass. xvi. 194—233.

301. (*not in* b, a.) *Synnen,* sin, is clearly the right reading; it means to sin against the seventh commandment.

304. (*not in* b, a.) *For a kytte*, because of a Kit, i. e. because of a wife. *Kit* was no doubt a common name enough; but the point of the allusion is to be found in the fact that it was the name of the poet's *own* wife; see Pass. vi. 2; xxi. 473.

305. (*not in* b, a.) "Though I may suffer tribulation."

307. (b. 6. 1; a. 7. 1.) "But the way is so bad, unless one were to have a guide." Cf. *wikkede weyes* in Pass. x. 31.

The two last lines of this Passus (in the C-text) are at the beginning of a new Passus in the two older texts.

308. (b. 6. 2; a. 7. 2.) *Ech fot*, i. e. every step of the way.

SCHEME OF C. PASSUS IX. (B. Pass. VI.; A. Pass. VII.)

(See Wright's edition, pp. 117—137; ll. 3798—4464.)

N. B. Lines B. vi. 1, 2, and A. vi. 1, 2 belong to the end of C. Pass. viii. The minor variations between the three Texts are very numerous throughout this Passus.

C-TEXT.	B-TEXT.	A-TEXT.
ix. 1—6	vi. 3—8	vii. 3—8
7	—	—
8	9	9
—	—	10—13
(a) 9—11	(a) 10—12	(a) [18—20]
12, 13	13, 14	
14		
—	15, 16	—
15	17	14, 15
—	18	16
16	19	17
(a) [9—11]	(a) [10—12]	(a) 18—20
17	20	21
18—20	21—23	22—24
21, 22	*like* 24	*like* 25, 26
23—34	25—36	27—38
—	37	—
35, 36	38, 39	39, 40
37, 38	40, 41	—
39—41	42—44	41—43
—	45	44
42	46	45
43, 44	47, 48	—
—	49	—
45, 46	50, 51	—
47		—
48—52	52—56	46—50

C-TEXT.	B-TEXT.	A-TEXT.
ix. 53		
54—62	vi. 57—65	vii. 51—59
63	66	
(b) 64, 65	(b) [105, 106]	(b) [96, 97]
66—71	67—72	60—65
72, 73	73, 74	
74		
75—83	75—83	66—74
84, 85		
86	84	75
87—91		
92—111	85—104	76—95
(b) [64, 65]	(b) 105, 106	(b) 96, 97
112—130	107—125	98—116
(c) [135]	(c) 126	(c) 117
131—134	127—130	118—121
(c) 135	(c) [126]	(c) [117]
	131	122
136—138		
139	like 132	123
	133, 134	124, 125
140	like 135	like 126
141	136	127
		128, 129
142, 143	137, 138	130, 131
	139, 140	like 132, 133
	141—146	
144, 145		
146	147	134
147, 148		
	148—153	like 135—139
149—158	154—163	140—149
159, 160	like 164, 165	
161—176	like 166—181	`like 150—166
		167—171
	182	172
177, 178	like 183—185	
179—183	186—190	173—177
184		
185, 186	191, 192	
187, 188	like 193, 194	like 178, 179
		180—186
	195	
189—191		
192	196	
	197—199	
193—196		
197 (see 203	200	187
198—202		
203—207	like 200—203	187—190
208	204	
209—213	205—209	191—195

C-TEXT.	B-TEXT.	A-TEXT.
ix. 214—216	——	——
217—221	vi. 210—214	vii. 196—200
222		
223—233	like 215—226	201—212
——		213—215
	227—230	
234, 235	——	——
236—246	like 231—239	like 216—224
247—259	like 240—248	like 225—233
	249—254	234—239
260—266		
267—272	255—260	240—245
——	261	246
(d) [278]	(d) 262	(d) 247
273—277	263—267	248—252
(d) 278	(d) [262]	(d) [247]
	268, 269	253, 254
279—290	——	——
291—310	like 270—288	like 255—273
(e) 311	(e) [296]	(e) [281]
312—318	289—295	274—280
(e) [311]	(e) 296	(e) 281
319—337	297—315	282—301
338, 339	316, and Latin	——
	317	
340—347	318—325	302—309
348, 349	327, 326	311, 310
——	328, 329	
350—352	——	——
353—355	330—332	——

NOTES TO C. PASSUS IX. (B. Pass. VI.; A. Pass. VII.).

N.B. The two first lines of B. Pass. vi. and A. Pass. vii. belong to C. Pass. viii. See notes to C. viii. 307, 308; p. 154.

C. ix. 1. [B. vi. 3; A. vii. 3.] *Perken*, i. e. Peterkin, the diminutive of Peter; hence the names Perkins, Parkinson, &c.; cf. l. 112 below. Concerning the oath by St Peter, see note to Pass. viii. 182.

2. (b. 6. 4; a. 7. 4.) *An half-acre*, i. e. a small piece of ground. This term was used generally, without *special* reference to the exact size of the 'field. It occurs, for example, in Gammer Gurton's Needle, Act i., sc. 2, where "Tom Tankard's cow" is described as "flinging about his *halfe aker*, fisking with her tail." Mr Hazlitt, in reprinting this play amongst the rest in Dodley's Collection, was much puzzled by this expression, as he unluckily printed it in the form *halse aker*. As a consequence, he proposed to read *halse anker*, because "a *halse* (?) or *halser* was a particular kind of cable." But though a *cow's* tail may resemble a rope, the word *his* must refer to *Tom*. *Eren*, to plough; as in Deut. xxi. 4; 1 Sam. viii. 12; Is. xxx. 24. See Eastword and Wright's Bible Word-book; and cf. Pass. xxii. 268.

It is often wrongly said to be 'derived' from the Lat. *arare*, it being merely *cognate* with it.   Fick cites the Lithuanian form *ariù*, Church-Slavonic *orja*, Mœso-Goth. *arjan* (cf. A.S. *erian*), Old High German *erjan* or *erran*, as forms cognate with the Lat. *arare* and the Gk. ἀρόειν.   Chaucer has a similar expression—"I have, God wot, a large feld to *ere* ;" Knightes Tale, l. 28.

8. (b. 6. 9; a. 7. 9.) *For shedynge,* i. e. to prevent the shedding or spilling of wheat; alluding to the loss of grain when sacks are badly sewn or are out of repair.   Cf. *for colde*, B. 6. 62, commented on in the note to l. 59 below.

11. (b. 6. 12; a. 7. 20.)   Compare Ancren Riwle, p. 421—"Make no purses, to gain friends therewith, nor blodbendes of silk; but shape, and sew, and mend church vestments, and poor people's clothes."   Embroidering of stoles is mentioned in the life of St Dunstan, and the working of a stole and amice in silk and gold is mentioned in the Roman de la Violette; see Wright, Homes of Other Days, pp. 67, 250.   For a full description of a chasuble, often ornamented with "a mass of rich golden needlework," see Rock, Church of our Fathers, i. 314—371.   And see Cutts, Scenes and Characters of the Middle Ages, p. 238.

15. (b. 6. 17; a. 7. 16.)   "For I shall give them (the poor) their sustenance, unless the land fail to yield produce;" i. e. as long as I can afford it : with a reference to the frequent dearths that happened about this time.

16. (b. 6. 19; a. 7. 17.) *For oure lordes loue in* (*of*) *heuene* ; for love of our Lord in heaven.   Observe the difference of arrangement, especially when *of* is used, as in [b, a].   So, in Chaucer, *the Grekis hors Sinon*, is *the horse of Sinon the Greek* ; see other instances in the note to Pass. xvi. 131.   Cf. b. 6. 223 below.

26. (b. 6. 28; a. 7. 30.) Lord Cobham, speaking of the duties of knights, said—"In knighthood are all they which beare sword by law of office.   These should defend God's lawes, and see that the gospell were purely taught, conforming their lives to the same, and secluding all false preachers . . . . They ought also to preserve Gods people from oppressors, tyrants, and thieves; and to see the Clergy supported, so long as they teach purely, pray rightly, and minister the sacraments freely ;" Wordsworth's Eccl. Biog. i. 362.   The context of Cobham's speech shews that he was following the old threefold division of the church into the Oratores (priests), Bellatores (warriors), and Laboratores (commons); and he had no doubt learnt this from Wyclif, who has very similar expressions.   See Wyclif's Works, ed. Arnold, iii. 130, 131, 145, 206.   See also Polit. Songs, ed. Wright, p. 334, and the notes at pp. 365, 366; An Old Eng. Miscellany, ed. Morris, pp. 106, 108; Gower's Conf. Amantis (ed. Pauli), iii. 380; The World and the Child, in Hazlitt's Old Plays, i. 258.   Cf. note to l. 36.

29. (b. 6. 31; a. 7. 33.) *Bockes*, bucks [c, a]; *brockes*, badgers [b].   See *Brock* in Halliwell's Dict., and *Brok* in Prompt. Parv.   A badger had three names, viz. a *bawsin*, a *brock*, and a *gray* ; Juliana Berners, Book of St Alban's, sig. D. vi. ; Dyce's Skelton, ii. 303.

30. (b. 6. 32; a. 7. 34.) "And tame thy falcons" [c]; "And go and tame for thyself falcons" [b]; "And fetch home for thyself falcons" [a].

32. (b. 6. 34; a. 7. 36.) This line much resembles Rich. Redeles, iv. 35.

36. (b. 6. 39; a. 7. 40.) Probably borrowed from Wyclif; compare the following passage from his works, ed. Arnold, iii. 206. "If þou be a lord ... governe wel þi tenantis, and maynteyne hem in riȝt and reson, and be merciful to hem in þer rentys and worldly mercimentis, and suffere not þi officeris to do hem wrong ne extorcions, and chastice in good manere hem þat ben rebel aȝens Goddis hestis and vertuous lyvyng, more þan for rebelte agens þin owne cause or persone;" &c.   See also the tale of the Knight who robbed a Poor Man, as told by Robert of Brunne, Handlyng Synne, ll. 2223, seqq.; and Chaucer's discourse on "hard lordships," "amercementes," and "thraldome" in the Persones Tale, *De Avaritia.*

37. (b. 6. 40; *not in* a.) "When you fine any man, let Mercy be the assessor of the fine;" i. e. let the fine be a light one.   The next line means — "and let Meekness be your master (i. e. rule over you), in spite of all that Meed can do."   The expression "maugre mede chekes," lit. in spite of Meed's cheeks, is to the same effect as the modern expression "in spite of his teeth."   Cf. Chaucer's use of "maugre his heed;" Kn. Tale, 311, 1760.

40. (b. 6. 43; a. 7. 42.) "Take it (i. e. the present) not, in case you may not be deserving of it; for you will have to repay it, it may be, and to pay somewhat dearly for it."   The end of the latter line slightly varies in [b] and [a].   The line following, having reference to purgatory, does not appear in the C-text.

42. (b. 6. 46; a. 7. 45.) See a tale about a Knight and a Bondman in Robert of Brunne, Handl. Synne, 8671, seqq.

45. (b. 6. 50; *not in* a.) *Vuel to knowe,* hard to discern; just as *vuel to defye* means hard to digest; Pass. vii. 87.   The idea is, that all are equal in the grave.   A very similar expression is used with reference to heaven in An Old Eng. Miscellany, ed. Morris, p. 143—"þer wûrth euenyng carle and cnyht," there shall churl and knight be equal.   The state of things in the present life is very different; "uor euere me schal þene cheorl pilken and peolien;" Ancren Riwle, p. 86.

46. (b. 6. 51; *not in* a.) The last part of the line varies in [b].   In [c] it means—"or a *quean* from a *queen.*"   We make a difference of spelling in these words, but they are, of course, mere doublets, and both mean the same thing, viz. a woman.   The MSS. have, in the first case, *queyne,* P; *queene,* EG; *quene,* IMS: and in the second, *queene,* PIMS; *quene,* EG.   It is obviously impossible to tell which is which; nor is it material.

47. (*not in* b, a.) A knight was, above all things, expected to be courteous and true; cf. Chaucer, Prol. 46.   Hence the excellence and fame of Sir Gawain; cf. Chaucer, Sq. Tale, 95.

50. (b. 6. 54; a. 7. 48.) *Hold nat of* is the same as *holde with none* [b], or *hold not þou with* [a]; i. e. do not encourage.

Harlotes, ribalds; a term here applied to tellers of loose stories, whence our author calls them 'the devil s *disours*,' i. e. the devil's story-tellers. They held forth in the hall 'atte mete,' whilst their employers were eating. They were *men*, as said in l. 51; see also note to Pass. v. 113. See Warton's Hist. of Eng. Poet. i. 68 (ed. 1840). Cf. Pass. xvi. 171; see *Diseur* in Cotgrave; and *disour* in Gower, Conf. Amantis, ed. Pauli, iii. 167.

54. (b. 6. 57; a. 7. 51.) *Seynt Gyle*, saint Giles or Ægidius. His day was Sept. 1; see an account of him in Chambers' Book of Days, ii. 296; and see note to B. 15. 267. In [b] and [a] the knight swears by saint James; see note to Pass. i. 48.

59. (b. 6. 62; a. 7. 56.) Halliwell explains *Cockers* as "a kind of rustic high shoes, or half-boots, fastened with laces or buttons. Old stockings without feet are also so called." Probably it means old stockings without feet, worn as gaiters. Jamieson tells us that coarse stockings without feet are called *hoggers* in Rosshire. Compare the following lines from the ballad of Dowsabell in Percy's Reliques, written by Drayton; where *cockers* seems to mean buskins or gaiters.

> "The shepheard ware a sheepe-gray cloake,
> Which was of the finest loke [*fleece*]
>   That could be cut with sheere:
> His mittens were of bauzens [*badger's*] skinne,
> His *cockers* were of cordiwin [*Cordovan leather*],
>   His hood of miniveere."

For colde [b, a] means—as a protection against cold. A good parallel instance of this use of *for* occurs in Chaucer's Sir Thopas, "for percinge of his herte;" C. T. Group B., l. 2052. See also B. 1. 24. above.

60. (b. 6. 63; a. 7. 57.) *Hoper*, a seed-basket. "Vas cum quo seminatores seminant, a sedelepe or a hopere;" MS. Gloss., pr. in Rel. Antiq. i. 7. Observe the gloss in the Oriel MS.—"i. a seed leep;" B-text, footnote. "*Leap, Lib*, half a bushel; *Sussex*. In *Essex*, a *seed-leap* or *lib*, is a vessel or basket to carry corn in, on the arm, to sow. Ab A.S. *sæd-leap*, a seed-basket;" Ray's South-country Words. It was also called a *cob* or *seed-cob*; id., s. v. *Cob*. The 'hoper' here mentioned held a bushel; see the next line.

61. (b. 6. 64; a. 7. 58.) In his Glossary of certain Lincolnshire words (Eng. Dial. Soc.) Mr Peacock has—"*Breadcorn*, corn to be ground into *breadmeal* (i. e. flour with only a portion of the bran taken out, from which brown bread is made); not to be used for finer purposes. It is a common custom of farmers, when they engage a bailiff, to give him a certain sum of money per annum, and to allow him also his *bread-corn*, at 40s. per quarter." In this case, Piers uses some of this for sowing. See the next note.

62. (b. 6. 65; a. 7. 59.) "I have never found any separate payment made for the labour of sowing, and am disposed to believe that this duty was performed by the bailiff himself. Fifty years ago it was generally done by the small farmer in person;" Hist. of Agric. in England, by J. E. T. Rogers, i. 16; see also p. 539 of the same volume.

68. (b. 6. 69; a. 7. 62.) *Maugre ho by-grucche*, in spite of him that grumble. See the variations in [b] and [a].

71. (b. 6. 72; a. 7. 65.) *Iogelour*, juggler; Lat. *ioculator*. See Tyrwhitt's note to Chaucer, C. T. l. 11453 :—" The name of *Jogelour* was, in a manner, appropriated to those, who, by sleight of hand and machines, produced such illusions of the senses as are usually supposed to be effected by enchantment. This species of *jogelour* is [also] called a *Tregetour*." Cf. Chaucer's House of Fame, iii. 169—

> " There saugh I pleyen *jugelours*,
>   Magiciens, and *tregetours*," &c.

Tyrwhitt's note is long and full. See also Ritson, Metrical Romances, i. pp. clix, ccv of Preface, where he insists that *jougleour* ought never to be misspelt *jongleur*, as is often done; but this is a question of chronology, the form *jongleur* being the later one; see *Iougleur* and *Iongleur* in Cotgrave. And compare—

> " There myghtist thou see these flowtours,
>   Mynstrales, and eke *jogelours*,
>   That wel to synge dide her peyne."
>   .Romaunt of the Rose, 763.

See also Warton, Hist. Eng. Poet. ed. 1840, i. 82; ii. 10, 168; and the remarks against *ioculatores* in Bernardus, de Cura Rei Famuliaris, ed. Lumby, pp. 9, 10. There is an old play called Jack Juggler; see Dodsley's Old Plays, ed. Hazlitt, vol. ii. The expression " And ye Ianettes of the stewys" occurs in the Towneley Mysteries, p. 314.

77. (b. 6. 77; a. 7. 68.) " Deleantur de libro uiuentium, et cum iustis non scribantur," Ps. lxviii. 29 (Vulgate). William interprets the last part of the quotation to mean, that churchmen ought not to receive tithes from such people. ·Cf. Pass. vii. 306. On the subject of *tithes*, see Wordsworth, Eccl. Biog. i. 319.

79. (b. 6. 79; a. 7. 70.) *Thei ben ascaped*, &c. Dr Whitaker paraphrases this by—" they have escaped payment by good luck "—which is probably right. For *aunter*, the Vernon MS. reads *thrift*, success.

84. (*not in* b, a.) Here Piers again begins speaking. In [b], he begins at l. 84; in [a], at l. 75.

86. (b. 6. 84; a. 7. 75.) *Let god worthe*, may God be with all, &c.

90. (*not in* b, a.) Dr Whitaker rightly suggests that all the MSS. are wrong here. It is obvious that *worchyng* is an error for *wording*, or for some equivalent expression. This has been already noted in the Crit. Notes to C-text, p. 456.

95. (b. 6. 88; a. 7. 79.) Lines 95—111 contain Piers' *biqueste*, i. e. his will. It begins with a common formula—*In dei nomine*. He bequeaths his soul to his Maker, his body to the church to which he paid tithes, his money to his wife and children. Whitaker remarks upon this passage—" To commit the soul to Him who made it, was, in the course of a century and a half after this time, accounted so heretical, that the church would not have kept the testator's bones. For this **very** offence, and for omitting the names of

the Virgin Mary and other saints, as joint legatees, the body of a Mr Tracy
was dug up out of his grave." See Tracie's will in Massingberd, Eng. Ref.
p. 165; also in Chambers, Book of Days, ii. 429.

101. (b. 6. 94; a. 7. 85.) The word *he* clearly refers, as in l. 103, to the
persona ecclesiæ, the parson. The Vernon MS. has *heo*, the feminine form,
with reference to the word *chirche* preceding it.

103. (b. 6. 96; a. 7. 87.) Instead of *holden* [b, a], we find in [c] the form
holdinge. This represents a common corruption, which appears also in *beholding*, as used for *beholden* by Shakespeare and others. See Rich. III. ii.
1. 129; Jul. Cæsar, iii. 2. 70; and Abbott, Shak. Grammar, 3rd ed.,
sect. 372.

104. (b. 6. 97; a. 7. 88.) "And mention me in his commemoration."
See note to Pass. viii. 27; also Grindal's Works, 136 (note), and Pilkington's Works, 535 (Parker Society).

109. (b. 6. 102; a. 7. 93.) For *Lukes*, MSS. of the A-type have *Chestre*;
cf. B. 5. 467. *Lukes* is Lucca (as in Pass. v. 194), formerly also spelt *Luca*,
where there was a famous cross; see Mr Wright's note. He adds—"the
peculiar oath of William Rufus was by the holy face at Lucca." This had
reference to a vernicle which was there preserved; cf. note to Pass. viii. 168.
Luke (for Lucca) occurs in Jewel's works, ii. 917 (Parker Soc.).

——(b. 6. 105; a. 7. 96.) "My plough-foot shall be my pike-staff, and
pick (peck, or pierce) in two the roots" [b]; "My plough-put shall be my
pike, and push at the roots" [a]. To understand this, it must be remembered that the pike-staff (or pike) means the pilgrim's spiked staff, as explained in note to Pass. vii. 329. Piers says that, instead of carrying a
pike-staff like a pilgrim, he will make good use of his plough-foot, so as to
push aside or pierce through the roots that are in the soil. In [a], the reading is *plouh-pote* (i. e. plough-put), where *pote* is used in the sense of something to poke or push with; see "*Pote*, (1) to push, or kick; (2) a broad
piece of wood used by thatchers to open the old thatch and *thrust in* the new
straw," in Halliwell; cf. *puten*, to push, in Stratmann. The parts of a plough,
according to Gervase Markham's Complete Husbandman (quoted in Prof.
Roger's Hist. Agric. in England, i. 534), are (1) the plough-beam; (2) the
skeath; (3) the plough's principal hale, on the left; (4) the plough-head;
(5) the plough-spindles; (6) the right-hand hale; (7) the plough-rest; (8)
the shelboard; (9) the coulter; (10) the share; (11) the plough-foot. The
plough-foot is explained to be "an iron implement, passed through a mortise-
hole, and fastened at the farther end of the beam by a wedge or two, so that
the husbandman may, at his discretion, set it higher or lower; the use being
to give the plough earth, or put it from the earth, for the more it is driven
downward the more it raises the beam from the ground, and makes the beam
forsake the earth; and the more it is driven upward, the more it lets down
the beam, and makes the irons bite the ground." It was also called a *plough-
shoe*, or *ferripedalis*; id. p. 537. A similar definition of a ploughfoot, as
being "a staye to order of what depenes the ploughe shall go," is given in

Fitzherbert's Boke of Husbandry, fol. 2, back.   In a modern plough, small wheels are generally used instead of it.

I may remark that the reading *plough-pote* occurs in at least two MSS. of the B-type, viz. MS. R (Rawlinson) and the MS. in Corpus Christi College, Oxford.   It may also be observed that, in the A-text, MS. H (Harleian 875) reads *plowbat*.   I suppose the *plowbat* is not the same as the *ploughfoot*, but is rather to be identified with the *ploughstaff* or *ploughpaddle*, which was no fixed part of the plough at all, but a sort of paddle sometimes used for cleaning a plough, or clearing it of weeds, or for breaking very large clods.   This is alluded to by Strutt (Manners and Customs, ii. 12), where he says—"The ploughman yoketh oxen to the plough, and he holdeth the plough-stilt [i. e. principal hale or handle] in his left hand, and in his right the *plough-stuff* to break the clods."   See plate 32 (vol. i.) in Strutt, and the picture of a plough at work prefixed to Mr Wright's edition of Piers the Plowman, copied from MS. T, described in my preface to the A-text, p. xviii, q. v.

112. (b. 6. 107; a. 7. 98.) *Perkyn*, little Piers or Peter; the same as Peterkin.   It is merely a familiar term for Piers in this passage, as in l. 1.

119. (b. 6. 114; a. 7. 105.) *Hye pryme*.   This expression occurs in a poem by Lydgate, which is better known, perhaps, than any other of his, named "The London Lickpeny:"

"Then to Westmynster gate I presently went,
When the sonn was at *hyghe pryme*."—MS. Harl. 367:

It seems to mean, when *prime was ended*, and it certainly marks the first break in the day's work.   Cotgrave explains *prime* as the first hour of the 'artificial day' (or day according to the sun) which begins at about 8 in winter, 4 in summer, and at 6 only at the equinoxes; but Mr Brae, in his edition of Chaucer's Astrolabe, pp. 90—101, makes it clear that, in Chaucer's time, the word was not used with reference to the artificial day, but with reference to the 'natural day,' or day as marked by a clock.   Again, some explain *prime* to be the *fourth part* of the natural day, viz. from 6 o'clock till 9 A.M.; see Tyrwhitt's note, Cant. Tales, l. 3904.   Others again explain *prime* to mean 6 A.M.   It is easy to reconcile these variations by supposing that reference was made sometimes to the *beginning*, sometimes to the *end* of the period from 6 to 9, or again, sometimes to the *whole* of that period. By putting together the various passages where Chaucer uses the word *prime*, I have shewn, in my edition of Chaucer's Astrolabe, p. lxii., that the term was commonly used in the sense suggested by Tyrwhitt, viz. as denoting the period from 6 to 9 A.M.; but, when restricted to a particular moment, it meant the *end* of that period, or 9 A.M. only.   Mr Brae identifies this with the Italian *terza*, since we find in Florio's Dictionary—"Terza, the third in order; also the hour that Priests call *Prime*"—and he goes on to say—"the true time of terza seems to be as much a matter of uncertainty with the Italians as prime is with us.   In their great national dictionary, Della Crusca, it is presented with the same unsatisfactory explanation—

'una dell' ore canoniche'—word for word the explanation of prime by our own dictionaries. But in the old French translation of the Decameron by Antoine Le Maçon, which went through so many editions in the sixteenth century, terza is invariably rendered by *neuf heures;*" Brae's ed. of Chaucer's Astrolabe, p. 94. I think we may explain the connection with *terza* by supposing 9 A.M. to be the time when prime ended, and tierce began. It was probably to avoid the usual vagueness in the use of the word that the phrase *high prime* is here employed; since the latter clearly means that the period of prime was ended, or that it was 9 o'clock exactly. In like manner I should explain Chaucer's *fully pryme*, in Sir Thopas; Cant. Tales, Group B. 2015; whilst in the Squyeres Tale, l. 360, the expression *pryme large* may very well mean a little past the hour of prime, a little past nine; in which case we must suppose that Chaucer is mentioning the very latest hour for rising, even after a night of unusual revelry. Mr Dyce says—"concerning this word see Du Cange's Gloss. in Prima and Horæ Canonicæ, Tyrwhitt's Gloss. to Canterbury Tales, Sibbald's Gloss. to Chron. of Scot. Poetry, and Sir F. Madden's Gloss. to Syr Gawayne." See also Timbs, Nooks and Corners of English Life, p. 222.

It is clear from ll. 120 and 121, that Piers was a "head harvest-man." See Knight's Pictorial Hist. of England, i. 840; the notice of the "head-reaper" on p. 179 below; and a good article on the duties of a ploughman in Chambers' Book of Days, i. 96.

122. (b. 6. 117; a. 7. 108.) *Atte nale* [b] = *atten ale* [c], or *at then ale*, i.e. at the ale. In the same way *at then ende* or *atten ende* (at the end) was afterwards corrupted into *at the nende*. See note to Pass. i. 43; also Warton, Hist. E. P., vol. ii. p. 79, note.

123. (b. 6. 118; a. 7. 109.) *Hoy troly lolly* is the burden of a song, answering nearly to the modern *tol de rol*. In Ritson's Ancient Songs, vol. ii. p. 7, is a song, with a burden of *trolly loley* occurring at every third line; whilst in Hickscorner (Dodsley's Old Plays, ed. Hazlitt, i. 179) we find the same exclamation of *hey, troly, loly*. "*Lullay* is a common burden to old songs, partaking of what may be called a nursery character; as in—'Lollai, lollai, litill child, why wepistou so sore;' MS. Harl. 913, fol. 30;"—T. Sharp, Dissertation on Pageants, p. 123. So in the Chester Plays (ed. Wright, p. 136), when the shepherds sing, we find the direction—
          "Singe troly loly, troly loe."
And Skelton (ed. Dyce, i. 15) says—
          "Wyth *hey troly loly, lo*, whip here, Jak."
Here is meant, that all which some of the men did towards ploughing the half-acre was to sit and sing choruses over their cups.

127. (b. 6. 122; a. 7. 113.) *Haue that recche*, take him who cares. *Recche* = may reck, as explained in the Critical Note (C-text), p. 456.

128. (b. 6. 123; a. 7. 114.) "Then were *faitours* afraid"; see the remarks on *faitours* in the note to l. 179 below, where the former half of this line is repeated.

See also Pass. x. 61—218, and notes to Pass. ix. 188, x. 169.

138. (*not in* b, a.) *Gon abegged*, go a-begging. This construction was first, I believe, explained by myself, in my preface to the C-text, p. lxxxvii, which see. I have there said that *gon abegged* is a corruption of the older reading *gon abeggeth* in the Ilchester MS. The *-ed* is a corruption of *-eth*, answering to the A.S. suffix *-að* or *-oð*, used in what are called verbal substantives, i. e. substantives derived from verbs. Thus, in Robert of Gloucester (in Specimens of English, Part ii, ed. Morris and Skeat, p. 14) we find—

  "As he rod *an hontep* · & par-auntre is hors spurnde"—
i. e. as he rode *a-hunting*, and his horse accidentally stumbled.

I omitted to mention that there is another example of this construction only a few lines further on, viz. in l. 216 (C-text), where we have 'gon abrybep' in two MSS., but 'gon abribed (*or* abribid)' in two others; and where the Ilchester MS. even has—'And gon abribeth and abeggeth.'

When once the ending *-ed* was thus sometimes used in place of the uncommon ending *-eth*, it was easily perpetuated, on account of its coincidence in form with that of the past participle. It was used, in particular, with the verb *to go*. I give four clear examples of it in Chaucer and Gower.

In the Wyf of Bathes Prologue (Cant. Tales, ed. Tyrwhitt, l. 5936) we have the expression *gon a caterwawed*, which clearly means 'to go a-caterwauling.'

In the Pardoneres Tale, Group C, l. 406 (ed. Tyrwhitt, l. 12340), we have the expression *gon a blakeberied*, which simply means go a-blackberrying, i. e. go where they list. Tyrwhitt gave up this expression as inexplicable, but it is really very simple when the right key is thus applied to it.

So in Gower's Confessio Amantis, bk. i, we find a tale about a king of Hungary :—

  "And so befel, vpon a daye,
  (And that was in the month of Maye)
  As thilke tyme it was vsance,
  This king with noble purueiance
  Hath for him-selfe his char arayed
  Wherin he wolde *ryde amayed*
  Out of the city, for to pleye," &c.

Here to 'ryde amayed' means 'to ride a-Maying,' for we are expressly told that the month was May; cf. Chaucer, Kn. Tale, 642—646.

And in Conf. Amant. bk. vi. we read of a priest who is drunk, and 'goth astrayed,' i. e. goes wandering about.

Here are seven examples of this construction. I leave it to the reader to find more.

146. (b. 6. 147; a. 7. 134.) *Ancres and hermits.* See notes to Pass. i. 30, 51. I add here a quotation from the Reply of Friar Daw Topias, in Polit. Poems, ed. Wright, ii. 64—

  "For sum fleen from the world and closen hemsilf in wallis,
  And steken hem in stones, and litil wole thei speken,
  To fleen sich occasiouns as foly wole fynden;
  And thees we clepen *ancres* in the comoun speche."

And again, at the same reference—

> " Also in contemplacion ther ben many other,
> That drawen hem to disert and drye [*endure*] muche peyne,
> By eerbis, rootes, and fruyte lyven for her goddis love,
> And this maner of folk men callen *hermytes*."

It is certain that *nones* originally meant about three o'clock in the afternoon, though it was afterwards shifted so as to mean midday, our modern *noon*. See Wedgwood, s. v. *Noon*. There seem to have been two principal meal-times, viz. dinner at about nine or ten A.M., and supper at about five or six P.M.; cf. ll. 275, 278. See Wright's Hist. of Domestic Manners, p. 155. We have reference to two meals in the day in Pass. vii. 429 (see note to that line), and in l. 434 Glutton is made to confess that he had wrongly eaten, on fasting-days, 'before none;' cf. Pass. iii. 100. The question of the time meant in this passage is not easy to settle. Taken in connection with the passages just referred to, and remembering the use of 'none' in other passages, I think that the hour meant is what we now call noon, viz. 12 o'clock; and that we are to understand the anchorites and hermits as having but *one* meal; that meal being taken at the hour of twelve, because the 'dinner-time' was at 12 instead of 9 on fasting-days. In Our English Home, p. 34, we read—"In the rules for the regulation of the household of the Princess Cecil, mother of Edward the Fourth, it is laid down, that upon ordinary days dinner was to be held at eleven, but upon fasting-days at twelve." So in The Myrour of Our Lady, ed. Blunt, p. 15, we read— "At houre of tyerse [here 9 A.M.] labourers desyre to haue theyr dyner.... At houre of none the sonne is hiest." The hours varied at different dates, as may be seen in Our Eng. Home; and in Chambers, Book of Days, i. 96, we read that Gervase Markham, in 1653, makes the ploughman have three meals, viz. breakfast at 6 A.M., dinner at half past 3 P.M., and supper at 6 P.M. But, in our author's time, dinner and supper were the only meals. Observe the reading *at non* in [a]; and see the extra lines, A. vii. 137—139. ·

In Riley's Memorials of London, p. 265, note 7, we learn that certain donations for drink to workmen are called in the Letter-book G, fol. iv (27 Edw. III.), *nonechenche*. This is the modern *nuncheon;* and the spelling shews at once that the derivation is from *none*, noon, and *schenche*, a pouring out or dispensing of drink, from A.S. *scencan*, to pour out drink, to 'skink.'

——(b. 6. 151; *not in* c, a.) The word *posteles* is only another spelling of *apostles*, and is not to be confused with *postills*, i. e. commentaries. Crowley actually has the reading *apostles;* and perhaps it is to the point to observe that the word *apostle* is written *postuli* in Icelandic. We have here possibly an allusion to Wyclif's 'poor priests,' as they were called; cf. Massingberd's English Reformation, p. 133. In any case, the word is clearly used with the sense of 'preachers.'

158. (b. 6. 163; a. 7. 149.) *Wolveskynnes* [b], of the kind or nature of a wolf. Cf. ·

"Thei ben wilde werwolves · that wiln the folk robben."

P. Ploughman's Crede, l. 459.

160. (b. 6. 165; *not in* a.) "There will be no plenty, quoth Piers, if the plough lie idle" [c]; "Shall never any plenty be among the people, whilst my plough lies idle" [b].

165. (b. 6. 170; a. 7. 154.) This line much resembles Rich. Redeles, iii. 284.

166. (b. 6. 171; a. 7. 155.) *Sette peers at a pese*, accounted Piers at the value of a pea; i. e. set him at naught. The form *pese* or *pees* (Lat. *pisum*) is quite correct; the plural is *pesen* or *peses*; see ll. 176, 307; and A. 7. 176. The *singular* (!) form *pea* really exhibits as great a blunder as if we were to develop *chee* as the singular of *cheese*; yet it is not a solitary instance, since we have "that heathen Chinee" as a formation from *Chinese*, *cherry* from *cherris* (Lat. *cerasus*), *sherry* from *sherris* (Span. *Xeres*), &c.; see an article on the words Chinee, Maltee, Portuguee, Yankee, Pea, Cherry, Sherry, and Shay, by Danby P. Fry, Esq.; Phil. Soc. Trans. 1873-4, p. 253.

168. (b. 7. 174; a. 7. 159.) "And whooped after (i. e. called loudly for) Hunger, who heard him at the (very) first." The explanation "hopped" in Crit. Note to A-text is quite wrong, and was corrected in Crit. Note to B-text. Whitaker well remarks that the very phrase occurs in Cowper (The Timepiece)—

> "He *calls for* Famine, and the meagre fiend
> Blows mildew from between his shrivel'd lips,
> And taints the golden ear."

The reader should notice that *hunger* has here a very strong meaning, and is nearly equivalent to *famine*. Trench, in his Select Glossary, s. v. *Hunger*, says—"it was long before this and 'famine' were desynonymized, and indeed the great famine year is still spoken of in Ireland as 'the year of the hunger.' · Still, in the main, they are distinguished, 'famine' expressing an outward fact, the dearth of food, and 'hunger' the inward sense and experience of this fact." See his quotations from Wyclif's Bible, Luke xv. 14, Acts xi. 28; Coverdale's Bible, Amos viii. 11; and Hampole's Pricke of Conscience, l. 4035. Cf. ll. 171, 342 below.

174. (b. 6. 179; a. 7. 164.) The phrase "lene as lanterne" occurs in an alliterative poem on the Destruction of Jerusalem, MS. Laud 656, fol. 16 *b*, l. 8 from bottom of the leaf. With this we may compare Chaucer's "lene as a rake;" Prol. 287. The expression in the text, "lyk a lanterne" is very graphic. The effect of Hunger's attack upon the Britoner was such that one could see through him. Cf. *Lantern-leeght* in F. K. Robinson's Whitby Glossary (E. D. S.).

——(b. 6. 182; a. 7. 172.) *Doluen*, buried; as shewn by [a].

178. This resembles l. 192; see note to that line.

179. (b. 6. 186; a. 7. 173.) *Faitours* has occurred before, Pass. iii. 193, ix. 128; it is equivalent to lying vagabonds, or canting rogues. The following extract is from The Athenæum of Feb. 27, 1869. "In a MS. of the early

part of the fifteenth century—William of Nassington's translation of John Waldby's treatise on the Paternoster, &c.—we find an earlier notice than we had expected of shamming beggars in England. Their trade must have been a well-known one, as they had a special name—*Faytours*—slugs or lazy scoundrels :—

'*ffaytours* wynnes mete and moné
Of þaim þat has mercy and pyte;
ffore lyther whyles cane þai fynde,
To make þaim seme crokede and blynde,
Ore seke, or mysays, to mennes syght;
So cane þai þaire lymes dyght,
ffor men suld þaim mysays deme;
Bote þai are noght swilke als þai seme.'"

185. (b. 6. 191; *not in* a.) "They cut their copes, and made them into jackets." The cope was "a kind of cloak worn during divine service by the clergy. It reaches from the neck nearly to the feet, and is open in the front, except at the top, where it is united by a band or clasp;" Hook's Church Dictionary. The clergy were specially distinguished by the use of such 'long clothes,' as William calls them; see Pass. vi. 41. And accordingly Myrk, in his Instructions to Parish Priests (ed. Peacock, l. 43), warns them to avoid "cuttede clothes and pyked schone." But long clothes were unsuited for hard manual labour, and are therefore here described as being cut short. Camden (Remaines concerning Britain, p. 196, ed. 1657) says of our ancestors—"They had also a kind of gown called a *git*, a jacket without sleeves called a *haketon*; a loose jacket like an heralds coat of armes, called a *tabard*; a short gabbardin called a *court-pie*; a gorget called a *chevesail*, for as yet they used no bands about their neck; a pouche called a *gipser*" [misprinted *gisper*]. Cf. Strutt, Manners and Customs, ii. 85; and see *courtepy* in Chaucer's Prol. 290.

188. (b. 6. 194; a. 7. 179.) *Bedreden* [b], bedridden; see the Glossary. "Also freris seyn in dede, þat hit is medeful to leeve þe comaundement of Crist, of gyvynge of almes to pore feble men, to pore croked men, to pore blynde men, and to *bedraden* men, and gif þis almes to ypocritis, þat feynen hem holy and nedy;" Wyclif's Works, iii. 372. "þe poore & þe *beedered* loke þou not loþe;" Babees Book, p. 37, l. 19. *He botnede*, he cured [c]; *were botened*, were cured [b]. The word *botnede* is not very correctly used. The right distinction is that *boten* means to better, to cure, but *botnen* is to become better, to recover, to be cured, according to the analogy of Mæsogothic verbs ending in -*nan*: but such a difference is seldom made at this date. See Stratmann, and cf. Will. of Palerne, l. 1055. This incorrect use of the word so puzzled Dr Whitaker that he proposed to explain *he botnede* by he *buttoned* (!) them, i. e. "bound them up or cured them of their pretended ailments." It is to be noted, however, that our author is, in this line, speaking of *real* ailments, not pretended ones.

191. (*not in* b, a.) This mention of *five* orders of friars is very remarkable, and is peculiar to MSS. of the C-class. It occurs again in Pass. x.

343, and xvi. 81. In most other passages we have mention of *four* orders only; see note to Pass. i. 56. The *fifth* order was that of the Crutched Friars, and the mention of them is an indication, probably, of the date of this latest version of the poem; but, unfortunately, it does not afford a clue that can be worked out. "Confluxerant in.ædes quatuor ordines Mendicantium; .his adjunxit sese *quintus Cruciferorum*, adversus hunc, ceu nothum, quatuòr illi magno tumulto coorti sunt; rogabant ubi vidissent unquam plaustrum quinque rotarum;" &c. Erasmus, Funus, Colloq. ii. 59.

192. (b. 6. 196; *not in* a.) *Bayarde*, a common name for a horse; used by Chaucer, Gower, and Skelton. William refers to the custom of giving horses *bread* to eat, as is still common on the continent. Cf. l. 225. A statute of Edw. III. orders—that horsebread be made only of beans and peas, without other mixture. The making of horsebread was formerly a regular part of a baker's business. See Toulmin Smith's English Gilds, p. 366. T. Sharp, in his Dissertation on Pageants, p. 164, gives the following item, from an account dated 1474 :—" Item, for horsbreed to the horsses, iij *d*." Skelton (ed. Dyce, i. 15) says—

> " A swete suger lofe and sowre bayardys bun
> Be sumdele lyke in forme and shap."

In Horman's Vulgaria, leaf 170, I find—" Horsis that muste runne for a wager or for a great erande be fedde with chaffe and barly-bredde, *Barbarici palea et zeatico aluntur*. Geue my horse .III. horseloues, *Da equo meo tres panes farragineos*." Sometimes poor people had no better fare. In Gammer Gurton's Needle, Act i. sc. 2, Hodge says he has had nothing to eat the whole day "save this pece of dry horsbred." See also notes to ll. 225, 304 below.

207. (b. 6. 203; a. 7. 190.) *Erthe* [c]; *erde* [b]; *hurde* [a]. The best reading is *erde*, A.S. *earde*. The sense is well illustrated by the A.S. version of S. Luke iv. 23—"do hér on þinum *earde*," &c., i. e. do here in thy *country*.

216. (*not in* b, a.) *Final*, complete, full, perfect. Gower has the expression 'final pees,' i. e. perfect peace, in the Prologue to his Confessio Amantis; ed. Pauli, i. 36. Whitaker misprints it *smal*, and explains 'no smal' as 'little,' simply ignoring the negative.

217. (b. 6. 210; a. 7. 196.) *Hit ben* [c] is the common phrase, and is equivalent to *They are* [b] or *heo beoþ* [a]; cf. l. 52. *Blody broþren*, brethren by blood or birth; the sense is obvious, but this use of *bloody* is extremely rare. Compare—"*Bloody*, well-bred, coming of a good stock. 'He comes of a *bloody* stock; that's why he's good to poor folks'"; Peacock's Linc. Gloss. (E. D. S.)

221. (b. 6. 214; a. 7. 200.) After the pestilence of 1349, there was a want of labourers. Edward published a proclamation, compelling men and women, in good health, and under sixty years of age, to work at stated wages. But it was evaded, and in harvest-time especially, exorbitant wages were both demanded and given. See Lingard, Hist. Eng. (3rd ed.), iv. 89; Th. Walsingham, ed. Riley, i. 276, 277; and Liber Albus, pp. 584, 634.

225. (b. 6. 207.; a. 7. 203.) *Houndes bred*. The Prioresse in Chaucer

(Prol. 147) fed her hounds with "wastel breed." The "chippings of trencher-brede" in Lord Percy's household were used "for the fedyinge of my lords houndis;" Percy Household Book, p. 353. On *hors-bred*, see note to l. 192 above.

226. (b. 6. 218; a. 7. 204.) *Abane hem*, give them disease, lit. poison them [c]; *Abate hem*, reduce them, keep them thin [b]; *bamme hem*, cozen them [a]. *For bollynge of here wombe*, to prevent swelling of their bellies, to keep them from growing fat. On this use of *for*, see notes to ll. 8 and 59 above. Cf. "Bean-belly Leicestershire," in Hazlitt's Eng. Proverbs, p. 81.

231. (b. 6. 224; a. 7. 210.) *Lene hem*, give to them; lit. lend to them.

233. (b. 6. 226; a. 7. 212.) "In misfortune or disease, if thou canst help them" [c].

Naughty [b], having naught.

"She had an idea from the very sound
That people *with naught* were *naughty*."

Hood; Miss Kilmansegg.

——(b. 6. 228; *not in* a.) *Late god yworthe*, let God alone; see note to Pass. i. 201. *Michi vindicta*, &c.: Rom. xii. 19. *Vindictam* is the reading of the MSS., and, though the Vulgate has *Mihi vindicta*, yet the same reading—*mihi vindictam*—will be found in the Ancren Riwle, pp. 184, 286; at p. 178 of Old Eng. Homilies, 2nd Series, ed. Morris; and at p. 112 of Albertani Brixiensis Liber Consolationis, ed. Thor Sundby. So that we should not be warranted in making the "correction."

——(b. 6. 230; *cf.* a. 7. 215.) See Crit. Note to B-text, p. 402.

246. (b. 6. 238; a. 7. 223.) "Propter frigus piger arare noluit; mendicabit ergo æstate, et non dabitur illi;" Prov. xx. 4. *Sapience* (b. 6. 237) means the book of Wisdom; William frequently refers to the wrong book of the Bible for his quotations. In [c], the MSS. mostly read *hyeme* for *estate*, which is found in MS. E only, a variation which I have marked in the footnote with a note of admiration. However, *estate* is right, and the reading *hyeme* is an adaptation, to suit our own climate. On the word *abrybeþ* [c], see note to l. 138 above.

247. (b. 6. 240; a. 7. 225.) *With mannes face* [b, a]. An allusion to a common representation of the evangelists, which likens Matthew to a *man*, Mark to a *lion*, Luke to a *bull*, and John to an *eagle*: cf. Ezekiel i. 10, Rev. iv. 7. Sometimes the arrangement varied; see the Ormulum, vol. i. p. 201. Of course *face* has no special force here; yet it is rather curious that we find in one case, and in addition to the usual symbol of St Matthew, a *man's head*. A striking example of this occurs in the splendid Lindisfarne MS. of the Gospels (MS. Cotton, Nero D. 4), where St Matthew is depicted writing, with a man's head peering at him from behind a curtain. See Plate 13 in Facsimiles of Miniatures and Ornaments of Anglo-Saxon and Irish MSS., by Prof. Westwood.

——(b. 6. 241; a. 7. 226.) *Nam*, a mina. It is glossed in the Laud MS. by the words—'a besaunt;' and in the Vernon MS. [a] by the word 'talentum.' Wyclif's version has 'besaunt' in Luke xix. 16. The parable occurs both in Matt. xxv. and Luke xix.; but the use of the word *nam* shews that our author was thinking rather of St Luke's account, where the word μνᾶ is used, from the Hebrew *maneh*. See the article on *Weights* in Smith's Bible Dictionary. In l. 243 [b], we have the better spelling *mnam*. For the value of a *besant*, see Ormulum, ed. White, ii. 390.

——(b. 6. 251; a. 7. 236.) Richard Rolle de Hampole, amongst others, carefully distinguishes between *active life*, or *bodily* service of God, and *contemplative life* or *ghostly* (i. e. spiritual) service. See his prose treatises, ed. Perry (E. E. T. S. 1866), p. 19; and see p. xi. of Mr Perry's preface.

The distinction between these two kinds of life seems to have been founded upon St James's epistle, especially (I suppose) the last verse of the first chapter. In the Reply of Frier Daw Topias (printed in Polit. Poems, ed. Wright, ii. 63) is the following passage:—

"Iack, in Iames pistles · al religioun is groundid,
For there is made mencion · of two perfit lyves,
That actif and contemplatif · comounli ben callid,
Fulli figurid by Marie · and Martha hir sister,
By Peter and bi Ioon · by Rachel and by Lya."

The two kinds of life are typified by Martha and Mary in a homily on the Assumption of the Virgin, found both in Wyclif's Works i. 383, and in the Homilies of Ælfric, ii. 443.

——(b. 6. 252; a. 7. 237.) The Psalm of *Beati omnes* begins thus; "Beati omnes, qui timent Dominum; qui ambulant in uiis eius. Labores manuum tuarum quia manducabis : beatus es, et bene tibi erit." Ps. cxxvii. 1, 2 (Vulgate). See the quotation at l. 262 [c].

273. (b. 6. 263; a. 7. 248.) See a paraphrase of A. vii. 248—259 in the Introduction to the A-text, p. vii.

——(b. 6. 269; a. 7. 254.) *Afyngred*, greatly hungry. It is corrupted from the A.S. *of-hingrian*, to be very hungry. The word occurs in the Vox and Wolf, in Hazlitt's Early Popular Poetry, vol. i. p. 58 (printed also in Reliq. Antiq. ii. 272, from MS. Digby 86), where the fox is described as *afingret*. In [a] we have the equivalent word *a-longet = of-longet*, i. e. filled with longing, very greedy. Other examples of the word will be found in Polit. Songs, ed. Wright, p. 342, l. 418; and in a note on "The Tale of the Basyn and the Frere and the Boy;" (Pickering, 1836.)

283. (*not in* b, a.) See the parable of Dives in Pass. xx. 229—246, and the mention of Lazarus "in Abraham's lap" in Pass. xix. 273.

286. (*not in* b, a.) On *souel*, see note to B. xvi. 11.

288. (*not in* b, a.) *Lacchedrawers*, thieves; also called *drawlacches*. See note to Pass. i. 45. *Lolleres*, vagabonds; see note to Pass. x. 213.

289. (*not in* b, a.) *Tyl the bord be drawe*, till the table be removed. The "board" or table was laid upon trestles, and removed after meals; see Our English Home, p. 30.

290. (*not in* b, a.) *None*, the noon-tide meal. See note to l. 146 above.

292. (b. 6. 271; a. 7. 256.) Cf.

> " And ȝit ther is another craft that toucheth the clergie, .
> That ben thise false fisiciens that helpen men to die."
> · Polit. Songs (Camd. Soc.), p. 333.

See Chaucer's Prologue, ll. 411—414, where the Doctour of Phisik is described; the description of physicians in Barclay's Ship of Fools, ed. Jamieson, i. 263; and that of the Potecary in Heywood's Four P's, in Hazlitt's Old Plays, i. 356.

293. (b. 6. 272; a. 7. 257.) A 'cloke of calabre' means a cloak trimmed with Calabrian fur. In the Coventry Mysteries, p. 242, we read—"Here colere splayed, and furryd with ermyn, *calabere*, or satan." A person who wore an amice trimmed with calabre was *himself* called a 'calaber amyse,' as appears from an extract from a Chapter Minute of Christ Church, Dublin, quoted in Todd's introduction to The Book of Obits, &c. of Christ Church, p. xcii. *Cf.* Notes and Queries, 3rd S. vol. xi.; pp. 224, 307. It appears that calabre was a *grey* fur, the belly of which was *black.*—Riley, Memorials of London, pp. 329, 331.

295. (b. 6. 274; a. 7. 259.) This line is nearly repeated in Rich. Redeles, iii. 253.

304. (b. 6. 282; a. 7. 267.) "In the parish of Hawsted, Suffolk, the allowance of food to the labourer in harvest was, two herrings per day, milk from the manor dairy to make cheese, and a loaf of bread, of which fifteen were made from a bushel of wheat. Messes of potage made their frequent appearance at the rustic board."—Knight, Pict. Hist. England, i. 839. Mr Knight obtained this information from the Rev. Sir John Cullum's History of Hawsted; and, as this book is not in every one's hands, I give a long extract from pp. 212—224 of the second edition, as it gives a great number of exact and curious details concerning the farm life of the period at which our author wrote. See the ADDITIONAL NOTE at the end of this Passus, p. 175.

I may remark here that a paraphrase of A. vii. 267—282 will be found in the Introduction to the A-text, pp. vii, viii.

The following passage from the Chester Plays (ed. Wright, p. 123) was evidently intended to describe and record the usual food of shepherds. One of the shepherds of Bethlehem is made to say :—

> " Here is bread this daie was baken,
> Onyans, garlicke, and leickes,
> Butter that boughte was in Blackon,
> And *green cheese* that will greese your cheekes.
> And heare [*here*] ale of Halton I have,
> And whotte [*hot*] meate I hade to my hier;
> A puddinge, may no man deprave,
> And a jannacke [*oaten loaf*] of Lancaster-shire.
> Loe! heares a sheepes heade sawsed in ale,
> And a grayne to laye on the greene,
> And sower mylke my wife hade ordened,
> A noble supper, as well is seene . . . .
> Gammons and other good meate in-feare [*together*],
> A puddinge with a pricke [*skewer*] in the ende;" &c.

Mr Wright, in his Homes of Other Days, p. 190, remarks that "a French moral poem of the 14th century, entitled Le 'Chemin de Pauvreto et de Richesse,' represents the poor labourers as having no other food than bread, garlic, and salt, with water to drink." Harrison, in his Description of England (bk. ii. ch. 13), referring to a later period, says that a poor man "thinketh himselfe verie frendlie dealt withall, if he may haue an acre of ground assigned vnto him, whereon to keepe a cow, or wherein to set cabbages, radishes, parsneps, carrets, melons, pompons, or such like stuffe, by which he and his poore household liueth as by their principall food, sith they can doo no better. And as for wheaten bread, they eat it when they can reach vnto the price of it, contenting themselues in the meane time with bread made of otes or barleie." See also Andrew Boorde's Introduction of Knowledge, ed. Furnivall, especially pp. 253—282, whence I make the following extracts :—

Boorde says that bread made of wheat and barley mixed, or of rye and barley mixed, "shall neuer do good to man, no more than horse-breade, or breade made of beanes and peason shall do ;" p. 259.

"Yf a man haue a lust or a sensuall appetyd (sic) to eate and drynke of a grayne bysyde malte or barlye, let hym eate and drynke of it the whiche maye be made of otes ; for hauer-cakes in Scotlande is many a good ·lordes dysshe ; and yf it wyll make good hauer-cakes, consequently it wyll do make goode drynke," &c. ; p. 259.

"Potage is not so moch vsed in al Crystendom as it is vsed in Englande. Potage is made of the lyquor in the whiche flesshe is soden in, with puttyng-to chopped herbes, and otemel, and salt ;" p. 262.

"Pease potage is better than beane potage, for it is sooner dygested," &c. ; p. 263.

"Grene chese is not called grene by reason of colour, but for the newnes of it ; for the whey is not halfe pressed out of it ; and in operacyon it is colde and moyste ;" p. 266.

"Clowtyd crayme and rawe crayme put togyther, is eaten more for a sensuall appetyde than for any good nowrysshement. Rawe crayme vndecocted, eaten with strawberyes or huttes [whortle-berries], is a rurall mannes banket ;" p. 267.

"A henne in wynter is goode and nutrytyue. And so is a chyken in somer, specyallye cockrellys [young cocks] and polettes [young hens]," &c. ; p. 270.

"Bacon is good for carters and plowmen ;" p. 273. To which he adds that "coloppes and egges" is very unwholesome for them. At p. 278, he recommends "the rootes of percelly [parsley] soden tender ;" also "turnepes eaten rawe moderatly ;" and at p. 279, he speaks of "onyons," of "leekes," and of "garlyke," &c.

With respect to the prices of provisions, some idea may be gained from those mentioned in Memorials of London, ed. Riley, p. 312, viz. :—"best goose, 6d. ; best sucking-pig, 8d. ; best capon, 6d. ; a hen, 4d. ; best rabbit, 4d. ; a roast goose, 7d. ;" &c. This was in the year 1363. The reader may find most minute details in the History of Prices and Agriculture in England, by J. E. T. Rogers.

305. (b. 6. 283; a. 7. 268.) *Grys*, pig; see Pass. i. 227. *Green cheses*, i. e. fresh cheeses; see the quotation from Boorde in the last note. The following curious account of a shepherds' breakfast occurs in The Complaint of Scotland, ed. Murray, pp. 42, 43. "[Thai] syne sat doune al to-gyddir to tak there refectione, quhar thai maid gret cheir of euyrie sort of mylk, baytht of ky mylk and ȝoue mylk, sueit mylk and sour mylk, *curdis* and quhaye, sourkittis [*clouted cream*], fresche buttir ande salt buttir, *reyme* [*cream*], fiot quhaye [*float whey, whey brose*], grene cheis, kyrn mylk; . . . thai hed na breyd bot ry-caikis and fustean skonnis [*puffy scones*] maid of flour."

306. (b. 6. 284; a. 7. 269.) *A cake of otes*, an oat-cake [c]; *an hauer cake*, an oaten-cake [b]; *a therf cake*, an unleavened cake [a]. "Panis sine fermento, *therf breed*." MS. Glos. pr. in Rel. Antiq. i. 6. "Thei make the sacrament of *therf breed*;" Maundeville's Travels, ed. Halliwell, p. 121. "Fadris maden þerfe brede for to ete þer Pask lomb;" Wyclif's Works; ii. 237. And see the Wycliffite Glossary, and Dr White's note in the Ormulum, vol. ii. p. 629. A late instance of the use of *therfe* is in Pilkington's Works (Parker Soc.), p. 54.

309. (b. 6. 287; a. 7. 272.) We find mention of "colopys of venyson" and "colopes of the wyld-dere" in Hazlitt's Early Pop. Poetry, vol. i. pp. 24, 28. Brand says, "Slices of this kind of meat (i. e. salted and dried) are to this day termed *collops* in the north, whereas they are called *steaks* when cut off from fresh or unsalted flesh."—Pop. Antiq. vol. i. p. 62. "Bacon and *colhoppes*" are mentioned in Pass. xvi. 67, q. v. Cotgrave has—"*Riblette*, a collop, or slice of bacon. *Des œufs à la riblette*, egges and collops; or, an omelet or pancake of egges and slices of bacon mingled, and fried together." For *cokeney*, see the Glossary.

311. (b. 6. 296; a. 7. 281.) From this passage, and the frequent allusions to *cherry-faire* in our old authors (see note to Pass. vii. 136), it is clear that cherries were a common fruit. It is certain that Sir Henry Ellis is right in his opinion (printed in a note to this line in Wright's edition) that Gough must have made some blunder in supposing that cherries were at this time unknown in England.

314. (b. 6. 291; a. 7. 276.) *Lammasse*, i. e. Loaf-mass, Aug. 1. In Anglo-Saxon times, a *loaf* was offered on this day, as an offering of first-fruits. See Chambers' Book of Days, ii. 154.

328. (b. 6. 306; a. 7. 292.) "Panis de *coket*" is mentioned in a MS. of Jesus Coll. Oxford, 1 Arch. i. 29, fol. 268, as being slightly inferior to *wastel* bread. See the whole passage, now printed in Munimenta Academica, ed. Ansley, i. 180. The fine kinds of white bread were called simnel bread or *pain demaigne*, wastel bread, coket, clere matyn, and manchet bread. The common kinds of brown bread were tourte, trete, and bis. Cf. Riley, Memorials of London, p. 644; Chambers' Book of Days, i. 119; Strutt, Manners and Customs, iii. 57; Liber Albus (*Cocket* and *Bread* in the Index);

and see *Coket* in the Glossary. In Arnold's Chronicle (ed. 1811), pp. 49—56, will be found the "Assize of Bred," and various information concerning all kinds of loaves, &c. In Andrew Boorde's Introduction of Knowledge, ed. Furnivall, will be found a chapter that "treateth of breade," p. 253; another that "treateth of potage," p. 262; &c., &c.

329. (b. 6. 307; a. 7. 293.) *Halpeny ale.* See note to Pass. vii. 226, and cf. l. 383 below.

331. (b. 6. 309; a. 7. 295.) See a paraphrase of A. vii. 295—302 in the Introduction to the A-text, p. viii.

336. (b. 6. 314; a. 7. 300.) As to the high wages of labourers, see note to l. 221 above. The statutes concerning them are alluded to in l. 341 below.

338. (b. 6. 316; *not in* a.) Dionysius Cato is the name commonly assigned to the author of a Latin work in four books, entitled Dionysii Catonis Disticha de Moribus ad Filium. The real author is unknown, but the work may perhaps be referred to the fourth century. It was very popular, both in Latin, and in English and French versions. William here quotes part of the 21st distich of the first book, which runs thus:—

> "Infantem nudum quum te natura crearit,
>   Paupertatis onus patienter ferre memento."

346. (b. 6. 324; a. 7. 308.) *Water,* i.e. floods, cf. l. 349.

348. (b. 6. 327; a. 7. 311.) Great disasters were often attributed to the malign influence of the planet Saturn. Besides this, great foresight was attributed to the god Saturn. This is very well illustrated by Chaucer's Knightes Tale, ll. 1585—1620. We may note also the following passage in the Commentary to book iii. c. xi. of the prophecies of John of Bridlington (ed. Wright). "Primo est notandum, quod Saturnus est stella maxima nociva terræ et inductiva pestilenciarum; unde, secundum Misaelem, Saturnus est planeta malevolus, frigidus, siccus, ponderosus, et nocturnus; et, secundum Catholicon, in iudiciis signat mœrorem et tristitiam." It may be added that this remark was made with especial reference to the pestilence of 1361-2, and was the expression of the generally received opinion. Mr Wright, in his Preface to Piers Plowman, p. xii, says, "This terrible calamity [the Black Death of 1349] was said by the astrologers to have been brought about by an extraordinary conjunction of Saturn with the other planets, which happened scarcely once in a thousand years." He refers us to a poem of Symon de Covino, *De Iudicio Solis in Conuiuiis Saturni.* Symon especially notes that the famine chiefly attacked the poor, because they were ill-fed, but spared the rich; see Bibliothèque de l'École des Chartres, tom. ii. p. 236. So also in the Shepheard's Kalender, ed. 1656, fol. O l;—"Saturne is the highest planet of all the seven, he is mighty of himself; he giveth all the great *colds* and *waters;* yet is he dry and cold of nature. . . . When he reigneth, there is much theft used, and little charity . . . [and] great travell on the earth; and old folk shall be very sickly, many diseases shall reigne among the people, &c. . . . . This planet is cause of hasty death," &c. In the Book of Quinte Essence, ed. Furnivall, p. 24, we find alcohol recom-

mended as a cure for "alle opere maner of feueris pestilence þat god suffriþ to come to mankynde by perilous influence of yuele plauctis."

In the A-text (earliest version), the Passus ends with this line. Ll. 349—355 (b. 328—332) were added afterwards; wherein William imitates, not perhaps without ridicule, the mysterious prophecies which were then popular; such as, for instance, the prophecies of John of Bridlington. Lines 351, 352, are, of course, inexplicable (cf. Pass. iv. 481—483, and Crit. Note to C. ix. 351); but the rest is clear enough. By *deth* is meant such a great pestilence as that which earned the name of the Black Death, and which was sometimes called simply "the dethe," as in Political, Religious, and Love Poems, ed. Furnivall, p. 98, l. 153. "The pestilence shall withdraw, Famine· shall then be the judge, and Dawe the ditcher (cf. Pass. vii. 369) shall die for hunger, unless God, of His goodness, grant us a truce." As regards famines and dearths cf. Polit. Songs (Camd. Soc.), p. 399.

ADDITIONAL NOTE TO C. PASSUS IX. 304.

(Extracts from Sir J. Cullum's History of Hawsted, 2nd edition, pp. 212—224.)

"In the year 1281, the prices of various kinds of grain, the produce of this village, were as follows:—Of wheat, about the Conversion of St. Paul (25 January), from 4*s*. 3*d*. to 4*s*. 5*d*. a quarter; in Lent, 4*s*. 6*d*., afterwards, 4*s*. 8*d*.; of siligo (a kind of light and white wheat), from 2*s*. 8*d*. to 2*s*. 10*d*.; of barley, 3*s*. 6½*d*.; of new pease, from 2*s*. 9¼*d*. to 2*s*. 11½*d*.; of old pease, 2*s*. 4½*d*.; of draget (oats and barley mixed together), 2*s*. 8*d*.; of oats, from 2*s*. 2*d*. to 2*s*. 4*d*.

"This was a year of moderate plenty, and therefore may be considered as the standard of the prices of grain, about this period; for in turning over the Chron. Pret. I find, that at different times, from 1246 to 1270, wheat sold at what were then all esteemed the enormous rates of 13*s*. 4*d*.; 16*s*.; 4*l*. 16*s*. and even 6*l*. 8*s*. a quarter, if the author may be credited, who says at the same time, that provisions were so scarce, that parents ate their children. In 1243, it sold at 2*s*. a quarter; in 1286, at 2*s*. 8*d*.; in 1288, it sunk to 1*s*., and in the North and West parts, even to 8*d*. Supposing then 4*s*. 6*d*. to be about the mean price of a quarter of wheat, and 4*d*. a year's rent of an acre of land, the disproportion between the produce of the land and its rent, is almost incredible; for, if (as I suspect) an acre produced, in general, only 1½ quarter, it would, if the ground was cropped only two years together, give the husbandman 13 times the rent of his land one year with another; a profit, which the best farmers, in the present state of improved agriculture, can rarely, I believe, reach. That lands should be thus rated, can only be attributed to the frequent and almost entire failures of their crops, unknown in modern times, in well cultivated countries; and which must have been owing to an ill-managed husbandry, that sunk entirely under an unfavourable season. At one time we are told, the ground was so hard that it could not be tilled; at another, that the rain and hail destroyed the crops; the consequence was, not only a scarcity, but often a famine. Even so late as the reign of Queen Mary, Bullein tells us, that 'bread was so skant, insomuch that the plain poor people did make very much of acorns; and a sickness of a strong fever did sore molest the commons;' Bulwark of Defence, fol. 30.

"Not that we are to imagine, that good husbandry was not now known; for some writers, even before this period, have shewn the contrary; but to know and to practise are very different things. Are there not invincible prejudices, even in this enlightened age, with which agriculture has to contend? In how many parts of this island do turnips still remain unhoed?

"The same year, 1281, the price of a bullock was 8s. 6d.; of a hog, 2s. 6d.; of a pig, 6d.; of threshing a quarter of wheat, 3d.; of siligo, 2½d.; of barley, 1¼d.; of pease, 2d.; of draget, 1d.; of oats, 1d.; a man's wages for cutting firewood for two days was 4d., which seems great pay. A carter was allowed for his Easter-day's repast 1d. Another had four bushels of siligo for six weeks work of various kinds; and a girl for winnowing corn, and keeping the young heiffers, geese, and poultry of the manor, for fourteen weeks, 1 quarter of the same grain. A servant called a *Daye* had 12d. for the same employment, from Michaelmas to Easter."

[I suppose *daye* = *deye*, a dairyman; cf. *deye* in Chaucer. Sir J. Cullum thought it meant a day-labourer, and says, "he occurs sometimes as an attendant upon the carter." But he adds, "Sometimes it should seem as if he belonged to the dairy, by having calves to sell."]

"In 1359, the lord of the principal manor held in his own hands 572 acres of arable land, estimated from 4d. to 8d. an acre; and eight pieces of meadow, or mowing-ground, valued at 202s. 4d. a year; the quantity of which was probably about 50 acres. For though the larger parcels are each valued in the gross at so many shillings a year, yet the quantities of three of the smaller are specified; one piece of three acres was valued at 10s. a year; one of 1 acre at 5s.; and another of 1 acre at 4s. Taking therefore the mean price of 4s., the 202s. 4d. was probably the annual value of about 50 acres. He had besides, in *Circuitu Broci* [of a brook], pasture for 24 cows, worth 36s.; as also for 12 horses, and as many oxen, worth 48s. a year. He held also 40 acres of wood, valued at 1s. an acre; and the croppings of the trees and hedges about his fields, at 6s. 8d. a year.

"Though, from the increased quantity of grass-grounds, the consumption of fleshmeat was probably increased; yet the poor landholders, who were obliged by their tenures to work for the lord so many days in haytime and harvest, had, at this time, no other allowance of animal food than two herrings a day each, and some milk from the manor dairy to make them cheese; they had besides each man a loaf, of which 15 made a bushel, and an allowance of drink, not specified. Of these there were eleven, who were to perform, amongst them, 42 days work in haytime, and 60 in harvest.

"The great inferiority of arable land to meadow, in point of value, about the proportion of 1 to 8, may be accounted for from the small quantity of the latter, at a time when hay was so great a part of the support of the live stock in winter. Why there was so small a quantity of it, may not be so easy to say.

"In 1386, the produce of the farm, which the lady of the manor held in her own hands, was, according to the bailiff's account (which was always from Michaelmas to Michaelmas), 69 quarters 5½ bushels of wheat; 54 quarters 4 bushels of barley; 11 quarters 7 bushels of pease; 29 quarters of haras;[1] and 65 quarters 4 bushels of oats.

"Oat-meal was part of the food of servants. This year, 12 bushels were used for the broth of seven. Tusser, a Suffolk farmer, tells us :—

'Though never so much a good huswife doth care
That such as do labour have husbandly fare,
Yet feed them and cram them till purse doth lack chinke,
No spoon-meat, no bellyfull, labourers thinke.'

This is not the case now. Pork and bacon are the Suffolk labourer's delicacies; and bread and cheese his ordinary diet.

"In 1387, 66 acres were sown with wheat, allowing 2 bushels to an acre; 26 acres with barley, allowing 4 bushels to an acre; 25 acres with pease; 25 acres with haras; 62 acres with oats, allowing 2½ bushels of oats to an acre.

"The stock was 4 cart-horses (equi carectarii), 6 stone-horses (stotti), 10 oxen, 1 bull, 26 cows, 6 heifers, 6 calves, 92 muttons, 10 score of hogerells (sheep of the 2nd year), 1 gander, 4 geese, 30 capons, 1 cock, 26 hens.

"The quantity of arable land in tillage, this year, appears, from the above account, to have been 214 acres. The whole, therefore, supposing one-third lay fallow, was 321; a great decrease from 572, which was the arable part of the demesnes in 1359. The dairy is rather increased; and a flock of near 300 sheep is now mentioned. There was nothing said of a flock before, though doubtless there was one; but if it had been of the consequence of that at present, it would hardly have been passed over in silence. . . .

"The dairy of 26 cows was let for 8 pounds a year, ad plenam firmam; the lactage of a cow with its calf, and a hen, being rated at 6s. 8d., and 2 cows thrown into the bargain. Wheat was sold for 4s. a quarter; oats for 2s.; 2 stone-horses (I suppose entirely worn out) for 5s.; a cart-horse for 21s.; a cow for 4s.; an ox for 13s. 6d.; a boar for 1s. 8d.; a capon for 4d.

1 "What particular grain this was, I cannot say; but its name implies, that it was a horse-corn, from Lat. haracium, Fr. haras, which signify a stud of horses; and the accounts before me shew, that horses were served with it, both threshed and in sheaves: and one year the sheep, in winter, had 120 sheaves of it, 12 of which made a bushel. It was threshed at the same price as pease and oats, which was 2d. a quarter, while wheat was threshed at 4d."

"A cart-horse was bought for 30s.; 30 fowls to be made capons, for 2s. 3d.; a goose for 6d.; a hen for 2d. Wheat was threshed for 4d. a quarter, and other grain for 2d. A reaper had 4d. a day. 1s. 11d. was paid for cutting and tying up 3 acres of wheat, *per taskam;* and 3s. 4d. for cutting and tying up 6 acres of bolymong; a pair of cart-wheels cost 6s.

"In 1388, the produce of the farm was 69 quarters 2 bushels of wheat; 52 qrs. 2 bu. of barley, 23 qrs. 3 bu. of pease; 28 qrs. of haras; 40 qrs. 4 bu. of oats.

"In 1389, 57 acres were sown with wheat; 24 with barley; 22 with pease; 38 with haras; 54¼ acres with oats.

"Wheat sold for 4s. and 5s. a quarter; barley for 3s.; oats for 2s. An old stallion, grown useless, for 12s.; a cow, for 3s. 8d.; another for 4s. 6d.; a pig or porker, for 1s. 4d.; a capon for 4d.; a cartload of hay for 5s.; a cow's hide for 1s. 8d.

"A horse's hide tawed (*dealbatum*) was bought for 1s.; bulmong (a word still familiar with us, meaning peas and oats sown together) for 2s. a quarter; a stone-horse for 15s.; a calf for 1s. Wheat was threshed for 4d. a quarter; barley, pease, and haras, for 2d. . . 60 persons, hired for 1 day to weed the corn, had 2d. each. Meadow ground was mown for 6d. an acre; malt made for 6d. a quarter; and 6 yards of canevas for table-cloths cost 12d.

"In 1390, the produce of the farm was 42 qrs. 1 bu. of wheat, from 57 acres, which is less than 6 bu. an acre; 38 qrs. 2 bu. of barley, from 24 acres, which is better than 12 bu. an acre; 34 qrs. 2½ bu. of pease, from 22 acres, which is better than 12 bu. an acre; 33 qrs. 2 bu. of oats, from 54¼ acres, which is about 5 bu. an acre.

"Either of the two first-mentioned crops, of 1386 and 1388, would ruin a modern farmer. For in 3 nearly successive years there were 183 acres sown with wheat; we may therefore conclude that the annual number was about 61; yet in neither of the best years did the quantity of wheat reach 70 qrs. However, no particular dearness followed; so that, probably, those very scanty crops were the usual and ordinary effects of the imperfect husbandry then practised. And this too, as being the manor farm, was likely to be at least as well cultivated as any in the village. But the produce of the present year [i. e. 1390] bears a more melancholy aspect; less than 6 bu. of wheat from an acre is not only a crop by which a tolerably managed farm is now rarely or never disgraced, in the most unfavourable season; but it even then produced a great scarcity; for wheat rose from 4s. and 5s. a quarter, to 13s. 4d.; barley, from 3s. to 5s. 6d.; oats from 2s. to 6s. 8d.; pease were sold at 8s. a quarter; and of wheat there were sold only 3 qrs., whereas in one of the former years there were 18, in the other 24. An ox was sold for 12s.; 5 acres of wheat-stubble for 1s. 6d.; a cow's hide for 1s. 2d.; the pease of the garden for 6s.

"A cow, with her calf, was bought for 10s.; another for 6s.; a third for 7s. 3d.; two cows, before calving, for 15s. 1d.; a boar for 2s. 7d.; and 6 calves, the property of the *daye,* for 6s. . .

"A carpenter's wages was 4*d.* a day. A man hired for 3½ days to fill the dung-cart had 10*d.*; a carter's wages were 10*s.* a year; a ploughman's, 10*s.*; a ploughdriver's, 6*s.* 8*d.*; a shepherd's, 10*s.* 4*d.*; a *daye's,* 5*s.* . . .

"The outgoings [in harvest] were called the costs of autumn, and are thus stated.

"In 1388, [we find] the expences of a ploughman, head reaper, baker, cook, brewer, *deye,* 244½ reapers (*sic*) hired for 1 day; 30 bedrepes (days of work performed in harvest-time by the customary tenants, at the *bidding* of their lord), the men [being] fed, according to custom, with bread and herring; 3 qrs. 3 bu. of wheat from the stock; 5 qrs. 3 bu. of malt from the stock; meat bought, 10*s.* 10*d.*; 5 sheep from the stock; fish and herrings bought, 5*s.*; herrings bought for the customary tenants, 7*d.*; cheese, milk, and butter bought (the dairy being let), 9*s.* 6*d.*; salt, 3*d.*; candles, 5*d.*; pepper, 3*d.*; spoons, dishes, and faucets, 5*d.*

"30 bedrepes, as before; 19 reapers, hired for 1 day, at their own board, 4*d.* each; 80 men, for 1 day, and kept at the lady's board, 4*d.* each; 140½ men (*sic*) hired for 1 day, at 3*d.* each; the wages of the head-reaper, 6*s.* 8*d.*; of the brewer, 3*s.* 4*d.*; of the cook, 3*s.* 4*d.* 30 acres of oats tied up by the job (*per taskam*), 1*s.* 8*d.*; 6 acres of bolymong cut and tied up by the job, 3*s.* 4*d.*; 16 acres of pease, cut by the job, 8*s.*; 5 acres of pease and bolymong, cut and tied up by the job, 2*s.* 6*d.*; 3 acres of wheat, cut and tied up by the job, 1*s.* 11*d.*"

[Here follow similar details for 1389, including a mention of 5 pairs of harvest-gloves, 10*d.*]

"What a scene of bustling industry was this! for, exclusive of the baker, cook, and brewer, who, we may presume, were fully engaged in their own offices, here were 553 persons employed in the first year; in the second, 520; and in a third, 538; yet the annual number of acres, of all sorts of corn, did not much exceed 200. From this prodigious number of hands, the whole business must have been soon finished. There were probably 2 principal days; for two large parties were hired, every year, for 1 day each. . . .

"These antient harvest-days must have exhibited one of the most cheerful spectacles in the world. One can hardly imagine a more animated scene than that of between 200 and 300 harvest-people all busily employed at once, and enlivened with the expectation of a festivity, which perhaps they experienced but this one season in the year. All the inhabitants of the village, of both sexes, and all ages, that could work, must have been assembled on the occasion; a muster that, in the present state of things, would be impossible. The success of thus compressing so much business into so short a time must have depended on the weather. But dispatch seems to have been the plan of agriculture at this time, at least in this village. We have seen before, that 60 persons were hired for 1 day, to weed the corn.

"These throngs of harvest-people were superintended by a person who was called the head-reaper (*supermessor,* or *præpositus*), who was annually elected, and presented to the lord, by the inhabitants; and it should seem that, in this village at least, he was always one of the customary tenants. The year he was in office, he was exempt from all or half of his usual rents and services, according to his tenure; he was to have his victuals and drink at the lord's table, if the lord kept house (*si dominus hospitium tenuerit*); if he did not, he was to have a livery of corn, as other domestics had; and his horse was to be kept in the manor-stable.   He was next in dignity to the steward and bailiff.

"The hay-harvest was an affair of no great importance.   There were but 30 acres of grass annually mown at this period.   This was done, or paid for, by the customary tenants.   The price of mowing an acre was 6*d*."

The following remarks are also very much to the point.

"Under the social system of our ancestors, six centuries ago and onwards, land was the cheapest kind of property.   The art of agriculture was so little developed that a fourfold return to seed was a good average.   The farmer knew nothing of winter-roots, of artificial grasses, and, except in its most rudimentary form, of the rotation of crops.   As the produce was scanty, so the stock was poor. . . . The best arable land was let at sixpence an acre in money of the time; land which now lets for fifty shillings.   You will best understand the growth of productiveness in England, when I state that while corn has risen in price about nine times over that which formed an average five or six centuries ago, the rent of land has risen a hundred times.   The rise and growth of rent are the result of prodigious improvements in the art of agriculture. . . . .

"Then came, like a hurricane, the terrible visitation of the Great Plague. The price of common labour instantly doubled, and the landowner could no more cultivate his large farm at a profit.   I have seen and examined many landlords' accounts of the time I refer to, and find that while, before this visitation, the profits of an owner who farmed his own land were, deducting rent, as high as 18 per cent., the rate of profit after the plague instantly sunk to 3 per cent.   It was impossible to carry on farming on such disadvantageous terms."   Historical Gleanings, by J. E. Thorold Rogers, 2nd Series, pp. 44—46.

For fuller details, the reader is referred to Prof. Thorold Rogers's History of Agriculture and Prices in England, which deals thoroughly with the whole subject.

SCHEME OF THE CONTENTS OF PASSUS X.
(B. Pass. VII; A. Pass. VIII.)

Cf. Wright's edition; pp. 138—150; ll. 4465—4899.

C-TEXT.	B-TEXT.	A-TEXT.
x. 1—13	vii. 1—13	viii. 1—13
——		14—17
14—16	*like* 14, 15	——
17—19	——	
20—33	16—29	18—31
34, 35	*like* 30, 31	*like* 32—34
36—38	32—34	35—37
	35	
39	36	38
——		39—41
40	——	——
41	37	42
	——	43, 44
42	38	——
43	——	
44	39	45
45	——	*like* 46
——.	40—43	*like* 47, 48
		49
——	44, 45	——
46—49	*like* 46—49	50—53
	50, 51	54, 55
50, 51	——	
(a) 52—54	(a) [*like* 56—58]	(a) [*like* 60, 61]
55		
56, 57	*like* 52, 53	*like* 56, 57
	54, 55	58, 59
——		
(a) [52—54]	(a) *like* 56—58	(a) *like* 60, 61
——	59—61	*like* 62, 63
58—60	*like* 62—65	64—67
61—65	66—70	68—72
66—69	*like* 71—74	——
	75—87	——
——	——	
70—161		——
162—165	*like* 88	——
166, 167	89, 90	73, 74
	91	75
168—173	92—97	76—81
	98	82
——	——	
174		——
175—177	99—101	83—85
178—182	——	
183	102	86
	103	87
——		
184, 185	104, 105	88, 89

C-TEXT.	B-TEXT.	A-TEXT.
x. 186—281		
282—291	vii. 106—115	viii. 90—99
——	116—125	*like* 100—110
——		111
——	126—128	112—114
——		115
——	129—137	116—124
		125, 126
292—297	138—143	127—132
298, 299	144, 145	134, 133
300—302	146—148	——
303	*like* 149, 150	*like* 135, 136
304—306	151—153	137—139
	154—158	140—144
307	——	
308, 309	159, 160	*like* 145—147
310	161	
311—314	162—165	148—151
315, 316	*like* 166	
317	167	152
		153, 154
318—351	168—200	155—187

NOTES TO C. PASSUS X. (B. Pass. VII; A. Pass. VIII.)

C. 10. 1. (B. 7. 1; A. 8. 1.) It has already been explained that *Truth* signifies God the Father. Cf. Pass. ii. 12; viii. 204; and see ll. 27, 37 below

3. (b. 7. 3; a. 8. 3.) *A pena et culpa.* On this expression Mr Arnold remarks (note to Wyclif's Works, i. 136)—"The ordinary indulgence absolved *pœna, sed non culpa.* In theory, the guilt of sins, and the *eternal* punishment due to them, were remitted in the sacrament of penance; it was the temporal punishment only, the *pœna,* which the indulgence professed to remit, in whole or in part. But it is well known that, during the 14th and 15th centuries, a great laxity prevailed, if not in the actual wording of indulgences, at any rate in the language of those to whom their distribution was entrusted." See also vol. iii. p. 362 of the same work, and Milman, Hist. of Lat. Christianity, vi. 254 (note), 2nd edit. See l. 23 below, where it clearly means *plenary* remission.

The phrase 'pœna et culpa' repeatedly occurs in the Parker Society publications; Becon, ii. 174; iii. 144, 233, 605; Ridley, 55, 418; Tyndale, i. 271, 342; iii. 103, 141, 154; and Bullinger (iii. 90) says that Peter Lombard distinguishes between the terms 'pœna' and 'culpa.'

——(b. 7. 14; a. 8. 13.) *Bothe the lawes,* i. e. our duty towards God, and towards our neighbours.

——(a. 8. 17; *not in* c, b.) See a similar passage in ll. 264—268 of this Passus; C-text, p. 172.

17. (*not in* b, a.) *By here powere*, as far as lies in their power; a not uncommon phrase. We must not make the mistake of supposing *by* to signify *by means of* in this passage. Cf. note to Pass. vii. 297.

21. (b. 7. 17; a. 8. 19.) "And, together with them, to judge both quick and dead at doomsday" [c]; "And at the day of doom, to sit at the high daïs" [b]; or, "to sit with them at the daïs" [a]. Tyrwhitt, in a long note on Chaucer, Prol. 372, gives an account of the word daïs, in which he seems to have been misled by a false etymology. The account in Wedgwood, s. v. *Daïs*, is rather to be followed; cf. *dois* in Burguy. The daïs was, in fact, the table *itself* (Lat. *discus*), and the high daïs was the high table at the upper end of the hall. In later times, the name was transferred, sometimes to the platform on which the table stood, and sometimes to the canopy overhanging the table. See Cotgrave.

22. (b. 7. 18; a. 8. 20.) *Menye yeres*, i. e. many years' remisssion of purgatory.

30. (b. 7. 26; a. 8. 28.) *Mesondieux*, put for *maisons de dieu*, houses of God. A hospital was called a *maison-dieu* or *masondewe*. Halliwell remarks that, till within the last few years, there was an ancient hospital at Newcastle so called. There was another, says Whitaker, at Ospringe, Kent.

31. (b. 7. 27; a. 8. 29.) *Wikkede weyes*, i. e. bad roads [c, b]; *wikkede wones*, bad dwellings, ruinous cottages [a]. Cf. "þe wey ys so wickede," i. e. the road is so bad; Pass. viii. 307. *With here good*, i. e. with their property or wealth.

32. (b. 7. 28; a. 8. 30.) The making and repairing of bridges was an excellent work of charity. Wyclif notices it;—"But we speken over litel for to visete and offre to pore men, and maken [i. e. repair] broken briges and causeis [causeways], where men and bestis and catel perischen ofte;" Works, iii. 283. For examples, see Rock, Church of Our Fathers, iii. 201, 202.

33. (b. 7. 29; a. 8. 31.) In the ordinances of the Gild of the Palmers, at Ludlow, we find provision for making a contribution out of the common chest, to enable any good poor girl of the gild "either to go into a religious house or to marry, whichever she wishes to do;" English Gilds, ed. Toulmin Smith, p. 194. Dr Rock, in his Church of Our Fathers, gives other examples; vol. iii. p. 35; and at p. 53 quotes a will of Johanne Beauchamp, Lady of Abergavenny, who devised "to the marriage of poer maydens dwellyng withyn my lordships, c. *l.*, and to makyng and emendyng of febull brugges and foul weyes, c. *l.*;" Test. Vet. i. 226; Dugdale's Warwickshire, ii. 1031.

35. (b. 7. 31; a. 8. 34.) *Fauntekynes (scoleres) to scole*. To pay for the education of poor scholars, especially at Oxford, was justly esteemed an excellent form of charity. Cf. Chaucer, Prol. 301, 302. In later times, the demand of poor scholars for money was a tax that fell rather heavily upon the poorer class of farmers—

"Than commeth clerkys of Oxford and make their mone,
To her scole hire they most haue money."

God Spede the Plough, 75.

38. (b. 7. 34; a. 8. 37.) To understand this passage, we must remember that it was the common belief that a dying man saw devils all around him, seeking to terrify him and make him despair.   This is most clearly shewn by the following passage from Hampole's Pricke of Conscience, ed. Morris, ll. 2220—2231, &c.

> "For when the lyf sal pas fra a man,
> Deuels sal gadir obout hym than,
> To rauissche the saul with tham away
> Tyl pyne of helle, if thai may.
> Als wode lyons [*like mad lions*] thai sal than fare,
> And raumpe on hym, and skoul, and stare,
> And grymly gryn on hym and blere,
> And hydus braydes [*grimaces*] mak, hym to fere.
> Thai sal fande at his last endyng
> Hym into wanhope for to bring
> Thurgh thretynges that thai sal mak,
> And thurgh the ferdnes [*fear*] that he sal tak."

Observe, too, that the word *fere* in this passage means to terrify, as in our text, B. vii. 34; and that *wanhope* is used for *despair*, as also in our text, C. viii. 59.   In old woodcuts, it is not uncommon to see representations of devils gathering round the bed of a dying man; see, e. g. Wright's Hist. of Caricature, p. 68.   The power of St Michael over evil spirits is inferred from Rev. xii. 7, 8.   It was thought that "unto Michael alone belonged the office of leading each soul from earth to the judgment-seat of Christ;" Rock, Church of Our Fathers, iii. 149; see also p. 210.

——(a. 8. 39; *not in* b, c.) "And form (i. e. prepare) your seats before the face of My Father."   Here *Truth* is, for the moment, identified with Christ instead of with God the Father, as elsewhere.   The reference is obviously to John xiv. 2, 3.

——(a. 8. 43; *not in* b, c.) "And gave Will, for his writing, some woollen clothes; and, because he thus copied out the clause for them, they gave him many thanks."   For *Cause* (Vernon MS.), the reading *clause* (see footnotes) is a great improvement.

This interesting variation affords us yet one more instance in which the author mentions himself by name.   He represents himself as writing out a new form of indulgence, coming (not from the Pope, but) from God Himself; and this new form was received with delight by the merchants.   It is indeed very probable that William, during his life in London, received encouragement from some of its merchants.   They certainly gave good support to his namesake—William Tyndale.

We also see that our author was sometimes employed as a scribe, and that he received payment in clothes instead of money from some of his employers.

45. (cf. b. 7. 39; a. 8. 46.) *Pre manibus*, in advance.   See Pass. iv. 301, and the note.

——(b. 7. 41; a. 8. 47.) "Qui pecuniam suam non dedit ad usuram, et munera super innocentem non accepit;" Ps. xiv. 5. (Vulgate).   The first verse of the same Psalm, which in English Bibles is Ps. xv., is quoted below, at l. 51 [b].

——(b. 7. 43; a. 8. 47.) I do not know the source of this quotation. It somewhat resembles Ecclus. xxxviii. 2—"A Deo est enim omnis medela, et a rege accipiet donationem."

——(b. 7. 44; *not in* c, a.) *Johan* would seem to be, at first sight, some great personage, such as John of Gaunt; see note to Pass. i. 165. If, however, we consider the passage a little more carefully, there is reason to suppose that "Johan" was neither one of the "pryuces" who were expected to reward *honest* lawyers, nor yet one of the innocent poor. It would hence follow that the name may stand for some unscrupulous fellow of middle rank, and we should get very good sense by supposing that he was a cook like the "master Johan" mentioned in Pass. xxii. 288, whose crowning merit was that he could make spiced meat acceptably.

——(b. 7. 50; a. 8. 54.) "No devil, at his deathday, shall harm him a mite, so that he will not be safe, and his soul too." *Worth* is here a verb. The construction is awkward to express. Cf. note to l. 38 above.

52. (b. 7. 56; cf. a. 8. 60.) Ʒe [c] refers to the *wise men* (l. 51); and, similarly, *Thei* [b] refers to the *legistres and lawyeres*, mentioned in l. 59 [b].

53. (b. 7. 57; a. 8. 60.) *Hus* [c] = *his* [a] is used generally, and is equivalent to *her* = their [b]. *Partynge hennes*, departure hence, i. e. death.

55. (b. 7. 52; a. 8. 56.) "For it is simony to sell that which is sent (us) by grace; that is to say, wit, and water, and wind, and fire, which is the fourth thing," &c. [c]. "But to buy water, nor wind, nor wit, nor fire, which is the fourth thing, *is a thing which Holy Writ never permitted*" [b]; where the words in italics are supplied from [a], to complete the sense, and *ne* (nor) would be better expressed in modern English by "or." Again— "But to buy water, nor wind, nor wit (which is the third thing) Holy Writ never permitted; God knows the truth [a]. The constructions are awkward, but the sense is clear. *Wit* here takes the place of *earth*, along with three of the four elements; and the meaning is—"Human intelligence is a gift of God, like three at least of the four elements, and is free for all men to profit by. Just as we should accord the free use of fire, water, and air to all men, so should we help them with our counsel and advice." If we take this in its most literal sense, i. e. in the sense that lawyers ought to do all their work for nothing, it is a most startling doctrine; but, fairly considered, it is in accordance with Christianity and common sense. I suppose that our author is merely insisting that one form of charity (and a very good form of it) is to give sound advice and kindly counsel *even* to those who cannot afford to pay for it. There can be no doubt that, in his day, the poor were most unjustly oppressed and unfairly dealt with. One gross form of cruelty practised by some lawyers was to exact from a poor man all he could afford to pay, and then to pay no attention whatever to his case.

In the A-text, we have but *three* things mentioned, viz. wit, water, and wind. In l. 58 [a], they are called "thralls," i. e. servants, or things which are at all men's service.

.*.* *For notes to* B. 7. 56, 57 (A. 8. 60), *see notes to ll.* 52, 53.

58. (b. 7. 62; a. 8. 64.) *With* [c, b] = *bi* [a] = by means of; cf. Pass. ix. 331.

66. (cf. b. 7. 70; *not in* a.) *Hus thankus*, of his own choice, of his own free will; lit. of his thank. It is a very old phrase, and found, e. g. in Alfred's translation of Boethius, chap. viii., in the form "þines agenes þonces" = of thine own choice. The very phrase "his thankes" occurs twice in Chaucer's Knightes Tale; ll. 768, 1249.

69. (b. 7. 73; *not in* a.) *Caton*, Cato. See note to Pass. ix. 338. Prefixed to Cato's Distiches are some 'Breves sententiæ,' of which the twenty-third consists only of the words—*Cui des, videto*. Mr Wright says that by *the clerk of the stories* [b] is meant Peter Comestor (died A.D. 1198), to whom Lydgate, in his Minor Poems (p. 102, ed. Halliwell), gives the title of *maister of storyes*; and I find him mentioned again by the same title in Pecock's Repressor, ii. 529; cf. i. 17. For some account of him, see Nouvelle Biographie Générale, tom. xi. col. 332; Paris, 1855. The title *clerk of stories* would then refer to the Historia Scholastica, of which Peter Comestor was the author. The Historia Scholastica is an account of all the chief events recorded in the Old and New Testaments, with additions from profane authors; and, since it is composed of many parts to each of which the title *historia* is given (as, e. g. Historia Libri Genesis, Historia Euangelica, etc.), it would naturally be called "stories" in English. In all probability Mr Wright's suggestion is correct, and the passage which our author had in his mind was, I suspect, the following passage in Comestor's Historia Libri Tobie:—"De substantia tua fac elemosynas, quia elemosyna ab omni peccata liberat, et magnam prestat fiduciam coram deo omnibus facientibus eam;" which is abridged from Tobit iv. 7—11. This is the more likely, because, in Pass. xviii. 40, our author quotes a passage from Tobit ii. 21, which is also in Comestor; see the note to that passage. There are remarks on almsgiving, very similar to this, in the Compendium by Peter Cantor, who was bishop of Tournay, A.D. 1191; they may be found at p. 150, vol. 205, of Migne's Patrologiæ Cursus Completus. Peter Cantor also quotes the sentence—*cui des, videto*. Cf. "Si benefeceris, scito cui feceris;" Ecclus. xii. 1. "Circumstantiæ eleemosynarum hæ sunt—quis, quid, quantum, cui, ubi, quando, quare;" Alani de Insulis Summa de Arte Prædicatoria, ed. Migne, col. 175. "Idem in beneficio faciam; uidebo quando dem, cui dem, quemadmodum, quare;" Seneca, De Beneficiis, l. iv. cap. x.

——(b. 7. 76; *not in* c, a.) Gregory the Great was pope from A.D. 590 to 604. I doubt if the quotation is really from his works. It seems rather to be from the following. "Ne eligas cui bene facias. . . . Incertum est enim quod opus magis placeat Deo;" S. Eusebii Hieronymi Comment. in Ecclesiasten, cap. xi. 6; vol. 23, col. 1103, of Migne's edition: and see the text itself, viz. Eccles. xi. 6. Instead of "Gregory," William should have said

"Jerome." The four chief "Latin Fathers" were S. Gregory, S. Jerome, S. Augustine, and S. Ambrose; they are mentioned in Pass. xxii. 269, 270.

——(b. 7. 85; *not in* c, a.) *Hath to buggen hym bred*, hath (enough) to buy himself bread.

——(b. 7. 86; *not in* c, a.) This quotation. is not from the Bible: A similar statement is that of St Paul, in 1 Tim. vi. 8. Burton, in his Anatomy of Melancholy, pt. 2. sect. 3. mem. 3, attributes it to St Jerome, saying— "S. Hierome esteems him rich that hath bread to eat; and a potent man, that is not compelled to be a slave; hunger is not ambitious, so that it have to eat; and thirst doth not prefer a cup of gold." Burton is right, though a part of his sentence is from another source. The original passage is— "Satis diues, qui pane non indiget. Nimium potens est, qui seruire non cogitur;" S. Hieronymi Epist. cxxv, ed. Migne, vol. i. col. 1085.

70—161. This long passage (92 lines long) is peculiar to the C-text. So also is the passage contained in ll. 186—281 (96 lines long). Both passages are well worthy of attention.

71. (*not in* b, a.) *And we nyme*, if we take. *And* (= if) occurs in all the best MSS.

72. (*not in* b, a.) *Prisones*, prisoners; as explained in the note to Pass. i. 2; so also in l. 180 below. *Puttes*, pits, i. e. dungeons.

74. (*not in* b, a.) "That which, by their spinning, they manage to save up, that they spend in house-rent." *Hit* is the antecedent to *That*.

75. (*not in* b, a.) "Both in milk and meal, to make messes of porridge with, to satisfy their children with, that cry for food." Here we note the peculiar situation of the preposition *with* (see note to Pass. i. 133; and the use of *gurles* for children of either sex (see note to Pass. ii. 29). *Papelote* is evidently a sort of porridge, being made with meal and milk, and used as food for children.

79. (*not in* b, a.) *Ruel* is the Fr. *ruelle*, a little street, or lane. Cotgrave has—"la ruelle du lict, the space between the bed and the wall;" and this is the sense here, with reference to the place where the cradle was placed. See Wright's Homes of Other Days, p. 412, where we find the remark—"the space thus left between the bed and the curtains was perhaps what was originally called in French the *ruelle* (lit. the "little street") of the bed, a term which was afterwards given to the space between the curtains of the bed and the wall." Miss L. Toulmin Smith kindly sent me the following note—"there are some woods near Arundel called the Ruelle or Rewel woods; it is supposed because they are full of narrow carefully cut lanes or alleys, cut out among the trees."

80, 81. (*not in* b, a.) "Both to card and comb, to patch (or mend) and to wash, to rub and to reel, and to peel rushes." The operations of carding and combing wool are well understood. To "reel" means to wind the yarn or thread from the spindle upon a reel; see "Relyn wyth a reele, *Alabrizo*," Prompt. Parv. p. 429; and "*Deoider*, to wind (as yarn, &c.) . . . to reele;" Cotgrave. The peeling of rushes was for the purpose of making rushlights, for use in the long winter evenings; see Notes and Queries, 4 S. iii. 552, iv. 43.   Palsgrave has—"I pyll rysshes, *Ie pille des ioncz*.   In wynter tyme good houswyues pyll risshes to burne in stede of candles, *en hyuer les bonnes mesnaigieres pillent des ioncz pour les brusler en lieu de chandelles.*"

85. (*not in* b, a.) *Afyngrede and afurst*, hungry and thirsty; see note to B. vi. 269.   *To turne the fayre outwarde*, to keep up appearances, to keep up a look of respectability; a truly expressive phrase.   This description of the struggling life of the honest well-conducted poor who are "abashed for to beg, and will not acknowledge what help they need from their neighbours," is in William's best manner, and is of undying interest.   It is obviously drawn from the life, and especially from life in the poor districts of London.

91. (*not in* b, a.) "And (there are) many to grasp thereat (i. e. at his earnings), and he receives but few pence (for his work)."   The poor man has many mouths to feed with his small and hardly earned wages.

92. (*not in* b, a.) "There bread and penny-ale (we should now say "small beer ") are accepted in place of a pittance."   In other words, they are as glad to get a piece of bread and some common ale as a friar is to receive "a good pittaunce," to use Chaucer's expression (Prologue to Cant. Tales, l. 224). The modern sense of *pittance* is misleading; it was a really good thing, and Tyrwhitt well remarks, in his Glossary, that it meant "an extraordinary allowance of victuals, given to monastics in addition to their usual commons."   See *Pictantiu* in Ducange.

Thus this line runs exactly parallel to ll. 93—95, which tell us that "cold flesh and cold fish are, in their eyes, as good as roast venison; and, on Fridays and fasting-days, a farthing's worth of mussels, or as many cockles, would be quite a feast for such folks."

In the Liber Albus, p. 240, mention is made of "scallops, mussels, whelks, and cockles" being brought in ships for sale.   In the Memorials of London, p. 666, it is ordered (A.D. 1418), that "oysters and mussels should be sold at 4*d.* the bushel, 2*d.* the half bushel, one penny the *pec*, and the half *pec* at one half penny."   In 1390, mussels were sold at 8 bushels for 5*d.*; Hist. Agric. and Prices in England, by J. E. Thorold Rogers, ii. 558.   At this rate, a farthing's worth would be more than 12 quarts; a sufficient quantity.

98. (*not in* b, a.) "But beggars with bags—which brewhouses are their churches."   This remarkable use of *which* is still common in London, as is well known.   The beggars "bags" have been already noticed; see note to Pass. i. 42, and cf. l. 120 below.   The following additional illustration is worth notice.

> "If the begger haue his staf and his hode,
> One bagge behynde and another before,
> Than thynkes he hym in the myddes of his goode,
> Thoughe that his clothes be raggyd and to-tore,
> His body nere bare; he hath no thought therfore."
>
> Barclay, Ship of Fools; ed. Jamieson, i. 305.

103. (*not in* b, a.) *Lolleres lyf*, the life of a vagabond. The word *loller* occurs frequently in this passage; see ll. 107, 137, 140, 158, 159, 192, 213, 240. See note to l. 213.

103. (*not in* b, a.) "And more or less mad, according as the moon sits;" i. e. according to the moon's phases. "*Lunacy*, a species of insanity or madness; properly, the kind of insanity which is broken by intervals of reason, formerly supposed to be influenced by the changes of the moon," &c.; Webster's Dictionary. So in l. 110 below, the phrase "after the mone" means "according to the moon."

118. (*not in* b, a.) "They are like His apostles." This singular belief, that idiots were more or less inspired, was no doubt common at a time when the "fool" was an established attendant at great men's tables. Perhaps it still lingers in country places. Dean Ramsay, in his Anecdotes of Scottish Life, chap. vi., gives many curious anecdotes of idiot wit, which he introduces in the following words. "We find in the conversation of old people frequent mention of parochial functionaries, now either become common-place, like the rest of the world, or removed altogether and shut up in poor-houses or mad-houses—I mean *parish-idiots*—eccentric, or somewhat crazy, useless, idle creatures, who used to wander about from house to house, and sometimes made very shrewd, sarcastic remarks upon what was going on in the parish. They used to take great liberty of speech regarding the conduct and disposition of those with whom they came in contact; and many odd sayings which emanated from the parish idiots *were traditionary in country localities;*" 21st ed. 1872, p. 188.

122. (*not in* b, a.) William tells us that he was himself considered as a lunatic by some, because he did not reverently salute persons of authority whom he met in the streets. See B. Pass. xv. 5—10.

127. (*not in* b, a.) *Boyes*, servants, followers; not here used in a bad sense, as is often the case elsewhere. *Bordiours*, jesters; Fr. *bourdeurs* (Cotgrave); see l. 136.

128. (*not in* b, a.) See a fragment of what was probably the original version of ll. 128—140, quoted in Pref. III. (C-text), pp. xxxiv, xxxv. Some of the various readings are quoted in the footnotes, and denoted by an italic *I*. We may note, e. g. the curious variation in l. 144, viz.
    "Reste hym, and roste hym · by þe rede gledes."

129. (*not in* b, a.) "To receive them liberally is the duty of the rich." It was a point of courtesy to be liberal to the minstrels. "Expended at Cauntebrigge . . on bread, ale, &c. . . and in gifts to the *minstrels* of the king, and of other lords, &c.;" Riley's Memorials of London, p. 512. Cf. Pass. viii. 97; also B. xiii. 227, xiv. 24.

131. (*not in* b, a.) "Men allow all that such men say to pass, and consider it as entertaining."

140. (*not in* b, a.) "Which is the life of lollers, and of ignorant hermits." *Lollaren* is the genitive plural; cf. *kingene*, B. i. 105; *klerken*, C. v. 114. See note to l. 213.

153. (*not in* b, a.) *Fisketh,* wanders, roams. As this word is scarce, I give all the instances of it that I can find.

In Sir Gawayne and the Grene Knight, ed. Morris, l, 1704, there is a description of a foxhunt, where the fox and the hounds are thus mentioned :—

"& he *fyskez* hem by-fore · þay foundeñ hym sone"—

i. e. and he (the fox) runs on before them (the hounds); but they soon found him.

"Fyscare abowte ydylly; Discursor, discursatrix, vagulus vel vagator, vagatrix;" Prompt. Parv., p. 162. "Fiskin abowte yn ydilnesse; Vago, giro, girovago;" ibid.

"Such serviture also deserveth a check,
That runneth out *fisking,* with meat in his beck [*mouth*];"
            Tusser; Five Hundred Points, &c., ed. Mavor, p. 286.

"Then had every flock his shepherd, or else shepherds; now they do not only run *fisking about* from place to place, . . . but covetously join living to living;" Whitgift's Works, L 528.

"I *fyske,* ie fretille. I praye you se howe she *fysketh* aboute;" Palsgrave.

"*Trotière,* a raumpe, fisgig, *fisking* huswife, raunging damsell;" Cotgrave.

"Then in cave, then in a field of corn,
Creeps to and fro, and *fisketh* in and out."
            Dubartas (in Nares).

"His roving eyes rolde to and fro,
He *fiskyng* fine, did mincyng go."
            Kendalls' Flowers of Epigrammes, 1577 (Nares).

"Tom Tankard's cow . . . .
Flinging about his halfe aker, *fisking* with her tail."
            Gammer Gurton's Needle, i. 2.

"*Fieska,* to *fisk* the tail about; to *fisk* up and down;" Swedish Dictionary, by J. Serenius.

"*Fjeska,* v. n. to fidge, to fidget, to *fisk*;" Swed. Dict. (Tauchnitz).

154. (*not in* b, a.) *A begeneldes wyse,* in the guise of a beggar. The word *begeneld* does not seem to occur elsewhere, but we may compare it with the form *beggilde,* which occurs in two MSS. as a various reading for *beggares* in the following extract :—"Hit is *beggares* rihte uorte beren *bagge on bac,* and burgeises for to beren purses;" Ancren Riwle, ed. Morton, p. 168. It thus appears that *begeneld, beggild,* and *beggare* are nearly equivalent forms; *beggilde* (with -*e* suffixed) being either a genitive plural or a genitive sing. *feminine.* The *bag* was the beggar's constant appendage; see note to Pass. i. 42

——(b. 7. 91; a. 8. 75.) *With wehe,* with a neighing noise, as explained in the note to Pass. v. 20, and with reference to Jer. v. 8. Probably *wo* in [a] has a similar meaning; see Crit. Notes to A-text, p. 148.

157. (*not in* b, a.) "And moreover to a garment, to cover his bones with."

168. (b. 7. 92; a. 8. 76.) *Beggers of kynde,* beggars by nature, "born beggars," as we should say. In [b] and [a] we have a different reading.

169. (b. 7. 93; a. 8. 77.) In [b], the word *he* is used quite indefinitely, so that *he* = one of you; cf. *heo* = they [a]. Neither in [a] or [b] is it

made quite clear whether the breaking of the child's bone is accidental or not; but in [c] we find an explicit statement that there were parents so detestably wicked as to break a bone of one of their own children, in order to appeal more powerfully to the sympathy of those from whom they begged. William was not likely to make any mistake upon this point, as he was so well acquainted with the home lives of the poor. Indeed, we find the same statement made at other periods. Thus, in Barclay's Ship of Fools, ed. Jamieson, i. 304, we find—

" Some other beggers falsly for the nonys
  Disfygure theyr children, got wot, vnhappely,
  Manglynge theyr facys, and brekynge theyr bonys,
  To stere the people to pety that passe by ;
  There stande they beggynge with tedyous shout and cry,
  ·There owne bodyes tournynge to a strange fassion
  To moue suche as passe to pyte and compassyon."

Mr Wright remarks that "the roads, in the Middle Ages, appear to have been infested with beggars of all descriptions, many of whom were cripples, and persons mutilated in the most revolting manner, the result of feudal wantonness and feudal vengeance;" Homes of Other Days, p. 338. Many of the cripples, however, were merely lazy tramps who shammed lameness; see the chapter on Gipsies, Tramps, and Beggars in P. Lacroix, Manners, Customs, and Dress during the Middle Ages, especially the pictures of the sham lame beggars, p. 469; also, at p. 471, the description of the Cour des Miracles, so called because the sham cripples who resorted thither at night to feast and enjoy themselves were *miraculously* restored to health. Compare Burns's poem of The Jolly Beggars. For notices of sham beggars in London, see Riley's Memorials of London, pp. 390, 445. Cf. Pass. ix. 138.

170. (b. 7. 94; a. 8. 78.) *Gooth afaytyng*, they go abegging [c]; *gon faiten*, ye go and beg [b]; *goth fayteth*, they go and beg [a]. If the reader considers the given instances of the construction explained in the note to Pass. ix. 138 (p. 164), he may perhaps see reason for thinking that the original reading in this passage was *goth afayteth*, of which the recorded readings are modifications.

——(b. 7. 98; a. 8. 82.) *Man wrought*, created as a man [b]; *men i-wrouȝt*, created as men [a]. *Hennes fare*, depart hence; i. e. die; cf. l. 53 above.

177. (b. 7. 101; a. 8. 85.) *Bedreden*. Dr Rock (Church of our Fathers, iii. 34) gives many instances of bequests to bed-ridden poor people. See also Stow's Survey of London, ed. Strype, i. B. ii. p. 23. Cf. note to Pass. ix. 188, p. 167.

178. (*not in* b, a.) *Apayed of godes sonde*, resigned to God's visitation.

179. (b. 7. 102; a. 8. 86.) *Mesels*, lepers. In a note to Amis and Amiloun, l. 1259, Mr Weber says—"About the time this story was originally invented, the loathsome disease of leprosy was in full force. According to Le Grand (Fabliaux, vol. v. p. 138), it was imported into France during the period of the first and second race of kings, by trade from Egypt, Pales-

tine, and Syria. During the reign of Louis le Jeune (1137—1180), lepers were so common, that that monarch bequeathed legacies to no less than two thousand hospitals for their reception. The degradation of lepers was excessive in those times. According to the ancient custom of Normandy, they could not inherit any property during the continuance of their malady; and in the 'Coutume de Beauvoisis' (chap. 39), they were debarred from being witness[es] in any case. They were expelled from all intercourse with men, banished to small huts by the side of the highways, and furnished with a gray mantle, a cap, and a wallet. They were obliged to give warning to the approaching traveller by their clapperdish;" Weber's Metrical Romances, iii. 365. The famous Robert Bruce died of leprosy in 1329. In 1346, an ordinance was made to exclude lepers from the City of London; Riley's Memorials of London, p. 230. In the time of Elizabeth, the "clap-dish" was often used by beggars who were not lepers, as being a convenient way of attracting attention, and there are frequent allusions to it; see Nares's Glossary. Compare—"Peine is sent by the rightwise *sonde* of God, and bi his suffrance, be it *meselrie*, or maime, or maladie;" Chaucer, Persones Tale, De Ira.

186. (*not in* b, a.) Here is another long and important passage peculiar to the latest version (ll. 186—281), on the subjects of hermits, lollers, religious duties, and negligent bishops.

188. (*not in* b, a.) I beg leave to refer the reader to Cutts's Scenes and Characters of the Middle Ages, which contains four chapters on the Hermits and Recluses of those times. The present passage (ll. 188—211) is quoted and commented upon at pp. 100, 101; and again, at pp. 95, 97, 102, the author cites, in illustration, Pass. i. 1—4 (which is compared with xi. 1, 2), Pass. i. 27—32, 51, 53—55; ix. 146, 147; and B. xv. 267—273. See the note to Pass. i. 51. See also Mrs Jameson's Sacred and Legendary Art, Malory's Morte Darthur, bk. xii. c. 3, bk. xiii. c. 16, bk. xv. c. 4, bk. xvi. c. 3—6, bk. xviii. c. 22, bk. xxi. c. 10; Mr Perry's preface to the English Prose Treatises of Richard Rolle de Hampole (E. E. T. S.); Spenser's Faerie Queene, i. 1. 29—35; Percy's Hermit of Warkworth; Kingsley's The Hermits; art. *Hermitages* in English Cyclopædia (Supplement to "Arts and Sciences"), &c. Two good examples of lives of English hermits are afforded by the A.S. version of the Life of St Guthlac, hermit of Crowland (ed. C. W. Goodwin), and the life of Richard Rolle de Hampole.

190. (*not in* b, a.) The construction is awkward, but the sense readily appears by taking 'þe contrarie' in l. 193 as an adverbial phrase, with the force of 'contrariwise.' There is a pause at the end of l. 189, and "These lolleres" is in apposition with the "eremites" in l. 188. The sense is—"These lollers, &c., contrariwise covet all that the old holy hermits hated and despised, viz. riches, and reverences, and rich men's alms." The passage seems to have been written in hot haste, under the influence of strong feelings of indignation. It is clear that the "lollers" did not covet the contrary of riches, but the contrary of what holy hermits hated. There is no

real difficulty here; the grammatical construction is certainly awkward, but the language strong and intelligible.

194. (*not in* b, a.) Here *boyes* is used contemptuously, as it probably is in Pass. i. 78, and not as in l. 127 above. *Bollers*, drunkards, men who were too fond of the *bolle* (bowl). Cf. "Thise cokkers [cockfighters] and thise *bollars;*" Towneley Myst. p. 242. "Both *bollers* of wyne and eche a gadlyng;" Meditations on the Supper of our Lord, ed. J. M. Cowper (E. E. T. S.), l. 477. "And I would to God, that in our time also we had not just cause to complain of this vicious plant of unmeasurable *Bolling*," i. e. hard drinking; Lambarde's Perambulation of Kent, ed. 1656, p. 386.

195. (*not in* b, a.) *Lyf-holy*, holy of life. Mr Way seldom made a mistake, but he misunderstood and misprinted this word. At p. 303 of his edition of the Promptorium Parvulórum, read "LYYF-HOLY, *Devotus, sanctus.*"

196. (*not in* b, a.) See Pass. xviii. 6—8, and 28—31.

197. (*not in* b, a.) "Some received their sustenance from their relatives, and from no one else." Here *lyf* = a person, man; as in other passages.

200. (*not in* b, a.) See the same statement in Pass. xviii. 11.

203. (*not in* b, a.) See another version of ll. 203—281, printed at length in Pref. III (C-text), pp. xxxv, xxxvi. The reading *howsen* is much to be preferred to *edefyen.* "Many of the hermitages were erected along the great highways of the country, and especially at bridges and fords, apparently with the express view of their being serviceable to travellers;" Cutts, Scenes and Characters, p. 103. "It is to be observed that hermitages were erected, for the most part, near great bridges and high roads," &c.; Blomefield, Hist. of Norfolk, i. 534. Hence the knights-errant, in the Morte Darthur, frequently come to a hermitage, and pass a night there; see note to l. 188.

204. (*not in* b, a.) That the ranks of the monks and friars were recruited from amongst the very poorest of the working-classes, is notorious.

> "And commouly soche ben comen
>   Of poore peple, and of hem begete,
> That this perfection han inomen,
>   Her fathers riden nat but on her fete,
> And traunilen sore for that thei eate," &c.
>
> Plowman's Tale, pt. iii.

See also P. Pl. Crede, 744—753.

211. (*not in* b, a.) "Or one of some order (of friars), or else a prophet." *Prophet* is probably here synonymous with *hermit*, as Mr Cutts suggests; otherwise, it refers to the privileged idiots who are described as prophecying in l. 114. See note to l. 118 above.

212. (*not in* b, a.) The Latin means—"It is not lawful for you to conform the law to your will, but it is for you to conform your will to the law." I do not know whence it is quoted.

213. (*not in* b, a.) *Kyndeliche*, naturally, properly, rightly. The argument is that the term *loller* as a term of reproach may be rightly applied to these false hermits. A man who lolls about must be one who is lame or maimed;

for "it hints at some accident;" l. 216. Just so do these hermits "loll" against right belief and law, offering but a lame and maimed obedience to the ordinances of the church. William proceeds to shew this by an enquiry into their conduct, and lays stress upon the word "obedience," which occurs four times, viz. in ll. 220, 222, 235, 241.

This passage throws much light upon the word *loller*. It proves beyond all doubt that the true sense of the word, in "englisch of oure eldres," was one who lolls about, or in other words, a lazy vagabond. Moreover, our English word, though purposely confused with the Low-Latin term *lollardus*, originally existed independently of it. To make the confusion still greater, the Latin term *lollardus* and the Old English *loller* were mixed up with jests about *lolia*, or tares, which the Wycliffites were accused of sowing amongst the good wheat of the church's doctrines. For further information, see note to Pass. vi. 2. In the Towneley Mysteries, p. 310, the demon Tutivillus is made to say—

> " Now am I master-lollar,
> And of sich men I melle me."

It is to be regretted that no very early example of *lolle* in its old sense has yet been found. Still we may note the examples of it in Pass. vii. 199; xv. 153; and in P. Pl. Crede, 224. And see the note to l. 218 below.

I believe this is the sole instance in which our author bears *direct* witness to the sense of an old English word.

216. (*not in* b, a.) "Or maimed in some member; for it hints at (lit. sounds like) some accident." *Meschief* means some mischance or accident, as in l. 179 above. For *souneth*, cf. Chaucer, Prol. 307, &c.

218. (*not in* b, a.) *Lollen*, i. e. offend by disobedience; see note to Pass. vi. 2. The sense is greatly cleared up by the extra line preceding this in the fragment printed in Pref. III (C-text), p. xxxv., viz.—

> "So þise lewed lollers · as lame men þey walken."

226. (*not in* b, a.) This is evidence that wolves were still found in England at this period, though probably only "in waste places." They are called "wilde woluves" in the version of this passage printed in the Pref. to C-text, p. xxxvi.

228. (*not in* b, a.) For *mete*, the reading *noon* occurs in the fragment printed in Pref. III (C-text), p. xxxvi. Cf. the expression "at mydday meel-tyme," l. 246; and see Pass. vii. 429, 434; and note to Pass. ix. 146. In this passage, our author is expressly speaking of Sunday. The whole of this passage is important, as shewing what was expected of well-conducted people.

233. (*not in* b, a.) "And fulfil those fasts, unless infirmity has caused it to be otherwise." This curious use of *make* occurs several times; cf. Pass. viii. 4, 28, 65.

238. (*not in* b, a.) *And*, if (see footnote). *Worth*, will be.

240. (*not in* b, a.) *Where*, whether. In l. 242, it may mean either *whether* or *where*; probably the latter.

243. (*not in* b, a.) All the MSS. read *As*, signifying 'as for instance.'
We might think that "*At* matyns" would be a simpler reading, but it would
be quite a mistake to substitute a modern idiom for an old one against all
authority.

249. (*not in* b, a.) The conduct of a friar at table is described at length in
Pass. xvi. 30—175, q. v. Cf. P. Pl. Crede, 760—774.

251. (*not in* b, a.) *In this worlde*, at a worldly occupation.

255. (*not in* b, a.) Compare the following:—

> "The cause why so many prestis lackyth wyt
> Is in you bysshops, if I durst trouth expresse,
> Which nat consyder what men that ye admyt
> Of lyuynge, cunnynge, person, and godlynes;
> But who so euer hymself therto wyll dresse,
> If an angell be his brokar to the scribe,
> He is admyttyd, howebeit he be wytles;
> Thus solde is presthode for an vnhappy brybe."
>
> Barclay's Ship of Fools, ed. Jamieson, ii. 63.

257. (*not in* b, a.) "Certainly, if one durst say so, Simon is as it were
asleep; it were better for thee to keep watch, for thou hast a heavy responsibility." The allusion is to Mark xiv. 37, 38—"Et ait Petro, Simon,
dormis? non potuisti una hora uigilare? Uigilate et orate," &c. William
here addresses a bishop, whom he calls Simon, as being a successor of Simon
Peter. He also insinuates a satirical hint at Simon Magus; see note to Pass.
vi. 79. Compare Gower, in the Prol. to Conf. Amantis—

> "And that thei mighten flee the vice
> Which *Symon* hath in his office."

Cf. Rich. Redeles, iv. 55, and the note.

260. (*not in* b, a.) "Thy barkers (i. e. dogs) that conduct thy lambs are
all blind." Suggested by Isaiah lvi. 10—"Speculatores eius caeci omnes,
nescierunt uniuersi: canes muti, non ualentes latrare." In the next line the
quotation is from Zech. xiii. 7—"Percute pastorem, et dispergentur oues."

262. (*not in* b, a.) Every shepherd used to carry a tar-box, called a *tarre-
boyste* in the Chester Plays, p. 121, or a *terre-powghe* (tar-pouch) in P. Pl.
Crede, l. 618. It held a salve containing tar, which was used for anointing
sores in sheep. See the Chester Plays, at the above reference, and compare
the shepherd's remark at p. 120 of the same—

> "Heare is tarre in a potte,
> To heale from the rotte."

And again, in a carol in Balliol MS. 354—

> "The sheperd vpon a hille he satt,
> he had on hym his tabard & his hat,
> hys *tarbox*, hys pype, & hys flagat;" &c.

263. (*not in* b, a.) "Their salue (i. e. the sheeps' salve) is made of *supersedeas*, and (carried about) in sompnours' boxes." That is, all the healing
which the sheep receive is that they are smothered with writs of *supersedeas*,
at the pleasure of meddling sompnours. See note to Pass. iii. 187. The word
boxes refers to the shepherds' tar-boxes; see note above.

264. (*not in* b, a.) *Ner aȝ shabbyd,* nearly all scabby. "Among the diseases peculiar to sheep, the *scab* is very frequently mentioned. This disease made its appearance at or about the year 1288, and became endemic. It was at first treated with copperas and verdigris, but in time ... it was discovered that tar ... was a specific for the complaint. Shortly after this, the purchase of tar is a regular entry. It is clear that the remedy was mixed with butter or lard, and then rubbed in."—Hist. of Agriculture and Prices in England, by J. E. Thorold Rogers, vol. i. p. 31. In the same work, ii. 608, it is noted that, in the year 1389, scab and sickness were very prevalent among sheep, at Alton Barnes in Wiltshire and at Leatherhead in Surrey.

265. (*not in* b, a.) Chaucer seems to allude to the same passage in his Doctoures Tale, where he says—

"Under a shepherd softe and negligent
The wolf hath many a sheep and lamb to-rent."

In his edition of Salomon and Saturn, at p. 63, Kemble quotes the Old French form of the proverb thus :—"a mol pasteur lou lui chie laine"; at p. 54, in prov. 76, we have it in Latin—"molli bergario lupus nou caccat lanam," where the word *non* is plainly inserted by mistake, and must be struck out; and lastly, at p. 46, prov. 89, he gives the same in Old High German.

273. (*not in* b, a.) "And (when) the wool shall be weighed, wo is thee then!" The reference is to the day of judgment.

275. (*not in* b, a.) *Hope,* expect, fear. So also *hope thow,* i. e. expect, in l. 290.

277. (*not in* b, a.) Here *toke* = didst bestow; cf. note to Pass. iv. 47. The sense is—"But (thou wilt hear a voice, saying)—receive this (punishment) in return for that (conduct); when (i. e. since) thou didst bestow indulgence for hire, and didst break my law," &c.

288. (b. 7. 112; a. 8. 96.) *Peter!* i. e. by Saint Peter; as in Pass. viii. 182. See also B. vii. 130.

——(b. 7. 120; a. 8. 105.) "And I will weep when I should sleep, though wheaten bread fail me (in consequence of my watching)" [b]; "And I will look loweringly upon that whereon I formerly smiled, ere my life fail" [a].

——(b. 7. 121; a. 8. 106.) *His payn ete,* i. e. ate his bread.

——(b. 7. 122; a. 8. 107.) "According to what the Psalter says, so did many others as well." Cf. "Multæ tribulationes iustorum"; Ps. xxxiii. 20 (Vulgate).

——(b. 7. 123; a. 8. 108.) "He that truly loves God, his sustenance is very easily procured" [b]; or, "is very considerable" [a]. The text alluded to here is certainly Ps. xxxiii. 11 (Vulgate), quoted a little further on, in Pass. xi. 201.

——(b. 7. 124; a. 8. 109.) *Luke.* But the reference is really to Mat. vi. 25. In another place, William makes just the reverse error; see note to B. vi. 241.

——(b. 7. 125 ; a. 8. 110.) This line recurs, very slightly altered from its form in [b]; see B. xiv. 33, with the same reference to Mat. vi. 25.

——(b. 7. 128 ; a. 8. 114.) " The birds in the field, who supplies them with food in winter? Though they have no garner to go to, yet God provides for them all." The punning motto of the Corbet family is " Deus pascit coruos." *Fynt*, findeth, provides for, as in Pass. vi. 88 ; so *fynde* in xvi. 251.

——(b. 7. 135; a. 8. 122.) The priest contemptuously suggests that Piers might *suitably* take for his text either "The *fool* hath spoken," Ps. xiv. 1 or xiii. 1, Vulgate [b]; or else " Quia literaturam non cognoui" (Ps. lxx. 15, Vulg.), i. e. for I know no learning [a]. The corresponding verse in the English version in the latter instance is quite differently expressed, being " for I know not the numbers thereof;" Ps. lxxi. 15.

——(b. 7. 136; a. 8. 123.) *Lewed lorel*, ignorant reprobate. " I play the *lorell* or the loyterer, *Ie loricarde*. . . . It is a goodly syght to se a yonge lourdayne [sluggard] play the *lorell* on this facyon ; " Palsgrave. Chaucer translates " perditissimum quemque " in Boethius, De Cons. Phil. Lib. i. pr. 4, by " euery lorel ; " see Morris's edition, p. 21. It is also spelt *losel ;* thus in P. Pl. Crede, l. 750, we have " losells," but in l. 755 the word is " lorels." In the ' Glosse' to Spenser's Shep. Kal. (July) is the odd explanation—" Lorrell, a losell ; " shewing that *lorel* was then looked upon as the older form. The Prompt. Parv. has—" Lorel or losel, *lurco ;* " see Way's note. And compare—

> " For thou canst no cattell gete,
> But liuest in londe *as a lorell ;*
> With glosing gettest thou thy mete," &c.

Plowman's Tale, in Chaucer's Works, ed. 1561, fol. xcv, back.

——(a. 8. 125, 126.) These lines are probably spurious, and introduced in the Harleian MS. as a translation of the Latin quotation. They mean— " Cast out these scorners with their cursed scolding, for I do not readily consent (*or* care) to dwell with them."

——(b. 7. 137; a. 8. 126.) I have remarked (Crit. Notes to B-text, p. 402) that *Eice* is the usual spelling of *Eiice* or *Ejice* in MSS. of the fourteenth century. Nearly all the MSS. wrongly read *Ecce*, as in Crowley's edition. The quotation is from Prov. xxii. 10—" Eiice derisorem, et exibit cum eo iurgium, cessabuntque causæ et contumeliæ."

295. (b. 7. 141; a. 8. 130.) *Meteles*, meat-less, without food ; see the passage quoted in note to Pass. vii. 159. It is a totally different word from the *meteles* in the next line, which signifies *a dream*. See the Glossary. In this line we have the third and last reference to the Malvern hills, mentioned before in Pass. i. 6, 163.

300. (b. 7. 146; *not in* a.) *Which a*, what sort of a. This is the usual idiom ; cf. Ch. Knyghtes Tale, 1817.

302. (b. 7. 148; *not in* a.) *Setten nat by songewarie*, value not the interpretation of dreams. A Metrical Treatise on Dreams (MS. Harl. 2253, fol. 119) is printed in Reliq. Antiq. i. 261. There is a chapter on Dreams in

Brand, Pop. Antiq. ed. Ellis, iii. 127; and see some curious examples of dreams in Chambers, Book of Days, i. 276, 394, 617; ii. 188. Robert of Brunne, Handl. Synne, ll. 387 scqq., says that dreams are of six kinds; and the cock in Chaucer's Nonne Prestes Tale discourses eloquently upon this subject. See also Batman upon Bartholomè, addition to lib. vi. c. 27, ed. 1582, fol. 84; and Burton, Anat. of Melancholy.

303. (b. 7. 149; a. 8. 135.) *Caton*, i.e. Dionysius Cato; cf. note to Pass. ix. 338. The quotation is from the following:—

"Somnia ne cures, nam mens humana quod optans [*vel* optat],
      Dum uigilat, sperat, per somnum cernit id ipsum."
                                        Dion. Cato; Distich. ii. 31.

This Rob. of Brunne (Handl. Synne) translates by—"ȝeue no charge to dremys;" and Chaucer (Non. Pr. Ta. 121) by—"ne do no fors of dremes."

306. (b. 7. 153; a. 8. 139.) The Vulgate has the spelling *Nabuchodonosor*, but the spelling *Nabugodonosor* is found in the MSS. of Chaucer, Wyclif, and Gower; our version has Nebuchadnezzar. The reference is properly to Dan. ii. 39, but it is tolerably clear that our author, in his two earlier versions, was really thinking of Belshazzar and the handwriting on the wall; Dan. v. 28. In the latest version, he seems to have partly perceived his mistake, as he leaves out five or six lines, and inserts l. 307 in place of them. It is remarkable that this new line does not much mend the matter, as the poet inadvertently writes the plural for the singular. He should have written *sone, him*, and *he*, instead of *sones, hem*, and *thei*.

——(b. 7. 158; a. 8. 144.) The best reading is *lees* (see footnotes to B-text); it means 'lost.' The same spelling occurs in Joseph of Arimathie, ed. Skeat, l. 125; and in Seven Sages, ed. Wright, l. 3425.

309. (b. 7. 160; a. 8. 147.) *Hailsede*, saluted; cf. B. v. 101. See Gen. xxxvii. 9, 10.

311. (b. 7. 162; a. 8. 149.) *Beau fitz*, fair son. This is a singular version of the story; for the Bible-account shews that Jacob hardly expected the dream to be fulfilled.

319. (b. 7. 169; a. 8. 156.) *Indulgences.* "When indulgences came to be sold, the pope made them a part of his ordinary revenue, and according to the usual way in those, and even in much later times, of farming the revenue, he let them out usually to the Dominican friars;" Massingberd, Hist. Ref. p. 126. Wyclif declared them to be futile; Works, i. 60; iii. 256, 362, 459; and declaims against the friars for being "moste privy and sotil procuratours of symonye and foule wynnynge, and biggynge [buying] of beneficis, of indulgensis and trinels, pardouns, and veyne privilegies;" iii. 400.

320. (b. 7. 170; a. 8. 157.) Wyclif (Works, iii. 398) uses the word *quienals*, on which Mr Arnold has the note—"*Quienal* seems to be a corruption of *quinquennale*, by which was meant an arrangement for saying mass for a departed soul during the period of five years. *Triennale* (Engl. *trinal* or *trienal*) and *annuale* are similar arrangements for three years or one

year." To which may be added, that *biennale* was a similar arrangement for the space of two years. The most common word of this description was *trental*, which meant the saying of thirty masses for the dead, usually on thirty different days. In the curious poem of 'St Gregory's Trental', pr. in Polit. Relig. and Love Poems, ed. Furnivall, pp. 83—92, the trental is directed to be performed by singing three masses on ten of the chief festivals of the year; p. 87. In the Archæologia, vol. i. c. 4, p. 11, we find the trental, annual, and biennial spoken of as "the monthes mind [i. e. remembrance], the yeares minde, the two yeares minde," &c. In Cullum's History of Hawsted, 2nd ed. p. 16, we read—"A trental of masses was, as its name implies, thirty masses, performed either one a day for 30 days together, immediately after the burial; or all together, on the thirtieth day. When the testator was so poor that he could not afford a whole trental, he sometimes ordered half a one." And, on the same page, we read that "In 1480, John Meryell left . . to the friars of Babwell, to pray for his soul a trental of masses, x *s*." "A trental of masses used to be offered up for almost every one on the burial-day;" Rock, Ch. of our Fathers, ii. 504 (note). "Why make ye men beleeue that your golden trentall sung of you, to take therefore ten shillings, or at least fiue shillings, woll bring souls out of hell, or out of purgatorie?" Jack Upland, sect. 12. Cf. Chaucer, Sompn. Ta. l. 9; Wyclif's Works, iii. 374.

322. (b. 7. 171; a. 8. 158.) *Worth faire vnderfonge*, will be well received [c]; *is dignelich vnderfongen*, is worthily received [b]; *is digneliche ipreiset*, is worthily praised [a]. By *dowel* [a, b] is meant "do-well," i. e. doing well, or the doing of good works. See note to l. 351 below. Compare Pass. xvii. 37—39.

324. (b. 7. 173; a. 8. 160.) See a paraphrase of ll. 160—187 of the A-text in Pref. I (A-text), p. x. In the Prick of Conscience, ed. Morris, pp. 104, 105, we find an explanation of "pardon;" that it is a remission of pain, and a part of the treasure of holy church, gathered together by the merits of the saints. The pope (says Richard Rolle) bears the keys of this treasure, and is God's vicar on earth, having, by succession, the power of the keys as delivered to St Peter; and not only the pope, but every bishop (though in a less degree) has the power of granting pardon. This throws some light upon the "bishops' letters" mentioned in l. 320.

342. (b. 7. 191; a. 8. 178.) *Poke-ful*, pouch-ful, a bagful or sackful. *Prouincials letteres*, provincial letters, or letters provincial. We frequently find, in Middle English, that an adjective of Romance origin takes an *-s* (or *-es*) in the plural; indeed, we have already had an instance of this in the case of the word *cardinales*, Pass. i. 132. Dr Morris draws attention to this in his Hist. Outlines of English Accidence, p. 104, sect. 105; but he adds the restriction, that the adjective is then placed after its substantive, of which he gives several examples. Such is certainly the usual arrangement, but there are a few exceptions, as in the present instance. A very clear example occurs in Chaucer's Treatise on the Astrolabe (ed. Skeat). In pt.

1, sect. 5, l. 7, the four quarters of the firmament are called the "four principals plages," but in pt. 2, sect. 31, l. 10, they are called the "four plages principalx." Again, in pt. 1, sect. 16, l. 8, we find "lettres capitals," but in pt. 2, sect. 3, l. 20, we have "capitalles lettres." See also Note to Pass. xiv. 128. In the present case, the reader may, if he prefers it, take *provincials* to be the genitive case plural of a substantive, thus making the phrase to mean "provincials' letters." Either way, the sense will be the same; the "provincial letters" referred to are evidently letters of indulgence granted by a *provincial*, which was a name given to the monastic superior, who had the direction of all the religious houses of the same fraternity in a given district termed the *province* of that order. See the term "priour prouincial" in Pass. xiii. 10; and cf. Pierce Pl. Crede, l. 328.

343. (b. 7. 192; a. 8. 179.) Here is another allusion to the "letters of fraternity." Wealthy people could, by means of these charters of fraternization, granted to them on the payment of so much money, become entitled to the prayers, masses, and merits of the order to which they thus belonged. Cf. Pass. iv. 67, and the note; xiii. 9, and the note; xxiii. 367. The present passage shews that the same rich man could belong to all the orders of friars at once; as is shewn also by the friar's remonstrance in Chaucer's Sompn. Tale,

> " What nedeth you diuerse freres to seche ?
> What nedeth him that hath a perfit leche
> To secchen other leches in the toun ? "

I give an example of the form of bequest for such a purpose. In a will dated Jan. 20, 1493, of Roger Drury, of Hawsted, we find—"if it please the abbot of Bury, and his convent, to keep a deryge [*dirige*] for me in the quere [*choir*], and masse of requiem on the next at the hey aultar, because it pleased them to make me a *brother of their chapter*, I will that the said abbot have xx *s.*, the prior vi *s.* viij *d.*," &c.; Cullum's Hist. of Hawsted, 2nd ed. p. 136.

For "fyue orders" the earlier texts have "foure ordres." On this variation, see note to Pass. ix. 191, and cf. Pref. III (C-text), p. lxxi.

345. (b. 7. 194; a. 8. 181.) "I value not the pardon at the value of a pea, or of a pie-heel." What a *pie-heel* means in this place it is not quite easy to say, nor is it of much importance, as it is obviously something of small value. It might mean a magpie's heel, or it might mean a pie-crust. The former is the more obvious interpretation, only it is rather a strange expression; the latter, though less obvious, is quite possible and (I think) much more likely, since *heel* is used provincially to mean the rind of cheese or the crust of bread; see *Heel* in Halliwell. Nearly all the MSS. agree in writing "pye hele;" but the scribe of C (Camb. MS., quoted in foot-notes to B-text) has evaded the difficulty by substituting "pese hule," and the scribe of B (Bodley MS., same text) has written "peese hole." Both these words mean a *pea-shell*, called "hoole of pesyn" in Prompt. Parv., p. 242, q. v. Though this substitution gives an easier expression, I am convinced that it is not the original reading.

The opinion expressed here was doubtless derived from Wyclif, whose words are equally explicit. "Therfore iche man do vercy penaunce for his synnes, kepe Goddis hestis, and do werkis of charite; ande ye schul have parte of alle Gods dedis in al holy chirche, als myche as Gods mercye and rightwisnesse wille, thof alle popis ande her bullis were fynally laide to slepe. And more then [i. e. than] a man disserves by gode lyif ending in charite schal he never have, for alle tho bullis on erthe;" Works, iii. 460.

347. (b. 7. 196; a. 8. 183.) It is worth while to notice how Crowley altered this line, in order to eliminate the name of Mary; see Crit. Notes to B-text, p. 403. Dr Rock comments upon this passage, in his Church of Our Fathers, iii. 341.

350. (b. 7. 199; a. 8. 186.) "That, after our death-day, Do-well may declare, at the day of doom, that we did as he bade us." Here Do-well is personified, as in l. 344.

351. (b. 7. 200; a. 8. 187.) Here terminates that part of the poem which is properly called the Vision of Piers the Plowman. (I beg leave to repeat here, on account of its importance, the Critical Note printed in the A-text, at p. 149.)

It is pretty clear that William had intended to wind up his poem here by discoursing on the excellencies of Doing Well; and, in this concluding passage, the word Do-wel accordingly occurs four times (ll. 319, 331, 344, 350), without any hint of Doing Better or Doing Best. But an afterthought suggested that Do-well, if supplemented by Do-bet and Do-best, deserved that much more should be said about it; and that, in fact, here was matter for a whole new poem. The opening lines of A. Pass. ix (which, it should be remembered, is only a prologue, and therefore, like the first prologue, much shorter than the other Passus) seem to indicate a short lapse of time between the conclusion of one poem and the commencement of the other. The poet's adventure with the two Minorite friars may possibly have had some foundation in fact; at any rate, it is very naturally inserted, and serves admirably to introduce a new Vision.

To this I must add here, that, in the C-text, all the Prologues are done away with, and Passus XI is lengthened out till it is very nearly of the same length as Passus XII.

NOTES TO DO-WEL, DO-BET, AND DO-BEST.

SCHEME OF THE CONTENTS OF C. PASSUS XI.

(B. Pass. VIII, IX; A. Pass. IX, X.)

(Wright, pp. 151—172; ll. 4900—5595.)

C-TEXT.	B-TEXT.	A-TEXT.
xi. 1—13	viii. 1—13	ix. 1—13
14—17	14—17	——
18—21	18—21	14—16
22	——	——
23—26	*like* 22, 23	17, 18
27—37	24—34	19—29
——	35—38	30—33
38—43	——	——
44—49	39—44	34—39
——	45—49	40—44
——	——	45
——	50, 51	46, 47
——	52—56	——
50—55	——	——
56—66	57—67	48—58
67	68, 69	59, 60
68—77	70—79	61—70
——	——	71
78—90	80—92	72—84
——	93	85
91	——	——
92—94	*like* 94—96	86—88
——	97—100	*like* 89—92
——	——	93
——	101	*like* 94
——	——	95
——	102	96
95—101	——	——
102—107	103—108	97—103
108, 109	*like* 109	104
110—120	110—120	105—115
121	121	——
122—124	122—124	116—118
——	125, 126	——
125, 126		

(*Here begins* B. Pass. IX; A. Pass. X.)

127—139	ix. 1—13	x. 1—13
——	——	14, 15
140	14	——
——	15	——

C-TEXT.	B-TEXT.	A-TEXT.
xi. 141.	ix. 16	———
142—148	17—23	x. 16—22
———	———	23
149	24	24
———	———	25
150—156	25—31	26—32
———	32	33
———	———	34
———	33	like 35
———	34—44	———
———	45—51	like 36—41
157—169	———	———
170	52	42
———	53—55	like 43—45
171, 172	———	———
———	———	46, 47
———	(a) [58]	(a) 48
173	like 56	like 49
———	57	———
———	(a) 58	(a) [48]
174	59	50—80
———	60—65	———
175—181	———	———
182, 183	like 66, 67	———
184	———	———
———	68—92	———
———	93	like 81
———	———	82—126
———	94—96	———
185	like 97	———
———	98—106	———
186—201	———	———
202, 203	like 107, 108	like 127—130
204	109	131
———	110, 111	133, 132
———	———	134
———	112—117	———
205—210	———	———
———	118—120	135, 136
———	———	137—144
211	like 121	like 145
212—219	———	———
220	like 122	like 146
———	———	147—151
[cf. 249—251]	123—129	like 152—158
221—232	130—141	159—170
———	———	171
233—235	142—144	———
———	145—150	———
236—248	———	———
249—251	[cf. 123—125]	[cf. 152, 153]

C-TEXT.	B-TEXT.	A-TEXT.
xi. 252, 253		
—		
254, 255	ix. 151—157	x. 172—179
	158, 159	
	160—163	180—183
256—269		
(b) 270	(b) [166]	(b) 184
271		
272	164	185
273		
274	165	186
(b) [270]	(b) 166	(b) [184]
275	167	187
276—282	168—174	188—194
283	like 175	
—	176	like 195
284—292	177—185	
293—295	like 186—189	196—199
—		200—203
	190, 191	—
296		
297—303	192—198	204—210
304	199	
305		—
306—308	200—202	
—	203—205	211—213
	206	—
309, 310	—	

NOTES TO C. PASSUS XI.

(B. Pass. VIII, IX; A. Pass. IX, X.)

1. (b. 8. 1; a. 9. 1.) *Thus robed in russett.* In the Pref. to B-text, p. xxviii, it is noted that MS. 201 in Corpus Christi College, Oxford, has two spurious lines at the commencement of this Passus, and begins thus :—

> And wanne y awaked was · y wondred were y were,
> Til þat y be-þowhte me · what þyng y dremede,
> & y-Robet in russet · gan rome a-bowhte.

In the footnote at the same page, it is suggested that the scribe seems to have meant us to read "& y, Robert, in russet," as he writes the word "Robt," with a stroke through the *b*. It is easy to see how such a mis-reading may have given rise to the fiction that the author's name was *Robert*. Cf. Pref. to B-text, p. xxii, last line but one.

All three texts agree in making the Vision of Do-well begin here. We also see that the author's original idea was to consider this Passus as an *introductory* one, or a mere Prologue; and this is why Passus IX of the A-text and Passus VIII of the B-text are both rather short; the former containing but 118, and the latter but 126 lines. But, in the C-text, he gave up the idea of introductory Prologues, which occasioned two alterations. The former was, that he called the opening Passus of the whole poem by the name of *Passus I*, instead of by the name of *Prologus*. The latter was, that, being no longer bound to the idea of inserting an introductory Prologue at the beginning of the poem of Do-well, he more than doubled the length of the present Passus, by putting Passus VIII and IX of the B-text together, and writing some new lines. Thus it came about that the divisions of the poem are much less distinctly marked in the C-text, and we may consider the whole work, in that form, as *continuous*, viz. from Pass. I (the first) to Pass. XXIII (the last).

I have already remarked (Pref. I, p. xxxii) that the opening lines of this Passus seem to imply that a short interval elapsed between the first composition of Piers the Plowman (properly so called, viz. A-text, Prol. and Pass. i—viii) and of the Vision of Do-wel (A. Pass. ix—xii).

It is well worth remark, that the opening lines of the present Passus certainly gave the key-note to the remarkable poem by another hand, known as Pierce the Ploughman's Crede; see my edition of that poem, Pref. p. xii.

I would also direct attention to the note to Pass. x. 351, on p. 201.

A long passage, beginning with the first line of the present Passus, is quoted, with notes, in Warton's Hist. of Eng. Poetry, ed. 1840, vol. ii. pp. 45 and 66; ed. 1871, vol. ii. pp. 251. The notes in the edition of 1840 are not much to be trusted.

Russet was a name given to a coarse woollen cloth, of a reddish brown colour. "*Russet, birrus* or *burreau* [or *boret*], *cordetum*, and *sarcilis* are quoted by the indefatigable Strutt, as coarse woollen cloths used for the garments of the lower orders during the thirteenth century;" British Costume, p. 120. Russet was the usual colour of hermits' robes; Cutts, Scenes and Characters of the Middle Ages, p. 97. We learn from the short poem on Arther, ed. Furnivall (E. E. T. S. 1864), l. 582, that a "russet cote" was the outer dress of a nun. In an Act passed in 1363, to restrict the dress of the peasantry, it was ordered that all people not possessing 40 shillings' worth of goods and chattels "ne usent nule manere de drap, si noun blanket et *russet* laune de xii*d*," i. e. shall not wear any manner of cloth, except blanket and russet wool of twelvepence; Stat. Realm, i. 381; see Bardsley's Eng. Surnames, p. 394; Our English Home, p. 108. To be "clad in russet" became an almost proverbial phrase for wearing homely garments; see Pass. xvii. 298, 342. Wyclif's followers, according to Knighton, were commonly "dressed in russet, that is, in unbleached and undyed cloth;" Historical Gleanings, by J. E. T. Rogers, 2nd Ser. p. 37; Hist. Agric. and Prices, by the same, i. 575. And lastly, russet was especially used by shepherds, and this is what our author chiefly refers to in the present passage, since he tells us that he was arrayed like a shepherd; cf. note to Pass. i. 2. Bp. Hall (Satires, bk. i. sat. 3) has the phrase *vile russetings*, applied to country clowns; see *Russet* in Richardson.

2. (b. 8. 2; a. 9. 2.) *Al a somer seson*, all the summer; alluding to the Visions which he saw "on a May morning," Pass. i. 6; B. v. 9. In the two

earlier texts, the poet sees two visions in one morning (B. i. 6; v. 9), and wakes at noon (B. vii. 140); after which he here describes himself as wandering about all the succeeding summer. In the C-text, a long interval occurs between those two visions, during which the poet talks with Reason "in a hot harvest;" Pass. vi. 7.

4. (b. 8. 4; a. 9. 4.) "If any one knew where Do-well lodged, and what sort of a personage he might be, I enquired of many a man." For *what* = what sort of a, cf. note to Pass. iii. 17. The notion of *Do-well* was suggested by the 'two lines' of which 'the pardon of Piers the Plowman consisted;' see Pass. x. 286, 289. The poet having once learnt that Do-well leads to life eternal, dwells upon the idea (see Pass. x. 318, 319, 321, 323, 331, 344, 350), and now determines to find out what Do-well is, and where he resides.

8. (b. 8. 8; a. 9. 8.) *Two freres*, two friars. There is a special reason for the mention of *two*, viz. that the friars often went about in pairs. See Chaucer, Sompn. Tale, l. 32. Compare—"What betokeneth that ye [freres] go tweine and tweine togethir?" Jack Upland, sect. 23.

9. (b. 8. 9; a. 9. 9.) "Masters of the Minorites;" i.e. masters, or men of superior learning, belonging to the order of the Minorites or Grey Friars. There is, too, a special force in the word *Maisteres*, as it signifies that these two Minorites were both 'masters of divinity,' a title much coveted by some of the order, who wore caps to signify that they had obtained it, as explained in Wyclif's Works, iii. 376. Compare the following passage from The Praier and Complaint of the Ploweman, pr. in Harl. Misc. vi. 110.—"But, Lorde, these glosers seggeth, that they ne desyren nat the state of *mastrie* to ben worschuped thereby, but to profite the more to thy puple, when they prechen thy worde. For, as they seggen, the peple wolden leven more the prechinge of a *mayster* that hath y-taken a state of scole [i.e. a degree] than the preching-inge of a-nother man that hath not y-take the state of *maystrye*." See note to P. Pl. Crede, l. 29, and see ll. 33, 276—301, 574—584, and 831—840 of that poem.

13. (b. 8. 13; a. 9. 13.) The words *doth me to wytene*, i.e. cause me to know [b], must be supposed to be uttered by William to the Minorites.

20. (b. 8. 20; a. 9. 16.) *Contra*, i.e. I dispute that. The author speaks 'as a clerk,' because he uses a Latin word common in the schools.

21. (b. 8. 21; a. 9. 16.) The full text is—"Septies enim cadit iustus, et resurget: impii autem corruent in malum;" Prov. xxiv. 16. But, for *enim*, our author has *in die;* and the same reading is quoted in Hampole's Pricke of Conscience, l. 3432; ed. Morris, p. 94. Hampole renders the passage by—

"Seven sythes [*times*] at the lest of the day
The ryghtwys falles; that es to say,
In sere [*various*] syns that er veniel,
But som er mare, and som les to fel."

32. (b. 8. 29; a. 9. 24.) *A forbusene*, an example, similitude; i.e.

parable; cf. Pass. xviii. 277, and the note. The following parable, of the man in the wagging boat, is well illustrated by the curious book called the Shepherds Kalender. In an edition printed in 1656, at signature H 6, there is a picture of a man in a ship, steering with a paddle; behind him is portrayed a demon, who tries to rock the boat; in front of him, above, is God the Father (or perhaps Christ), who encourages him to proceed. The text has—"Chap. XIII. Hereafter followeth of the man in the Ship, that sheweth the unstablenesse of the world . . .

> Nos sumus in hoc mundo, sicut navis super mare,
> Semper est in periculo, semper timet accubare,
> Prævigilanti nos oportet remigare," &c.

See further information in Strutt's Manners and Customs, ii. 111, and an explanation of the corresponding picture and passage of the French Kalendrier des Bergers in Lacroix; Manners, Customs, and Dress during the Middle Ages, p. 254. The idea here referred to is the very common one to which an allusion may be found in our Baptismal Service—"that he . . . may be received into the ark of Christ's Church; and . . . may so pass the waves of this troublesome world," &c. In the Metrical Homilies edited by Mr Small, at p. 134, is a homily upon the miraculous stilling of the tempest upon the sea of Galilee; and the homilist goes on to compare the ship in which were Christ and His disciples to holy church—

> "For schip fletes on the flode,
> And hali kirc, wit costes gode,
> Fletes abouen this werldes se,
> Flouand wit sin and caitifte."

See Specimens of English, 1298 to 1393, ed. Morris and Skeat, p. 90. In the Old English Homilies ed. by Dr Morris, 2nd Series, there are at least three allusions to the comparison of the world to the sea; see p. 42, l. 4; p. 142, l. 1; and p. 160, l. 6. In Barclay's Ship of Fools (ed. Jamieson, i. 18) we read—"This boke is named the Shyp of foles of the worlde; for this worlde is nought els but a tempestous se in the whiche we dayly wander." In Ælfric's Homilies, ed. Thorpe, ii. 385, this similitude, as deduced from the account of the stilling of the tempest, is attributed to St Augustine. Accordingly, we find in his works the source of all these allusions, in the words—"Interea nauis portans discipulos, i. e. ecclesia, fluctuat et quatitur tempestatibus tentationum; et non quiescit uentus contrarius, i. e. aduersarius ei diabolus, et impedire nititur ne perueniat ad quietem," &c.; S. Aug. Sermo lxxv. cap. iii, ed. Migne, v. 475. See other passages from the fathers cited in Trench on the Miracles, 6th ed., pp. 148, 149.

34. (b. 8. 31; a. 9. 26.) In a MS. Glossary, printed in Reliq. Antiq. i. 6, we find—"vacillare, to wagge, sicut navis in aqua."

35. (b. 8. 32; a. 9. 27.) "Causes the man often to stumble, if he stands up" [c]; or, "to fall, and again to stand up" [b]; or, "to stumble and fall" [a]. The notes in Warton, ed. 1840, ii. 46, 67, are not much to the purpose. Mr Wright well shews that the reading of the B-text, though rather awkward, is not wrong; "to falle and to stonde" means "to fall,

and again to rise," and is justified by the text quoted in the note to l. 21—
"cadit iustus, *et resurget*." See note to l. 52 below.

42. (*not in* b, a.) *Foxdinge*, temptation; not 'folly,' as wrongly explained
by Whitaker.

44. (b. 8. 39; a. 9. 34.) This comparison of the world to the sea is to be
found in the continuation of the Metrical Homily quoted in the note to l.
32 :—

> " Bi salte water of the se .
> Ful gratheli mai bisend be
> This werldes welth, auht, and catel,
> That werdes men lufes ful wel ;
> For salte water geres men threst,
> And werdes catel geres men brest," &c.

See the whole passage, quoted in Specimens of English, 1298—1393, ed.
Morris and Skeat, p. 92. Cf. note to l. 32 above.

46. (b. 8. 41; a. 9. 36.) "That move about (or fluctuate), just as the
winds and storms do." There is no necessity for inserting *aren* after
wederes, as proposed in Warton, ed. 1840, ii. 68; neither is there any
authority for it.

——(b. 8. 52; *not in* c, a.) "For He (God) gave thee, as a year's-gift,
the means of taking good care of yourself; that is, (He gave you) instinct
and free will, to every creature a portion." Here *to yereszyne* means, by
way of present, or as a free gift. For *yereszyue*, see note to B. iii. 99. At
p. 83 of Cooper's Memoir of the Lady Margaret, we find—"Item, to Bygot,
servaunt to my lady the kinges moder, for bringing a *newe yeres gift* to the
quene, lxvjs. viijd." And at p. 245 of the same, Prof. Mayor says—"*A newe
yeres gift.* See Rog. Ascham *Scholemaster*, ed. 1863, xix. 206. *Autobiogr.
of Matt. Robinson*, Cambr. 1856, 22, 105. Sir H. Ellis *Orig. Letters* ser. 3
I 221. ind. to Nicolas *Privy Purse Expenses of Hen. VIII* and Madden *Privy
Purse Expenses of Mary*. Read Nichols *Progresses of Elizabeth* under each
new year, or Cooper's *Ath. Cant.* I under any statesman or bishop of her
reign. Wood-Bliss *A. O.* I 200."

52. (*not in* b, a.) Compare Chaucer, Pers. Tale (near beginning)—"But
natheles, men shulde hope that, at euery tyme that man falleth, be it neuer
so ofte, that he may aryse through penaunce, if he haue grace : but certain,
it is gret doute."

54. (*not in* b, a.) *Rather*, sooner; referring to *ende* in the previous line.
" Sooner than our death, we have no rest."

57. (b. 8. 58; a. 9. 49.) In Warton's Hist. E. P. ed. 1840, ii. 68, it is
pointed out that William here uses "one of those primitive figures which
are common to the poetry of every country; " and the following parallel is
quoted from Homer, Il. i. 88 :—

> Οὔτις, ἐμεῦ ζῶντος καὶ ἐπὶ χθονὶ δερκομένοιο,
> Σοὶ κοίλῃς παρὰ νηυσὶ βαρείας χεῖρας ἐποίσει.

It occurs elsewhere in our poem. Cf. " Al þat *lyueth* other *loketh*," xxi.
29; "And *lyues* and *lokynge*," xxii. 159; "And now art *lynynge* and

lokynge," xxii. 175. The phrase clearly means—" if I may live and have the use of my faculties;" and Dr Whitaker was quite wrong in explaining it to mean—" if I have space to live and *look in the book.*"

58. (b. 8. 59; a. 9. 50.) *Ich bykenne the Crist,* I commit thee to Christ; and the same is the sense of *I beo-take you to crist* [a]; see Pass. iii. 51. Dr Whitaker misinterprets this, and Price (in Warton) corrects him.

61. (b. 8. 62; a. 9. 54.) *Walkynge myn one,* walking alone, walking by myself. Observe the reading of F [c], viz. *al myn oone.* I will merely observe here, in passing, that all who are really conversant with Middle-English MSS. must be well aware that the word *alone* is constantly written *al one,* and that the insertion of a word like *myn* between *al* and *one* is sufficiently common, so that there can be no doubt about the derivation of the mod. Eng. *alone* from *al* (all) and *one.* A good example is in Gower's Confessio Amantis, bk. i (ed. Chalmers, p. 42)—" Within a garden *al him one.*" Some have expressed a different opinion, and amongst others, I believe, Dr Dasent; who has unadvisedly identified the present expression with the Lowland Scotch *my lane, her lane,* &c. The two expressions have only an accidental resemblance; and whilst it is quite right to connect *my lane,* and the English *lone* (lonely, lonesome) with the Icel. *laun,* none of these words have any connection with *alone.* It is a singular coincidence, certainly, that the Icel. *á laun* means nearly the same as our *alone,* but it is, at the same time, quite clear that the expressions are wholly unconnected. It furnishes us, in fact, with an excellent caution against rushing to conclusions, however specious. See examples under *án* in Grein and Stratmann; and under *one* in Gloss. to Will. of Palerne, where we find *al himself one,* l. 3316; *himself one,* l. 657; *bi hereself one,* l. 3101; *him one,* ll. 17, 4112; &c.

63. (b. 8. 64; a. 9. 58.) See Crit. Note to B-text, at p. 403. We must make [b] agree with [c] rather than with [a].

68. (b. 8. 70; a. 9. 61.) *A muche man,* i. e. a big or tall man. Cf. " He was *mike,* he was strong;" Havelok, 960. Price (in Warton) quotes from the Chronicle of England, l. 14—

" A *moche mon* com with him also,
Corineus yclepud was tho."

In the legend of St Christopher, who was of gigantic stature, we read that people were afraid of him because " he was so *moche* ;" Early Eng. Poems and Lives of Saints, ed. Furnivall, p. 63, l. 128. We may draw the conclusion that the poet was himself of large stature (cf. Pass. vi. 24); whence his nickname of 'Long Will,' B. xv. 148. We learn from l. 72 that the stranger whom the poet meets is named Thought; and he is, in fact, merely William's double, the personification of his own contemplative power, who had " followed him about these seven years," and was therefore like himself in all respects.

69. (b. 8. 71; a. 9. 62.) *By my kynde name,* by my right name, the name to which I was accustomed. He called him " Wille;" see l. 71. The same name occurs elsewhere, as in A. xii. 94; B. v. 62, viii. 124, xv. 148; C. ii. 5, &c.

73. (b. 8. 75; a. 9. 66.) "I have followed thee these seven years; sawest thou me no sooner?" Of course "these seven years" is mere indefinite expression, signifying a long while; see notes to Pass. v. 82; vii. 214.

80. (b. 8. 82; a. 9. 74.) *Trewe of hus tail,* true in his reckoning; i. e. careful never to defraud. *Tail* (French *taille*) here means *a tally;* in [b] and [a] we have *tailende,* i. e. tallying, or reckoning kept by a tally. See *tailende* in the Glossary. *Halt wel his handes,* restrains well his hands, i. e. 'keeps them from picking and stealing.'

84. (b. 8. 86; *cf.* a. 9. 78.) "And helps all men heartily, out of that which he has to spare" [c]; "And helps all men, according to what is lacking to them" [b].

85. (b. 8. 87; a. 9. 79.) *Bygurdeles,* purses; so called because they used to hang at the girdle. The word occurs in the A.S. version of Matt. x. 9— "Næbbe ge gold, ne seolfer, ne feoh on eowrum *bigyrdlum,*" have not gold, nor silver, nor money in your purses. Cf. Chaucer, Prol. 358, where we read that the "gipser" (or purse) "hung at the girdle." Hence arose the name of *cut-purse,* which, in our days, has given place to *pick-pocket.*

To-broke, broken them in twain, destroyed them. On the force of the prefix *to-,* see *to-* in the Glossary.

86. (b. 8. 88; a. 9. 80.) "Which the earl named Avarous (i. e. avaricious one) and his heirs had possession of." The Vernon MS. omits the word *Erl;* but it should have been inserted in [a] on the authority of the other MSS., which rightly omit the words *eny of.* Read, in [a], the line thus—

þat þe [Erl] Auerous · hedde, or his heires.

87. (b. 8. 89; a. 9. 81.) "And has made for himself many friends, by means of the money of Mammon." Our author seems to take Mammon to be a man's name; cf. Mat. vi. 24. His use of the word *of* here is an excellent illustration of the language of our Authorised Version in Luke xvi. 9, where also *of* = by means of. The Greek has—ἐκ τοῦ μαμωνᾶ τῆς ἀδικίας; the Latin Vulgate has—de mammona iniquitatis.

88. (b. 8. 90; a. 9. 82.) *Is ronne into religion* probably means—"has entered into the ministry," or "has entered the service of Christ." The word *religion* was frequently used to signify a religious order, as in Wyclif's Works, iii. 437, l. 8; and the word *religious* was applied to any one who had entered a religious order. Cotgrave gives "a religious house" as one of the meanings of *religion* in French. But it is difficult to imagine that our author should so deliberately recommend entry into a religious house, unless perhaps it were a house for *monks,* and not for *friars.* We must also bear in mind that Wyclif was at great pains to extend the meaning of the word *religion* beyond its old narrow limits. His tract on the Fifty Heresies of Friars begins with a protest upon this very point. He says—"First, freris seyn þat her religioun, founden of synful men, is more perfite þen þat *religion or ordir þe whiche Crist hymself made....* Cristen men sey þat þe *religion and ordir* þat Crist made for his disciplis and *prestes,* is moste perfite, moste esy, and moste siker;" Works, iii. 367. Again, in Pass. xviii. l. 47,

we find *religiouse* used quite generally, as equivalent to *men of holy churche* in l. 41 above. Whence it is clear that, whilst the words *religion* and *order* were considered as nearly synonymous, they were understood by the Wycliffites as at least including secular priests, and need not be so restricted in their sense as would at first sight appear.

Rendreþ, translates [c]; *hath rendred*, has translated [b, a]. In reading this line, the reader is sure to be reminded of Wyclif; yet the expression occurs in the A-text, written A.D. 1362; whilst the Wycliffite translation of the Bible does not appear to have been completed till about 1380. But the apparent inconsistency is easily removed by observing that our author has probably no distinct reference to Wyclif in particular, but rather to the *idea* of which Wyclif's work was the successful realisation. He is praising the conduct of those who were persuaded that a translation of the Bible was necessary; and we may readily suppose that, even as early as 1360, many were in the habit of translating portions of the Bible for the use of the unlearned in a more systematic way than it had been done before. The Wycliffite version itself was not the work of a short period only, nor of one man. Our extant Early English homilies shew that, whilst the preachers invariably quoted the Latin version of the Bible, they commonly gave a translation of the passage at the same time. Neither were metrical English versions of parts of the Bible at all uncommon at an early period. The reader who wishes for further information should consult the admirable Preface to the Wycliffite Versions, by Sir F. Madden and Mr Forshall.

One conclusion may be drawn, at any rate, with much confidence. If the word *religion* in this line is to be taken (which I doubt) in its strictest sense of "religious order," then there can be no reference here to Wyclif, the enemy of all monks and friars.

90. (b. 8. 92; a. 9. 84.) It will be observed that William mistranslates the Latin text, taking *suffertis* as if it were in the imperative mood. It is not, however, so much a mistranslation as due to a variation of reading, since the MSS. of the A-text actually have *sufferte*.

92. (b. 8. 94; a. 9. 86.) *Croce*, crosier [c]; badly spelt *crosse* or *cros* [b, a]. William goes on to describe the bishop's crosier as furnished with a hook at the upper end, and a spike at the lower. In the French prose romance of the Seynt Graal (ed. Furnivall, p. 78), a bishop is described as holding "the staff of Vengeance-and-Mercy," the latter being denoted by the bend at the top, the former by the spiked end; see my note to the alliterative version of Joseph of Arimathie, l. 300 (where, however, I have unluckily reversed the significations of the symbols, by a slip which may be corrected). The 17th line of Chaucer's Freres Tale alludes to a bishop catching offenders "with his crook." So here the bishop is described as drawing men to good life by the hook of the crosier, whilst he strikes down hardened transgressors with the spike. *Croce* means a crook, and is a different word from *cross*; see *Croce* in Prompt. Parv., p. 103, and note 5, *which consult*. On the bishop's crosier, see Rock, Church of Our Fathers, ii. 181—198.

94. (b. 8. 96; a. 9. 88.) *Potent*, properly a crutch, but here used as a synonym for crosier. "Potent, or crotche. *Podium*," Prompt. Parv. Way's note says—"'*Potence*, a gibbit; also a crutch for a lame man;' Cotgrave. See Ducange, v. *Potentia*.' Chaucer termed the 'tipped staf,' carried by the itinerant limitour, a 'potent;' Sompn. Tale, 7358. Cf. R. of Rose, 368, 7417; Vision of P. Ploughman (ed. Wright), 5092." A cross-potent, in heraldry, signifies a cross whose arms have ends shaped like a crutch. Lydgate uses it of the crutch with which a man walks when he goes on three feet, according to the riddle of the Sphinx; Siege of Thebes, pt. i.

95. (*not in* b, a.) This line is in explanation of the words *preuaricatores legis*, i. e. wilful evaders or misinterpreters of the law. It means—"Lords who live as it pleases them, and respect no law."

96. (*not in* b, a.) "Such men (i. e. the lords mentioned above) think that, because of their muck (i. e. wealth) and their movable property, no bishop ought to oppose their request (*or*, their command)." Whitaker's interpretation is quite wrong, as Price (in Warton) remarks; I have already given it in the Critical Notes to the C-text, p. 457.

110. (b. 8. 110; a. 9. 105.) "Only Wit will teach thee" [c]; *or*, "can teach thee" [b, a].

112. (b. 8. 112; a. 9. 107.) The curious word *þroly* occurs only in the Vernon MS. [a]. I suspect that it was the original word, but afterwards altered because our author found that many did not know what it meant. It was used most, I think, in the North and West; and its genuineness is, accordingly, the better attested by its being preserved in the Vernon MS., written out by a Southern scribe. It means quickly, earnestly; see William of Palerne, 612, 3518; Joseph of Arimathie, 91; and Stratmann's Dictionary. I draw attention to it because I think it will be found that the A-text contains several provincial words which were afterwards eliminated in order to make the poem more widely understood. William's residence in London enabled him to realize that some of the words of his native county were not known there.

118. (b. 8. 118; a. 9. 113.) "I durst propose no subject, to make him talk freely, but only so far as I then besought Thought to be a mediator between us, and to propose some matter to prove his abilities." Compare— "Of *maters* þat I thenke · to *meve* for the best;" Rich. Redeles, i. 84.

124. (b. 8. 124; a. 9. 118.) *Here is on*, here is one [c]; *Here is wille*, here is Will [b]; *Oure wille*, Our Will [a.] On the expression "our Will," see Preface to A-text, p. xxxvi, ll. 1—6.

——(b. 8. 125; *not in* c, a.) See Crit. note, B-text, p. 403.

Here begins B. Passus IX (A. Pass. X).

127. (b. 9. 1; a. 10. 1.) *Nat a daye hennes*, not a day's journey from this place.

128. (b. 9. 2; a. 10. 2.) "In a castle that Nature made, out of things of four kinds." Properly *kyne* (*kynnes*, b) is a genitive case singular in form,

though oddly used with the numeral *four*; see *cyn* in Grein's A.S. Dictionary. Indeed, we find in [a] (see footnotes) the curious form *foure skynnes*, a variation of *foures kynnes*. Compare—"Clerkes and other kynnes men," i. e. clerks and men of another sort, B. x. 69. The awkwardness of the phrase led to the dropping of the genitive sign (-*s*), and people came to regard the words as to be construed in the order in which they stood. Hence we no longer say "things of four kinds," but "four kinds of things." It is remarkable that, in some instances, the B-text preserves the genitive suffix, where the C-text drops it. Thus we have—none kynnes riche, B. xi. 185; no kyne ryche, C. xiii. 102; any kynnes catel, B. xix. 73; eny kynne catel, C. xxii. 77; many kynnes maneres, B. xvii. 193; menye kynne manere, C. xx. 158. Cf. alkin, B. prol. 222; alle kynne, C. ix. 69. We find also— þre kynne kynges, B. xix. 91; any kynnes wise, B. v. 273.

There is a note upon the word *kynnes* or *cunnes* in Weymouth's edition of the Castle of Love, p. 40, where several examples will be found. In Laȝamon, for instance, we have—on aiȝes cunnes wisan, iii. 23; monies kunnes folc, i. 73; a summes kunnes wisen, i. 168; on ælches cunnes wise, i. 344; anes kunnes iweden, iii. 207. So also "alkyns trees," Allit. Morte Arthur, ed. Brock, 3244; "what kyns schappe;" Rob. of Brunne's Chron. prol. l. 155. Other forms are—moni kunne, allirkin, this kin, what kin, &c. Several good examples will be found in the Cursor Mundi, as "sumkins," 115; "tuinkyn," 512; "serekin," 1016; &c.

See also the note to l. 150 below; and cf. note to Will. of Palerne, l. 4061.

The idea intended in this passage is the following. "Sir Dowel" is the type of perfect humanity, afterwards exemplified in the person of Christ. This humanity or human nature dwells in a castle, that is, in the body or in the flesh, as is explained in B. ix. 48 (*not in* o), where the name of the castle is said to be *Caro*. Moreover, this body is formed of four things, i. e. of the four elements.

The notion of the four elements being earth, air, fire, and water, is alluded to by Ovid, Metamorphoseon, lib. i. 26—31; but William either took it from Peter Comestor's account of the Creation, or simply adopted it as being familiar to every physician of the day who had studied (as all did) the works of Galen. See the life of Galenus in the English Cyclopædia. Dr White, in a note to the Ormulum, ii. 406, quotes a passage from St Augustine, where he says it is notorious that man's body is composed of the four elements—"notissima enim sunt quatuor primordia quibus corpus constat;" Serm. li. De Concord. Matth. et Luc. § 34. In the same passage St Augustine reminds us that there are four parts of the world, meaning the four quarters of the compass. In English we find very frequent allusions to these elements; see the Anglo-Saxon Exameron, p. 22 (ed. Norman); an Anglo-Saxon Manual of Astronomy, printed in Wright's Popular Treatises on Science, p. 17; some Middle-English verses printed in the same volume, at p. 138; Ormulum, ll. 17605—17608; Cursor Mundi, ed. Morris, pp. 23, 38; Dialogue between Solomon and Saturn, printed in Thorpe's Analecta Saxonica, 2nd ed. p. 110, and in Kemble's edition of Solomon and Saturn (Ælfric Society), p. 180; and the Questions bitwene the Master of Oxinford and his Scoler, printed in Reliquiæ Antiquæ, vol. i. p. 230.   Mr Wright quotes some of these passages in the note to l. 5157 of his edition of Piers Plowman. One of the most curious of these accounts occurs in Old Friesic, and is as follows.   "God scop thene eresta meneska, thet was Adam, fon achta wendem; that benete fon tha stene, thet flask fon there erthe, thet blod fon tha wetere, tha lierta fon tha winde, thene togta fon ta wolken, the suet fon tha dewe, tha lokkar fon tha gerse, tha agene fon there sunna; and tha blerem on thene helga om; and tha scope Eua fon sine ribbe, adames liana;" Friesische Rechtsquellen, ed. Richtofen, p. 211.   The meaning of the passage is—"God created the first man, that was Adam, of eight elements; the bone of stone, the flesh of earth, the blood of water, the heart of wind, the thought of cloud, the sweat of dew, the locks (of hair) of grass, the eyes of the sun; and then blew into him the holy breath; and then created Eve from his rib, (who was) Adam's bride."   An account of this notion in later times will be found in Nares's Glossary, s. v. Elements.   The four "humours" or "complexions" of men were connected by Galen with the four elements.   Those of a *sanguine* temperament have an excess of *blood*, due to *air*; those of a phlegmatic temperament, an excess of phlegm, or *water*; those of a melancholy temperament, an excess of the dull *earth*; and lastly, those of a choleric temperament, an excess of *fire*.   Nares well refers us to Twelfth Night, ii. 3. 10; Julius Cæsar, v. 5. 73; Ant. and Cleop. v. 2. 292; Shak. Sonnets, 44 and 45.   He also quotes from Browne, Brit. Past. i. 1, p. 8; Higgins, Mirror for Magistrates, Ferrex and Porrex, p. 76; Massinger, Renegado, iii. 2; Beaum. and Fletcher, Nice Valour, Act i. p. 312; Sir John Davies, Im. of Soul, Exordium; &c.   Similar quotations may easily be found; see Milton, Par. Lost, ii. 897.

The remark of St Augustine, that there are *four* elements as there are *four* quarters of the world, will explain an otherwise obscure passage in Solomon and Saturn, ed. Kemble, p. 178.   "Saga me, hwanon wæs Adames nama gesceapen? Ic ðe secge, from iiii steorrum.   Saga me, hwæt hátton ðage? Ic ðe secge, *Arthox, Dux, Arótholem, Minsymbrie.*"   That is—"Tell me, whence Adam's name was formed? I tell thee, of four stars.   Tell me, what they are called? I tell thee, *Arthox, Dux, Arótholem, Minsymbrie.*"   In the Reliquiæ Antiquæ, i. 288, we find these words slightly varied.

"Anothole dedit A; disis D; contulit arthos
A, messembris M.   Collige, fiat ADAM."

The simple solution is that we have here corrupted forms of the Greek words for East, West, North, and South, viz. *anatole, dusis, arctos, mesembria;* as is fully proved in a note to Dr White's edition of the Ormulum, vol. ii. p. 425.   See S. Cypriani Opera (fol. Paris, 1726), Inter Opusc. v. adscripta S. Cypr. p. xxvi; S. August. in Johan. Evang. c. ii. Tract. ix.   And this solution completely explains a passage in the Cursor Mundi, ed. Morris, p. 42, which is otherwise unintelligible.

> " Here now the resun of his nam,
> Qui þat he was cald adam.
> In þis nam er four letters laid,
> þat o þe four ȝates er said ;
> Sua micul es adam for to muth,
> Als est, and west, and north, and south."

Throughout the account of Dowel, William is partly following the traditional explanation concerning man's body, as being guarded by Conscience, and served by the Five Wits. See the Homily entitled Soul's Ward, in Early English Homilies, ed. Morris, i. 244. A similar account will be found in the Pricke of Conscience, pp. 157, 158; which presents several points of resemblance to the present passage.

130. (b. 9. 4; a. 10. 4.) It is very remarkable that William gives the names of the four elements as earth, air, *wind*, and water; putting *wind* in the place of *fire*. Whitaker coolly proposed to turn *eyre* into *fyre*, not observing that the MSS. all agree. Price (in Warton) says it is a mistake, due to the exigencies of alliteration, and calls attention to the mention of " wit, water, wind, and fire " in Pass. x. 56. I do not think it is a mistake at all, but a deliberate statement ; and that some plain distinction between *air* and *wind* was intended. William must have been thinking of some explanation similar to that given in the Cursor Mundi, ed. Morris, p. 38 ; where, after telling us that Adam was made of the four elements (l. 518), we find, at l. 539—

> " þe ouer *fir* gis man his sight,
> þat ouer *air*, of hering might ;
> þis vnder *wynd* him gis his aand,
> þe *erth*, þe tast, to fele and faand."

Here is a clear distinction between the " upper air " and the " under (or lower) wind ;" and we may, accordingly, consider that William means by " wind " that which we call *air*, but by " air " that which is expressed by the Latin *aër*, which he confuses with *æther*, and this again with *fire*. Indeed, we find him elsewhere describing the four elements as being *welkin, wind, water*, and *earth ;* B. xvii. 160; see note to that line. A similar distinction between *wind* and *air* occurs in Gower, Conf. Amantis, bk. v. In the story of Medea renewing Æson's youth, Ovid has the line—

Auræque et uenti, montesque, amnesque, lacusque ; Met. vii. 197.

But Gower turns this into what looks very like a similar allusion to the four elements. He writes—

> " To *wynd*, to *air*, to *see*, to *lond*
> Sche preide, and ek hield vp hir hond."

Whatever may be the right interpretation of the passage, it is surely best to suppose that the text is uncorrupt. It is, moreover, not a little remarkable that, in Sanskrit literature, *five* elements (or *Bhūtas*) are enumerated, viz. fire, water, earth, *air, and æther ;* see Benfey's Sansk. Dict. p. 658, col. 2.

133. (b. 9. 7; a. 10. 7.) *Anima*, the soul ; which is described as placed

within the body by Nature, and as being a "lemman" or favourite, whom
Nature loves. Similarly, in the Pricke of Conscience, l. 6707, the soul is
described as being God's daughter who is "leve and dere" to Him; and in
the Soul's Ward (in Early Eng. Hom. ed. Morris, i. 246), we are told that
within the house of man's body is the treasure that God gave Himself for,
that is, man's soul. Cf. note to l. 173.

To hure hath enuye, &c., i. e. the Prince of this world has envy (or feels
spite) towards her. Price (in Warton) remarks—"The reader will not consider the idiom of the text to be a literal translation of a modern Gallicism,
à lui a envie ; for in Early English poetry this term is never applied except
in malam partem." Cf. Pass. viii. 262.

134. (b. 9. 8 ; a. 10. 8.) "A proud pricker (or horseman) of France,
viz. the Prince of this World." To *prick* is to spur, to ride ; see Spenser,
F. Q. i. 1. 1. Dr Whitaker calls attention to this instance of "ancient
national prejudice ; for this proud pricker of France is the devil." See a
similar insinuation in All's Well, iv. 5. 40. The expression *princeps huius
mundi* is from St John, xvi. 11 ; Vulgate. version. It is perhaps worth
noting that this text is quoted very near the beginning of Peter Comestor's
Historia Scholastica, which our author may very well have consulted for his
account of the Creation in ll. 151—156, &c. Mr Wright remarks that
"until the fifteenth century there appears to have been a strong prejudice
among the lower orders against horses and horsemen ; their name was connected with oppressors and foreigners." This he exemplifies by a quotation
from his edition of Political Songs, p. 240—

> "Whil God wes on erthe and wondrede [*wandered*] wyde,
> Whet was the resoun why he nolde ryde ?
> For he nolde no grom to go by ys syde,
> Ne grucchyng of no gedelyng to chaule ne to chyde . . . .
> Herkneth hiderward, horsmen, a tidyng ich ou telle,
> That ye shulen hougen, ant herbarewen in helle !"

In Monumenta Franciscana, p. 572, we find that "the 3de [rule of the
Franciscan order] is, that the bretherne shal not *ride* withoute a grete mani-
fest necessite." Cf. Pass. vi. 158, 160.

137. (b. 9. 11 ; a. 10. 11.) *Dooth hure*, places her [c] ; *hath do hir*, hath
placed her [b, a]. *Thes marches*, these borders, these parts. *Is duke*, who
is duke [b] ; the relative being omitted, as is frequently the case. Cf. *Is*
(= which is), B. x. 369 ; *Was* (= who was), B. x. 453.

143. (b. 9. 18 ; a. 10. 17.) *Inwit*, Conscience. Cf. the "Ayenbite of
Inwyt," i. e. Remorse (lit. Again-biting) of Conscience ; the name of a
treatise by Dan Michel of Northgate, written A.D. 1340. Conscience is
represented as the keeper of the castle of man's body. In the Homily
named Soul's Ward, already referred to (upon the text Matt. xxiv. 43), the
"house-lord" or *paterfamilias* is named Wit. "Deafnesse is priuation and
let of hearing, that is the gate of the *inwit*, as Constantine saith ; " Batman
upon Bartholome, lib. vii. c. 21.

146. (b. 9. 20 ; a. 10. 19.) Here William makes the five sons of Con-

science to be See-well, Say-well, Hear-well, Work-well, and Goodfaith Go-well. This is a deviation from the original idea, which made the five guardians to be the Five Wits or Five Senses (cf. l. 170); as is (by the way) so admirably illustrated in Bunyan's allegory of the Holy War. Thus we find in the Ancren Riwle, ed. Morton, p. 48—"Omni custodia serua cor tuum, quia ex ipso uita procedit. 'Mid alle cunne warde, dohter,' seith Salomon the wise, 'wite wel thine heorte, uor soule lif is in hire,' yif heo is wel iwust. The heorte wardeins beoth the vif wittes, sihthe and herunge, smecchunge and smellunge, and eueriches limes uelunge;" &c. I. e. "With protection of every kind, daughter—saith Solomon the wise—guard well thy heart, for the soul's life is in it, if it is well guarded. The heart's wardens are the five wits, sight and hearing, tasting and smelling, and the feeling of every limb."· So in the Sermon called Sawles Warde, in Old Eng. Homilies, ed. Morris, Ser. i. p. 245, the servants of Wit are said to be the five wits; and the same account is repeated in the Ayenbyte of Inwit, pp. 154, 263. Cf. Prov. iv. 23; and see B. xiv. 54, and the note to Pass. ii. 15.

150. (b. 9. 25; a. 10. 26.) *What lyues þyng*, what thing alive, i. e. what living thing [c]; *What kynnes thyng*, a thing of what kind, i. e. what kind of thing [b, a]. For the phrase *what kynnes*, see note to l. 128 above. The word *lyues*, properly the gen. case of *lyf* (life), is often used adverbially, in the sense of *alive*; and here, it is boldly used as an adjective, as in Pass. xxii. 159, q. v. The footnotes to [c] shew that it occurs in at least five MSS.; and I can well believe that it was the author's own substitution, not-withstanding that it detracts from the alliteration, as to which he is often extremely indifferent.

151. (b. 9. 26; a. 10. 27.) *Kind*, i. e. Nature, is here explained to mean the God of nature, or the First Person of the Trinity. Cf. l. 168.

155. (b. 9. 30; a. 10. 31.) Observe the use of *aren* here, not *ben*; the Northern form, as distinguished from the Southern. We know with certainty that *aren* is here the author's own word, as the whole stress of the alliteration falls upon the initial *a*.

——(b. 9. 32; a. 10. 33.) This line is repeated further on; see B. xiv. 60.

——(b. 9. 35; *not in* c, a.) "God was singular (i. e. sole) by Himself; and yet He said *faciamus*;" i. e. He used the plural number. Our author probably made use of Peter Comestor's Historia Scholastica, where, in the account of the Creation, is the remark—"*Faciamus hominem, &c.* Et loqui-tur pater ad filium et spiritum sanctum. Uel est quasi communis vox trium personarum." See Gen. i. 26.

——(b. 9. 38; *not in* c, a.) "Just as if a lord had to write a letter, and could get no parchment—though he could write never so well, yet, if he had no pen—the letter, I believe, would never be written, for all the lord's ability." In this curious illustration of the Trinity, the Father is signified by the ability to write, and the other two Persons by the pen and parchment. In the Critical Notes to the B-text, p. 404, I have already noted that the word *lettres* (like Lat. *literœ*) has a singular sense.   See a passage (there quoted) in Barbour's Bruce, ii. 80—83.

The mention of *parchment* is interesting. "The earliest English specimen of *paper* from linen-rags which I have seen, is a small piece having an account of the Merton College larder, 1337;" Hist. Agric. and Prices in England, by J. E. T. Rogers, ii. pref. p. xvii.

157. (*not in* b, a.) *Bote yf synne hit make,* unless sin cause it (to be otherwise). Cf. Pass. viii. 4, 8, 65; x. 233.

163. (*not in* b, a.) "God will not know of (regard) them, but lets them be (lets them alone), as the Psalter says with regard to such sinful wretches." For *by* (= with regard to), see note to Pass. i. 78.

168. (*not in* b, a.) *Kynde,* the God of nature; see note to l. 151.

170. (b. 9. 52; a. 10. 42.) "Conscience and all the (five) senses are enclosed therein." Here the word *therein* must be referred back to "þat castel," in l. 142. The fact is that the author, in revising the text for the last time, inadvertently omitted the line which contains the true antecedent to *therein;* that line being B. ix. 48 (A. x. 38).

——(b. 9. 54; a. 10. 44.) *He* [b] is for *heo,* and means *she,* as already noted in the Critical Notes to B-text, p. 404; see *hir* in the next line, and *heo* in A. x. 46. But in B. ix. 56, the same form (*he*) is masculine.

173. (b. 9. 55, 56; a. 10. 45 *and* 49.) The B-text means—"But in the heart is her home, and her chief abode. But Conscience is in the head, and looks after (i. e. watches over) the heart; and, at his will, he assents to whatever is pleasing or displeasing to the Soul." This notion, that *anima* or "life" is in the heart, is derived from the text already quoted in the note to l. 146, viz. Prov. iv. 23—"Keep thy heart with all diligence; for out of it are the issues of life." In a dialogue between Solomon and Saturn, ed. Kemble, p. 189, we find—"Saga me, hwær restað ðæs mannes sáwul ðonne se líchama slépð? Ic ðe secge, on þrim stówum heó bið; on ðám brægene, oððe on ðære heortan, oððe on ðám blóde." The same idea occurs again at p. 219 of the same volume, in The Master of Oxford's Catechism—"Where resteth a manys soule, whan he shall slepe? In the brayne, or in the blode, or in the herte."

Here, again, we see the influence of Galen's doctrines. "He divided the functions into three great classes. The *vital* functions are those whose continuance is essential to life; the *animal* are those which are perceived, and for the most part are *subject to the will;* whilst the *natural* are performed without consciousness or control. He then assumed certain abstract principles upon which these functions were supposed to depend. He conceived the first to have their seat in the *heart,* the second in the *brain,* and the third in the *liver;*" Eng. Cyclopædia, s. v. Galenus.

In the Crit. Note to B. ix. 57 (B-text, p. 404), I have noted Crowley's reading of *ledyth* for *lat;* adding that *lat* may be a contraction of *ledeth.* But it may equally well be considered as a contraction for *leteth,* i. e. lets, permits, assents to.

——(a. 10. 55 ; *not in* c, b.) "There is he (i. e. Conscience) most active; unless blood cause it (to be otherwise); for when blood (i. e. animal passion) is more active (*or* fiercer) than the brain, then Conscience is fettered, and becomes also wanton and wild, and devoid of reason." This alludes to the idea in the last note, of the difference between the Brain, the Blood, and the Heart, considered as residences of the Soul. See a curious poem on the subject of the three Souls in man, which reside respectively in the Brain, the Heart, and the Liver, printed in Treatises on Popular Science, ed. Wright, pp. 138—140.

——(a. 10. 62 ; *not in* c, b.) "Sir Prince of this world" is the devil, as already explained; see note to l. 134. The same is therefore the meaning of "þe Pouke," as is equally evident from B. xiv. 190; C. xix. 50. Compare——   "I wene that knyght was a *pouke*,"

i. e. I believe that knight was a demon; Rich. Cœur de Lion, l. 566, in Weber's Met. Rom. ii. 25. The word is the Icelandic *púki*, an imp, or the devil. Hence Shakespeare's *Puck*. See *Puck* in Halliwell, and consult Keightley's Fairy Mythology.

——(a. 10. 73—75 ; *not in* c, b.) "And keep himself clear from all imputation, when he grows beyond childhood, and save himself from sin, as is his duty; for, whether he work well or ill, the blame is his own." The word *wit* = *wyte*, blame; see the reading of MS. U in the footnote to l. 75.

——(a. 10. 78 ; *not in* c, a.) *Route*, to slumber, lit. to snore; *reste*, to take rest, remain; *rooten*, to take root.

174. (b. 9. 59 ; *not in* a.) "And great woe will be to him, who misspends (*or* misrules, *b*) his Conscience." William proceeds to cite the examples of Lot, as in Pass. ii. 25; of Noah (see Gen. ix. 21); and of Herod, whom Chaucer couples with Lot in a similar manner in his Pardoner's Tale.

——(b. 9. 63 ; *not in* c, a.) The introduction of the text "Qui manet in caritate" is seen to be much more natural here than it might at first appear to be, if we remember that it was commonly quoted in the Graces before and after meat. See Babees Book, ed. Furnivall, p. 382; and cf. Pass. xvi. 266.

——(b. 9. 64, 65 ; *not in* c, a.) "Allas! that drink shall destroy them that God redeemed at a dear price; and that it causes God to forsake them that He created in His likeness!"

181. (*not in* b, a.) *To fynde with hym-selue*, to provide for himself therewith.

——(b. 9. 70 ; *not in* c, a.) "All these lack responsibility, and teaching is necessary (for them)." Cf. B. v. 38.

——(b. 9. 72 ; *not in* c, a.) The "four doctors" are St Gregory, St Jerome, St Augustine, and St Ambrose. See Pass. xxii. 269, 270.

——(b. 9. 80 ; *not in* c, a.) "Nor lack bread nor pottage, if prelates did as they ought." *And* = *an*, if. So also in l. 82.

——(b. 9. 84 ; *not in* c, a.) "Since Jews, whom we esteem as comrades of Judas." See note to Pass. i. 56; and cf. B. prol. 35.

——(b. 9. 86; *not in* c, a.) "Why will not we Christians be as charitable with Christ's property as Jews, who are our teachers, are (with theirs)? Shame upon us all!" The commons, for their uncharitableness, I fear, shall pay the penalty."

——(b. 9. 91; *not in* c, a.) *Broke*, torn; as in B. v. 108; see note above, p. 108. The Latin quotations may be compared with those in B. xv. 336. I cannot find the exact words here quoted, but the reference may be to the following passage in the Compendium by Peter Cantor, cap. xlvii, in vol. 205 of Migne's Patrologiæ Cursus Completus, at col. 135. "Sic dantibus objici potest, quod similes sunt Judæ . . . quanto magis furtum et sacrilegium committit, qui patrimonium crucifixi, pauperibus erogandum, non dico ad horam, dat carni et sanguini, sed officium dispensandi res pauperum, dum vixerit, nepoti committit." And again, at col. 150—"Malum est indignis de patrimonio Christi dare, periculosum est, de illis dispensatores rerum pauperum constituere." For "*minus* distribuit," Mr Wright reads "*mimis* distribuit," but the majority of MSS. plainly have "min," followed by the mark of contraction for "us;" so that this reading must be rejected. In the only MS. (W) which has a word resembling "mimis," the word may equally well be read as "minus," and no doubt ought to be read so.

——(b. 9. 92; *not in* c, a.) *Drat = dredeth*, which actually occurs in l. 94. See footnotes to ll. 92, 94.

——(b. 9. 93; a. 10. 81.) "Nor loves the sayings of Solomon, who taught wisdom." We find the saying four times. "Initium sapientiæ, timor domini;" Ps. cx. 10 (Vulg.); Ecclus. i. 16. "Timor domini, principium sapientiæ;" Prov. i. 7. "Principium sapientiæ, timor domini;" Prov. ix. 10.

——(a. 10. 82; *not in* c, b.) "For fear, men do better," &c.

——(a. 10. 92; *not in* c, b.) Observe the distinction between "God's word" and "holy writ;" by the latter is meant the works of the fathers of the church. I do not know whence the quotation is taken. The reference to the Bible may be to Heb. x. 26, 27.

——(a. 10. 95; *not in* c, b.) *Catoun*, Dionysius Cato. The passage is—

" Cum recte uiuas, ne cures uerba malorum,
Arbitrium non est nostri, quid quisque loquatur."
Distich. liber iii. dist. 3.

——(a. 10. 98; *not in* c, b.) *Coueyte herre*, covet to climb still higher. Cf. *furre* = further, in l. 96.

——(a. 10. 101; *not in* c, b.) *Selden moseth*, seldom becomes moss-covered.

" Syldon mossyth the stone
þat oftyn ys tornnyd & wende."
How the Good-wife taught her daughter; pr. in
Qu. Elizabeth's Achademy, ed. Furnivall, p. 39.

" The Proverb says, and who'd a Proverb cross,
That Stones, when rolling, gather little moss."
Vade Mecum for Malt Worms, 1720, p. 6, Part (2).

"Saxum uolutum non obducitur musco.   Λίθος κυλινδόμενος τὸ φῦκος οὐ ποιεῖ.   Pietra mossa non fa muschio.   La pierre souvent remuée n'amasse pas volontiers mousse.   To which is parallel that of Quintus Fabius, Planta quæ sæpius transfertur non coalescit; A plant often removed cannot thrive."—Ray's Proverbs, under "A rolling Stone gathers no moss."

———(a. 10. 115; *not in* c, b.) "For thou mayst see how sovereigns arise (i. e. how men come to power) by means of patience."   See Luke xiv. 11.

———(a. 10. 117; *not in* c, b.) "Thus Do-best arises out of the dread of God (which is Do-wel), and out of its effect on the conduct (which is Do-bet); and hence it is like flower and fruit, being fostered by them both." William then proceeds to say that the red and sweet rose, much prized by spice-sellers (and representing Do-best), springs out of a ragged root (Do-well) and rough briars (Do-bet).   Cf. Myrour of our Lady, ed. Blunt, p. 283.

———(b. 9. 105; *not in* c, a.) *Lent* = *leneth*, i. e. lends, gives, grants. *Loude other stille*, whether loudly or silently; a proverbial phrase, formerly very common, signifying "under all circumstances," or "at all times," "always."   See *Loud-and-still* in Halliwell.

———(b. 9. 106; *not in* c, a.) I. e. "our Lord grants them grace, (permitting it) to enter into them, and (helping them) to obtain their livelihood."

189. (*not in* b, a.) "And it would be still best of all to be busy about (this endeavour), and to effect this one result, viz. that all lands should love (one another), and should believe in one law."   To *bringe to hepe* means to put into one heap, to collect into one result.   We find *to hepe* used in the sense of *together*, or *in one*, by Chaucer.   Thus, in his translation of Boethius, ed. Morris, p. 140, we find—"god ȝeueþ and departiþ to oþer folk prosperites and aduersites ymedeled to hepe," i. e. mingled in one.   Again—"And lost were all, that Love halt now to hepe," i. e. which Love now holds together; Troil. and Cress. iii. 1764 (ed. Tyrwhitt).   And again—"a litel wegge, . . . þat streyneth alle thise parties to hepe," i. e. a little wedge, that fastens all these parts together; Treatise on the Astrolabe, ed. Skeat, part 1, sect. 14.   See also l. 191 below.

193. (*not in* b, a.) The expression "thre clothes," i. e. three pieces of cloth, is merely indefinite.   The fullest account is that in St John xix. 23, 24, which says there were four soldiers, who cast lots for His coat, but divided the rest of His garments amongst them by rending them.

195. (*not in* b, a.) "After that, He lost his life, in order that law should increase to love," i. e. that the dispensation of the Law should give way to the greater dispensation of the Gospel of love.

———(b. 9. 117; *not in* c, a.) "The heaven (of wedlock) is upon earth; God Himself was the witness."   The reading of the text is probably right, as our author uses the phrase "heaven upon earth" in another passage; see Pass. vi. 153.   The alternative reading is—"in earth and in heaven;" see footnote and Crit. Note to B-text, p. 405.   The reference in the words "God Himself was the witness" is to the marriage at Cana; John ii. 2.   See also Gen. i. 28; ix. 1, 7.

206. (*not in* b, a.) The reference is to Matt. vii. 18.   Cf. Pass. iii. 29; xi. 244; xix. 61—70.

209. (*not in* b, a.) To obtain the full sense, the word *of* must be understood as repeated before *moillere*, which William uses in the sense of "lawful wife;" see Pass. xix. 222, 236.   Thus the line means—"Out of wedlock, not by a lawful wife."

212. (cf. b. 9. 120; a. 10. 136.) Mr Wright's note is—"According to a very curious legend, which was popular in the middle ages, Cain was born during the period of penitence and fasting to which our first parents were condemned for their breach of obedience."   Peter Comestor says—"Adam cognouit vxorem suam, sed non in paradiso, sed iam reus et eiectus."

220. (b. 9. 122; a. 10. 146.) The notion that Cain's children were exceedingly wicked is frequently alluded to in the middle ages; insomuch that "to be of Cain's kin" or "to be of Judas' kin" was a proverbial expression equivalent to the Scriptural expression "sons of Belial."   It is due to Josephus, who enlarges upon the extreme wickedness of Cain's posterity, and whose account is partly repeated in Peter Comestor's Hist. Scholastica, cap. xxviii.   Cf. Cursor Mundi, ll. 1559—1588; Beowulf, ed. Thorpe, p. 8; Alisaunder, ed. Weber, Metrical Romances, i. 84, l. 1933; Havelok, l. 2045. The usual spelling of *Cain* was *Caym* or *Caim*, which enable Wyclif to say that the friars were denoted by the word *Caim*, since the four orders of them were the Carmelites, Augustines, Jacobins, and Minorites, the initials of which compose that word.   See my note to P. Plowm. Crede, l. 486; and note to Pass. i. 56.

Compare—"And als the karl of Kaymes kin;" Ywain and Gawain, 559; in Ritson, Met. Rom. i. 24.

.*.* *For note to* b. 9. 123 (a. 10. 152), *see note to l.* 249, *on p.* 226.

222. (b. 9. 131; a. 10. 160.) Compare with this the descriptions of the ark in Allit. Poems, ed. Morris, B. 309—344; Genesis and Exodus, ed. Morris, 561—574; Cursor Mundi, ed. Morris, 1664—1722; Chester Plays, ed. Wright, p. 243.

232. (b. 9. 141; a. 10. 170.) The word *scingles* occurs in the Land of Cokaygne, l. 57, and King Alisaunder, ed. Weber, l. 2210.   "*Scingles*, wooden tiles, for which those of clay were afterwards substituted.   Those ships in which the edges of the planks cover each other like tiles, and which we now ... call *clinkerbuilt* vessels, were formerly called *shingled ships*, as in P. Plowman;" Ellis, Specimens of Early Poets, i. 87.   "*Shyngles*, hyllyng of an house;" Palsgrave.   "*Shyngle*, whyche be tyles of woode suche as churches and steples be covered wyth, *scandulæ;*" Huloct.   See Levins, Manip. Vocab.; Bardsley's Eng. Surnames, p. 212; and Prompt. Parv., p. 446.

233. (b. 9. 142; *not in* a.) "Here the son paid the penalty for the sins of his ancestor."   See Crit. Note to C-text, p. 458.

235. (b. 9. 144; *not in* a.) The word "godspel" is used by mistake.   See Ezek. xviii. 20.

——(b. 9. 146; *not in* c, a.) Compare—"Sith all children be *tached* with euill manners;" Batman on Bartholome, lib. vi. c. 6. See *Tuche* in Halliwell.

240. (*not in* b, a.) The attainder of felony caused 'corruption of blood;' i. e. the felon's goods were escheated to the feudal lord instead of going to his heirs. See *Felony*, and *Corruption of Blood*, in Blount's Law Dictionary.

249. (b. 9. 123; a. 10. 152.) William may have derived this command of God to Seth from Peter Comestor, who says:—"Methodius causam diluuii hominum, scilicet peccata, diffusius exequitur dicens ... Mortuo adam, seth separauit cognationem suam a cognatione Cain, qui redierat ad natale solum. Nam et pater viuens prohibuerat ne commiscerentur ... Septingentesimo anno secunde ciliadis filii seth concupierunt filias Cain, et inde orti sunt gigantes;" Hist. Schol. Genesis, cap. xxxi. A similar account, also attributed to Methodius, and perhaps merely borrowed from Comestor, appears in The Story of Genesis and Exodus, ed. Morris, ll. 517—554.

In most MSS. of the B-text, and some of those of the A-text, the name *Seth* is miswritten *Sem* or *Seem*, i. e. Shem; which was a more familiar name.

254. (b. 9. 158; *not in* a.) "For good men should wed good women, though they should have no goods;" i. e. though they be poor. See the glosses to the line in the B-text.

——(b. 9. 160; a. 10. 180.) See Wyclif's Works, iii. 191. One sentence agrees very closely with our text. "Also this contract [of matrimony] shulde nat be maade bitwixe a yonge man and an olde bareyne widewe, passid child-berynge, for love of worldly muk, as men ful of coveitise usen sumtyme;" &c. Compare the chapter in Barclay's Ship of Fools (ed. Jamieson, i. 247) entitled—"Of yonge folys that take olde wymen to theyr wyues for theyr ryches." See note to l. 272.

——(b. 9. 163; a. 10. 183.) "Who shall never bear a child, except it be (by carrying it) in her arms." A pun on the two senses of *to bear*.

263. (*not in* b, a.) *A bounde on*, a bound one, i. e. one who is a bondwoman. In l. 267, we have the spelling *that bonde*. For the word *begeneldes*, see Pass. x. 154, and the note.

269. (*not in* b, a.) The wish here alluded to, that an ugly bride might be turned into wax, is easily explained. Wax was much used for churches, to which it was frequently offered, and was very costly. It was also usual to offer as much wax as was *equivalent to the weight of the person* in whose behalf it was given; see note to Pass. i. 52 (page 11, l. 5). Hence it was easy to find a use even for a large quantity of it.

271. (*not in* b, a.) "They live their life in an unloving manner, till death parts them." It is interesting to remember that the phrase "til deth us departe" (altered in 1661 to "till death us *do* part") was formerly used in the Marriage-Service, even at an early period. It is found, for instance, in the Sarum Manual.

272. (b. 9. 164; a. 10. 185.) Mr Wright (note to l. 5507 of his edition)

quotes a passage from the Continuator of William de Nangis (in Dacherii Spicileg. iii. 110, ed. 1723) which gives a very different account of the results of the hasty marriages which followed upon the great pestilence; but the remarks refer to the continent. He says that many twins, and sometimes three at a birth, were born, and that few women were barren. He complains, however, of a great increase in iniquity and ignorance. See Wyclif's discourse Of Weddid Men and Wifis in his Works, ed. Arnold, vol. iii, pp. 188—201; especially p. 191; and Blomefield's Norfolk, ii. 69, note *e*. The great pestilence was that of 1369; see note to Pass. vi. 115.

275. (b. 9. 167; a. 10. 187.) "They have no children except strife, and exchanges (of reproaches) between them." That is, the sole result of their marriage is continual quarreling.

> "But they that marien hem for mukke and goode
> Onely, and not for love of the persone,
> Not have I wist they ony while stoode
> In rest[e]; but of strife is there suche wone [*abundance*],
> As for the more part, betwixt hem everychone,
> That alle her lives they leden in hevynesse;
> Suche is the fruyte to wedde for richesse."
>
>   Occleve; De Regim. Princ. ed. Wright, p. 59.

276. (b. 9. 168; a. 10. 188.) *Don hem*, do themselves; i. e. betake themselves, go.

In the present passage, we have the earliest known allusion to the singular custom known as that of "the Dunmow flitch of Bacon." The custom was—"that if any pair could, after a twelvemonth of matrimony, come forward, and make oath at Dunmow [co. Essex] that, during the whole time, they had never had a quarrel, never regretted their marriage, and, if again open to an engagement, would make exactly that they had made, they should be rewarded with a flitch of Bacon;" Chambers, Book of Days, i. 749; which see for a good article on the subject.

The custom is said, on slight authority, to have been instituted by Lord Fitzwalter, a favourite of king John; see Blount's Jocular Tenures, ed. 1784, p..296; Brand's Pop. Antiq. ed. Ellis, ii. 178; Strutt, Manners and Customs, iii. 155. A similar practice prevailed at Whichenover; see Plott's Hist. of Staffordshire. And Tyrwhitt, note to Cant. Tales, l. 5799, remarks that there was a similar custom at St. Melaine, near Rennes, in Bretagne. The allusion to the custom in Chaucer is in the Prol. to the Wyf of Bathes Tale, where she says of her three old husbands whom she kept under by her perpetual fault-finding—

> The bacoun was not fet for hem, I trowe,
> That som men haue in Essex, at Dunmowe.

Another allusion is the following, in a poem found in MS. Laud 416, written about 1460, and printed in Reliquiæ Antiquæ, ii. 29.

> I can fynd no man now that wille enquere
> The parfyte wais unto Dunmow;
> For they repent hem within a yere,
> And many within a weke, and sonner, men trow;

That causith the weis to be rowgh and over-grow,
That no man, may fynd path or gap
The world is turnyd to another shap.
Befe and moton wylle serve wele enow;
And for to seche so ferre a lytill bakon flyk
Which hath long hanggid, resty and tow;
And the wey, I telle you, is comborous and thyk,
And thou might stomble, and take the cryk;
Therefore bide at home, what so ever hap,
Tylle the world be turnyd into another shap.

In Eastern England, by Walter White, vol. ii. p. 225, is the following account. "The old Priory, much disguised and debased by modern bricks and mortar, shows but little of its former beauty. . . . The woman who opened the door showed us, as the most interesting relic, the square-seated wooden chair in which the lucky winners of the flitch used to be carried in triumph about the neighbourhood. It must have been a very tight fit for any two of comfortable rotundity; that is, if they sat side by side."

The grotesque oath formerly exacted of the claimants was, says Mr White, as follows:—

"You shall swear, by custom of confession,
If ever you made nuptial transgression.
Be you either married man or wife,
If you have brawls or contentious strife,
Or otherwise, at bed or at board,
Offended each other in deed or word;
Or, since the parish-clerk said *Amen*,
You wished yourselves unmarried again;
Or in a twelvemonth and a day
Repented not in thought any way;
But continued true in thought and desire
As when you joined hands in the quire.
If to these conditions, without all fear,
Of your own accord you will freely swear,
A whole gammon of bacon shall you receive,
And bear it home with love and good leave;
For this is our custom at Dunmow well-known,
Though the pleasure be ours, the Bacon's your own."

A similar version, but with some variations, is given by Chambers.

Halliwell, in his Dictionary, s. v. *Dunmow*, gives further references to Howell's Eng. Proverbs, p. 21; MS. Sloane 1946, fol. 23; Edwards's Old English Customs, p. 1; Lelandi Itin. iii. 5—9; MS. Ashmole 860, p. 117; MS. Savil. 47, fol. 63; Selections from Gent. Mag. i. 140-2. Chambers gives some account of the various occasions on which the flitch was claimed, viz. in 1445, 1467, 1701, 1751, and 1763, after which year the custom was formally discontinued. The flitch was, however, claimed again in 1772, 1851, 1855, and 1876! In 1772 no flitch of bacon was forthcoming, but in 1851 and 1855 it was supplied by some who wished to see the custom retained.

278. (b. 9. 170; a. 10. 190.) "Unless they are both forsworn (i. e. for-swear themselves), they lose the bacon."

281. (b. 9. 173; a. 10. 193.) Here *maydenes* is used of both sexes; *maydenes and maydenes* = bachelors and spinsters. We find something like this in Chaucer, Cant. Tales, 3227—3230; see Tyrwhitt's note to C. T. 3227.

284. (b. 9. 177; *not in* a.) The allusion is obviously to the advice of St Paul—"Quod si non se continent, nubant. Melius est enim nubere, quam uri;" ad Corinth. i. 7. 9. The expression "eucrech manere seculer man" was, no doubt, intended to include the secular clergy; and the passage is important, as shewing that many were of opinion that the secular clergy, at least, should be allowed lawfully to marry. In his Notes to Myrc, Mr Peacock says, at p. 66, that in 1450, "the Church of England had long refused its sanction to the marriage of persons in holy orders. Though it was contrary to the theory of the Western Church from very early days, there is the most positive evidence that, before the Norman conquest, English priests were frequently married. In the North of England, celibacy was the exception rather than the rule. A clerical family, whose pedigree has been compiled by Mr Raine (Priory of Hexham, Surtees Soc., vol. i. p. li.) held the office of Priest of Hexham from father to son for several generations." "To priests of common order it is ordained, according to the teaching of St Gregory, that they may chastely enjoy wedlock;" Ælfric's Homilies, ed. Thorpe, ii. 95. See S. Gregorii Curæ Pastoralis Liber, cap. xxvii (answering to cap. li of the 'A.S. version). So in Wyclif's Works, ed. Arnold, iii. 190, we find—"God ordeynede prestis in the olde lawe to have wyves, and nevere forbede it in the newe lawe, neither bi Crist ne bi his apostlis, but rathere aprovede it." See also vol. i. p. 59, 364; and Massingberd's History of the Reformation, pp. 81, 242. Compare the note above (pp. 113, 114) to Pass. vii. 135; and Chaucer's statement in Cant. Tales, l 3941—"The persone of the toun hire father was."

286. (b. 9. 179; *not in* a.) *A lykynge thyng*, a pleasant (or enticing) thing [c]; *in likyng*, in sensual pleasure [b]. *Lymyerde*, lime-rod or lime-twig; in allusion to the twig covered with birdlime by which birds are sometimes caught. This line was, to some extent, imitated by the author of the Ploughman's Crede, who says—" I likne it to a lym-yerde · to drawen men to helle;" l. 564. Whitaker actually explains *lykynge* by "licking or sticking fast" (!) See Crit. Notes, C-text, p. 458.

287. (b. 9. 180; *not in* a.) ȝep, active, vigorous [c]; omitted here in [b], though it occurs in B. xi. 17. See ȝeap in Stratmann, and *Yep* in Halliwell.

289. (b. 9. 182; *not in* a.) John of Bridlington, whose Latin verses are printed in Polit. Poems, ed. Wright, vol. i. has the two lines following—

" Dedita gens scortis morietur fulmine sortis,
    Scribitur in portis, meretrix est ianua mortis;" p. 159.

These are Leonine verses, and probably at one time well known, as these citations seem to shew. Cf. Prov. vii. 27.

291. (b. 9. 184; cf. a. 10. 196.) Compare Old Eng. Homilies, ed. Morris, Ser. 1, p. 133; Ælfric's Homilies, ed. Thorpe, ii. 94; Ayenbite of Inwyt,

ed. Morris, p. 224. *Out of tyme*, at an unseasonable time. In l. 186 [b] =
196 [a], we have the curious equivalent phrase *in vntyme*. In Ratis Raving,
ed. Lumby, at p. 18, l. 590, there is a passage copied from Eccles. v. 12,
where it is said of the rich man that his wealth often "lattis hyme to slep,"
i. e. prevents him from sleeping, so that he "walkis in *vntymis*," i. e. lies
awake at unseasonable hours; (*walk* being the usual Lowland-Scotch form
of *wake*).

And again, in Ratis Raving, book iii. l. 187, we have—

"Tak not delyt in morne-slepinge,
Wntymous eting na drynkynge."

304. (b. 9. 199; a. 10. 211.) "And so, my friend, Do-well is to do what
the law ordains" [c, b]; and [c] adds—"to love and to humble thyself, and
to grieve no one." Whitaker, not perceiving the words *my friend* to be in
the vocative case, was unable to interpret this passage. The definitions of
Dowell, Dobet, and Dobest in this passage should be compared with those
in Pass. xvi. 125—127. It will be observed that the C-text differs here from
the two previous ones.

——(b. 9. 204; a. 10. 212.) "And so Do-best comes from both (the
others), and subdues the obstinate (nature of man), that is to say, the wicked
self-will that spoils many a (good) work."

SCHEME OF THE CONTENTS OF C. PASSUS XII.

(B. Pass. X—XI. 42; A. Pass. XI.)

(See Wright's edition, pp. 173—204; ll. 5596—6657.)

C-TEXT.	B-TEXT.	A-TEXT.
xii. 1—6	x. 1—6	xi. 1—6
——	7, 8	7, 8
7—18	9—21	9—21
——		·22
19—22	22	——
23	23	23
——	24, 25	——
·24	——	——
25—27	*like* 26—28	——
——	29	——
28	30	——
——	31	·——
29, 30	——	——
31—34	*like* 32—36	*like* 24—29
——	37	*like* 30
——	38—44	——
——	45—50	*like* 31—37
35, 36	*like* 52, 51	38, 39

C-TEXT.	B-TEXT.	A-TEXT.
xii. 37—44	x. 53—61	xi. 40—48
45, 46	——	
47—50	62—65	49—52
——	66, 67	53, 54
51—55	68—72	55—59
56—60	73—77	——
61, 62	——	——
63—70	78—85	——
71—75	*like* 86—88	——
76—83		——
——	89—100	——
——	——	60—63
——	101, 102	——
——	103—108	*like* 64—69
——	109—112	——
——	113—128	*like* 70—85
——	——	86
——	129	——
——	130—134	*like* 87—91
84	135	92
——	136—138	93—95
85—94	139—148	96—104
95, 96	——	
97—99	*like* 149, 150	105, 106
——	151, 152	107, 108
100—102	——	——
103—110	153—160	109—116
111—115	161—167	117—123
116—126	——	——
127, 128	168—178	124—134
129—136	*like* 179	135
——	*like* 180—188	136—144
——	189—191	145
——	192—194	——
——	195—199	146—150
——	——	151
——	200—206	——
——	207—212	152—157
——	——	158
. ——	213—215	159—161
——	——	162
——	216, 217	——
——	218	163
137	219	164
——	——	165
138, 139	*like* 220, 221	166, 167
——	222—227	168—173
——	——	. 174, 175
140, 141	*like* 228, 229	*like* 176—178
——	——	179—200
——	230—240	——
144—148	——	——

xii. C-TEXT.	x. B-TEXT.	A-TEXT.
149	241	——
——	242	——
150	*like* 243	——
——	244	——
151—156	——	——
157—160	245—248	——
161, 162	——	——
——	249—291	——

Here comes a passage, in A and B, which has already occurred in C.
Pass. VI. See Scheme, *p.* 85 ; *and* Notes, *pp.* 93—98.

vi. 147—160	*like* x. 292—308	xi. 201—210
vi. 161—180	*like* x. 309—329	——

Here is a return to the original order.

——	——	xi. 211—220
——	330, 331	

Here there is again a transposition of matter ; see B. XI. 1—35.

xii. 163	xi. 1	——
164	——	——
165—167	xi. 2—4	——
——	xi. 5	——
168—186	xi. 6—24	——
187	*like* xi. 25	——
188—197	xi. 26—35	——
198—204	——	——

Here is a return to the original order ; see B. X. 332.

——	x. 332—336	xi. 221—225
——	337—341	——
——	342—344	*like* 226, 227
——	345—353	228—235
——	——	236—242
——	354—363	——
——	364—371	*like* 243—249
——	——	250—252
——	372—374	——
205, 206	375, 376	253, 254
207, 208	——	——
209—212	377—380	255—258
213	——	——
214, 215	381, 382	259, 260
——	——	261
216—223	*like* 383—389	262—270
224—227	——	——
228—232	390—394	——
233—237	*like* 395—398	——
238—245	399—406	——
——	407, 408	——
246, 247	——	——
248—253	*like* 409—413	——
254—263	414—422	271—279

C-TEXT.	B-TEXT.	A-TEXT.
xii. 264 ·	——	
265	*like* x. 423	xi. 280
266, 267		
268—270	424—427	281—284
271—273	*like* 428—430	
——	431—441	
		285
274, 275		
276—280	*like* 442—447	*like* 286—292
281, 282	448, 449	
283		——
284, 285	450, 451	
286—296	*like* 452—463	*like* 293—303
	464—468	
297—302	*like* 469—473	——
303		
——	474	——

Here begins B. Pass. xi. *The passage in* B. xi. 1—35 *has already occurred.*
See above; ll. 163—197 (C-text).

304, 305	xi. 36, 37	——
306—311	xi. 38—42	——
312	[xi. 47]	——
313	——	——

NOTES TO C. PASS. XII. (B. Passus X—XI. 42;
A. Passus XI.)

2. (b. 10. 2; a. 11. 2.) "Who looked very lean, and appeared austere"
[c]; "Who was lean in face, and in body too" [b]; "Who was lean of
body, and of humble look" [a]. *Lere* commonly means complexion, face,
look; see *hleor* in Stratmann. As regards *liche*, see *lic* and *liche* in Stratmann, who attempts a distinction between these forms. In this view, *lic* or
lich = A.S. *líc*, a corpse, a body, whilst *liche* = A.S. *líca*, likeness, form.
If this be correct, we have here the former of these words. The term *lic* or
lich is often understood of a dead body, or corpse, as in *lich-gate*, and in
Chaucer's *liche-wake*, Kn. Ta. 2100; but instances are not wanting in which
it is applied to the living form. Thus in Kyng Alisaunder, ed. Weber, l. 3482,
we have—"The armure he dude on his *liche*," i. e. on his body. Corresponding to the A.S. *líca*, we have "inn an manness *like*," in the form of a man,
Ormulum, 5813; "ine the *liche* of man;" Shoreham's Poems, ed. Wright,
p. 20, l. 3.

——(b. 10. 7; a. 11. 7.) *And banned him*, and severely rebuked him [b];
for his beere, for his noisiness, or loudness of speech [a].

7. (b. 10. 9; a. 11. 9.) "Nolite dare sanctum canibus, neque mittatis
margaritas uestras ante porcos," Matt. vii. 6; where the Greek text has
μαργαρίτας. The expression "margery-pearl" is therefore a reduplicated
one; it occurs again in Palsgrave, who has—"Margery-perle, *nacle*." The

A.S. form of the word is most ingenious; it was turned into *mere-grót*, i. e. a *meer-grit*, or small particle found in the sea. Thus our ancestors succeeded in giving it a sense of their own.

In the Testament of Love, near the beginning of Book iii, is a curious passage in which the forms 'Margery perle' and 'Margarit perle' both occur; the passage itself seems to be corrupt. In P. Lacroix, Manners, Customs, and Dress during the Middle Ages, fig. 86, p. 120, is a picture of a stall of carved wood representing the casting of pearls before swine, from Rouen cathedral. In st. 44 of Hermes Bird (pr. in Ashmole's Theatrum Chemicum, p. 222) is the passage—

> "Men shalle not put a precius *Margareyt*
>   As Rubeys, Saferys, and other Stonys ynde,
> Emeraudys, nor rownde Perlys whyte
>   Before rude Swyne that love[n] *draffe* of kynde."

See also Wyclif's description of *margarites:* Works, i. 286.

8. (b. 10. 10; a. 11. 10.) Repeated below (see l. 82); where "haws" are explained to mean pleasure and love of the world.

9. (b. 10. 11; a. 11. 11.) "Draff would be more acceptable to them." In Skelton's Elinor Rummyng, ll. 170, 171, we have—

> "Get me a staffe,
>   The swyne eate my *draffe*."

Mr Dyce seems uncertain whether it means a coarse liquor, i. e. hogwash, or brewers' grains. It is a general term for refuse, and also bears the meaning of husks and chaff, the refuse of thrashed corn; which may be intended here. See Mr Way's note on "Draffe" in the Prompt. Parv.; where he cites Chaucer's "Why shuld I sowen *draf* out of my fist" (Persones Prol.), and the expression "*draf*-sak" in the Reve's Tale. "Still swine eat all the draff" is a common proverb, and is cited by Shakespeare; Merry Wives, iv. 2.·105.

10. (b. 10. 12; a. 11. 12.) "Than all the precious stones, that any prince is master of" [c]; *or*, "that grow in Paradise" [b]; *or*, "pearls, that grow in Paradise" [a]. The allusion to *Paradise* is readily understood by referring to Gen. ii. 12. Note also the old belief, that stones could *grow*.

14. (b. 10. 17; a. 11. 17.) *Nat worth a carse*, not worth a cress [c, b]; not worth a rush [a]. Chaucer has—"ne raught he not a *kers;*" C. T. 3754. And in Allit. Poems, ed. Morris, A. 343, we have—"For anger gayne; the not a *cresse*," i. e. avails thee not a cress. A "cress" means a plant of cress (not necessarily water-cress, as some say), i. e. a thing of small value. Hence, by an odd corruption, the modern expression—"not worth a *curse*." Just as *cress* was formerly spelt *carse* or *kers*, we find the Mid. Eng. form of *grass* to be *gres* or *gers; A.S. gærs*. Chaucer has several equivalent expressions, as, e.g. "Ne sette I nought the mountance of a *tare;*" Kn. Tale, 712.

15. (b. 10. 18; a. 11. 18.) "Unless it be carded by means of Covetousness, just as clothiers comb wool." The sense is, that Wisdom and Intelli-

gence are not now esteemed when rightly employed; to be appreciated, they
must suffer themselves to be 'dressed' over by the workings of Avarice, so
that they may be employed to deceive, cajole, and beguile; see l. 80 below.
The simile is an excellent one when its force is perceived. We may put it
more shortly thus. Ability, to be appreciated in these days, must allow itself to be 'dressed' by Avarice, as wool is when it is carded. In Horman's
Vulgaria, leaf 149, back, is the expression—"I can bothe carde wolle and
kembe it, Noui lanam et carminare et pectere." In Riley's Liber Albus, p. 530,
the importance of wool-carding thistles is shewn by the "Letter of the King,
that *thistles*, butter, madder, woad, and *fuller's earth*, shall not be taken out of
the realm;" i. e. they might not be exported. In his Flowers of the Field,
at p. 314, the Rev. C. A. Johns says—"*Dipsacus Fullonum* is the Clothiers'
Teazel, a plant with large heads of flowers, which are imbedded in stiff,
hooked bracts. These heads are set in frames and used in the dressing of
broad-cloth, the hooks catching up and removing all loose particles of wool,
but giving way when held fast by the substance of the cloth. This is almost
the only process in the manufacture of cloth, which it has been found impossible to execute by machinery."

17. (b. 10. 20; a. 11. 20.) "And hinder truth, and beguile it, by means
of a love-day" [c]; "And preside over a love-day, to hinder truth thereby"
[b]; "And presides over a love-day, to hinder truth thereby" [a]. The
word *love-day* has been already explained; note to Pass. iv. 196, p. 67.

19, 20. (*not in* b, a.) "They who understand trifles and slanders are
called in (to help) by the law; but the law bids them to be off, who are
truly wise." I do not know the source of this quotation.

22. (*not in* b, a.) *Fallas*, trickery, deceit. It occurs in the Tale of
Beryn.
    " But now shull ye here the most sotill *fallace*,
      That ever man wrought till other, and highest trechery."
Again, in the Testament of Love, book ii (near the end), we find—"Mylke of
fallas is venym of disceite." And again, in the Dispute between the Soul
and Body (Vernon MS.), pr. in Walter Mapes, ed. Wright (Camden Society),
p. 342, col. 2—
    " A thou foule flesch, unseete,
      Ful of falsnesse and *fallas*."
Fallaces is used as a plural adjective in Pass. xvii. 231.

26, 27. (b. 10. 27, 28; *not in* a.) These two lines are a loose translation
of the text above, quoted at length in [b]. The A. V. has—"Behold, these
are the ungodly, who prosper in the world; they increase in riches;" Ps.
lxxiii. 12.

28. (b. 10. 30; *not in* a.) "And ribalds, for the sake of their ribaldry,
are helped (with gifts) before the needy poor" [c]; "Ribalds, for their
ribaldry, may receive of their goods" [b]; i. e. may receive presents out of
the wealth of the wicked. See note to Pass. v. 113, p. 81.

32. (b. 10. 33; a. 11. 25.) *Tobye*, i. e. Tobit [b, a]; see l. 70 below, and
cf. Pass. xviii. 37.

34. (b. 10. 36; a. 11. 29.) *Alowed*, praised [c]; *loued*, loved [b]; *loued or leten bi*, loved or esteemed [a].   *He* = such a one.

——(b. 10. 42; *not in* c, a.) "Liken men (to various objects of ridicule), and lie against them that give them no gifts." To *liken* is to compare; in this case, for the purpose of exciting ridicule. See B. x. 277.

——(b. 10. 44; *not in* c, a.) "Munde the miller" has been mentioned before; see note to Pass. iii. 113. I regret to say that I know no more than Munde did what is the precise reference in the words *multa fecit Deus;* unless it be to Ps. xxxix. 6—"Multa fecisti tu, Domine Deus," &c.

——(a. 11. 32; *not in* c, b.) *Makyng of Crist*, the composing of verses concerning Christ.

——(b. 10. 47; a. 11. 34.) *Yeresyiue*, year's-gift; see notes to B. iii. 99, B. viii. 52. I may add here, in confirmation of the explanation that it means a gift given on New-year's day, that, in this passage, Crowley altered the reading *yeres gyfte* (as it stood at first) to *newyeres gyfte*, in his third impression. See Crit. Notes to B-text, at p. 405.

35. (b. 10. 52; a. 11. 39.) "When the minstrels are silent." The minstrels played to the guests during the feasts in the great halls; and, whenever they paused for a while, the time 'was' often filled up, as we are told here, by jesting disputes on very sacred subjects. See more on this subject below, B. x. 92—134, C. xvi. 194—210. Cf. Monumenta Franciscana, p. 634.

38. (b. 10. 54; a. 11. 41.) *Ballede resones*, bald reasons; not, as Whitaker would have it, reasons "worthy of a ballad!" The expression occurs again in Richard Redeles, iv. 70, which is more explicit, viz :—

"So blynde and so *ballid* · and bare was the reson."

Chaucer has the same spelling—"His heed was *balled;*" Prol. 198. Our author has it also, with reference to the head; see Pass. xxiii. 184. There is surely no difficulty in the expression, and Hotspur's celebrated speech has something very like it; 1 Hen. IV. i. 3. 65—

"This *bald* unjointed chat of his, my lord,
I answer'd indirectly, as I said."

"They take Bernard to witness;" i. e. they quote from St Bernard such passages as they think will suit their arguments. It is easy to wrest the sense of passages in argument, so that we need not be surprised at finding (as Price, in Warton, remarks) that "the abbot of Clairvaux was a zealous opponent of the scholastic subtleties satirized in the text." For example, he says—"Mulier insipiens, audax hereticorum uanitas, prurientes auribus ad talia discutienda sollicitat, cum Deus credendus sit, non discutiendus;" S. Bern. in die Ascensionis domini Sermo; ed. Migne, vol. iv. col. 153.

40. (b. 10. 56; a. 11. 43.) *Atte deyes*, at the daïs or high table; see note to Pass. x. 21.

41. (b. 10. 57; a. 11. 44.) "And gnaw God with their throat (defame Him with their words), when their bellies are full." A forcibly indignant rebuke. Cf. B. x. 66.

42. (b. 10. 58; a. 11. 45.) Compare the following from Rob. of Brunne's Handlyng Synne, ll. 6896—6900.

> " Also hyt ys grete curteysye
> To ȝyue ȝoure almes hastelye ;
> Nat for to make long delay,
> To late a wreeche stonde al day
> Cryyng at þy gate yn colde."

43. (b. 10. 59; a. 11. 46.) The alliteration is made by the treble recurrence of *f*. Hence the spellings *afyngred* and *afurst*, as in [c], are the best. These are, however, corruptions of *of-hyngred* and *of-thurst*, i. e. exceedingly plagued by hunger and thirst. The word *afyngred* has occurred before; see B. vi. 269, and the note (p. 170); cf. also l. 50 below. And the whole phrase occurs again; see Pass. xvii. 15.

With *afurst*, compare *of-thurste*, King Horn, 1120; *hof-thurst*, Vox and Wolf, 273; *of-thurst*, Ancren Riwle, p. 240; *afurst*, Joseph of Arimathie, ed. Skeat, l. 553.

44. (b. 10. 60, 61; a. 11. 47, 48.) " There is no one so generous as to have him indoors, but he bids him go where God is," i. e. to heaven [c]; " There is no one to take him near himself, to remedy his annoyance (*or* suffering); but only to cry ho! upon him, as at a dog, and bid him go thence " [b]; " There is no man nigh him, to remedy his suffering; but only to chase him away like a dog," &c.; [a]. The words *hoen, honesschen* may be either in the infinitive mood, or in the pres. pl. indicative, with the word *they* understood; it matters little which. *Hoen* is to cry ho! to hoot at; see *Howen, How, Hoo, Ho*, in Halliwell's Dict. Cf. note to Pass. iii. 228.

Honesschen is spelt *honysche* in MS. U, and *hunsen* in MS. T (footnote to A-text); we find also the pp. *honsched*, in the phrase "*honsched* as an hounde," A. ii. 194, footnote. It is a rare word, but I suspect it to be merely a variation of *hunch*. To *hunch* is to give a push, to shove (see three examples in the edition of Nares by Wright and Halliwell); Bailey explains it by—" to give a thrust with the elbow." Here it may well mean " to push out," or " to chase away," or " dismiss with violence." Hence may perhaps be explained two passages in the Allit. Romance of Alexander, ll. 3004 and 3792, which have never been explained till now. In the first passage we are told that Alexander tried to cross a frozen river, when the ice gave way, the result being that

> "His hors it *hunyschist* [*sic*; an error for *hunyschit*] for euire · & he with
> hard schapid;"

i. e. it dismissed (did away with) his horse for ever, and he himself hardly escaped.

In the other passage we are told that it was so hot in the month of August, when Alexander went against the Indian king Porus, that it made an end of some of his soldiers, oppressed as they were with their armour.

> "Sum in þaire harnais for hete · was [*sic*] *honest* for euire ;"

i. e. some of them, in their armour, owing to the heat, were dismissed (or thrust out of this world) for ever. The notion of *thrusting out* will suit all the passages; and the sense of *thrust* will suit the sense of *hunch*. See also Halliwell's Dictionary, which gives—"*Hunch*, to shove; to heave up; to gore with the horns." Forby, in his East-Anglian Glossary, gives an example which is to the point. "*Hunch*, a lift, a shove. 'Give me a *hunch*, Tom,' said an elderly East-Anglian matron, somewhat corpulent, to her stout footman, who stood grinning behind her, while she was endeavouring to climb into her carriage." So, in the present passage, when the rich man finds the poor man quaking for cold at his gate, he "gives him a hunch."

I have found one more passage in the (unprinted) Alliterative poem on the Wars of the Jews (MS. Laud 656, leaf 14, back) in which this somewhat rare word occurs. It is as follows.

> "For y haue heylych hey3t · here forto lenge,
> Tille I þis toured dou*n* [? toun] · han taken at wille,
> & me þe 3ates ben 3et · & 3olden þe keyes,
> & suþ *honsched* on hem · þat þis hold kepyn,
> brosten & betyn dou*n* · þis britages heye,
> þat neue*r* ston i*n* þat stede · stond vpon oþere."

i. e. For I have firmly (lit. highly) promised to linger here, till I have taken, at my pleasure, this towered down [*better* town], and till the gates be given up to me, and the keys yielded, and afterwards (I have) *driven away* them that keep this hold, and broken (lit. burst) and beaten down these high battlements, so that no stone in that stead may ever again stand upon another.

51. (b. 10. 68; a. 11. 55.) By *memento* is meant Ps. cxxxi, beginning with "Memento, Domine, David, et omnis mansuetudinis eius;" the sixth verse being—"Ecce audiuimus eam in Ephratah," &c. The word *eam* refers to the ark of the covenant; but our author, by inserting the gloss "i..[= id est] caritatem" *intends* us to understand it as referring to Christian love. He seems to take the whole verse as signifying—"we can most easily find Christian charity amongst the poor, and in country-places."

52. (b. 10. 69; a. 11. 56.) "Clerks and knights" [c]; "Clerks and men of another kind," i. e. clerks and others [b]; "Clerks and intelligent men" [a]. The word *kete* seems to signify keen of wits, acute, in this passage; see the note upon it in my glossary to William of Palerne. Other MSS. read *kid* (footnote to A-text), which means famous, being the pp. of *kithen*, to make known; see numerous examples of the use of *kid* in the same glossary.

56. (b. 10. 73; *not in* a.) Note this allusion to the preaching of the friars at St Paul's; see it again, Pass. xvi. 70. The preaching-place was in the open air, at St Paul's Cross. Latimer preached there in fine weather, and in the 'Shrouds,' a place of shelter, in less favourable weather. "In foul and rainy weather, these solemn sermons were preached in a place called *The Shrouds;* which was, as it seems, by the side of the cathedral church, where was covering and shelter. Now, long since, both the Cross and Shrouds are disused, and neither of them extant. But the sermons are preached in the cathedral it-self, though they be still called *Paul's Cross Sermons.*"—John Strype, ed. of Stow's Survey of London, 1720, p. 149.

63. (b. 10. 78; *not in* a.) "And yet, as for these wretches who are devoted to this world, not one of them takes warning by the other."

64. (b. 10. 79; *not in* a.) An instance of the minute care with which the text was revised. The C-text has *eny deth*, a general expression; but [b] has *the deth*, i. e. the great pestilence emphatically called "the Death;" see note to Pass. ix. 348. The expression was made more general because that event was, at the time of revision, less recent. Similarly, in ll. 55, 60, we have the plural *pestilences*, where the B-text has the singular.

65. (b. 10. 80; *not in* a.) "Nor share their goods with the poor" [c]; "Nor are bountiful to the poor" [b].

67. (b. 10. 82; *not in* a.) It is worth observing that this quotation from Isaiah was a familiar one, because it was repeated in the Latin grace on fish-days during Lent; see Babees Boke, ed. Furnivall, p. 383.

68. (b. 10. 83; *not in* a.) The reading *hath* [c] is not so good as *welt* [b]. *Welt* is equivalent to *weldeth*, which actually occurs just below, l. 72, and in B. x. 88; the sense is wields, commands, makes use of; see l. 12 above, and B. x. 24, 29. These contracted forms of the 3rd pers. sing. pres. indicative are very common; just above we have *to-grynt* for *to-gryndeth*, l. 62; and just below, *lust* for *lusteth*, l. 76.

69. (b. 10. 84; *not in* a.) "And (the more he) is landlord of tenements, the less property he gives away." For *leedes*, the B-text has the nearly equivalent word *londes*; the common phrase being *leedes and londes*, which actually occurs in MS. B (footnote to B-text), and of which examples may be seen in my glossary to William of Palerne, s. v. *Lud*, which see. The word *leedes*, often used by Robert of Brunne in the sense of *tenements*, or *rents*, appears to be quite distinct (at any rate in use) from the more common word *leedes* in the sense of *men*; which, curiously enough, occurs almost immediately below, in l. 73. The latter is the A.S. *leód*, G. *leute*; the former seems rather to be connected with *leet* and *lease*.

74. (cf. b. 10. 88; *not in* a.) "If thou have but little, dear son, take care, by thy manner of life, to get love thereby, though thou fare the worse for it." The sense of B. x. 88 is much the same—"And who-so commands but little, let him rule himself accordingly."

79. (*not in* b, a.) "For no intelligence is esteemed now, unless it tend to gain." Compare Chaucer, Prol. 275—
    "Sowninge alwey thencrees of his winninge."
And see note to l. 15 above.

80. (*not in* b, a.) "And (unless it be) capped with learning, in order to plot wrong-doing." The word 'capped' refers to the caps worn by masters of divinity, as a mark of their degree; see note to Pass. xi. 9.

82. (*not in* b, a.) Repeated from l. 8; see note to that line.

——(b. 10. 91; *not in* c, a.) "And how he might, in a hospitable manner, provide for the greatest number of people." *Manliche*, hospitable, has occurred before; B. v. 260. *Fynde*, to provide for, has occurred several times; see, e. g. B. vii. 128. *Meyne* is spelt *meynee* in MS. W (see footnote), and is the usual word for "household."

——(b. 10. 92; *not in* c, a.) An allusion to the "feast-finding minstrels," as Shakespeare calls them; Lucrece, 817. The friars were equally celebrated for haunting the feasts of the rich; see Pass. xvi. 30, 47; and Pierce the Ploughman's Crede, 554—557.

——(b. 10. 94; *not in* c, a.) "Dull is the hall, every day of the week, where neither the lord nor lady likes to sit." See note on *elyng*, Pass. i. 204 (p. 24). I have observed another example of it in the Tale of Beryn, l. 967— "And seyd[e], sir, why do yee thus? this is an *elyng* fare."

I here transcribe Mr Wright's excellent note upon the present passage. "This is a curious illustration of contemporary manners. The *hall* was the apartment in which originally the lord of the household and the male portion of the family passed their time when at home, and where they lived in a manner in public. The chambers were only used for sleeping, and as places of retirement for the ladies, and had, at first, no fire-places (*chymenees*), which were added, in course of time, for their comfort.

"The *parlour* was an apartment introduced also at a comparatively late period, and was, as its name indicates, a place for private conferences or conversation. As society advanced in refinement, people sought to live less and less in public, and the heads of the household gradually deserted the hall, except on special occasions, and lived more in the parlour and in the 'chambre with a chymence.' With the absence of the lord from the hall, its festive character and indiscriminate hospitality began to diminish; and the popular agitators declaimed against this as an unmistakeable sign of the debasement of the times."

Observe that the word *chymneye* (l. 98) means properly a fireplace at this period, in accordance with its derivation from the Lat. *caminus*. Cf. '*chimney's* length' in L'Allegro, l. 111; "the *chimney* is south the chamber;" Cymbeline, ii. 4. 80. In the instructions of the Primate to the Abbot of Thorney concerning the treatment of Reginald Pecock, we find it provided that Pecock was to have "a secret enclosed chamber, having a *chimney*;" Pecock's Repressor, ed. Babington, vol. i. p. lvii. See the article on "The Englishman's Fireside" in Timbs's Nooks and Corners of England, p. 135. What we now call chimneys were not very common before the time of Elizabeth. Harrison, in his Description of England, p. 212, says—"Now have we manie *chimnies*, and yet our tenderlings complaine of rheumes, catarrhs, and poses [*colds in the head*]; then had we none but *reredosses*, and our heads did never ake." See Halliwell's Dict., who gives this quotation s. v. *reredosse*, which he explains as an open fire-hearth. The author of the Ploughman's Crede thus describes a Dominican convent; ll. 204.

> "An halle for an hey3 kinge · an housholde to holden,
> With brode bordes aboute · y-benched wel clene,
> With windowes of glas · wrou3t as a chirche;
> Thanne walkede y ferrer · & went all abouten,
> And sei3 [*saw*] halles full hy3e · & houses full noble,
> Chambers with chymneyes · & chapells gaie."

——(b. 10. 100; *not in* c, a.) "And all in order to refrain from expending that which another will spend afterwards." Many misers leave their money to spendthrift heirs.

———(b. 10. 103; a. 11. 64.) See the modern rendering of this passage in the Introduction to the A-text, p. ix.

———(b. 10. 105; a. 11. 66.) "Why was our Saviour pleased to suffer such a serpent to enter His (place of) bliss," i. e. the garden of Eden? Observe the use of *worm* for a large serpent; it is the usual old term; cf. Ant. and Cleopatra, v. 2, and see Pass. xiv. 137 (C-text).

———(b. 10. 115; *not in* c, a.) This is a very curious allusion; the author is referring, by anticipation, to a later passage of his poem. The speaker in this passage is Dame Study; she is addressing the poet himself, and says— "One named Imaginative shall, hereafter, give an answer to your question." The *question* is about Do-well, &c., and is proposed in C. xi. 121 (being expressly called a *purpos* in the preceding line). The *answer* is actually given, as Dame Study promised, by one Imaginative, in C. xv. 1—22. See B. viii. 120, 121; xi. 399—402; xii. 1, 26, 30.

———(b. 10. 116; a. 11. 72.) Perhaps our author refers to the following passage in St Augustine. "Unde aliquid sapere quam res se habet, humana tentatio est. Nimis autem amando sententiam suam, uel inuidendo melioribus, usque ad praecidendae communionis et condendi schismatis vel hæresis sacrilegium peruenire, diabolica praesumptio est. In nullo autem aliter sapere quam res se habet, angelica perfectio est;" De Baptismo, contra Donatistas, lib. 2, cap. 5. See also St Jerome's commentary on the text cited, viz. Rom. xii. 3.

———(b. 10. 120; a. 11. 77.) Here *penance* is considered as a gift of God's grace. The line means—"But pray to Him for (the graces of) pardon and penance, during your life."

———(b. 10. 128; a. 11. 85.) *Worth*, shall be; as opposed to *was* in the preceding line.

———(a. 11. 86; *not in* c, b.) Compare Rich. Redeles, iii. 45—

"Thanne cometh ther a *congioun* · with a grey cote."

See my note to the line (C-text, p. 514), shewing that the word occurs four times in the Chester Plays, spelt *congeon, counjon, congion*. The question as to whether the third letter in the word is *n* or *u* is pretty well settled by the form here used, and by the form *counjon*; it is not likely that *counjon* ought to be *couujon*, nor that the form in the A-text is meant for *couioun*, with five consecutive vowels. But I can now adduce further evidence on the point, having observed the line "Thou liest, thou black *conjoun*," quoted (from the romance of Merlin) in Ellis's Metrical Romances, ed. Halliwell, p. 89. Compare also the following. "Bisih þe, seli meiden, beo þe cnot ienute anes of wedlac, beo he *cangun* oðer crupel, beo he hwuch se he eauer beo; þu most to him halden;" i. e. "Look around, seely maiden, if the knot of wedlock be once knotted, let the man be a dump or a cripple, be he whatever he may be, thou must keep to him;" Hali Meidenhad, ed. Cockayne, p. 33. In Mr Cockayne's Glossary is the following explanation. "*Cangun*, a broad

short built man." "*Congeon*, one of low stature, or a dwarf;" Bailey (1759).
"The cammede *kongons* cryen after col, col, And blowen here bellowys that
al here brayn brestes," the crooked *conguns* cry after coal, coal, And blow
their bellows till their brains crack; Reliq. Antiq. i. 240. Mr Wedgwood
has kindly suggested to me that, in the form *congioun*, the *n* is inserted, as
in *jongleur* from O.Fr. *jogleur* or *jougleur*, and that the word is really identical
with *cullion*, which he derives from "the Fr. *coion*, Span. *cojon*, Ital. *coglione*,
a scoundrel." Compare—"*Coion*, *cohion*, *coyon*, lâche, poltron;" Roquefort. It may be so, but it may not be amiss to observe on the other hand
that Roquefort gives "*Canche*, boiteux, boiteuse," and that the difficult
words *cang*, *cangliche*, *kangschipe*, *cangen*, are also found in the Ancren Riwle;
see the examples in Stratmann. In particular, at p. 62 of the Ancren Riwle,
we have *cangun* as a various reading of *cang*. Stratmann gives *foolish* as the
sense of *cang*, but a better sense is *perverse*; so also *cangliche* is *perversely*,
sidelong, Ancren Riwle, p. 56; *kangschipe* is *perversity*, id. p. 338. For these
words, a likely root seems to be the common Celtic (Welsh and Gaelic) *cam*,
crooked, perverse; compare *cangun* in the sense of *dwarf* with the Gaelic *caim-
dacan*, a hump-backed person. It is plain that *conioun* is used as a term of
contempt; and this, perhaps, may suffice.

——(b. 10. 129; *not in* c, a.) "And those that use these wiles, to blind
men's wits." The term *hanelon* is used in the same sense in Peter Langtoft,
ed. Hearne, p. 308;—"with *hanelon* tham led," he led them with guile.
Hearne misprints it as *hauelon*, and explains it by "howling, yelling!" In
Sir Gawayn and the Grene Knyght, l. 1708, it is said of a fox that he
"*Hamlounez*, & herkenez · bi heggez ful ofte;" i.e. he winds about, and
often listens beside hedges. In Sir F. Madden's Glossary to Sir Gawayn
we find the following note. "So in the Boke of St Albans, l. 1496.

> And yf your houndes at a chace · renne there ye hunto,
> And the beest begyn to renne · as hartes ben wonte,
> Or for to *hanylon*, as dooth · the foxe wyth his gyle,
> Or for to crosse, as the roo · doth otherwhyle.

And in the older treatise of Twety, MS. Cotton, Vesp. A. xii., fol. 6, *b*—
'*Sohow* goth to alle maner of chases . . but if yowre houndes renne to one
chace, that is to seye, ruse3t, or *hamylone*, or croisethe, or dwelle,' &c."

Hence it is clear that the sb. *hanilon* means the winding course or wile
of a fox, and the vb. means to wind about in order to beguile. Cf. "*Hanni-
crochemens*, subtilties, intanglements."—Cotgrave.

94—98. (cf. b. 10. 149; a. 11. 105.) This passage is rather hazy in [c],
as already noted; see Crit. Note to C. xii. 97, p. 458 (C-text). In [b] it
means—"He hath wedded a wife, within the last six months, who is akin
to the Seven Arts; Scripture is her name." In [c] the word *scripture* is
either governed by *comsynges*, as suggested in the Crit. Note; or perhaps a
better sense is obtained by supplying *is* before *of scripture*, so that the sentence will mean—"I will recommend you to Clergy, my cousin, who knows
all the arts and beginnings of Do-well, Do-bet, and Do-best; for he is cele-

brated as a doctor (*or*, teacher); and he is the skilful (one) in Scripture, if only scriveners would be correct." *And* (in l. 97) = *an*, if; *were* = would be, as often elsewhere. See note to B. x. 332 below; p. 251.

The *seven arts* or *seven sciences* were contained in the so-called trivium and quadrivium. The trivium contained grammar, logic (or dialectics), and rhetoric; the quadrivium, music, arithmetic, geometry, and astronomy; according to the mnemonic lines—

　　Gram. loquitur; *Dia.* vera docet; *Rhet.* verba colorat.
　　Mus. canit; *Ar.* numerat; *Geo.* ponderat; *Ast.* colit astra.

See a somewhat lengthy note upon the subject in Marco Polo, ed. Yule, i. 13; Hallam's Introd. to the Lit. of Europe, i. 3 (ed. 1860); Dante, Convito, Trat. ii. c. 14; Chester Plays, ed. Wright, p. 241, where a quotation from the French "Image du Monde" is given, asserting that these sciences were first taught to Adam in Paradise by his Creator; Wright's note to his edition of Walter Mapes, p. 2. In Lydgate's description of the entry of Henry V into London after the battle of Agincourt (printed from MS. Harl. 565, at p. 242 of A Chronicle of London) there is an account of a spectacle representing the Seven Sciences. Here the teaching of Grammar is attributed to Priscian; of Logic, to Aristotle; of Rhetoric, to Cicero; of Music, to Boëthius; of Arithmetic, to Pythagoras; of Geometry, to Euclid; and of Astronomy, to Albumasar. But this means no more than that these names were known in connection with their respective sciences.

Our poet expressly mentions the "seven arts" below; Pass. xiii. 93 (b. 11. 166).

103. (b. 10. 153; a. 11. 109.) *Foul*, bird. "As glad as a bird is of a fine morning" is the meaning of the proverbial expression here used. It was once quite a common proverb. In Hazlitt's English Proverbs it is given in the form—"As glad as fowl of a fair day;" where "glad" should rather be "fain," to preserve the alliteration. Cf. "As fayn as foul is of the brighte sonne;" Chaucer, Kn. Ta. 1579; and "As foul is fayn, whan that the sonne vp ryseth;" Shipm. Tale, 51.

104. (b. 10. 154; a. 11. 110.) *To gyfte*, for a gift, as a gift [c, b].

107. (b. 10. 157; a. 11. 113.) This passage is in much the same strain as one in Pass. viii. 204—234; q. v.

118. (b. 10. 170; a. 11. 126.) *Sapience*, the book of Wisdom. *Sauter glosed*, the Psalter with a commentary or gloss, such as that by Nicholas de Lyra. It is Dame Study (see l. 86) who is the speaker; she taught men the seven sciences; see note to l. 94. Of these, Logic is alluded to in l. 119, Music in l. 120, Grammar in l. 123, and Geometry in l. 127.

120. (b. 10. 172; a. 11. 128.) *Masons*, measures. The etymology is easier than the exact use of it. It is the F. *moison*, from Lat. acc. *mensionem*, a measuring. Cotgrave has—"*Moyson*, size, bignesse, quantity, full length." Roquefort gives—"*Maison*, mesure;" but adds a false etymology. Burguy has—"*moison*, mesure, forme; de *mensio*." In a Poem on Learning to Sing, printed in Reliquiæ Antiq. i. 292, we find a definition of it.

" Qwan ilke note til other lepes, and makes hem a sawt,
    That we calles a *moyson* in gesolreutz en hawt."

Here " a sawt," i. e. a leap, is printed " a-sawt," as if it meant " assault;"
and *gesolreutz* is printed *gesolrentz*, which makes no sense. It plainly means
G-sol-re-ut (all musical terms) with *z* added to denote the plural;, and " en
hawt" is the French *en haut*.

On application to Mr Chappell, I received from him the following explanation, which he kindly gave me at once.

" The meaning of 'measures' is the time and rhythm of *mensurable*
music, as opposed to plain chant, which was *immensurable*. The measures
were denoted by signs at the commencement, which were puzzling to learn.
A circle meant 'perfect' or triple time; a semi-circle 'imperfect' or common time. To these were added bars (1, 2, or 3) across certain lines of the
staff, and the meaning depended upon which of the lines were thus crossed.
They denoted whether the *mode* was major or minor, and the 'probation' or
division into minims. For a printed book in which to see them exemplified,
refer to Piero Aron's 'Toscanello in Musica,' fol. Vineggia, 1539.

" There are two G-sol-re-uts in the Guidonian scale, therefore the upper
one was distinguished as G-sol-re-ut *the haut*. A third G in the scale was
the lowest note, called Gamma-ut, or gamut, written Γ. Thus G-sol-re-ut
the haut is the mark of the *treble clef* (now a corruption of the letter G), in
which all music for women and boys was written; and I understand the
quotation from Reliquiæ Antiquæ to mean—'That (skipping music) we call
a *measure* (or mensurable music),' fit for a boy's voice·(and not for a man's).
[Give us the *tenor* to hold on with, whilst they *skip*.] The tenor did not
then mean a high-voice part, but rather the low one that held on the plain
chant, while higher voices made 'division' or variation upon it."

Since *muson* meant measure, it was easily extended to signify measure-
ment or dimension. Thus, in Riley's Memorials of London, p. 563, anno
1406, mention is made of some boxes, that might be made " of nine different
dimensions [orig. *mewsons*] in length, and breadth, and depth within."

123. (b. 10. 175; a. 11. 131.) *Gurles*, children; boys rather than girls;
see note to Pass. ii. 29, on p. 30; and cf. A. 10. 155; B. 10. 77 (footnote).

124. (b. 10. 176; a. 11. 132.) *Baleyse*, a rod; see note to Pass. vii. 157,
on p. 115.

133. (b. 10. 185; a. 11. 141.) "But because it teaches men to love, I
believe in it the more " [c]; "But because it sets the highest value on love,
I love it the more " [b]; *or,* "I believe it the more " [a].

——(b. 10. 189; a. 11. 145.) *Catoun*, Dionysius Cato; see his Disticha,
lib. i. 26. For *simile*, another reading is *simules*, for the improvement of the
prosody. Cf. Pass. xxi. 166.

——(b. 10. 192; *not in* c, a.) "Whoever speaks fairly (yet deceitfully),
as flatterers do, let men resort to the same (plan)." This line and the next
is a translation of the two Latin lines above. The expression *go me* is for
go men, i. e. let men go, or resort to. Crowley has the same reading, which

is that of the three best MSS. Four other MSS. (see footnote) read *do* (or *don*) *hem the same*, i. e. do the same to them, which gives precisely the same sense, and is a gloss, since it does not preserve the alliteration. The shortened form *me* for *men* occurs but seldom in Piers the Plowman; other instances are in C. xii. 174; xiii. 112. It is well-known that *me* or *men* was used in Middle English (only with a singular verb) with the force of the Fr. *on*. See Morris's Hist. Accidence, p. 143; and p. 144, note 1. Sir F. Madden remarks, in his edition of Layamon, iii. 455, note to l. 2124—"*me* is used in Layamon as *man* or *mon* in A.S., and as *on* in French. The same form occurs in the Sax. Chron. anno 1137, and often afterwards, and in the poem of the Grave, in Thorpe's Analecta, p. 142." The verb *go* is in the 3 p. s. imperative. The chiefly remarkable point about this passage is the late date of this use of *me*, which is more usually found in the twelfth and thirteenth centuries. Still, it occurs in Trevisa, A.D. 1387; see Specimens of English, 1298—1393, ed. Morris and Skeat, p. 236, l. 15. Cf. the form *go we* = let us go; Pass. i. 227.

——(b. 10. 204; *not in* c, a.) For a note upon "Michi vindictam," see note to B. vi. 228, on p. 169. In addition to the examples there given, I find *Michi vindictam* in the margin of Occleve, De Regim. Princ., ed. Wright, p. 112.

——(b. 10. 203; a. 11. 153.) "Geometry and geomancy are guileful of speech," i. e. full of deceit in the terms employed by their professors. *Geomesye* should rather be *geomensye*; see A-text, and the footnote. For further remarks, see note to A. xi. 158, on the next page.

——(b. 10. 211; a. 11. 156.) "Yet are there contrivances (?) in caskets of many men's making" [b]; "Yet are there contrivances (?) of boxes, of many men's inventions" [a]. The word *fybicches*, *febicchis*, *fibeches*, or *febucches*, is plainly written in the MSS., but I cannot trace any such word in English, French, or Scandinavian. The nearest are the Icel. *fipa*, to confuse, *fipla*, to handle, fumble with, *fipling* or *fifling*, beguilement. I cannot even feel sure of the meaning; perhaps "contrivances" or "cheating tricks" suits the context; or it may have been a technical name for some compound substance employed by sorcerers and pretenders to witchcraft. A *forcer* is a casket or coffer; a *forel* is a box, or chest, or case; both these words are well illustrated by Mr Way. See his notes to the Prompt. Parv. p. 170, note 2, and p. 171, note 2. *Forel* is the mod. Fr. *fourreau*, a sheath, case, scabbard.

——(b. 10. 212; a. 11. 157.) *Alkenamye*, alchemy. The various spellings are *alkenamye*, *alkenemye*, *alconomye*, *alknamye*, and, in one MS. only (but probably by a writer's error), *alkamye*. It is clear that William meant the word to be spelt as above; but for what reason, does not appear. Roquefort gives the Old Fr. as *alkemie*, *alquemie*, *arquemie*. *Of Alberdes making*, of Albert's doing. The allusion is to the celebrated Albertus Magnus (died A.D. 1280), whose attainments were of the most varied kind, and who was ranked with Roger Bacon and Raymond Lully as an authority upon the occult sciences; see Warton, Hist. E. P. ed. 1840, ii. 337. In a note to his translation of Dante, Paradise, c. x., Mr Cary observes that "the absurd imputation of his [Albert's] having dealt in the magical art is well known; and his biographers take some pains to clear him of it." He refers to Scriptores Ordinis Prædicatorum, by Quetif and Echard, Lut. Par. 1719, fol. tom. i. p. 162.

——(a. 11. 158; *not in* c, b.) *Nigromancye,* necromancy. Archbishop Trench, in his English Past and Present, 4th ed., p. 244, has a note upon this word, which should be consulted. He rightly tells us, that "the Latin mediæval writers, whose Greek was either little or none, spelt the word *nigromantia,* as if its first syllables had been Latin." Hence, he says, the origin of the term "the *Black* Art" as applied to necromancy. Just as necromancy signifies divination by means of the dead (cf. 1 Sam. xxviii. 8; Lucan, Pharsalia, vi. 720—830), so pyromancy (here spelt *perimancie*) signifies divination by means of fire; and *geomancy,* divination by means of the earth. See these and similar terms in Brand's Pop. Antiq. ed. Ellis, iii. 329; and Burton's Anat. of Melancholy. See also, for *pyromancy,* Gower's Conf. Amant. ed. Chalmers, p. 194; and for *geomancy,* Dante, Purg. xix. 4, on which see Cary's note. In a treatise called an Apology, attributed (perhaps wrongly) to Wyclif, edited by Dr Todd for the Camden Society, we find the following, at p. 95. "*Nigramauncers* are thei that bi figeris or markyngis vpon the dead body of best or of man, thus enforcith to geit wityng, or to wirk, or thus to bow God .... And thus are callid *geománceris,* that werkun bi the ȝerth." See the quotations in Richardson, s. v. *Necromancy.* Compare also—"that horrible swering of adiuration and coniuracion, as don thise false enchauntours and *nigromancers* in basins ful of water, or in a bright swerd, in a cercle, or in a fire, or in a sholder-bone of a sheep. .... What say we of hem that beleuen on diuinales, as by flight or by noise of briddes or of bestes, or by sorte of *geomancie,* by dremes, by chirking of dores, or craking of houses, by gnawing of rattes, and swiche maner wrecchednesse?" Ch. Pers. Tale, *De Ira.* Hugo de S. Victore (Eruditionis Didascalicæ lib. vi. c. 15; ed. Migne, ii. 810) tells us that 'mantice' or divination is of five species, viz. *necromantia, gæomantia, hydromantia, aerimantia,* and *pyromantia.* Of these, the divination "in mortuis" is infernal; the other four kinds depend upon the four elements.

The pouke to rise maketh, cause the devil to rise, raise the devil; a result commonly supposed, in former times, to be within the power of magic; see 2 Hen. VI. i. 4. 24; 1 Hen. VI. v. 3. 2; and Marlowe's Doctor Faustus. On the word *pouke,* see note to A. x. 62, on p. 222.

——(b. 10. 230; cf. a. 11. 179.) Here the word *It* refers to Do-well. "Do-well is a common mode of life, quoth Clergy, viz. to believe in holy church," [b]; "Do-well is a very upright life, quoth she, among the common people," [a]. The definitions of Do-well in the two texts vary considerably. In [b], it is made to depend upon orthodox belief in the Trinity; but in [a], it is identified with the Active Life, according to the favourite distinction

between the Active Life and the Contemplative one; see Pass. xvi. 194, and
B. vi. 251.

——(a. 11. 180; *not in* c, b.) "It (i. e. the life) is called the Active
life; husbandmen lead it, and all other true tillers upon earth; tailors and
cobblers, and craftsmen of every-kind, that know how to earn their food, or
to toil for it with any true labour, or to ditch or dig; (such a life) is called
Do-well." At the end of l. 184, there should be a full stop; it was omitted
only by a misprint. Line 185 begins a new sentence; see the side-note.

——(a. 11. 198; *not in* c, b.) "For the sake of beggars who have fallen
into misfortune were such men endowed."

——(b. 10. 238; *not in* c, a.) The Latin line "Deus pater," &c. is quoted
from the Athanasian Creed.

157. (b. 10. 245; *not in* a.) "Not all the clerks under Christ could explain this; but thus it behoves all to believe who approve of Do-well" [c];
or, "but thus it behoves all the unlearned, who desire to Do Well, to
believe" [b]. Whitaker's Paraphrase is quite wrong.

159. (b. 10. 247; *not in* a.) "For, had no man ever a subtle wit, to dispute against the faith, no man could have any merit in faith, if it could all
be proved." Here Whitaker's Paraphrase is again wrong. Line 160 is,
however, merely a translation of the Latin sentence following, which
means—"Faith has no good desert, where the human reason supplies proof."
The sentence is from S. Gregorii xl. Homil. in Evang. lib. ii. homil. xxvi.;
in St Gregory's Works, ed. Migne, vol. 2, col. 1197; where we find—"Sed
sciendum nobis est quod divina operatio, si ratione comprehenditur, non est
admirabilis; nec fides humana habet meritum cui humana ratio præbet experimentum." This is frequently quoted by our old authors. Thus, in the
Legend of the Three Kings (MS. Harl. 1704), quoted in Wright's edition
of the Chester Plays, p. 279, we find—"Seint Gregorie saith in an Omelie,
si divina operacio humana ratione comprehendi posset, non esset admirabilis, nec fides haberet meritum, cui humana ratio prebet experimentum;
that is to seye, yf the workys myght be comprehendid in mannes wit by
reason, it were no wonder; also no hath [it] no mede, yf kyndely reason
shewet it to a man." Occleve translates it thus; De Regim. Princ. ed.
Wright, p. 13—

"Our feithe were not to us meritorie,
Yf that we myght[e] by resoun it preeve."

In Reliq. Antiq. i. 207, is the following from MS. Harl. 541, fol. 207
verso—

Wytte hath wonder how reson telle can
That mayd is mother and God is man,
Our noble sacrament, yn thre thinges on.
In this leeve reson, beleve thou the woudre;
There faith is lord, reson gothe undre.
Gregorius : Fides non habet," &c.

At p. 127 of the same volume, these lines (excepting the third line) reappear,
with the name of "Pecok" prefixed, and four Latin hexameters above them;

it would seem that they were translated from the Latin by Reginald Pecock. The same four English lines were printed by Caxton, without the Latin, in his edition of Lydgate's Stans Puer ad Mensam, leaf 4, back.

——(b. 10. 253; *not in* c, a.) "Be found, upon trial, to be in reality such as thou seemest to be. Appear like what thou art, or be what thou appearest." I do not know whence this is quoted.

——(b. 10. 259; *not in* c, a.) "If thou wouldst blame, take heed not to be blameworthy; for thine instruction is contemptible, when thine own fault makes thee feel remorse." I do not know the source of these lines; the rime in the latter shews them to be of no very early date.

——(b. 10. 262; *not in* c, a.) "All that blame any person, and have defects themselves." *Lyf* = person; see the Glossary.

——(b. 10. 263; *not in* c, a.) "Why excitest thou thy wrath because of a mote," &c. *Meuestow* = *meuest thou*, movest thou. Chaucer quotes the same text at the end of the Reeve's Prologue; see also Pierce the Pl. Crede, ll. 141, 142. See some curious illustrations of this parable (representing the *beam* as being several feet in length) in the woodcuts at pp. 157 and 158 of Wright's Hist. of Caricature.

——(b. 10. 266; *not in* c, a.) "I advise every blind buzzard to amend himself." A *buzzard* here means a worthless fellow. It is properly the name of an inferior kind of hawk, useless for hawking. Thus, in the Romaunt of the Rose, l. 4031, we have—

> " This have I herde ofte in saying
> That man ne maie for no daunting [*taming*]
> Make a sperhauke of a *bosarde*."

The original has—

> " Ce oï dire en reprovier
> Que l'en ne puet fere espervier
> En nule guise d'ung *bosart*."

A note on the passage in Bell's Chaucer, vol. vii. 137, says—"The proverb is still in use in France—'On ne saurait faire d'une *buse* une épervier.' The buzzard is a lazy, cowardly hawk, feeding on vermin, and utterly unfit for falconry; the *épervier*, or sparrow-hawk, on the contrary, is the most fierce and courageous, for its size, of all the hawks, and was highly esteemed. The corresponding proverb in English is not so refined—You cannot make a silk purse of a sow's ear."

So, too, in Weber's edition of King Alisaunder, l. 3047—

> " Nultow never, late ne skete [*soon*],
> A goshawk maken of a kete [*kite*],
> Ne faucon mak[en] of *busard*,
> Ne hardy knyght mak[e] of coward."

The epithet *blind* means dull of sight. We have the expression again in the Answer to the Reply of Frere Daw Topias, Polit. Poems, ed. Wright, ii. 98—"But of other thou bluudyrst as a *blynde buserde*." And again, in Bradford's Works, ii. 43 (Parker Soc.), the expression "*blind buzzard* Sir John" occurs as a contemptuous title for a priest.

" More pity that the eagle should be mewed,
  While kites and *buzzards* prey at liberty."

Rich. III. i. 1. 132.

——(b. 10. 271; *not in* c, a.) " That ye should be such as ye spoke of,
in order to heal others with." *To salue with othere* = *to salve othere with*,
to heal (or anoint) others with. Compare Chaucer's Sq. Tale, 639—

" and make *salues* newe
Of herbes precious, and fyne of hewe,
To *helen with* this hauk."

——(b. 10. 276; *not in* c, a.) *Marke* is an error of the author's; he
means *Matthew*. See Crit. Note (B-text), p. 406.

——(b. 10. 277; *not in* c, a.) " Unlearned men may make this comparison
about you; that the beam lies in your eyes, and the mote, through your defect, is fallen into the eyes of men of every kind, by means of cursed priests."
Festu is the right word here; see " Quid consideras *festucam*," &c. at l. 262
above. " Festue to spell with, *festeu*;" Palsgrave. Cf. *festu* in Prompt.
Parv. and Cotgrave; *fescue* in Halliwell, and Nares; also *feasestraw* in Halliwell, *vester* in Jennings' Gloss. of West Country Words; and the note on
fescu in Milton's Areopagitica, p. 30, l. 19, ed. Hales.

——(b. 10. 281; *not in* c, a.) " Bitterly paid for the sins," &c. This
reference to Hophni and Phineas was afterwards introduced into the C-text,
at greater length, but near the beginning of the poem. See Pass. i. 105—
123.

——(b. 10. 284; *not in* c, a.) " Therefore, ye correctors, seize hold of
this advice, and first correct yourselves."

——(b. 10. 285; *not in* c, a.) The text " Existimasti, &c." is quoted
again below; C. xiii. 30 (B. xi. 91).

——(b. 10. 286; *not in* c, a.) *Borel clerkes* no doubt means, as Tyrwhitt
suggested, lay-clerks, i. e. learned laymen, laymen who could read. *Borel*
was a coarse cloth of a brown colour; see *Burellus* in Ducange, and *bureau*
in Cotgrave. Hence the phrases—*a borel man*, a plain man; Chaucer, C. T.
11028; *borel folk*, lay people, id. 7453; *borel men*, laymen, id. 13961.
William is referring to the laymen whose reading enabled them to attack
the priests, by calling them " dumb dogs," &c. Cf. Pass. x. 260 (C-text).

**Here comes a passage (B. x. 292—329, A. xi. 201—210), which
has already occurred; see Notes to Pass. vi. 147—179, on pp.
93—98; and cf. Crit. Note to B. x. 291, at p. 406 (B-text).**

**Next comes the passage in A. xi. 211—220, B. x. 330, 331,
upon which I give the notes here following.**

——(a. 11. 211; *not in* c, b.) *Bidowe*, a curved dagger. Ducange gives
" *Bidubium*, ferramentum rusticum, i. q. *fulcastrum*;" and " *Dubio*, instru-
mentum incurvum." The *fulcastrum* was a sickle at the end of a long pole,
used for cutting brushwood. Soldiers armed with weapons resembling it
were called in Old French *bidaux* (Roquefort); and Roquefort also gives us
—" *Bedoil*, sorte d'armo, courbée comme une serpe." The prefix *bi* probably

meant that the weapon was double-edged; and it is clear, that in the present case, the handle was a short one. The word *baselard* has been already explained; see note to Pass. iv. 461, on p. 72.

——(a. 11. 212; *not in* c, b.) The reference here is to the horrible oaths in which even the "religious" indulged; cf. Chaucer's Pard. Tale, and Pers. Tale, *De Ira*.

——(b. 10. 330; *not in* c, a:) The word *dominus*, here used merely for the alliteration, is exactly equivalent to *kinghed* (i. e. the kingly estate) in A. xi. 216, q. v.

Next we return to C. xii. 163, where there is again a transposition of the B-text; see B. xi. 1; not in A.

Here comes a portion of B. Pass. xi., viz. B. xi. 1—35.

163. (b. 11. 1; cf. a. 12. 1.) *Many skyles*, many reasons [c]; *a skile*, a reason [b]. This answers to A. xii. 12, but the resemblance here to the A-text is so slight that A. Pass. xii. will be considered, by itself, further on.

164. (*not in* b, a.) "And made a gesture to (*or*, gave a look at) Clergy, to dismiss me, as it seemed."

165. (b. 11. 2; *not in* a.) "And blamed me in Latin, and set light by me," i. e. lightly esteemed me. The quotation is from the first words of S. Bernardi Cogitationes Piissimæ de cognitione humanæ conditionis, cap. i; see St Bernard's Works, ed. 1839, vol. ii. p. 660. It is quoted in the margin to Gower's Confessio Amantis, ed. Pauli, iii. 54, in the form—"Plures plura sciunt, et seipsos nesciunt;" which Gower translates—

Men sain, a man hath knouleching
Save of himself, of alle thing.

167. (b. 11. 4; *not in* a.) "And I fell (lit. became) into a sleepiness, and wonderfully I dreamt" [c]; "And, in a sleepy sullenness, I fell asleep" [b]. The word *wynkyng* is an adjective in [b], but a substantive in [c]. It means *sleepy*, or *sleepiness*. Dr Morris translates "lokinge withuten *winkunge*" by "sight without *sleepiness;*" Old Eng. Homilies, 1 Series, p. 144. Cf. Crit. Note to B. xi. 4, p. 408 (B-text).

170. (b. 11. 8; *not in* a.) "And she caused me to gaze into a mirror, named Middle-earth;" i. e. upon the mirror of the World; wherein he would behold all the world's delights; see l. 181. Poets seem to have been fond of the notion of seeing things in a mirror; we have the Mirror for Magistrates, Gascoigne's Steel Glass (or Mirror), the magic mirror in Chaucer's Squire's Tale, &c. See a long note by Warton, Hist. Eng. Poetry, where he treats of the Squire's Tale; the passage is reprinted in my Introduction to Chaucer's Prioresses Tale, &c. (Clarendon Press, Oxford). The notion is probably Eastern; Warton remarks that "the title of an Arabian book translated from the Persian is The Mirror which reflects the World." There is an old French poem entitled L'Image du Monde.

173. (b. 11. 12; *not in* a.) William really introduces us to *three* persons; the two damsels who accompany Fortune, and who personate the Lust-of-the-Flesh and the Lust-of-the-Eyes, and a third personage named the Pride

of-Life; according to a common exposition of the three kinds of temptation addressed to our Lord. "Hoc modo tria sunt illa notata; nam concupiscentia carnis, voluptatis infimæ amatores significat; concupiscentia oculorum, curiosos; ambitio sæculi, superbos." S. August. De Vera Religione, cap. 38, § 70.

188. (b. 11. 26; *not in* a.) "Then there was one named Old-age, who was mournful of look." Cf. *heny-chered*, downcast; Pass. xxiii. 2.

194. (b. 11. 32; *not in* a.) Before *brynge* supply the word *shal* (see *shalt* in l. 192). "And Pride-of-perfect-life shall bring thee to much peril."

195. (b. 11. 33; *not in* a.) *Stod*, i. e. who stood; the relative is omitted. In the B-text, Recklessness only speaks eight lines, and soon after we have a long discourse by Loyalty, beginning at xi. 148, and ending at l. 308. In the C-text, the discourse is delivered by Recklessness, ll. 200—309, a change which necessitated several modifications in the wording.

197. (b. 11. 35; *not in* a.) *The corone*, the crown of hair left on the head of those who had received the tonsure; see note to Pass. i. 86. *To tyne the corone*, i. e. to lose the crown, was to lose this hair; in other words, to become wholly bald, through the effect of age. Recklessness advises the poet to amuse himself while he may, and not to bend his back by stooping to do hard labour (cf. Pass. vi. 24); for, when he goes bald, and grows old, he will stoop easily enough then; in allusion to another common effect of age. There is a slight variation between *tyme ynowe*, i. e. time enough, soon enough [c], and *tymes ynow*, i. e. times enough, often enough [b].

The careful reader will observe (what no one seems to have observed hitherto) that the poet clearly implies, in this passage, that he had *himself* received the tonsure.

200. (*not in* b, a.) *Go ich*, whether I go. *Myn one*, by myself, alone.

Here is a return to the original order; beginning with B. x. 332; A. xi. 221.

——(b. 10. 332; a. 11. 221.) "I will not speak scornfully, quoth Scripture, unless scriveners lie." This expression (which somewhat resembles C. xii. 97) means that the writings of divines will not be found to use scoffing language, unless scribes wilfully corrupt their meaning. Before the invention of printing, the author was much at the mercy of the scrivener whom he employed; as Chaucer's Lines to Adam Scrivener plainly shew.

——(b. 10. 334; a. 11. 223.) "Help (men) not heavenward (to the extent of) a hair's end" [b]; *or*, "at the end of a whole year" [a]. The former expression denotes a very *small quantity*; the latter, a *large* space of time.

——(b. 10. 330; *not in* c, a.) Dionysius Cato, Distich. lib. iv. dist. 4, has—

> "Dilige denarî, sed parce dilige, formam;
> Quem nemo sanctus nec honestus captat ab ære."

Our MSS., however, read *denarium*. *Srt* for *sed* is very common.

Perhaps our author sometimes quoted Cato at second-hand; he has much the same selections from that author as are to be found in Vincent of Beauvais, Spec. Hist. v. 108—110; and it is remarkable that Vincent has the reading *denarium*.

———(b. 10. 344; a. 11. 227.) "Where rich men may claim no right (of entrance), except by (God's) mercy and grace" [b]. Remember *there* = where.

———(b. 10. 346; a. 11. 229.) "And prove it both by Peter and Paul." William does not make this good; for he really refers to Mark xvi. 16; see [a]. Perhaps he was thinking also of 1 Pet. iii. 21; Eph. v. 26, 27.

———(b. 10. 348; a. 11. 230.) "That text refers to extreme cases; such as the baptism of Saracens or Jews." The words *in extremis* probably refer to the case of people lying at the point of death. See the next note.

———(b. 10. 350; a. 11. 232.) "That even an infidel (*or* pagan) in that case (i. e. in a case of extreme need) may baptize a heathen; and he (i. e. the baptized person) may, for his true belief, when he loses his life, have the inheritance of heaven, just like any other baptized person." This seems a little startling at first, but William had doubtless good authority for his statement. Professor Pearson, whom I consulted about this question, at once gave me the following quotations. At the council of Florence, in 1438, it was ruled as follows. "In casu autem necessitatis non solum sacerdos vel diaconus sed etiam laicus vel mulier, imo *paganus et hereticus* baptizare potest, dummodo formam servet ecclesiæ et facere intendat quod facit ecclesia;" Eugenius ad Armenos; Concilia, Tom. 33, p. 575 (ed. Paris). "Casus. *Paganus* quidam baptizavit hominem in forma ecclesiæ; quare quæsitum fuit, quid erat faciendum. Et respondit Isidorus, quod Papa non attendit baptizantem hominem, sed Dei virtutem in baptismo."—Gratiani Decreta; De Baptismo, pars iii. distinctio 4, col. 2073, ed. Antverpiæ, 1573.

See also Hook's Church Dictionary, art. *Baptism, Lay;* where we read that in the Constitutions of Archbishop Peckham, in 1281, it is ruled that infants baptized by laymen or women (when in imminent danger of death) shall not be baptized again; and the priest shall afterwards supply the rest. But it would appear that lay baptism is expressly excluded by the present rubrics of the Church of England. The baptism of children by midwives is certainly recognised in the Poems of William de Shoreham, ed. Wright, p. 12. In Myrc's Instructions for Parish Priests, ed. Peacock, p. 5, we are told that either the father or the mother may baptize the child, if no one else be at hand; and, at p. 4, the midwife is directed, in case of need, to baptize the child even if only half-born; and the form of words used might be either in English or in Latin. Compare B. xi. 82; xv. 448—450; 490, 491; 594, 595.

———(b. 10. 355; *not in* c, a.) The text is—"Igitur, si consurrexistis cum Christo, quæ sursum sunt quærite, ubi Christus est in dextera Dei sedens;" Coloss. iii. 1.

———(b. 10. 356; *not in* c, a.) "He should love and believe, and fulfil the law." *Leue* = believe; see l. 359, which means—"And thus it behoves him to love, who believes he is saved."

——(b. 10. 361; *not in* c, a.) "It shall oppress us very bitterly, (viz. such wealth as is in) the silver that we hoard, and our clothes that are moth-eaten (by being stored away), while we see beggars go naked; or if we delight in wine and wild fowl, and know any to be in want." *Bisitten* = to sit close to, oppress; from *sitten*, to sit, to fit closely. *Soure* = sourly, bitterly; see note to Pass. iii. 154. The expression *moth-eaten* clearly refers to the text in Matt. vi. 19.

The word *bakkes* is correctly glossed by *panni*. A *bakke* had two senses: (1) the human back; and (2) a covering for the back; somewhat as when we speak of the *arm* of a coat, or the *leg* of a pair of trousers. The latter odd use of the word appears in Chaucer, Group G, l. 881, Six-text edition, where five MSS. have *bak*, whilst the Ellesmere MS. alone reads *bratt*. The passage is in the Canon's Yeoman's Prologue (l. 328), and, in the Hengwrt MS., is as follows:—

> "So semeth it; for, ne had thei but a shete
> Which [that] thei myghte wrappe hem in a nyght,
> And a *bak* to walken in[ne] by day-light,
> They wolde hem selle, and spenden on the craft."

Bratt = Welsh *brat*, a clout, a rag, &c.; and Chaucer clearly means, by *bak*, some kind of coarse cloak or mantle. William, however, uses it of a rich man's dress. We may hence conclude that it was a general term; and probably the nearest modern equivalent is the word *cloak*; which will suit both passages. I may observe that *bakke* has yet a third sense in Middle-English, viz. the animal commonly called a *bat*; for this, see Halliwell's Dictionary.

From the sb. *bak*, a cloak, was formed the verb *bakken*, to clothe with a mantle, which occurs in A. xi. 185, q. v.

——(b. 10. 368, 369; a. 11. 247.) *But if*, unless. Here our author commits a very curious mistake; he actually quotes *non mecaberis* for the purpose of translating it by "slay not." I fear we must lay the mistake upon William himself, as it stands the same in so many MSS. of both the A-type and B-type. Mr Wright's note really goes to prove that such odd mistakes may easily occur. He says—"A mistake in the original MS. for *necaberis*, as it is rightly printed in Crowley's edition." But we know that it is *not* "rightly printed;" for the reason that *necare* is not a deponent verb, and *non necaberis* = "thou shalt not *be killed*." A better suggestion is the *non necabis* of the Oriel MS.; but against this we must set the fact that the Vulgate version does not use the verb *necare* at all, but gives the command in the form "non occides." Obviously, the right explanation is, that the author, at the moment of composing, thought of the *words* of what is now the 7th commandment whilst thinking of the *meaning* of the one preceding it. In these cases, the text is likely to be right. In this very passage I ventured to correct the reading "Michi vindictam" of the Vernon MS. [a]

to the form "Michi vindicta;" only to discover afterwards that all the MSS. have "vindictam" here, and that the reading can be justified. See note to B. vi. 228. Elsewhere, William quotes the text correctly; see Pass. xxii. 448 (b. 19. 443).

—(b. 10. 371; a. 11. 249.) *But mercy it lette*, unless Mercy hinder it [b]; *but mercy it make*, unless Mercy cause it to be otherwise [a].

206. (b. 10. 376; a. 11. 254.) *Legende of lif*, the Book of Life; see Rev. xx. 12, 15. Referring to the doctrine of predestination.

208. (*not in* b, a.) "Or else they preach (that their hearers are) imperfect, and thrust out from grace." *Ypull*, thrust; lit. put.

209. (b. 10. 377; a. 11. 255.) *Vnwryten*, not written down [c, b]; *vndirwriten for wykkid*, written (*or* marked) under as being wicked [a].

215. (b. 10. 382; a. 11. 260.) "And to judge well and wisely, as women bear witness" [c]; "He judged well and wisely, as Holy Writ tells" [b]; "Did he not well and wisely, as Holy Church tells?" [a]. Alluding to the famous judgment of Solomon; whence the expression—"as women bear witness," because he decided the dispute between them. The text quoted in [c] is from the saying of the woman who was in the wrong—" Nec mihi, nec tibi sit; sed diuidatur;" 1 Kings iii. 26.

220. (b. 10. 386; a. 11. 263.) Aristotle was supposed to be in hell for lack of baptism. But Dante places him in the first circle, or place of least punishment; see Inferno, iv. 131. It seems to have been a general belief that Solomon also was condemned to hell; but Dante speaks of it as being a disputed point; he says of it—

"che tutto il mondo
Laggiù ne gola di saper novella,"

i. e. that all the world there below (on earth) desires to have information about it; Paradiso, x. 110. The notion of Solomon's condemnation may have been founded upon the tone of despair in his writings; see Eccles. i. 2, 14, 17, 18; ii. 11, 18, 20; vii. 16; viii. 8. But see Eccles. ix. 1 (quoted at l. 273 below), which tells us that we know nothing of the matter.

230. (b. 10. 392; *not in* a.) Whitaker wrongly explains *molde* by *stamp*, as it were a *mould;* but it is a common phrase for the *mould* of the earth, or the earth in general. *Men of this molde* = men of this earth or world; hence the B-text reads *men on this molde*, men upon this earth; which comes to the same thing. The phrase is common; see the Glossary.

232. (*not in* b, a.) This means that if we wish for mercy ourselves, we must shew mercy to others; then our mercifulness will win for us God's compassion.*

239. (b. 10. 400; *not in* a.) See Pass. xi. 222.

244. (b. 10. 405; *not in* a.) "God grant that it may not be so with them that teach the faith."

245. (b. 10. 406; *not in* a.) In [c], the word *churche* should be *kirke*, to suit the alliteration; see l. 249. Our author uses either form; for in Pass. xiii. 51, we must have the form *churche*. The Ilchester MS., which has

kirke in l. 249, is deficient here, which was my sole reason for not venturing on the emendation.

247. (cf. b. 10. 406; *not in* a.) *Herbergh*, a harbour, a safe shelter. The phrase "the ark of Christ's church" occurs in our Baptismal Service; it was suggested by 1 Pet. iii. 20, 21.

248. (b. 10. 409; *not in* a.) "The end of this clause (*or* argument) has reference to curators (*or* curates)." In other words, the sequel of my argument refers to men who have cure of souls, whom I liken to the carpenters or "wrights" who assisted Noah in making the ark.

251. (b. 10. 411; *not in* a.) "At doom's day there shall be a flood of death and fire at once." *Dyluuye* = Lat. *diluuium*, the deluge. That is, the world was once destroyed by a deluge of water; it shall hereafter be destroyed by a deluge of deadly fire. See 2 Pet. iii. 10.

252. (b. 10. 413; *not in* a.) In [b], the sense is—"Work ye such works as ye see recommended in writing, lest ye be not found therein;" where by "therein" is meant "in holy church," in the ark of safety.

256. (b. 10. 416; a. 11. 273.) *Byknew on*, acknowledged. The Trinity MS., printed by Mr Wright, has the inferior reading *beknede to*, beckoned to, which neither accords with the fact, nor makes good sense. *Byknowe* = to confess; Pass. i. 209; Pass. vii. 206. Hence *byknew on* = confessed in, i. e. confessed belief in, acknowledged. The penitent thief is here said to have been saved before John the Baptist and others, because it was said to him—"To-day shalt thou be with Me in paradise;" and it was believed that when Christ had descended into hell, fetching thence the souls of John the Baptist, of Adam, Isaiah, and other saints, He led them to Paradise, when they found that the penitent thief had already obtained entrance there. Such is the account given in the apocryphal gospel of Nicodemus, which is discussed more fully in the Notes to Pass. xxi.; which see. Cf. Pass. xxi. 369, 370.

260. (b. 10. 420; a. 11. 277.) *Rather*, sooner; solely with reference to *time*. Cf. *sonnere* in l. 257.

263. (b. 10. 422; a. 11. 279.) The Gospels merely say of Mary Magdalene—"out of whom went seven devils;" Luke viii. 2; Mark xvi. 9. There is not a word to connect her with the account in the preceding chapter of St Luke, viz. Luke vii. 37—50. We are quite at liberty to reject the once prevalent notion, which has found its way even into our Bibles, viz. in the heading to Luke vii., where we read—"Mary Magdalene anointeth Christ's feet." But it is very clear that our author took Mary Magdalene to have been the same with "the woman that was a sinner;" hence it is that he says—"who could have done worse in fondness for lechery, for she refused no man." (For *lyf* = man, see the Glossary.) This belief was so general that the name of Magdalen has (probably with great injustice) become proverbially significant in a bad sense. The spelling *maudeleyn* in [a] is worthy of notice; it shews that the pronunciation of the word as *Maudlin* is of early date.

265. (b. 10. 423; a. 11. 280.) *Vrye*, Uriah. See 2 Sam. xi. 14, 15. The C-text means—"who devised how Uriah might be most slily slain, and sent him to war, truly, as to all appearance, but provided with a deceitful letter." *As by hus lok* = to judge by his (David's) look.

——(b. 10. 431; *not in* c, a.) Translated from Eccles. ix. 1—"Sunt iusti atque sapientes, et opera eorum in manu dei; et tamen nescit homo, utrum amore an odio dignus sit." *Wel-libbynge*, living a good life; a translation of "iusti."

——(b. 10. 433; *not in* c, a.) "Whether a man shall be esteemed there for his love and his true deeds, or whether he shall be esteemed, for his ill will and envy of heart, in accordance with the way in which he lived; for, by (observing) the bad, men discern the good."

——(b. 10. 438; *not in* c, a.) "Therefore let us continue to live with wicked men (*or*, as wicked men do); I believe few are good." This is not a very proper sentiment; but it is hardly William's own. He is following up a particular line of argument, which, in the C-text, he puts into the mouth of *Recklessness*.

——(b. 10. 439; *not in* c, a.) "For when the word 'must' comes forward, there is nothing for it but to suffer." A proverbial expression; we now say—"What can't be cured, must be endured." The mixture of Latin and Old French is curious. The spelling *qant* for *quant* was common; see Burguy's Glossaire. *Ny* was written for *n'y*. *Ad* should rather be *at*, the old spelling of the 3rd pers. sing. indic. of *avoir*; *at* being for *habet*. It is now written *a*, except in the phrase *y at il*, which is ridiculously written *y a-t-il*, as if the *t* belonged to nothing. Indeed, many still believe that the *t* is "inserted for euphony," though why a *t* is more "euphonious" than another letter, they cannot tell us. The whole line becomes, in modern spelling—For, "quand *oportet* vient en place, il n'y a que *pati*." See a similar French proverb in Pass. xiv. 205, 206.

In a short poem on Grammatical Rules, printed in Reliquiæ Antiquæ, ii. 14, we find the proverb again in the form following :—

"And, when *oportet* cums in plas,
   Thou knawys *miserere* has no gras."

275. (*not in* b; a. 11. 285.) "And, in faith, to tell the truth, I never found that learning was ever commended by the mouth of Christ" [c]; "And moreover I further forget [i. e. cannot remember], as far as the teaching of my five wits goes, that learning," &c. [a]. The B-text has but *one* line (10. 442), viz. "Learning was then little commended by Christ's mouth."

280. (b. 10. 446; a. 11. 292.) *Conclude*, refute [c, b]; *answere*, reply to [a]. In the Examination of W. Thorpe, printed in Wordsworth's Eccl. Biog. i. 266, we read—"In all those temptations Christ *concluded* the fiend, and withstood him." Bp. Wordsworth remarks that *conclude* occurs, with the same sense of *confute*, in Sir Thos. More's Works, p. 1429.

287. (b. 10. 453; a. 11. 294.) *That euere man wiste*, that ever man

knew [c]; and highest of the four [b, a]. By "the four" is meant the four chief "Latin Fathers;" see Pass. xxii. 269, 270.

288. (b. 10. 454; a. 11. 295.) St Augustine did not say this "in a sermon," but in his Confessions. The passage runs thus—"Surgunt indocti et cœlum rapiunt, et nos cum doctrinis nostris sine corde, ecce ubi uolutamur in carne et sanguine;" S. Aug. Confess. Lib. viii. c. 8; ed. Migne, vol. 32, col. 757. Cf. Matt. xi. 12; xxi. 31. Mr Wright printed "idiotæ irapiunt" in his text, but in his note says:—"for *idiotæ irupiunt*, read *idiotæ vi rapiunt*." I notice this because the correction is wrong; the MS. which he printed has *idioti*, and omits *vi* altogether. The spelling *idioti* occurs in several MSS., and Ducange gives *idiotus* as well as *idiota*. See the word *Idiot* fully explained in Trench's Select Glossary. The Greek ἰδιώτης meant a private person, one not in public life; and secondly, an uneducated person. It is used here in the latter sense, and there are several instances of a similar use of it in our older writers. Thus—"images be the laymen's books, and pictures are the Scripture of *idiots* and simple persons;" Homilies: Against Perils of Idolatry. "The plain places of Scripture are sufficient to all laics, and all *idiots* or private persons;" J. Taylor; A Dissuasive from Popery, pt. ii. bk. i., § 1. See also Becon's Works, ii. 568, and Bullinger's Works, i. 71; ii. 3 (Parker Society).

294. (b. 10. 460; a. 11. 301.) "And ignorant true-hearted labourers and land-tilling people" [c]; "Cobblers and shepherds [*or* sewers, i. e. men who sew, *A-text*], such ignorant fellows" [b]. The word *soware* is given as a variation of "sewstare or sowstare, *sutrix*" in the Prompt. Parv. We have had the verb *sewen*, to sew, in Pass. ix. 8, 10. Thus *souter* (= Lat. *sutor*) is really the very same word, etymologically, as *sewer* (from A.S. *seówian*). Cf. "*Hic sutor*, a sowter;" Wright's Vocabularies, i. 212. In the Apology ascribed to Wyclif, ed. Todd, Camden Soc., p. 106, we find the words *sewars* and *sowtars* used, apparently as synonymous terms.

295. (b. 10. 461; a. 11. 302.) *Persen*, pierce, force their way into; cf. Matt. xi. 12. *A pater-noster*, just one short prayer.

Dr Rock says—"That the souls of the good are carried to heaven instantly after death, is a truth expressed repeatedly in our old literature;" Church of Our Fathers, iii. 204. He gives several examples. Thus, in the Golden Legend, ed. 1527, fol. cccix., we find—"And they that ben ryght good, been they that anone flee to heuen and ben quyte of the fyre of purgatorye, and of helle also." Cf. Polit. Songs, ed. Wright, p. 127, last stanza. And see B. x. 421 above.

296. (b. 10. 463; a. 11. 303.) Here ends A. Pass. xi. See A-text, Pref. pp. xviii., xxi., xxiv.; Crit. Notes to A-text, p. 154. The A-text is continued in Pass. xii., on the pages marked 137*—141*.

Here ends A. Pass. xi. For notes to A. Pass. xii., see p. 259.

298. (b. 10. 470.) *The reyue.* Comp. Chaucer, Prol. 587—622, especially l. 602—

"Ther couthe no man bringe him in arrerage."

302. (b. 10. 473.) "As clerks of holy church, who ought to keep and save unlearned people in true belief, and give them (things) in their need" [c]; "As clerks of holy church, who keep Christ's treasure, that is to say, man's soul, in order to save it," &c. [b].   Cf. B. xv. 491.

Here ends B. Pass. x.   For notes to B. xi. 1—35, see notes to ll. 163—197 above ; p. 250.   Pass on here to B. xi. 36.

304. (b. 11. 36.) "Homo proponit, sed Deus disponit;" De Imitatione Christi, lib. i. c. 19. The proverb is quoted again, Pass. xxiii. 34; it is also mentioned in the Chronicle of Battle Abbey, ed. Lower, p. 27. The attribution of it to Plato is probably a mistake; the obvious source of it is— "Cor hominis disponit uiam suam; sed Domini est dirigere grossus eius;" Prov. xvi. 9. Ray gives the following forms of it—"Man proposes, God disposes. Humana consilia diuinitus gubernantur. Homme propose, mais Dieu dispose; *French.* El hombre pone, y Dios dispone; *Spanish.*"

310. (b. 11. 41.) "'Yea, farewell, Phip!' quoth Childishness." Here *fauntelet* = a little child [c], which is equivalent in sense to *fauntelle* = childishness [b]. Roquefort gives—"*fantiliarga*, enfance, premier âge, enfantillage;" and Cotgrave—"*Enfantiller*, to play the child," &c. Childishness is here introduced in opposition to Elde (old age), l. 188. Elde gives the poet good advice, but Recklessness (l. 195) and Childishness tell him to despise that advice, which, for a time, he does. Moreover, Childishness dismisses the good advice of Elde in the most flippant and contemptuous manner, viz. by the expression—"Well, farewell, Phip!" i. e. good bye to you, be off! you may go! Compare the phrase—"Go farewell, felde fare!" in the Romaunt of the Rose, 5513, which must be considered in connection with its context; see also Chaucer's Troilus and Cress. iii. 861—"The harme is done, and farewel feldefare." So also in the Cant. Tales—

And *farewel*, al the reuel is ago; l. 11516.
The pot to-breketh, and *farewel*, al is go; l. 16376.

By consulting all these passages, it will be found that "farewel" was used much as we should use the phrase—"it's all over, and it's of no good to talk about it." "Farewel, feldefare" was marked by Tyrwhitt as a phrase not understood by him, but it is clearly an ironical way of dismissing a profitless or unpleasant subject. The fieldfare visits England in the winter, from November to April; its departure is therefore observed with pleasure, as a sign of the beginning of milder weather. See Hazlitt's Eng. Prov. p. 128.

Fyppe or *phippe* is for *Phip*, the contracted form of Philip, and is often used in Skelton's Phyllyp Sparowe. It was a pet name for a sparrow, given to it because its note was supposed to resemble the sound of the word. Cf. Lat. *pipire*, to chirp; whence, by the way, is derived the word *pigeon.* Hence "farewell, Phip" is "good bye, you sparrow!" also a form of contemptuous dismissal.

In Mr F. K. Robinson's Whitby Glossary (E. D. S.) we find the entry—

" *Oula.* ' When they got all they could, it was—"fare thee well, *oula.*" '
Query, the meaning of *oula;* but the phrase, which is frequently heard, points
to the selfish and ungrateful." Perhaps *oula* is here the Icel. *ugla,* an owl.

NOTES TO A. PASSUS XII; (NOT IN C, B.)

1. This twelfth Passus, printed on pp. 137*—141*, is very scarce. Of
ll. 1—19 there are but two copies extant, and of the remainder, but one.
See the Notes to A-text, pp. 154 and 142*. At p. 143* I have stated my
belief in the entire genuineness of ll. 1—100 of this Passus. To that belief
I still adhere in the main, but now admit that I have my doubts about the
last seven lines, ll. 94—100. If these lines are not William's, I suppose
they are John But's, who certainly wrote ll. 101—112. Let the reader have
it his own way. See note to l. 94.

6. " It would please you to learn, but displease you to study; " i. e. you
do not mind learning when you can be *told* a thing, but you are too lazy to
find out *by yourself.* This state of mind is still common.

7. " You would like to know all that I know, so as to be able to retail it
to others."

8. " In order, perhaps, to question so many people in a presumptuous
manner, that it might do harm to your fellow-men, and to the study of
Theology also. If I knew for certain that you would do according to my
teaching, I would explain all you ask me."

14, 15. An explanation of these obscure lines is attempted at p. 155
(A-text), l. 10.

18. *Defendeth,* forbids; as in C. iv. 68 (B. iii. 64; A. iii. 55).

19. " Vidi praeuaricantes, et tabescebam: quia eloquia tua non costo-
dierunt;" Ps. cxviii. 158 (Vulgate). It is clear that William translates
tabescebam as if it were *tacebam;* see l. 20.

28. " What is truth? said jesting Pilate, and would not stay for an
answer;" Bacon's Essays, i. William, on the other hand, suggests that
Christ did not deem Pilate deserving of an answer.

33. Alluding to A. xi. 286, where William says that Christ never commended " Clergy;" accordingly, Clergy now retorts, saying ironically, " I
am such as he says," i. e. I am not to be commended; and declines to say
more.

34. *Wyt y-sheued,* shewed her wit (at my expence).

35. This resembles the line—

Creptest into a caban · for colde of thi nayles;
A. iii. 184 (B. iii. 190).

39. " To be her servant, if I might, for ever after." We often find
moste = might; thus *myghte* (C. v. 107) is written for *moste* (B. iv. 112;
A. iv. 99).

40. *With that,* on the condition that. *Me wisse,* instruct me. *Were,*
might be, was.

42. *Low*, laughed. *Laughthe*, written for *laughte*, i. e. caught, seized; see l. 91.

49. "She called, to shew me the way, a young chorister named *omnia-probate*." *Clerioun* is Chaucer's *clergeon*, Cant. Tales, Group B. 1693; see my note on the line, in The Prioresses Tale, &c., ed. for the Clarendon Press. "Omnia probate; quod bonum est tenete;" 1 Thess. v. 21; a text quoted again in B. iii. 335, 339 (C. iv. 492, 496).

55. *Laughthe* (= *laughte*) *oure leue*, took our leave; cf. A. iii. 26.

58. This line has occurred before; A. Prol. 62 (B. Prol. 65; C. i. 63).

59. *A-fyngrid* = *of-hungred*, extremely hungry; see the Glossary. Cf. l. 63.

66. *Hendeth* = *henteth*, seizeth. Cf.—"a feyntise me hente," A. v. 5, 6 (B. v. 5).

75. *When*, put for *whenne*, whence; *wheder*, whither. "Whence he had come, and whither he meant to go."

77. "My name is Fever; on the fourth day I am always thirsty." An allusion to the so-called quartan fever, which "grieueth from the fourth daye to the fourth daye;" see Batman upon Bartholome, lib. vii. c. 40— "Of the feauer quartane, his signes and remedies." The two preceding chapters treat "Of the Feauer Cotidian," which "vexeth daylye," and "Of the Feauer Tertian, his signes and cure," which "vexeth euery second daye." See ll. 79 and 80.

81. *Letteres of lyf*, i. e. a letter belonging to Life, directed to Life, or (as we should now say) a letter *for* Life. Fever is bringing a letter from his master Death, to tell Life that he must die; cf. C. xxiii. 168—179. *Letteres* = a letter; see note above, to B. ix. 38, on p. 220.

83. "If I might do so, God knows I should like to go your way;" i. e. to accompany you.

86. "Thou wilt tumble as if caught in a pit-fall, if thou follow my track." *Tomblest* is the present used for the future, as in Anglo-Saxon. *Trepget* is the Fr. *trebuchet*, from the O. Fr. *tresbucher*, to overthrow. Cotgrave gives—"*Trebuchet*, m. a pit-fall for birds; a pit, with a trap-door, for wild beasts; also, a pair of gold weights; also, an old fashioned engine of wood, from which great and battering stones were most violently thrown." Halliwell gives the spelling *trepeget*. For "*Trase* (1) a trace, path; (2) a track," see Halliwell.

87. *Wrouʒþ* is certainly a mistake for *worth*, which the scribe might not have understood, as it is a rather uncommon word. *Worth* = shall be; see the Glossary. The reading *wrouʒþ* is impossible, because the future tense is absolutely required. The sense is—"man's joy shall not be greater than he deserves (by his life) here."

91. *Laughth* is for *laught*, caught, taken up. *Lyghth* = light, i. e. heaven. *Loking of an eye*, glance of an eye; i. e. in the twinkling of an eye; cf. 1 Cor. xv. 52.

94. The rest of this Passus is paraphrased at p. 144*. If ll. 94—100

are genuine, then we must regard the mention of his death as a mere flourish; but perhaps they are spurious, and added by John But (see l. 101). If so, then they express John But's belief that the author was dead. In this, I suspect he was mistaken, when we observe the loyal mention of Richard II. in l. 109. For most assuredly our author wrote "Richard the Redeles" in 1399, when there were but few lords left who could love Richard "loyally in heart." The passage may perhaps shew that the author's *real* name and position were no better known in his own time than they are now.

100. *Clom*, clay; it is the A.S. *clam*, mud, clay; cf. A.S. *lam*, loam. In Devonshire, *cloam* means earthen-ware.

101. Nothing is known of John But except from this passage; he lived in the time of Richard II. (l. 108), and in l. 104 he says that he "medleþ of makyng," i. e. he was accustomed to dabble in the composition of verses.

SCHEME OF THE CONTENTS OF C. PASSUS XIII.

(B. Pass. XI. 43—277.)

(Cf. Wright's edition, pp. 204—219.)

C-TEXT.	B-TEXT.	C-TEXT.	B-TEXT.
xiii. 1—3	xi. 43—45	xiii. 92—94	xi. 165—167
	46	95—97	
(xii. 312)	47		168, 169
	48—51	98	170
4—7	*like* 52, 53	99, 100	
8—16	54—62		171—183
17—19		101—104	*like* 184—187
	63—70	105	
20—23	71—74		188
	75—83	106, 107	*like* 189, 190
24, 25	84, 85		191—193
26—30		108—111	194—197
	86, 87	112	198, 199
31—33	88—90	113—115	200—202
	91—96	116	*like* 203, 204
34—42	97—105	117	205
43		118	
44	106		206—221
45		119	222
46—81	107—142	120	
82—84	*like* 143, 144		223, 224
85	145	121—131	225—235
86—88	*like* 146—148		236
	149—151	132	*like* 237
89, 90	152, 153		238, 239
91		133, 134	*like* 240, 241
	154—164	135, 136	242, 243

C-TEXT.	B-TEXT.	C-TEXT.	B-TEXT.
xiii. 137, 138 *like* xi. 244		xiii. 154—161	
——	245	——	xi. 262—266
139—147	246—254	162, 163	*like* 267, 268
148, 149 *like* 255—257		——	269—277
150—153	258—261	164—247	——

NOTES TO C. PASSUS XIII. (B. PASS. XI. 43—277.)

The references within a parenthesis refer to the B-text.

13. 1. (11. 43.) *Eye*, an interjection denoting astonishment, answering nearly to our "eh!" It is spelt *ey* in Tyrwhitt's Chaucer, C. T. 3766, 10165. Cf. G. *ei*.

2. (11. 44.) *For welthe*, &c.; because Wealth does all that he pleases [c]; but in [b] we have—*for wille to haue his lykynge*, in order for Will to have his pleasure. And here *Will* may either denote the mind's desire, or the poet himself, with reference to his name of "Will." The latter interpretation suits the context very well; see *me* in l. 41, *my* in l. 42, and *me* again in l. 45 of the B-text.

——(11. 46; *not in c.*) *Wynter*, years. It is well known that our ancestors commonly calculated by *winters*, as being, to them, the most serious part of the year to provide for. See numberless instances in the Anglo-Saxon Chronicle; also Chaucer, Cant. Tales, B. 3249, F. 43.

And a fyfte more, and a fifth (year) besides. That is, the poet was 45 years old, as he again tells us in B. xii. 3. Taking A.D. 1377 as the date of the B-text (see Pref. B. pp. ii—v), we thus get A.D. 1332 as the year of his birth.

Observe that the next line of [b] corresponds to C. xii. 312.

4. (11. 52.) In the C-text, we must suppose that Lust-of-the-Eyes addresses Recklessness in l. 4, but in l. 5 turns to the poet and addresses him in a like strain. William has, at the moment, identified his opinions with those of Recklessness, whose arguments he for the time adopts. See the speeches of Recklessness in C. xii. 195—197, 200—309, and observe that he is mentioned by name in C. xii. 274 and 283. The B-text is clearer, because no mention is made of Recklessness after l. 40.

6. (11. 52.) Here, *to come to good* means to arrive at the possession of property, to acquire wealth. *Morally* speaking, it would be a "going to the bad."

With reference to confession to *friars*, see notes to Pass. iv. 38 and vii. 120.

9. (11. 55.) *Fraternite*. This alludes to the "letters of fraternity" or "provincial letters." See notes to Pass. iv. 67; x. 342, 343.

The following illustrations are from Jack Upland. "Why aske ye no letters of bretherheads of other mens praiers, as ye desire that other men should aske letters of you? If your letters be good, why grant ye them not generally to all manner of men for the more charitie?"   And again—"Why be ye so hardie to grant by letters of fraternitie to men and wommen that they shall haue part and merite of all your good deeds, and ye weten neuer whether God be apayed with your deeds because of your sin?"   And again— "Freer, what charitie is this, to prease vpon a rich man, and to intice him to bee buried among you from his parish-church, and to such rich men giue letters of fraternity confirmed by your general seale, and therby to bear him in hand [i. e. make him believe] that he shall haue part of all your masses, metteus [*read* mattins], preachings, fastings, wakings, and all other good deeds done by your brethren of your order."

11. (11. 57.) *Pol by pol*, head by head; i. e. severally, separately. Each sinner who had made the proper payment would have a separate mass said for his benefit.

21. (11. 72.) "That desireth the widow, only to be married to her wealth" [c]; "That marry no widows, except in order to command (*lit.* wield) their goods" [b]. We frequently find similar charges against the friars.

> " And if the riche man deie that was of eny mihte, ·
>   Than wolen the freres for the cors fihte" . . .
> " For als ich evere brouke min hod under min hat,
>   The frere wole to the *direge*, if the cors is fat;
>   Ac, bi the feith I owe to God, if the cors is lene,
>   He wole wagge aboute the cloistre and kepen hise fet clene."
>   Polit. Poems, ed. Wright, pp. 331, 332.

" Why busie ye not to heare to shrift of poor folke, as well as of riche lords and ladies? . . . Why couet ye not to bury poor folk among you? . . . Why will ye not be at their *diriges* as ye haue been at rich mens?" Jack Upland, sectt. 16, 17.

" Freris drawen to hem confessioun and birying of riche men by mony sotil meenes, and messe pens, and trentals; bot thei wil not cum to pore mennis *dirige*, ne resseyve hem to be biryed amonge hem;" Wyclif's Works, iii. 374. And see Pierce the Ploughmans Crede, ll. 113—117, 318—329, 393—397, 408—417, 705—716.

——(11. 77; *not in* c.) *Catekumelynges*, i. e. catechumens. In Hook's Church Dictionary we find—" *Catechumens*; a name given, in the first ages of Christianity, to the Jews or Gentiles who were being prepared and instructed to receive baptism," &c. See the whole article. Richardson gives a quotation shewing the form *catechumenists*, viz.—" Hence their forenamed authors assume, that the children of the faithfull dying without baptisme, may be thought to receive the baptisme of the Spirit, as well as those *catechumenists* spoken of;" Bp. Morton, Cath. Appeale, p. 248.

——(11. 81; *not in* c.) I do not know where to find the quotation "sola contritio," &c. Chaucer has the same remark. "I say that contrition somtime delivereth man fro sinne," &c.; Pers. Tale, Prima Pars Penitentiæ. Cf. Ps. xxxii. 5; 1 John i. 9.

——(11. 82; *not in* c.) See B. xv. 448—450, and note to B. x. 350.

24. (11. 84.) Love and Loyalty are mentioned, as persons, in Pass. v. 36, 156; since which we have had no more mention of them. In this line Loyalty is suddenly brought before us again, without any introduction. "Then laughed Loyalty, because I frowned upon the friar" [c]; or, "And Loyalty looked on me, and I frowned afterwards" [b].

30. (*not in* b, *but compare* 11. 92.) The expression *and saue onliche prestes* means that the only exception to the duty of publicly rebuking sinners is in the case of priests who have learnt the existence of sins in the course of confessions made to them. See note below, to B. xi. 92.

——(11. 87; *not in* c, *but compare* xi. 34.) It would not be very easy to support the duty, of rebuking sinning brethren publicly, from St Peter's epistles, but our author may have been thinking rather of certain passages in those of St Paul; especially Gal. ii. 11, 1 Tim. v. 20, Titus i. 13, ii. 15. Or, indeed, the reference to St Peter may very easily point to St Paul's open rebuke of him; Gal. ii. 11. The text "non oderis" is from Levit. xix. 17— "Non oderis fratrem tuum in corde tuo, sed publice argue eum, ne habeas super illo peccatum."

It is particularly to be noted that there is a pun upon the word *fratres*. Literally, it means· *brethren*, but our author tells us plainly that it also means *friars*; see note to Pass. xvi. 75, and observe l. 90 [b] below.

31. (11. 88.) Here William uses a counter argument. "But they (the friars) will quote a text to a different effect, viz. Mat. vii. 1."

32. (11. 89.) Loyalty replies—"Of what use then were the law, if no man ever reproved falsehood and deceit? Surely it was for some good reason that the apostle said *non oderis fratrem.*"

Lyf, a living person, a man; see the Glossary. *Vndertoke*, rebuked, reproved. This sense is required by the context, and is justified by our author's use of *vndernymeth* in the same sense, that of *reproveth*, in B. v. 115; since *nyme* and *take* are words of the same power and sense.

William is verbally wrong in using the word "apostle" here, since the text occurs in Levit. xix. 17, as above noted; but perhaps he considered that St Paul practically quoted that text in 1 Tim. v. 20, which bears the very same sense, though worded differently.

——(11. 92; *not in* c, *but compare* xiii. 30.) *Licitum*, permitted. The argument is—every law permits laymen to speak the truth openly in all cases; but parsons and priests must not utter "tales," i. e. matters recounted to them in confession. At first sight, this looks like an argument in favour of the supposition that the author was himself a layman; but it is clearly meant that the clergy were *likewise* permitted to speak freely, with the sole exception that they must not utter sins admitted to them in the confessional. And the reader will further observe the advice in ll. 36—39, and the argument, in l. 34, that the misdeeds of the friars were *so notorious* that it could not be wrong to speak against them. That the author was in orders (probably only in minor orders) is so clearly told us in Passus vi. (C-text) that we cannot doubt it; cf. note to Pass. xii. 197. Neither may we suppose that he took orders *after* the B-text was written; both because that would make him more than 45 years old before doing so, and because ll. 16 and 17 of Passus ii. (B-text) expressly contradict that supposition. In other words, we must not lay stress upon the *three lines* in B. xi. 92—94, apart from their context, but fairly read and ponder the *whole* of that Text.

——(11. 96.) *And*, if. "Though the recital were true, if it touched upon sinful conduct."

46. (11. 107.) The use of the words *multi* and *pauci* is not out of place; for though no such words occur in the parable itself, as told in Mat. xxii. 1—13, they occur in the very next verse, in what is the moral lesson drawn from that parable. The Vulgate version has—"*Multi* enim sunt uocati, *pauci* uero electi."

Mangerie, a feast; lit. an eating. Wyclif uses the very same word with respect to this same parable of the Great Supper. He says—"þis grete soper is þe grete *mangery* þat seintis in hevene shal eten of Goddis bord;" Works, i. 4. The word occurs at least thrice in the Tale of Gamelyn; ed. Wright, ll. 341, 430, 460. In Sir Amadace, st. lv, a wedding-feast is called a *maungery*, and lasted 40 days; Early Eng. Met. Romances, ed. Robson, p. 49.

51. (11. 112.) Holy-church, it may be remembered, was introduced as a person in Pass. ii. 72, and was made to say, in the next line—

"Ich *vnderfeng* þe formest · and fre man þe made."

With respect to ll. 53—73, Whitaker remarks—"the, best theology of modern times will scarcely furnish a better refutation of the doctrine of absolute election and reprobation, than this admirable passage."

61. (11. 122.) This is one of the frequent allusions which shew that William was familiar with legal matters. The reference is to the legal condition of "villeins," which is illustrated by Littleton's Book of Tenures, sect. 172—208. There were two principal classes of villeins, viz. "villeins in gross," who were of the lowest class, and could be sold by their lords; and a rather higher class, named "villeins regardant," here referred to, who were attached to the soil, and specially engaged in agriculture. "These were in a better condition than villeins in gross, were allowed many indulgences, and even, in some cases, a limited kind of property; yet the law held that the person and property of the villein belonged entirely to his lord, the rule being the same as that in the Roman law, that whatever was acquired through the slave was acquired by the lord;" English Cyclopædia, Arts and Sciences, s. v. Villein. In further illustration of the condition of the *cherl* or peasant, Mr Wright refers to the Descriptio Norfolcensium, in his Early Mysteries and other Latin Poems of the Twelfth and Thirteenth Centuries, p. 94; and to a poem on the Constitution of Masonry, ed. Halliwell, p. 14, wherein it is stated that a bondman could not be apprenticed without the leave of his lord. See also the remarks on thraldom in Cursor Mundi, ed. Morris, p. 546; and Bruce, ed. Skeat, i. 229—274.

74. (11. 135.) *Baw*, an expression of great contempt, used again in Pass.

xxii. 398. It is clearly the word which is spelt *buf* in Chaucer's Sompnours Tale, Group D, l. 1934; and it was obviously intended to represent the sound of an eructation.

"Lo, *buf* they seye, cor meum eructauit."

Chaucer refers here to the somewhat strange beginning of Ps. xliv. (or xlv.) in the Vulgate version—"Eructauit cor meum uerbum bonum."

Whitaker notes that it is "still used [A.D. 1813] in Lancashire as an interjection of contempt and abhorrence."

75. (11. 136.) *Troianus* means Trajan, whose name seems to have been unfamiliar to the scribes, and probably was somewhat so to the poet himself; only two MSS. (see C-text, footnotes) give the right spelling—*traianus*. In B. xi. 155, we are expressly referred to the Legenda Sanctorum for the story. Bacon alludes to it in his Advancement of Learning, ed. W. Aldis Wright, pp. 54, 55, in these words:—"On the other side, how much Trajan's virtue and government was admired and renowned, surely no testimony of grave and faithful history doth more lively set forth, than that legend tale of Gregorius Magnus, bishop of Rome, who was noted for the extreme hatred he bare towards all heathen excellency; and yet he is reported, out of the love and estimation of Trajan's moral virtues, to have made unto God passionate and fervent prayers for the delivery of his soul out of hell; and to have obtained, with a caveat that he should make no more such petitions." Mr W. A. Wright adds a note—"This story is told of Gregory the Great in his life by Paulus Diaconus, c. 27, and in that by Joannes Diaconus, lib. ii. c. 44; and is referred to by Joannes Damascenus, De iis qui in Fide Dormierunt, c. 16." Dante refers to the story twice; Purg. x. 73; Par. xx. 40. See Mrs Jameson's Sacred and Legendary Art, i. 307. Compare also the story of St Gregory's Treutal, in Polit., Religious, and Love Poems, ed. Furnivall, p. 83. The following is the version of the story as given in the life of Gregory in Caxton's translation of the Golden Legend, fol. lxxxxvii.

"In the tyme that Trayan themperour regned, and on a tyme as he wente toward a batayll out of Rome, it happed that in hys waye as he shold ryde, a woman a wydowe came to hym wepyng and sayd : I praye thee, syre, that thou auenge the deth of one my sone, whyche innocently and wythout cause hath ben slayn. Themperour answerd: yf I come agayn fro the batayll hool and sounde, then I shall do justyce for the deth of thy sone. Thenne sayd the wydowe : Syre, and yf thou deye in the bataylle, who shall thenne avenge hys deth for me ? And the wydowe sayd, is it not better that thou do to me justice, and have the meryte thereof of God, than another have it for thee ? Then had Trayan pyte, and descended fro his horse, and dyde justyce in avengynge the deth of her sone. On a tyme saynt Gregory went by the marked of Rome whyche is called the marked of Trayan. And thenne he remembred of the justyce and other good dedes of Trayan, and how he had ben pyteous and debonayr, and was moche sorowfull that he had ben a paynem ; and he tourned to the chyrche of saynt Peter waylyng for thorrour

of the mescreaunce of Trayan.   Thenne answerd a voys fro God, sayng: I
haue now herd thy prayer, and haue spared Trayan fro the payne perpetuelly.
By thys thus, as somme saye, the payne perpetuell due to Trayan as a mes-
creaunt was somme dele take awaye, but for all that was he not quyte fro
the pryson of helle; for the sowle may well be in helle, and fele ther no
payne, by the mercy of God."   The legend is alluded to by Bradford, ii. 290,
and Coverdale, ii. 269; in the editions by the Parker Society.

87. (*see* b. 11. 151.)   *Surrasyn*, Saracen, i. e. unbeliever, idolater.   In B.
xi. 157, he is called a "paynym of Rome."   The terms Saracen and Pagan
were often used as synonymous with Mahommedan, and it was a universal
belief with Christians in the middle ages that Mahommedans were idolaters.
Cf. Pass. iv. 484, xviii. 123, 132, 150—186.

——(11. 147.)   *There no biddyng myghte*, where no prayer could do so.
Here *biddyng* is used in the restricted sense of a mass offered for a soul in
purgatory; see C. xiii. 85 (b. 11. 145).   Trajan could not have been released
by prayers offered in the usual manner; only by a special grace.   For
there = where, cf. B. xi. 160 below.

88. (11. 148.)   Let the reader observe the inverted commas at the beginning of this line.   In the B-text the speech is spoken by Loyalty, and
extends to 163 lines, ending with l. 310.   In the C-text, it is spoken by
Recklessness, and consists of no less than 283 lines, ending with C.
xiv. 128.

"See, ye lords, what Loyalty effected, and true judgment as practised by
him" [c]; "See, ye lords, what Loyalty did with respect to an emperor
of Rome."   On this use of *by*, see note to Pass. i. 78.

——(11. 164.) "And gave it to Moses on the mount, to teach all men."
See the note on *took*; Pass. iv. 47; p. 58.

92. (11. 165.) "As for Law without Loyalty (i. e. Truth), stake but a
bean on it!" [c]; "As for Law without Love, saith Trajan, stake but a bean
on it" [b].   William is fond of this theme; cf. Pass. iv. 447—450, v. 144,
145, 156, &c.

93. (11. 166.)   *Seuene ars*, seven arts; see note to Pass. xii. 98.

——(11. 173.) "Should each of them love the other, and lend to them
(*or* give to them) as they would to themselves."   *Lene*, lend, give; cf. l. 190
below, where *ȝiueth* is used as an equivalent word; and observe the context,
especially C. xiii. 116.   The word cannot be *leue*, believe, as that would make
nonsense.

——(11. 180.)   Surely a beautiful line; cf. Mat. xxv. 40.   See C. xii.
121 below.

103. (11. 186.)   *Carful*, full of care, wretched; cf. Pass. xii. 42, and see
Luke xiv. 13.

105. (*not in* b.)   *Manshupes*, courtesies, honours, compliments.   In the
Ormulum, l. 19014, *mannshipe* means dignity.   In Layamon, *monscipe* occurs
repeatedly; and Sir F. Madden remarks (vol. iii. p. 439)—"This word does
not occur in Bosworth's A.S. Dictionary, although it is difficult to suppose

it did not exist. It is used very frequently in both texts of Layamon, and its usual meaning undoubtedly is *honor, worship, dignity*. The synonyms are *menscu* (l. 2535) and *mahþe* (l. 6234); and, in the French text of Wace, *los, dignité*. In the later text we have the adverb *mansipliche*, honourably; l. 20743." In William of Palerne, ll. 2076, 3337, *manchip* means courage; which is also the sense of the Icel. *mannskapr*. It is clear that, in the present passage, the sense is nearly that of the Lowland-Scotch *mensk* or *mense* (which see in Jamieson), from the A.S. *mennisc*, humane.

106. (ll. 189.) In [c], *for* is a conjunction, meaning *because*; in [b], it is the common preposition.

107. (ll. 190.) *That*, those who [c]; who [b].

109. (ll. 109.) *Blod-breþrene*, brethren by blood; written *blody bretheren* in [b]. See l. 115 below, and the phrase *bretheren as of o blode* in B. xi. 193; and see note to Pass. ix. 217; p. 168.

110. (ll. 196.) *Quasi modo geniti* was a familiar phrase, and used as a name for Low Sunday, or the octave of Easter, because, in the Sarum Missal, the Office for that day begins with the text 1 Pet. ii. 2; viz. "quasi modo geniti infantes, rationabile sine dolo lac concupiscite."

111. (ll. 197.) *Bote yf synne hit make*, unless sin cause it to be so [c]; *or*, unless sin caused it to be so [b]; cf. Pass. viii. 4, 28, 65.

112. (ll. 199.) *Me*, i.e. men, people; the usual indefinite pronoun, common in Middle-English. See Morris, Outlines of Eng. Accidence, p. 144, note 1. Thus *me calde vs* = we were called. The B-text has the form *men*. See note to B. x. 192; p. 244.

Considering that William had no access to a concordance, he is remarkably correct in his argument. The phrase "children of men" occurs 19 times in the Old Testament, but, in the New, not at all; whilst "children of God" occurs 10 times in the New Testament, but not once in the Old.

116. (ll. 203.) "Therefore let us love (one another) as dear children, and give to them that need" [c]; "Therefore let us love as dear brethren ought to do, and let each man smile upon another; and, out of what each man can spare, let him give alms where it is necessary" [b].

117. (ll. 205.) "For we shall all (depart) hence."

——(ll. 207.) "For no man knows how nigh is the time for him to be taken away from both (property and skill). Therefore let no living being blame another, though he know more Latin, nor reprove him foully, since there is none faultless."

——(ll. 216.) "For it is very long before logic can explain thoroughly a moral discourse." *Lessoun* seems to mean a "lesson" taken out of the Legenda Sanctorum. To *assoille* is to resolve, explain, answer, satisfy, &c.; lit. to absolve; see *asoilede* in C. xiii. 137 below.

137. (ll. 244.) "And God quickly made answer with respect to the desire of each of them" [c]; "And God quickly answered, and followed (i.e. acceded to) the wish of each" [b].

——(11. 245.) *Mathew*. A mistake; St Matthew does not mention them; see Luke x. 40—42.

146. (11. 253.) *Kynde*, natural vigour. In The Book of Quinte Essence, ed. Furnivall, p. 1, we have the expression—"how þat olde men, and feble in *kynde*, myȝte be *restorid.*" And again, at p. 15 of the same—"The first medecyn is to reduce [*bring back*] an oold feble euangelik man to þe firste strenkþe of ȝongþe [ȝougþe?]; also to *restore* aȝen his *nature* þat is lost." It is rather odd that so much virtue should here be attributed to walnuts, but it was no doubt a common belief. It is sufficiently verified by the words of Andrew Boorde, in his Introduction of Knowledge, ed. Furnivall, p. 283; where, speaking "of nuttes, great and smale," he says—"The *walnut* and the banocke be of one operacyon. They be tarde and slow of digestyon, yet they doth *comforte the brayn if the pyth or skyn be pylled of, and than they be nutrytyue.* Fylberdes be better than hasell nuttes; yf they be newe; and taken from the tree, *and the skyn or the pyth pulled of, they be nutrytyue, & doth increase fatnes.*" A *banocke*, by the way, is the West-of-England *bannut*. Halliwell says—" the growing tree is called a *bannut* tree, but the converted timber *walnut.*" An explanation given me in Shropshire affords a further light. I was told that a *bannut* was the ordinary walnut such as is commonly seen there, but a *walnut* was a similar nut of a larger size, imported from abroad, in accordance with the well-known derivation of the word.

151. (11. 259.) *Drat*, a contracted form of *dredeth* [b].

——(11. 262.) *Salamon*. But, strictly speaking, the text (Prov. xxx. 8) is not Solomon's; it occurs in the proverbs of Agur, son of Jakeh; Prov. xxx. 1.

——(11. 265.) The text in St Luke is—"Adhuc unum tibi deest : omnia quæcunque habes uende, et da pauperibus;" Lu. xviii. 22. William really quotes the parallel passage, in Mat. xix. 21. He seems to have observed the mistake, as it does not appear in the C-text.

——(11. 277.) *And þei her deuoir dede*, if they did their duty. William refers us to Ps. xlii. 1 (Vulgate), i. e. to Ps. xliii. 1 (A. V.), which does not seem to be much connected with the subject. But no doubt he meant us to consider the general tenor of the whole Psalm, which has language suitable for priests in verses 3 and 4, and breathes the true spirit of reliance upon God's protecting care.

☞ **A long insertion here in the C-text ; B. 11. 278 corresponds to C. xiv. 101.**

173. (*not in* b.) *Poetes*. The poets (or rather authors) here mentioned are merely named at random, just as in Pass. xv. 190. It would be useless to point out what these authors have really said in praise of poverty. The reader may consult what is said of it in Burton's Anatomy of Melancholy, where sufficient references may be found.

Porfirie of course represents the celebrated Greek philosopher Porphyrius (died A.D. 306), many of whose works are extant, including a life of Pythagoras, though his greatest work, written against Christianity, was purposely destroyed by Theodosius. The reference cannot be to the poet Porphyrius, who wrote a panegyric of Constantine, as his works were little known.

175. (*not in* b.) *Tullius,* i. e. M. Tullius Cicero. *Tholomeus,* i. e. Ptolemæus the astronomer (floruit A.D. 130—160), author of the Almagest, &c. The reader may remember that the Wife of Bath cites him in such a manner as to have drawn from Tyrwhitt the remark (note to C. T. 5764) that her copy of Ptolemy "was very different from any I have been able to meet with." In another place (C. T. 5906) Chaucer cites a passage which may very well be the one here intended.

179, 180. (*not in* b.) "Unless the seed that is sown die in the slough (*or* mould), no blade will ever spring up, nor any ear of corn harden to grain upon the straw." Palsgrave has—"*Spyre* of corne, *barbe du ble;*" and again, "I *spyer,* as corne dothe whan it begynneth to waxe rype, *Ie espie.*" So Chaucer, Troil. and Cress. ii. 1335, has—

> "Or as an ook comth of a litel *spyre.*"

"What thinge is thilke *spire* that in-to a tree shoulde wexe?" Test. of Love, Bk. iii.; in Chaucer's Works, ed. 1561, fol. 314. "*Spyre* of corne or herbe, *Hastula;*" Prompt. Parv. And see Skelton, ed. Dyce, ii. 251. *Spike* is the Lat. *spica,* an ear of corn; cf. Icel. *spik,* a spike, a sprig. To *curne* is to form grain, to granulate; cf. G. *körnen.*

> "The thridde time, tho grene corn in somer ssolde *curne,*
> To foule wormes muchedel the eres gonne turne."
>   Rob. of Gl. ed. Hearne, p. 490.

"*Kerned,* formed into corns; Jewel's Works, ii. 1017;" Index to Parker Society's Publications. See Critical Notes to C-text, p. 459.

187. (*not in* b.) "Are more seasonable and hardier (lit. tougher) for man's behoof." William's father is said to have been a farmer; and this is one of the innumerable passages that prove him to have been qualified to sing of "The Plowman."

188. (*not in* b.) Observe *with* = against, as in l. 192. *Mowe nouht,* may not endure, cannot hold out.

192. (*not in* b.) "Cannot so well hold out against the frost, in the open field, if it freeze long."

193, 194. (*not in* b.) *That,* they that. *Worth alowed of,* will be approved by. The whole passage is good.

204—207. I repeat here, for convenience, the Critical Note to these lines; C-text, p. 460. This passage is the only incomplete one in the C-text. Line 206 is from the Ilchester MS., and is incomplete because the rats have eaten the end of it. The missing portion must have been like what I have suggested in the footnote. The sense is—"For Christ said to his saints, that for His sake suffered poverty, penance, and persecution of body, (they) shall have the more honour for their reward, and be esteemed more worthy than angels; in their affliction, He greeted them in this wise,

viz. your sorrow shall be turned into joy." It deserves to be particularly
noted that, in our author, as in Hampole, the word *anger* means *affliction* or
distress, and just answers to the Latin *tristitia*. See the Glossary.

209. *Wyrdes*, weirds, fates, destinies. See Critical Note, C-text, p. 460.

211. *Foul towname*, evil "to-name," evil nickname; alluding to the word
stulte below. Some MSS. read *fool to name*, i. e. fool as a name; see the
footnote. Stratmann gives three examples of *toname*, as meaning *cognomen;*
viz. Wycl. Ecclus. xlvii. 19; Manning, l. 7000; Layamon, l. 9383.

212. (*not in* b.) "And that his spirit shall depart hence, and his wealth
remain behind." See *bilæfen* in Stratmann.

215. (*not in* b.) Here the person is changed, from the third to the second.
"Thou that art so loath to leave that which thou must needs leave." The
whole text in Ps. xxxviii. 7 (Vulgate) is—"Thesaurizat, et ignorat cui con-
gregabit ea."

216, 217. (*not in* b.) *Unredy*, void of counsel, improvident. Æthelred
was named the Unready because he was void of counsel and imprudent;
from A.S. *unrad*, bad advice. The sense is—"an improvident reeve shall
spend what thou leavest; (he shall spend) in a moment that (wealth) in
which many a moth was master;" i. e. in which many a moth revelled. Cf.
B. x. 362. *Mynte-while*, a moment; this form is clearly due to the confusion
between *mite* and *minute*, on which see Way's note to "Mynute, myte,
minutum" in Prompt. Parv. p. 340. See also Pass. xiv. 200, where the
B-text (xi. 372) has *minute-while*. It must be remembered, too, that *mites*
are called *mints* in the West of England. It is clear that *mint* (from the
root *min*, small), was the old spelling of *mite*, just as the verb *to mince* (from
the same root) is represented by *meizan* in Old High German. *Minute* is
also from the same root; and as *mite* and *minute* meant just the same thing,
viz. that which is small, they were easily confused.

218. (*not in* b.) *Vpholderes*, dealers in second-hand articles; as in Pass.
vii. 374. *The hul*, the hill; which, beyond all doubt, means Cornhill. This
will be obvious on reference to the note to Pass. vii. 377, and to the context
of that passage.

221. (*not in* b.) *Pees-coddes*, pods of peas.

> " The *peascod* greene oft with no litle toyle
> Hee'd seeke for *in the fattest fertil'st soile*."
> Browne's Britannia's Pastorals, p. 71.

Pere-ionettes, evidently pears that were soon ripe. "In *July* come . . .
early peares, and plummes in fruit, *ginnitings*, quadlins;" Bacon, Essay 46.
The *genniting* is an early apple. Cotgrave has—"Pomme de S. Jean, S.
John's apple, a kind of soon-ripe sweeting;" and again—"Hastiveau, a
hasting apple or peare;" and—"Hastivel, as Hastiveau; or, a soon-ripe
apple, called the St John's apple." P. Lacroix (Manners, Customs, &c.
during the Middle Ages, p. 116) tells us that, in the 13th century, one of
the best esteemed pears was the *hastiveau*, which was "an early sort, and no
doubt the golden pear now called St Jean." I have no doubt that the term

ionelle (and probably *genniting*) is ultimately derived from *Jean*, and that the reference is to St John's day, June 24. Cf. F. *Jeaunot* (O.F. *Jeannet*) as a diminutive of *Jean*.

222. (*not in* b.) "Soon ripe, soon rotten;" Heywood's Proverbs. On which Ray notes—"Cito maturum, cito putridum . . . As trees that bear double flowers, viz. cherries, peaches, &c., bring forth no fruit, but spend all in the blossom. Presto maturo, presto marzo."

224. (*not in* b.) "Most subject is the fattest soil to weeds;" 2 Hen. IV. iv. 4, 54.

229. *Wose*, i. e. ooze, slime, mud. It occurs in the Tale of Beryn— "They [the ships] been nat yit ysetelid, ne fixid in the *wose.*" Also thrice in the Ayenbite of Inwyt, pp. 87, 89, 186. And see Prompt. Parv., p. 532, note 3.

230. (*not in* b.) "So out of riches, (heaped) upon riches, arise all vices."

232. (*not in* b.) *Worth lygge*, will lie down; will be "laid" by its own over-weight.

244. (*not in* b.) *Hus harde holdynge*, his close keeping (of his wealth), his parsimonious grasping, his 'closefistedness.'

246. (*not in* b.) "See how money has (often) purchased both fair mansions and, at the same time, terror; money, which is the root of robbers; I mean, the riches that is kept within-doors." The sense is clear, but the construction is very awkward. A *place* often means a manor-house or squire's mansion, as in Chaucer's Sir Thopas, first stanza. Money is called the "root" of robbers, as being productive of robbery.

SCHEME OF THE CONTENTS OF PASSUS XIV.

(B. PASS. XI. 278—END. Cf. Wright's edition, pp. 219—227.)

C-TEXT.	B-TEXT.		C-TEXT.	B-TEXT.
xiv. 198	———		xiv. 220	*like* xi. 400
	xi. 369, 370		221—230	401—410
199—201	371—373		231—233	*like* 411—413
202—204			234	414
	374, 375		235	*like* 415, 416
205—211	376—382		236—240	417—421
	383—391		241	*like* 422, 423
212—219	392—399		242—249	424—431

NOTES TO PASSUS XIV. (B. Pass. XI. 278—END.)

Lines 1—100 are peculiar to the C-text. For a brief abstract of their contents, see Pref. to C-text, p. xc.

1. (*not in* b.) "But well may it be for poverty." *Wel worth*, well be it, is the opposite of *wo worth*, which is much more common. - Cf. "O *well* is thee;" Ps. cxxviii. 2 (Pr. Book). In a poetical epistle to Henry IV., Gower begins stanza 22 with—"A, *wel* is him that shedde neuer blode."

5. (*not in* b.) *Men rat*, people read, one reads. *Men*, being indefinite, takes the singular verb. *Rat* is short for *redeth*, as in Pass. iv. 410, 416.

10. (*not in* b.) Understand *was*. "And Abraham (was) not bold enough once to hinder him."

18. (*not in* b.) *Do we so mala*, let us also receive evil.

23. (*not in* b.) *Thorgh grace*, by God's favour, or blessing. Whitaker cites the second stanza of Chaucer's Sir Thopas—

> "His fader was a man ful free,
> And lord he was of that contree,
>   As it was *goddes grace*"—

where *goddes grace* means no more than 'God's pleasure.'

45. (*not in* b.) This is interesting testimony. It shews that messengers were sometimes privileged, and might take a short cut without trespass. It also shews that the hayward, in case of trespass, used to exact a pledge (such as a hat, or a pair of gloves, see l. 48 below) from the trespasser. A similar allusion occurs in a burlesque song about the Man in the Moon, of whom it is said that—

> "He hath hewe sumwher a burthen of brere,
> Therefore *sum hayward hath taken ys wed;*"
>
> Ritson's Ancient Songs, i. 69.

In this case, the allusion is to committing trespass for the purpose of cutting some briars for fuel. Perhaps a hayward was sometimes chosen to act as overseer or foreman in harvest-time; cf. Pecock's Repressor, ii. 383—"as whanne money is take and paied to a man forto go and fynde him-silf and his hors, that he be an hayward or an ouerseer thoruȝ al an haruest-cesoun vpon repe-men, that thei repe bisili and clenli." For further remarks, see Note to Pass. vi. 16. Whitaker remarks upon this line—"It was an ancient custom in cases of trespass, to distrain upon some personal chattel of the trespasser, a summary mode of redress, which, though it might lead to breaches of the peace, was surely preferable to a lawsuit. But this representation gives a striking idea of the wild state of manners, when the whole country lay open, and messengers riding express might abridge their way, without penalty or complaint, by riding over the most valuable fields of corn."

"Necessity has no law;" quoted as "Need hath no law" in Pass. xxiii. 10. Skelton, in his Colin Clout, ll. 864, 865, says—

> "But it is an olde sayd sawe,
> That nede hath no lawe."

The same form occurs in Heywood. Mr Hunter, in his Hallamshire Glossary, says that *law* is used, provincially, to signify liberty, advantage, or license (which is true); and that it has the same sense in this proverb (which is false). Of course, it does not mean that "necessity has no liberty," but the exact converse, viz. that it knows of no restraint, and indulges in a license not permitted under ordinary circumstances, according to our poet's own excellent illustrations in Pass. xxiii. 6—22. Mr Hunter has made the mistake through the confusion of mind which is sometimes caused by clauses involving a negative; and Mr Hazlitt, in his English Proverbs, has unthinkingly accepted his explanation. The proverb is an old one, and often cited. Ray compares it with the Greek "Ἀνάγκῃ οὐδὲ Θεοὶ μάχονται;" with the Italian "La necessita non ha legge;" and with the Latin "Ingens telum necessitas" in Cicero's De Amicitia.

52. (*not in* b.) Winchester fair. See Note to Pass. vii. 211.

55. *Breuet*, a letter or note. Cotgrave has—"*Brevet*, m.: a briefe, note, breviate, little writing," &c. See Hist. Agriculture in England, by J. E. T. Rogers, i. 666, for examples of messengers being sent with a scroll. He observes—"Parchment, though not very cheap, was quite within the use of most persons of any substance. The letter was written on a slip of this material, a narrow piece being cut half way through at the bottom to which the seal was annexed, and the whole rolled round and tied with thread, or in some cases silk."

In the present passage, the letter is described as enclosed in a box. So also, in Nicholas Trivet's Life of Constance (Originals and Analogues published by the Chaucer Society, pt. i. p. 27) we find—"Puis ouery la *boiste* le messagier et ouery les lettres," i. e. then she opened the messenger's box, and opened the letter.

69. (*not in* b.) "Both to love, and to give alms (lit. lend) to the true and the false."

71. (*not in* b.) *By hus power*, as far as lies in his power.

72. (*not in* b.) *Backes*, clothes for the back, cloaks; see B. x. 362, and the Note. *For the colde*, as a protection against the cold; see B. vi. 62, and the Note on p. 159.

73. (*not in* b.) "Truly to pay tithes of their property; which tithe, as it seems, is a sort of toll (or payment) which our Lord expects from every living creature that makes money without fraud or wrong-dealing, or without keeping women in brothels (as the brothel-keepers do)."

Loketh after, looks for, expects to have. *Lyf*, creature; see the Glossary. But our author remarks that men ought not to presume to offer tithes of gains that they have obtained by fraudulent means, neither ought brothel-keepers to offer of the money paid them by those who lodge with them. See Pass. vii. 287—308.

77. (*not in* b.) *Spele*, to spare, hoard; *see* Pass. vii. 432, and the Note.

80. (*not in* b.) *The two lawes, i. e.* the duty to God and to our neighbour. William means that the poor beggars could not carry out some parts of these duties, especially the giving of alms, the imparting of instruction, and fasting during Lent. They could not clothe the naked, they were excused from paying tithes and serving on inquests, and they were permitted to work on saints'-days and vigils to earn food.

85. (*not in* b.) *Contumax*, contumacious, a despiser of authority. "*Contumax* is he that thurgh his indignation is ayenst euery auctoritee or power of hem that ben his soueraines;" Chaucer, Pers. Tale, *De Superbia.*

90. (*not in* b.) "Confesses himself to be a Christian, and of holy-church's belief."

91. (*not in* b.) "There is no law, in my belief, that will hinder him in his way, where God is the porter Himself, and knows every one (who enters). The Porter, out of pure compassion, may fulfil the law (by admitting him), inasmuch as he (the poor beggar) desires (to do) and would (do) to each man as to himself." It is clear from what follows that *he* (l. 94) refers to the beggar, not to the porter.

96. (*not in* b.) *Reyme*, clutch, seize, grasp, obtain, acquire. Such I take to be the sense of this difficult word. Cf. Icel. *hremma*, to clutch, *hrammr*, a bear's paw, lit. that which clutches; Swed. *rama*, to paw, to lay hold of an opportunity. Halliwell gives "*Rame*, to reach, or stretch after. 'To rame, *pandiculor*'; Coles' Dict.;" and again, "*Rame*, to rob or plunder. Lincolnshire;" also, "*Ream*, to hold out the hand for taking or receiving; North." So in Polit. Songs, ed. Wright, p. 150—

"Thus me pileth the pore and pyketh ful clene,
    The ryche *raymeth* withouten eny ryght."

Here the same meaning applies, and Mr Wright merely made a bad guess in translating the word by "lord it;" a mistake which is copied into H. Coleridge's Glossarial Index. So again, in Political, Religious, and Love Poems, ed. Furnivall, p. 231, it is said of Cupidity, that "hit falseth, hit *reymeth*, hit falleth, hit shendeth;" i. e. it cheats, *grasps*, fells (?), and disgraces. In Mr Furnivall's Glossary the mistaken explanation re-appears, with Coleridge's authority. Thus it is that errors are spread.

This word is totally distinct from *rayme* in A. i. 93, which is the same as "*Rame*, to rove, or ramble; Yorkshire," as given in Halliwell's Dictionary. I take the present opportunity of illustrating this word also—

"This souerayn with his seggis thurȝe Sycile he wyndes,
    Thoȝt to ride and to *rayme* the regions of Barbres."
                    Allit. Rom. of Alexander (ed. Stevenson), L 2487.

"Why thow has *redyne* and *raymede*, & raunsound the pople."
Morte Arthure (ed. Brock), 1. 100.

Dr Stratmann gives the references to *reyme* and *rayme* under the same heading—*raimen;* which tends to confusion.

101. (11. 278.) This is an obvious and interesting allusion to Wyclif's so-called "Poor Priests." See Wyclif's Works, i. 63, 176, 177; iii. 272, 293, &c. By 'Spera-in-deo' is meant part of Ps. xxxvi (Vulgate) or Ps. xxxvii (A. V.); the third verse of which is—"Spera in Domino, et fac bonitatem; et inhabita terram, et pasceris in diuitiis eius." The whole of the rest of the psalm, verses 4—40, is full of encouragement to welldoers

104. (11. 281.) "The title (of 'priest') by which you take orders proclaims that you are advanced," i. e are set in authority. The very word *priest* or *presbyter*, i. e. elder, entitles the man who bears the name to some respect. This would be still more marked in days when the orders (exclusive of the bishop) were reckoned as being *seven* in number, the order of priest being the highest of these. See Note to B. v. 138, on p. 112.

106. (11. 283.) *Tok*, gave; as elsewhere. "He that gave you the title should give you your wages ; or else the bishop should do so who ordained you, and anointed your fingers." In l. 106, the person intended by *he* is probably the pope himself, as is suggested by his being likened to a king in l. 108.

112. (11. 289.) *By*, with reference to; as elsewhere.

113. (11. 290.) "Who have neither skill nor relationship (to great men), but only the tonsure, and the title of priest, a thing of no account, to live upon, as it were." *Corone* means the tonsure; see l. 125, and cf. Pass. i. 86, and the Note. *A tale of nouht*, a reckoning of no value, a thing of no account; because the title, though in some degree a sign of rank (see l. 104), is often slightly esteemed, and does not go for much in the way of supporting the man who bears it. The opposite to "a tale of nouht" is expressed by the Icel. *talsverðr* (lit. tale-worthy), worth counting or worth speaking of, considerable.

118. (11. 297.) "If false Latin be in that document, the law impugns it." This clearly shews, I think, that William had often drawn up, or at least copied out, legal documents.

119. (11. 298.) *Peynted parentrelignarie*, "i. e. interlined; for I cannot think that mere interlineary flourishes would vitiate a charter;" Whitaker.

123. (11. 302.) The advice of David is contained in the word *sapienter;* or, in our English version, "sing ye praises *with understanding;*" Ps. xlvii. 7. William is declaiming against "ouerskippers," or those who skipped over passages in reciting masses or other services. In Reliq. Antiq. i. 90, there is a distich which is remarkable for preserving the epithets bestowed on those who either *mumbled*, *skipped*, or *leaped over* the Psalms in chauting.

"Ecclesiæ sunt tres qui servitium male fallunt ;
Momyllers, forscyppers, ouerlepers, non bene psallunt."

Compare also the following, from Rel. Ant. i. 290—

> " Psallite devote, distincte metra tenete,
> Vocibus estote concordes, vana cavete;
> Nunquam posterior versus prius incipiatur
> Quam finis anterior perfecto fine fruatur.
> Hii sunt qui psalmos corrumpunt nequitur almos,
> *Dangler*, cum *jasper*, *lepar*, *galper*, quoque *draggar*,
> *Momeler*, *forskypper*, *forereynner*, sic et *overlepar*;
> Fragmina verborum Tutivillus colligit horum."

Perhaps "Dangler" should be "jangler;" else it means one who loiters. "Jasper" is "gasper;" "galper" is "gaper;" the other words are easily intelligible. Another version is given in the Poems of Walter Mapes, ed. Wright, p. 148, viz.—

> " Hii sunt qui psalmos corrumpunt nequiter almos,
> *Momler*, *forscypper*, *stumler*, *scaterer*, *overhipper*."

The word *overhipped*, i. e. hopped over, occurs in Jewel's Works, i. 363 (Parker Society). Gower (Conf. Amant. bk. v.) has—"But euer he somwhat *ouerhippeth*." Palsgrave has—"I *Ouerhyppe* a thyng in redyng or suche lyke, *Ie trespasse:* you haue *ouer-hypped* a lyne, *vous auez trespasse vne ligne*." See *ouerhuppen* in B. xiii. 68.

Concerning Tutivillus a few lines are printed also in Reliq. Antiq., i. 257, from MS. Douce 104, which is MS. xxxviii of Piers the Ploughman, described in Pref. C, p. xlv. He is also mentioned in the Towneley Mysteries, pp. 310, 319. Mr Wright says—"According to an old legend, a hermit walking out met one of the devils bearing a large sack, very full, under the load of which he seemed to labour. The hermit asked him what he carried in his sack. He answered that it was filled with the fragments of words which the clerks had skipped over or mutilated in the performance of the service, and that he was carrying them to hell to be deposited among the stores there." This legend is told at length in the Myrour of Our Lady, ed. Blunt; see pp. 53, 54, and 342.

125. (11. 304.) *Coroneþ*, marks with the tonsure, shaves in a priestly manner. See note to l. 113, and compare—

> "With *croune* and berde al fresh and newe yshaue."
> Chaucer; C. T. 13239.

The term *knightes* is correctly used, since it meant servants. Cf. A.S. *leorning-cniht*, a disciple, lit. a learning-servant. Mr Cutts, in his Scenes and Characters of the Middle Ages, p. 247, quotes this passage, and reminds us that priests commonly had the title of *Sir*, which is another reason for the use of the term *knight*.

128. (11. 307, 308.) "For either of them is indicted, and that by reason of the statement, that ignorance does not excuse bishops, nor unlearned priests" [b]. The word *idiotes* is here used as an adjective, with the French plural ending. Cf. *cardinales*, Pass. i. 132; *prouincials*, Pass. x. 342, and see the Note to the latter line, at p. 199. So in Pecock's Repressor, ii. 478, we have, as a translation of 2 Pet. ii. 1—"False prophetis weren in the peple,

as in ʒou schulen be *maistris liers.*" Again, in the same work, at p. 523, we
have "religiosis persoones." The passage referred to is probably one of the
following. "Inscitia sacerdotum nec excusatione est digna, nec uenia;"
and—"Non omnis ignorans immunis est a poena;" Decret. Gratiani, Pars
i. Distinctio xxxviii., and Distinctio xxvii. c. 16.

With respect to the word *idiot,* see Note to Pass. xii. 288; p. 257.

With this line is concluded the long speech which, in [c], is spoken by
Recklessness, and begins at xiii. 88. In [b], it ends two lines further on,
and is spoken by Loyalty, who begins at B. xi. 148.

150. (11. 333.) *Bere,* make a noise, low [c]; *belwe,* bellow [b].

156. (11. 336.) Compare Bacon's Advancement of Learning, ed. W.
Aldis Wright, p. 151—"Quis psittaco docuit suum χαῖρε? Who taught the
raven in a drought to throw pebbles into an hollow tree, where she spied
water, that the water might rise so as she might come to it? Who taught
the bee to sail through such a vast sea of air, and to find the way from a field
in flower a great way off to her hive? Who taught the ant to bite every
grain of corn that she burieth in her hill, lest it should take root and grow?"
Mr Thomas Wright aptly quotes a favourite passage from Hurdis's Poems.

> "But most of all it wins my admiration
> To view the structure of this little work,
> A bird's nest. Mark it well, within, without;
> No tool had he that wrought, no knife to cut,
> No nail to fix, no bodkin to insert,
> No glue to join. His little beak was all.
> And yet how neatly finished! What nice hand,
> With every implement and means of art,
> And twenty years' apprenticeship to boot,
> Could make me such another? Fondly then
> We boast of excellence, where noblest skill
> Instinctive genius foils."

161. (11. 341.) "If any mason were to make a mould for it with all her
(the pie's) wise contrivances, it seems to me a wonder!" See remarks on
the magpie's nest in The Architecture of Birds, p. 325. In the same work
will be found examples of various places of concealment or modes of protection adopted by birds in nest-building; see pp. 91, 129, 151, 189, &c.

169. (*not in b.*) *Dompynges* (spelt *doppynges* in MS. E), is clearly only
another name for the *dab-chick,* called by Drayton "the diving *dobchick,*"
Polyolbion, s. 25. We also find *didapper,* spelt *dice-dapper* by Middleton;
see Nares. Halliwell gives *dopchicken* as the Lincolnshire name. In the
Prompt. Parv. p. 127, we have the entry—"Doppar, or dydoppar, watyr-
byrde. *Mergulus,*" immediately followed by "Doppynge," which is left
unexplained. As we here see that *doppynge* means the same as *doppar,* we
can now tell *why* it was left unexplained. Cf. A.S. *dopened,* fulica; *dop-
fugel,* mergus. The word *doppettan,* with the sense "to dive," occurs in
Ælfric's Homilies, ii. 516, though Dr Bosworth explains it only as "to
sink;" it is a longer form of *dyppan,* to dip. I do not know where else the
form *domping* occurs; but the sense of it is obvious.

——(11. 349.) This curious idea was derived from Aristotle. "The pregnancy and conception of barren eggs is quick in most birds, as in the partridge, on account of the violence of their sexual desires; for if the hen stands in the way of the *breath* of the male she conceives, and immediately becomes of no use for fowling; for the partridge appears to have a very distinct smell;" Arist. Hist. of Animals, bk. vi. c. ii. § 9; tr. by Creswell (Bohn's Library).

171. (11. 350.) Cotgrave gives—"*Cuuquer,* to tread a hen, as a cock doth;" and Palsgrave—"I trede, as a cocke dothe an henne, *Ie cauque.*" It is the Lat. *calcare,* and is the same word as is used when we speak of *calking* or *caulking* a ship; see *Calk* in Wedgwood. In the St Alban's Book of Hawking, ed. 1496, sig. A i, we find—"And in the tyme of their [the hawkes'] love, they calle, and not *cauke.*" With respect to the peacock we find the following account in Batman vppon Bartholomè, lib. 12. c. 31. "And the Pecock is a bird that loueth not his young: for the male searcheth out the female, and secketh out her egges for to breake them, that he may so occupy him the more in his lecherie." Cf. note to Pass. xv. 184.

181. (11. 361.) "Was the fact that I saw Reason follow all animals" [c]; "Because Reason regarded and ruled all animals" [b]. Observe *rewarded* for 'regarded.' So, too, in the Romans of Partenay, ed. Skeat, l. 1190, *rewarde* is used to translate the French *regarder.*

192. (*not in* b.) *Reason.* "He should have said by *instinct,* which would have removed the difficulty;" Whitaker.

197. (11. 368.) The B-text means—"Why I suffer (it to be so), or suffer it not; thou thyself hast naught to do (with it). Amend it if thou canst, for *my* time is to be waited for. Patience is a sovereign virtue, and is (really) a swift vengeance." The apparent paradox in the last line is an evident reference to Luke xviii. 7—"And shall not God avenge his own elect, which cry day and night unto him, though he bear *long* with them? I tell you that he will avenge them *speedily.*"

199. (11. 371.) "Who is more long-suffering than God? quoth he; no one, as I believe."

204. (11. 375.) "And so the wise man witnesseth, and so the French proverb instructs us" [c]; "French men and free men thus train their children" [b]. The conjunction of "Frenchmen" with "free men" is striking, and points to the French-speaking habits of the upper classes. Observe how "free man" is opposed to "cherl;" Pass. xxiii. 146. *Affcyteth* means literally *tame,* and was used, in French, with respect to hawks; it here means *train, tutor,* or *discipline.* For the opinion of "the wise man," see Eccles. vii. 8—"the patient in spirit is better than the proud in spirit;" also Ecclus. xi. 9, quoted at C. xiv. 198, B. xi. 385.

205. (11. 376.) "A fair virtue is Patience; evil speaking is a petty vengeance. To speak well of others and to endure things patiently make the patient man come to a good end." These two lines are really four short lines, in rime. The word *suffrable* is rare, and less intelligible than the form

soffrant of the B-text, which I have adopted in the above translation. The form *ly* or *li* (better than *lui*) was used in Old French as an article; see Burguy's Grammaire, I. 46, 53.

Chaucer has some lines much resembling ll. 202—208 of the present passage; see his Frankeleyn's Tale, C. T. 11085—11092—,

"Patience is an hey vertue certein," &c.

Observe that we have a quotation from Ecclus. xi. 9 at l. 198 above; hence we may be sure that ll. 207, 208, were suggested by Ecclus. xi. 7, 8, the two preceding verses, which are as follows—"Priusquam interroges, ne uituperes quemquam; et cum interrogaueris, corripe iuste. Priusquam audias, ne respondeas uerbum; et in medio sermonum ne adiicias loqui."

211. (11. 382.) "Each man would be blameless, believe thou none otherwise!" With *lacles*, blameless, cf. *lakke*, to blame, in l. 208.

——(11. 389.) "And bade every created thing multiply according to its kind, and all to please man with, who must endure wo, through the temptation of the flesh and of the fiend also."

213. (11. 393.) *Tid*, for *tideth* [c]; *bitit*, for *bitideth* [b]; i. e. it betides or happens to him.

214. (11. 394.) The reference is to Dionysius Cato, Distichorum liber, i. 5—

"Si uitam inspicias, hominum si denique mores,
    Cum culpant alios, nemo sine crimine uiuit."

In an edition of Cato, printed at Amsterdam in 1759, there are references to somewhat similar passages in Horace, lib. i. Serm. Sat. iii. 23; Catullus, Carm. xxii. 11; Persius, Sat. iv. 23; Phædrus, lib. iv. fab. ix.; &c.

216. (11. 396.) *And awaked.* Here ends the Fourth Vision; see Pref. to C-text, p. xcix., Pref. to B-text, p. liii.

217. (11. 397.) Whitaker refers us to a similar passage in the Tempest, iii. 2. 149—

——"and then, in dreaming,
The clouds, methought, would open and shew riches
Ready to drop upon me, that, when I waked,
I cried to dream again!' "

220. (11. 400.) "And then there appeared a wight, who he was I knew not" [c]; "And, as I lifted up mine eyes, one looked at me, and asked me" [b]. The stranger's name is Imaginative; Pass. xv. 1. Here, in fact, begins the Fifth Vision, or the Vision of Imaginative; ending, in both texts, at the conclusion of the Passus next following. See Pref. to C-text, p. xcix; Pref. to B-text, p. liii.

226. (11. 406.) *Entermetyng*, intermeddling, with reference to the text Ecclus. xi. 9, quoted at l. 198 above. See the verb *entermeted* in l. 408 of the B-text. Cotgrave has—"*S'entremettre de*, to meddle, or deal with, to thrust himself into." In Pecock's Repressor, i. 145, we have—"Who euer schewith him lewid . . . he is worthi to be forbode fro *entermeting* with the Bible in eny party ther-of." In King Alisaunder, ed. Weber, l. 4025, *entermetyd of* = meddled with, interfered with. And in Barclay's Ship of Fools,

ed. Jamieson, ii. 33, is the heading—"Of folys that vnderstonde nat game, and can no thynge take in sport, and yet *intermyt them* with Folys." The quotation "philosophus esses, si tacuisses" is from Boethius, de Cons. Phil. lib. ii. prosa 7. The story is thus told in Chaucer's translation of Boethius, ed. Morris, p. 59. "Somtyme there was a man that hadde assaied with striuyng wordes an other man, the whiche, nat for vsage of verrey vertue but for proude veyne glorie, hadde taken vpon hym falsly the name of a philosopher. This rather man that I speke of thou₃te he wolde assaye where he thilke were a philosopher or no; that is to seyne, yif he wolde han suffred ly₃tly in patience the wronges that weren don vnto hym. This feinede philosophre took patience a litel while; and, whan he hadde receiued wordes of outerage, he, as in stryuynge a₃eine and reioysynge of hym-self, seide at the laste ry₃t thus—'vnderstondest thou nat that I am a philosophere' [Lat. *intelligis me esse philosophum*]? That other man answerede a₃ein ful bityngy and seide—'I hadde wel vndirstonden yt, yf thou haddest holden thi tonge stille'" [Lat. *intellexeram*, inquit, *si tacuisses*]. Compare the ending of Chaucer's Manciples Tale. "Stullus quoque si tacuerit, sapiens reputabitur;" Prov. xvii. 28. "In multiloquio non deerit peccatum; qui autem moderabitur labia sua prudentissimus est;" Prov. x. 19. So also Cato, lib. i. dist. 3—

"Virtutem primam esse puta, compescere linguam,
　Proximus ille Deo est, qui scit ratione tenere."
Also—　　　"With an O and an I, *si tunc tacuisses,*
　Tu nunc, stulto similis, *philosophus fuisses.*"
　　　　　　　　　　　　　　　　Monumenta Franciscana, p. 600.

The quotation "Locutum me aliquando penituit, tacuisse nunquam" is possibly a prose rendering, from memory, of Cato, lib. i. dist. 12—

"Rumorem fuge, ne incipias nouus auctor haberi,
　Nam nulli tacuisse nocet, nocet esse locutum."

228. (11. 408.) *Mamelede aboute mete*, prated about food, viz. the forbidden fruit. Cf. *mamely*, B. v. 21. See Adam's speech in Milton, P. L. ix. 921.

234. (11. 414.) "Nor doth Clergy care to shew thee (some) of his cunning" [c]: "That Clergy careth not to follow thy company" [b]. The double negative in *ne kepeth nat* is equivalent to no more than a single negative; but is more emphatic. I. e. the sense is—"And Clergy does not *at all* care," &c.

235. (*cf.* 11. 416.) Cf.—"Uerecundia pars est magna penitentiæ;" quoted from S. Augustin in the Ancren Riwle, p. 331.

247. (11. 429.) "Yea, certainly, that is true; and he got ready to set off walking." So in Gower, Conf. Amant. iii. 62—

"She *shope her* for to riden out."
See note to Pass. i. 2.

SCHEME OF THE CONTENTS OF C. PASSUS XV.

(B. Pass. XII.)

(Cf. Wright's edition, pp. 228—245 ; ll. 7435—8024.)

C-TEXT.	B-TEXT.	C-TEXT.	B-TEXT.
1—3	1—3	——	166—169
4—16	——	109—120	170—181
——	4—56	121, 122	182
17, 18	57, 58	123—132	183—192
19—22	——	133—135	like 193—195
——	59, 60	136—157	196—217
23, 24	61, 62	158	——
25—29	——	——	218
——	63—65	159	219
30	like 66	——	220—224
31, 32	——	160, 161	like 225, 226
——	67—69	——	227, 228
33—35	like 70—72	162, 163	like 229, 230
36	——	164—168	——
——	73	——	231—235
37	74	169, 170	like 236, 237
38—42	——	171, 172	238, 239
——	75—93	173, 174	like 240
43	94	175—182	like 241—245
——	95—100	183	——
44—62	101—119	——	246—259
——	120, 121	184, 185	like 260, 261
63	like 122	186	262
64—68	123—127	187	like 263, 264
69	——	188	265
70, 71	like 128, 129	189, 190	——
72—74	——	——	266
——	130—132	191—193	267—269
75—79	133—137	194	——
80	——	195—214	270—289
81—87	138—144	215, 216	——
88	like 145	——	290—292
89—108	146—165	217	like 293

NOTES TO C. PASS. XV. · (B. Pass. XII.)

1. (12. 1.) By *ymaginatyf* is represented what we should call Imagination or Fancy. William means, in particular, *his own* power of Imagination; see l. 3. Line 2 describes Imagination as a lonely power, ever busy ; *to which* [*b*] *adds*—in all states of health. And see note to B. x. 115, on p. 241, which accounts for the introduction of Imaginative in the present passage.

3. (12. 3.) This is an important line, as fixing the poet's age. In the B-text, he is 45, in the year 1377, and so born about 1332; as discussed in the Note to B. xi. 46 ; p. 262. In the C-text, William has altered it to the purposely

vague form "more than forty years." He was 49 years old in 1381, in which
year he was probably employed in recasting his poem. But he certainly
took many years over the work, and it was probably still incomplete in 1391,
when he was "more than fifty," viz. 59, and even in 1393, when he was
"more than sixty." From the exact expression in the B-text we may fairly
deduce his age, but from the vague expression in the C-text no exact conclusion can be drawn.

7. (*not in* b.) "Nor to waste speech, as, e. g., by speaking idly."

9. (*not in* b.) "Humble thyself to continue to live," &c.

——(12. 14.) This is rather a singular interpretation of "thy rod and
thy staff, they comfort me;" Ps. xxiii. 4. William takes it to mean that
God's corrections turn to consolations.

——(12. 16.) *Makynges*, poems; so *make*, to write poetry, to compose,
in l. 22 below; and in C. Pass. vi. 5. Trench, in his Select Glossary, s. v.
Make, observes—"The very early use of *maker*, as equivalent to poet, and
to make as applied to the exercise of the poet's art, is evidence that the
words are of genuine home growth, and not mere imitations of the Greek
ποιητής and ποιεῖν, which Sir Philip Sydney [Apologie for Poetrie, ed. Arber,
p. 24] suggests as possible. The words, like the French *trouvère* and *troubadour*, the O.H.G. *scof*, and the A.S. *scop*, mark men's sense that invention,
and in a certain sense creation, is the essential character of the poet. The
quotation from Chaucer [last line of the Complaint of Mars and Venus] will
sufficiently prove how entirely mistaken Sir John Harrington was, when he
affirmed (Apology for Poetry, p. 2) that Puttenham in his Art of English
Poesie, 1589 [ed. Arber, p. 94], was the first who gave *make* and *maker* this
meaning. Sir Walter Scott somewhere claims them as Scotticisms, but ex-
clusively such they certainly are not." Indeed, so far is the term from
being "Scottish," that one of the earliest instances of the use of *makyere* in
the sense of "author" occurs in the Kentish Ayenbyte of Inwyt, ed. Morris,
p. 269; written A.D. 1340. The A.S. *scóp* and O.H.G. *scof* mean a "shaper."
The German *dichter* means an "arranger," from *dichten* (A.S. *dihtan*), to
arrange or *dight*. The Fr. *trouvère*, Provençal *troubadour*, and Ital. *trovatore*
mean a "finder." With the expression *sey thi sauter*, compare C. Pass. vi.
45—52.

——(12. 19.) *Peyre freres*, pair of friars. *Peyre* often means a set, as in
a peire of bedes, Ch. Prol. 159; but here it most likely means *pair*. The
friars often went about in pairs; see Ch. Somp. Ta. l. 32, and cf. C. Pass.
xi. 8. For the omission of the word *of* after *peyre*, cf. "a peyre tables" in
Chaucer's Astrolabe, ed. Skeat, ii. 40. 18.

——(12. 21.) *His sone.* The title of Cato's book is Dionysii Catonis
Disticha de Moribus *ad Filium*, and the short preface contains the words
"fili charissime."

——(12. 23.) The quotation is from Distich. iii. 7—
> "Interpone tuis interdum gaudia curis,
> Ut possis animo quemuis sufferre laborem."

——(12. 30.) "Nunc autem. manent fides, spes, charitas, tria hæc; maior autem horum est charitas;" 1 Cor. xiii. 13.

——(12. 37.) *Rochemadore*. In Zedler's Universal Lexicon, Roquemadour or Roquemadou (Rupes Amatoris) is said to be a town in Guienne, on the river Dordogne, formerly called also Rocamacorus or Rochemindour. Zedler refers to Baudrand, P. 1, p. 135. In the Knight de la Tour-Landry, ed. Wright, p. 70, mention is made of "miracles that hathe be done in the chirche of oure lady of Rochemadame," where the original has "nostre Dame de Rochemadour." Mr Wright observes (note, p. 213) that Rochemadour "was a well-known place of pilgrimage near Cahors, famous in the middle ages for the miracles performed there." It is not marked in Black's General Atlas, so that, probably, it is no longer a place of any note. The name commemorates St Amadour (Lat. Amator) as will be seen from the following quotation :—

"The Virgin of Rocamadour was famous as early as the eighth century, for, if tradition is to be believed, Charlemagne and his brave followers came to pay it homage on their return from an expedition against the Gascons; and the sword of Roland, deposited as an offering upon the altar of the chapel of St Michael, is still [1874] to be seen. Around this sanctuary, dedicated to the Virgin, were seventeen chapels hewn *in the rock* [note the name of the place]; they were dedicated to Jesus Christ, to the Twelve Apostles, to St John the Baptist, to St Anne, to St Michael, and to *St Amadour*, whose hermitage was here, and who had no doubt brought from the East the black Virgin who has been venerated there for twelve or fifteen centuries."—Lacroix, Military and Religious Life in the Middle Ages, p. 388. Froissart (cap. cclxiii) narrates how Roquemadour was besieged and taken by the English under Sir John Chandos.

——(12. 39.) This line is very difficult. It seems that *mayden to marye* must be an expression meaning "a maiden as regards marriage," i. e. unmarried; and the rest of the line then means—"and mightest well continue (such)." That it was so understood is rendered probable by the reading *contene* (i. e. contain) of the Oriel MS., just as two MSS. have *conteyne* for *contynue* in C. Pass. xi. 284, which see. Though the author speaks strongly in favour of marriage in Pass. xi. 281—288, he yet puts the unmarried life above it, as in Pass. xix. 89, 90. I think this is, accordingly, the right interpretation; and agree with Mr Wright in placing no comma after *mayden*.

——(12. 41.) William is arguing in praise of Loyalty or obedience. Lucifer fell through pride and consequent disobedience; see Note to Pass. ii. 105. Solomon and Samson were disloyal to chastity.

——(12. 43.) "Job the Jew bought his joy very dearly;" or, "paid dearly for his prosperity." William here really changes his subject. Having mentioned the examples of Lucifer, Solomon, and Samson, he proceeds to adduce further examples of such as fell from great prosperity into subsequent adversity. This was a favourite theme with the writers of the time, as exemplified by Boccaccio's De Casibus Virorum Illustrium, Chaucer's Monkes Tale, and Lydgate's Falls of Princes. At a later period, the Mirror for Magistrates treated of the same subject.

——(12. 44.) Mr Wright has a note here which I quote. "These three names were the great representatives of ancient science and literature in the middle ages. Aristotle represented philosophy, in its most general sense; Virgil represented literature in general, and more particularly the ancient writers who formed the *grammar* course of scholastic learning, whether verse or prose; Ypocras, or Hippocrates, represented medicine. They are here introduced to illustrate the fact that men of science and learning, as well as warriors and rich men, experience the vicissitudes of fortune." It remains, however, to be explained in what sense these three worthies experienced adversity. This is not to be explained from the history of their lives on earth, but by the universal belief of the time that their souls were lost, as was also that of Solomon; see this expressly declared in Pass. xii. 211—220. The spelling *ypocras*, for Hippocrates, occurs in some MSS. of Chaucer, Prol. 431. There is a legend concerning him, which brings him to an evil end, in The Seven Sages, ed. Wright, 1046—1153; see also Weber's Metrical Romances, iii. 41. It describes him as having been jealous of the knowlege of his nephew Galien (i. e. Galen), whom he murdered treacherously, dying himself soon afterwards from remorse. Virgil was chiefly celebrated, in the middle ages, as having been a great magician, who, according to Vincent of Beauvais, fabricated certain magical statues at Rome. See ch. lvii. of the Gesta Romanorum, analysed by Warton, Hist. E. P., ed. Hazlitt, i. 254, 327; and the introduction to the Seven Sages, ed. Wright, pp. lviii, lx. Also Weber's Metrical Romances, iii. 77, 368.

——(12. 45.) *Elengelich*, sadly, miserably; see notes to Pass. i. 204; B. x. 94; and The Land of Cockayne, l. 15, in Mätzner's Altenglische Sprachproben, i. 148. So in Occleve, De Regim. Principum, ed. Wright, p. 37, the comparative *elengere* signifies more miserable. Alexander's sad and early death is well described by Plutarch, who asserts that he had, shortly before, "left his trust and confidence in the gods;" North's Plutarch, ed. 1612, p. 710. Most likely William adopted the current notion that Alexander died by poison, as told, e. g., in the Romance of Alexander, ed. Weber, ll. 7850—7893. The same notion appears in Chaucer's Monkes Tale, and in Barbour's Bruce, i. 533; also in Ælfred's tr. of Orosius, iii. 9.

——(12. 46.) "Wealth and natural intelligence became a source of ruin to them all." In all the above examples, their fall was due either to riches or to pride of knowledge. This remark shews that William adopted the legendary tales about Hippocrates and Virgil that have been indicated above. Strict grammar would require the use of *or*, not *and*, in this line. See nearly the same expression below, C. xv. 17; B. xii. 57.

——(12. 47.) *Felyce hir fayrnesse*. For remarks on this use of *hir*, see note to Pass. xix. 236. "Felice's fairness became altogether a disgrace to her." I cannot suppose, with Mr Wright, that this name was merely in-

troduced for the sake of alliteration. Our author is somewhat careless of
his alliteration, but never writes without an object. It is possible that we
have here a reference to some particular version of the famous romance of
Guy of Warwick, mentioned not only by Chaucer, in his Rime of Sir Thopas,
but even at an earlier date, as, e. g., in the Romance of Richard Cœur de
Lion, l. 6664, in Weber's Metrical Romances, vol. ii. For notices of Sir
Guy, see Warton, Hist. Eng. Poetry, ed. Hazlitt, i. 285, ii. 143, 162; and
The Percy Folio MS., ed. Hales and Furnivall, ii. 509, 515. Note particularly
the quotation at the last reference, viz.—"Dame *Felys*, daughter and heire
to Erle Rohand, for her beauty called *Felyse belle*, or *Felys the faire* by true
enheritance, was countesse of Warwyke, and lady and wyfe to the most
victoriouse Knight, Sir Guy, to whome in his woinge tyme she made greate
straungenes, and caused him, for her sake, to put himselfe in meny greate
distresse, dangers, and perills ; but when they wer wedded and been but a
litle season togither, he departed from her to her greate hevynes, and never
was conversaunt with her after, to her vnderstandinge ;" &c. See the story
as narrated in the same work, in the ballad of Guy and Colbrande, especially
at p. 548. William's reference is expressed in exact language. The conduct
of dame Felice had been disdainful ; and, when Sir Guy quitted her at the
end of the fortieth day, she must have felt it as a great disgrace. Her fairness had but brought slander and scandal upon her. She even thought of
suicide. Amongst other misfortunes, her son was stolen from her, according to one version of the story. The Romance of Sir Guy was edited by
Mr Turnbull for the Abbotsford Club; another edition, by Dr Zupitza, is
being edited for the E. E. T. S. See the description of Felice's despair in this
edition; ll. 7276—7308. I may add that the name was often spelt *Phyllis*,
by confusion of sound; the words were, of course, quite distinct. Skelton
uses the name of *Felyse* to signify a woman of indifferent repute; Works, ed.
Dyce, i. 44; ii. 116.

The alternative solution is that the allusion is to the well-known story
of Phillis, who was betrayed by Demophon, and slew herself. See Chaucer,
Leg. of Good Women; Ovid, Heroides, Ep. ii.

——(12. 48.) "And Rosamund, in like manner, pitiably bestowed herself," i. e. sacrificed herself. The word *bysette* is properly active, meaning
to employ, as in C. vii. 254; we must supply *her*, i. e. herself. The name
of Rosamund is but too notorious. A very curious account of her is given
in The French Chronicle of London, ed. G. J. Aungier, for the Camden
Society, 1844; a translation of which is given by Mr Riley, in his Chronicles
of London, and in Mr Timbs's Nooks and Corners of English Life, pp.
274—277. See also Warton, Hist. E. P., ed. 1840, ii. 84, 100, 371, 408;
ed. 1871, iii. 176, 177, 182.

——(12. 52.) I do not know whence this is quoted. It is not in Cato's
Distiches.

17. (12. 57.) Nearly repeated from above; B. xii. 46.

——(12. 60.) *But if the rote be trewe*, unless the root (or foundation) of it be true; *i.e.* unless the wealth be acquired by perfectly just and fair means. Otherwise, the wealth is rather "a root of robbers," i. e. productive of thieves; because what has been untruly obtained deserves to be untruly taken away; see Pass. xiii. 247, and the Note.

20, 21. (*not in* b.) These two lines are parenthetical, and explanatory of the expression *vnkynde rychesse*, which means wealth unnaturally acquired, wrongful gains. They mean—"As, for instance, when abandoned wretches come to be lords, and ignorant men set up as teachers, and holy church becomes a giver to harlots and is avaricious and covetous." *Horen* is the genitive plural, and presents no difficulty; but Dr Whitaker was wholly unable to make it out.

23. (12. 61.) There is a pun here on the words *grace* and *grass*, which must have been pronounced very much the same at this period. The latter is used, in this passage, in the sense of *a herb of healing virtue*, as in William of Palerne, ed. Skeat, ll. 636, 644, 799, 1030. Compare the pun by which *rue*, to repent, caused the herb *rue* to be called the "herb of grace;" Hamlet, iv. 5. 181. Hemp was sometimes called "Gallow-grasse;" see Babees Boke, ed. Furnivall, p. 240.

24. (12. 62.) "Till good-will begin to rain (upon it)" [c]; "but amongst the humble" [b]. For the various readings in the C-text, see the footnote.

25. (*not in* b.) *Wokie*, moisten, soften. The sense is, that grace is like a healing herb; but it grows not till good-will rains upon it, and moistens (*or* softens) men's wicked hearts by means of good works. Though I am unable to produce another instance of the use of *wokie* in this sense (unless it be the same word as *woketh* in Pass. xvii. 332, and *woke* in B. xv. 332, see Notes to those lines), I have little doubt as to the meaning of it. Perhaps we may connect it with the Icel. *vökva*, to moisten, to water; Icel. *vökna*, to become wet; both of which verbs seem to be related to Icel. *vök* (also *vaka*), a hole or gap in ice; cf. Swed. *vak*, Dan. *vaage*, with the same sense. Similarly, the Dutch *wak* means both (1) moist, damp; and (2) a hole in ice. Halliwell gives "*wokey*, moist, sappy," as a Durham word; also "*Weaky*, moist, watery. *North*." Cf. G. *weichen*, to soak, to macerate.

40. (cf. 12. 80.) The *sygne* [c], or *carectus*, i. e. characters [b], has reference to the words written by Christ upon the ground. See this illustrated in the Coventry Mysteries, ed. Halliwell, pp. 220, 221, where Christ is represented as writing upon the ground the sins of the accusers. So also in the Chester Plays, ed. Wright, p. 211, a doctor is made to quote Saint Augustine's homily upon the text, to the effect that Christ

> ———"wrote in claye, leeve you me,
> Ther owine synnes, that ye may se,
> That eichone fayne was to fleye [*flee*],
> And the[r] lefte her aloone."

What St Augustine really says (Homil. on St John, vi. 6) is that Christ, by writing on the ground, signified that he was the Lawgiver; it was to remind the Jews that The Law had at first been written on tables of stone; and this reminded the Pharisees of the Law, and how *each one ought to judge himself.* It is clear that William was thinking of this interpretation, since he refers to the Law of Moses just above. It is also easy to see how St Augustine's remark was changed into the statement that Christ wrote each man's *sins* upon the ground. Peter Comestor, after relating the circumstance as told in St John's Gospel, adds—" Hieronymus in quadam epistola ad studiosum uidetur illum uelle scripsisse—' terra, terra, scribe hos uiros abdicatos;' vel—' terra terram accusat,' in epistola ad Hyreneum."

The word *sygne* (*carectus*, b) is curious. It seems to indicate that Christ's words upon the ground were supposed to have been denoted rather by special characters or signs than by ordinary letters. See the Chapter on "Characts" in Brand's Popular Antiquities (ed. Ellis, iii. 319), shewing that Gower uses *carect* in the sense of a charm—" With his *carect* would him enchaunt;" Conf. Amant. bk. i. *Charect* occurs again in the same sense in the Dialogue of Dives and Pauper, printed by Pynson, 1493. In old French, *caracte* meant a mark, sign; also, a written charm, rendering the wearer of it invulnerable; also, a magic rite; see Vie de Seint Auban, ed. R. Atkinson, l. 1006, and note at p. 104. Lydgate uses *carectes* to signify the marks or scars left by old wounds, viz. upon the feet of Œdipus; Siege of Thebes, Part I. See also *Caractes* in Halliwell's Dictionary.

The following passage from Ashmole's Theatrum Chemicum, p. 463, well illustrates that learned author's belief in charms, in the year 1652. "What I have further to say, shall onely be to shew what Naturall powers Sigills, &c. graved or imprest with proper Characters and figures, and made under certaine peculiar constellations, may have. Albumazar, Zahel, Haly, Albategnus, and divers other Arabians give us severall examples of such as have been cured of the biting of Serpents, Scorpents, Mad dogs, &c. by Talismanicall Figures," &c.

50. (12. 107.) It seems reasonable to suppose that this comparison of an untaught man to a "blind man in battle" may have been suggested by the well-known yet unusual instance of such an occurrence at the' battle of Creçy, A.D. 1346, in which the blind king of Bohemia was slain. See Froissart, Chron., bk. i. c. 129.

65. (12. 124.) "Nor think lightly of their science, whatever they do themselves."

66. (12. 125.) "Let us take their words at their (true) worth, for their witnesses are true."

68. (12. 127.) "Lest strife should thus enrage us, and each man should aim blows at another." Cf. *choppe adoun*, strike down, Pass. i. 64.

88. (cf. 12. 145.) "But of cleanness and of clerks, and keepers of beasts" [c]; "Nor of lords that were ignorant men, but of the most learned men existing" (lit. the highest lettered men out) [b]. This use of *oute* with a superlative is very remarkable. It sounds like a modern slang phrase; for we can still say "the last thing *out.*" It occurs again below; xv. 191.

91. (12. 148.) This seems a strange version of the Bible narrative in Luke ii. 7. But the notion would hardly be one which William invented; I have no doubt he merely adopted some opinion which he had met with. If we could trace the quotation—"et pauper non habet diuersorium," we should probably have the clue. The reasoning is that Joseph and Mary sought for an inn, or *diuersorium*, which was no poor place, but a large house, unsuited for poor people. It is true that St Luke expressly says that "there was *no place for them* in the inn," but some commentators are in strange confusion upon this point, because St Matthew, in speaking of the visit of the Magi, uses the term *domum*; Mat. ii. 11, Vulgate version. Thus Peter Comestor writes—"Ingressi vero magi *domum*, quam *diuersorium* lucas nominat." This plainly shews how the notion might arise. The Magi entered a *house*; this house was wrongly identified with the *inn*; and the *inn* was imagined to be the best house in the town. See Dict. of the Bible, s. v. *Inn*.

92. (12. 149.) *Poetes.* This idea was possibly founded upon the words of St Luke, that "the shepherds returned, glorifying and praising God." The passages relating to the Shepherds in the Chester and Towneley Mysteries are very curious. We are reminded, too, of Cædmon, the neatherd and poet. The very name of *pastoral* poetry suggests the same combination of ideas, and needs no illustration.

96. (12. 153.) *Tho*, when. *Hit.* i. e. "the glory of the Lord;" Luke ii. 9. *Shewere;* not "a shower of glory," as Whitaker oddly explains it, but a "shewer," i. e. a revealer or discloser. *Shewere* is the usual Middle-English word for *a mirror*; see the examples in Stratmann, of which I here cite a few. "*Shewers, Sheweres*, mirrors, Exod. xxxviii. 8; Is. iii. 23;" Wycliffite Glossary. Also—

> "He putfyth in hys pawtener [*bag*]
> A kerchyf and a comb,
> A *shewer*, and a coyf
> To bynd with hys loks," &c.

This passage occurs in A Poem on the Times of Edward II., ed. Hardwick, stanza 16; where another version, printed in Polit. Songs, ed. Wright, p. 327, has—

> "He put in his pautener an honne (*sic*) and a komb,
> A *myroar* and a koeverchef to binde with his crok."

(I here note, by the way, that Mr Wright failed to explain *honne*, and no wonder; it is plainly a misprint for *houue*, a hood, which see in Pass. xxiii. 172, *footnote*.) So also—"asc ine *schauwere*," as in a mirror; Ancren Riwle, p. 92; "ane sseawere," a mirror, Ayenbyte of Inwyt, ed. Morris, p. 84. And in King Alisaunder, l. 18, in Weber's Metrical Romances, the word 'schewere' means a mirror rather than 'an example,' as explained by Weber.

97. (12. 154.) *Clerkes*, learned men, viz. the Magi. *Comete;* see Note to Pass. xxi. 243.

100. (12. 157.) *Crabbede*, harsh, cross, peevish. The reference is to Pass. xii. 275—303; B. x. 442—474. In the B-text, the poet speaks the

" crabbed words " himself; see B. x. 372. In the C-text, they are put into the mouth of Recklessness (see xii. 200); who is the poet's confidential friend and adviser for the time being.

104. (12. 161.) The illustration here given is imitated from Boëthius, lib. 4, pr. 2. See Chaucer's translation, ed. Morris, p. 114, ll. 9—16.

· *Temese,* the Thames. This use of the name of a river (without the definite article preceding it) is still common in many parts of England, and sounds well; it seems to add to the dignity of the river. I take the opportunity of recording here that I heard a good instance of it at Cleobury Mortimer. One boy said to another—" if yo dunna take care, yo'll fall into Severn." I did not overhear the rest of the conversation, which must have referred to some adventure at a distance, since the Severn does not come at all near to Cleobury. The interesting point was the use of William's idiom at the supposed place of his birth.

105. (12. 162.) " And both naked as a needle, neither of them heavier than the other; " where, for " heavier," the B-text has *sykerer,* i.e. safer, or in a less dangerous position. The curious proverbial expression here used is not to be found in the usual collections of proverbs; but I once observed it, in the form " naked as nedel," in MS. Laud 656, fol. 6 b, line 2.

120. (12. 181.) *Loketh after lente,* waits for Lent.

124. (12. 184.) *After,* according to, according to the instructions of. Observe the distinction here between a parson and a parish-priest. The former was properly a rector, the latter might be a vicar or perpetual curate. See *Parson* in Hook's Church Dictionary. William is here very severe upon their frequent ignorance. See this illustrated in Myrc's Instructions for Parish Priests, ed. Peacock, which begins with an allusion to the very text here cited.

> " God seyth hym-self, as wryten we fynde,
> That whenne the blynde ledeth the blynde,
> In-to the dyche they fallen boo [*both*],
> For they ne sen whare-by to go.
> So faren prestes now by dawe [*day*] ; " &c.

Mr Wright cites a very similar passage from a French poem, apparently written in England in the fourteenth century, entitled Le Miroir de l'Ome (Speculum Hominis).

125. (12. 185.) *Luk,* Luke. See Luke vi. 39; but William's words are somewhat nearer to Mat. xv. 14.

126. (12. 186.) " For much woe was marked out (allotted) to him that has to wade with the ignorant." The image refers to a man who employs a guide to conduct him over a ford, and finds that he is unacquainted with the depth of the stream.

127. (12. 187.) " Well may the child bless him that set him to his book," i.e. taught him to read. *That* = him that.

128. (12. 188.) *After letterure,* according to written precepts.

129. (12. 189.) " *Verset,* a versicle, or short verse ; " Cotgrave. The allusion is to the " benefit of clergy," and to the " neckverse."

Such allusions are very numerous. Thus, in Marlowe's Jew of Malta, A. iv.
sc. 4, we have—"within forty foot of the gallows, conning his neck-verse."
A note on the passage, in Cunningham's edition, says—"The words used
by a criminal to establish his right to 'benefit of clergy.' The fifty-first
Psalm was generally selected, and the opening words *Miserere mei Deus*
came to be considered the neck-verse, *par excellence*. The ceremony was
not abolished till the reign of Queen Anne." In Hudibras, part iii. c. 1, we
find—

> "And if they cannot read one verse
> I' th' psalms, must sing it, and that's worse."

"In Hudibras's days," observes Dr Grey, "they used to sing a psalm at
the gallows; and therefore he that, by not being able to *read* a verse in the
Psalms, was condemned to be hanged, must *sing*, or at least hear a verse
sung, under the gallows before he was turned off. This custom arose from
the practice of what was called benefit of clergy. In the times when book-
learning was a rare accomplishment, a person who was tried for any capital
crime, except treason or sacrilege, might obtain an acquittal by 'praying his
clergy;' the meaning of which was, to call for a Latin bible, and read a
passage in it, generally selected from the Psalms. 'If he exhibited this
capacity, he was saved as a person of learning, who might be useful to the
state; if he could not read, however, he was hanged. Hence the common
saying among the people, that if they could not read their neck-verse at
sessions, they must sing it at the gallows." See a very graphic description
of such an ordeal in Sir F. Palgrave's Merchant and Friar, at p. 175. The
benefit merely saved the man's life; he could still be subjected to fine or
imprisonment; see ll. 146, 147 below. See also Strutt, Manners and
Customs, iii. 44; who refers to Hollingshead's [Harrison's] Description of
Britain, p. 108; also *Neck-Verse* in Halliwell's Dictionary. Cf. Lay of the
Last Minstrel, i. 24. It is clear from the present passage that *Dominus pars
hereditatis* was also in use as a neck-verse in the time of Richard II. as well
as *Miserere mei*.

In the Praier and Complaint of the Ploweman, printed in the Harleian
Miscellany, vi. 105, we find the following protest. "Lord, what dome ys it
to slene [*slay*] an vnkunnynge lewed man for hys synne, and suffren a prest,
'other a clerke, that doth the same synne, scapen alyve?'"

131. (12. 191.) "Where ignorant thieves are hung, see how they (the
clerks) are saved!" The sense is clear, though Dr Whitaker contrived to
misunderstand it.

133. (12. 193.) *Yelde hym creaunt*, yielded himself as a believer. The
more usual phrase is exemplified in *yelt him recreaunt*, yields himself as a
coward, which occurs in Pass. xxi. 105. The form *yelde* is here weak, but
the verb was originally a strong one; hence we find *yald* in the second
Trinity MS. (C-text, footnote), and in two other MSS. (B-text, footnote).
See other examples in Stratmann, with which compare the use of *yolde*
as a past participle in Lancelot of the Laik, ed. Skeat, ll. 291, 380, 951,
1088.

135. (*not in* b.) The quotation is inexact. The Vulgate has—"nolo mortem impii, sed ut conuertatur impius a uia sua et uiuat;" Ezek. xxxiii. 11.

136. (12. 196.) That there are degrees of bliss in heaven has been at all times a prevalent belief. See Dante's Divina Commedia; Ayenbyté of Inwyt, ed. Morris, p. 267; Hampole's Pricke of Conscience, l. 7876 (where the "maners of blysses" are said to be "seuen"); &c. Cf. Matt. v. 19; xi. 11; xviii.; 2 Cor. xii. 2; &c.

138. (12. 198.) In like manner King Horn, when disguised, enters the hall, and sits upon the ground like a beggar. See King Horn, ed. Lumby, ll. 1115—1133. The "sovereigns of the hall" were those who sat at the high table, generally raised upon a daïs.

145. (12. 205.) *A soleyn*, a solitary person. *Soleyn* is our modern *sullen ;* see examples in Stratmann; to which add—"In *solein* place by my-selue;" Gower, Conf. Amant. iii. 6:

146. (12. 206.) See Note to l. 129 above. The quotation is from Ecclus. v. 5—"De propitiato peccato noli esse sine metu, neque adiicias peccatum super peccatum."

150. (12. 210.) See the Note to Pass. xiii. 75. *Tulde*, dwelt; lit. pitched his tent. The verb is *telden*, to pitch a tent, which see in Stratmann. It is a derivative of A.S. *teld*, a tent; cf. the "*tilt* of a cart," which is cognate with G. *zelt*. So, in Icelandic, we have *tjald*, a tent, *tjalda*, to pitch a tent. To the examples in Stratmann, add—"Ther they *teilde* paveloune;" King Alisaunder, ed. Weber, 1975; "The king ther *teildid* his pavelons;" id. 3470.

153. (12. 213.) See Ps. lxi. 13 (Vulgate); Matt. xvi. 27.

156. (12. 216.) Cf. Ps. cxxxiv. 6 (Vulgate); "Omnia quæcunque uoluit, Dominus fecit in cælo, in terra, in mari, et in omnibus abyssis." See the "Thyrde Lesson" in the Monday service used by the nuns of Sion, in the Myrour of our Lady, ed. Blunt, p. 182, where the question is discussed why God gave free will to angels and men :—"*Placuit igitur*, Therfore yt plesed that verteu, that ys god hymselfe, to gyue them fredome to do what they wolde." So in Peter Comestor's Historia Scolastica, at the end of cap. xxiv.—"Iterum si queritur, quare permisit hominem tentari, cum cum sciret lapsurum, et de multis in hunc modum dicimus quantum ad presens attinet opus, *quia sic voluit*. Si queritur *cur voluit*, insipida est questio querere causam diuine voluntatis, cum ipsa sit summa causa omnium causarum."

157. (12. 217.) *By thee*, with respect to thee. *Weyes*, ways [c]; *the whyes*, the reasons why, lit. the why's [b].

158. (12. 218.) See Pass. xiv. 170—193.

——(12. 228.) "The nest [of the magpie] is usually placed conspicuous enough, either in the middle of some hawthorn bush, or on the top of some high tree. The place, however, is always found difficult of access, for the tree pitched upon generally grows in some thick hedgerow, fenced by brambles at the root, or sometimes one of the higher bushes is fixed upon for the purpose;" Goldsmith's Animated Nature, iii. 170. See also The

Architecture of Birds, p. 327. "Its nest, well fortified with blackthorn twigs, is a curiosity;" Eng. Cyclopædia, s. v. Corvidæ; Pica caudata. Cf. Note to Pass. xiv. 156.

——(12. 233.) *Hiled*, covered. Cf. Pass. xii. 35—41.

171. (12. 238.) "That the fairest bird (i. e. the peacock) engenders in the foulest manner." Cf. Pass. xiv. 171—173, and the Note.

179. (12. 243, 244.) See the description of the peacock's long tail, ugly feet, and harsh cry in Laurence Andrewe's Noble Life, cap. xci, quoted in The Babees Boke, ed. Furnivall, p. 219. Though the flesh is here called "foul flesh" [b], or "loathsome" [e], peacock was, as Mr Wright remarks, a very celebrated dish at table. In Manners, Customs, and Dress in the Middle Ages, by P. Lacroix, p. 130, we are told that the peacock was much esteemed in the thirteenth century. "In the fourteenth century the poultry-yards were still stocked with these birds; but the turkey and the pheasant gradually replaced them, as their flesh was considered somewhat hard and stringy." He adds that, in 1581, a peacock was only worth $2\frac{1}{3}$ sous, or about 3 francs of present money. Yet Andrewe says—"it is euyll flesshe to disiest [*digest*], for it can nat lightely be rosted or soden ynogh." See Horace, Sat. lib. i. 2. 116; lib. ii. 2. 23—30. For an account of the use made of the peacock in feasts, Mr Wright refers us to Le Grand d'Aussy, Histoire de la Vie privée des Français, tom. i. pp. 299—301, and 361. See also the Note to l. 184 below.

——(12. 253.) *Chiteryng*, chattering, chirping. In Trevisa's translation of Higden's Polychronicon, i. 239, the word is used of the note of the starling—"With mouth than *chetereth* the stare." And in the Ancren Riwle, p. 152—"Sparuwe is a *cheaterinde* bird; *cheatereth* euer ant chirmeth." Chaucer has—"As eny swalwe *chiteryng* on a berne," Milleres Tale, l. 72 (C. T. 3258; Harl. MS.); and again, "They may wel *chateren* [or *chyteren*] as don thise iayes;" C. T. 16865; and again, "the swalwe Progne" is said to make a "*chiteringe*," Troil. and Cress., bk. ii. st. 3, where Tyrwhitt has a "waimenting." Wyclif says that a confused noise is "as ȝyf iayes and pyes *chateriden*;" Works, iii. 479, last line. Palsgrave has—"I *chytter*, I make a charme as a flocke of small byrdes do whan they be together, *Ie iargonne*." Barclay mentions "the *chatrynge* pie;" Ship of Fools, ed. Jamieson, i. 109. Two more examples are in Halliwell's Dict. s. v. *Chitre*. Robert of Brunne (Handlyng Synne, ll. 355—360), amongst warnings against various kinds of witchcraft, says—

> "Beleue nouȝt yn þe *pyys cheteryng;*
> Hit ys no trouþe, but fals beleuyng.
> Many beleuyn yn þe pye:
> Whan she comþ lowe or hye
> *Cheteryng*, and haþ no reste,
> þan sey þey—'we shul haue geste.'"

I. e. we shall have news. The original has only—

> "Si il oient la pie iangler,
> Quident sanz dute noucles auer."

Perhaps this illustrates Macbeth's remarks about the disclosure of murder by "magot-pies;" see Macb. iii. 4. 125.

——(12. 255.) *Flaumbe :* 3 p. s. subj. used with a future sense. "I believe it will contaminate very foully all the earth around it." *Flaumbe* is the same word as *flame*, from the O.Fr. *flamber*, to blaze, burn, throw out flames. It is here curiously used in the sense to spread a taint, to contaminate. The same verb occurs, in a neuter sense, in MS. Laud 656, fol. 4 b, where we have—

"A flauo*ur flambeþ* þer-fro · þey felleden hit alle ;"

i. e. a scent is exhaled from it, they all perceived it. In the same MS., fol. 10, we have the verb in its usual sense—

"Quarels *flambande* of fure · flowen out harde ;"

i. e. crossbow-bolts,' blazing with fire, flew out fast. The connection in idea is easily perceived ; a burning piece of wood emits blaze, smoke, heat; and smell, all at once. So the Lat. *flagrare* is to burn, to glow ; but its derivative is the Fr. *flairer*, to scent; cf. *flayre*, a sweet smell, in Hampole's Pricke of Conscience, l. 9017.

——(12. 257.) "By the peacock's feet is meant," &c. *Auynete*, a certain collection of fables. Mr Wright says—"In the fourteenth and fifteenth centuries, as any grammar was called a *Donet* [see Note to Pass. vii. 215] because the treatise of Donatus was the main foundation of them all, so, from Æsop and Avianus, from whom the materials were taken, any collection of fables was called an *Avionet* or an *Esopet*. The title of one of these collections in a MS. of the Bibl. du Roi at Paris is—Compilacio Ysopi alata cum Avionetto, cum quibusdam addicionibus et moralitatibus. (Robert, *Fabl. Inéd. Essay*, p. clxv.) Perhaps the reference in the present case is to the fable of the Peacock who complained of his voice, the 39th in the collection which M. Robert calls *Ysopet*, in the morality to which are the following lines :—

'Les riches conteront	[The rich will boast
Des biens qu'il aront	Of the wealth they will hav
En ce siecle conquis.	Acquired in this world.
Cil qui petit ara	He who will have little
De petit contera	Will boast of little
Au Roy de paradis.	To the king of Paradise.
Qui vit en povreté	He who lives in poverty
Sans point d'iniquité	Without any iniquity
Moult ara grant richesse	Will have great riches
Es cieux, en paradis.	In heaven, in Paradise.
O dieux et ses amis	With God and their friends
Seront joyeux et aise.' "	They will be joyous and happy.]

In Warton's Hist. Eng. Poetry, ed. 1873, iii. 136, note 3, there is a list of authors in vogue in the 13th century. It includes—"Cato the moralist, . . . Flavius Avianus, a writer of Latin fables or apologues, Æsop, or the Latin fabulist, printed among the *Octo Morales*, Lugd. Bat. 1505, . . . Boethius, . . . Virgil, Horace, Ovid, Lucan, Statius, Juvenal, Persius ;" &c. Avianus flourished about the fourth century, and wrote 42 Æsopic fables in Latin elegiac verse, of no great merit.

——(12. 253.) Robert of Brunne (Handlyng Synne, ll. 6259—6264) says—

> "Of alle fals þat beryn name
> Fals executours are moste to blame.
> þe pope of þe courte of Rome,
> Aȝens hem ȝyfþ he harde dome,
> And curseþ hem yn cherchys here
> Foure tymes yn þe ȝere."

184. (12. 260.) *The poete*, the author, the writer. William would have called a poet a *maker* (see Note to B. xii. 16); he uses *poet* to denote any writer, whether in prose or verse, as when he speaks of Plato as being such (Pass. xii. 304), or Cicero and Aristotle (Pass. xiii. 173—175; and see l. 190 below). In the present passage, I have no doubt that the writer meant is Aristotle; see below, B. xii. 266. Thus in Batman vpon Bartholome, lib. xii. c. 31, we read—"And Aristotle sayth, that the Pecocke hath an vnstedfast and euill-shapen head, as it were the head of a serpent, and with a crest. And he hath a simple pace, and small necke and areared, and a blew breast, and a taile ful of bewty, distinguished on high with wonderful fairnesse; and he hath foulest feet and riueled [*wrinkled*]. And he wondereth of the fairenesse of his fethers, and areareth them vp, as it were a circle about his head; and then he looketh to the foulenesse of his feete, and lyke as he wer ashamed, he letteth his fethers fall sodeinlye: and all the taile downeward, as though he tooke no heed of the fairenesse of his fethers: and he hath an horrible voice." And see note to Pass. xiv. 171.

The original passage in Aristotle, Hist. of Animals, bk. vi. cap. 9, says but little about the peacock's tail or feet. Cf. Note to l. 179 above. See also Holland's tr. of Pliny, bk. x. c. 20; quoted by Richardson (s. v. *Peacock*).

190. (*not in* b.) The authors Porphyry and Plato are cited at random, as in Pass. xii. 304; xiii. 173. It is hopeless to verify such references; the names are merely introduced as a sort of flourish. The alliteration has, for once, much to do with the selection of the names; like *poet*, they begin with *p*. In the B-text, the author referred to is Aristotle; see next Note.

——(12. 266.) I doubt if the comparison of poor men to larks is to be found in Aristotle; see his Hist. of Animals, for a description of the lark.

Aristotle is here called "the great clerk." The real reason of the great influence of Aristotle's writings from the eleventh to the sixteenth centuries is pointed out in Milman's Hist. of Lat. Christianity, vi. 443. Aristotle's authority was indeed considered supreme, but it was because he was regarded as "the teacher of logic, the master of dialectics." Observe the occurrence of *logyk* in the next line.

191. (12. 267.) "The least bird existing;" a hyperbolical expression. On *oute*, see Note to l. 88 above.

192. (12. 268.) See this discussed in Pass. xii. 216—223.

193. (12. 269.) *Sortes* is, probably, a mere corruption of Socrates, as Mr Wright supposes. His reference to Walter Map's Poems, p. 251, is much to the point. The passage is—

> " Adest ei bajulus cui nomen Gnato,
> Praecedebat logicum gressu fatigato,
> Dorso ferens sarcinam ventre tensam lato,
> Plenam vestro dogmate, *o Sortes et Plato !* "

Speaking of logic, Barclay (in his Ship of Fools, ed. Jamieson, i. 144) says—

> " Now Sortes *currit*, now is in hand Plato ;
> Another comyth in with *bocardo* and *pheryson*,
> And out goeth agayn a fole, in conclusyon."

Here *bocardo* and *pheryson* are said to be terms in logic, but Sortes goes with Plato, as above.

In Œuvres de Rutebeuf, ed. Jubinal, ii. 428, is the line—"Mès dans *Sortes* la fist repondre ; " but the word is not explained, nor does the context help us.

From the use of *thei* in the following line in the C-text, it is clear that *Sortes* is the name of a man. There is no allusion here to the mode of divination known as *sortes sanctorum* (see Ducange), which I mention only that it may not be supposed that I have overlooked that supposition.

204. (12. 279.) The right quotation is—"Et si iustus uix saluabitur, impius et peccator ubi parebunt ?" 1 Pet. iv. 18. William lays a stress upon *uix*, and says—"since the just man shall *scarcely* be saved, it follows that he *shall* be saved." See Pass. xvi. 23, and the note, for a still clearer statement of the same opinion. On the other hand, Whitgift (iii. 499, Parker Society) says that *uix* sometimes means *non*. For the story of Trajan, see Pass. xiii. 75, and the Note.

207. (12. 282.) *Follyng*, baptism. See Matt. iii. 11; Acts ii. 3.

208. (12. 283.) Compare—"Ignis enim triplicem uim habet, scilicet, illuminandi, calefaciendi, consumendi," &c. ; Old Eng. Homilies, ed. Morris, ii. 118.

209. (12. 284.) *Treuthe* here signifies a true man, a righteous man ; see *he* in l. 211. *Transuersede*, transgressed, lit. traversed. See *Traverser* in Cotgrave. Cf. Testament of Love, bk. i. (in Chaucer's Works, ed. 1561, fol. 287, back), where *transuers* means to 'gainsay :'—"I trowe the strongest and the best that maie be founde woll not *transuers* thy wordes."

210. (12. 285.) "But (ever) lived as his own law taught (him), and believes there is no better (law); and if there were (a better law made known to him), he would (have kept it), and in such a desire dieth—surely the true God would never (permit) but that (such) true truth were commended. And whether it shall be so or shall not be so, the faith of the true man is great; and a hope ever depends upon that faith, that he shall have what he deserves." In [b], l. 286, the reading is—"he would amend ; " and in l. 289—"to have a reward for his truth." The sentence is terse and elliptical, but the sense is clear ; the argument is that of St Paul, in Rom. ii. 13—15.

The first quotation in [b] probably refers to John xvii. 2—"Sicut dedisti ei potestatem omnis carnis, ut omne quod dedisti ei, det eis uitam æternam."

The second quotation is from Ps. xxii. 4 (Vulgate)—"Nam, et si ambulauero in medio umbræ mortis, non timebo mala : quoniam tu mecum es." The rest of the verse has been already quoted above; B. xii. 13.

216. (*not in* b.) "And a present beyond what was agreed for, whatever clerks may say." Cf. Pass. iv. 317.

217. (*not in* b.) "For all shall be as God will." Cf. l. 213 above.

——(12. 290.) "The gloss on that verse grants a large reward to true men." See note to l. 209 above for the sense of *treulhe* here, and note to l. 210 for the whole verse from Psalm xxii. The Glosa Ordinaria contains the following remark on the words *mecum es*. "I. e. in corde per fidem, vt post umbram mortis ego tecum sim." This shows that the "meed" spoken of is, that true men shall dwell with God hereafter.

——(12. 292.) "To keep (*or* maintain) a community with; no (sort of) wealth was considered better."

Here ends the Fifth Vision, or the Vision of Imaginative. The Sixth Vision follows almost immediately.

SCHEME OF THE CONTENTS OF C. PASSUS XVI.

(B. Pass. XIII.—XIV. 131.)

Cf. Wright's edition ; pp. 246—281.

N.B. See also the Schemes of C. Passus VII. and VIII.

C-TEXT.	B-TEXT.	C-TEXT.	B-TEXT.
xvi. 1—6	xiii. 1—6	xvi. 52	——
7, 8	——	53—55	*like* xiii. 46, 47
9—13	7—11	56—59	48—51
14	——	——	52—56
15—19	12—16	60	——
20	*like* 17, 18	61—66	57—62
21—23	*like* 19	67	——
24	20	——	63
25—27	*like* 21—23	68—70	64—66
28—30	*like* 24—26	71—73	——
31, 32	27, 28	——	67
33	——	74—76	*like* 68—70
34—36	*like* 29, 30	——	71, 72
37, 38	——	77—79	——
39	*like* 31, 32	80	73
40	33	81	——
	——	82—84	——
41—51	34	85. 86	*like* 74—79
	35—45		

C-TEXT.	B-TEXT.	C-TEXT.	B-TEXT.
xvi. 87—89	xiii. 78—80	xvi. 154	xiii. 149
90, 91	*like* 81, 82	155—157	——
92, 93	83, 84	——	150—157'
94	——	158, 159	158, 159
——	85	(*a*) 160	(*a*) [163]
95—112	86—103	161—163	——
113	*like* 104	——	160
114	——	164, 165	161, 162
115, 116	*like* 105	(*a*) [160]	(*a*) 163
117	——	166—170	*like* 164—171
——	106, 107	171—173	172—174
118	*like* 108	——	175
119	——	174, 175	176, 177
——	109, 110	——	178—197
120—123	111—114	176—180	*like* 198—201
124, 125	*like* 115	181—185	——
126, 127	*like* 116, 117	——	202—215
128	118	186—194	216—224
129, 130	——	——	225
——	119—122	195—198	——
131	123	199	*like* 226
132	——	200, 201	——
133	*like* 124	202—210	227—235
134, 135	125, 126	211—214	*like* 236—238
136—140	——	215	——
——	127—135	——	239
141	*like* 136	216	240
——	137—142	——	241, 242
142	*like* 143	217	*like* 243
143	144	218—222	——
144	*like* 145	——	244—249
145, 146	——	223, 224	*like* 250—253
147, 148	146, 147	225—231	254—260
149—153	——	——	261—277
——	148		

(*Here is a break. Some portions of the* B-text *have appeared at a much earlier place in the* C-text, *and have been already commented on. See notes to* C. Pass. vii. 30—viii. 117, *on pp.* 104—142. *The complete scheme of this portion is here given.*)

C-TEXT.	B-TEXT.	C-TEXT.	B-TEXT.
vii. 30	xiii. 278	——	xiii. 299—302
31—34	*like* 279—281	vii. 49, 50	*like* 303, 304
35	——	51	*like* 305
——	282	52	——
36, 37	283, 284	——	306
38—40	——	53—60	307—313
——	285—291	61, 62	——
41—44	292—295	——	314—323
45	——		

(*Here is a break; see* C. vii. 63—68.)

C-TEXT	B-TEXT	C-TEXT	B-TEXT
46	*like* 297, 298	vii. 69—75	325—331
47, 48	——	76	——

C-TEXT	B-TEXT	C-TEXT	B-TEXT
——	xiii. 332, 333	——	xiii. 458—460
vii. 77—85	334—342		xiv. 1—27
(Here is a break; see C. vii. 86—177.)		xvi. 232, 233	[*cf.* xiv. 75, 76]
——	343, 344	234—236	*like* 28
vii. 178—185	345—352	237, 238	
——	353—361		29—37
(Here is a break; see C. vii. 186—259.)		239—242	38—41
vii. 260—266	362—368	243	*like* 42, 43
	369, 370	244—246	44—46
267—271	371—375	247—249	——
——	376—383	250, 251	*like* 47, 48
272—277	384—389	252—262	49—59
——	390, 391	263	——
278—285	392—399	264—275	60—71
(Here is a break; see C. vii. 286—429.)			72—74
——	xiii. 400—403	[*cf.* 232, 233]	75, 76
vii. 430	*like* 404		77
——	405—409	276—278	——
(Here is a break; see C. vii. 431—viii. 69.)		——	78—99
viii. 70—74	410—414	279	*like* 100
	415	280	——
75, 76	*like* 416	281—286	101—106
77—117	417—457	287, 288	——
(Here is a break; and the original order is reverted to.)			107
		289—303	108—122
		304—309	——
			123—129
		310	*like* 130, 131

NOTES TO C. PASS. XVI. (B. Pass. XIII.—XIV. 131.)

2. (13. 2.) *Feye*, fated to die [c]; *fre*, at liberty [b]. A remarkable variation.

3. (13. 3.) *Mendinaunt*, mendicant friar. The spelling is peculiar, but is the same in all the MSS.; see also l. 81 below, and Pass. xiv. 79. In Chaucer, C. T. 7488, Tyrwhitt prints *mendiants*, but he has the following note. "In MS. A. it is *mendinants*, both here and below, verse 7494, which reading, though not agreeable to analogy, is perhaps the true one, as I find the word constantly so spelled in the Stat. 12 R. II. c. 7, 8, 9, 10." In the Six-text edition of Chaucer, Group D, l. 1906, the first five MSS. have the readings *mendynantz, mendynauntis, mendinantz,* and *mendenauntz*. The word occurs also in Pierce the Plowman's Crede, l. 66, where it is spelt *mendynauns*.

Meny ȝeres after. This expression may, after all, mean nothing. At the same time, we know that the recensions of the poem occupied many years, and it is quite possible that the expression is literally true. If so, some time must have elapsed between the first composition of Passus XV. and of Passus XVI., i. e. between Passus XII. and XIII. of the B-text. See note to l. 173 below.

5. (13. 5.) Here our author recapitulates a part of the Vision of Do-wel. The references are to Pass. xiii. 14—27, 233—247, xiv. 112—128, xv. 120—126, 157—168, 203—217.

7. (*not in* b.) There is an awkward change of construction here; the word *þat* should be followed by a subjunctive mood, but *leue* is the infinitive, governed by *manacede*, whilst *vanshie* appears to be used as a transitive verb. Thus the sense is—"And how Old-age threatened me, (that) it might so happen, that, if I lived long—(he threatened, I say,) to leave me behind, and to consume all my powers, and my fair locks."

23. (*cf.* 13. 19.) See the note to Pass. xv. 204. The expression here used in the C-text, viz. "but *vis* help," refers to a curious popular exposition which, as Wyclif informs us, was then current. His words are—"And, *as men seien*, in this word 'unneþe shal þe just man be saved,' is menyd þis word Iesus, whoso coude undirstonde it. For in þis word VIX ben but þree lettris, V, and I, and X. And V bitokeneþ fyue; I betokeneth Iesus; and X bitokeneþ Crist. [Cf. Gk. Χριστος.] And so þis resoun sciþ þat þe just man shal be saved by þe V woundis of Iesus Crist oure Lord."—Works, i. 337.

26. (13. 22.) Here begins the Sixth Vision, viz. of Conscience, Patience, and Activa-Vita (called Haukyn the Active Man in the B-text). It properly terminates at Pass. xvii. 157 (or at the end of B. xiv.).

27. (13. 23.) In [c], William dines with Conscience, Clergy, Reason, and Patience; in [b], Reason is omitted.

——(13. 24.) "And because Conscience spake of Clergy, I came all the sooner."

30. (13. 25.) *What man he was I neste*, I knew not what sort of a man he was [b]. But the C-text is more explicit, saying—"a man like a friar." *Mayster* means a master of divinity; in l. 65 he is called a *doctor;* see Note to that line. Compare—

'"And also þis myster men ben *maysters* icalled;"
Pierce Pl. Crede, l. 574; cf. l. 838.
" No *maister*, sir (quod he), but scruitour,
Though I haue had in scole such honour; "
Ch. Sompnoures Tale, l. 485.

Soo too in the Complaint of the Ploughman, in Political Poems, ed. Wright, i. 337; and see Pass. xi. 9, and the Note. Accordingly, Mr Wright notes that the word *maister* "was generally used in the scholastic ages in a restricted sense, to signify one who had taken his degree in the schools—a master of arts." In Jack Upland, we find the question—"why make ye so many *maisters* among you [friars], sith it is against the teaching of Christ and his apostles?"

40. (*not in* b.) *Stihlede*, arranged every thing, set all in order. See the various spellings in the footnote. It is commonly spelt with *t* after the *h*, as in P. Pl. Crede, l. 315; see further examples in Stratmann.

41. (13. 35.) *Mettes*, companions at table [c]; *macches*, mates [b]. The same variation occurs below, in l. 55 (b. 13. 47). With the former cf. A.S.

"*gemettan*, comestores," in Lye and Manning's A.S. Dictionary; and with the latter cf. A.S. *gemæcca*, a companion.

43. (13. 37.) *Calde after*, called for, expressed a wish for.

45. (13. 39.) The dishes have very singular names; see especially l. 61, and B. xiii. 52—55. The guests have before them, for their consumption, portions of the writings of the fathers and various texts of Scripture, and even the drink was called *diu-perseuerans*. The friar turned away from these uninviting viands, and regaled himself with "meat of more cost;" but even so, he did not quite escape. The sauce which he chose had been made from ingredients ground in a mortar named *post-mortem*, which is a way of saying that after death he would suffer for his gluttony.

The use of such names for the dishes is an important matter, as we are able to tell whence William derived the idea of describing so strange a feast. Warton (Hist. E. P. ed. Hazlitt, ii. 263) has noted William's obligations, in another passage, to Huon de Meri's Tornoiment de l'Antichrist. In this poem, now printed by P. Tarbó, in his Poètes de Champagne, xv. 13, is a description of a feast in which the dishes are named after various *sins;* and the author says—

> "De divers mès, de divers vins
> Fumes plenièrement servi.
> Et sachiez bien qu'oncques ni vi
> Fèves et pois, oes ne harenc;
> Tuz les mès Raoul de Hodenc
> Eumes sans faire riot."

I. e. we had plenty of different dishes and wines; but we did not have beans and peas, nor goose, nor herring, but all the dishes described by Raoul de Hodenc. This shews that Huon de Meri himself borrowed the idea, viz. from Le Songe d'Enfer of Raoul de Houdans (or Hodenc), also printed by M. Tarbé in the same volume, pp. 134—148. See also the description of the Abbot of Gloucester's Feast in Reliq. Antiq., i. 140.

47. (13. 41.) *Mortrewes and potages;* and in l. 66 we have *mortrews and poddynges.* "*Mortrewes*, a dish in ancient cookery, very frequently mentioned in early works; see Reliq. Antiq., i. 81, 85, 86; Pr. Parv., pp. 13, 70; Ord. and Reg., pp. 438, 454;" Halliwell's Dictionary.

The making of *mortrewes* was one of the qualifications of Chaucer's Cook; Prol. 386. Tyrwhitt's note on the line tells us that "Lord Bacon, in his Nat. Hist., i. 48, speaks of 'a *mortress* made with the brawn of capons stamped and strained' . . . It seems to have been a rich broth or soupe, in the preparation of which the flesh was stamped, or beat, in a mortar; from whence it probably derived its name, *une mortreuse;* though I cannot say that I have ever met with the French word."

Roquefort gives—"*Mortreur*, mélange de pain et de lait." The term occurs in Prompt. Parv., p. 13, note 1; p. 70, note 5, as above noted by Halliwell; but there is a much fuller notice of it at p. 314, note 2, where Mr Way says— "*Mortrews*, according to various recipes given in Harl. MS. 279, Cotton MS Jul. D. VIII., and Sloane MS. 1986, seems to have been fish or white meat ground small, and mixed with crumbs, rice flour, &c. See in the last-mentioned compilation 'mortrews de chare, blanchyd mortrews, and mortrews of-fysche,' pp. 55, 60, 66, given under the head *de potagiis.*" See also Babees Book, pp. 151, 170, 172; a Recipe for "mortrewes de chare" in Liber Cure Cocorum, p. 9; "of fysche," p. 19; and see Houschold Ord., pp. 438, 454, 470; Archæologia, vol. xi. pp. 421, 422. Dr Morris (note to Ch. Prol. 384) explains *mortrewes de chare* as a soup in which chickens, fresh pork, crumbs of bread, yolks of eggs, and saffron formed the chief ingredients; and *mortrewes of fysche* as a soup containing the roe (or milt) and liver of fish, bread, pepper, and ale. In Sir J. Cullum's Hist. of Hawsted, 2nd ed. p. 11, there is an entry of *morterels*, which were made of wastel-bread and milk; and Sir J. Cullum remarks that it was one of the messes for the poor people of St Cross's near Winchester; Lowth's Life of Wykeham, p. 68. This last sort agrees with Roquefort's definition. In Migne's edition of Ducange we have—"*Mortea*, pulmenti genus ex pane et lacte; *soupe au lait;* ol. *mortreux;*." also "*Mortarius, Mortarium*, vas in quo aliquod feritur:" The derivation suggested by Tyrwhitt is certainly right, and no doubt our author himself was aware of it, as he at once goes on to speak of the *morter* in which the ingredients had been prepared. Compare—

"Thise cokes, how they stampe, and streine, and grinde," &c.
Ch. Pard. Tale; C. T. 12474.

48. (13. 42.) "They made themselves well at ease with that which men had won amiss," i. e. gained by cheating.

50. (13. 44.) The whole expression, from *post-mortem* down to *teeres*, is the allegorical name of the mortar. This name signifies—"after death they shall suffer many bitter pains, unless they sing for those souls and weep salt tears for them." The expression *tho soules* means the souls of the men who had "mis-won" their wealth. The passage requires to be pondered before its full sense is perceived; yet a little thought will shew that it is of some satirical force. The friars (he would say) fared sumptuously, paying for their rich fare with the money which wealthy cheats had left to them when in present fear of death; but they must bear in mind that they will suffer bitterly hereafter for their gluttony, unless they actually perform that which they have solemnly engaged to do, viz. sing masses for the souls of such wealthy persons. Hence the aptness of the Latin quotation (the source of which I know not) which signifies—"Ye who feast upon the sins of men, unless ye pour out tears on their behalf, ye shall vomit up those meats amid torments which ye feast upon amid pleasures."

57. (13. 49.) "And then he drew for us a drink, the name of which was *Long-enduring.*" This line was omitted in Mr Wright's edition by mere accident; it may be found in the MS. which he used, and also in Crowley's edition. The allusion is to the text—"qui autem perseuerauerit usque in finem, hic saluus erit;" Mat. x. 22.

58. (13. 50.) *Quod I* [b], changed to *quath he* [c]; an improvement. In the B-text, it looks like a poor joke, as if the author expresses his readiness to drink as long as he lives.

——(13. 54, 55.) See Critical Note, B-text, p. 410.

61. (13. 57.) See Critical Note to B. xiii. 57; B-text, p. 410.

65. (13. 61.) *A doctor* [c]; *this doctor* [b]. Note that the word *a* is not indefinite here; it is the same idiom as we should still use if we were to say—"I was sorry to see a doctor drink wine so fast." *For* = because; and assigns the reason of William's mourning. See *þis doctor* in l. 69, and again in l. 85. In l. 90 he is called *that master;* he is, in fact, the friar who sat at the head of the table (ll. 30, 39).

——(13. 63.) *Wombe-cloutes,* tripes; lit. belly-rags. Halliwell notes that it is explained by *omentum* in the Nominale MS. *Yfryed,* fried; the second *y* in this word has lost its tail in some of the copies of my edition. But see the footnote, where it is correctly printed.

70. (13. 65.) The friar preached "at St Paul's" [c]; or "before the dean of St Paul's" [b]. Latimer preached his famous Sermon on the Ploughers, 18 Jan. 1549, in the "shrowds" of St Paul's, having previously preached at St Paul's. Cross, Jan. 1, 1548. "In foul and rainy weather, these solemn sermons were preached in a place called *the Shrowds ;* which was, as it seems, by the side of the cathedral church, where was covering and shelter. Now, long since, both the Cross and Shrouds are disused, and neither of them extant. But the Sermons are preached in the cathedral itself, though they be still called *Paul's Cross Sermons;*" John Strype's ed. of Stow's Survey of London, 1720, p. 149.

——(13. 68.) *Ouerhuppen,* hop over, skip over, omit; see note to Pass. xiv. 123.

75. (13. 69.) "Peril among false brethren," 2 Cor. xi. 26. I have already noted the pun upon "brethren" and "friars;" see Note to B. xi. 87; p. 264. The jest is a venerable one; in the Poems of Walter Mapes, ed. Wright, p. 206, there is a poem on the false friars—*De Falsis Fratribus*—containing the lines following:—

> "A falsis fratribus et fraudis glutino
> Ut me protegere cura sit Domino!"

Wyclif says, with reference to the same text—"The peril of *freris* is þe laste of eght, that falles to men in this waye, as seynt Poule telles;" Works, ed. Arnold, iii. 233.

81. (*not in* b.) *Fyue mendynauns,* five mendicant orders; see Notes to l. 3 above, to Pass. ix. 191, p. 167, and to Pass. x. 343, p. 200.

85. (*not in* b.) *Decretistre of canon,* student of the decretals and canon law. Ducange gives—"*Decretista,* qui studet in decretis. *Magistri de-cretistæ,* professores juris canonici." See B. v. 428, and the note (p. 140). The odd termination *-istre* occurs again in Chaucer's *diuinistre,* C. T. 2813; perhaps it is a mere corruption of Lat. *-ista,* by confusion with *-ister.*

86. (13. 77.) *Gnedy,* niggardly [c]; *goddes,* God's (ironically) [b]. *Gnedy* is connected with A.S. *gneðen,* frugal (Bosworth), and A.S. *gneáð,* sparing (Grein); see *gnede* in Glossary to Havelok, and in Halliwell.

91. (13. 81.) *Dobeleres,* platters. William wishes the doctor, who had

so greedily 'swallowed all the eatables, had swallowed dishes and platters
too! *"Dobeler,* vesselle; *Parapses;"* Prompt. Parv. Mr Way notes—
"The Medulla gives the following explanation of *Parapsis*—'proprie est
discus sive vas quadrangulum; ex omni parte habens latera equalia, a *do-
buler;'"* and he refers us to Ray and Brockett. Ray has—*"Doubler,* a platter
(*North*); so called also in the *South."* Tomlinson (in Ray) says—"A *Dubler,*
or *Doubler,* a dish;" and Lloyd (also in Ray) says—*"Dwbler* in Cardigan-
shire signifies the same." The French *doublier* meant (1) a cloth or napkin;
(2) a purse or bag; (3) a platter; see Roquefort.

——(13. 82.) In the B-text, William wishes that the plates and dishes
had turned to molten lead within the glutton's stomach. So in the Ancren
Riwle, p. 216, we find—"Gif the gulchecuppe weallinde bres to drincken,
and geot in his wide throte that he aswelte withinnen," i. e. give the toss-
pot boiling brass to drink, and pour it in his wide throat that he be suffocated
within." So too in Hampole's Pricke of Conscience (l. 9433) the throats of
the wicked are filled

> " Of molten bras and lede with-alle,
>   Aud of other welland metalle."

The expression "and Mahoun amyddes" is equivalent to "and the devil in
the midst of them." *Mahoun* is Mahomet, often used as a name for an idol,
and idols were supposed to be tenanted by devils. See note to Pass. i. 119;
and cf. Joseph of Arimathie, ed. Skeat, ll. 373—402.

92. (13. 83.) "I shall argue with this chamber-pot, with his bottle-like
belly."

Jordan is used both by Chaucer and Shakespeare, and is fully explained
in the Prompt. Parv., p. 267, note 1. Considering the connection, I think
there can be no doubt that the word *Iuste* is not to be explained as *just*
(which would make poor sense), and still less as a tournament (which is Mr
Wright's solution, making no sense at all); but is the word *juste,* in its
signification of flagon, bottle, or wine-jar. The Prompt. Parv. has—*"Iuste,*
potte, *Oenoforum, justa."* Mr Way notes—"' *Obba, quidam vas liquidorum,*
Anglicè a iuste;' Medulla . . According to Ducange, the term *justa demesuralis* occurs in the signification of a certain measure by which wine was
served to the monks. So likewise in the Consuetudinary of Evesham, printed
by Dugdale from the document in the Augmentation office, the *justa* is named
as the measure by which drinks were at certain seasons to be served by the
cellarer; Mon. Angl. i. 149. Roquefort states that the *Iuste* contained about
a pint; but the *Iuta,* which Ducange considers as synonymous, is accounted
to hold two quarts." No doubt it did so; and I may add that Ducange's
explanation is worth being given in full. He has—*"Iusta demesuralis,* seu
tertiera, mensura uini aliquantulum maior consueta, quæ monachis *in festis
solennioribus* dabatur." Halliwell explains *Juste* as "a kind of vessel with
a wide body and long straight neck." Surely this proposed interpretation
must be right, and the word is happily employed. Observe that the Trinity
MS. (C-text, footnote) has the adjectival form *iusty,* i. e. like a *juste.*

————(13. 85.) The alliteration suggests that the word *wynked* (so in all the MSS.) is miswritten for the unusual word *preynte*, which occurs just below, in C. xvi. 121, B. xiii. 112. See note to l. 121 below.

95. (13. 86.) *May na more*, can do no more, can eat and drink no longer; cf. *til we myghte no more*, C. vii. 185; B. xiii. 352.

97. (13. 88.) *Godelen*, rumble; see Note to Pass. vii. 398, p. 131.

99. (13. 90.) *Here apocalips*, their 'Apocalypse. The use of the word *their* is most significant; the reference is not to St John, but to the Apocalypse of the gluttons, i. e. to the Apocalipsis Goliæ by Walter Mapes, a sort of parody upon St John, the argument of which may be read in Morley's Eng. Writers, i. 587—590. The following extract from that argument will fully explain the allusion. "Then I read of the Morals and the Deeds of Abbots, who declare by their base shaving, vile habit, and watery eyes, that they scorn delights and carry contrite hearts; but whose throats when they dine are open sepulchres, whose stomachs are whirlpools, and their fingers rakes. At supper with his brethren, the Abbot extols the wine-cup lifted in both hands, crying with loud voice—'O how glorious a lantern of the Lord is the cup of drunkenness in the brisk hand.'.. So they decree that none shall leave the cup undrained, empty the full and fill the empty, without rest to bellies or to hands. Each monk becomes demoniac. As pye with pye, parrot with parrot, the brothers chatter and feed, eat till their jaws swell, drink till there is a deluge in their stomachs." See the Latin Poems of Walter Mapes, ed. Wright, Camden Society, 1841.

The next reference is bitterly satirical, if, as I suppose, it relates to an instance of extreme and rigid abstinence. There is no saint named *Averey* or *Averay*; the word is possibly a corruption of *Aurea*. The day of St Aurea is Oct. 4, and the following extract from a notice of her in Vincent of Beauvais, Spec. Hist., lib. 23, cap. lxx, will perhaps shew the point of the allusion. "Nunquam carnem comedens aut uinum uel siceram bibens, sed pro uino potabat stillicidium cineribus expressum. Estimabat *tamen* sororum quedam eam aliud bibe*re*, vnde quedam temeraria experiri cupiens, et allis propalare q*u*od biberet, latenter intrauit loculum vbi colaba*n*tur cine*re* potus eius. Apponens a*u*tem ori suo tentatrix exemplo percussa est paralysi in vultu, ita vt auric*u*le bu*c*ca iung*atu*r : sicque se ream agnoscens ante pedes sacre virginis ve*n*iam postulauit, quam pariter et medela*m* obtinuit." St Aurea drank, it appears, only such drink as she could distil from cinders, but there was one rash sister who doubted the fact, and was consequently punished by palsy. Probably the doctor in our text was ready to declare that the "mortrews" which he ate was prepared with cinders instead of marrow-bones!

A friend has suggested that perhaps *St Afra* is meant, whose day is Aug. 5. After all, the allusion may be to a burlesque piece on some saint who had no real existence; and I cannot pretend to say that I have cleared up this matter satisfactorily.

100. (13. 91.) *Blammanger* is Chaucer's *blancmanger*, Prol. 389. Tyrwhitt, in his Glossary, remarks that it "seems to have been a very different dish in

the time of Chaucer, from that which is now called by the same name. There is a receipt for making it in MS. Harl. 4016. One of the ingredients is 'the brawne of a capon, tesed small.'" Mr Furnivall says—"*Blanch-manger*, a made dish of Cream, Eggs, and Sugar, put into an open puff paste bottom, with a loose cover." He also quotes—"*Blamanger* is a Capon roast, or boile, minced small, planched (*sic*) Almonds beaten to paste, Cream, Eggs, Grated Bread, Sugar and Spices boiled to a pap.—R. Holme." See Babees Book, p. 217; and the Glossary to that volume.

103. (13. 94.) "What he (i. e. his fellow) really found in a case, belonging to a friar's living," t. e. provisions [c]; *or*, "What he really found in a basket, according to a friar's living " [b]. The meaning is that the doctor was ready to bring forward his companion as a witness; and the said companion was ready to state what very poor fare he had often found in a poor friar's provision-box.

Forel has been explained above; see Note to B. x. 211, p. 245. Mr Wright explains it as the "Low-Latin *forellus*, a bag, sack, or purse;" but it rather means a case, sheath, box, scabbard, and sometimes a book-cover; see Prompt. Parv. Mr Halliwell gives the same explanation as Mr Wright, having perhaps accepted it from him; yet Migne's edition of Ducange merely has—"*Forellus*, vagina; *fourreau*; olim *forel*."

Freyel is the Low-Latin *frælum*, a rush-basket or mat-basket, especially used for containing figs and raisins. See "Frayle of frute, *Palata, carica*" in Prompt. Parv., and Mr Way's note. To the examples there given I can add the following. "Bere out the duste in this *fygge-frayle*, Asporta cinerem in hoc syrisco;" Hormanni Vulgaria, leaf 149. *Frail* is still used in Essex to mean a rush-basket; as noted by Mr Jephson. Also, in Kennett's Parochial Antiquities, the glossary has—"*Frayle*, a basket in which figs are brought from Spain and other parts." He cites the phrase "in uno frayle ficuum" from an account dated 1424-6. Palsgrave has—"Frayle for fygges, *cabas, cabache*." See *cabas, cabasser* in Cotgrave. Also Babees Book, ed. Furnivall, p. 200, note to l. 74.

Of means "belonging to" [c]; *after* means "in accordance with " [b].

112. (13. 103.) "This portrait of gluttony and hypocrisy combined, is in Langland's best manner, strong and indignant. There is genuine humour in this line; the doctor, beginning to discourse on good works, only utters a single word before he interrupts the sentence to drink;" Whitaker's note. Cowper has hit off the very same trait, in his poem on Hope.

> "Adieu, Vinosa cries, ere yet he sips
> The purple bumper trembling at his lips,
> Adieu to all morality, if Grace
> Make works a vain ingredient in the case.
> The Christian hope is—Waiter, draw the cork—
> If I mistake not—Blockhead, with a fork!
> Without good works, whatever some may boast,
> Mere folly and delusion—Sir, your toast."

No modern poet comes so near to our author in tone and subject-matter as Cowper does.

113. (13. 104.) "Do no evil to thy fellow-Christian, that is, not as far as your power goes" [b]. *By þi powere*, to the extent of your power; a common phrase.

. ——(13. 107.) *Morsel* is the better spelling; the reading *mussel* points a provincial pronunciation, which may still be heard, though *mossel* (*in glossic—*mos'l) is more common.

118. (13. 108.) "If ye so treat your sick friars, it seems to me a wonder unless Do-well accuses you in the day of judgment" [c]; "And if ye act thus in your infirmary, it seems to me a wonder unless strife exists where love ought rather to exist, if only young children dared complain" [b]. This speech was obviously a very bold one, because Conscience immediately advises him to be silent. I cannot help thinking that strange rumours were afloat as to the treatment of sick friars by their companions, as shewn by the very curious passage in P. Pl. Crede, l. 614; see my note on the line. It was clearly a sore subject with the doctor.

Compare also Wycliff's charge against the friars, that they imprisoned, and even tortured, members of their own order; Works, iii. 383.

121. (13. 112.) *Preynte*, winked. Just as Chaucer has *spreynd*, from *springen*, to sprinkle, so *preynte* is from the verb *prinken*. The traces of this word are slight. Lye, in his A.S. Dict., gives "*Prince eages*, nictus vel ictus oculi;" but without a reference; Halliwell gives "*Prink*, to look at, to gaze upon. *West*." It is not to be confused with *prink* or *prick*, used in the same sense as *prank*, to trim. Cf. note to B. xiii. 85, just above.

125. (13. 115.) Crowley inserts *is* before *do* in [b]. It is required for the sense, but is omitted in all the MSS.

129. (*not in* b.) Whitaker has a note here—to quote which would be unprofitable—shewing that he completely mistook this passage. Clergy, having heard the doctor's very correct explanation, declines to explain the matter himself in a scholastic manner, on the ground that he is not now in the schools, and chiefly because of his love for Piers the Plowman (Christ). The doctor's explanation was just; for, though acting as a sinner, he could talk as a saint. Accordingly, Clergy declines to explain the matter scholastically, but at the same time hints that there is a higher law—the law of Love, the law taught by Christ—which excels all the teaching of the schools.

——(13. 119.) *Seuene sones*. Clergy's seven sons are the seven sciences, as Crowley rightly observes here in a sidenote. Still, William is hardly consistent with himself, since in B. x. 150 (q. v.) he says that the Seven Sciences are *relations* merely of Scripture, who is Clergy's wife. He now calls them *sons*.

131. (13. 123.) "For love of Piers the Plowman, who once impugned sciences and crafts of every kind except love, loyalty, and humility" [c]; "For a certain Piers the Plowman hath impugned us all, and counted all sciences as worth a mere sop, except Love only" [b].

Note the construction in "peers loue þe plouhman," repeated in xxiii. 77. We have it again in "peers prentys þe plouhman," i. e. the apprentice of Piers the Plowman, xvi. 195; in "peers pardon þe plouhman," i. e. the pardon of Piers the Plowman, xxii. 187, 392; and in "peers bern þe plouh-man," i. e. the barn of Piers the Plowman, xxii. 360.   So Chaucer, Sq. Ta. 209, has "the Grekes hors Sinon," i. e. the horse of Sinon the Greek; and in a note to that line I have given other instances of this common idiom, which I here repeat.   They are :—"The kinges meting Pharao," the dream of king Pharaoh; Book of the Duchesse, 282.   "The erles wif Alein," the wife of earl Alein; Rob. of Glouc., in Spec. of English, ed. Morris and Skeat, p. 11, l. 303.   "Themperours moder William," the mother of the emperor William;" Will. of Palerne, l. 5437.   Readers ignorant of this idiom might suppose that Chaucer thought Sinon was the name of the wooden horse, or that William was the name of an emperor's mother.

138. (13. 134.) The saying *patientes vincunt* is attributed to Piers the Plowman in [c], and to Christ in [b], shewing that the immediate reference is to the Gospels.   Yet they contain no such words, though fairly expressing the sense of Mat. x. 22—"qui autem perseuerauerit usque in finem, hic saluus erit."   A more usual form of the proverb is—"uincit qui patitur;" see Hazlitt's Eng. Proverbs, pp. 175, 450.

I suspect that William was thinking of the words of Dionysius Cato, who, in his Breves Sententiæ, gives the advice—"Parentes patientia uince;" Sent. xl.   And again, in his Distiches, lib. i. 38, he says—

> "Quem superare potes, interdum uince ferendo,
> Maxima enim morum semper patientia uirtus."

Cf. Virgil, Æn., v. 710; Ovid, Art. Am. ii. 197, Am. iii. 11. 7, Am. i. 2. 10. Compare also Chaucer's Frank. Ta., 45—47—

> "Patience is a hy vertue certein,
> For it venquisheth, as thise clerkes seyn,
> Thinges that rigour neuer sholde atteine."

And again, in Old Eng. Homilies, ed. Morris, 2nd Ser., p. 80, we have what looks very like a new version of Cato, viz.—"Quem superare nequis, patienter uince ferendo."   In the Ayenbite of Inwyt, ed. Morris, p. 232 (bottom), a similar saying, to the effect that perseverance wins the crown of heaven, is attributed to St Bernard.

By comparing the two texts, we see that Piers the Plowman is already, at this point, identified with Christ; and the reader should bear in mind that this identification is adhered to, for the most part, throughout nearly all the remainder of the poem.   In the C-text, Christ himself here appears upon the scene, unannounced, at this line; and after speaking but one sentence, again vanishes; see l. 150.   In the B-text, the sentence is attributed to Love, who was beloved by Patience.

143. (13. 144.) "Cast upon his head the hot coals of all kind speech." See Rom. xii. 20; Prov. xxv. 22; a passage which is usually explained as having reference to the melting of metals by fire, and to the melting of an enemy's heart by kindness.   This interpretation occurs, for example, in the Ancren Riwle, p. 407.

148. (13. 147.) "Unless he become obedient through this sort of beating, may he become blind!" *Bowe* has reference to the common word *buxom* (lit. *bow-some*), which means obedient.

150. (*not in* b.) *Where he by-cam*, where he had gone to; see Note to B. v. 651.

155. (*not in* b.) "I would (i. e. I could) easily, if I had the will, conquer all France without destruction of men or any bloodshed; I take to my witness a portion of holy writ—'the patient conquer.'" See note to l. 138 above. Whitaker's paraphrase is full of errors here, as shewn in the Critical Notes, C-text, p. 461.

——(13. 150.) "Natural affection covets nothing (from thee) but speech," i. e. asks only for kind words from thee.

——(13. 151.) This line *is* a complete riddle. I merely offer a wild guess at the sense of it. Suppose "a lamp-line in Latin" to be a Latin inscription on such a lamp as was often kept burning in old churches; as when, e. g. J. Cowper, A.D. 1503, provided for finding "a lampe before the roode in the cherche of Hawsted;" see Sir J. Cullum, Hist. of Hawsted, p. 17. Suppose such an inscription to have been a verse from the Bible expressive of good-will, as, e. g. "Gloria in altissimis Deo, et in terra pax hominibus bonæ uoluntatis," Lu. ii. 14; a verse which is still not seldom seen inscribed within a church. Then the sentence might mean—"Natural affection expects from you no wealthy gift, but only kindly words; it expects merely some kindly expression, such as *pax hominibus*." This still leaves *ex vi transicionis* unexplained; nor can I explain it.

——(13. 152.) Here are riddles upon riddles; the passage is purposely obscure, though no doubt contemporary readers understood it. In the first place, the word *there-inne* refers to nothing that has preceded; but we can explain it. It is clear, from l. 157 [b], that Patience is here supposed to hold up a bundle before the company, and to say—"See! herein I have Do-well, fast tied up." Moreover, the bundle is clearly supposed to contain *Caritas*, or Charity; see ll. 163, 164. This explains why Patience says, in l. 156— "and herewith I am welcome, wherever I have it with me." The general solution of the riddle (it is called *redeles* in l. 167), is Charity, exercised with Patience. Hence, in ll. 153—155, we are told that Charity "is betokened by the Saturday that first set the calendar, and by the signification (wit) of the Wednesday of the week next after it; the full moon being that which causes the might of both." Now the full moon is the Paschal full moon, as in a former enigmatic passage; see Note to Pass. iv. 481, p. 73. Mr A. P. Cooke has sent me the following suggestion. "The sign of the Saturday seems to me to mean Holy Baptism, the font having anciently been hallowed on Easter Eve. The epistle of Easter Wednesday was Acts iii. 12—19, and so the wit of this day may be Repentance; the force of both Baptism and Repentance depending upon the Cross, which was set up in the middle of the Paschal month." I certainly think that the Saturday can be no other than Holy Saturday, or Easter Eve. And it may well have been said to have set first the Calendar; for, Adam having been created on Friday (cf. Salomon and Saturn, ed. Kemble, p. 198) the Saturday was to him the first complete day, and the first Sabbath. Besides, there was an idea that the particular Saturday which was the first Sabbath was nearly at the Paschal season; since it was supposed that the world was created at the time of the vernal equinox. Compare—

> " Swylce eác rímcræftige
> On þá ylcan tíd emniht healdaδ,
> Forþan wealdend god worhte æt frymδe,
> On þú sylfan dœge sunnan and mónan."
>
> Menologium, ed. Grein, l. 44.

I. e. "as also the clever calculators consider the equinox to be at that same season, because God the Ruler created, at the beginning, on that very day both sun and moon." The chief things in connection with Saturday are Holy Baptism, wherein the font "denoteth the holy sepulchre" (Old Eng. Homilies, ed. Morris, 2nd Ser., p. 94), and the Assumption of the Virgin; see Myrour of Our Lady, ed. Blunt, p. 257. The Wednesday service was sometimes connected with the birth of the Virgin and with her Conception; "thus in the feastes of the Concepcyon and of the Natyuyte of oure lady, ye saye the story of the wednesday;" Myr. of Our Lady, p. 277. Again, we learn from the same volume, pp. 212, 213, that the Incarnation was particularly celebrated in the Wednesday service, with special reference to 'charyte' or divine Love. The fact that the word 'charyte' occurs so repeatedly in the 'thyrde lesson' of this Wednesday service surely points to the right solution. I therefore agree with Mr Cooke in explaining the 'sign of the Saturday' as Holy Baptism, but prefer to interpret the 'wit of the Wednesday' as meaning the Incarnation; and I would refer to the Myrour of Our Lady (q. v.) in support of this view.

That the passage has, at any rate, a general reference to the great events of Christianity, cannot admit of any doubt. From Christ it is that we learn the lessons of Love and Patience.

162. (*not in* b.) This odd line is probably genuine, as it is preserved in five MSS. out of seven. It probably alludes to some saying which has not been preserved.

164. (13. 161.) *Helle pouke*, goblin of hell; *helle* being the genitive case. In other passages, e. g. in Pass. xix. 282 (which compare with l. 284), the word *pouke* means the devil. It is the same word as Puck, but used here in a bad sense. Cf. Icel. *púki*, the devil, commonly with the notion of a wee devil, an imp; Dan. *pokker*, the devil; Welsh *pwca*, or *pwci*, hobgoblin, fiend; Gaelic *bocan*, a hobgoblin, a spectre; cf. the name Pug in Ben Jonson's "The Devil is an Ass."

"*Púki*, in Icelandic, is an evil spirit. The writer in the Quarterly Review, vol. xxii., gives a long list of words which he regards as connected with *Puck*; the editor of Warton [ed. 1840, vol. i. p. (31)] adds the German *Spuk* and the Danish *Spögelse*; we will contribute the Scottish *Pauky*, and the Devonshire *Pixies*;" Keightley, Fairy Mythology, ii. 118. See also pp. 119, 121 of the same. I am bound to add that I think Price's etymologies, above alluded to, are open to doubt. Puck is often identified with Robin Goodfellow; thus, Mr Hazlitt says (Fairy Tales, &c., p. 33)—"Puck, *alias* Robin Goodfellow, is the most active and extraordinary fellow of a fairy that we anywhere meet with; and it is believed we find him nowhere but in our own country, and peradventure also, only in the South. Spenser, it would seem, is the first that alludes to his name of Puck—

> Ne let the *pouke*, nor other evill sprights, ...
> Ne let Hob-goblins, names whose sence we see not,
> Fray us with things that be not; *Epithalamion*, l. 341."

I quote this for the reader's convenience, but doubt its accuracy. The idea of a Puck is much more widely spread than is here implied, and Spenser (as our text shews) is far from being the first to employ the name. It occurs before Spenser yet again, in Golding's Translation of Ovid. The Herefordshire form of the word is *Pout;* see Sir G. C. Lewis's Herefordshire Glossary. Professor Morley, in his Library of English Lit., p. 234, has a note on the word, reminding us that one of "Three Notelets on Shakespeare, by Mr W. J. Thoms," is on the "Folk-Lore of Shakespeare," including a section "of Puck's several names." Some of the etymological remarks of various writers upon this word seem to me of extremely doubtful value.

For further examples of the use of the word, see *Puck* and *Pouke* in Nares. I may add, that even our author was *not* the first writer who uses the form *pouke*, as it is found in l. 566 of Richard Coer de Lion, in Weber's Met. Rom., ii. 25.

——(13. 170.) "To give all that they can give to thee, as being the best guardian." This makes good sense, and is no doubt right, though the MS. transposes *the* and *for*, as noted in the footnote. See Crit. Note, B-text, p. 411, l. 152; and cf. C. xvi. 168—170.   .

171. (13. 172.) See Critical Note, C-text, p. 462.

173. (13. 174.) This line stands nearly the same in both texts. In the Preface to the B-text, pp. ii—v, I have discussed the date of that text, coming (at p. v) to the conclusion that the expression here used is hardly strong enough for us to be sure that the reference is to the famous Schism of the Popes, Sept. 20, 1378. If, on the contrary, the reference be to that event, it only proves that the B-text was in hand for some time, having been commenced in 1377. See note to l. 3 above.

——(13. 175.) This line, be it noted, was omitted in the C-text, no doubt because the allusion was to an event that was then too far in the past. A truce had been concluded with France in 1389, to last till 1392; it was renewed in 1392, to last till 1393, and a four years' truce was again concluded on May 27, 1394. This truce was firmly established by Richard's marriage with Isabella of France, Oct. 31, 1396. The conclusion is that the C-text was written *after* 1389, as was certainly the case; see Preface to C-text, pp. xvii—xix.

Gower, writing in 1393, says in his Prologue to the Confessio Amantis—

> " But whyle the lawe is ruled so
>   That clerkes to the werre intende,
>   I not how that thei shal amende
>   The woful werlde in other thinges
>   To make pees betwene kinges
>   After the lawe of charitce,   ·
>   Whiche is the proper dewtee
>   Belonged unto the priesthode."

In the B-text, commenced in 1377, the allusion is clearly to such events as are recorded in the following quotations.

"1372. This same yere ... too cardinalx were sent fro the pope to entrete for the pees betwen the two reaumes;" A Chronicle of London, p. 69.

"1374. In this yere, at the town of Bruges in Flaundres, was tretyd upon diverses articles hangyng betwen the pope and kyng Edward. Also the same yere was treted at Bruges for the pees betwen the too reaumes;" id. p. 70.

"Edward [in 1374] obtained a truce ... The pope continually exhorted the kings to convert the truce into a peace; but their resentments were too violent, their pretensions too high, to allow of any adjustment;" Lingard, Hist. Eng., iv. 140.

We may note Occleve's excellent exhortation to the kings of England and France to make peace with each other; De Regim. Princip., ed. Wright, p. 191.

174. (13. 176.) *Put the bord fram him;* "that is, pushed away the table in a passion, which accounts for the following reflection, on the want of patience in learned men."—Whitaker. For *bord*, [b] has *table*.

——(13. 178.) Cf. Pass. i. 50, and the note.

——(13. 184.) *Yeresyyues*, new year's gifts. They were given both *by* the sovereign, and *to* him; see Brand, Pop. Antiq., ed. Ellis, i. 14. They were also given to secure favours; see note to B. iii. 99, p. 63.

——(13. 204.) *Forwalked*, tired out with walking; cf. *forwandred*, B. prol. 7. *Wilne me to consaille*, to desire to have me to counsel you, i.e. when you will be glad to ask my counsel. *Wilne* seems to be in the infinitive mood, governed by the sentence "thou shalt see the time."

——(13. 209.) *Surre*, Syria; cf. the form *Surrye* in the first line of Chaucer's Man of Lawes Tale. *Forth*, by way of continuance; it is the positive degree of *further*. William looked forward to a time when Saracens and Jews should all be converted to Christianity; see Pass. iv. 458, 484; xviii. 317.

191. (13. 221.) The description here given of a minstrel should be noted. See note to Pass. i. 35, and cf. Pass. viii. 82—119. Mr Wright refers us, for a sketch of such a character, to Shaw's Dresses and Decorations of the Middle Ages, the Introduction to Percy's Reliques, and Chappell's History of National Airs. I have already referred to Ritson's Ancient Romances, and Warton's Hist. of Eng. Poetry. See also Ritson's Ancient Songs, p. xvi, where he reminds us that they were commonly classed with vagabonds.

Thus the phrase "westours, rymours, ministralx, et autres vacabondes" occurs in Stat. 4 Hen. iv. c. 27; and in the 39th of Elizabeth, a statute was passed, ranking them with "rogues and vagabonds."

There is a passage somewhat resembling the text, and enumerating the accomplishments of a minstrel, in a poem (of the thirteenth century) called Les Deux Troveors Ribaux, printed in an Appendix to the poems of Rutebuef, ed. Jubinal, i. 337.   Part of it is as follows—

> " Ge suis juglères de viele,
> Si sai de muse et de frestele,
> Et de harpe et de chifonie,
> De la gigue, de l'armonie,
> De l'salteire, et en la rote
> Sai ge bien chanter une note."

194. (13. 224.) *Actiua uita,* Active life.   See note to B. vi. 251, p. 170. "This is clepid actif liif, whanne men travailen for worldli goodis, and kepen hem in rightwisnesse;" Wyclif, Works, i. 384.   It will be seen, however, that the minstrel here described was very far from being an honest man, and was hardly justified in giving himself so honest a name.

195. (*not in* b.) *Peers prentys the plouhman,* an apprentice of Piers the Plowman; i. e. a true servant of Christ; see note to l. 131 above.   But the minstrel's claim to this character was of the slightest; it turns out that his sole point of connection with a religious life was that he made or sold wafers for a holy use !

199. (13. 226.) *Godes gistes,* God's guests; i. e. guests at the Table of the Lord, communicants.   A *waferer* answers very nearly to what we now call a *confectioner;* see Our English Home, pp. 70—72.   One of the chief triumphs of their art was the manufacture of "soteltees" or ornamental dishes, exhibiting castles, warriors, beasts, and birds constructed of sugar, &c.   They sold ornamented cakes and eucharistic wafers.   Among other gifts that Absolom the clerk gave Alison, Chaucer hints of—

> 'wafres piping hot out of the glede'

and the Pardoner, in enumerating the company of lewd folk of Flanders, speaks of 'fruitsters,' 'singers with harps,' and 'waferers.'   [The author of] Piers Plowman puts them amid still more disreputable associates;" Bardsley's English Surnames, p. 324; cf. Chaucer, C. T. 3379, 12413.   Mr Bardsley also cites an entry from the Issues of the Exchequer, 26 Henry III. —"Pay to Ralph Crast the *waferer,* 40s. of our gift."   See *Wafer-woman* in Nares.   I may add that cakes named "wafers" were used even at funerals, as appears from an entry quoted by Brand (Pop. Antiq., ii. 244) from Peck's Desiderata Curiosa, ii. 549.   "1671. Jan. 2, died Mr. Cornelius Bee, bookseller in Little Britain.   Buried 4 Jan. at St. Bartholomew's, without sermon, without wine or *wafers;* onely gloves and rosemary."

The fem. form *wafestre* has already occurred; see Pass. viii. 285.

202. (13. 227.) Robes and furred gowns were common gifts to minstrels, from the great men before whom they exhibited; see B. xiv. 24; and cf. C. Pass. viii. 82—109.   Some minstrels were not itinerant, but were retained

by rich men as jesters; these are the "lords' minstrels" mentioned in
l. 204. "At first, and down to the thirteenth century, they [i. e. jugglers and
minstrels] frequently retired from business loaded with presents, such as
riding-horses, carriage-horses, jewels, cloaks, fur robes, clothing of violet·or
scarlet cloth, and above all, with large sums of money;" P. Lacroix; Manners, Customs, &c. during the Middle Ages, p. 225.

205. (13. 230.) *Tabre*, play upon the tabor; *trompe*, play·upon the
trumpet. "In a poem against the growing taste for the tabor, printed in
M. Jubinal's volume entitled Jougleurs et Trouvères, the low state into
which the minstrel's art had fallen is ascribed to a growing love for instruments of an undignified character, such as the *tabor*, which is said to have
been brought to us from the Arabs, and the *pipe;*" Homes of Other Days,
by T. Wright, p. 200. See the whole passage; also p. 209. Compare—

> "Entyrludes, or syngynge,
> Or *tabure* bete, or other *pypynge*,
> All swyche thyng forbodyn es,
> Whyle the prest stondeth at messe."
> Rob. of Brunne, Hand. Synne, l. 8993.

"Dost thou live by thy *tabor*?" Twelfth Night, Act iii. sc. 1. See also
Spenser, Shep. Kal. May, l. 22. The *taborer* was one of the morris-dancers;
in the morris described in The Two Noble Kinsmen, Act iii. sc. 5. Small
drums were known to the Egyptians; Chappell, Hist. of Music, i. 292.

Gestes, tales, romances. See Warton, Hist. Eng. Poetry, ed. Hazlitt, ii.
85, note.

206. (13. 231.) This passage is sufficiently exemplified by comparison
with a note which Warton prefers "to give in Latin;" see his Hist. Eng.
Poetry, ed. 1840, ii. 393, note *w*; or ed. 1871, iii. 162, note 3; cf. Ritson,
Met. Rom., vol. i., p. clxxxi. I have little doubt that William had himself
witnessed the Coventry Mysteries, and is here alluding to them; see Halliwell's edition of the Cov. Myst., pp. 21, 29.

Fithelen, play the fiddle. See the picture of the Anglo-Saxon *fithele* in
Wright's Homes of Other Days, p. 46; and, at p. 197, note the story of
John de Raunpayne, a minstrel, who "knew enough of tabor, harp, fiddle,
citole, and joglery." See also Wackerbath's Account of Anglo-Saxon Music;
Strutt's Sports and Pastimes; Hart's History of the Violin.

207. (13. 232.) *Iapen*, play tricks, act as buffoon. "Summe iuglers
beoð þet ne kunnen seruen of none oþer gleo buten makien cheres, and
wrenchen mis hore muð, and schulen mid hore eien;" i. e. there be some
jugglers that know no other way of causing fun except to make faces, and
distort their mouth, and scowl with their eyes; Ancren Riwle, p. 210.

208. (13. 233.) *Sailen*, dance; *sautrien*, play on the psaltery [c]; *saute*,
leap, bound [b]. Cf. Rom. of the Rose, l. 769—

> "There was many a timbestere,
> And *sailours*, that I dar wel swere
> Couthe hir craft ful parfitly;"

where *sailours* means *dancers*, whatever may be the sense of the disputed word *timbestere*, which I should suppose to mean a female player upon the timbrel or tambourine, which was thrown up in the air now and then and caught upon the point of the finger, as described; see *Timbre* in Burguy's Glossaire, and observe the use of *tymbres* for "timbrels" in Kyng Alisaunder, ed. Weber, l. 191.   Cotgrave gives—"*Saillir*, to go out, issue forth; appear above, stand out beyond others; also, to leap, jump, bound, skip, hop." Also—"*Sailleur*, m. a leaper, jumper," &c.   *Giterne*, a kind of stringed instrument or guitar, used (as is evident from the text) to accompany the voice in singing.   Cf. Chaucer, C. T. 3333, 3363, 4394.   "*Gittern*, a cittern. Stanihurst, p. 16.   Spelt *gittron* in Leighton's Teares or Lamentations, 4to. London, 1613;" Halliwell.   "*Gyterne*, samba, citolla, quinterna;" Prompt. Parv.; see Mr Way's long note, p. 196.   Ritson tries to distinguish between the *gittern* and *cittern;* Ancient Songs, p. lxii.   So does Ben Jonson; see *Gittern* and *Citterne* in Nares, who gives many examples, shewing that Ben Jonson had small reason for attempting to make the distinction.

209. (13. 234.) Concerning gifts to minstrels, cf. notes to Pass. viii. 97; x. 129; xvi. 202; and to B. xiv. 24.

210. (13. 235.) In the B-text, at least, there is surely an allusion here to the *holy-bread*, i. e. "ordinary leavened bread cut into small pieces, blessed, and given to the people;" as explained in the note to Peacock's edition of Myrc's Instructions to Parish Priests, p. 89; q. v.   He refers us to Bingham, Antiq., ed. 1834, v. 300, 322; Rock, Church of our Fathers, i. 135—140; Becon, Catech. ed. 1844, 260; Cranmer's Works, ed. Fox, ii. 158, 503; Wilkins, Concilia, i. 714; Peacock, Church Furniture, 86, 96; Gent. Maga. 1837, i. 492; Hart, Eccl. Records, 204, 294.   Cf. Pass. vii. 146.

213. (13. 237.) *Peers plouhman* seems to be used here in the sense of the Church of Christ upon earth, as in Pass. xxii.   We still use a Prayer for the Church Militant.

And that hym profite wayten, and them that look after profit for him [b].

216. (13. 240.) From Michaelmas to Michaelmas, i. e. from year to year, year by year.   In Chambers, Book of Days, ii. 389, will be found a list of saints who were supposed to guard men from various evils.   After which we read—"It will be learned, with some surprise, that these notions of presiding angels and saints are what have led to the custom of choosing magistracies on the 29th of September. . . . The idea must have been extensively prevalent, for the custom of electing magistrates on this day is very extensive."   We may suppose that the waferer in our text found it convenient, accordingly, to keep his accounts from one Michaelmas to another.   The Chamberlain of London, for example, who is the treasurer of the corporation, seems to have made up his accounts from Michaelmas to Michaelmas, since we learn that he was expected to "give in his account each year, between the Feasts of Saint Michael and of Saint Simon and St Jude, 28 October;" Liber Albus, ed. Riley, p. 42.   The accounts of farm-bailiffs were kept from Michaelmas to Michaelmas; see note above, p. 177, l. 10.

——(13. 242.) *With brode crounes,* i. e. wearing the tonsure, as in other passages.

217. (13. 243.) The expression "provender for his palfrey" [b] alludes to the custom of giving bread to horses; see Pass. ix. 225. The statement that the waferer provided "bread for the pope" is to be taken in a satirical sense. It clearly alludes, I think, to the money contributed to the Pope under the name of Peter's-pence; see note to Pass. v. 125. Thus the waferer complains that, though he has contributed to the support of the pope, the pope has done nothing for *him;* and, in the B-text, by a play upon the word *prouendre,* he says that, whilst he has provided provender (horse-bread) for the pope's palfrey, the pope has found no provender (or *prebend*) for himself in return.

——(13. 246.) All that he had ever received was a pardon with a leaden weight on it, bearing two heads in the middle of it. Mr Wright remarks that "the papal bulls, &c., had seals of lead, instead of wax." The very name *bull* (from *bulla,* a leaden seal) reminds us of this. See *Bulls* in Hook's Church Dictionary.

The two "polls" or heads are those of St Peter and St Paul. The *bulla* was round and flat, like a coin, and bore impressions on both sides. An example of one (used by Pope Boniface VIII) is figured at p. 273 of Lacroix' Military and Religious Life of the Middle Ages. On the one side is the inscription "BONIFATIVS·PP: VIII;" on the other are the heads of St Peter and St Paul, marked "S. PE." and "S. PA." respectively. Three similar *bullæ,* of Urban III., Gregory XII., and Leo II. respectively, are engraved in the Engl. Cyclop. Arts and Sciences, Supplement, p. 387; s. v. *Bulla.* There is a paper "indulgence" preserved in Trinity College Library, on which are painted full-length representations of the same saints.

——(13. 247.) "Had I a clerk that could write, I would send him in a petition." The waferer could not write himself, and seems to have had a difficulty in finding a professional scribe. A *bylle* is a petition; see note to Pass. v. 45; p. 77.

220, 221. (*cf.* b. 13. 248, 249; *also* 252, 253.) *Founde ich,* if I could find, if I found. *Letten this luther eir,* put a stop to this pestilential air. This must refer to some pestilence that was prevailing at the time, and I have supposed that the date of the C-text is about A.D. 1393. A glance at Haydn's Dictionary of Dates, s. v. *Plague,* will shew that the so-called four great pestilences of 1349, 1362, 1369, and 1376 were not the only ones; such plagues were of constant recurrence. Some, for instance, give the name of *fourth* pestilence to that of 1383; and 30,000 people died in London of a pestilence in 1407. In the B-text, the allusion is clearly to the pestilence of 1376, as shewn in the Preface to that text, p. iv, which see.

Whitaker remarks that—"the irony of these lines is exquisite. If, saith the poet, the promise of miraculous gifts of healing bestowed on the Apostles is not extended to their successor the pope, the reason is, because mankind are unworthy of such a blessing, for in another essential circumstance, the pope exactly resembles his first predecessor, St Peter—'Silver and gold hath he none.' The whole account of Active Life, and of the indisposition of the great to reward useful services, while they pay liberally for mere entertainment, is excellent."

I suppose Whitaker means that the resemblance of the Pope to St Peter in the matter of poverty is an ironical expression, the actual fact being that he was notoriously wealthy. In the life of Thomas Aquinas in the Encyclopædia Britannica, there is an anecdote which is exactly to the point. "Aquinas found the Holy Father [Innocent IV.] seated by a table covered with piles of indulgence-money. 'You see,' said the Pontiff, 'the church is no longer in the days when she could say—Silver and gold have I none.' 'True, holy Father,' said Aquinas, 'and she is as little able to say to the sick of the palsy—Rise up and walk.'"

I would add that the notion of trying to buy a "salve for the pestilence" from the pope was a fine idea for an unscrupulous quack. If Haukyn the waferer could have obtained it, beyond all doubt he would have made a good thing of it. But even this idea was surpassed by that of the quack, who, according to Horace Walpole, sold pills "as good against an earthquake;" see Chambers, Book of Days, i. 233.

231. (13. 260.) "Till pride be entirely destroyed, and that (will be) through lack of bread." The pestilences produce famines, which were considered as God's judgments against pride; see Pass. vi. 115—118.

——(13. 267.) *Stretforth*, Stratford; Chaucer's "Stratford-atte-Bowe." Here lived numerous bakers, who supplied some part of London with bread. In Riley's Memorials of London, p. 291, we read that, in 1356, carts bringing wheat and flour from Stratford to the City, had to pay 3*d.* per week; also that, in 1310, and again in 1316, some of the Stratford bread was seized, as being short of weight; id. pp. 71, 121. It may be added that, in 1371, it was ordered that oxen and sheep were to be slaughtered, not in the city, but at Stratford. Cf. Liber Albus, pp. 204, 205.

But the most explicit note is that in Stow's Survey of London, p. 159, who refers to the very passage in our text. This is quoted by Mr Wright, who observes that Stowe seems to have altered the date mentioned in l. 270; the fact being, however, that Stowe is quite right. See note to l. 270 below. Stowe's remarks are as follows :—"And because I have here before spoken of the bread-carts comming from Stratford at the Bow, ye shall understand that of olde time the bakers of breade at Stratford were allowed to bring dayly (except the Sabbaoth and principall feast) diverse long cartes laden with bread, the same being two ounces in the pennie wheate-loafe heavier then the penny wheate-loafe baked in the citie, the same to be solde in Cheape, three or foure carts standing there, betweene Gutherans lane and Fausters lane ende, one cart on Cornehill, by the conduit, and one other in Grasse streete. And I have reade that in the fourth yere of Edward the second, Richard Reffeham being maior, a baker named John of Stratforde, for making bread lesser than the assise, was with a fooles whoode on his head, and loaves of bread about his necke, drawne on a hurdle through the streets of this citie. Moreover in the 44. of Edward the third, John Chichester being maior of London, I read in the visions of Pierce Plowman, a booke so called, as followeth. 'There was a carefull commune when no cart came to towne with baked bread from Stratford: tho gan beggers weepe, and workemen were agast a little, this will be thought long, in the date of our Drite, in a drie Averell, a thousand and three hundred, twise thirtie and ten,' &c. I read also in the 20. of Henrie the eight, Sir James Spencer being maior, six bakers of Stratford were merced [*fined*] in the Guildhall of London, for baking under the sizo appoynted. These bakers of Stratford left serving of this citie, I know not uppon what occasion, about 30 yeares since" [i. e. about 1570].

——(13. 268.) "And workmen were somewhat terrified ; this will be long remembered." Here *thoughte* is used in the sense of *thought on ;* which is, indeed, the reading of the Bodley MS., as noted.

——(13. 269.) Mr Wright, misled by the reading of the Trinity MS., identifies this mention of "a dry April" with Fabyan's mention of "the drie sommer" in the 27th year of Edward the third, which year Mr Wright considers to be 1351. However, Fabyan calculates the years of that reign wrongly, as shewn in my Preface to the B-text, p. ii, note 3, and the year which he really means is the 26 Edw. III., from Jan. 25, 1352, to Jan. 24, 1353; cf. Chron. of London, p. 61. It is obvious, then, that this identification of a supposed dry April in 1351 with the mention of a hot summer in 1352 must be given up. The year really meant here is 1370, as in the text, and that there was "a dry April" in that year is rendered exceedingly probable by the mention by Fabyan of "excessyvenes of rayne" in the previous autumn of 1369; see the passage quoted in Pref. to B-text, p. iii. That there was an extraordinary dearth in 1370, Fabyan expressly testifies; wheat, he tells us, sold at .xld. a bushel. No wonder that "the commons were filled with anxiety, and the workmen were a little aghast," as described in ll. 266, 267. See the next note.

——(13. 270.) "My cakes were scarce there, when Chichester was mayor."

Geson, scarce, rare. *Geason* occurs in this sense in Jewel's Works, iv. 723; and (spelt *geson*) in the same, iii. 622 (Parker Society). *Gesoun* has the same meaning in John Russell's Boke of Nurture, l. 803, printed in the Babees Boke, ed. Furnivall, p. 170. Mr Furnivall gives it the opposite meaning of "plentiful" in his Glossary, but by mistake. See five more examples in Halliwell, s. vv. *Geason, Geson.* Ray notes "*Geazon*, scarce, hard to come by" as an Essex word. Gascoigne says—"grafts of suche a stocke are very *geason* in these dayes;" Supposes, Act I, sc. 2. Skelton has it twice; see his Why Come Ye Nat To Courte, l. 997, and another passage in Dyce's edition, i. 123, l. 129. So too Puttenham, Arte of Eng. Poesie, ed. Arber, p. 222. For early examples of it, see *gæsne* in Grein's A.S. Dictionary.

The difficulty about this date, mentioned in Pref. to A-text, p. xxxii, note 2, is cleared up in Pref. to B-text, pp. ii, iii. Much trouble has been caused by Fabyan's curious error of omitting all mention of the sixth year of Edward III, and by his confusion of the regnal year (beginning Jan. 25) with the year of the mayor of London (beginning Oct. 28). The final result is that our author, as might be expected, is perfectly correct. Chichester was elected in 1369 (probably in October) and was still mayor in 1370. In Riley's Memorials of London, p. 344, he is mentioned as being mayor in that very month of April in that very year in the words—"Afterwards, on the 25th day of April in the year above-mentioned, it was agreed by John de Chichestre, Mayor," &c. It is important to insist upon this, because the MS. followed by Mr Wright, in company with many inferior ones, has a corrupt reading which turns the words—"A þousande and thre hondreth · tweis *thretty* and ten" into "twice *twenty* and ten," occasioning a great difficulty, and misleading many modern writers and readers, since the same mistake occurs in Crowley's edition. Fortunately, the Laud MS. 581 and MS. Rawl. Poet. 38 set us right here, and all difficulty now vanishes; for it is easily ascertained that Chichester was mayor in 1369-70, and at no other time, having never been re-elected. Stowe and other old writers have the right date. See the quotation from Stowe in note to l. 267.

Another result is, that Stowe did not follow *any of the printed copies*, but some MS. Now there are but two good MSS. now extant, which have the right reading, viz. the two above mentioned; and again, of these two, only the Rawlinson MS. has the spelling "auerel" for April. Consequently, if Stowe obtained his information from any of the sources now extant, it was from this very Rawlinson MS.

There are several notices of John de Chichestre in Riley's Memorials of London. It appears that he was a goldsmith, and a wealthy man. He is mentioned as being mayor of London, Feb. 14, 1370 (p. 341); April 25, 1370 (p. 344); Aug. 10, 1370 (p. 344); Sept. 21, 1370 (p. 345). His year lasted from Oct. 28, 1369, to Oct. 27, 1370. In 1371, a great quantity of plate was bought from him (p. 350); and he was still alive in 1376 (p. 404). He is noticed also in A Chronicle of London, p. 68, in the words :—"John Chichestre, mayor, goldsmyth. In this yere was so gret derthe of corne in Engelond that a busshell of whete was worth xld."

☞ Here is a break. Some portions of the B-text have already appeared at an earlier place in the C-text, and have been already commented on. See notes to C. Pass. vii. 30—viii. 117 (pp. 104, 105, 109, 116, 123, 124, 132, 133, 141, 142), and the Schemes of C. Pass. vii., viii., and xvi. above. The notes here following refer to B. xiv. 1—131, and to C. xvi. 232—310.

——(14. 1.) *Hatere*, garment. This word is miswritten as *batere* in the Assumpcioun de notre Dame, l. 149, printed in King Horn, ed. Lumby, p.

48; see Mr Lumby's note at p. 121. See several examples in Stratmann, s. v. *hatre*, to which add the following.

> "He sauh kyng Philip als he lay in þe watre,
> 'Sir kyng, rise vp and skip, for þou has wette þi *hater.*'"
> Rob. of Brunne, Chron., ed. Hearne, i. 204.

"They drewe him by the *hatere;*" Owayne Miles, MS. Cott. Cal. A. ii., fol. 91, back; qu. by Wright, St Patrick's Purgatory, p. 74. See *haterynge* below, B. xv. 76. "The cloak, robe, or gown of the day was often the coverlet at night;" and again—"Shirts were, in fact, such valuable articles, that they are often the subject of charitable or ostentatious doles, and we find them not unfrequently . . . devised by will;" Hist. of Agriculture and Prices in England, by J. E. Thorold Rogers, i. 120, and 66.

——(14. 2.) "I sleep in it at night." This may mean that Haukyn used his garment at night as a coverlet. If it is to be taken literally, it is somewhat at variance with the usual custom, which was, as Mr Wright remarks, for all classes of society to go to bed quite naked. Strange as this may seem, it is so well ascertained that it is hardly worth while to multiply instances of it; indeed, it is expressly asserted in our text elsewhere, viz. in Pass. xxiii. 196. The reader may look at Plates XIV, XV, and XVI in the Babees Book. See also *Naked-bed* in Nares; Our English Home, p. 92; Chambers, Book of Days, ii. 232.

——(14. 5.) "It has been washed both during Lent, and out of Lent." The whole passage is a kind of parable. Haukyn's one garment symbolises the carnal nature of man, which requires shrift in the same way that a garment needs to be washed. He has been shriven, he tells us, both in Lent and out of it; he has been washed with the soap of sickness, and purified by the loss of worldly wealth. See this idea worked out in an old sermon on Shrift in Old English Homilies, ed. Morris, 2nd. Ser., p. 56. Cf. Ps. li. 2, 7; Isaiah i. 16, 18; Jerem. ii. 22. "Omnia confessione lavantur;" Ancren Riwle, p. 300. A "washing-day" in olden times was, doubtless, a great event. See Our Eng. Home, p. 92; Babees Boke, ed. Furnivall, p. lxiii.

——(14. 15.) *Flober*, sully, dirty; see *beflobered* above, B. xiii. 401; and the note to the line, p. 133.

——(14. 16.) *Contrition* was divided into three parts or acts, viz. contrition of heart, confession of mouth, and satisfaction of deed; see Pass. xvii. 25—32. The penitent is to be sorry in thought, word, and deed; to feel sorrow, to express it, and to prove it by doing penance, or by making restitution. "For which sayth Seint John Chrisostome: penance distreineth a man to accepte benignely every peine that him is enjoined, with *contrition of herte*, and *shrift of mouth*, with *satisfaction, and werking* of all maner humilitee;" Ch. Pers. Tale, first part. In fact, the whole of the Persones Tale is really upon this subject of Shrift. So likewise in Old Eng. Homilies, ed. Morris, 1st Ser. pp. 49, 51—"Cordis contritione moritur peccatum, oris confessione defertur ad tumulum, operis satisfactione tumu-

latur in perpetuum;" which resembles the quotation below, B. xiv. 91.
Such is the usual formula; thus we find in Peter Cantor, ed. Migne, Cursus
Patrologicus, vol. 205, col. 342—"Post confessionem cordis sequitur de con-
fessione oris. Est enim triplex confessio; cordis, . . . oris, et operis." In a
Poem on the Seven Deadly Sins, several herbs are named as remedies for
sin :—

> "Other erbys ther ben alsoo,
> That suffer the sores they may nat swell;
> *Orys confescio* is on of thoo,
> He wyll nat suffre no ded flessche for to dwell;
> *Cordys contrycio* ys the too,
> A wasshyth the woundes as doth a well;
> *Operys satisfaccio* the souereyne sauetyff,
> For soth as I yow tell."
>
> Polit. Rel. and Love Poems, ed. Furnivall, p. 218.

See also Ancren Riwle, pp. 299—343; Barclay, Ship of Fools, ed. Jamieson,
i. 196, and the article *Penance* in the Index to the Parker Society's publications.

——(14. 19.) "Do-bet shall beat and buck it." "I Bucke lynen clothes
to scoure of their fylthe, & make them whyte, *Ie bue.* Bucke these shyrtes,
for they be to foule to be wasshed by hande, *Buez ces chemises, car elles sont
trop sallies de les lauer a sauon;*" Palsgrave. "*Buée*, lie wherewith clothes
are scowred; also, a buck of clothes;"—"*Buer*, to wash a buck; to scowre
with lie;"—"*Buandiere*, f. a laundresse, or buck washer;" Cotgrave. To
buck is to cleanse clothes by steeping them in lye; see *Buck* in Webster,
Nares, Halliwell, Wedgwood, and Richardson. See *bouketh* in Pass. xvii.
331. The various processes are accurately described. First of all, some of
the dirt is to be "clawed" or scraped off; next, Do-well is to wash the
garment and wring it, so as to remove such part of the dirt as could be
easily removed by water; next, Do-bet is to beat it thoroughly with a
washing-beetle and then to soak it in lye, so as to restore its original
colour; it was then to be re-dyed in grain, for which purpose (if not before)
it would be taken to pieces; after which, Do-best was to sew it all together
again, and it would be as good as new.

——(14. 20.) *Engreynen it*, dye it in grain, i. e. of a fast colour. The
word was misprinted *engreyven* in Mr Wright's edition, and left unexplained.
In another passage, B. ii. 15, Mr Wright wrongly explains *engreyned* by
"powdered." See note to C. iii. 14, on p. 44 above, and cf. note to
Chaucer, C. T. Group B, l. 1917, in my edition of The Prioresses Tale, &c.
(Clar. Press).

——(14. 24.) Heralds and harpers often had *new* garments given them;
see notes above, C. xvi. 202, 209.

——(14. 27.) "Than the wife of Haukyn the waferer;" see note above,
C. xvi. 131, pp. 307, 308.

232—236. Lines 232, 233 have some resemblance to B. xiv. 75, 76; and
l. 236 has the same ending as B. xiv. 23. See note below, to B. xiv. 76.

——(14. 33.) This line closely resembles B. vii. 125, 126.

240. (14. 39.) The sense is much the same as that of the proverb— "God never sendeth mouth but he sendeth meat" (Heywood); on which Ray well remarks—"This proverb is much in the mouth of poor people, who get children, but take no care to maintain them. Rather it intimates, that God never sends children, but he gives the parents the means of providing for them."

243. (14. 42, 43.) The cricket is here said to live in the fire. Usually, this fabulous story is spoken of the salamander, called *Grylio* in the Bestiary. of Philip de Thaun; see Wright's Popular Treatises on Science, p. 97, and Ayenbite of Inwyt, ed. Morris, p. 167 (near the bottom). The cricket's Latin name was *gryllus ;* hence, possibly, a confusion between the animals. Indeed, we find in the Prompt. Parv. the entry—"*Crykette*, salamandra, crillus, grillus." Still, the notion of a cricket living in the fire is the more reasonable, on account of its partiality for the domestic hearth. The salamander was even said to extinguish fire; see English Cyclopædia, Nat. Hist. art. Amphibia, p. 178, where references are given to Aristotle, Hist. Animals, v. 19; Ælian, ii. 31; Pliny, Nat. Hist. xxix. 4.

Our author seems to assert here that the curlew lived upon air, a fable generally told of the chameleon. "The food of this well-known and wary bird (*Numenius arquatus*), which is called in Scotland the Whaup, consists of earth-worms, slugs, small testaceans, and insects ;" Eng. Cycl. Nat. Hist. art. Scolopacidæ, p. 718. However, Gower (Conf. Amant. bk. vi.) has the lines—

> "And, as the plover doth of the eire,
> I liue, and am in good espeire," &c.

And P. Lacroix, in his Manners, Customs, &c. during the Middle Ages, p. 132, quotes from an old author the statement that "plovers feed on air." In Nashe's Lenten Stuffe, printed in the Harleian Miscellany, vi. 179, we find—"as the cameleon liveth by the ayre, and the salamander by the fire."

251. (14. 48.) *Fynde vs alle*, provide for us all.

253. (14. 50.) *Clomsest for colde*, art benumbed with cold. Cf. Du. *kleumen*, to be benumbed with cold; *kleumer*, a chilly person; *kleumsch*, chilly. See *Clumsy* in Wedgwood, who cites several examples. Ray has— "*Clumps, Clumpst*, idle, lazy, unhandy; *Lincolnshire* . . . *Clumpst* with cold, i. e. benummed;" also—"*Clussumed ;* as, 'a *clussum'd* hand,' a clumsie hand. *Cheshire*." The sense of Mid. Eng. *clomsen* is, I suppose, *to become torpid*, or *useless*, especially from the effect of cold, with ultimate reference to the verb *clemmen*, to pinch. Hence, I should translate—"He is outher *clomsed*, or wode" in the Pricke of Conscience, l. 1651, by "he is either stupefied or mad." And I should suppose the quotation given in Dr Morris's Glos. to Pr. of Cons., p. 287, from the Gospel of Nichodemus, fol. 213, viz. "we er *clomsed* gret and smalle," to mean "we are stupefied, great and small;" for it is an expression used by the fiends to express their state of amazement and confusion at Christ's approach. Dr Morris explains *clomsed* in one passage by *cursed*, and in the other by *confined, bound ;*

whereas the single meaning of *stupefied* will serve for both. A person is *clumsy* who has no more use of his fingers than if they were benumbed. Surely, too, "*clumsid* hondis" in Wyclif, Isaiah xxxv. 3, means "clumsy or weak hands," rather than "unloosed," as in the Wycl. Glos.; and answers equally well to the Lat. *dissolutas*. See *Acomelyd* in Prompt. Parv., and Way's note; and especially *Comelyd* in the same, with Way's note; pp. 6, note 3, and 88, note 6.

Clyngest for drouthe, art pined with thirst; see *clingen* and *clengen* in Stratmann, and cf. the Lancashire *clem* or *clam*, to starve for want of food. Shakespeare has—"Till famine *cling* thee," i. e. pine thee, shrivel thee up; Macb. v. 5. 40.

257. (14. 54.) *Ondyng*, smelling [c]; *etynge*, eating [b]. *Fyue wittes*, five senses; the B-text, by the repetition of idea in *tonge* and *etynge*, mentions but three of them; the revised C-text mentions all but the sense of hearing. See note to Pass. ii. 15, p. 29. The true sense of *onding* is "breathing;" see "*Ondyn* or brethyn, *aspiro, anelo*," in Prompt. Parv., p. 364, and Way's excellent note. Here it is used of sniffing, or drawing in the breath in the act of smelling.

263. (*not in* b.) This line is found in one MS. only. I cannot trace the origin of these Leonine verses; William may have composed them himself.

266. (14. 62.) Whoever will turn to the Babees Book, ed. Furnivall, pp. 382, 386, will see at once that the text "Aperis tu manum tuam" was repeated daily in saying grace, and was therefore very familiar to every one. It is well worth noting that William has quoted several texts which were used in graces, viz. "Qui in caritate," &c., Pass. iv. 406; "Frange esurienti," &c., Pass. xii. 67; "Dispersit, dedit pauperibus," &c., B. xv. 320; "Iustitia eius manet," &c., Pass. xviii. 65.

I am now able to complete the quotation at Pass. iv. 342, which I failed to find at the time of printing the notes to Passus iv. The whole sentence will be found at p. 390 of the Babees Book, being part of a Latin grace, and runs thus:—"Retribuere dignare, domine deus, omnibus nobis bona facientibus, propter nomen sanctum tuum, uitam eternam. Amen." This well agrees with William's loose translation of it in the three lines above it.

267. (14. 63.) This of course refers to the 40 years' wandering of the Israelites in the wilderness, and to the issue of water from the smitten rock; Numb. xx. 11; Deut. viii. 15.

269. (14. 65.) *Elyes*, Elias's, Elijah's. See James v. 17; 1 Kings xvii. 1.

270. (14. 66.) *Reynede*, rained [c]; *rone*, rained [b]. The use of the strong preterite of this verb is very rare.

271. (14. 67.) *Wynter*, years; according to the usual A.S. idiom. *Of no mete telden*, made account of no food, i. e. made no special provision [c]; *no mete ne tulyeden*, earned no food by tilling the ground [b]. *Telden* is from *tellen*; cf. the readings *tolden, toolden*; but the earlier C-text MSS. (viz. I and T) read *ne tiled* or *ne tilide*, like the B-text.

272. (14. 68.) *The book* is the Legenda Aurea of Jacobus de Voragine. The allusion is to the legend of the Seven Sleepers of Ephesus, told at length in the Legenda Aurea, in Gregory of Tours, De Gloria Martyrum, i. 9; and in Baring Gould's Curious Myths of the Middle Ages, Ser. i. p. 88. See also Gibbon's Decline and Fall of the Roman Empire; Wheeler, Noted Names of Fiction, art. Seven Sleepers; Chambers, Book of Days, ii. 127; Homilies of Ælfric, ed. Thorpe, ii. 425; Mrs Jameson's Sacred and Legendary Art, 3rd ed., p. 581. The day on which they are commemorated is July 27, and the supposed date of their "sleep" is A.D. 250. The legend is often alluded to. In Hazlitt's ed. of Warton, Hist. Eng. Poet., ii. 62, note 5, is a note of a French copy of the legend, MS. Cotton, Calig. A. ix. fol. 213, back—"Ici commence la vie de Set Dormanz." Heywood, in his Four Ps, makes the Pardoner offer "a slipper of one of the Seven Sleepers" as a relic.

In the B-text, they are said to have slept for 700 years; in [c], for more than 60 years; Jacobus de Voragine says 360 years, though he also says it was from the time of the Decian persecution (A.D. 250) to the 30th year of Theodosius II. (A.D. 432), less than 200 years. Yet the common account says their sleep was from A.D. 250 to A.D. 479, a period of 229 years. What Mr Baring-Gould means by "the discovery and translation of their relics under Theodosius, in 479," I am unable to say; since Theodosius died A.D. 450. The emperor of the East in 479 was named Zeno. In no way can the chronology be brought right.

——(14. 72.) "But dearth causes unkindness." *Caristia* is here the nominative case, and the reading *caristiam* is wrong. The word was in common use in the 14th century. We find the entry "magna caristia ferri" four times, under the dates, 1353, 1354, 1355, and 1371, in Prof. J. E. Thorold Rogers, Hist. of Agric. and Prices in England, ii. 607. William refers to *mesure* (moderation) as being the priceless mean between dearth and plenty.

——(14. 76.) The Latin quotation here is differently worded from that at C. xvi. 231. It resembles a sentence in Peter Cantor, ed. Migne, col. 331—"Et abundantia panis causa fuit peccati Sodomorum;" see also col. 333. So also in the Ancren Riwle, p. 422—"Of idelnesse awakeneð muchel flesshes fondunge. Iniquitas Sodome saturitas panis et ocium." And again —"hæc [Sodoma] propter abundantiam panis, et per luxuriæ magnitudinem excessit modum libidinis;" S. Hieronymi Dialogus adv. Pelagianos, lib. i. sect. 17; ed. Migne, t. ii. col. 511. The ultimate reference is clearly to Ezek. xvi. 49.

——(14. 80.) "They sunk into hell, those cities, each one of them." This was the accepted account. "The cytees [of Sodom, Gomorrah, Admah, and Zeboim] and the lond weren brent and sonken into helle;" Mandeville, ed. Halliwell, p. 101.

"Al tho citees & her sydes sunkken to helle;"

Allit. Poems, ed. Morris, B. 968.

——(14. 81.) "Therefore let us act with great moderation, and make our faith our defence." William uses the word in the old sense; cf. A.S. *scýld-truma*, a strong shield, lit. a troop-shield. The later and commoner sense is an armed company, a body of troops, battalion; in which sense it occurs frequently in Barbour's Bruce. For further examples, see Stratmann, s. v. *schild*. To which add—"ar the *scheltroms* come to-gedders," i. e. before the troops were engaged, in Trevisa's description of the Battle of Hastings; Spec. of English, ed. Morris and Skeat, p. 246. Note that William's use of the word exactly accounts for our word *shelter*, which I take to be a mere corruption of *sheltrom* or *sheltron;* for various spellings, see the footnote.

——(14. 91.) Here William again recognises the three acts of Shrift, mentioned in note above, B. xiv. 16. He here says—*Contrition of heart* merely turns a deadly sin into a venial one; but *confession of mouth* slays the sin; and thirdly, *satisfaction of deed* removes and puts away the slain sin, as if it had never been. The idea is much the same as in the first Latin quotation given in the note to B. xiv. 16 above, but differs in its degrees.

283. (14: 103.) *Ye*, yea, is used in expressing mere assent, like the modern *aye*. See note on ʒ*is* in Glos. to Will. of Palerne; and Marsh, Lectures, 1st Series, p. 579. The point of this satirical line is easily seen. The question (in ll. 281, 282) is put in such a form as to suggest that the patient endurance of poverty is not so meritorious as a rightful expenditure of wealth. To which the reply is—"Aye, but *who* is that righteous rich man? Only point him out, and we will soon praise him!"

299. (14. 118.) *Bote*, unless. *Sende*, may send [c]; *sent*, sendeth [b]. ·

301. (14. 120.) "For he was wrought to evil fortune, who was never created for joy;" *or perhaps*, "for whom joy was never prepared." The curious expression *to wrotherhele* is composed of the preposition *to*, followed by *wrother*, the dat. fem. of *wroth*, and the dat. of the fem. sb. *hele* (A.S. *hǽlu*). *Hele* means *health, condition*, as usual; *wroth* means angry, and hence *bad, evil*. The suffix *-er* corresponds to the A.S. dat. fem. adjectival suffix *-re*. "It was evidently not originally a compound word, .. but afterwards became so," says Sir F. Madden; see his remarks in his edition of Layamon, vol. iii. p. 444. Instances occur in Layamon, l. 29556; the Legend of St Juliane, MS. Reg. 17 A. xxvii. fol. 58, back (where it is miswritten *wrathel heale*); Rob. of Glouc., ed. Hearne, pp: 143, 164; Rob. of Brunne, pp. 104, 201, 221; Squire of Lowe Degree, ap. Ritson, iii. 157. All these instances are adduced by Sir F. Madden. Add these :—Debate of the Body and the Soul, pr. in Wright's edition of Mapes, p. 339; and in Mätzner, Alteng. Sprachproben, i. 103, l. 450, where we find much the same expression as in our text, viz. :—

"Thouʒ that wistest al bifor, wʒi schope thou me *to wrother hele?* "

And again, in an Old Eng. Misc., ed. Morris, p. 148—

"*To wrothere hele* he wes ibore
That for sunnes is for-lore." ·

Also in Ancren Riwle, p. 102; and in Early Eng. Poems and Lives of Saints, ed. Furnivall, xxiv. 189. The opposite expression, *to goder hele*, with the sense of "fortunately," is also common, and exhibits the same dat. fem. suffix. See Layamon, l. 3597; Rob. of Glouc., p. 368; Dame Siriz, l. 261.

303. (14. 122.) *Douce uye*, luxurious life; Fr. *douce vie*. Luke xvi. 19.

304. (*not in* b.) *Buyeth hit ful bitere*, pays very dearly for it.

306. (*not in* b.) *Leudes*, tenements, possessions. The phrase "londes and leedes" occurs in Will. of Palerne, l. 4001; frag. of Alisaunder (in the same volume), l. 12. I quote the following from my Glossary to Wm. of Palerne, s. v. *Lud*. "On this difficult phrase see Sir F. Madden's reply to Mr Singer's remarks on Havelok. It seems to mean 'lands and leases,' or 'lands and tenements,' as Rob. of Brunne uses it frequently to mean *tenements, rents*, or *fees*. The older form of the word is *lethe* or *lithe*;" &c. In Havelok, l. 2515, we have—"Lond and *lith*, and other catel." So also— "No asked he lond no *lithe*;" Sir Tristrem, p. 101;—"Ther wille not be went, ne lete ther lond ne *lith*;" Rob. of Brunne, p. 194, where it answers to the French "Ne volent lesser tere ne *tenement*;"—"Who schall us now geve londes or *lythe*;" Le Bone Florence, l. 841;—"Al the londis and the *lithis*;" Sir Gawain and Sir Golagros, ii. 27.

307. (*not in* b.) Here the life of the rich is likened to a pleasant slumber, with dreams of perpetual summer, from which death is the harsh awakening.

309. (*not in* b.) *Than aren hit*, lit. then are it, i. e. then are they. The usual idiom; see note to Pass. vi. 59, p. 89.

SCHEME OF C. PASSUS XVII.

(B. Pass. XIV. 132—XV. 252.)

(Cf. Wright's edition, pp. 281—310; ll. 9181—10130.)

C-TEXT.	B-TEXT.	C-TEXT.	B-TEXT.
xvii. 1—5	xiv. 132—136	xvii. 116—118	xiv. 274—276
6	137, 138	119, 120	*like* 277, 278
7—9	139—141	121	279
——	142—156	122, 123	*like* 280
10, 11	158, 159	——	281—285
12	157	124—131	286—293
13—17	160—164	132	——
18—20	*like* 165—167	133—136	294—297
21—37	——	137, 138	*like* 298, 299
——	168—194	139—143	*like* 300—304
38—78	195—235	——	305
79	*like* 236, 237	144—157	*like* 306—319
80—114	238—272	——	320—332
115	*unlike* 273	——	xv. 1—14

C-text.	B-text.	C-text.	B-text.
xvii. 158—165	—	xvii. 297—300	xv. 161—164
166—172	xv. 15—21	301, 302	—
173	like 22	—	165, 166
174—182	—	303	like 168
183—192	23—32	304—306	—
193, 194	—	307	like 167
195—218	33—56	308, 309	like 169
219, 220	like 57, 58	310—312	—
221—225	59—63	—	170
226—229	—	313—316	171—173
—	64—67	317, 318	like 174
230—232	68—70	319	—
—	71	—	175
233	like 72	320—322	176—178
—	73	323—327	—
234—239	74—79	—	179—181
—	80—84	(a) [330]	(a) 182
240	like 85, 86	328	like 183
241	—	329	184
—	87—89	(a) 330	(a) [182]
242—244	like 90, 91	331	185
245—248	92—95	[like 330]	186
249	—	332, 333	187, 188
250—256	96—102	334	like 189
257	—	335	—
258—263	103—108	—	190
264	—	336	191
265—269	109—113	—	192
270	—	337	193
—	114	—	194—202
271	115	338, 339	203, 204
—	116—123	—	205—210
272	124	340	211
273	—	—	212
274—278	125—129	341—345	213—217
—	130, 131	346	—
279, 280	132, 133	—	218
281—283	—	347—351	219—223
—	134—144	—	224
284	like 145	352—362	225—235
—	146	—	236—238
285—287	like 147—149	363	like 239
288, 289	—	—	240, 241
—	150—152	364	like 242
290—292	like 153—155	365—368	—
293, 294	—	—	243—250
—	156, 157	369	251
295	158	370, 371	—
296	[145]	—	252
—	159, 160		

NOTES TO C. PASSUS XVII. (B. XIV. 132—XV. 252.)

2. (14. 133.) *At hus laste ende*, at his death; referring to *mannes* in l. 1.

5. (14. 136.) *Deuer*, duty; F. *devoir*. This word seems only to occur in the phrase "to do one's dever," i. e. to do one's duty. Examples are—

"Doth now your deuoir, yonge knyghtes proude;" Kn. Tale, 1740.

"And doth nought but his deuer;" Will. of Palerne, l. 474.

"For he has don his deuere · dignely as he ou[gh]t;" id., l. 520.

"Seide—do thi deuer · that thow hast to done;" id. 2546.

"And has donne thy deuer with [i. e. against] my dere knyghttes;"
Morte Arthur, 1940.

"When he his deuer hade done," &c.; Troy Book, 797; cf. ll. 234, 590.

"Also, yif eny of the brethren of the forsaid bretherhede be chosen wardein in the bretherhede, . . he shal take the charge al-sone as he is warned therof, and do his deuer as a wardein of the bretherhede ought to do;" English Gilds, ed. Toulmin Smith, p. 5. At a later period, this word was confused with its derivative *endeavour*, and to "do one's dever" came to signify to do one's endeavour, to do one's best at anything. In this sense it is used in Shropshire to this day, and in the West of Scotland, as noted in Jamieson and by Mr Donaldson in his note to the Troy-book, at p. 475. I am of opinion, however, that this latter sense is *not the right one* in the Troy-book, nor in any other of the passages above cited. Cf. B. xiv. 150, 153.

Daies iourne, i. e. day's work, day's task. Hence our word *journeyman*. William little thought that *day* and *journey* are from the same root, and that he was repeating the same idea!

This passage should be compared with Pass. iv. 294—305.

8. (14. 140.) *By*, with reference to. *Hit semeth nat*, it befits not, it is not seemly.

——(14. 148.) "And reward with double riches all that have pitying hearts." So *rewarde wel* = pay good wages, in B. xiv. 145, just above; and see ll. 153, 154 below.

——(14. 152.) *Rewfullich lybbeth*, live a life of compassion, live mercifully. Cf. the expression "reuful hertes" just above, l. 148.

13. (14. 160.) The best time for the poor was, no doubt, harvest-time; see Pass. ix. 323. Compare Chaucer's Prologue to the Man of Law's Tale.

14. (14. 161.) *Wet-shood*, wet-shoe'd, with wet shoes, wet-footed. Halliwell gives "*Watched*, wet-shod;" and in Oxfordshire *watcherd* is used; both *watched* and *watcherd* being mere corruptions of the word here employed. William has it again, Pass. xxi. 1. The Icelandic term is *skó-vátr*, lit. shoe-wet; Cleasby and Vigfusson. In a fragment termed "Arthur," ed. Furnivall, E. E. T. S. (1864), l. 469, there is a description of a battle in which men's shoes were soaked in brains and blood.

"There men were wetschoede
Alle of brayn and of blode."

15. (14. 162.) *Afurst and afyngred*, oppressed by thirst and hunger; see notes to Pass. xii. 43 (p. 237), and to B. vi. 269 (p. 170).

20. (14. 167.) "And all equally intelligent and wise, and (have made them to) live without penury" [c]; *or*, "if it had well pleased Thee" [b].

21. (*not in* b.) "But it is all for the best, as I hope, that some are poor and some rich."

25. (*not in* b.) See note to B. xiv. 91. *To clanse with oure soules*, to cleanse our souls with; the usual idiom.

27. (*not in* b.) *The fadres will of heuene*, the will of the Father in heaven; see note above to Pass. xvi. 131; p. 307.

29. (*not in* b.) See note to B. xiv. 91, p. 325.

37. (*not in* b.) *Bote*, unless, except. Cf. Pass. x. 338—345.

——(14. 171.) "For no dearth, nor drought, nor (excessive) wet can be any injury to them;" viz. to the wealthy. *Dere* is here a substantive; see several instances in Stratmann. The Oriel MS. omits *ben*, in which case *hem dere =* injure them, giving precisely the same sense.

——(14. 172.) *Haue thei here hele*, if they have their health.

——(14. 179.) *Thi careful*, Thy people who are full of care and misery. See *care =* misery in l. 175 above; and see *careful* in Wright's Bible Word-book and Trench's Select Glossary.

——(14. 181.) *In genere of his gentrice*, in the nature of [i. e. by reason of] His gentle birth, *or* humanity. *Gentrise* is gentleness or nobility of birth or disposition; it occurs in l. 52 of the later life of St Juliana.

"And thench on hire heie kunne and hire owe *gentrise* ; "

i. e. they bade her think upon her noble kindred and her own nobleness; St Juliana, ed. Cockayne, p. 82, l. 52. So also in the Troy-book, ed. Donaldson, l. 131—

"This Jason, for his *gentris*, was ioyfull till all."

Cf. *genterie* and *gentillesse*, as explained in the Wyf of Bathes Tale; with which compare the Romaunt of the Rose, ll. 2187—2197; Chaucer's tr. of Boethius, ed. Morris, Book 3, pr. 6, p. 78; and the "generall signes of gen-tilnesse" enumerated in the Persones Tale, near the end of the section *De Superbia*.

——(14. 188.) "But if the devil would plead against this," &c. *The pouke* has been explained before; see notes to A. x. 62, p. 222; and to Pass. xvi. 164, p. 310. It is very remarkable that nearly all the scribes have strangely inserted the word *pope* instead of *pouke*, as observed in the foot-note. However, the Rawlinson MS. has the right reading, and in l. 190 the word has not been thus altered. See the next note. Cf. Crit. Note, B-text, p. 413.

——(14. 189.) *He*, i. e. Christ; cf. ll. 179, 181. *As quik*, as quickly as possible, immediately. We have the very same idiom in the phrase *as tyte*, B. xiii. 319; xvi. 61. In Cambridgeshire, the ordinary phrase "very hot" is expressed by "*as hot as hot*," or sometimes (but more rarely) by "*as hot*" alone; and the same with other adjectives and adverbs.

The qued, the Evil One; see the Glossary. Of course this proves the absurdity of the reading *pope* in the line above.

——(14. 190.) "And so put off (repel) the devil, and prove us to be under a security." The Passion of Christ is the pledge of Redemption.

——(14. 191.) *Be moste*, ought to be, lit. must be. *Moste* is disyllabic, and thus the rhythm of the line is preserved; the Oriel MS. has the spelling *muste*. *Be* is the infinitive mood.

——(14. 193.) *Decorreth*, discourseth; not "discovers," as in Mr Wright's Glossary. Our author has here confused two words; he uses *decorreth* for *discorreth*. The O.Fr. *decorre* is to flow down, Lat. *decurrere;* but the O.Fr. *descorrer* or *discourir* (Lat. *discurrere*) is the word he was intending to employ. Cotgrave has—"*Discourir*, to discourse of, to relate, report, recite, rehearse; *to particularize point after point;*" &c. This last is the very best possible explanation. The general sense is—"(if we hope for pardon), the heavenly record of our deeds should enlarge upon our poverty, our patience, and our faith. But alas! in too many cases, that record does but *particularize instances* of pomp and pride."

41, 42. (14. 198, 199.) "Lo! how men write upon the windows in the friars' chapels! if the foundation be false (it is all in vain)." Mr Wright remarks—"Both in the Vision of Piers Ploughman and in the Creed, there are frequent expressions of indignation at the extravagant expenditure in painting the windows of the abbeys and churches. It must not be forgotten that, a little later, the same feeling as that exhibited in these satires led to the destruction of many of the noblest monuments of medieval art." See P. Pl. Crede, ll. 120—129, 162, 175, 206, and cf. Pass. iv. 64—74 above.

44. (14. 201.) *Seuene synnes*, the Seven Deadly Sins, so fully described above; see note to Pass. vii. 3.

46. (14. 203.) *With richesse*, by means of riches. It is not meant that Riches is a sin, but that it is the allurement to it; indeed, to all the Seven Sins, as is more particularly explained below. *Tho ribaudes*, those evil ones, i. e. the Seven Sins [c]; *that ribaude*, that Evil One [b]. The sense is—"and those evil ones [*or*, that Evil One] soonest beguile men by means of Riches."

50. (14. 207.) *Can more*, knows more.

54. (14. 211.) *Heye wey*, high road. The quotation in [b] is intended to refer to Mat. xix. 23—"quia diues difficile intrabit in regnum cælorum."

56. (14. 213.) *Batauntlyche*, hastily; or rather, with noisy and eager haste. This is rather a clumsy compound, and does not appear to occur elsewhere. *Bataunt* is the O.Fr. *batant*, properly the pres. part. of *batre* or *battre*, to beat. Burguy has—"Batre, Battre, de *batuere; venir batant*, ii. 376 [i. e. vol. ii. p. 376 of Burguy's Grammaire de la Langue d'oïl]; *tot batant*, battant, tout courant, en toute hâte." Cotgrave has—"*Batant*, beating, battering, thrashing. *Il arriua tout batant*, he came very hastily. . . *Il les chassa tout batant*, he pursued them very hard." Also—"*Batre les chemins*, to belay the way, as purse-takers and boot-halers do." Thus *batant* clearly refers to the noisy and eager way in which beggars beset and

clamour round an almsgiver, thronging and pushing against one another, and even crushing one another to death. Mr Furnivall sends me a good illustration of this from Hall's Chronicle, ed. 1809, p. 630. "The kynges highnes kept this year (1521-2) his Easter at his manour of Richemont, and caused his amner [almoner] to make enquire eight miles round about the said manour, what poore people was in euery parish. And for the eschuyng of murther, *that moste commonly fortuned euery goodfridaie, by reason of the great resort of poore people,* his grace caused them to be refreshed with his almose [alms] at home at their houses."

58. (14. 215.) William now discusses the enticements of Riches to the Seven Sins. *Pride* is discussed in ll. 58—66; *Wrath,* ll. 67—71; *Gluttony,* ll. 72—79; *Avarice,* ll. 80—90; *Lechery,* ll. 91—94; *Sloth,* ll. 95—105. There does not seem to be any mention of *Envy,* unless it be in ll. 69—71; but perhaps it would not have been easy to shew that the poor are more free from this vice than the rich.

59. (14. 216.) This line is slightly, but remarkably, varied in the two texts. In [b], William says of Pride, that "he hath some dwelling rather in the master than in the man." Afterwards, calling to mind the arrogant manners of the retainers in a great household, who were themselves well-fed and well-clothed, he altered it to—"Either in the master or in the man he shews some abiding."

70—79. (14. 227—237.) Only found in one MS. of the B-text; see Crit. Note [b], p. 413.

76. (14. 233.) This line is an allusion to an old proverb, quoted by Mr Riley (Memorials of London, p. 8, note 4) from the Book of Husbandry, attributed to Robert Grosteste, bp. of Lincoln :—"Whoso streket his fot forthere than the whitel will reche, he schal streken in the straw," i. e. he that stretches his foot further than the blanket, will stretch into the straw. In fact, as Mr Riley remarks, "the bed of those days, among the humbler people, was nothing but a whitel, or blanket, thrown upon a heap of straw." Hence William says that the poor man, stretching himself, finds that part of his blanket [*or* of his sheets, b] is nothing but straw. This is also well illustrated by the following passage from Harrison's Description of England—"As for servants, if they had anie sheete above them it was well; for seldom had they anie under their bodies to keep them from the pricking straws than ran oft through the canvas of the pallet, and rased their hardened hides." This passage relates to a later time, but shews no great improvement. The words *whitel* (A.S. *hwitel*) and *blanket* are equivalent, and denote the *white* colour of the material; see Prompt. Parv., p. 38, note 1; also *Whittle* in Halliwell's Dictionary.

77. (14. 234.) Compare—"The king of gluttony hath no jollity, There [i. e. where] poverty is pight;" The World and the Child, in Hazlitt's Old Plays, i. 249.

81. (14. 239.) *Nameliche,* especially. *Her neither,* neither of them [c]; *her none,* neither (lit. none) of them [b].

84. (14. 242.) *Apereth nat*, &c., and hardly comes up to (reaches to) his navel.

85. (14. 243.) *A loueliche laik*, a good struggle, a satisfactory bout, good sport, a real 'lark;' the last word being the A.S. *lác*.

89. (14. 247.) "And which of the two is easier to break open; which is it that makes less noise?" *or*, "it makes less noise" [b]. "*Boost*, a noise; a provincial word still familiar [1813] in the midland counties;" Whitaker. In Rich. Coer de Lion, l. 4237, ed. Weber, the context clearly shews that "no *bost* gan make" means "made no noise."

93. (14. 251.) *A straw for*, i. e. small indeed would be the value of.

"*Straw* for your gentillesse, quod our host."

Chaucer; C. T. Group F, l. 695.

Hy stod nat, they would not stand, would not exist. *Stod* is here in the subjunctive mood.

94. (14. 252.) "If they had no other use but by poor people" [c]; *or*, "If they received nothing except from poor men, their houses would be roofless" [b]. In the latter case, for *untyled*, i. e. without a tiled roof, the Oriel MS. has the good reading *vnhiled*, uncovered. *Vnhiled* occurs in the Tale of Gamelyn, l. 87; and *unhuled* in Jos. of Arimathie, ed. Skeat, l. 515.

96. (14. 254.) *Meschief*, adversity. *Mene*, mean, instrument [c]; *his maister*, his teacher [b].

98. (14. 256.) *Secte*, retinue, train, company of followers. The form *sute* [b] has the same sense; see note to Pass. viii. 130, p. 143, which closely resembles l. 100 in the present passage. Only note that *secte*, in l. 100, has rather the sense of *suit* or apparel.

106. (14. 264.) Whitaker remarks—"Never was a more unhappy illustration. The saints of the Church of Rome who forsook lands and lordships for the love of Christ, are here compared to young women, who leave their father and mother to run away with a lover; that is, to indulge a much stronger animal passion." I believe this comment to be a mistaken one. Whitaker was misled by the word *paramour* in l. 107, which is not at all intended in a bad sense, but is used, like the modern *lover*, with reference to an honourable affection. This is clear, both from the expression "kynde loue of the mariage" in l. 111, and from the B-text, which has the equivalent word *make* (mate). Surely, it is clear that William was not inventing a new illustration for himself, but is quoting from St Paul, Eph. v. 31; and his illustration is also very nearly that of St Paul, Eph. v. 25, 29. As a maiden who quits her home to be honourably married to the man of her choice, so (says our author) are those who forsake wealth for the love of Christ. This is little else than an inversion of St Paul's simile in Eph. v. 25, as if he had said—"wives, love your husbands, even as the church also loveth Christ." There is also, of course, a reference to Mat. xix. 29; and any weakness of our author's argument really rests upon the question as to whether those who, in his time, embraced voluntary poverty, did so in such a manner as truly to fulfil the intention of that text.

108. (14. 266.) The sense is—"greatly ought such a maiden to be loved by him that marries one of her character."

109. (14. 267.) *Brocage*, treaty by an agent.

"He woeth hire by menes and *brocage;*" Ch. C. T. 3375.

> "I dele with no wight but he
> Haue golde and tresour gret plente ;
> Hire acqueintance wel love I ;
> This moche [is] my desyr shortly,
> I entremet me of *brocages,*
> I make pees and *mariages,*" &c.
>
>   Rom. of the Rose ; 6967—6972.

112. (14. 270.) For *persone*, Crowley's text has *parson* (B-text, Crit. Note, p. 413). Such is the meaning intended here; see note to B. v. 144, p. 113.

114. (14. 272.) *Semblable bothe*, like Him also [c]; *so to his seyntes*, and likewise to His saints [b].

117. (14. 275.) Very near the end of the Wyf of Bathes Tale is this passage—

> "Pouerte is hateful good ; and, as I gesse,
> A ful gret bringer out of bisynesse ;
> A gret amender eek of sapience
> To him that taketh it in patience ;
> Pouerte is this, although it seme elenge,
> Possessioun that no wight wol chalenge."

In the margin of the Ellesmere MS. is the note:—"Secundus Philosophus. Paupertas est odibile bonum, sanitatis mater, curarum remocio, sapientie reparatrix, possessio sine calumpnia." It will be seen that Chaucer's lines are a mere paraphrase of this, with the omission of "sanitatis mater." Tyrwhitt's note is—"In this commendation of Poverty, our author seems plainly to have had in view the following passage of a fabulous conference between the emperor Adrian and Secundus the philosopher, reported by Vincent of Beauvais, *Speculum Historiale*, lib. x. cap. 71. 'Quid est Paupertas? Odibile bonum; sanitatis mater; remotio curarum; sapientiæ repertrix; negotium sine damno; possessio absque calumnia; sine sollicitudine felicitas.' What Vincent has there published appears to have been extracted from a larger collection of *Gnomæ* under the name of Secundus, which are still extant in Greek and in Latin. See Fabric. Bib. Gr., l. vi. c. x. and MS. Harl. 399. The author of *Pierce Ploughman* has quoted and paraphrased the same passage." I may add that, in an edition of Vincent printed in 1624, the reading "temperatrix" occurs instead of "repertrix," exactly as in our text. Mr Wright, in his note on the present passage, copies the quotation from MS. Reg. 9 A. xiv. fol. 140, back, with the reading "reparatrix," and with the insertions of "absque sollicitudine semita" before "sapientiæ," of "intractabilis substantia" after "damno," and of "incerta fortuna" before "sine sollicitudine felicitas." He further refers us to Vincent of Beauvais, as above, and to Roger de Hoveden, p. 816. None of these versions include the clause "donum dei," for which see the note to l. 136 below. The reader may find a large cluster of quotations in praise of poverty in Burton's Anatomy of Melancholy, pt. 2, sec. 3, mem. 3.

120. (14. 278.) *By so*, provided that [b].

128. (14. 290.) The "commandment" is in Matt. vii. 1—"Nolite iudicare, ut non iudicemini."

130. (14. 292.) *Vnseled*, unsealed. Gallons, pottles, and quarts, used by brewsters and taverners, were to be "sealed with the seal of the Alderman;" Liber Albus, p. 233. See also the statute "Of Sealed Measures," id. p. 290. Cf. note to Pass. iv. 87, p. 62.

136. (14. 297.) *Sonde*, sending, gift [c]; *yifte*, gift [b]. The clause "Donum dei" (as noted in note to l. 117) is not contained in the sentence from Secundus, as given by Vincent of Beauvais. In speaking of poverty, Burton observes—"Though it be *donum dei*, a blessed estate, the way to heaven, as Chrysostome calls it (Comment. ad Hebræos), *God's gift*, the mother of modesty, and much to be preferred before riches," &c.; Anatomy of Melancholy, pt. 1, sec. 2, mem. 4, subsec. 6. The passage in St Chrysostom occurs in his Commentary on the Epistle to the Hebrews, cap. x. homil. 18, sec. 3 (ed. Migne); where we find—"Tantum bonum est paupertas; est enim quædam deductio ad cælum, unctio athletica, magna quædam et admirabilis exercitatio, portus tranquillus." I do not find the actual words "donum Dei," but just above, sec. 2, St Chrysostom says—"diuitiæ et paupertas sunt a Domino."

139. (14. 300.) *Altoun*, Alton in Hampshire; not Halton, in Cheshire, as suggested by Whitaker. His mistake was due to the reading *haultone* in the Phillipps MS.; but this is certainly wrong, as all other MSS., both of the B-type and C-type, read *altoun* (or some variation of *altoun*) without an initial *h*. This point was completely cleared up by a discussion in Notes and Queries, due to Mr James Kendrick, who raised the question under the signature of "M.D." See N. and Q., 3rd Ser., xii. 373, 468; 4th Ser., i. 277, 464. The most material parts of this correspondence are as follows. M. D. tells us that "the rock upon which Halton castle (Cheshire) is built stands in the midst of a long marshy district, affording no shelter for robbers, and was never a place of much resort." "William Wickham" objected that "the town of Alton (Hampshire) lies in a broad valley, to which the word 'pass' is quite inapplicable." This objection was overruled by W. H. R. M., who shewed that the word "pass" *has been* applied to it, and cited the following extract from p. 107 of the late T. Hudson Turner's Account of Domestic Architecture of the Thirteenth Century. "The wooded pass of Alton, on the borders of Surrey and Hampshire, which was not disafforested until the end of Henry's reign, was a favourite ambush for outlaws, who there awaited the merchants and their trains of sumpter-horses travelling to or from Winchester: even in the fourteenth century the wardens of the great fair of St Giles, held in that city, paid five mounted sergeants-at-arms to keep the *pass of Alton* during the continuance of the

fair, 'according to custom.' Mr Turner refers, in a footnote, to Feriæ S. Egidii Winton., 17 Edw. II., Chapter House, Westminster." "W. Chapman" says—"The district (of Alton) is known to have been for a very long period the resort of robbers. There is a spot in the parish of Bentley, and close to the forest of Alice Holt, to which the word 'pass' would not be inapplicable; but it is more than probable that the word is used in the sense of road or passage, as ordinarily applied at the present day. The abode of Adam Gurdon, who was disinherited and outlawed with other adherents of Simon, Earl of Leicester . . has been described as 'a woody height in a valley near the road, between the town of Alton and the castle of Farnham.' It was here that Gurdon, in 1267, withdrew with his men, infesting the country with rapine . . The story of his combat with the Prince of Wales, afterwards Edward I., in this same locality, is well known. The celebrated robber-chieftain seems to have possessed qualities of humanity similar to those attributed to Robin Hood . . . robbing the rich, and sparing the poor; and it is evidently to some such personage that the allusion is made in the quotation—

'Pouerte myghte passe with-oute peril of robbynge.'"

The above explanation, I may add, is made quite certain by William's allusions to Winchester fair; see Pass. vii. 211, xiv. 52, and especially the parallel passage to the present one in Pass. v. 51—54, where Peace is described as being robbed on his way to St Giles's down, whereon Winchester Fair was held.

143. (14. 304.) I do not see why reference is here made to Seneca, as the quotation given is a part of the longer one at l. 117. Perhaps the name of Seneca was added by the scribes, because his name occurs in the parallel passage in Chaucer (note to l. 117 above).

"Glad pouerte is an honest thing certeyn;
This wol Senek and othere clerkes seyn."

Here the allusion is to a passage in Seneca's second Epistle, where he professes to quote Epicurus—"Honesta (inquit) res est, læta paupertas. Illa vero non est paupertas, si læta est. Non qui parum habet, sed qui plus cupit, pauper est." Similar sentiments may be found frequently in Seneca. Thus, in his Letters (Epist. xvii.) he says—"Paupertas expedita est, secura est . . . Si uis uacare animo, aut pauper sis oportet, aut pauperi similis." And again (Epist. lxxx)—"compara inter se pauperum et diuitum uultus. Sæpius pauper et fidelius ridet: nulla sollicitudo in alto est [i. e. is deeply seated within him]; etiamsi qua incidit cura, uelut nubes leuis transit." And again—"Cui cum paupertate bene conuenit, diues est;" Epist. iv. Burton (Anat. Mel. ii. 3, 3) slily observes that Seneca, though he praised poverty, was himself a rich man

——(14. 305.) The quotation is from Juvenal, Sat. x. 22, as marked in the margin. The second word in the line should, of course, be uacuus, but most MSS. have paupertas. I have adopted the reading pauper of the Oriel MS., because it scans, and comes nearer to the true reading.

Chaucer, in his Wyf of Bathes Tale (Group D, l. 1191) alludes to the same passage.

> "Verray pouerte it singeth proprely;
> Iuuenal seith of pouerte, myrily
> The poure man, whan he goth by the weye,
> Bifore the theues he may singe and pleye."

Juvenal's line is quoted in the margin of the Ellesmere MS. The same thought is in Boethius, bk. 2, pr. 5; see Chaucer's translation, ed. Morris, p. 50, l. 3. Compare Occleve, de Regim. Princ., ed. Wright, p. 40—

> "The poore man slepeth fulle sikerly
> On nyghtes, thoughe his dore be not shette."

151. (14. 313.) *Paneter*, keeper of the pantry. From the Lat. *panis*, Fr. *pain*, are derived the F. *panetier* and *paneterie*, respectively explained by Cotgrave to mean "a pantler" and "a pantry." The keeper of the pantry was, at a later period, generally called a *pantler*; sometimes a *panterer* (see Halliwell), with an unnecessary reduplication of the last syllable. The B-text has *payn*, i. e. bread.

153. (14. 315, 316.) The B-text is rather obscure, as pointed out in the Critical Note to B. xiv. 316, at p. 413 of that text, where an explanation is given. It is easily made out, however, by comparing it with the C-text, which shews that *Seynt austin* is a nominative case, in apposition with *a lettred man*. The reference to Saint Augustine probably means no more than that similar praise of poverty is to be found in his writings. For example, in his De Civitate Dei, lib. iv. c. 3, he compares the conditions of a rich and poor man, saying of the latter—"mediocrem uero illum re familiari parua atque succincta sibi sufficientem, charissimum suis, cum cognatis, uicinis, amicis dulcissima pace gaudentem, pietate religiosum, benignum mente, sanum corpore, uita parcum, moribus castum, conscientia securum" (Opera, ed. Migne, vii. 114).

——(14. 322.) This line is discussed in the Critical Notes [b], where Mr Wright's unauthorised introduction of the word *no* is shewn to be needless. *Harde* here means wretched, miserable, perilous. The general sense is—"So wretched (*or* perilous) is it to continue in sin, and yet sin pursueth us ever."

——(14. 325.) *Dede dede*, did deed; three MSS. read *dide* for the first *dede*.

——(14. 328.) "Or more mastery over any man than over himself." Cf. Prov. xvi. 32.

——(14. 332.) Here ends the Sixth Vision, as clearly marked in [b]. See Pref. to C-text, p. c., note 2.

Here begins B. Pass. xv.

——(15. 1.) Here, in [b], begins the poem of Do-bet; but, in [c], it does not begin till farther on, at Pass. xviii. 1, corresponding to B. xv. 253 nearly.

158. (*see* 15. 12.) Here begins the Seventh Vision, which may be called

the Vision of *Anima* and of the Tree of Charity [b], or that of *Liberum Arbitrium* (Free Will) and of the Tree of Charity [c]. The various names of *Anima* (as given in the quotation at l. 201) are considered, in the C-text, as various names of *Liberum Arbitrium*.   See note to l. 201.

169. (15. 18.) St Peter is generally represented with a key or keys, in allusion to Matt. xvi. 19.   He is here described as the porter of heaven, but Dante makes him rather the porter of purgatory, saying that an angel deputed by him keeps the gate of purgatory, bearing two keys, a golden and a silver one; Purg. ix. 118 (and Cary's note).   Milton gives him a golden and an iron key; Lycidas, 111.   St Paul is generally represented with a sword, in allusion to his martyrdom; but Cary suggests that Dante (Purg. xxix. 140) represents St Paul with a sword in allusion to the power of his style, and Bianchi well suggests that the allusion is to the "sword of the Spirit" mentioned by St. Paul in Eph. vi. 17; Heb. iv. 12.

179. (*not in* b.) No doubt this refers to the favourite Poem, perhaps by Walter Map, called Dialogus inter Corpus et Animam.   The Latin version is printed at p. 95 of Mr Wright's edition of Mapes (Camden Soc.); a French version at p. 321, and an English version at p. 334 of the same. The last is reprinted, with notes, in Mätzner's Altenglische Sprachproben, i. 92. In the course of this Dialogue the question is debated, whether the Body or the Soul has the higher authority, and each accuses the other of causing their common misery.   Our poet likens them to a piece of wood on fire. The Body is the wood, the Soul the flame; and the two together contribute to the burning.

183. (15. 23.) For an account of these various names, see the Latin quotation at l. 201, and the note to that line.

186. (15. 26.) "And when I make my moan (i. e. complain) to God, I am called Memory."   The expression *maden mone* has occurred before, Pass. ix. 130.   The author seems to have misunderstood the Latin original— "dum recolit, memoria est."   I suppose that *recolit* here means remembers, recollects; but William has either taken it in another sense, or adopted another reading, or else has varied the phrase to suit the requirements of alliteration.

191. (15. 31.) "And when I claim or claim not, buy or refuse to buy." The reader will miss the sense unless he remembers the old sense of *challenge*.   No better instance of this can be found than in the words of Henry IV, whose claim to the throne appears thus on the Rolls of Parliament: "In the name of the Father, Son, and Holy Ghost I, Henry of Lancaster, *challenge* the realm of England," &c. (Annals of England, p. 210).

193, 194. (*not in* b.) These two lines do not appear in the B-text; neither do we find there the corresponding Latin clause (dum declinat a malo ad bonum, liberum arbitrium est).   Still it is evident that William attached much importance to this inserted clause, as he now makes *Liberum Arbitrium* to be the principal name of the Soul.

201. (15. 39.) In l. 199 we are referred to St Augustine and Isidore as authorities for the Latin quotation here given.   It is to be found in Isidore, *Etymologiarum Liber* xi [not xl, as in Mr Wright's note] cap. 1; also in his *Differentiarum Liber* ii. cap. 29.   Mr Wright adds—"They are repeated by Alcuin, De Anim. Rat. N. x. p. 149—*Animus* est, dum vivificat; dum contemplatur, *spiritus* est; dum sentit, *sensus* est; dum sapit, *animus* est; dum intelligit, *mens* est; dum discernit, *ratio* est; dum consentit, *voluntas* est; dum recordatur, *memoria* est."   A translation of Alcuin's definition will be found in Political, Religious, & Love Poems, ed. Furnivall, p. 37, from Lambeth MS. 306, fol. 118, as follows : "And whylth it noryssh the body, it is cawlyd *Anima*, the sowle.   This word *Anima* hath many significacions : for when it is in contemplacyon, it is sayde a spyryt, *Spiritus*.   And when it savyrth, it is saide Reson or wytte, *Animus*.   And when it felith, it is sayde felyng, *Sensus*.   And when it vnderstondyth, it is callyd mynde, *Mens*.   And when it demyth, it is called Reson, *Racis*.   And when it consentyth, it is callyd wylle, *Voluntas*. And when it recordyth, it is sayde mynde, *Memoria*."

Between the quotations as given in [b] and [c] there are two variations. The first is that [c] omits the clause "dum scit, mens est."   This omission must have been a mere accident, as the translation of the clause is retained in l. 185.   The other is that [c] inserts the clause "dum declinat a malo ad bonum, liberum arbitrium est," which is translated in ll. 193, 194, whilst at the same time the name of the allegorical personage seen in the vision is changed from *Anima* to *Liberum Arbitrium*.   There seems to be small reason for this change, which is no improvement.   It is hard to see how all these various names can be applied to Free Will.

It is clear from Drayton's Works that he had read William's Vision, and it is very likely that it was from this very passage that he derived his Sonnet to the Soul, which runs as follows :—

> "That learned father, which so firmly proves
> The Soul of Man immortal and divine,
> And doth the several offices define,

Anima.	Gives her that name, as she the body moves ;
Amor.	Then is the love, embracing charity ;
Animus.	Moving a will in us, it is the mind ;
Mens.	Retaining knowledge, still the same in kind ;
Memoria.	As intellectual, it is memory ;
Ratio.	In judging, reason is her only name ;
Sensus.	In speedy apprehension, it is sense ;
Conscientia.	In right or wrong, they call her conscience ;
Spiritus.	The spirit, when it to Godward doth inflame.

> These of the soul the several functions be,
> Which my heart, lighten'd by thy love, doth see."

In Hickscorner (Hazlitt's Old Plays, i. 154) Free Will is introduced as one of the personages, and is made to describe himself after this sort :—

> "What, sirs, I tell you my name is Free Will ;
> I may choose whether I do good or ill ;
> But for all that, I will do as me list.
> My conditions ye know not, perdè.

> I can fight, chide, and be merry;
> Full soon of my company ye would be weary
>   And ye knew all!
> What! fill the cup, and make good cheer!
> I trow I have a noble here.
> Who lent it me?   By Christ, a frere,
>   And I lent him a fall."

He proceeds to describe his intemperance and other failings.

216. (15. 54.) This saying (from Prov. xxv. 27) is attributed to Solomon in Prov. xxv. 1. The B-text has the reading *opprimitur*, the C-text *opprimatur;* but the ordinary reading of the Vulgate is *opprimetur*. Chaucer quotes this saying in his Tale of Melibeus: "And Salomon sayth, if thou hast founden hony, ete of it that suffyceth; for if thou ete of it out of mesure, thou shalt spewe, and be nedy and poure." Hampole also refers to it in his English Prose Treatises, ed. Perry, 1866 (E. E. T. S.), p. 42: "For the wyse man saise thus; *Scrutator maiestatis opprimetur a gloria;* that es to say, Raunsaker of the myghte of Godd and of His maieste withowttene gret clennes and meknes sall be ouerlayde and oppresside of hymselfe."

220. (*not in* b.) "The more dearly he shall pay for it, unless he act rightly." On the phrase *abygge bitere*, see note to Pass. xxi. 448.

221. (15. 59.) The following passage from St Bernard has nearly the same force as the expression in the text, though differently worded. "Ut opera tua uerbis concinant, immo uerba operibus, ut cures uidelicet plus facere quam docere;" S. Bernardi Epistolæ; Epist. cci., vol. i. p. 370 (ed. Migne).

224. (15. 62.) See Pass. xiv. 227—229.

225. (15. 63.) *Vuel to defie*, difficult to digest. For this use of *defie*, see Pass. i. 230, and the note on p. 27. See l. 218 above.

227. (*not in* b.) *Deynous*, disdainful, contemptuous. *Deme that*, judge them that. *That* is often used for *he that* or *they that*.

231. (15. 69.) *Meuen*, discuss; lit. move. Both in [b] and [c] we have examples of French plural adjectives terminating in *s*. Thus *materes inmesurables* [b] means immeasurable or infinite subjects; and *motifs insolibles* [c] means insoluble questions or problems. *Fallaces* may be construed either as an adjective or a substantive. If the former, the sense is "insoluble and fallacious problems." If the latter, it is "insoluble problems and falsehoods." The former is better. For *fallas*, when used as a substantive, see note to Pass. xii. 22, p. 235.

——(15. 71.) "It were better for many doctors to abandon such teaching." *Byleue* sometimes means to leave off, abandon, quit, forsake; as in the 1st line of a poem on the Birth of Jesus, printed in Altenglische Legenden, ed. Horstmann:—"Of joie and blisse is al my song, kare to *bileue;*" p. 64. Chaucer uses *bileue* intransitively, in the sense of *to remain behind;* Squ. Tale, F. 583. See further examples in Stratmann, s. v. *bilæfan*.

——(15. 73.) The Seven Deadly Sins were supposed to have several off-shoots or branches. Thus Chaucer, in his Persones Tale, speaking "De

Septem Peccatis mortalibus," says—"Now ben they cleped chiefetains, for as moche as they be chiefe, and of hem springen all other sinnes. The *rote* of thise sinnes than is pride, the general rote of all harmes. For of this rote springen certain *braunches;* as ire, envie, accidie or slouthe, avarice (or coveitise, to commun understonding), glotonie, and lecherie : and eche of thise chief sinnes hath his *braunches* and his *twigges,* as shal be declared in hir chapitres folowing." Compare the descriptions of the several Boughs of the Seven Deadly Sins (as, e. g. that of the Seven Boughs of Pride, each with its Twigs) in the Ayenbite of Inwyt, ed. Morris, p. 17 ; and see note above, to Pass. viii. 70, p. 141.

234. (15. 74.) *Fif wittes,* five senses; see note to Pass. ii. 15, p. 29.

——(15. 80.) *Glose,* the comment. Perhaps the allusion is to St Augustine, in Psalm iv. 3 (Opera, v. iv. col. 79, ed. Migne) :—"Utquid ergo temporalium rerum amore detinemini? utquid tanquam prima, extrema sectamini?... Cupitis enim permanere uobiscum quæ omnia transeunt tanquam umbra."

——(15. 81.) "If I lie against you, as far as my ignorant wit is concerned, lead me to the burning." This interesting passage, in which there is a clear allusion to the burning of heretics, has been fully discussed in Pref. II (B-text), p. v, and in Pref. III (C-text), pp. xi—xiv. The net result is that the common opinion, that no man was burnt for his religion in England before 1401, can be proved to be wrong; so that the present allusion does not in any way contradict the date 1377, which I have assigned for the composition of the B-text. Similarly, the Complaint of the Ploughman, pr. in Harl. Misc. vol. vi, seems to have been written before A.D. 1400; yet we find (p. 106) the expression—"But, Lorde, if a man ones breke her lawes [i. e. the priests' laws] or speke aȝenst hem, he maie done penaunce but ones, and aftur ben *brunt.*"

240. (15. 86.) It is difficult to find in the gospels the words here quoted. William was probably thinking of the 1st verse of the 2nd chapter of St James—"Fratres mei, nolite in personarum acceptione habere fidem Domini nostri Jesu Christi gloriæ." See also Deut. i. 17; xvi. 19; Levit. xix. 15; Prov. xxiv. 23 ; Ecclus. xlii. 1. Or perhaps the text in Luke xiv. 12 may be meant, owing to the mention of "the rich" in l. 239.

——(15. 89.) This line might be considered as the poet's own motto. It exactly expresses the spirit in which he wrote.

250. (15. 96.) "There is a disease in the root of such kind of stems ;" or "of boughs" [b]. *More,* a root, is still in use, especially in Hampshire, and was used by one of the witnesses in the Titchborne Trial, to the perplexity of judge and jury. See Pass. xviii. 21, and the note. Aubrey notes it as a Wiltshire word; see Halliwell. Marshall gives it as a West Devonshire word; Eng. Dialect Society, Gloss. B. 6, p. 73. See several examples in Stratmann. The Sanskrit form of the word is *múla,* occurring in the compound *phala-múláni,* i. e. fruits and roots, in the Tale of Nala, ix. 11. There is even a verb *moren,* to take root; it occurs in Old Eng. Homilies,

ed. Morris, ii. 163, l. 10; and in Legends of the Holy Rood, ed. Morris, p. 28, l. 126.   Hence the "myschif in the more" comes to the same thing as "the rote is roten" in l. 253.

264. (*not in* b.) In the Ayenbite of Inwyt, ed. Morris, p. 25, Hypocrisy is called the Sixth Bough of Pride.   Chaucer (Persones Tale, De Superbia) enumerates "inobedience, avaunting, *ipocrisie*, despit, arrogance," &c., among the "twigges and harmes that comen of pride."

265. (15. 109.) *In latyn.*   Mr Wright remarks—"The monks had collections of comparisons, similitudes, proverbs, &c., to be introduced in their sermons, and even when preaching in English they generally quoted them in Latin.   This I suppose to be the meaning of the expression here."   The reader who turns to Dr Morris's edition of Old English Homilies will at once see how freely Latin was quoted in English Sermons.

Chaucer has a passage closely resembling this, Sq. Tale, Group F, 512—520, where he compares a "ypocrite" to a serpent hidden under flowers, or to a fair tomb above a corpse.   These similes were probably suggested by Christ's description of the hypocritical Pharisees, Matt. xxiii. 27, and by St Paul's expression "thou whited wall" (paries dealbate); Acts xxiii. 3.

269. (15. 113.) *Bele paroles,* fair words; as glossed in the margin of MS. C.

271. (15. 115.) The passage here attributed to St John Chrysostom is not to be found in his genuine works.   It occurs in the 38th of a set of Homilies on the Gospel of St Matthew, a work of an uncertain author, sometimes called "Opus Imperfectum" from its incomplete state, and printed in some editions of St Chrysostom's works as an Appendix to his Homilies on St Matthew.   The text commented on is contained in Matt. xxi. 12—20, and the comment is as follows.   "Nam sicut de templo omne bonum egreditur, sic et de templo omne malum procedit . . . . Sic si aliquis Christianorum peccauerit, non omnino peccant et sacerdotes; si autem et sacerdotes fuerint in peccatis, totus populus conuertitur in peccandum. Uidit arborem pallentibus foliis marcidam, et intellexit studiosus agricola, quia læsuram in radicibus haberet.   Nam uere quemadmodum cum uideris arborem pallentibus foliis, marcidam intelligis, quia aliquam culpam habet circa radicem : ita cum uideris populum indisciplinatum et irreligiosum, sine dubio cognosce, quia sacerdotium eius non est sanum;" Incerti authoris Hom. 38 in Matt. ex cap. xxi; in S. Chrysost. Op., Parisiis, 1570, tom. ii. col. 877.   The first sentence, to the effect that "as every good thing proceeds from the temple, so every ill thing proceeds likewise from the temple" is quoted as from Chrysostom in the Works of Bp Jewel, iii. 596 (Parker Society).   It is obvious that William's quotation was made from memory.

It is clear, too, that the author of the Opus Imperfectum was thinking of Isaiah xxiv. 2—"Ut populus, sic sacerdos."   Compare—

> "Crescit malorum cumulus,
> Est sacerdos ut populus," &c.

> Polit. Songs, ed. Wright, p. 9.

"Þat sore wepyng seyþ Isaye,
  ' Ryȝt swych shal be þe prest
  As þe lewede man lyue þou sest.' "
          Rob. of Brunne, Handlyng Synne, l. 10064.

——(15. 118.) *But if*, except, unless. *Bere*, were to bear; past tense, subjunctive mood. The sense is—"I should be very much surprised unless many priests were to carry a set of beads in their hand and a book under their arm, instead of their baselards and their brooches."

For a note on *baselard*, see note to l. 121, on the opposite page.

——(15. 119.) *A peyre bedes*, a set of beads. Chaucer represents the Prioresses as carrying a "peyre of bedes;" Prol. 159. A *pair* (from Lat. *par*) is often used of a set of things of *equal* size. Thus "a pair of stairs" is a flight of stairs; and "a pair of cards" is a pack of cards; see Nares and Halliwell. Also "a pair of organs" means a set of pipes, or an organ; see note to Pass. xxi. 7.

Observe the curious variation here in the Oriel MS., which also has *heer* for *bere* in the line above, giving the sense—"unless many priests here, instead of (having) their baselards and their brooches, should go and sing, where there is no service, along with Sir Philip the sparrow." That is, they would be turned out of their employment as priests, and be obliged to sing out of doors with the sparrows. The same reading is in MS. Camb. Ll. 4. 14, as noted in the Preface to B-text, p. xxi.

The epithet "sir" is playfully applied to the sparrow as if he too were a priest, and could sing mass. Skelton's poem on "Phyllyp Sparowe" shews clearly that Philip or Phip was a name for a pet sparrow, probably because it somewhat resembles the bird's chirp. Thus Legonidec, in his Dictionary of Breton words, has—"*Filip*, s. m. passereau ou moineau, oiseau. Ce nom est une onomatopée, étant formé de l'imitation du cri de l'oiseau qu'il désigne. On le nomme aussi *chilip* et *golven*." So in Shakespeare's King John, i. 1. 231, we find—"Good leave, good Philip;" with the answer— "Philip! sparrow." And in Lyly's Mother Bombie, we find that "sparrows, as they fly" are said to "cry Phip! Phip!" See note to Pass. xii. 310, p. 258.

——(15. 120.) "Sir John and Sir Geoffrey." The title "sir" was the common title of respect, chiefly used in the three instances of "sir king," "sir knight," and "sir priest," as noted by Bradford, vol. i. p. 589 (Parker Society). Priests especially were so called; Bradford, vol. ii. p. 7, note. See further under "Sir" in the Parker Society's Index. From the same Index, we learn that "Sir John" was a familiar title for a priest; Bradford, i. 71, 589, ii. 120, 313; Cranmer, ii. 306; Latimer, i. 317; Ridley, 104; Tyndale, i. 146, 277, ii. 249, &c. Bradford speaks of "singing Sir Johns," i. 391; of "blind buzzard Sir John," ii. 43; of "Sir John Masser," ii. 324. Pilkington speaks of "Sir John Lack-Latin," 20, 160, 271; of "Sir John Mumble-matins," 26; and of "Sir John Smell-smoke," 255. See also Chaucer, Group B. 4000, and my note in The Prioresses Tale, &c. (Clarendon Press); Wordsworth's Eccl. Biography, i. 392, note. Of course, John is a very common name. We may also infer from the present passage that *Geoffrey* was also formerly a common name. For example, it was Chaucer's name; and Mr Bardsley well remarks (Eng. Surnames, p. 42) that "such surnames as Jeffries, Jefferson, Jeffs, Jeffcock, Jeffkins, Jephson, and Jepson still record the share it had obtained in English esteem." Cf. note to Pass. xiv. 125.

——(15. 121.) *Basellarde*, a kind of sword, which priests were particularly forbidden to wear, an injunction which they commonly disregarded. Compare—

> " Bucklers brode and sweardes long,
>   Baudrike, with *baselardes* kene,
> Soche toles about her necke they hong;
>   With Antichrist soche priestes been."
>   Ploughman's Tale; in Polit. Poems, ed. Wright, i. 331.

Compare also—

> " For thise wantoune prestes that pleien here nice game
>   Bi nihte,
> Hii gon with swerd and bokeler, as men that wolde fighte."
>   Polit. Songs, ed. Wright, p. 328.

Priests were forbidden to wear knives at all; see Cutts, Scenes and Characters of the Middle Ages, p. 243. See notes to Pass. iv. l. 461 (p. 72), and to l. 467 (p. 73), for further information.

Ballokknyf, probably a large knife, such as were worn suspended from the girdle; cf. note to Pass. xxiii. 219. *With botoxes ouergylte*, with gilt studs on the handle or sheath. The following passages illustrate the meaning.

> " Here knyfes were i-chaped nat with bras,
>   But al with siluer wrought ful clene and wel."
>   Chaucer, Prol. 366.

The two following items are taken from an inventory of Sir John Fastolf, A.D. 1459; Paston Letters, ed. Gairdner, i. 478, 488. "Item, j. bollok-hafted dager, harnesyd wyth sylver, and j. chape thertoo." "Item, iij. kneyves in a schcythe, the haftys of every withe naylys gilt."

——(15. 122.) *Portous*, a breviary. Also spelt *portasse, portesse, poortos, portous*, &c., all from Lat. *portiforium*, which see in Ducange. "Poortos, booke, *portiforium, breviarium ;*" Prompt. Parv. "The *Portous*, or Breviary, contained whatever was to be said by all beneficed clerks, and those in holy orders, either in choir, or privately by themselves, as they recited their daily canonical hours; no musical notation was put into these books."—Rock; Church of our Fathers, v. iii. pt. 2, p. 212; see also v. iii. pt. 1, p. 55. See Tyrwhitt's note to Chaucer, C. T. 13061; Kitchen's Gloss. to Spenser (see F. Q. i. 4. 9); *Portasse* in Index to Parker Society's publications; *Portuous* in Gloss. to Cooper's Memoir of Lady Margaret, &c. The expression "a breviary that should be his plough for saying *placebo*" means that he should be diligent in using the breviary. There is a parallel passage in Pass. iv. 467 ; see the note to that line, and cf. Wyclif's Works, iii. 374, note.

The passage means—"but, as for a breviary that should be his plough to say *placebo* with, unless he had some service (to say) in order to save some silver in addition, he says it with an ill will." The priests used to continue to say *Placebo*, and *Dirige* and masses all through the month following a funeral; Rock, Church of our Fathers, ii. 516. They said these with a better will when well paid, or when money was left for additional masses.

Dirige came to mean the morning-service for the dead, *Placebo* the evening-service, and *Requiem* the mass for the same; see Rock, Ch. of our Fathers, ii. 502, 503.

272. (15. 124.) *Leese ye*, ye lose [c]; *lese ye on*, ye lose by, spend on [b]. *Fynden*, provide for.

277. (15. 128.) *Sodenes*, sub-deans; see note to Pass. iii. 187, p. 52.

278. (15. 129.) See a similar description of the evil ways of some priests in Old Eng. Homilies, ed. Morris, 2nd Ser., p. 162; the preacher there quotes the very text *erit sicut populus sacerdos;* see note to l. 271.

280. (15. 133.) "That which they leave, profligates readily devour it" [c]; *or*, "get it" [b].

——(15. 141.) "Thus depart their goods, when the spirit has fled."

284. (15. 145.) The B-text says—"What is charity? said I. A child-like thing, said he; a free liberal will, free from puerility and folly." The corresponding line in [c] is really l. 296.

286. (15. 148.) "I have lived in London many long years" [c]; "I have lived in the country, quoth I, my name is Long Will" [b]. This is an important line, in both versions. We hence learn that the author lived a long while in London, and that he was commonly known by the name of Long Will, obviously with reference to his tallness of stature; cf. note to Pass. xi. 68; p. 212. This nickname may be parallelled from Mr Riley's Memorials of London, p. 457, where we read of John Edward, "otherwise called Long Jacke," under the date 1382. Similarly, the poet Gascoigne, a tall man, was commonly called "Long George."

——(15. 151.) "And will lend (*or* give) where they expect to be faithfully repaid."

291. (15. 154.) *Hus* [c] = *his* [b]. *Askede after hus*, asked for his dues.

295. (15. 158.) *By that*, with reference to what people say about charity.

298. (15. 162.) *Russet* was the name of a coarse and common cloth; see l. 342 below, and note to Pass. xi. 1, p. 208.

299. (15. 163.) *Cammoka.* Halliwell has—"*Camaca*, a kind of silk or rich cloth. Curtains were often made of this material. See the Squyr of Lowe Degre, 835; Test. Vetust., p. 14; Coventry Mysteries, p. 163." Migne's edition of Ducange has—"*Camoca*, panni serici vel pretiosioris species; étoffe fine de poil de chameau ou de chèvre sauvage; olim *camocas*" [i. e. O.Fr. *camocas*]. Roquefort has—"*Camocas*, étoffe fine faite de poil de chameau ou de chévre sauvage; en bas Latin *camoca, camucum*.

Si ont ceulx qui de camelos
Sont vestus et de *camocas*,

Qui dient qu'ilz sont advocas,
Mais pourtant ne le sont ilz mye.   *Pathelin.*"

There seems to be a doubt whether the name is due to the *camel* or to the *chamois*. If the former, *cammoka* cannot have been very different from *camlet*, a word of much more frequent occurrence, and still in use. See *Camlet* in Webster.

Tarse [b] was the name of a kind of silken stuff formerly much esteemed, and said to have come from a country called *Tharsia* adjoining Cathay (China). See Chaucer, Kn. Ta., 1302. Ducange explains *Tarsicus* as "panni preciosioris species," and quotes (says Mr Wright) a visitation of the treasury of St Paul's, London, in 1295, where there is mention of "Tunica et dalmatica de panno Indico Tarsico besantato de auro," and of a "casula de panno Tarsico." Roquefort gives "*Tartaire*, sorte d'étoffe de Tartarie;" and if *Tars* be the same as *Tartarie* (as stated in Migne's edition of Ducange), then *Tharsia* is merely another name for *Tartary*, which is very probable. Further, as the people of Tartary were called, in Old French, *Tartarins* (see Roquefort), it is clear that the O.Fr. *Tartaire* is the same as *Tartarin*, defined by Halliwell to be "a kind of silk." The only difficulty caused by this identification is that it is not at first clear why the word *tarse* should be used here, whilst in B. xv. 224 (just below) we have *tartaryne*. The most probable explanation of the difference is to suppose that the latter line (omitted in the three best MSS. and in Crowley's edition) is spurious, in which case it is easy to see that *tartaryne* was suggested by the mention of *tarse*, and is, in fact, a gloss upon it. I add some further examples of the word.

"The rich stuff called cloth of Tars is mentioned in this reign [Edw. I.]. It was latinized *tarsicus* and *tartarinus*, and we read of dalmaticas and tunics of slate-colour, and light-blue cloth of *tars* embroidered with branches and bezants of gold; Visit. Thesaur. S. Paul, London. sub anno 1295;" British Costume, p. 105, note; cf. Ducange, as above.

A.D. 1382, it was agreed "that all the aldermen of London, for the dignity of the said city, should be arrayed upon the feast of Pentecost . . . , in cloaks of green lined with green taffata or *tartaryn*," &c.; Riley, Memorials of London, p. 466. Mr Riley explains it as "a thin silk."

"On every trumpe hanging a broad banere
Of fine *tartarium* were full richely bete."
                            The Flower and the Leaf; st. 31.

Tartaryn is mentioned as being bought at Oxford, A.D. 1379; Hist. of Agriculture, &c., by J. E. Thorold Rogers, ii. 541. And see note in Warton, Hist. Eng. Poetry, 1840, ii. 146; or ed. 1873, ii. 315.

In his edition of Marco Polo (i. 259), Col. Yule, speaking of the cloths called *nakh* and *nasij*, says—"these stuffs, or such as these were, I believe, what the medieval writers called *Tartary cloth*, not because they were made in Tartary, but because they were brought from China and its borders through the Tartar dominions. Dante alludes to the supposed skill of the Turks and Tartars in weaving gorgeous stuffs (*Inf.* xvii. 17); and see Mandeville's Travels, pp. 175, 247."

Trye [b] means *choice;* and the allusion is, of course, to robes of expensive material and splendid colour.

——(15. 165.) *Leueth,* believes;˙answering to *let it soth,* considers it true, in l. 168 [b].

317. (*not in* b.) "One named 'Thou-openest-thine-hand' provides all things for him." Compare Pass. xvi. 266, and see note to that line; p. 323.

318. (15. 174.) Compare Pass. xvi. 251 (b. 14. 48).

321. (15. 177.) The reader must not for a moment suppose that William here commends pilgrimages. The next line tells us that he only means such pilgrimages as conduct the charitable man to˙the cottages of the poor and to prisons. See the parallel passage, Pass. v. 122, 123; and see l. 327 below.

328. (15. 182.) "Then he enters (lit. runs) into thoughtfulness (*or* anxiety), and eagerly seeks out Pride, with all its appurtenances, and packs them up together, and (afterwards) washes them in the laundry called *Laboraui,* and soaks them in his breast, and often beats it, and with warm tears he moistens it till it becomes white" [c]. The passage is, of course, highly figurative. Charity is represented as first visiting the poor people and wretched prisoners, with the hope of alleviating their sufferings. This done, the charitable man turns his thoughts inward. Having helped others, he has more leisure for self-examination. He becomes anxious for himself; he collects all his proud feelings, and cleanses them by the groanings of prayer. He "buck-washes" them, or cleanses yet more thoroughly, within his own breast, which he beats in self-condemnation. With tears of contrition he washes his breast white, and becomes whiter than snow.

It must be remembered that to beat one's breast was one of the olden modes of penitence; see Pass. viii. 61.

˙The B-text runs differently, viz.—"He will labour in a laundry nearly the length of a mile [i. e. for a very long time], and enter into the thoughts of his youth (lit. run into youth), and eagerly address Pride, with all its appurtenances, and pack them together, and soak them in his breast, and beat them clean, and lay upon them (i. e. labour upon them) long with *Laboraui* (i. e. penitential groans), and afterwards wash them with tears." Here the word *them* represents proud thoughts and feelings.

The word *ȝerne,* meaning here to run, hasten, must not be confounded with *ȝerne,* to desire. William uses the latter in B. i. 35, as equivalent to *wylne* in C. ii. 33. But the sense is settled here by the expression "ȝorn into elde," Pass. xiii. 13; and we certainly have *ȝernynge* for running in Pass. xxii. 380. Several examples of *ȝerne,* to run (A.S. *yrnan*) may be found in the Glossary to the Ayenbite of Inwyt; and *ȝerner,* a runner, occurs in The Praier and Complaint of the Ploughman, Harl. Miscellany, vi. 114. It is remarkable that William also uses the form *rennen,* Pass. xvii. 348; he simply adopts that form which best suits the alliteration at the moment.

The word *ȝouthe* (B. 15. 183) was ill-chosen; accordingly, in [c], the poet gave up the alliteration for the sake of the better word *þouht*, meaning inward care, anxiety. He also changed the inexpressive *speke* into the more intelligible *secheth*. The word *bouketh* or *bouken* has been commented on before, in the parallel passage to the present; see B. 14. 5—21, and note to B. 14. 19, p. 321. For *woketh*, see note to Pass. xv. 25, p. 287.

336. (15. 191.) *Wher*, whether; the usual contraction. It is equivalent to—"is it the case that?"

337. (15. 193.) Here *Piers the Plowman* is completely identified with *Jesus Christ*; cf. B. 15. 205.

——(15. 197.) *Han peper in the nose*, conduct themselves superciliously. To "have pepper in the nose" is to take offence, to be angry; see the examples in Halliwell, to which add the following :—"I take peper in the nose, *Ie me courouce;*" Palsgrave. "*Se courroucer*, to fret, fume, chafe, be angry, take pet, or *pepper in the nose;*" Cotgrave. Also in Skelton's "Why Come Ye Nat To Courte," l. 381; on which see Dyce's note. Cotgrave, s. v. *Chevre*, has—"Prendre le chevre, to take pepper in the nose; to take a thing in dudgeon, or in snuffe." Cf. 1 Henry IV., i. 3. 41; Dodsley's Old Plays, ed. Hazlitt, xiii. 166.

——(15. 198.) *As a lyoun*, i. e. proudly; see B. 13. 302, and note to Pass. vii. 3, p. 102. *There*, where, when.

——(15. 206.) See note to l. 337, just above. The text is misquoted; it is—"petra autem erat Christus;" 1 Cor. x. 4. It has evidently been taken in connection with Mat. xvi. 18—"tu es Petrus, et super hanc petram," &c. Whence *Piers = Petrus = petra = Christus*.

——(15. 208.) *Landeleperes hermytes*, vagabond hermits; observe the nominatives in apposition. On *landeleper*, see note to B. 5. 483, under that to C. vii. 329, p. 126.

——(15. 208.) *At ancres*, among anchorites. *Box*, an alms-box; see note to Pass. i. 96, p. 16.

——(15. 209.) "Fie upon hypocrites, and upon them that favour them!"

343. (15. 215.) "Both in (sober) grey and in (costly) fur, and in gilt armour." Charity is found among all classes; sometimes clad in homely russet or grey, sometimes in furs and armour.

345. (15. 217.) *Seyntes*, saints [c]; *kynges*, kings [b]. They were both. The reference is, of course, to St Edmund, the martyr, king of East Anglia, died Nov. 20, 870, from whom Bury St Edmund's takes its name, and who is often represented on rood-screens in East-Anglian churches; and to St Edward the Confessor, died Jan. 5, 1066, whose shrine is in Westminster Abbey. St Edmund's day is Nov. 20, still marked in our prayer-books. St Edward "was esteemed the patron-saint of England until superseded in the 13th century by Saint George; the translation of his relics from the old to his new shrine at Westminster, in 1263, still finds a place, on the 13th of October, in the English calendar;" Chambers, Book of Days, i. 54.

347. (15. 219.) "Sing and read;" i.e. discharge the duties of a priest.

350. (15. 222.) *Rathest,* soonest. Whitaker is quite wrong in saying that there should be a full stop at the end of this line.

351. (15. 223.) " Wearing a cap and with crimped hair, and having his crown shaven." The "kelle" or caul was chiefly used with reference to the ornamental network worn over the hair by women; but it sometimes meant, as here, a man's cap. Another instance of this is in Chaucer, Troil. and Cress., iii. 775 (ed. Tyrwhitt), or iii. 727 (ed. Morris). The right reading in that line is—"And maken hym a howue aboue a calle," as in Morris's edition. Tyrwhitt has—"a howne above to call;" but, in his note to the Cant. Ta. 3909, he corrects this, and rightly says that "an howue aboue a calle" signifies *a hood over a cap.* I suppose that a man's *calle* was a sort of skull-cap; this would admit of a hood being thrown over it, and would shew the crimped or waved hair upon that part of the head which was left unshorn. For *kelle* in the more usual sense, see Way's excellent note in the Prompt. Parv., p. 270. The person here spoken of as an embodiment of Charity seems to be meant for a rich ecclesiastic, of a kindly and liberal nature.

——(15. 224.) This line, being found in only a few MSS. of the B-class, is probably spurious; still it is in keeping with the context. See the note to l. 299 above, p. 345.

353. (15. 226.) St Francis, the founder of the Franciscan or Grey Friars, or Minorites, was *himself* held in great reverence, though his followers were, in course of time, so much disliked. "For if men speken of Fraunceys, he usid and tauȝte myche mekenesse, povert, and penaunce, and Menoures now usen the contrarie;" Wyclif's Works, iii. 375.

"And Frauncis founded his folke · fulliche on trewthe," &c.

P. Pl. Crede, 511.

And see below, B. 15. 413.

355. (15. 228.) "He commends rich men and receives robes (i. e. presents) from them, of such as live truly, and love and believe" [c]; or, "of such as lead guileless lives" [b]. Compare—

" Þe ryche myd iwisse
Wel myghte cume to blisse
    If he hit wolde of-seruie;
Þe poure may wel mysse,
Bute he his pouernesse
    Mid mylde heorte þolye."

Old Eng. Misc., ed. Morris, p. 75.

——(15. 237.) *That,* that which, viz. marriage.

——(15. 244.) "But I blame nobody." *Lyf,* a living being; as elsewhere.

SCHEME OF THE CONTENTS OF C. PASSUS XVIII.

(B. Pass. XV. 253—601.)

Cf. Wright's edition, pp. 310—329; ll. 10131—10793.

C-TEXT.	B-TEXT.	C-TEXT.	B-TEXT.
—	xv. 253—267	135	387
(a) [28]	(a) 268	136—158	—
1—8	—	—	388
—	269—273	159	like 389
9, 10	274, 275	160—164	—
11, 12	—	—	390
—	276—280	165	like 391
13—21	281—289	166—168	—
22—24	—	169, 170	like 392
—	290	171	393
25, 26	291, 292	172, 173	like 394
27	—	174—176	395—397
(a) 28	(a) [268]	177, 178	like 398—400
29—43	—	179, 180	—
—	293—303	—	401
44, 45	304, 305	181—184	402—404
46—52	—	—	like 405
—	306—312	185, 186	—
53—55	313—316	—	406—483
—	317, 318	187—189	484—486
56	like 319	190, 191	like 487
57—71	—	192, 193	488, 489
—	320—341	—	490, 491
72—75	like 342, 343	(b) [252—254]	(b) 492—494
76—79	344—347	194—201	495—502
80—93	—	202	—
—	348, 349	203—211	503—511
94—99	350—355	212	—
—	356	213—227	512—526
100—102	357—359	228	—
103	like 360, 361	229	527
104—110	362—368	230	—
—	369	231, 232	528, 529
111	370	233—249	—
112	like 371, 372	250, 251	530, 531
113	373	(b) 252—254	(b) [492—494]
114	like 374, 375	255—272	532—549
115, 116	like 377, 376	273	—
117	—	—	550
—	378	274, 275	like 551, 552
118—121	379—382	—	553
122	—	276—284	554—562
123	383	—	563
124—134	—	285	like 564
—	384—386	286—294	—

C-TEXT.	B-TEXT.	C-TEXT.	B-TEXT.
——	565—568	305	——
295	*like* 569	——	584, 585
296	——	306—308	586—588
——	570, 571	——	589
297	*like* 572	309—311	*like* 590
——	573, 574	312—314	591—593
298—303	*like* 575—580	——	594, 595
——	581, 582	315, 316	——
304	583	317—322	596—601

NOTES TO C. PASS. XVIII.   (B. XV. 253—601.)

——(15. 254.) *Angres*, afflictions, trials; see C. xiii. 207, and the note.

——(15. 258.) "For every one may well know, that, if God Himself had so willed, neither Judas nor any Jew could have placed Jesus on the cross."

——(15. 264.) The reference is probably to the Aurea Legenda of Jacobus de Voragine, but there are numerous other collections. In Ælfric's Homilies, ed. Thorpe, i. 545, is some account of the early anchorites, where it is said that—"Seo bóc þe is gehåten Uitæ Patrum sprecð menigfealdlice embe þyssera ancersetlena;" i. e. the book that is called Uitæ Patrum speaks manifoldly concerning the lives of these hermits. See the note on Lives of Saints in Warton, Hist. Eng. Poetry, ed. 1840, i. 13; ed. 1871, ii. 58.

——(15. 267; *cf.* c. 18. 12.) St Anthony, reputed as one of the first of anchorites, and the founder of Monachism, was born in Egypt, about A.D. 251, or later, and died Jan. 17, 356. His day is Jan. 17, and an excellent account of him may be found in Chambers, Book of Days, i. 124, 126. He was the first to live a solitary life in a desert, but his mode of life was soon imitated by multitudes. See also Mrs Jameson's Sacred and Legendary Art, ii. 370 (or 3rd ed. p. 740); S. Augustini Confessiones, lib. 8, cap. 6; the description of Anthony in the life of S. Hilarion written by St Jerome; Cutts, Scenes and Characters of the Middle Ages, p. 95; Kingsley's The Hermits; &c. Seven of St Anthony's letters, originally written in Coptic, are extant. His life was written by St Athanasius. St Ægidius, better known as St Giles, died about 700; his day is Sept. 1. "Giles, or Ægidius, a very eminent saint of the seventh century, is believed to have been a Greek who migrated to France, . . . [and settled] in a hermitage, first in one of the deserts near the mouth of the Rhone, finally in a forest in the diocese of Nismes. . . . There is a romantic story of his being partly indebted for his subsistence to a Heaven-directed hind, which came daily to give him its milk; and it is added that his retirement was discovered by the king of the country, who, starting this animal in the chase, followed it till it took refuge at the feet of the holy anchorite. . . . To this day, on one side of the coat-armorial of the city of Edinburgh, you see figuring, as a supporter, the hind which ancient legend represents as nurturing the holy anchorite in the forests of Languedoc 1200 years ago;" Chambers, Book of Days, ii. 296. And see Mrs Jameson's Sacred and Legendary Art, 3rd ed. p. 770.

St Arsenius [c] was, says Mr Wright, "a noble Roman who, at the end of the fourth century, retired to Egypt to live the life of an anchorite in the desert." He died July 19, 449; his day is July 19. The story of his hearing voices from heaven, saying "Arseni, fuge homines et saluaberis," and "Arseni, fuge, tace, quiesce" is given in the Ancren Riwle, p. 163. See further in the note to l. 17 below, p. 352.

——(15. 268.) See note to l. 28 below.

——(15. 270.) *Spekes an spelonkes*, caves and caverns. The word *speke* probably occurs nowhere else as an English word, and does not appear in any Glossary, to my knowledge. If it were not for the context, it were hard to guess the sense. However, it is clear that *spelonke* is the Lat. *spelunca*, from which it follows that *speke* is the Lat. *specus*. William, though probably the only author who uses *speke*, is not the only author to use *spelonke*. The phrase "double *spelunke*, or double cave" occurs in Mandeville's Travels, ed. Halliwell, p. 66. "Who knoweth not that our recluses have grates of yron in their *spelunckes* and dennes?" Reliques of Rome, by T. Becon, 1563, fol. 53; quoted in Rock, Ch. of Our Fathers, iii. 118. The following notable etymology, almost on a par with some of modern times, is given in Batman vpon Bartholome, lib. 14, c. 56. "Of Spelunca. Spelunca is a ditch or hollowness under the earth, and hath that name, Spelunca, of *Speculando*, waiting and espieing. For because of widenesse therof it is an able place to abide in, and to behold and look about." Cf. also—"*Spelonque:* f. A hole in a rock; a wild beast's den;" Cotgrave.

——(15. 273.) *Foules that fleeth*, birds that fly. So in Ælfric's Homilies, ed. Thorpe, i. 547—"Sume hí leofodon be ófete and wyrtum, sume be agenum geswince, sumum ðenodon englas, sumum *fugelas*, oðþæt englas eft on eaðelicum forðsiðe hí to Gode feredon;" i. e. Some of them lived on fruit and herbs, some by their own labour, some were served by angels, some by *birds*, until angels afterwards by an easy departure [death] bore them to God. See note to B. 15. 279 below.

9. (15. 274.) For this story of the hind, see note to B. 15. 267 above.

——(15. 279.) Mr Wright observes that this story does not occur in the usual accounts of St Anthony. The fact is that our poet has made a slight mistake. In the next line he says—"and though the man had a guest, God provided for them both." He is right as to St Anthony and St Paul being fed by a bird, but it was St Anthony who was the *guest*, and St Paul the hermit who was the *host*. The story is, in fact, to be found in the life of St Paul. In Mrs Jameson's Sacred and Legendary Art, ii. 370 (or 3rd ed. p. 747), she relates (following an account in Il Perfetto Legendario), that St Anthony once went to visit St Paul the hermit, and, whilst they were conversing, a raven let fall a loaf between them; and Paul said—"For sixty years, every day, hath this raven brought me half a loaf; but, because thou hast come, my brother, lo! the portion is doubled, and we are fed as Elijah was fed in the wilderness." Again—"Inter has sermocinationes suscipiunt alitem corvum in ramo arboris consedisse, qui inde leniter subvolabat, et integrum panem ante ora mirantium deposuit," &c.; Vita S. Pauli, cap. 10; v. S. Hieronymi Opera, ed. Migne, vol. ii. Cf. Martyrologium Romanum, Jan. 10; Breviar. Rom. Jan. 15.

13. (15. 281.) St Paul (of Thebes) is here called the first hermit. He and St Anthony were the first to lead a heremitic life; and St Jerome calls the former the *author* of that mode of life, the latter its *illustrator*—"huius uitæ auctor Paulus, illustrator etiam Antonius;" Epist. 22, ad Eustochiam, cap. 16. During the persecution under Decius, Paul fled to a desert on the East of the Nile, and there became the founder of the anchorites or solitary hermits. "Paulus *primus eremita* semper ieiunauit, quousque de cœlis sibi panis mitteretur, qui duplicatus est cum ad eum ueniret Antoninus" (*sic*); Peter Cantor, ed. Migne, col. 328. See Mrs Jameson's Sacred and Legendary Art, ii. 368; Kingsley's The Hermits; Vita S. Pauli, by St Jerome (Opera, ed. Migne, ii.); and the article *Monachism* in the English Cyclopædia, Arts and Sciences, v. 722. He died A.D. 342; and his day is Jan. 15.

It is one of the marks by which the author of the "Crede" is seen to have copied our author, that he copies this line with but slight alteration.

"Paul *primus heremita* · put vs himselue
Awey into wildernes · þe werlde to dispisen;" l. 308.

Parroked, enclosed; lit. imparked; see Pass. vii. 144.

15. (15. 284.) *Frere austyn*, Augustine the friar. A general term for the Augustine or Austin Friars; see B-text. The four orders of friars fiercely disputed as to the priority of their respective foundations, and each sought to shew that their order was older than the rest. The Austin friars took their name from the celebrated St Augustine of Hippo; but, to prove their antiquity, maintained that their order was really due to St Paul, the *first* hermit; see this claim asserted by an Austin friar in P. Pl. Crede, ll. 306— 317. But even this was outdone; for the Carmelites said their order dated from the time *of the prophet Elijah!* See P. Pl. Crede, note to ll. 29, and 48.

17. (15. 285.) *Panyeres*, baskets; see Havelok, l. 813. The word is curiously chosen, as St Paul was a tentmaker; "erant autem *scenofactoriæ artis;*" Acts xviii. 3. Yet Chaucer seems to have the same idea.

"I wol nat do no labour with my hondes,
Ne make *baskettes*, and lyue therby . . . .
I wol non of the *apostles* counterfete."
Prol. to Pardoneres Tale.

However, it was St Paul who set the example of labouring with his hands; and, in imitation of him, we find an early example of *basket-making* by St Arsenius, "who, before he turned hermit, had been the tutor of the emperors Arcadius and Honorius," and who is represented in a fresco in the Campo Santo at Pisa, by Pietro Laurati, as "weaving baskets of palm-leaves;" whilst beside him another hermit is cutting wooden spoons, and a third is fishing. See Mrs Jameson's Sacred and Legendary Art, 3rd ed. p. 757; with the illustration.

19. (15. 287.) St Peter and St Andrew were fishers; Mat. iv. 18.

21. (15. 289.) "Mary Magdalen lived by roots (to eat) and dews (to drink)." *By mores* might also be translated "upon moors;" hence my side-note—"Mary Magdalen lived in desert places." But the use of the word "dewes" is against this, as well as the general sense of the passage; so that the sidenote is, in fact, wrong. Moreover, William uses *mores* in the same sense (that of *roots*) elsewhere; see the note to Pass. xvii. 250, p. 340, and observe the word *radicibus* in the Latin quotation in the next note.

The notion that St Mary Magdalen and Mary, the sister of Lazarus, were one and the same person is almost wholly unfounded, and indeed repulsive; but, in olden times, it was almost universal. See *Mary Magdalene* in The Concise Dictionary of the Bible, ed. W. Smith, p. 521. Tradition relates that St Mary Magdalen found her way to the South of Gaul, and retired to a solitary life in a desert not far from Marseilles. "It was a frightful barren wilderness, in the midst of horrid rocks and caves; and here, for thirty years, she devoted herself to solitary penance for the sins of her past life;" Mrs Jameson's Sacred and Legendary Art, i. 337. In the Knight of La Tour-Landry, ed. Wright, p. 132, Mary Magdalen is called the sister of Lazarus, and it is said that "she putte her lyff in the desert, and lyued in grete abstinence the space of .xx. wynter." See particularly the poem entitled The Lamentacioun of Marie Magdaleine, printed in the old copies of Chaucer's Works; and compare the account of the supposed relics of the saint at Vezelai and La Baume in Chambers, Book of Days, ii. 101. Her day is July 22.

23. (*not in* b.) "Sancta Maria Ægyptiaca quadraginta annis uixit de duobus panibus et radicibus;" Peter Cantor, ed. Migne, col. 328. The usual day assigned to St Mary of Egypt (S. Maria Egyptiaca) is April 9. She is said to have lived in the fifth century. In Mandeville's Travels (ed. Halliwell, p. 96), we are told that nigh unto mount Olivet is "a chirche of seynte Marie Egipcyane, and there sche lythe in a tombe." Rutebuef, a French trouvère of the 13th century, wrote a poem of some length, entitled La Vie de sainte Marie l'Egypcienne; see Œuvres Complètes de Rutebuef, ed. Jubinal, ii. 106—150. Chaucer alludes to her in the Man of Lawes Tale (Group B. 500)—

> "Who fedde the Egypcien Marie in the caue,
> Or in desert? no wight but Crist, sanz faille."

Her legend relates that, at the age of twelve, she went to Alexandria, where she lived a life of constant debauchery for seventeen years; after which, however, she was converted, and lived for the rest of her life (47 years more) in the wilderness beyond the Jordan. She had with her, says Rutebuef (p. 120) but two loaves and a half—

> "Or n'a que .ij. pains et demi"—

which William here speaks of as "three loaves." Two of the loaves lasted her more than 40 years (id. p. 122)—

"Plus de .xl. anz ala nue ;
Ij. petits pains non guères granz,
De cels vesqui par plusors anz.
Le premier an devindrent dur
Com se fussent pièrres de mur ;
Chascun jor en menja Marie,
Mès ce fu petite partie."

Skelton introduces her name to swear by, in his Garlande of Laurell, 1455.

" By *Mary Gipcy !*
Quod scripsi, scripsi."

Dyce well remarks, in a note on this (vol. ii. p. 333) that this was
shortened, in later writers, to the interjection *marry gip, marry gep, marry
guep,* or *marry gup.* Nares, s. v. *Marry,* quotes *marry gip* in Ben Jonson
(Barth. Fair, act. 1) and *marry guep* in Hudibras, i. 3. 202. Being misunderstood, it seems to have been interpreted as *marry, go up,* and finally, as *marry,
come up !* Sô says the theory.

We see also that *Gipsy* was, long ago, the accepted shortened form for
Egyptian.

24. (*not in* b.) "Love was her relish." See note to B. xvi. 11, p. 374.

28. (15. 268.) Owing to various alterations in the C-text, this line
corresponds to B. 15. 268. See the Scheme.

31. (15. 295.) Wild beasts are not uncommonly represented in early art
as associating with the saints on friendly terms. Compare the story of
Daniel in the lions' den, from which many other similar accounts may have
been imitated. Thus, in the aprocryphal book of Paul and Thecla (ed. Honc,
ix. 2) a fierce she-lion, who was to have devoured Thecla, ran to her, and
fell at her feet. "The lion will not touch the true prince ;" 1 Hen. IV. ii. 4.
Very similar is the story of Una and the lion, F. Q. i. 3. 5.

33. (15. 301.) *Trewe man,* a truthful man [c]; *meke þinge,* a meek creature
[b]. Birds, being supposed to be milder by nature than beasts, are here taken
to represent the better class of men. The idea of the excellence of birds seems
to have been due to the expression "uolucres cœli," the birds of *heaven,* in
Mat. viii. 20. See this exposition enlarged upon in the Ancren Riwle, p.
131, where true anchoresses are compared to birds. We may also observe the use of the dove as a symbol of the Holy Spirit. Cf. B. 15. 308,
below.

34. (15. 302.) *Fynde,* provide for, support. The B-text means—"as if
one should say that just men ought to provide for men of religious orders."

40. (*not in* b.) The story in the book of Tobit is that Tobit's wife Anna,
in receiving wages for some work done, received also a present of a kid from
her employers. Tobit was blind ; but, hearing the kid's cry, thought that it
must have been stolen, and compelled his wife to restore it, not believing
her account of it. His words were—" *Uidete, ne forte furtiuus sit ;* reddite
eum dominis suis, quia non licet nobis aut edere ex furto aliquid, aut con-
tingere ;" Tob. ii. 21 (Vulgate) ; ii. 13 (A. V.). Upon this, his wife taunts
him ; whereupon, being grieved, he laments his fate in being reproached,

concluding with the words—"*expedit enim mihi mori magis quam uiuere;*". Tob. iii. 6.

William gives both quotations inexactly; the latter is an improvement on the original. He has quoted it twice before; see Pass. ii. 144, and the note, p. 37; also Pass. vii. 290.

In the edition of Batman vpon Bartholome, printed at London by Thomas East in 1582, the colophon contains the motto—"Mieulx vault movrir en vertu que vivre en honte;" shewing that the phrase was a proverbial one.

41. (*not in* b.) Whitaker thinks the inference is not very obvious. But, the author's meaning is clear enough. Just as Tobit, being blind, thought himself in danger of having stolen goods brought into his house, so the clergy and other religious, being blind sometimes to the faults of the rich, were in danger of receiving from them things which had been stolen from the poor. Shameless extortion was the rule, and the clergy were naturally looked to as being the poor man's friends. If they did not refuse tithes on this account, they might refuse presents or offerings out of wealth that was known to be stolen. In the B-text the advice is particularly given to the friars (15. 306). See the parallel passage in Pass. vii. 300—302.

49. (*not in* b.) *Child*, i. e. chilled; note the reading *cold* in MSS. M and F. *Chaufen*, grow warm.

——(15. 306.) *Foude thei*, if they found. The reading *Foulde* (Wright's ed.) is a mere misprint; the Trin. MS. has *Founde*.

——(15. 310.) *Peny ale*, common ale. See note to Pass. vii. 226, p. 120.

52. (*cf.* 15. 312.) *Mesure*, moderation. The first part of the quotation is from Job vi. 5; the last part is probably from some comment on that text. There is something like it in the following: "Uel ipsa uos bruta animalia doceant, quæ quando necessariis abundant, neque rugiunt, neque mugiunt;" S. Brunonis Episcopi Signiensis Exp. in Job vi. 5.

54. (15. 315.) *Amorteisede*, granted in mortmain. Cotgrave gives, as one of the meanings of F. *amortir*, "to grant, alien, or pass away, in mortmain." "*Amortize*, to alien lands or tenements to any corporation, guild, or fraternity, and their successors; which cannot be done without licence of the king, and of the lord of the mannor. Anno 15 Rich. 2. cap. 5. See the statute of *Amortizing* lauds made temp. Edw. I.;" Blount's Nomolexicon.

56. (15. 319.) The B-text means—"and are (regularly) founded and endowed in order to pray for others." In the C-text the construction is inverted, the last half of the line coming first in the sense. The sense is—"to endow and feed such as are already fully founded, (to endow them, I say,) with the money that your children and kindred may lawfully claim."

64. (*not in* b.) *Largenesse*, liberality. The story of St Lawrence is that, by command of Bishop Xystus, he distributed to the poor all the wealth which was at that time in the treasury of the church of Rome. The emperor, attempting to seize these treasures, was told by St Lawrence that he should see the wealth of the church; and the saint then pointed to the poor of Rome, as being the true treasures of the Christian community. On this the

emperor revenged himself by commanding that St Lawrence should be roasted to death. Our poet has alluded to St Lawrence once before; see the note to Pass. iii. 130, p. 50. Since writing that note, I have found that, in that passage, William follows the account of St Lawrence given in the Aurea Legenda (cap. cxvii), which contains an expression closely resembling that in the text. "Et gratias agens dixit, 'gratias tibi ago, domine, quia *ianuas tuas ingredi merui ;*' et sic spiritum emisit."

The allusion to this story is continued in l. 68 below.

66. (*not in* b.) "He gave God's goods (i. e. the treasures of the church) to God's men (i. e. to the poor)."

71. (*not in* b.) *Purnele*, a common female name; hence, a concubine. See note to Pass. v. 111, p. 80; also Pass. vi. 129, and Pass. vii. 3.

——(15. 329.) *Robeth*, robe, clothe, give rich clothes to; and so in l. 333. The MSS. that read *robben* or *robbeth* are wrong.

——(15. 332.) *To woke with themese*, to moisten the Thames with. It is common to find *with* in this close conjunction with the verb. The word *woke* presents more difficulty; it is discussed above, in the note to Pass. xv. 25, p. 287. Hazlitt's collection of Proverbs has—"To cast water into the sea, *or*, into the Thames." Ray's comment is—"that is, to give to them who had plenty before; which, notwithstanding, is the dole general of the world. Lumen soli mutuari, &c."

Heywood has—

> "It is, to geue him, as muche almes or neede
> As cast water in tems."

And Barclay, Ship of Fools, ed. Jamieson, i. 166—

> "Or in the se cast water, thynkynge it to augment."

See also Barclay's Eclogue i., quoted in Jamieson's Introduction to Barclay, p. xlvi. On the use of *Thames* without the definite article, see note to Pass. xv. 104, p. 290. Add, as an illustration, "yn temse," i. e. in the Thames; Riley's Memor. of London, p. 629.

——(15. 336.) "Sacrilegium est res pauperum dare non pauperibus;" Peter Cantor, ed. Migne, cap. 47. "Maximum periculum est de patrimonio Christi pauperibus non dare;" id. "Pars sacrilegii est rem pauperum dare non pauperibus;" S. Hieron. Epist. 66. § 8. "Res pauperum non pauperibus dare, par sacrilegio crimen esse dignoscitur;" Gaufrid. Abb. Declam. ex Bernard. (inter S. Bernardi Opera, tom. ii. p. 612. The last of these is quoted by Pecock (Repressor, ii. 409), who translates it by—"For to not ʒeue to poor men the godis of poor men is euen synne with sacrilegie."

"Paria sunt et dare peccatoribus, et immolare demonibus;" Pet. Cantor, cap. 47. "Paria sunt histrionibus dare, et dæmonibus immolare;" id.; quoted, but inexactly, from St Jerome.

Peter Cantor, cap. 48, also quotes from St Jerome the words—"O monache, si indiges et accipis, potius das quam accipis; si non indiges et accipis, rapis, quia distribuenda pauperibus tibi usurpas."

See also Wyclif's Works, iii. 473, note. Cf. 1 Tim. vi. 8.

——(15. 339.) *Prisone*, prisoner; see Pass. x. 34; xxi. 59, &c.

72. (15. 342.) *Lussheborgh*, a light coin. Chaucer has, in the Monkes Prologue—

"God wot, no lussheburghes payen ye."

They were spurious coins imported into England from Luxembourg, whence the name. A "Writ as to the money called lussheburghe" is mentioned in the Liber Albus, ed. Riley, p. 495. "*Lushburgs*, al. *Luxenburghs*, was a base sort of money coyned beyond seas, to the likeness of English money, in the days of Edw. III., and brought in to deceive the king and his people. To avoid which, it was made treason for any man wittingly to bring in any such. Anno 25 Edw. 3. stat. 4. cap. 2. 3 Part Inst. fol. 1;" Blount's Nomolexicon. Mr Wright adds that they "were the subject of legislation in 1346, 1347, 1348, and 1351. . . . Many of these coins are preserved, and found in the cabinets of collectors; they are in general very much like the contemporary English coinage, and might easily be taken for it, but the metal is very base."

The spelling *Lusscheburghe* is used to denote the town of Luxemburg in the Allit. Morte Arthure, ed. Brock, l. 2388. There was an ordinance "that money, counterfeited after the sterling, if it be not good according to the old standard, shall be forfeited;" Liber Albus, p. 494.

77. (15. 345.) "The mark of the king of heaven." That is, the cross made in baptism. *Croune*, the tonsure [b].

78. (15. 346.) It is well to note that *of* [c] means *by*; i.e. the metal, man's soul, is by many of these teachers alloyed, &c. Whitaker translates it by *of*, and makes nonsense of the passage.

98. (15. 354.) *Shephurdes*. See a curious passage in the Complaynt of Scotlande, ed. Murray, pp. 46, 47, on the indebtedness of the science of astronomy to Shepherds. The Calendrier des Bergers deals with astronomy. So in the English translation—"Thus endeth the Astrology of Shepheards, with the knowledge that they have of the stars, planets, and movings of the skies;" Sheph. Kal., ed. 1656, sig. A 4, back. And again, at chap. xxxi— "Here followeth the Shepheards Astrology." To this day a work entitled "The Shepherd of Banbury's Rules to judge of the changes of the Weather," by John Claridge, Shepherd, is popular among the lower orders; an edition was published in 1744, and it was reprinted in 1827, and perhaps later. Marco Polo (ed. Yule, i. 399) describes how the 5000 astrologers in the city of Cambaluc observe and predict the weather. William again mentions the "seven stars" in Rich. Redeles, iii. 352. In my note on that line, I have suggested that it there seems to mean Charles's Wain; or it might mean the seven stars of the Lesser Bear, so as to give more exactly the sense of "above the pole." What was the exact meaning of the "seven stars" in William's time, we have perhaps hardly enough to decide by; cf. Lat. *septentriones*. The account of 'Arcthurus' in Batman vppon Bartholome, lib. 8. c. 35, is a mass of confusion, shewing how very vague people's ideas could be upon so simple a subject; the account follows that in

. Isidore, which is also somewhat vague. However, the same phrase, i. e. 'seven stars,' occurs in Shakespeare; and we know that, in Elizabethan English, it referred to neither Greater nor Lesser Bear, but was used of the Pleiades. Cotgrave has—"*Pleiade*, one of the seven stars," and his continuator Sherwood interprets "The seven starres" by, *pleiades*. He also gives—"*Estoille poussiniere*, the seven stars; called by some, the hen and her chickens." The last name refers to the closeness of the stars in that cluster.

In Puttenham's Arte of Poesie, lib. ii. c. 11, ed. Arber, p. 122, the 'seuen starres' are the *pleiades;* and even in Isidore's time the Pleiades were especially regarded as symbolical of good preachers, endowed with the sevenfold gifts of the Spirit. See S. Isidori de Natura Rerum liber, c. 26, sect. 6; ed. Migne (vol. 83), coll. 998, 999.

99. (15. 355.) On weather omens, see the chapter so headed in Brand, Pop. Antiq., ed. Ellis, iii. 241; Choice Notes, from Notes and Queries, on Folklore; &c.

103. (15. 360.) By comparing the texts, we see that "the folk of the flood" are sailors, and "the folk of the land" are sowers or husbandmen. Wyclif has a similar lament, in which he seems to attribute the dearths to the friars; "heven," he says, "lokes lesse to fruyt of þe erthe, monnes strength is lesse, here lyue is shortere, þe tyme is lesse sesounable, and charite withdrawen;" Works, iii. 416.

106. (15. 364.) *Clymat*, latitude [c]; *element*, air [b]. A *climate* was, at this time, a region of the earth between certain parallels of latitude. See *Climate* and *Element* in Trench's Select Glossary; and my note on *climates* in Chaucer's Treatise on the Astrolabe, Part ii., sect. 39, l. 19; ed. Skeat, p. 85.

. 107. (15. 365.) Grammar was considered as the first of the "seven arts," and as the foundation of the rest; see Pass. xii. 98, 122. Mr Wright refers us to his Essay on Anglo-Saxon Literature, introductory to vol. i. of the Biographia Britannica Literaria, p. 72; and quotes a passage on the importance of grammar from the Image du Monde of Gautier de Metz (thirteenth century):—

> "Gramaires si est fondemens
> De clergie et coumenchemens;
> Cou est li porte de science," &c.

Bygyleth, deceives, perplexes, leads astray.

——(15. 369.) This is an important line. It shews how common was some knowledge of Latin, and in what high esteem French was held. It is also remarkable as being omitted in the O-text; possibly because French was going out of fashion.

111. (15. 370.) *Gowe*, let us go; see note to Pass. i. 227, p. 26.

114. (*cf.* 15. 375.) *Seuene ars*, the "seven arts;" see note to Pass. xii. 98, p. 243. *Asoile ad quodlibet*, answer to any question, generally.

115, 116. (15. 376, 377.) "Unless they should fail in philosophy—that is to say, if there were any philosophers in existence who would carefully examine them—I should be much surprised" [c]. *Apposed*, questioned [b].

118. (15. 379.) *Ouerhuppe,* skip over parts of the service; see note to Pass. xiv. 123, p. 276.

120. (15. 381.) The feast of Corpus Christi was held on the Thursday after Trinity Sunday, in memory, as was supposed, of the miraculous confirmation of the doctrine of transubstantiation under Pope Urban IV.; it was instituted between 1262 and 1264, and confirmed by the council of Vienne in 1311. It was the favourite day for acting miracle-plays and mysteries, as is well known. See *Corpus Christi Day* in Nares; *Corpus Christi* in Haydn's Book of Dates; and Chambers, Book of Days, i. 686. Chambers inadvertently makes it a week too early. "Corpus Christi even" is mentioned in the alliterative poem of The Crowned King, l. 19, printed as an appendix to the C-text, at p. 525.

121. (15. 382.) William is quite right in referring us to the service for Corpus Christi day. In the Breviary, "in festo Corporis Christi," will be found the hymn beginning—

> "Pange, lingua, gloriosi
> Corporis mysterium."

The fourth stanza is—

> "Uerbum caro, panem uerum
> Uerbo carnem efficit,
> Fitque sanguis Christi merum
> Et si sensus deficit.
> Ad firmandum cor sincerum
> *Sola fides sufficit.*"

To saue with lewed peple, to save ignorant people with.

130. (*not in* b.) "The law of love without loyalty (or sincerity) was never praiseworthy." Here "loue lawe," lit. law of love, means law founded upon love. The expression is an awkward one, and would be obscure but for the expression in l. 136, where mention is made of "love that has law for a cause," i. e. an orderly love, a love founded on law, one that is in accord with God's will. Thus the general sense is—"God does not approve of law, even if founded on love, if loyalty or truth be excluded from it. He teaches none to love without a true cause. Jews, Gentiles, and Saracens, suppose that they believe truly, and honour, love, and believe in one God alike; but their law is different," &c. (Here William probably uses "Gentiles" as meaning other than Christians.) "But our Lord approves of no love but what is founded on law," &c. The whole passage is one of those uninteresting specimens of subtlety into which our author sometimes sinks. The Latin quotation at l. 140 is the best guide to the sense of this passage.

In the phrase "loue lawe," *loue* must be a genitive case; it cannot well be the infinitive mood, as that (at least in some of the MSS.) would have taken the form *louye;* see, e. g. l. 152 below.

148. (*not in* b.) This line is a repetition of l. 143, and has the same sense. William says that true Charity is to be *cher,* i. e. fond, concerning one's own soul; i. e. so to love one's own eternal welfare as to avoid sin and be kind to all. I have no doubt that he has here used the wrong word; he meant to

have said *chary*, i. e. to be chary (anxious, careful) over one's soul. He evidently took *chary* to be a corruption of the F. *cher*, and thought it would be more correct to use the F. form. Unluckily, *chary* has nothing to do with *cher*, being the A.S. *cearig*, careful, from *cearu* or *caru*, care, anxiety.

150. (*not in* b.) *Wher*, whether, whether is it the case that.

. 153. (*not in* b.) "It is a natural thing for a creature to honour his Creator."

157. (*not in* b.) *As by*, according to. They love not God with that love of which we read in the Legend of the Saints; i. e. in the Golden Legend.

158. (*not in* b.) "They live not in a true belief, for they believe in a (merely human) mediator."

167. (*cf.* 15. 391.) *Porsuede*, endeavoured. *Moste noughte be*, might not be, could not attain to being [b]. The true account of the career of Mohammed was very imperfectly known at this time in England. The phrase "souhte in-to surrye" (l. 169), lit. made his way to Syria, probably refers to the famous Hegira, or flight from Mecca to Medina, July 15, 622.

. The use of the words "pope" and "cardinal" seems strange here, but is justified by the current opinion of the time. This will best appear from Mr Wright's excellent note, which I here transcribe.

"This account of Mohammed was the one most popularly current in the middle ages. According to Hildebert, who wrote a life of the pseudo-prophet in Latin verse in the 12th century, Mohammed was a Christian, skilled in magical arts, who; on the death of the patriarch of Jerusalem, aspired to succeed him :—

> 'Nam male deuotus quidam baptismate lotus
> Plenus perfidia uixit in ecclesia . . . . ,
> Nam cum transisset Pater illius urbis, et isset
> In cœlum subito corpore disposito,
> Tunc exaltari magus hic et *pontificari*
> Affectans auide; se tamen hæc pauide
> Dixit facturum, nisi sciret non nociturum
> Si præsul fiat, cum Deus hoc cupiat.'

His intrigues being discovered, the emperor drives him away, and in revenge he goes and founds a new sect. The story of the pigeon, which is not in Hildebert, is found in Vincent of Beauvais, Spec. Hist. lib. xxiii. c. 40. This story is said to be founded in truth. Neither of them are found in the Roman de Mahomet, by Alexander du Pont, written in the 13th century, and edited by M.M. Reinaud and Michel, Paris, 1831, 8vo, a work which contains much information concerning the Christian notions relative to Mohammed in the middle ages." See note to l. 171 below.

168. (*not in* b.) *A lussheborgh*, a counterfeit coin. See note to l. 72 above, p. 357.

171. (15. 393.) *Enduuntede a douue*, tamed a dove. This story is from Vincent of Beauvais, as stated in the note to l. 167. William seems to have borrowed several things from that author.

"The Turkes hath a law called Macomites law, and the booke that there

lawc is wrytten in, is called the Alkaron. Macomyt, a false fellow, made it ;
he scdused the people vnder thys maner : he dyd bryng vp a doue, and would
put .ii. or thre pesen in his eare, & she would euery day come to his eare
and eate the peason, and then the people would thynke the holy goost, or
an Angell, did come & teache him what the people should do;" Andrew
Boorde, Introduction of Knowledge, c. 37.

"Was Mahomet inspired with a dove ?" 1st Pt. of Hen. VI. i. 2.
Staunton's note on this line is—"Mahomet, it is related, had a dove, 'which
he used to feed with wheat out of his ear; which dove, when it was hungry,
lighted on Mahomet's shoulder, and thrust its bill in to find its breakfast;
Mahomet persuading the rude and simple Arabians, that it was the Holy
Ghost that gave him advice.'—See Sir W. Raleigh's Hist. of the World, b.
i. pt. i. c. 6."

"He replied by pointing to the idle legend of Mahomet's pigeon, ..
which legend had been accredited and adopted by Grotius ; " De Quincey,
Confessions, p. 47.

——(15. 413.) *Antony*, the hermit ; see note to l. 12 above. *Dominik*, of
Castile, the founder of the Dominican or Black Friars, also known as the
Friars Preachers or Jacobins ; born April 5, 1170, died Aug. 6, 1221. His
day is Aug. 4. See Mrs Jameson's Legends of the Monastic Orders, p. 227 ;
Chambers, Book of Days, ii. 169; Dante, Paradiso, xii. 55—105. *Francis*,
of Assisi, founder of the Franciscan friars, or Minorites ; see Mrs Jameson's
Legends of the Monastic Orders; Chambers, Book of Days, ii. 413 ; Dante,
Paradiso, xi. 43—117. His day is Oct. 4. Cf. note to Pass. v. 117.

——(15. 414.) *Benet and Bernarde ;* see note to Pass. v. 117, p. 82.

——(15. 420.) *And*, if. And so in l. 422 [b].

——(15. 430.) Alluding to the eleven apostles. William forgets St
Matthias.

——(15. 436.) *Gregory*, the Great, born 544, died Mar. 12, 604. See
Chambers, Book of Days, i. 361, 679; and note to Pass. vi. 147. His day
is March 12.

——(15. 437.) St Augustine, the famous missionary to England, died
about 607. His day is May 26. He baptised Ethelberht, King of Kent, on
Whitsunday, June 2, 597. See Chambers, Book of Days, i. 681.

——(15. 445.) *Fulled.* In a note to the Ormulum, ii. 626, Dr White
says—"The connection of the A.S. *fulluht* (baptism) with the Lat. *fullo*
seems to have been held by William de Langloud, in the Vision of P. P., p.
322 (ed. Wright), where he compares the unbaptised infant with 'Clooth
that cometh fro the wevyng,' and is 'not yet fulled under foot,' nor 'in
fulling stokkes Wasshen wel with water.' A much more probable etymology
is suggested by a friend, who remarks—'I consider *fulluht* a compound of
full (full, perfect) and a derivative of *hlutor* (O.H.G. *hlutari*, puritas) ; the
prefix denoting the fulness of the act denoted by the substantive. We have
a like use of *full* in *fulfremian*. Hence the signification [of *fulluht*] will be
complete purification.'"

I have no faith in this derivation of *fulluht*, nor can I see how to turn *hlut-* into *-luht;* surely the position of the *-h* makes all the difference. *Fulluht* (spelt *fulwiht* in the Northumbrian version of Mat. xxi. 25) simply means baptism, and is obviously a mere derivative of the verb *fullian*, to baptise. Cf. "Ic *fullige* eow on wætere," I baptise you with water, Mk. i. 8. And the same notion of cleansing appears in Mark ix. 3, where the A.S. version has "swa nan *fullere* ofer eorðan ne mæg swa hwite gedon;" i. e. as no fuller on earth could whiten them. See also the mention of "fuller's sope" in Mal. iii. 2 (A. V.).

Our author uses *fullynge* for *baptism*, and *fulled* for *cleansed*, in the ordinary manner. We must, however, take care to keep the two senses of "to full" quite distinct. There were two distinct processes to which the name of *fulling* has been applied; one process is that of cleansing, the other is that of thickening the cloth, called in Middle-English *tacking*, referred to, not here, but two lines further on, in the word "ytouked." The A.S. *fullian*, to baptise, is clearly connected with the A.S. *fullere*, a cleanser of cloth, as above mentioned.

But the operation which is now generally understood by *fulling* is a very different one. It is a process of beating the wool so as to felt it together; and it happens that this process (formerly called *tucking*) is also connected with the Lat. *fullo*. Thus Cotgrave has—"*Foullonner, Fouller*, to full, or thicken cloath in a mill;" and Palsgrave—"I thycke clothe in thy [*sic;* read the] myll, *Ie feullonne.*" To understand this rightly, see the article *Woollen Manufactures* in the Engl. Cyclopædia, vol. viii. coll. 999—1001. The wool is sorted, scoured, washed, willowed, scribbled, slubbed, spun, woven, scoured again, stretched on tenters, and then picked over. "After this it is ready for the important process of *fulling*, or *felting*, which imparts to woollen goods that peculiarity of surface whereby they are distinguished from all others. A large mass of cloth folded into many plies is put into the *fulling-mill*, where it is exposed to the long-continued action of two heavy wooden mallets or stocks. . . . . This compacting process in the cloth manufacture is effected by beating, and is called *fulling*; in the hat-manufacture it is effected by pressure and rolling, and is called *felting*; but the two are clearly analogous in principle." I may add that our word *felt* is cognate with the Gk. πίλος, with its derivative verb πιλόω. I do not say that the A.S. *fullian* was not simply borrowed from Latin, but I think it clear that the primary notion in the Latin *fullo* was that of treading or stamping upon the cloth (cf. F. *fouler*, to tread, to stamp upon), whence both the notions of *cleansing* and *thickening by beating* took their origin; and I think further, that the A.S. *fullian* commonly ignores the latter meaning, and fixes upon that of cleansing only, with special reference to its metaphorical use, i. e. the cleansing of the soul in baptism. In modern English, however, we have nearly lost sight of a reference to mere cleansing, and have rather followed the sense of the Fr. *foullonner;* and this I take to be the simple explanation of the whole matter.

We may note the proper names *Fuller*, *Walker*, and *Tucker*, as being all derived from the different names for the process of felting cloth. It is worth noting that William mentions two ways in which the *cleansing* process was formerly effected. Sometimes it was "fulled under foot," by being trodden upon, much as when Scotch washerwomen wash clothes by stamping upon them with naked feet; or, at other times, thoroughly cleansed in some sort of frame which he appears to denote by "fulling-stock"; and which, moreover, must have materially differed from what is now called a fulling-stock, as employed in the modern process above described. The only gain from Dr White's note (which seems to me wrong in other respects) is in observing that he demolishes the comma which appears in my edition at the end of l. 415, and gives what is probably the correct sense in a simpler form. I conclude that ll. 445 and 446 mean—"till it is cleansed under foot, or well washed with water in fulling-stocks, and afterwards scratched over with teazles."

——(15. 446.) *Taseles*, teasles. A reference to the Engl. Cyclopædia (as in the last note) will best explain this. "In the fulled state the cloth presents a woolly and rough appearance, to improve which it goes through the processes of *teazling* or *raising*, and *shearing* or *cutting*. The object of the first is to raise the ends of the fibres above the surface, and of the second to cut them off to a uniform level. The raising of the fibres is effected by thistle-heads, teazling-cards, or wire brushes. Teazles are the seed-pods of the *dipsacus fullonum*, having small hooked points on their surfaces. They were formerly used in the cloth manufacture thus. A number of them were put into a small frame with handles, so as to form a kind of curry-comb; and this was worked by two men over the surface of the cloth, which was suspended horizontally. . . . . . In some machines the teazling-points are made of wire, to obviate the waste of 3000 natural teazles, which takes place in the dressing of one piece of cloth." It will be observed that William alludes to this process a little too early. The cloth was not teazled till it had been "tucked" (i. e. fulled) and "tented;" see the next note.

The result of the use of teazles for cloth was to make them extremely valuable. Thus, in 1326, we find mention of a writ—"that none of the thistles that in English are called *taseles*, and no fuller's earth, shall be carried out of the kingdom," &c.; Riley's Memorials of London, p. 150. "*Dipsacus Fullonum* is the Clothier's Teazel, a plant with large heads of flowers, which are imbedded in stiff, hooked bracts. These heads are set in frames and used in the dressing of broad-cloth, the hooks catching up and removing all loose particles of wool, but giving way when held fast by the substance of the cloth;" Rev. C. A. Johns, Flowers of the Field, p. 314.

——(15. 447.) *Ytouked*, tucked or thickened; this is the process which is *now* called *fulling*; see note to l. 445 above, p. 362. Hence the name of *Tucker*. Hence arose also the name of *Walker*, according to the explanation given in Ray's Glossary—"*Walker*, a fuller; *walkmill*, a fulling-mill." Cf. G. *walken*, to full. See note to Pass. i. 223, p. 26.

Ytented, stretched on tenter-hooks. This process, strictly speaking, precedes that of tucking. After the second scouring, it is carried "to the drying-room, or the tenter-ground, where it is stretched out by means of hooks on rails, and allowed to dry in a smooth and extended state;" Engl. Cycl., as above. After the tenting, it is picked over, fulled or tucked, teazled, sheared, brushed, and then finally smoothed; till it comes at last "under the tailor's hand."

——(15. 451.) *Hethene*, heathen. This derivation of *heathen* from *heath* is perfectly correct; and, as Archbp. Trench points out, in his Study of Words, is well paralleled by the Lat. *paganus*, Eng. *pagan*, from *pagus*, a village.

——(15. 455.) *Fesauntes*, pheasants. Mr Wright remarks—"The pheasant was formerly held in the same honour as the peacock, and was served at table in the same manner. It was considered one of the most precious dishes. See Le Grand d'Aussy, Hist. de la Vie privée des François; ii. 19." So in the Babees Book, ed. Furnivall, p. 278, after mention of "rosted capon," and "fruyters [fritters] or other bake metes," we read—"take hede to the *fesande*; he shal be arayed in the maner of a capon; but it shall be done drye, without ony moysture, and he shall be eten with salte and pouder of gynger."

——(15. 456.) *Fram hym nolde*, would not go away from him; i. e. were tame. See note to l. 467 [b] below.

——(15. 458.) The calf was a clean animal; Lev. xi. 3. See a somewhat similar passage in the Ormulum, ll. 1220—1249, where the ox is said to have cloven feet and to walk deliberately—

"& ȝifeþþ bisne off-þatt te birþ · all haȝhelike & faȝȝre
& dafttelike ledenn þe · wiþþutenn bracc & braþþe;"

i. e. "and he gives an example, that it behoves thee to conduct thyself all deliberately and fairly and deftly, without noise and anger."

——(15. 467.) This refers to the art of calling birds by the use of a pipe. "The pipe-call, mentioned by Burton, is noticed under a different denomination by Chaucer. 'Lo,' says he, 'the birde is begyled with the merry voice of the fowler's whistel, when it is closed in your nette'—alluding to the deceptive art of the bird-catchers in his time;" Strutt, Sports and Pastimes, p. 35. The quotation, however, is not from Chaucer, but from the anonymous Testament of Love, book ii, fol. 297, col. 2; appended to Chaucer's Works, ed. 1561.

At p. 212 of Lacroix (Manners, Customs, and Dress during the Middle Ages), there is an excellent illustration of "Bird-piping, or the manner of catching birds by piping," being a facsimile of a miniature in the MS. of the Livre du Roy Modus, of the fourteenth century. The picture shews a man, concealed within a bush, attracting wild birds by means of a pipe. In our text, however, the allusion is to *tame* birds, which, it would appear, were called to their food in a similar way, though probably by whistling with the lips only, without the use of a pipe.

Observe that ll. 464—477 are preserved *only* in the Rawlinson MS.; see pref. to B-text, pp. xi—xiii.

——(15. 472.) I have already suggested (Crit. Note to B. 15. 464, B-text, p. 415) that the word *whistlynge* at the end of this line may have been wrongly repeated; we should rather read *techynge*.

The general sense is—just as fowls are allured by whistling, so ignorant men are attracted heavenwards by wise teachers.

——(15. 473.) The nominative to *bymeneth* is *matheu* in l. 454. "And, by the man who made a feast [Mat. xxii] he signifies the majesty (of God)."

——(15. 475.) "By His tempests and His wonders He warns us, as by means of a whistler, wherever it is His will to honour us all, and to feed and feast us at the same time, for evermore."

——(15. 476.) *Worschipen*, to honour, shew regard to. We could hardly have a clearer instance of the difference between the old and modern senses of this word; for God is here said to "worship" men. So in Wyclif's translation of John xii. 26—"If ony man serve me, my fadir schal *worschip* him." See *Worship* in Trench's Select Glossary.

——(15. 478.) The argument goes back to l. 433, and the first part of this line is best taken interrogatively. "And who are they that excuse themselves (from attempting the work of conversion)? They are the parsons and priests."

——(15. 479.) *Han her wille*, obtain their wish, get what they want, viz. their tithes.

——(15. 482.) William's argument still refers to the conversion of the heathen, as in ll. 430—443. He therefore appeals to *Matheu*, i. e. Matt. xxviii. 19, and to *Marke*, i. e. Mark xvi. 15 (quoted below). He also refers to the psalm beginning with "Memento, domine, Dauid," i. e. Ps. cxxxi in the Vulgate version; the 6th verse being—"Ecce audiuimus eam in Ephrata; inuenimus eam in campis siluæ," which has already been quoted before; see note to Pass. xii. 51, p. 238. In that former place, *eam* is interpreted to mean *caritatem*, i. e. Christian love. So here, William clearly interprets the verse as meaning that Christian love is to be met with in unexpected places, from which he infers the duty of preaching to the heathen.

189. (15. 486.) See l. 538 [b] below for the mention of bishops of Bethlehem and Babylon. The pope used to appoint titular bishops *in partibus infidelium*, who were never intended to reside in their dioceses. "I have noticed," says Dean Milman, "the pluralist who held the archdeaconry of Thessalonica with benefices in Norfolk;" Hist. Lat. Christianity, vi. 379, note; with a reference to vol. iv. p. 308. By way of a modern example, I may observe that it was stated in the Daily Telegraph newspaper (Oct. 14, 1873), that the Abbot of the monastery of St Maurice, in the Canton Valais in Switzerland, was also a Bishop of Bethlehem in partibus. The famous Bedlam hospital for the insane owes its name to a similar circumstance. It was originally known as St Mary's of Bethlehem, and was "founded by Stephen Fitzmary, in 1247, for the pious purpose of sheltering and entertaining the *bishop of*

Bethlehem whenever he should be in London; " De Vere, Studies in English, p. 211. It was afterwards granted by Henry VIII., in 1545, to the city of London, and became a hospital for the reception of lunatics. Mention is made of a "Bishop of Bedlem" in 1298; Riley's Memorials of London, p. 39. Whitaker well remarks, that "these bishops in partibus, most of whom were abbots and priors, living at ease in the lazy plenty of their own well-endowed houses, were of all men least qualified for missionaries, and would be least inclined to hearken to this call of residence."

200. (15. 501.) *Red noble*, the gold coin so called. On the noble, see note to Pass. iv. 47, p. 59. There is an allusion here to the cross on the reverse of the coin; whence "rode" in ll. 201, 206, and "croys" in ll. 203, 205, 208. The same pun has occurred before, B. 5. 244, and is very common in old authors. See the engravings of the groat of Edward III, and the noble of Henry V, in Knight's Old England; figg. 862, 1179. An early example of a similar play upon words occurs in the poem "De Cruce Denarii," beginning—"Crux est denarii potens in sæculo," in the Poems of Walter Mapes, ed. Wright, p. 223. And again, at p. 38 of the same volume, we have—

> "Nummis in hac curia non est qui non vacet,
> *Crux* placet, rotunditas et albedo placet."

So also Occleve speaks of a fiend "hopping," i. e. dancing, in a *crossless* purse; De Regimine Principum, ed. Wright, p. 25. Many similar examples are cited in Warton, Hist. Eng. Poetry, ed. Hazlitt, iii. 278, note 7.

205. (15. 505.) "The answer is—because of greediness after the cross, the crown stands (i. e. is shewn) in the gold." This is a little obscure, but we may remember that, by the *crown*, William almost always means the tonsure; only here we have, probably, a pun upon the word. Men, covetous only of that *cross* which appears on money, are best satisfied with that *crown* which is seen on gold. Cf. note to Pass. xviii. 77, p. 357. Perhaps we may go so far as to see a reference here to the proverb—"no cross, no crown." If so, we may suppose William to say that, in order to accommodate the seekers after the cross on a piece of money, the crown is placed upon the coin also; so that they who have the cross, have the crown too. The cross, as has been said, was on the reverse of the coin; the crown was upon the king's head, on the obverse; see the engraving of the noble of Henry V, in Knight's Old England, fig. 1179.

I do not think *crown* is here to be taken in the sense of a piece of money. The English crowns only began with Henry VIII; and the foreign *écus* were called "sheeldes" in English, as in Chaucer's Prologue, l. 278.

209. (15. 509.) *Ouerturne*, perish, be suppressed [c]; *tourne*, change their lives, be converted; see l. 254 below [c]. The allusion is to the suppression of the order the Templars, which was still fresh in men's memories at that time. "The first military order of Knights of the Temple was founded in 1118 by Baldwin II., king of Jerusalem. The Templars were numerous in several countries, and came to England before 1185. Their wealth having excited the cupidity of the French kings, the order was suppressed by the council of

Vienne [Mar. 22, 1312], and part of its revenues were bestowed upon other orders in 1312. Numbers of the order were tried, condemned, and burned alive or hanged in 1308-10, and it suffered great persecutions throughout Europe; 68 were burnt at Paris, 1310. The grand-master Molay was burnt alive at Paris, March, 1314;" Haydn, Dict. of Dates. See some account of them in Ivanhoe, capp. 36, 37, 38, 44. In a note to cap. 38, Sir W. Scott refers us to the Rules of the Poor Military Brotherhood of the Temple, which occur in the works of St Bernard. There is an excellent article (with a list of books) on the Templars in the Engl. Cyclopædia, Div. Arts and Sciences, viii. 125. One of the most recent works is The History of the Knights Templars, &c. by C. G. Addison, 4to., London, 1842. Cf. Lacroix, Military and Religious Life of the Middle Ages, p. 172.

215. (15. 514.) *Demen*, judge, condemn. *Dos ecclesie*, the endowment of the church; see l. 223 below.

219. (15. 518.) *Leuitici*, the Levites; cf. Deut. xii. 6:—"Et offeretis in loco illo holocausta et uictimas uestras, *decimas et primitias* manuum uestrarum," &c.

220. (15. 519.) This story is thus alluded to in Pecock's Repressor, p. 323. "It is fablid to be trewe, that whanne greet Constantine the Emperour was baptisid of Siluester Pope, and hadde endewid [*endowed*] Siluester Pope with greet plente of londis of the empire, a voice of an aungel was herd in the eir, seiyng thus: 'In this dai venom is hildid [*poured*] into the chirche of God.' Wherfore the seid endewing bi immovable godis to the clergie is vnvertuose and yuel." Pecock gives this as a favourite story of the Lollards, and argues against the conclusion drawn from it by them. Prof. Babington's note is as follows. "Anno iii*. xv. Constantinus ·baptizatur a Sancto Silvestro, et tunc ditavit ecclesiam Romanam libertatibus, prædiis, et possessionibus, et dedit sedem suam imperialem Sancto Petro et suis successoribus. Et illo tempore Diabolus in aere volando clamavit, *Hodie venenum ecclesiis Dei infusum est*;" Sprot. *Chron.*, p. 43 (ed. Hearne). "Narrant chronica quod in dotatione ecclesiæ, vox audita est in aere angelica tunc temporis, sic dicentis, *Hodie effusum est venenum in ecclesia sancta Dei.*" Wicl. *Dial.* lib. iv. c. 18. "The angel said full sothe when the church was dowed, that this day is venym shed into the church." Wicl. *Of clerks possessioners*, MS. cited in Lewis's *Life of Wiclif*, p. 122. Professor Babington also refers to the present passage.

There are at least two more allusions in Wyclif's Works, ed. Arnold, iii. 341, 477; in the former of which the voice is that of a "fend" or fiend, in the latter that of an "aungel." Further remarks on the story occur in Prof. Babington's edition of Pecock's Repressor, in the Addenda, vol. ii. p. 699. It appears that it is also cited by Johannes de Parisiis, circa 1290, "who is rather an early authority for *angeli* in lieu of *diabolus*. 'Quod vero Dei displicuerit (Constantini donatio) ex hoc sumitur argumentum, quod legitur in vita B. Sylvestri Papæ, quod in donatione illa audita est vox angelorum, dicentium in aere, *Hodie in ecclesia venenam effusum est*'; De Pot. Reg. et

Pap. c. xxii, quoted by Dr Todd in notes to *Wycliffe's Three treatises*, p. 163." The story was known to Lord Cobham, who cited it in his examination; Foxe's *Martyrs*, s. a. 1413 (vol. iii. p. 333, ed. 1844; cf. Wordsworth, Eccl. Biog. i. 380. It is cited also by Higden, *Polychronicon*, lib. iv. c. 26; by Bale, Works (Parker Soc.), p. 35; and by Jewel, Works (Park. Soc.), vol. ii. p. 992. Gower alludes to it in his Conf. Amantis, bk. ii.

It is to be suspected that not only is the story of the angel's voice a fabrication, but also that upon which it was founded, viz. the pretended gift of the Lateran by Constantine to Sylvester. Dante mentions it (Inf. xix. 115), but, as Cary shews in a note, seems to have had his doubts about it. Ariosto refers to it, but not seriously; Orl. Furioso, c. xxxiv. st. 80. Milton translates both these passages in the lines—

> "Ah Constantine! of how much ill was cause,
> Not thy conversion, but those rich domains
> That the first wealthy pope received of thee."—

> "Then pass'd he to a flowery mountain green,
> Which once smelt sweet, now stinks as odiously;
> This was the gift, if you the truth will have,
> That Constantine to good Sylvester gave."

Massingberd (Eng. Ref., p. 53) remarks upon this—"It was believed in the middle ages that the emperor Constantine had given the Bishop of Rome his territory in Italy; though there was no truth in it, and no proof that there was any lordship belonging to the see before the age of Charlemagne."

Gower again alludes, in the Prologue to his Confessio Amantis, to—

> "The patrimonie and the richesse
> Which to Siluestre in pure almesse
> The firste Constantinus lefte."

There is actually a representation, in one of the grand frescoes in the Vatican, of Constantine bestowing the city of Rome upon pope Sylvester, A.D. 385; the date being as imaginary as the circumstance. See Mrs Jamieson's Sacred and Legendary Art, 3rd ed. pp. 687, 692.

Perhaps the most curious point about the story is that the death of Wyclif upon St Sylvester's day (Dec. 31, 1384) was interpreted as a judgment upon him for having defamed that pope.

227. (15. 526.) *Dymes*, tithes. Palsgrave has—"Dyme, tythe, *disme*." So in the Paston Letters, i. 543, the prior of Bromholm, speaking of "the commission that the Bysbop of Norwich sente us on Thursday laste paste to gader the *dymes*," complains that it "is a shrewde labour for us, a grete coste and a shrewde jupardy." It is worth noting that the term *dyme* was applied not only to the tithes due to the clergy, but to the tenths paid to a king by his subjects, or to a feudal lord by his vassals. Examples are:— "Tandem finis Parliamenti erat taxa levanda ad opus Regis, id est, *decima de clero*, et *quinta-decima* de populo laicali;" Walsingham, Hist. Anglic., ed. Riley, ii. 177. And Lacroix, in his Manners, Customs, and Dress during the Middle Ages, p. 35, observes that among the dues to the nobles were

"the *dime*, or tenth part of all the corn, wine," &c.   Cf. Lambarde, Perambulation of the County of Kent, ed. 1656, p. 55.

Wyclif appealed in strong terms to the temporal lords to take away from
the clergy all superfluous wealth; Works, iii. 478, 479. He also proposed
that the friars should be suppressed, because then "þe peple schulde better
paye her rentis to lordis, and *dymes* and offringis to curatis;" Works, iii.
401. He constantly maintained that tithes and offerings were amply sufficient
for the maintenance of priests; "for it were inowȝ to us to˙ have *offringis
and dymes*, siþ Crist and hise apostlis helden hem paied on lesse;" Works,
i. 199; see also i. 147, 282; iii. 513. His followers were of the same
opinion; see Historical Gleanings, 2nd Ser., p. 47, by J. E. Thorold Rogers.

234. (*not in* b.) This allusion has some bearing on the date of the C-
text. The expression is somewhat stronger than in the similar previous
passage; see note to Pass. xvi. 173, p. 311. The pope who is here spoken
of as engaging in war could hardly be Gregory XI., but it might very well
be Urban VI. or Boniface IX. The chronology is as follows:

Death of Gregory XI., and schism of the Popes, 1378.

The popes elected were Urban VI., recognised in England; and Clement
VII., anti-pope, recognised in France.   Urban VI. died in 1389.

Boniface IX. was elected in 1389.   Benedict, called the XIII., succeeded
Clement as anti-pope in 1394.

In 1379, Urban proclaimed a crusade against the anti-pope, and "took
into his pay the mercenary troop called the company of St George;" Engl.
Cyclopædia. This is most likely the circumstance referred to, and is consistent with the supposition that the date of the C-text is *after* 1379, whilst
that of the B-text is *before* it. Boniface was also involved in the Italian
wars, but these would be less known or cared about.

In any case, the present passage should be compared with Wyclif's Tract
De Pontificum Romanorum Schismate, whose remarks on the bull of pope
Urban, granting indulgences for the crusade against the anti-pope, seem to
be here, to some extent, followed. See Wyclif's Works, iii. 244, 246. The
date of Wyclif's tract appears to be 1382.

241. (*not in* b.) This assertion, that Mohammed's success was not
achieved by the sword, is remarkable for its wide deviation from the truth.
We must suppose that all the poet's knowledge about Mohammed was confined to the story of his teaching the dove; see notes to ll. 167, 171, p. 360.

252—254. These lines correspond to B. 15. 492—494.

258. (15. 535.) *In a false mene*, in a false mediator; see *mene* in Pass. x.
347, as compared with B. 7. 196. I note this because Dr Stratmann oddly
assigns to this word the sense of moan or complaint, with a reference to the
present passage. William's word for complaint is *mone*, which occurs in the
very line before this, and again in Pass. ix. 130 (b. 6. 125), which Dr Stratmann also cites, correctly.

261. (15. 538.) See note above, to l. 189.

267. (15. 545.) *Metropolitanus* was formerly commonly used as synony-

mous with *archiepiscopus;* see Ducange. It here seems to mean "chief
bishop" of all the world; Jerusalem being the original Christian metropolis.

274. (15. 551.) St Thomas of Canterbury, i. e. Thomas Becket, the most
famous of English saints. His shrine at Canterbury was continually visited
by crowds of pilgrims, not all of whom, as Chaucer testifies, were remarkable
for devotion. He was canonized in 1221, but at the Reformation his shrine
was dismantled, and the very name of the saint erased from the calendar.
So stringent were the orders to demolish the records of his name, that not
even the MSS. of Piers the Plowman have escaped. This line is much de-
faced in MSS. M and I (C-text), and in MS. R (B-text). For early notices
of him in English poetry, see Polit. Songs, ed. Wright, p. 325; and An Old
Eng. Miscellany, ed. Morris, p. 92.

276. (15. 554.) "And all holy church (was) honoured on account of that
death" [c]; "Holy church is highly honoured through his death" [b].

277. (15. 555.) *Forbusne,* example, pattern; in Pass. xi. 32, it means an
example or parable. I have inserted in the Critical Notes (C-text, p. 463)
Whitaker's odd misreading of this word.

278. (15. 556.) *Surrye,* Syria. This looks like a pointed personal allusion.

279. (15. 557.) *Huppe abowte,* dance about, skip from place to place.
Hoppen commonly means to dance in Middle English; indeed, a dance is
still called a *hop* in jocular speech. *Halewen menne auters,* to consecrate
men's altars. The allusion is to the very lucrative way in which titular
bishops could employ themselves, by consecrating churches, &c., and by
ordaining priests.

> "They halow no thing but for hire,
>   Church, ne font, ne vestement,
> And make orders in everie shire,
>   But priestes pay for the parchement."
> Ploughman's Tale; in Polit. Poems, ed. Wright, i. 311.

"Whate money get they by mortuaries, by hearing of confessions, . . . by
halowing of churches, altares, super-altares, chapelles, and belles?" A Suppli-
cacyon for the Beggers, by Simon Fish; ed. Furnivall (E. E. T. S.), p. 2.
See also Wyclif, Works, i. 282; and P. Plowm. Crede, l. 356.

280. (15. 558.) *Aȝen þe lawe,* against the law; i. e. contrary to the precept in the Mosaic law—"thou shalt not move a sickle into thy neighbour's
standing corn;" Deut. xxiii. 25. Cf. note to Pass. vii. 120, p. 111.

281. (15. 559.) *Among romaynes,* among the Romans [c]; *in Romanye,*
in Romania [b]. Romania, according to Ducange, was sometimes used
merely to signify Roman territory; and such, according to our author's own
interpretation, is the meaning here. St Paul and St Peter both suffered at
Rome, before Christianity was triumphant there. The argument is, that
missionaries must expect persecution, but ought not therefore to flinch from
their duties.

286. (*not in* b.) It would be difficult to trace whence these Leonine
verses are derived; indeed, William may himself have composed them. The
sense is—"In the shape of the crosier be this rule (evident) to thee, O

bishop; bear, lead, goad on the flock, preserving the law in all cases."
Presul is the vocative case; it often means a bishop (Ducange). The
allusion is to the bishop's staff or crosier; see note to Pass. xi. 92, p. 214.

——(15. 565.) *Osyas*, Hosea; called *Osee* in the Vulgate; the quotation,
however, is from Malachi, iii. 10; see l. 563.

——(15. 574.) "Love God and thy neighbour." The reference to Luke
x. 27 should have been added in the margin.

——(15. 575.) *Toke it moyses*, delivered it to Moses; see note to Pass.
iv. 47, p. 58; and cf. C. xx. 2, 74.

305. (*not in* b.) *Quatriduanus*, four days dead. The word is taken from
the Vulgate. "Domine, iam fetet, *quatriduanus* est enim;" Jo. xi. 39.

313. (15. 592.) *Hopen*, expect. "It signifies the mere expectation of a
future event, whether good or evil, as ἐλπίζω in Greek and *spero* in Latin
often do. So in Shakesp. Ant. and Cleop. (ii. 1. 38)—

> 'I cannot *hope*
> Cæsar and Anthony shall well greet together.' "
—Tyrwhitt's note to Chaucer, C. T. 4027.

See *Hope* in Nares, who cites the story of the Tanner of Tamworth (from
Puttenham's Arte of Poesie, bk. iii. c. 22, ed. Arber, p. 263), who said—"I
hope I shall be hanged tomorrow."

To comynge, to come; a corruption of the old gerundial form *to comenne*,
A.S. *to cumenne*. "Eart þu ðe *to cumenne* eart," art thou he that is to come?
Luke vii. 20.

315. (*not in* b.) "And have the expectation that they will be saved."

319. (15. 598.) "Prelates and priests (*or*, prelates of Christian provinces,
b) should endeavour, if they could, gradually to teach them the other
clauses."

*320. (15. 599.) *Lytulum and lytulum*, by littles and littles, gradually.
The first *lytulum* is miswritten *lytulhum* in the MS. here chiefly followed,
and is so printed in Whitaker's edition. Whitaker's amazing explanation,
perhaps seldom surpassed for boldness of guessing, is quoted in the Critical
Notes, C-text, p. 463. Compare—"On þæm wæron þreó clystru and ic
geseah þær on weaxende blósman *litlum and litlum;*" whereon were three
clusters, and I saw blossoms growing gradually thereon; Gen. xl. 10 (where
the Vulgate has *paulatim*).

SCHEME OF THE CONTENTS OF C. PASSUS XIX.
(B. Pass. XVI.)

Cf. Wright's Edition; pp. 330—347; ll. 10794—11368.

C-TEXT.	B-TEXT.	C-TEXT.	B-TEXT.
xix. 1—10	———	———	xvi. 105—109
———	xvi. 1—6	xix. 143	110
11	like 7	———	111, 112
12—30	———	144—148	113—117
———	8—26	149—151	like 118—120
31—41	27—37	———	121
———	38	152, 153	like 122, 123
42	like 39	———	124
43	40	154—156	125, 126
(a) 44	(a) [44]	157—161	———
45	41	———	127—131
———	42	162	132
46	43	163, 164	———
(a) [44]	(a) 44	———	133—135
47, 48	———	165	136
49	———	166, 167	———
———	45	———	137, 138
———	46—49	168	139
50	like 50, 51	———	140—150
51	———	169	———
52	52	170—175	151—156
53—84	———	176	———
———	53—66	———	157
85, 86	67, 68	177, 178	158, 159
87—89	———	179	———
———	69, 70	———	160—166
90	like 71	180	like 167
91—99	———	181, 182	———
100	72	———	168—171
101—103	———	183, 184	172, 173
———	73	185	like 174, 175
104	like 74	186, 187	176, 177
105—107	———	———	178, 179
108	like 75	188	like 180
109, 110	76, 77	189—194	———
———	78	———	181—185
111—117	79—85	195	186
118, 119	like 86	———	187
120—122	87—89	196	———
123	———	197	like 188
124—134	90—100	198—201	———
135, 136	———	———	189, 190
———	101	202—210	191—199
137	102	211—217	———
138	like 103, 104	———	200—204
139—142	———		

C-TEXT.	B-TEXT.		C-TEXT.	B-TEXT.
xix. 218, 219	*like* xvi. 205, 206			xvi. 229
220, 221	——		xix. 248—250	230—232
——	207—218		251	
222	219		252	*like* 233
223—234	——		——	234
235, 236	*like* 220, 221		253—259	235—241
237—241			260, 261	242
——	222—224		262, 263	243, 244
242	225		264—266	
243	——		——	245, 246
244	226		267, 268	247, 248
——	227		269	*like* 249, 250
245	228		——	251
246, 247	——		270—293	252—275

NOTES TO C. PASSUS XIX.   (B. PASS. XVI.)

19. 3. (*not in* b.) *Ladde—tales*, conducted me on my way, instructing me with tales as we went.

4. (*not in* b.) *Cor-hominis*, the heart of man; called "herte" in B. 16. 15. Man's heart is here likened to a garden in which the tree of Charity grows.

5. (cf. b. **16.** 15.) *Herber*, garden; Lat. *herbarium*, O.Fr. *herbier;* spelt *erber* in some MSS. of B-text; and in P. Pl. Crede, l. 166, we find the plural *erberes*. In Thomas of Erceldoune, ed. Murray, l. 177, is a description of a *herbere* in which grew pears, apples, dates, damsons, and figs. This word was afterwards confounded with *harbour* (Mid. E. *herberwe*), and, at a still later period, was misspelt *arbour* from a supposed connection with trees (*arbores*). See Dr Murray's note on the line.

6. (*not in* b.) *Ympe*, a graft, shoot, scion; but here used of a sapling or young tree. This tree, growing in Man's Heart, is called *Imago-Dei* (God's Image), otherwise "Trewe-loue," otherwise Patience [b]; its fruit is Charity, and it is supported on three props representing the three Persons of the Trinity. The blossoms of this tree are Kind Speech. Moreover, in the B-text, we are told that its root is Mercy, its stem is Ruth or Pity, and its leaves are the words that compose the Law of Holy Church.

The introduction of the three props betokening the Trinity (see ll. 20—26) shew that William had in his mind the old Legend of the Holy Rood, which tells us how the tree of which Christ's cross was made grew up from three stems, one of cedar, one of cypress, and one of pine. See Cursor Mundi, ll. 1417—1432, 6341—6343, 8005—8050, 8905—8976, 16547—16576, &c.; Legends of the Holy Rood, pp. 62—86, especially pp. 29, 77. See also a remarkable description of the Tree of the Trinity, in Joseph of Arimathea, ed. Skeat, ll. 181—201; The Legend of the Cross, in Curious Myths of the Middle Ages, by S. Baring-Gould, ii. 117, and the description of the Tree of Life, in the Ayenbite of Inwyt, p. 95. Cf. S. August. De Fide et Symbolo, ix. 17. Further references to articles on "The Tree of Life" will be found in Cowper's Apocryphal Gospels, pp. ci, cii.

——(16. 11.) *Saulee* (also spelt *saule, soule, saulees*) is rightly glossed by *edulium* in MS. Laud 581. Halliwell has—"*Sool*, anything eaten with bread; *North*. Anything used to flavour bread, such as butter, cheese, &c. is called *sowl* in Pembrokeshire. 'Tytter want ye *sowlle* then sorow;' Towneley Mysteries, p. 87. '*Edulium*, Anglice sowylle;' Nominale MS. And see *sowel* in Havelok, l. 767." *Souel* occurs in Wyclif's Works, i. 63, where it is misprinted *sonel*.

——(16. 25.) For *wyndes*, against winds. *To witen it*, to keep it. A mark of quotation should have been inserted before this latter phrase.

——(16. 26.) *Abite*, they bite (i. e. nip) the blossoms. The word *they* must be understood before *abite*; with reference to the winds.

The "three wicked winds" (c. 19. 29) are explained to mean the World, the Flesh, and the Devil. See the passage from The Myrour of Our Lady, p. 189 (already quoted in note to Pass. ii. 111, p. 35), where the north wind, being cold and *biting*, is compared to Lucifer.

32. (16. 28.) "Avarice comes from (is produced by) that wind (viz. the World), and it nips Charity" [c]; *or* "and creeps among the leaves" [b].

34. (16. 30.) "And with the first plank (*or* pile, b), which is the power of God the Father, I beat him down." The verb *palle* is very rare, but occurs in Joseph of Arimathea, ed. Skeat, 499, where it is said of a warrior that he "proude doun *pallede*," i. e. beat down the proud ones. The derivation may have been from the Latin *palus*, a stake, whence O.Fr. *pal*, a great stick, Eng. *pale*; in which case *palle* would mean to beat with such a stick. It is rather remarkable that, in the same poem of Joseph of Arimathea, the word *mallen*, to beat or hammer, occurs only 9 lines lower, l. 508. These words remind us of *Pall-Mall*, so named from its having been the place where the game of *pall-mall* (somewhat resembling the modern croquet) was played; see *Palemaille* in Cotgrave; and, for a representation of the old game, see Knight's Old England, vol. ii. fig. 2152. Yet it is well ascertained that the derivation of *pall-mall* is to be found in a partly different direction, and I only introduce this note to guard against a wrong inference. As a fact, the F. *palemaille* was borrowed from the Ital. *pallamaglio*; and, though *maglio* is really the Lat. *malleus*, the word *palla* means a ball, and was borrowed from the O. H. G. *palle*, a ball; whence also Ital. *pallone*.

44. (16. 44.) "And lays a ladder against it, the rungs of which consist of lies."

45. (16. 41.) *Waggeth the roote*, violently shakes the lower part of the trunk; as men do who try to shake fruit off a tree.

46. (16. 42, 43.) *Thorw*, by means of [c]. But in [b], the image is bolder. The devil is represented as throwing things up into the top of the tree of Charity, to knock the fruit down. (For *croppe* = top, see note to b. 16. 69, 376.) The things which he thus throws up are very remarkable; they are not ordinary sticks or brick-bats, but unkind neighbours,

backbiters, brawlers, and chiders. The word *breke-chesle* (written *breke þe chesle* in the Trinity MS.) is evidently used as an epithet of *backbiters*. As to the sense of it, I am thoroughly satisfied that it does not refer, as might appear at first sight, to any breaking open of chests or boxes. *Chesle* means here, as in several other passages (see Glossary), strife, dispute, quarrelling; compare Chaucer's Persones Tale, *De Ira*, where "the sinne of contumelie or strife and *cheste*" is spoken of not long before we are told that "homicide is also by *backbiting*." Whatever difficulty there may be in this epithet resides in the word *breke* rather than in *cheste*. We commonly speak of *breaking* the law, i. e. of offending against what is right; but *break* is also used in the sense of to vent, as in "to *break* one's mind," i. e. to declare it; "to *break* a jest," i. c. to utter a jest. See Todd's Johnson, ed. 1827; s. v. *Break*, in senses 13, 14, 23, 41. So here *breke-cheste* means, literally, an utterer of strife or debate, a venter of quarrelsome humour; or, since it is used as an adjective, we may equate it with "strife-venting," or, in more familiar language, "mischief-making." Thus *bakbiters breke-cheste* (or *breke the cheste*) simply means "mischief-making backbiters." Such men are the very ones to destroy neighbourly charity; cf. Prov. xvii. 14. That this is really the sense is, in my opinion, proved by comparing the parallel passage in B. xiii. 108, 109—

"And if ȝe fare so in ȝowre fermorie · ferly me þinketh
But *chest* be þere *charite shuld be* · & ȝonge childern dorste pleyne ! "

I. e. "and if ye go on like this in your infirmary, it seems to me a very strange thing if strife does not arise where charity ought rather to be found, if indeed young children might dare to utter complaints."

——(16. 46.) *Lelleth hym some tyme*, resists him for a while. So also *lelle* = resist, hinder, in l. 288 [c] below.

——(16. 47.) *Loken*, look to, guard; cf. B. i. 207. The second Latin sentence signifies—"This means the same as—he that sins by his own free will does not resist sin." Perhaps the reference is to Heb. xii. 4; see the discussion of this in the Critical Note, B-text, pp. 415, 416.

60. (*not in* b.) Compare Pass. xiii. 220—223.

63. (*not in* b.) "Nor gradually small, nor with one sweetness sweet." *Of sewynge*, in regular order, in perfect gradation or succession; from the verb *sewe*, or *sue*, to follow; see l. 72 below. The word *suant*, regular, is still used in Devonshire; see *souant* in Glos. B. 6, published by the Eng. Dialect Society. ·

78. (*not in* b.) "And more pleasing to our Lord than to live as nature suggests."

82. (*not in* b.) The Active Life and Contemplative Life are frequently contrasted in old authors. See note to Pass. xvi. 194, p. 313, and to B. vi. 251, p. 170.

84. (*not in* b.) *For a good skyle*, for a good reason. The three degrees or qualities of the fruit are explained to mean married life, widowhood, and virginity. This classification is clearly founded on Rev. xiv. 4, 5, and 1 Tim.

v. 3—14. So in a Fabliau entitled La Court de Paradis, quoted by Mr Wright at p. 50 of his St Patrick's Purgatory, there is a description of paradise, with its various mansions or chambers. One of these is "the chamber of virginity;" next which is that of such widows as had preserved their widowhood, and then that of married women. So also in Wyclif (Works, iii. 190)—"Neþeles, þouȝ matrimonye be good and gretly commendid of God, ȝit clene virgynite is moche betre, and wedlok [*read* widewehood] also, as Seynt Poul seiþ opynli." In Ælfric's Homilies, ed. Thorpe, ii. 93, 94, we find an exposition of the parable of the sower, attributed to St Augustine, which likens believing laymen, living in lawful wedlock, to the good seed that brought forth fruit thirtyfold; whilst those that continue in chaste widowhood are said to bring forth fruit sixtyfold, and pure virgins yield fruit an hundredfold. In Old Eng. Homilies, ed. Morris, 2nd Series, p. 44, we are told that the three Magi betoken the same three states. "Tres reges significant tres ordines in ecclesia, scilicet, Virginum, Coniugatorum, Continentium." See also Cutts, Scenes and Characters of the Middle Ages, p. 153, note.

——(16. 55.) "But I have a multitude of thoughts concerning these three supports."

——(16. 69.) "Then continence is nearer the top, like a bastard sweet pear." *Crop* = top, occurs in Chaucer's Kn. Tale, 674, and the 7th line of the Prologue, where it is very liable to be mistaken for "crops" in the modern sense. He also has *crop and rote*, top and root, in Troilus, ii. 348. See other examples in Stratmann.

Caleweis (plural) occurs in the Romaunt of the Rose, 7093, where the original has—"La poire du *cuillouel*," l. 12189 (Roquefort), or l. 12463 (Tyrwhitt). Roquefort has—"CAILLOS, *cailloel, caillouel :* Espèce de poire qui est remplie de grumelaux ou de petites pierres, et qui n'est bonne que cuite." This explanation is probably a mere guess, according to the method, too much in vogue, of falsifying or inventing an explanation in order to suggest an etymology. Burguy has—"*Caillou, chaillo, kaillo, caillau,* caillou ; Prov. *cahhau ;* dans le Berry *caille.* On a dérivé *caillou* de *calculus,* mais la disparition du premier *l* est inexplicable et contre la règle ;" after which follows a long and unsatisfactory discussion of the etymology. Cotgrave has—"*Caillouel,* the name of a very sweet pear." Also—"*Caillorosal,* a Lording apple; also, a certaine greene and great peare of a pleasant taste." It is clear that William meant a pear of this description, sweet and good to eat, and presumably soft, and not, as Roquefort absurdly suggests, one so stony as not to be fit for anything till cooked. The etymology is really very simple, but to be found in a very different direction. Lacroix, in his Manners, Customs, and Dress during the Middle Ages, p. 116, says—"Of pears, the most esteemed in the 13th century were the *hastiveau,* . . . the *caillou* or *chaillou,* a hard [?] pear, which came from Cailloux in Burgundy." Yet even here the epithet "hard" lingers, in accordance with Roquefort's suggestion. To me, it is clear that the hardness resided, not in the *pear*, but in the *soil* of Cailloux, which may very easily and reasonably have taken its name from the Fr. *caillou*, a flint.

Mr Furnivall sends me the following note, which seems conclusive. "*Chaillous*, poires de Cailloux en Bourgogne;" indeed, "Poires de Chaillou" occurs as a street-cry: see *Les Crieries de Paris*, par Guillaume de la Villeneuve (end of 13th century); in Fabliaux et Coutes, publiées par Barbazan, ed. Méon, 1808, ii. 279, l. 48.

The identity of *calewey* with the Fr. *caillouet* was pointed out by Herbert Coleridge, Phil. Soc. Trans. 1859, p. 72.

Why the epithet *bastard* was applied to this pear, I cannot say. Perhaps it may mean grafted, or cultivated. The former sense would suit with the notion of the engrafted portion being nearer the top. The latter sense is in accordance with Cotgrave's explanation of *Bastardiere* as "a seed-plot, nurse-garden, or nursery, wherein young trees are set to be afterwards removed." *Bastard*, in the sense of a sweet wine, is familiar to all readers of Shakespeare; see *Bastard* in Nares. Perhaps in this case also there is reference to some method of training the vines.

90. (16. 71.) *Angeles peer* [c]; *angeles peres* [b]. In [b], *peres* clearly means *pears*, from the context; see last note. In [c], the sense is less certain; *peer* may be the modern *peer* (Lat. *par*), a sense which is pointed to by the spelling and by the use of the equivalent word *euene*. Yet in l. 91 we have the word *frut*, fruit. On the whole, it seems fair to suppose that a pun was really intended on the words *peer* and *pear*; words which must once have been pronounced nearly alike. Indeed, we still keep *pair* as a doublet of *peer*, making a difference of sense and of sound where there was once no such difference.

In curious contrast to our text, let me quote Parolles—"Your virginity, your old virginity, is like one of our French withered pears, it looks ill, it eats drily; marry, 'tis a withered pear; it was formerly better; marry, yet 'tis a withered pear;" All's Well, i. 1. 174. Without pursuing the subject further, I may refer to the five pear-tree stories published for the Chaucer Society in Originals and Analogues, pt. ii. pp. 177—188.

93. (*not in* b.) *Fuireste þyng*, fairest work of creation, man; answering to *clennest creature* in the next line. So also *the furste þyng* must mean the Great First Cause, answering to *creatour* in the next line. See ll. 95—100.

97. (*not in* b.) *Hym*, to Christ; alluding to Luke viii. 3; xxiii. 56.

105. (*not in* b.) "Dear Free-Will, let somebody shake it." See *Lyf* in the Glossary.

107. (*not in* b.) *Ripen*, ripe ones; most MSS. have *ripe*. The retention of the final *n* is remarkable; it is the true old A.S. plural of the definite form of the adjective; *þe ripen* = A.S. *þá rípan*.

108. (16. 75.) "Old-age climbed towards the top," &c. [c]; "And Piers threw things towards the top," &c. [b]; that is, for the purpose of knocking down the fruit. In the top of the tree were placed the Virgins.

111. (16. 79.) "For ever, as soon as Old-Age had cast any down" [c];

"For ever, as they dropped down" [b]. The idea is, that the inhabitants of the tree retain life as long as they remain on it; but, by the attacks of Old Age, one after another drops off. Compare—

> "Meetest for death; the weakest kind of fruit
> Drops earliest to the ground;" Merch. of Venice, iv. 1. 115.

116. (16. 84.) *In limbo inferni*, in the verge of hell. "A *limbo* large and broad;" Paradise Lost, iii. 495. *Limbus patrum* was the name given to the supposed outermost circle of hell; from Lat. *limbus*, a border, hem of a garment. Dante describes it (Inferno iv. 45) as the residence of Virgil and of many good men who died unbaptized. The souls of the olden patriarchs, such as Adam, Abraham, Isaiah, Samuel, and Samson, above mentioned, were detained here till the descent of Christ into hell, when He released them, and led them to heaven. For the account of this, see Pass. xxi. 279—282, 451.

118. (cf. 16. 86.) "Then anger arose (bestirred itself) in the Majesty of God, so that God's Free-will seized the middle prop (the symbol of Christ), and hit after (i.e. struck in the direction of) the fiend, let the blow fall where it might." The graphic expression "hap how it might" means unsparingly, regardless of the consequence of the force of the blow.

122. (16. 89.) *Rageman* or *raggeman*, in this passage, means the devil. In Pass. i. 73 (see the note to that line) it means a papal bull. The fact is, that in Pass. i. it is a familiar abbreviation for *ragman-roll*, i.e. the devil's roll or the craven's roll, but in the present passage we have the word in its original form and sense. The best spelling is *ragman*, as in MS. Y [b], and the true sense seems to be a craven, a coward. Cf. Icel. *ragr*, craven, cowardly; *ragmenni*, a craven person; *ragmennska*, cowardice. To call a person *ragr* was to offer him the greatest possible insult; and *ragmæli* means an ignominious calumny, or the calling of a person *ragr*. "Ok bera þar upp *ragmæli* um Þorstein," i.e. and there to bring an ignominious accusation against Thorstein; Cleasby and Vigfusson's Icel. Dict. Then, as this was a term of the highest opprobrium, we find the Swedish *raggen* in common use for the devil. The successive senses may be thus arranged. *Rag*, cowardly; whence *ragman* (1) a craven, (2) the devil; whence again *ragman-roll*, (1) the craven's roll (which gives us the reason *why* the Scotch called the deeds of allegiance to Edward I. by that name); (2) a deed with seals, such as a papal bull, sometimes called *ragman* for the sake of brevity; (3) a game in which a roll was used, with strings supplying the place of the seals; (4) a long list or catalogue of names, as in P. Pl. Crede, 180 (unless it is there applied to the maker of such a list); (5) an unintelligible or tedious story, a sense preserved in the modern *rigmarole*. See *Rigmarole* in Wedgwood, and compare what I have already said above in the note to Pass. i. 73, p. 13.

See the long and interesting note on *Ragman* in Halliwell's Dictionary. He shews that the "blank charters" issued by Richard II. (see Shak. Rich. II. i. 4. 48) were also called *raggemans*. Also, that a good instance of *rag-*

man-roll in the sense of a pardoner's bull occurs in the Pardoner and Friar (Hazlitt's Old Plays, i. 234), where the Friar says to the parson—

> " Mayster parson, I marvayll ye wyll gyue lycence
> To this false knave in this audience
> To publish his *ragman-rolls* with lyes."

Further, a note to Collier's Preface to the World and the Child (Hazlitt's Old Plays, i. 241) speaks of a "last leaf of a tract, the running title of which is Ragmannes Rolle, and it purports to be a collection of the names and qualities of good and bad women in alternate stanzas."

I may add that Whitaker, in his short glossary, suggests that the word is properly *rage-man*, from *rage* and *man*. I will only say that "anger-man" is stark nonsense.

126. (16. 92.) *Iouken*, sleep, rest, slumber. This word, borrowed from the O.Fr. *jouchier*, F. *jucher*, is very rare in English. I believe it only occurs as a term in hawking. A hawk that went to roost was said to *jouke*. In the Termys of Haukyng, quoted by Strutt, Manners and Customs, ii. 123, we are told that it is proper to say "that your hauke *joketh*, and not sleepith." The same passage is quoted in Reliq. Antiq., i. 296.

Roquefort gives—" *Jouquer, jouquier :* se coucher, se reposer, percher, jucher." He also gives the form *jouchier*. Cotgrave has—" *Se jucher*, to roost, or pearch in a roost as pullein [poultry] do." He also spells it *joucher*.

127. (16. 93.) *Plenitudo temporis*, the fulness of time. "At ubi uenit plenitudo temporis, misit Deus Filium suum," &c.; Gal. iv. 4. See l. 139 below.

The narrative, up to l. 179, is full of allusions to the Gospels, but can so easily be followed that I need not point them out. See a similar enumeration of Christ's miracles in Castell of Love, ed. Weymouth, p. 61.

165. (16. 136.) *ȝorn*, ran; i. e. pervaded their minds, occupied their thoughts [c]; *was*, were [b]. In both texts, the verb is in the singular number. See similar examples in Shakespeare; Abbott's Shakespearian Grammar, 3rd ed., art. 336, p. 239.

166. (cf. 16. 137.) *Porsuede*, they pursued. Supply *they ;* cf. B-text.

168. (16. 139.) *Paske*, the Passover. Used by Wyclif, Matt. xxvi. 1. Hence Pask-flower, and Pask-eggs or Pace-eggs, i. e. Easter eggs. See Bardsley's Eng. Surnames, p. 34.

——(16. 140.) *There*, where. *Made his maundee*, i. e. washed His disciples' feet. "The Thursday before Easter is called *Maundy Thursday, dies mandati*, a name derived from the ancient custom of washing the feet of the poor on this day, and singing at the same time the anthem—'Mandatum novum,' &c.; John xiii. 34. . . . The notion was, that the washing of the feet was a fulfilling of this command; and it is so called in the rubric, *conveniunt clerici ad faciendum mandatum*. This rite, called *mandatum* or *lavipedium*, is of great antiquity, both in the Eastern and Western Church. During the middle ages, it was not only customary in monasteries, but with bishops, nobles, and even sovereigns, to wash the feet of the poor, and to distribute alms. In England, the rite of the Maundy continued to be performed by our sovereigns till the time of James II., who is said to have been the last sovereign who celebrated it in person. It is now customary for the Sovereign, through the Lord Almoner, to distribute alms at Whitehall chapel: and the form of prayer which is used on the occasion, and called 'the office for the Royal Maundy,' is given in the notes to Mr Stephens' edition of the Prayer Book, vol. i. p. 891, where may also be seen an account of the ceremonial in 1572, when Queen Elizabeth, being 39 years old, washed the feet of 39 poor persons on Maundy Thursday at the palace of Greenwich;" Humphrey on the Common Prayer, p. 179. See also *Maundy* in Wedgwood, and *Maundy Thursday* in the Index to the Parker Soc. publications. *Maundy*, for *mandatum*, occurs in Grindal's Works, p. 51; Hutchinson, p. 221, 259, 346; Tyndale, i. 259, iii. 236 (Parker Soc.). The derivation from *maund*, a basket, is wrong; it is given in Chambers, Book of Days, i. 411, q. v. Maundy Thursday was also called Shir Thursday or Sheer Thursday; see Wyclif's Works, i. 325, where the editor quotes the opinion of Nares, that it was so named from a custom of shearing heads on that day! But whatever the custom may have been in that respect, it has nothing to do with the name. Still worse is the explanation in the Index to the Parker Society's publications, that *sheer* is derived from *shrive*. The spelling *shir* shews at once that the word is our modern *sheer*, which formerly had the sense of pure, bright, clean, pure. Cf. Icel. *skírr*, clear, bright, pure, cleansed from guilt; *skíra*, to cleanse, to baptize; *Skír-dagr* or *Skíri-þórsdagr*, Maundy Thursday. See Rock, Church of Our Fathers, iii. pt. i. 235; pt. ii. 74, 84, 236; Wordsworth, Eccl. Biography, i. 617.

In the Coventry Mysteries, ed. Halliwell, p. 259, Peter says to Christ—"Lord, where wolte thou kepe thi maunde?"

178. (16. 159.) *Pees* [c] and *pays* [b] are merely different spellings of the same word, from O.Fr. *pais*, Lat. *pacem*, peace. The repetition of the words is a defect in the line, but we must remember that the two clauses are quite distinct. The line means—"Let my apostles remain undisturbed, and let them depart peaceably;" or, more briefly—"Let my apostles alone, and let them go in peace."

——(16. 165.) *Her botheres myghtes*, the powers of them both. *Her* = A.S. *hira*, of them. *Botheres* (also spelt *bother*, *beire*, see footnote) is the genitive plural. Cf. Pass. iii. 67; xxi. 374.

——(16. 166.) "Died, and destroyed death, and turned night into day." The last expression is explained by Pass. xxi. 129, 185, 369, 371, 454.

180. (16. 167.) Here the poet again awakes, and the Seventh Vision terminates. Immediately afterwards, the Eighth Vision begins, being the Vision of Faith, Hope, and Charity. It begins, namely, at l. 183 (b. 16. 172), where the dreamer is supposed to fall asleep upon Mid-lent Sunday, and at once to behold Abraham, the representative of Faith. Although no mention is here made of his falling asleep, the poet describes himself as awaking when the Vision ends; see Pass. xx. 332.

The subjects of the Eighth Vision are Abraham, representing Faith, ll. 184—289; Spes or Hope, ll. 290—xx. 46, and Charity (represented by the Good Samaritan), xx. 47—332.

183. (16. 172.) *Mydlentens Soneday,* Mid-lent Sunday; i. e. the fourth Sunday in Lent; Wheatley on the Common Prayer, p. 227.

188. (cf. 16. 180.) "What is his cognisance, as shewn on his coat-of-arms" [c]; *or,* "What (coat-of-arms) does that man bear? quoth I then; tell me; so may bliss betide you!" [b]. The person meant is Christ, or Piers the Plowman as he is called just above in the B-text (l. 171).

195. (16. 186.) *Sothfastnesse,* truth [b]. Compare the following. "I believe that there is not but one God almightie, and in this godhead, and of this godhead, are three persons, that is, the father, the sonne, and the *soothfast* holy ghost;" Examination of W. Thorpe; in Wordsworth, Eccl. Biog. p. 265.

199. (*not in* b.) "How one lord might live in three; I believe it not, I said." *A þre,* in three, occurs again in l. 214 below, which means "he is in three where he is."

218. (cf. 16. 205.) "Eve was of Adam, and taken out of him, and Abel proceeded from both; and all three are one nature" [c]. "Adam (was) the father of us all, Eve proceeded from him, and their issue was of them both; and each of them is the delight of the other, though in three separate persons" [b]. St Augustine, De Trinitate, lib. xii. c. 5 (Opera, ed. Migne, viii. 1000) mentions this comparison of the Trinity to husband, wife, and offspring; but he does not think it a good illustration.

224. (16. 219.) I can find no such text as this in the Bible; but it is clearly taken from the apocryphal gospel of the Nativity of Mary, to be found in the *Aurea Legenda,* very near the beginning. We there read that when Joachim (afterwards the father of Mary) appeared before the high priest, he was told that his offerings were unacceptable, as he had no children. The high priest added, that the Scripture says [which it does not], that "every one is accursed who hath not begotten male or female in Israel." See Cowper's Apoc. Gospels, p. 86. Accordingly, in the Cursor Mundi, l. 10265—10267, a passage which is taken from the same source, we find—

> "þan semis þe lagh, wit resun right,
> Biclepis þat man for maledight
> þat has na bairn, ne mai ne knaue "—

where *mai* = maid, female child.

The idea was no doubt founded on Gen. xxx. 23; 1 Sam. i. 6; Luke i. 25.

236. (16. 221.) *Moillere-is issue,* the wife's offspring [c]; the wife's children [b]. *Moillere* is Old French. Burguy gives—"*Moilier, moillier, muillier, muller, mouillier,* femme, épouse: *mulier.*" The ending *-is* (written a little apart from the word) is the suffix of the genitive case; and we may note here how completely words of foreign origin were subjected to English

grammar. The plan of writing the suffix a little apart from the word is not particularly uncommon in old MSS. Thus *sone-is* is put for *sones* = son's, in the Romans of Partenay, ed. Skeat, p. 9, l. 28. It also happens that *is* is often written for *his*, as in William of Palerne, ll. 8, 69, 181, &c. Hence arose a curious confusion, whereby such substitutions as *egle hys* for *egles* (eagle's) became common, towards the end of the fourteenth century; this particular example occurs A.D. 1387, in John of Trevisa's translation of Higden's Polychronicon, lib. i. cap. 41—"a-pon euerych rooch [*rock*] is an egle hys nest." See Specimens of English, 1298—1393, ed. Morris and Skeat, sect. xviii. *a.* l. 96, and the note. But besides this, the use of *his*, after a *proper name*, sprang up *independently*, for the sake of convenience of expression, as is apparent from the later text of Layamon; *in which case* it is not to be regarded as a mere mistake, but rather as an intentional periphrasis. See Sir F. Madden's Glossarial Remarks on Layamon, l. 1459; and an article in the Cambridge Philological Museum, vol. ii. p. 245. At a later period, the frequent use of *his* further suggested the use of *her* after feminine nouns, especially when proper names; see an example of this in the present poem, viz. *Felyce hir fayrnesse*, B. xii. 47. In the present passage, we have an excellent example of its use after an ordinary substantive, since the Laud MS. (B-text) has *moillere her*, as printed; though five MSS. omit the *her*, as noted. Lastly, the error arose, and is still current, of looking upon *his* as the *real origin* of the suffix of the genitive case, according to which odd notion *his* itself must be short for *he + his*, which again must be short for *he + he + his*, and so on, ad infinitum! Of course, such an explanation fails also in such words as *queen's*, *woman's*, and the like, and is inadmissible in Latin and German; so that it may safely be dismissed. With Eng. *fish's*, for example, from A.S. *fisces*, compare Ger. *fisches*, Mœso-Goth. *fiskis*, Old Frisian *fiskis* or *fiskes*, Icel. *fisks*, Lat. *piscis*.

242. (16. 225.) Compare Cursor Mundi, ll. 2703—2712.

> "Quen it was hate [*hot*], a-pon a tide,
> Abram satt his hus be-side,
> Bi-side þe wale of mont mambre,
> Loked him far and nere; sagh he
> Toward him com childir thre,
> Liknes o god in trinite;
> But on allan he honired o þaa [*of them*],
> As anfald [*one-fold*] godd and in na ma.
> The trinite he sagh bi þat sight;
> And gestend [*lodged*] þam wit him þat night."

The account followed seems to be that in Peter Comestor's Historia Scholastica, who says—"Apparuit dominus Abrae in conualle mambre. Cumque eleuasset oculos, *vidit tres* viros : et occurrens illis, *vnum ex eis adorauit*." He adds the explanation of Eusebius that the One adored by Abraham was God the Son, and that the other two were angels only. Cf. Gen. xviii. 2; John viii. 56. Compare—"And in that same place was Abrahames hous, and there he satt and saughe 3 persones, and worschipte but on, as holy writt seythe, *Tres vidit et unum adoravit*: that is to seyne, He saughe 3, and worschiped on;" Maundeville's Travels, ed. Halliwell, p. 66; copied from the narrative of Odoricus, p. 154; see Mätzner's note in his Engl. Sprachproben, ii. 184. The three angels have generally been regarded as a symbol of the Trinity; hence the expression in the text—"Where God came, going in three." But note the use of *he* (i. e. Christ) in l. 246. See Dict. of the Bible, s. v. *Angels*.

——(16. 229.) *Calues flesshe;* see Gen. xviii. 7, 8.

253. (16. 235.) *My sone,* i. e. Ishmael; Gen. xvii. 23.

257. (16. 239.) Cf. Gen. xii. 2; xiii. 16; xv. 5—16; xviii. 17, 18; Rom. iv. 13; Gal. iii. 8, 9; Luke i. 55.

263. (16. 244.) There is no such statement in the Bible; William was thinking of Melchizedek's offering of bread and wine; see Gen. xiv. 18. We are also told that Abraham built altars; Gen. xii. 7, 8; xiii. 18. Beyond this, there is no warrant for the expressions in the text. It is easy to see that William perceived, in the mention of "bread and wine" (Gen. xiv. 18), a token of the Holy Eucharist.

266. (*not in* b.) "I believe that that Lord is thinking of making a new law." *Thenke* is the 3rd pers. sing. of the pres. subjunctive.

267. (16. 247.) Abraham was God's herald here on earth, as being "the father of all them that believe;" Rom. iv. 11; cf. Gal. iii. 8. He is also called God's herald in hell, because, according to the belief that the early patriarchs dwelt in *limbo* till the time of Christ's descent into hell, it must have been his mission to announce to the rest the promise that in him should all families of the earth be blessed. See Gen. xii. 3; Gal. iii. 8, 16. His presence in hell is expressly alluded to in one version of the Apocryphal Gospel of Nicodemus; see Cowper's Apoc. Gospels, p. 301. Cf. note to l. 116 above.

273. (16. 255.) *Lazar,* a leper. Lepers were so named after Lazarus. Here, however, the reference is to no other than Lazarus himself, who is here said to be in Abraham's lap; as in Luke xvi. 22. The Lazarus of the parable can hardly be identified with the Lazarus (Eleazar) of Bethany. "The name of Lazarus has been perpetuated in an institution of the Christian church. The leper of the Middle Ages appears as a Lazzaro. Among the orders, half-military and half-monastic, of the 12th century, was one which bore the title of the Knights of St Lazarus (A.D. 1119), whose special work it was to minister to the lepers, first of Syria, and afterwards of Europe. The use of *lazaretto* and *lazar-house* for the leper-hospitals then founded in all parts of Western Christendom, no less than that of *lazzarone* for the mendicants of Italian towns, are indications of the effect of the parable upon the mind of Europe in the Middle Ages, and thence upon its later speech;" Dict. of the Bible. See the description of a "lazar-house" in Milton, P. L. xi. 479—493.

286. (16. 268.) *Or ligge,* or he must lie.

291. (16. 273.) "Quickly run the very way we went" [c]; "Quickly run forth; he went the same way" [b]. Or the line in [b] may mean—

"Quickly run forth the very way he (Abraham) went; which comes to the same thing."

The new object in William's vision is *Spes*, or Hope; see Pass. xx. 1.

SCHEME OF THE CONTENTS OF C. PASSUS XX.
(B. Pass. XVII.)

(Cf. Wright's edition, pp. 348—368; ll. 11369—12070.)

C-TEXT.	B-TEXT.	C-TEXT.	B-TEXT.
xx. 1—3	xvii. 1—3	xx. 107, 108 *like* xvii. 131, 132	
4, 5	——	——	133, 134
6—34	4—32	109, 110	135, 136
35, 36	*like* 33, 34	111, 112	——
37	——	——	137
38, 39	*like* 35	113—124	138—149
40, 41	——	125—127	——
——	36—42	——	150
42, 43	*like* 43, 44	128	151
44—51	45—52	129	——
52, 53	*like* 53	——	152—165
54—72	54—72	130	166
73	——	131—133	*like* 167
——	73—75	134	168
74, 75	*like* 76, 77	135, 136	*like* 169
76—78	78—80	137—139	——
——	81—83	——	170—172
79	*like* 84	140—145	173—178
——	85—87	146	——
80	*like* 88	147—156	179—188
——	89	——	189—191
81—83	90—92	157—172	192—207
84, 85	*like* 93	173	——
86	*like* 94	174—194	208—228
(a) [89]	(a) *like* 95	195, 196	*like* 229, 230
87, 88	96, 97	197—228	231—262
(a) 89	(a) [*like* 95]	229	——
90, 91	*like* 98—101	230, 231	263, 264
92, 93	——	232—246	——
——	102—123	247—272	265—290
94—97	124—127	273, 274	*like* 291
98—100	*like* 128—130	——	292
101—106	——	275—332	293—350

NOTES TO C. PASSUS XX. (B. Pass. XVII.)

C. 20. 1. (B. 17. 1.) *Spes*, Hope; the expectation of the Messiah's coming. Hence he is called "a spy," i. e. a scout. *Spire after*, enquire about, seek information concerning. *Knyght*, i. e. Christ; see l. 8.

In a note to the alliterative Troy-book, l. 823, Mr Donaldson remarks that to "spere *at*" a person, is to ask him (something); to "spere *for*" a person, is to inquire for him, or ask after his welfare; and "to spere *after*" a person, to ask for information regarding him, such as where and how he is, or what he is about.

2. (17. 2.) *Tooke*, gave; as in l. 74 below. *Maundement*, commandment, i. e. the Mosaic law; see l. 60 below.

4. (*not in* b.) *Latyn*, the Vulgate version. *Ebrew*, the Hebrew original.

7. (17. 5.) *Nay;* i. e. it is *not* sealed. The Law was to be fulfilled by the death of Christ, and its spirit confirmed by the giving of "a new commandment."

8. (17. 6.) Observe how the texts differ by transposing the words *criste* and *croys*. The B-text describes the seal as representing the cross and Christendom (i. e. baptism?) and the figure of Christ hanging upon the cross. In the C-text, it would seem that Christ is the keeper of the seal, Christendom the seal itself, and the cross the impression upon it; in which case the words "there-on to hang" refer to the seal with its impress, since the old seals hung down from the deeds to which they were attached.

10. (17. 8.) "That Lucifer's dominion would lie full low" [c]; *or,* "shall last no longer" [b]. The death of Christ destroyed Lucifer's power.

12. (17. 10.) "*Letters Patent* are writings, sealed with the Great Seal of England, whereby a man is enabled to do or enjoy that which otherwise of himself he could not. *Anno* 19 *Hen.* 7, *cap.* 7. And they are so called, because they are *open*, ready to be shewed for confirmation of the authority thereby given;" Blount's Law Dictionary. Thus a *patent* is like what we should now call a *license*.

A pece an harde roche; alluding to the tables of stone on which the Mosaic law was written.

13. (17. 11.) *Wordes*, i. e. precepts. *Glosede*, glossed, explained; see l. 15.

18. (17. 16.) "No devil shall harm him." See Pass. x. 38, and the note, p. 184.

21. (17. 19.) "Faith" [c]; "this herald" [b]. See Pass. xix. 267, and the note, p. 383.

22. (17. 20.) *In my lappe;* see Pass. xix. 273, and the note, p. 383. *That leyuede*, them that believed; cf. l. 30.

23. (17. 21.) See the apocryphal books of Judith and the Maccabees.

25. (17. 23.) *Wher eny of ȝow*, whether either of you? i. e. can it be that either of you? [c]; see [b].

27. (17. 25.) *Abraham;* see Pass. xix. 242.

30. (17. 28.) "And (hath) saved (them) that so believed, and (are) sorry for their sins."

33. (17. 31.) "So to believe and be saved" [c]; "for salvation and bliss" [b].

42, 43. (17. 43, 44.) The texts differ not only in language, but in argument. "But to believe in one Lord that dwells in Three Persons, and who moreover teaches us that we ought to love liars as much as true men" [c]. "It is easier to believe in Three lovely Persons than to love and believe rascals as much as true men" [b]. The passage is badly altered, and becomes inconsistent in [c]. Instead of declaring, as in [b], that Hope's law is harder than Abraham's, the author rather clumsily attributes to Hope an opinion which is a mixture of the two laws.

47. (17. 48.) *Samaritan.* This is the Good Samaritan of St Luke's parable. He here appears as the representative of *Charity,* since we have been already introduced to Faith and Hope. He is, in the C-text, little more than a mere abstraction, and not, as in the B-text, Christ himself veiled in human flesh by the Incarnation. Towards the end of the Passus, Charity degenerates into an uninteresting instructor in dogmatic theology.

49. (17. 50.) St Luke represents the unfortunate traveller as going *towards* Jericho. William here supposes the Samaritan to be coming *from* it, and to meet him. For the explanation of the parable, in a form like that which William adopts, see Old Eng. Homilies, ed. Morris, 1st Ser., pp. 78—85, in a homily "De Natali Domini." The traveller is Adam; the thieves, the devils; the priest, one of the patriarchs (here Abraham); the Levite, Moses; the Samaritan, the incarnate Saviour. See also Wyclif's Works, i. 33, and cf. note to l. 57 below.

50. (17. 51.) The Samaritan is characteristically represented, in the true fourteenth-century style, as going to Jerusalem for the purpose of taking part in a tournament. See the description of Christ's tournament with Death in Pass. xxi. *Iacede away,* jounced along, jaunced along. "*Jounce,* to bounce, thump, and jolt, as rough riders are wont to do;" Forby. Cf. Shakespeare's "*jauncing* Bolingbroke;" Richard II. v. 5. 94; and our *jaunt, jaunty.* Cotgrave has—"*Ianser vn cheval,* to stirre a horse in the stable till he sweat [*misprinted* swart] with-all; or as our to jaunt." See Bale, Pageant of Popes, fol. 127, as quoted in Richardson, for a quotation where *iaunted* = jolted (on a horse's back). The Prompt. Parv. has—"Iowncynge, or grete vngentylle mevynge, *Strepitus.*" At first, the poet wrote *chaced* [b]; in [c], he ventured on what seems to be a (partially) coined word, to make the alliteration more exact.

55. (17. 55.) *Semiuiuus,* half alive; Luke x. 30 (Vulgate). Our version has "half dead."

56. (17. 56.) The proverb "as naked as a needle" has occurred before; Pass. xv. 105; see note, p. 290.

57. (17. 57.) Here William identifies the "priest" of the parable with Faith or Abraham; the Levite, with Hope; and the Samaritan, with Charity. But he merely followed a received interpretation. See note to l. 49 above.

58. (17. 58.) *Nyne londes lengthe,* the length of nine fields, as we might now say; no definite distance, but rather far.

62. (17. 62.) *Dredfulliche,* in great terror. Observe the reading of [b]—"as the (wild) duck does from the falcon."

64. (17. 64.) *Lyarde*, a common name for a horse, properly of a gray colour; see "*liart, liarde*, gris, gris-pommelé," in Burguy, which corresponds clearly to Chaucer's "pomely gray;" Prol. l. 616. "Thou shalt ride sporeles [spur-less] o thy *lyard;*" Ballad on Rich. of Almaigne (Harl. MS. 2253), in Percy's Reliques. See *Liard* in Halliwell; Tyrwhitt's note to Cant. Tales, l. 7145; Richard Coer de Lion, l. 2330, and note in Weber's Met. Rom., iii. 355. Weber quotes an old Italian poem shewing that that colour was highly esteemed for horses.

> "Fra li colori il *liardò pomato*
> Ottien la palma," &c.

Burns uses *lyart* for gray; Holy Fair, st. 2; Cottar's Sat. Night, st. 12. And see a poem on "Lyarde" in Rel. Antiq., ii. 280. See also note to l. 70 below.

67. (17. 67.) "And unless he had a recovery very soon, he would never rise again."

68. (17. 68.) *Vnbokeled*, unbuckled, undid [c], as in Chaucer, Pers. Prol. 26; *breyde*, hastened [b]. *Atamede*, broached; see Prompt. Parv., p. 16.

70. (17. 70.) *Bayarde*, properly a bay horse [c]. As the same animal is called *lyarde* only six lines above, and again in six lines below, we see that both terms were used in a general sense. The B-text has—"and laid him in his lap."

71. (17. 71.) *Lauacrum*, a bath; probably in allusion to the baptismal font. William here, however, makes "Lauacrum Lex Dei" the name of a grange [c]; called "Lex Christi" in [b]. The grange of course represents the church of Christ. "What is this inn? It is holy church;" Old Eng. Hom., ed. Morris, 1st Ser., i. 84.

Graunge, a grange, a farm-house; especially a lone farm-house with its barns, stables, &c. "Graunge or a lytell thorpe, *hameau;*" Palsgrave. So many abbeys were (I suppose in Henry VIII.'s time) turned into granges that "to bring an abbey to a grange" passed into a proverb. See Skelton, ed. Dyce, i. 327; ii. 285. The word is used by Chaucer (C. T. 3668); Shakespeare (M. for M., iii. 1. 277; Wint. Ta., iv. 4. 309; Oth., i. 1. 106); &c. Massinger has it, for a solitary house.

> "No, sir, removed to a *grange* some two miles off;"
> Believe as You List, ii. 1. 18.

"*Grange* is a French word, meaning properly a barn, and was applied to outlying farms belonging to the abbeys. The manual labour on these farms was performed by an inferior class of monks, called lay-brothers, who were excused from many of the requirements of the monastic *rule* (see Fleury, *Eccl. Hist.*), but they were superintended by the monks themselves, who were allowed occasionally to spend some days at the grange for this purpose;" note in Bell's Chaucer (Milleres Tale).

72. (17. 72.) Introduced to express the solitary character of the grange. *Besyde*, i. e. away from. *Newe markett*, market-town.

74. (17. 76.) "And gave two pence to the inn-keeper, to take care of him" [c]; "and gave him two pence, for his nourishment, as it were" [b].

The pence were *silver* pennies; see line above in [b].   There was no copper coinage of pence in England till the seventeenth century.

75. (17. 77.) *That goth mor*, whatever more is required [c]; *he speneth more*, he spends more [b].   *Make the good*, make good to you, will repay you.

——(17. 81.) *Spaklich*, nimbly; see Pass. xxi. 10, and the note.

——(17. 85.) "And offered to become his servant."

88. (17. 97.) Of course an allusion to the Sacrament of the Lord's Supper.

89. (17. 95.) *And ȝut, &c.*, and moreover be plaistered with Patience, when temptations assail him [c].   Alluding probably to the proverb— "Patience is a plaister," i. e. is an excellent remedy.   Hazlitt gives it in the form—"Patience is a plaister for all sores."   Plaisters were much used at a time when sword-wounds, &c. were so common.   Canacee applied them to the falcon (Sq. Ta., 636)—"And softely in *plastres* gan hir wrappe."   Cf. Pass. xxiii. 310, 314.

90. (17. 99.) *Rifled*, robbed; i. e. deprived of grace by the assaults of the world, the flesh, and the devil.   "These three, like three robbers, fight against each believing man as long as we wander in the wilderness of this world;" Old Eng. Homilies, ed. Morris, 1st Ser., 242.   In [c], ll. 90, 91 are parenthetical.

——(17. 102.) *Lotyeth*, lurk.   The word *lotynge* in Chaucer (Group G. 186) is glossed by *latitantem* or *latitans* in four MSS.

——(17. 107.) "On my horse called Flesh."   Compare—"Then he [the Samaritan] brought him on his own beast, that is, a rude mare; which denoteth our vile flesh whensoever we have made the body subject to the soul;" Old Eng. Hom., ed. Morris, i. 84.

——(17. 108.) *Vnhardy*, timid, fearful; alluding to Satan.   *Harlot*, knave; see Trench's Select Glossary, and note to Pass. v. 113, p. 81.

——(17. 109.) *Thre dayes;* alluding to the texts Mat. xxvii. 63, Mark viii. 31.

94. (17. 124.) *Shul nat we,* are we not to? [c].   *Wher shal I*, whether shall I, am I to? [b].

96. (17. 126.) *A parceles*, in separate parts, i. e. Persons [c].   See l. 28 above.

101. (*not in* b.) *Noþer lacky ne alose*, neither to blame nor praise.

110. (17. 136.) This supposed proof of the Trinity, from a fancied analogy with the fist, palm, and fingers of the hand, was no doubt borrowed from an older source; but I am unable to point it out.

112. (17. 138.) *Ferde furst*, fared first, acted first.   *And ȝut is*, and still is like one.

"The line 'mundum pugillo continens' is the third line of the third stanza of the hymn 'Quem terra, pontus, sidera,' given in the Roman Breviary at Matins in the Office of the Blessed Virgin.   It is ascribed by Cornelius Schulting (ob. 1604) to Fortunatus, and by Michael Timotheus (flor. 1580) to Pope S. Gregory I [apud Gavanti, Thesaur. Sacror. Rit., t.

2. sect. 5. cap. 6]. In the Roman Breviary, the hymn appears in its modern form; in the 'prymer of Salysbury,' at Matins of the Blessed Virgin, it is given with the old readings and spellings;" note kindly communicated by Rev. J. A. Smith, Blair College, Aberdeen. See Daniel's Thesaur. Hymnolog., i. 172. The idea is taken from Isaiah xl. 12.

——(17. 160.) "Both sky and wind, water and earth." See note to Pass. xi. 130, p. 218.

——(17. 164.) *Serelepes*, separately. Or it may be the pl. adj. meaning "separate things;" but it is well known that the suffix *s* is seldom added to adjectives unless they are of *Latin* origin. Besides, *Serlepess* is clearly an adverb in the Ormulum, ed. White, p. 15, l. 513; p. 17, l. 573. See *sere* in the second line of the quotation in the note to l. 168 below, and consult the Glossary.

133. (17. 167.) *Shepper*, creator [b]. "The line 'Tu fabricator omnium' is the first line of the second stanza of the hymn 'Jesu saluator saeculi.' It appears in the office for Compline of the Salisbury Breviary, or of the Aberdeen Breviary;" note communicated by Rev. J. A. Smith.

139. (*not in* b.) The Latin line here quoted is the 10th line of the very well-known hymn beginning—"Ueni Creator Spiritus." See Daniel, Thesaur. Hymnolog., i. 213.

146. (*not in* b.) *Beo he*, if he be. *Let falle*, lets (it) fall, referring to *al þat* in the preceding line. *Let* is the 3 p. s. present, contracted from *leteth*, as in B. xv. 168. The sense is made a little clearer by altering the comma after *liketh* in l. 144 to a semi-colon.

159. (17. 194.) *Oken*, ached. Cf. "she said her head *oke;*" Knight of La Tour Landry, ed. Wright, p. 8. The glossary wrongly says "*oke*, to ache;" but it is the past tense. So also *oc*, Layamon, 6707; and in O. Eng. Hom., ed. Morris, ii. 21, l. 26; and *ok*, Rob. of Glouc., ed. Hearne, 68, 18.

168. (17. 203.) The Trinity was often likened to the sun. Thus, in Cursor Mundi, l. 291—

> " In the sune that schines clere
> Es a thing and thre thinges sere [*separate*];
> A bodi rond, and hete, and light,
> Thir thre we find al at a sight."

The same is said in Ælfric's Homilies, ed. Thorpe, i. 283 (cf. i. 279) in a sermon De Fide Catholica. This is probably from St Augustine, who says—"Ignis, splendor, et calor simul atque inseparabilia, nec distincte, sed æqualiter habitant unam lucernam, et una Trinitas Deus simul non potest inhabitare animam humanam?" S. Aug. Sermo de Quarta Feria, cap. vi; ed. Migne, vi. 692. And again—"Ecce in igue quædam tria conspicimus; ignem, splendorem et calorem; et cum sint tria, unum lumen est. . . . Et hæc non confuse unum sunt, nec disiuncte tria, sed cum unum sint, tria sunt . . . Nam cum ad ignem refers ustionem, ibi operatur et splendor et calor; &c." S. Aug. De Symbolo Sermo ad Catechumenos, cap. ix. ed. Migne, vi. 659; cf. 692.

But the following quotation comes still closer to our text. "For in the tapre be three things, the matter, and use, and disposition and shape; and the matter is treble, as Isidore saith, the waxe, wike, and fire. The wike is made of hempe thrid, and the ground and fundament of the taper; and the waxe compasseth the wike, and findeth [*provides for, sustains*] and nourisheth the fire, that is lyght, and is end and complement of either. For it worketh in the waxe and in the wike, and turneth them into his owne likenes; and things of diuers kinde haue within themselues wonderfull and most couenable vnitye;" Batman upon Bartholomè, lib. xix. cap. 62. This chapter is headed "De Cereo," with a reference to Isidore, lib. xx; but Isidore merely says—"Cereus per derivationem a *cera* nomen habet, ex quo formatur;" S. Isidori Hispalensis episcopi Etymologiarum lib. xx. c. 10.

A *torch* was a large twisted wreath of tow, or a twisted candle. "*Torche*, Cereus;" Prompt. Parv. "Cierges, *torchys*, priketz," &c.; Riley, Memorials of London, p. 301, where *Cierges* are wax-tapers: on the same page *wyke* occurs as the old spelling of *wick*.

179. (17. 213.) "Without flame and light, if fire lies (remains) in the match" [c]; *or*, "that burns away the match" [b].

180. (17. 214.) This line and the next are (nearly) repeated below; see l. 214 (b. 17. 248).

194. (17. 228.) Compare—"Lacrima compassionis est tepida sicut aqua nivis, quæ defluit ad calorem solis;" Old Eng. Hom., ed. Morris, ii. 150.

203. (17. 237.) *Aseth* [c]; *assetz* [b], i. e. assets. The spelling *aseth* or *asseth* is the usual one. We find *asseth*, Rom. Rose, 5600, where the original French has *assez*; *assethe*, i. e. restitution, recompense, compensation, in Relig. Pieces, ed. Perry, p. 6, l. 24; *assethe*, Pricke of Conscience, ll. 3610, 3747, where Dr Morris notes—"This is the earlier form of our 'assets.' We find other O.Eng. forms such as *assyth*, *syth*, *sithe*, &c. A.S. *sæd*, *sade*, satisfied; Germ. *satt*, full; Icel. *sætt*, reconciliation.

'And who so harmes any man in his nede,
Sal noȝt be safe, bot he make *asseth* at his power.'
Castle of Love, ed. Weymouth, p. 107."

Note also "Acethen (*or* acethe, *or* aceth) for trespas, *Satisfactio*:" Prompt. Parv., p. 5. Jamieson gives the verb to *assyth*, *syith*, or *sithe*, to compensate; and *assyth*, *syth*, or *assythment*, compensation. *Aseeth*, satisfaction, occurs in Wyclif's Bible, and in his Works, ed. Arnold, i. 17, 55.

In Dr Morris's note above, there is, I think, a contradiction. If *aseth* be connected with A.S. *sæd*, it cannot also be related (at any rate nearly) to Icel. *sætt*, which is A.S. *saht*, reconciliation. Rather is it to be referred to Icel. *seðja*, to satiate, Gothic *saths*, full; which accounts for the *th*. And this *th*, by Grimm's law, answers to the *t* in Lat. *satis*, and shews that *aseth* is not derived from Lat. *satis*, but is cognate with it. From the Low-German root *sath-* we get the Mid. Eng. *aseth*, and from the cognate Latin root *sat-*, we have the French *assez*.

214. (17. 248.) Repeated from above; see l. 180.

216. (17. 250.) *Beo*, i.e. if thou be. It is a supposition, not a command; cf. note to l. 146 above, p. 389.

218. (17. 252.) *Paumpelon*, Pampeluna, the old capital of the kingdom of Navarre.

232. (*not in* b.) Such was no doubt the usual view taken of the character of Dives. "And marke we how þis gospel telliþ þat þis riche man was not dampned for extorsioun or wrong þat he dide to his neiʒborp, but for he failide in werkes of mercy;" Wyclif's Works, i. 3.

240; 244. (*not in* b.) *Atemye*, attain. This curious spelling is borne out by the frequent occurrence of *manteme* or *manteym* in Lowland Scotch, where we should now write *maintain*. Thus Barbour has *manteym*, Bruce, x. 779; *manteyme*, xi. 318, 401; &c. Similarly, for *renowme* we now write *renown*.

247. (17. 265.) *Reward*, regard. "Take note of this" [c]; "pay regard to him" [b].

249. (17. 267.) *Hyse*, His (i. e. God's) servants; the final *e* denoting a plural; however [b] has *his*. *Hope*, expect; see note to Pass. xviii. 313, p. 371.

251. (17. 269.) *Kid*, manifested, made known [c].

259. (17. 277.) "To reverence the Trinity therewith." A taper represents the Trinity, and similarly good men may be represented by so excellent a symbol.

260. (17. 278.) *Morthereth*, murders. Walsingham has the remark— "occultus iugulator, quales *mordrerers* appellant Anglici;" Hist. Anglic., ed. Riley, ii. 196 (*sub anno* 1390).

274. (cf. 17. 291.) *Lyf*, man; as elsewhere. "Will love that man who destroys love and true charity." Here *destruyen* is the author's slip for *destruyeth*, due to the verb being near to *two* objective cases. Such slips are common in English authors.

275. (17. 293.) *Ich pose*, I put the case. *Shold nouthe deye*, had now to die, were now about to die.

284. (17. 302.) *Ther þat partye porsueth*, where the (injured) party prosecutes. *Apeel*, appeal, accusation; spelt *pele* [b], which is miswritten *peple* in several MSS.; see footnote in [b]. "Appeal (Fr. *Appel*) is as much as accusation with the civilians . . . *Appeal* is a lawful declaration of another man's crime (which, by *Bracton*, must be felony at least) before a competent judge, by one that sets his name to the declaration, and undertakes to prove it, upon the penalty that may ensue of the contrary;" Blount's Law Dictionary. Cf. Shak. Rich. II. i. 1. 9.

286. (17. 304.) This quotation has occurred before; see note to Pass. vii. 257, p. 123.

88. (17. 306.) *Til hem forsake synne*, till sin at last leaves them, viz. at death [c]; till life leaves them [b]. This rather curious use of *forsake* is exactly parallel to the expression in the last line of Chaucer's Doctours Tale :—

"Forsaketh sinne, or [*ere*] sinne yow forsake."

Chaucer, by the way, repeats the expression near the beginning of his Persones Tale, where he says—"And therfor repentant folk, that stinte for to sinne, and forlete sinne or that sinne forlete hem, holy chirche holdeth hem siker of her saluation."

292. (17. 310.) "Not through the non-power (i. e. lack of power) of God." *Nounpower* is opposed to *power* in Chaucer's translation of Boëthius, ed. Morris, p. 75. So too—"there as lacketh his power, his *nonpower* entereth;" Testament of Love, book ii; ed. 1561, fol. ccc, back, col. 2.

295. (17. 313.) *Restitucion hit maketh*, restitution causes it, *or* is the cause, viz. of God's justice turning to mercy [c]; "some restitution is necessary" [b].

297. (17. 315.) Perhaps the original form of this commonly quoted proverb is this:—"Tria sunt enim quæ non sinunt hominem in domo permanere : fumus, stillicidium, et mala uxor;" Innocens Papa, de Contemptu Mundi, i. 18. It is a mere compilation from Prov. x. 26, xix. 13, and xxvii. 15. Again—"Tria sunt, quæ expellunt hominem de domo, scilicet fumus et stillicidium et mala uxor; de quibus etiam Salomon dixit, 'Melius est habitare,' &c. (Prov. xxi. 19);" Albertani Brixiensis Liber Consolationis, ed. Sundby, p. 15. This work is the original of Chaucer's Tale of Melibeus, where we find—"of which women men sain that three things driven a man out of his hous, that is to say, smoke, dropping of raine, and wicked wives; and of swiche women Salomon sayth," &c. Chaucer again quotes it in his Prologue to the Wyf of Bathes Tale—

> "Thou saist, that dropping houses, and eek smoke
> And chyding wyues, maken men to flee
> Out of her owne hous."

And yet again, in his Pers. Tale, he quotes Solomon's parallel between "an hous that is uncouered in rayn and dropping, and a chyding wyf;" *De Ira.*

In Kemble's Salomon and Saturn, p. 43, we have in Old High German—

> "Eyn rynnende húss, eyn bósse wíp,
> Kortzent dem goden man sýnen líp."

I. e.
> A dropping house, an evil wife
> Cut short the goodman's weary life.

At p. 53 of the same, we have in Latin—"Domina irata fumus ad ratta patella perforata damnum sunt in casa." And at p. 63, Kemble further refers us to Collins, Span. Proverbs, p. 179; Grüter, p. 153, Prov. Ital.; Gartner, Dict. Prov., p. 34. b. See also Shakespeare, 1 Hen. IV. iii. 1. 160.

Walter Mapes (ed. Wright, p. 83, cf. p. 297) has it in his Latin poem entitled Golias de Uxore non ducenda—

> "Fumus, mulier, et stillicidia,
> Expellunt hominem a domo propria."

Mr Wright further quotes it in French—

> "Fumée, pluye, et femme sans raison
> Chassent l'homme de sa maison."

See also Hazlitt's Proverbs, pp. 114, 339; and, in particular, the collection of similar proverbs in the Sprichwörter der Germanischen und Romanischen Sprachen, by Ida von Düringsfeld, vol. i. sect. 303. Probably William took it from Peter Cantor, as he gives nearly the same interpretation of the three evils. "Eiiciunt enim hominem de domo·hæc tria: primo, litigiosa uxor, i. e. carnis tentatio; hinc fumus, peccatum ignorantiæ; deinde stillicidium, aliena quæque suggestio extrinseca;" ed. Migne, col. 331.

304. (17. 322.) *Wors to slepe*, to sleep worse, i. e. less. To understand this, we must remember the pungent-effects of the smoke of imperfectly dried wood in houses with no proper chimney; see the effects described in l. 306.

306. (17. 324.) *Bler-eyed*, blear-eyed [c]; *blere-nyed* [b]. The prefixing of an *n* is common in English, and is probably due in some cases to the *n* in the word *an*, as in *a newt* for *an ewt*. At any rate we find *neyes* for *eyes*, as when a bear is described "with his two pinke *neyes*" in a quotation given in Jesse's History of the British Dog, vol. ii. Halliwell's Dict. gives *nall*, an awl; *nangnail*, a hangnail; *nuye* (Mid. Eng. *ey*), an egg; *neme* (Mid. Eng. *eme*), an uncle; *nif* (clearly short for *an if*) if; *ningle*, an ingle; *nover*, high land above a precipitous bank, clearly from A.S. *ofer*, Mid. Eng. *over*, a bank; *nye*, an eye; *nynon*, eyes. So, too, *at the nale* for *at then ale*; *for the nonce* for *for then once*; and Nan, Ned, for Ann, Edward. Lydgate has *nasse* for *ass* in his Chorl and Bird, st. 47. Almost as often the initial *n* is dropped, as in *apron* for *napron*, *ouch* (Spenser) for *nouch*, *umpire* for *numpire* (Mid. Eng. *nompere*); *auger* for *nauger* (see *navegor* in Halliwell); *eyas hawk* for *nias hawk* (see *nias* in Halliwell); *orange* for *norange*, Spanish *naranja*; and probably *adder* for *nadder*, A.S. *nædre*, though Wedgwood seems to doubt this, and refers us to A.S. *atter*, poison, without explaining how the *tt* turned into *dd*. I would suggest that the word *really* derived from *atter* is *natter-jack*, a name given to a kind of toad, which may well have been once an *atter-jack*; cf. A.S. *atter-coppa*, a poison-head, i.e. a spider. Cf. note to Pass. i. 43, p. 8.

307. (17. 325.) "Coughs, and curses (saying) may Christ give them sorrow." Cf. B. v. 107.

312. (17. 330.) "And though it (lit. he, i. e. the flesh) fall into sin, it discovers reasons (excuses), as, e. g. that frailty caused it to fall."

327. (17. 345.) "But he may love, if it please him, and lend good will and a good word out of his heart, both to wish and desire mercy and forgiveness for all conditions of men."

SCHEME OF C. PASSUS XXI.   (B. Pass. XVIII.)

Cf. Wright's edition, pp. 369—395; ll. 12071—12959.

C-TEXT.	B-TEXT.	C-TEXT.	B-TEXT.
1—5	1—5	——	285—287
	6, 7	323—327	288—292
6—19	8—21	328—330	——
20	——	331—333	293—295
21—44	22—45	334, 335	296
45	——	336	*like* 297
46—54	46—54	337	——
55, 56	55		298, 299
57—61	56—60	338—340	300—302
62	*like* 61	341—343	
63, 64	——	——	303
65—93	62—90	344—348	304—308
94	——	349—352	*like* 309—312
95, 96	91, 92	353—361	——
97—99	*like* 93—95	362	313
100	——	363	*like* 314, 315
101—143	96—138	364—382	316—334
	139	383, 384	
144—156	140—152	——	335, 336
157	——	385	337 (*and* 358)
158—164	153—159	386—390	——
165, 166	160	391, 392	338, 339
167—188	161—182	——	340—342
189	*like* 183	393, 394	343, 344
190, 191		395	*like* 345
192—213	184—205	396, 397	*like* 346
214, 215	——	398	347
216, 217	206, 207	——	348—350
218, 219	——	399	351
220—254	208—242	——	352—355
255	——	400, 401	356, 357
256—264	243—251	[385]	358 (*and* 337)
265	——	402—407	359—364
266	252	408—410	——
——	253	411	365
267—282	254—269	412, 413	*like* 366
283—296		414—435	367—388
297—304	270—277	436, 437	——
305—310	——	——	389, 390
——	278—280	438—475	391—428
311—313	*like* 281, 282	476	——
314, 315	283, 284	477—479	429—431
316—322	——		

NOTES TO C. PASSUS XXI. (B. Pass. XVIII.)

(Cf. Wright's edition, pp. 369—395.)

N.B. This is, upon the whole, at once the best written and the most interesting Passus in the whole poem. The subject is the death, descent into hell, and resurrection of the Saviour of mankind.

The three chief sources of the subject-matter are (1) the Gospel narratives; (2) Grostête's Castel of Love; and (3) the apocryphal Gospel of Nicodemus, especially as cited in the chapter De Resurrectione Domini of the Aurea Legenda of Jacobus a Voragine. These sources will be commented on more particularly in their due places.

Besides these, the author constantly shews that he had in his mind some actual representation of the circumstances; so that the reader must throughout consult The Coventry Mysteries.

1. (18. 1.) " Wo-weary and wet-shod " [c]; " Woolward and wet-shod " [b]. " *Wetshod*, with water in the shoes. ' Are you not *wetshod?*' have not your shoes taken in water?"—Marshall's Glossary of Yorkshire Words, 2nd ed., 1796. Compare also—

> " þere men were wetschoede
> Alle of brayn & of blode;"
>> Arthur; ed. Furnivall, E. E. T. S., 1864, l. 469.

In Oxfordshire it is pronounced *Watcherd* [woch·urd], and used correctly by many who have no idea of what are the component parts of the word. The opposite form, *dryshod*, is better known; see Isaiah xi. 15. The corresponding Icelandic word is *skóvátr*, lit. shoe-wet.

Wolleward [b] is thus explained by Palsgrave. " *Wolwarde*, without any lynnen nexte ones body. *Sans chemyse.*" The sense of the word is clearly—with wool next to one's body. It is well discussed and explained by Nares, who says—" Dressed in wool only, without linen, often enjoined in times of superstition, by way of penance." See Love's Labour Lost, v. 2. 717, and the five other examples which Nares cites. To these examples add—

> " And do he penance with al his myght,
> And be in prayers, bathe day and uyght,
> And fast and ga *wolwarde*, and wake,
> And thole hardnes for Goddes sake."
>> Hampole's Pricke of Conscience, l. 3512.

" And werchen and *wolward* gon · as we wrecches vsen;".
>> Pierce the Ploughman's Crede, l. 788.

" Lynen cloth I shall none were," &c.; Squire of Lowe Degree, in Ritson's Metrical Romances, iii. 151. And see Rock, Church of Our Fathers, iii. 435.

The word was discussed also in Notes and Queries, 4 S. i. 65, 181, 254, 351, 425, but without any result beyond what is here given. Woolward or Woolard is still in use as a surname; Bardsley's Eng. Surnames, p. 406. A similar penance was the custom of wearing a hair-shirt; see note to Pass. vii. 6, p. 103.

4. (18. 4.) *Eft to slepe*, to sleep again.

Here begins the Ninth Vision, or the Vision of the Triumph of Piers the Plowman, which extends to the end of the Passus in each Text. See Pref. to C-text, p. ci; Pref. to B-text, p. liv. .

5. (18. 5.) "And leant about (idled about) till Lent-time" [c]; *or*, "till a Lent-time" [b]. The phrase is not very clear. *Lenede me* (lit. leant myself) probably means leant about or idled about; much as the verb to *loll* meant the same thing; cf. Pass. x. 215, 218. Cf. *reste me* in l. 7 [b].

——(18. 6, 7.) These two lines are very awkward. They are almost certainly misplaced, and should follow l. 8; yet all the MSS. agree. As they stand, we must at any rate understand (from l. 8) the words—"And *I dreamt* of Christ's passion and penance," &c.

Of-rauȝte, reached to, extended to. The sense is—"And I dreamt of Christ's passion and penance, that extended to the people;" with reference to the *effects* of the Passion. *Of-rauȝte* is the past tense of *ofrechen*, to reach to; of which see examples in Stratmann. He cites *ofreche*, King Horn, ed. Lumby, l. 1283; Rob. of Gloucester, ed. Hearne, p. 285, l. 6; William of Palerne, l. 3874; pt. t. *ofrahte*, Juliana, ed. Cockayne, p. 57; *ofrauȝte*, Sir Beves, ed. Turnbull, 867.

Reste me, rested myself; *reste* is the past tense, as in Layamon, l. 3511. *And rutte faste*, and snored fast, slept heavily. *Tyl ramis palmarum*, till Palm Sunday (came).

Palm Sunday was often called *dominica palmarum*, or more commonly *in ramis palmarum*. See Proctor's History of the Book of Common Prayer, 3rd ed. p. 279. Proctor observes—"The Quadrigesimal Fast was closed by the *Great Week, Passion Week,* or the *Holy Week*. It began on Palm Sunday, which was kept in commemoration of Christ's entry into Jerusalem." And see cap. ccxvii in the Legenda Aurea, ed. Grässe, 2nd ed., headed—"De dominica in ramis palmarum."

6. (18. 8.) "I dreamt much about children and *gloria laus*." *Gurles* here means children of both sexes, as opposed to *olde folk* in the next line; cf. notes to Pass. ii. 29, xii. 123. The allusion is to the children who, on Palm Sunday, used to sing a hymn in honour of Jesus, beginning with the words "Gloria, laus." An account of the Palm Sunday procession is given in Pecock's Repressor, i. 203, 269; see also Chambers, Book of Days, i. 395; Rock, Church of Our Fathers, iii. pt. 2, pp. 63, 227, 231; Ælfric's Homilies, i. 219; Wordsworth's Eccl. Biog., i. 617; Strutt, Manners and Customs, iii. 174; Brand's Pop. Antiquities, &c. There is a curious and minute description of the Palm Sunday pageantry in Becon's "Potation for Lent."

See, particularly, the Coventry Mystery of the Entry into Jerusalem, where we find the direction—"Here Cryst passyth forth, ther metyth with hym a serteyn of chylderyn with flowres, and cast beforn hym, and they synggyn *Gloria Laus*, and beforn on seyth—'Thow sone of Davyd, thou be our supporte,'" &c.—Coventry Myst., ed. Halliwell, p. 256.

7. (18. 9.) "And how the old folk sang Hosanna to instruments of

music," or, "to the organ." *Orgone* [c] or *orgonye* [b] answers to the Lat. *organa*, of which it is a mere corruption. *Organum* signified any mechanical instrument, and, in particular, an instrument of music; see Chappell, Hist. of Music, i. 327. Chaucer has—"And whyl the *organs* maden melodye;" Sec. Nonnes Tale, l. 134; where *organs* may either mean instruments of music, or what we now call *an organ*, in the singular. Most likely the latter is meant, both in Chaucer and in the present passage. "What we now call *an organ* was formerly styled *the organs;* and, so low as the last century, *a pair of organs;*" Pegge, Anecdotes of the Eng. Language, ed. 1844, p. 122. (Of course *a pair* here means *a set*, referring to the set of pipes; cf. "a paire of bedes" for a set of them, and *a pair of stairs* for a flight of them.) Pegge adds, in a footnote, that Mr Alleyne, founder of Dulwich College, paid £8 for *a pair of organs* in the year 1618. The expression "pair of organs" also occurs under the dates 1521, 1536, and 1637; see Cullum's Hist. of Hawsted, 2nd ed., p. 33. The clearest example is—"1521. To the organ-maker for a pair of new organs, and bringing them home, 10s. 8d." I reject both the suggestions in Cullum, (1) that a pair of organs means that churches had two organs, one portable and the other fixed; and (2) that the portable organs were divided into two parts. Both of these are mere guesses, and founded on the false assumption that *a pair*, in Middle English, meant *a couple*. It is clear that *organs* (without *pair*) also means a single instrument. Thus, in a burlesque Poem in Reliq. Antiq., i. 81, we read— "On the *orgons* playde the porpas;" and Cutts, in his Scenes and Characters of the Middle Ages, p. 285, quotes that 8d were "paied to a carpenter for makyng of a plaunche [*plank, platform*] to sette the *organs* on." Similarly, a single clavichord was called "a payre of clauycordys;" Skelton, ed. Dyce, ii. 94. Cf. a note in Wright's Vocabularies, i. 216; T. Sharp, Dissertation on Pageants, p. 74.

8. (18. 10.) *On was*, one who was [c]. Christ is here represented as riding into Jerusalem, and is said to be like the Good Samaritan described in Pass. xx. 63—77. He is also like Piers Plowman, as being the personification of Human Nature; see ll. 21—24 below.

9. (18. 11.) *Bootles*, without boots. Such is the sense really intended here; cf. 1 Hen. IV., iii. 1. 66, 67. *Cam prykye*, came riding; lit. came to ride. So in Layamon, l. 3625, we have—"þet Leir was cumen liðen;" i.e. that Leir was come travelling; lit. was come to travel.

10. (8. 12.) *Sprakliche*, sprightly, lively [c]; and it is probable that *spakliche* [b] is really the same word, with the *r* dropped. In fact, MS. R. (footnote, B-text) reads *spracliche*. The dropping of *r* is remarkably shewn in the common word *to speak*, which ought, of course, to be *spreak*, as it is from the A.S. *sprécan;* cf. G. *sprechen*, Du. *spreken*. The dropping of *r* in *sp(r)eak* can be dated; it was going out of use about A.D. 1000, since in the MSS. of the A.S. Gospels, written about that time, both forms are found; e. g. *spræcon* or *spræcun*, Luke xii. 3; *spæcon*, Luke xxiv. 14. The word *sprakliche* seems to be Scandinavian; cf. Icel. *sprækr*, *sprækligr*, sprightly;

sparkr, lively. It is found, however, in English dialects where the Scandinavian element is small. Thus, in Akermann's Wiltshire Glossary, we have—"*Sprack*, lively, active, intelligent. 'A *sprack* un,' a lively one. This word is not applied merely to the talkative, or it might be supposed to be derived from A.S. *spræc*." Halliwell also gives—"*Sprag*, the same as *Sprack*, quick, lively, active. *West*." Our common word *spark*, in the sense of a gay fellow, is also merely the Icel. *sparkr*. And I much suspect that our *sprightly* is a mere corruption of *sprakliche*, with a change of vowel due to confusion with *sprite*. Two things point to this; (1) that we retain the *gh* in the spelling; and (2) that the sense of *sprightly* is exactly that of *sprakliche*, and therefore different from *spritely*, which would mean *fairy-like*. I also think it clear that the form *spakliche*, used here in the B-text, and again in B. xvii. 81, (where MS. R. has the spelling *sparkliche*), is a mere variation of *sprakliche*, and therefore quite a different word from the adverb formed from the Middle English *spak*, mild, tame, borrowed from the Icel. *spakr*, quiet, gentle. Dr Stratmann mixes all the examples together under the heading *spac*; but I should arrange and illustrate them thus.

Sprak, lively, active (Icel. *sprækr*, lively), still current in Wiltshire; see Akermann's Glossary. Also *sprag*; see Halliwell. Spelt *spac*, quick, ready; O.E. Homilies, ed. Morris, i. 305; King of Tars (Ritson), 774; superl. *spakest*, boldest, Allit. Poems, ed. Morris, C. 169. Hence *sprakliche* (probably still preserved in *sprightly*) (1) sprightly, lively; or as an adverb, in a lively manner; P. Pl. C. xxi. 10; also spelt *spakliche*, P. Pl. B. xviii. 12. (2) adv. quickly, nimbly; P. Pl. B. xvii. 81; Will. of Palerne, 966, 3357, 3631, &c.; Allit. Poems, ed. Morris, C. 338; Spec. of Lyric Poetry, ed. Wright, p. 37. The comparative *spaklóker* occurs in MS. Laud 656, fol. 12, l. 10.

Spake, tame (Icel. *spakr*, mild, gentle); of rare occurrence; in Rob. of Brunne's Handling Synne, l. 7486, it is said of a bird—"For hyt sate by hym so *spake*," where the word *spake* is glossed by *tame*, written above it in an early hand. It is remarkable that this word is nearly opposite in sense to the former.

11. (18. 13.) The comparison of Christ to a knight is most curious, and is kept up throughout the Passus. The idea is old enough. Compare—"And he [Christ], ase noble woware [*wooer*], com forto preouen his luue, and scheawede þuruh *kniktscipe* þet he was luue-wurde [*love-worthy*]; as weren sumewhule knihtes iwuned for to donne. He dude him iue turnement," &c.; Ancren Riwle, p. 390. The ceremony of dubbing a knight is described with minuteness in Ly Beaus Desconus, l. 73; and see King Horn, ed. Lumby, ll. 495—504; and Havelok, l. 2314.

12. (18. 14.) It is well known that three very essential ceremonies were the dubbing the new-made knight with the flat of a sword, the girding on of a sword, and the buckling on of spurs; as humorously described in Don Quixote, ch. iii. Hence the phrase "to win one's spurs." But the last part of this line is extremely obscure, though I think *galoches y-couped* must

mean shoes cut down, alluding to some peculiarity in the make of the shoe
as used by knights.   I do not agree with Mr Halliwell in his explanation of
this passage under *Coppid*.   No doubt *coppid* means *peaked*, and it is
notorious, too, that shoes with peaked toes were in common use in the reign
of Richard II; and I am also aware that Way (Prompt. Parv., p. 184, note)
cites "*Milleus*, a coppid shoo" from the Ortus Vocabulorum.   But the
word *here* used is not *coppid*, peaked, but *couped*, cut; and the passage that
really throws most light on our text is one in the Romaunt of the Rose (l.
842), where Mirth is described as attired in a most elegant suit of
clothes—

> "And shode he was with great maistric,
> With shoone *decoped*, and with lace."

Here "shoone decoped" can only mean "shoes cut down;" for the French
prefix *de-* will not sort well with *coppid*, from the Welsh and A.S. *cop*.   Cotgrave gives—"Decoupé, cut down, cut off; pared, or cut away; slit, sliced."
Hence the reference is not at all to the *peaks* of the shoes, but to the
fashion of slashing or slitting them by way of ornament, just as Chaucer
(C. T. 3318) describes the clerk Absolon as having "Poules windowes coruen
on his shoos;" and just as Hamlet speaks of "razed shoes;" Act iii. sc. 2.
Steevens, in a note on Hamlet, quotes an apt passage from Stubbes's
Anatomie of Abuses, concerning shoes that are "razed, carued, cut, and
stitched all ouer with Silke."   I find, too, that Dr Stratmann inclines to
my view of the matter, as he gives—"*Coupen*, Fr. *couper?* couped shon,
Torrent of Portugal, 193 [page 51]; galoches icouped, Piers Pl. B.
xviii. 14."

As to *galoches*, we learn from Cotgrave that, in his time, the term was
restricted to the wooden clogs used by country clowns, a sense which appears
again in Riley's Memorials of London, p. 554, where mention is made of
galoches *of wood* under the date 1400.   But Way's note (Prompt. Parv., p.
184) clearly shews that the term was also formerly used of the expensive
shoes worn by the upper classes.   He says—"In the reign of Edw. IV a
statute was passed, by which the higher classes alone were permitted to
wear shoes, *galoges*, or boots, with a peak longer than 2 inches (Rot. Parl.,
v. 505, 566; Stat. of Realm, ii. 415); but, from certain allusions in ancient
romance, it would seem that the fashion was, at an earlier period, permitted
to none under the degree of a knight.   See Torrent of Portugal, 1193, &c.;
Sir Degore, 700.   The curious drawings in Cott. MS. Julius E. iv. (t. Hen.
VI), one of which, representing King John, has been given in Shaw's Dresses,
exhibit the *galache* in its most extravagant form."

I conclude, then, that the allusion is to such fashionably slashed or
"rased" shoes as were only worn by knights or those of still higher rank.

Our author alludes to the peaked shoes also, but it is *in another passage;*
see "pikede shoes," Pass. xxiii. 219.

13. (18. 15.) Alluding to Mat. xxi. 9—"Hosanna filio David," &c.

14. (18. 16.) The allusion is to the proclamation by the heralds of the

names and titles of the knights who come to the tournament. Cf. Rich. II. i. 3. 104.

Auntres [c] is almost certainly a mere misspelling of *auntrous* [b]; and the footnotes to the B-text shew that *auntrous* means *adventurous*, as usual in other authors. The substantive *knights* is understood, and the word *auntrous* means, accordingly, "adventurous knights;" or, as they were sometimes called, "knights adventurers." Chaucer's Sir Topas was one of these :—

<blockquote>
"And for he was a knyght <i>auntrous</i>,
He nolde slepen in noon hous,
But liggen in his hoode."
</blockquote>

The word *auntres* means *adventures*, and would make nonsense. MS. T (C-text, footnote) has the right reading.

18. (18. 20.) "And fetch that which the fiend claims, viz. the fruit of Piers the Plowman." The reference is to Pass. xix. 55—123, particularly to ll. 111, 122. Mankind are the apples of the tree of Charity, stolen by Satan and hid in hell, whence Christ recovered them by assuming the form of Piers Plowman, i. e. by His Incarnation and subsequent Passion. The idiom "peers frut þe plouhman" has been already explained; see note to Pass. xvi. 131, p. 307; and see another instance in l. 24 below.

19. (18. 21.) *Preynkte*, gazed, looked; see Pass. xvi. 121, and the note at p. 307. "*Prink*, to look at; to gaze upon. *West*;" Hall. Dict.

21. (18. 22.) *Of his gentrise*, as consistent with his noble birth. Douce, Illust. of Shak., ii. 262, says that "Gerard Leigh, one of the oldest writers on heraldry, speaks of Jesus Christ, a *gentleman* of great lineage, and king of the Jews." See Pass. xv. 90, 91.

In peers armes, in Piers' coat-armour, i. e. with the coat of arms which would indicate Piers. The next line explains clearly what is meant by Piers the Plowman in this Passus. It means Mankind, or Human Nature in its highest form; and Christ assumed Piers' armour by His Incarnation.

24. (18. 25.) *Plates*, plate-armour [c]; *paltok*, a kind of jacket [b]. "Habent etiam aliud indumentum sericum quod vulgo dicitur *paltok;* et si bene disponeretur, potius ad cultum ecclesiasticum cederet quam ad terrenum; unde dicitur in Libris Regum quod Salamon in tota vita sua talibus non est usus;" Eulogium Historiarum, ed. Haydon, iii. 230. This passage is cited in Camden's Remaines, and thence again by Strutt, Manners and Customs, ii. 84, who says—"They have another weed of silk, which they call a *paltock;*" and a footnote explains the word to mean "a close jacket, like a waistcoat." Observe that our author elsewhere speaks of *paltokes* as being worn by priests; Pass. xxiii. 219. We find "Paltok. *Baltheus*" in the Prompt. Parv., p. 380, on which see Way's long illustrative note. To this I will merely add that in Riley's Memorials of London, p. 283, a *paltoke* was valued at 5s. in 1356; and again, id. p. 418, we read that a John Grey bought of John Tilney, paltoke-maker, "2 paltokes called jackes, at 100s." Also, in Malory's Morte Arthur, bk. v. cap. 10, we find—"I am no knight,

said Gawaine, I have been brought up in the guard-robe with the noble king Arthur many years, for to take heed to his armour and his other array, and to point his *paltocks* that belong to himself." And see British Costume, p. 153 ; Dyce's Skelton, ii. 181; Chaucer's Prologue, ed. Morris, 3rd ed. p. vi; and Cotgrave, s. v. *Palletoc*.

28. (18. 29.) This and the subsequent lines clearly suggested the beautiful poem entitled Death and Liffe, printed in the Percy Folio MS., ed. Hales and Furnivall, p. 56, with an Introduction by myself (p. 49), in which I have discussed the points of resemblance between that poem and our text.

34. (18. 35.) "And beat thoroughly and bring down (to destruction) sorrow and death for ever." In the B-text, supply the marks of quotation after *tua*, at the end of the Latin text. This text (Hosea xiii. 14) is quoted and commented on in Old Eng. Homilies, ed. Morris, i. 122.

35. (18. 36.) "Sedente autem illo pro tribunali," &c. ; Matt. xxvii. 19.

36. (18. 37.) *And deme here beyer ryght,* and adjudge the right of them both ; cf. l. 374. *Beyer* [c] and *botheres* [b] are different forms of the genitive case of *both ;* we also find *buþre*, Ormulum, 2794; *beire*, Layamon, 5283; *bother* (see Hall. Dict.). *Beyer* and *beire* are from the A.S. gen. pl. *begra ; botheres* is formed from *bother* (Icel. *báðir*, gen. *báðra*), by the unnecessary addition of *-es*.

46. (18. 46.) *Wicchecrafte*. This was probably suggested by a passage in the Apocryphal Gospel of Nicodemus ; see Cowper's translation of the Apocryphal Gospels, p. 270—"And the Jews said, he is a *magician*, and therefore he doeth these things ;" and again, at p. 272—"us, who know well that he is a *magician*." See also S. John, xix. 15, where we find the words—"Illi autem clamabant: Tolle, tolle, crucifige eum." See *Witch* in Trench's Select Glossary.

50. (18. 50.) Suggested by Matt. xxvii. 29, 30—"posuerunt . . . arundinem in dextera eius. Et genu flexo ante eum, illudebant ei dicentes : *Aue rex Iudæorum*. Et expuentes in eum, *acceperunt arundinem, et percutiebant caput eius*." But the poet has translated this in a very odd way.

51. (18. 51.) *Thre nayles*. A long essay might be written on the wholly unimportant question whether *three* nails or *four* were used in the Crucifixion. "That there were four nails was maintained at one time, from a supposition that each foot was separately nailed, instead of both feet being transfixed by *one* nail; but as, by the latter mode, the disposition of the limbs looks better to the eye, the best painters decide in its favour, while the number *three* has rendered it convenient as an emblem of the Trinity;" Hone's Ancient Mysteries, p. 282. The question is discussed in Notes and Queries, 3rd Ser., iii. 315, and in Legends of the Holy Rood, ed. Morris, p. xix, which see. "St Cyprian, St Augustine, St Gregory of Tours, and Pope Innocent III., as also Rufinus, and Theodoret, reckon *four* nails ;" F. C. H., in N. and Q., 3rd S., iii. 392. So also in Ælfric, ed. Thorpe, i. 217 ; and Maundeville's Travels, ed. Halliwell, p. 78. The *three* nails are mentioned by St Gregory Nazianzen; by Nonnus (Greek poet, fifth century); in the

Ancren Riwle, p. 391; Polit. Rel. and Love Poems, ed. Furnivall, p. 111; Coventry Mysteries, ed. Halliwell, p. 315; Joseph of Arimathie, ed. Skeat, p. 59, l. 262.

In Godwin's Archæological Handbook, p. 270, is this summary. "*Before the eleventh* century, our Saviour on the cross was always represented with a robe. *Eleventh and twelfth century.* The robe became shorter, the sleeves ending at the elbow, and the skirt about the knees, and the body was attached to the cross by *four* nails. *Thirteenth century.* The robe was exchanged for a cloth about the loins, and the body was affixed by three nails only. *Fifteenth century.* The cloth was diminished in size." In Legends of the Holy Rood, ed. Morris, p. 184, we have a drawing of the *four* nails; but, at p. 185, a drawing of *three. Naked;* see Pass. xi. 193. So in the Ancren Riwle, p. 260—"Vor steorc-naked he was despuiled oðe rode" [*on the rood*]. Compare—

> "Cros, he stikeþ vppon þi steir,
> Naked in þe wylde wynde."
>   Legends of the Holy Rood, ed. Morris, p. 200.

53. (18. 53.) There is a most remarkable variation here; in the B-text, Christ is said to be asked to drink, to *shorten* his life; in the C-text, to *lengthen* it. The former opinion is in the Aurea Legenda, cap. liii.—"dederunt ei acetum cum myrrha et felle mixtum, ut ex aceto citius moreretur." See Smith's Dict. of the Bible, art. *Gall.*

57. (18. 56.) *That lyf þe louyeþ,* that Life loves thee; see l. 30 above.

59. (18. 58.) A magnificent line; there are many passages of real power and sublimity in this Passus.

Prison, a prisoner; as frequently in other authors. In the English version of the Castle of Love, ed. Weymouth, ll. 330—334, we actually find *prisoun* = a prisoner, and *prison* = a prison, in the same passage.

> "I besech þat þou here me,
>   þat þe wrecche prisoun [*prisoner*]
>   Mote come to sum rauӡsum,
>   þat amidden alle his fon [*foes*]
>   In strong *prison* þou hast i-don."

So too, in Gen. and Exodus, ed. Morris, we find *prisun,* a prison, ll. 2040, 2046; *prisunes,* prisoners, l. 2044; *prisuner,* a gaoler, keeper of a prison, l. 2042. And again, in Cursor Mundi, *prisun* means a prisoner in l. 9573, but a prison in l. 9576. Cf. Mid. Eng. *message,* a messenger; *hunte,* a hunter.

61. (18. 60.) Compare Legends of Holy Rood, ed. Morris, p. 144—

> "The dede worþily gan wake,
>   þe dai turned to nihtes donne,
>   þe merke mone gan mournyng make,
>   þe lyht out leop of þe sonne,
>   þe temple-walles gan chiuere and schake,
>   Veiles in þe temple a-two þei sponne."

See also Towneley Mysteries, p. 255.

79. (18. 76.) *Kynde forӡaf,* nature granted. *Kynde,* lit. Nature, here means the God of Nature, the Creator, as in Pass. xi. 128. *For-ӡaf* is here

merely the intensive of *ʒaf*, and means "fully gave," or "fully granted."
This sense is unusual, but we may compare the A.S. *forgeafe* = Lat. *dedisti*;
Gen. iii. 12.   And see l. 188 below.

Compare the words of Pilate in the Coventry Mysteries, p. 315—

    "That ther be no man xal towche ʒour kyng,
      But yf he be knyght or jentylman born."

82. (18. 79.) This story is from the Aurea Legenda, cap. xlvii. "Longinus fuit quidam centurio, qui cum aliis militibus cruci domini adstans iussu
Pylati latus domini lancea perforauit, et uidens signa quæ fiebant, solem
scilicet obscuratum et terræ motum, in Christum credidit. Maxime ut eo,
ut quidam dicunt, quod cum ex infirmitate uel senectute oculi eius caligas-
sent, de sanguine Christi per lanceam decurrente fortuito oculos suos tetigit
et protinus clare uidit." The day of S. Longinus is Mar. 15; see Chambers,
Book of Days. The name *Longinus* is most likely derived from λόγχη, a
lance, the word used in John xix. 34; and the legend was easily developed
from St John's narrative. The name Longinus first appears in the Apoc.
Gospel of Nicodemus. Allusions to it are common; see Legends of the
Holy Rood, ed. Morris, pp. xix, 106; Old Eng. Homilies, ed. Morris, i. 282;
Townely Mysteries, p. 231; Coventry Mysteries, pp. 334, 335; Hymns to
the Virgin and Christ, ed. Furnivall, p. 123; Castle of Love, ed. Weymouth,
p. 68; Chaucer's A, B, C, under the letter X; Lamentacion of Mary
Magdalen, l 176; Reliq. Antiq., i. 126; Jubinal, Mystères inédits du quin-
zième Siècle, tom. ii. pp. 254—257; Mrs Jameson's Sacred and Legendary
Art, 3rd ed., p. 788; Wordsworth's Eccl. Biography, i. 268 (where we learn
that Wm Thorpe believed the story); &c. Cf. note to l. 89.

83. (18. 80.) *Houede*, waited in readiness; see *hovin* in Stratmann. Cf.
"where that she *hoved* and abode;" Gower, Conf. Amant. iii. 63. But the
best example of the poet's use of the word is in Holinshed, where, referring
to the duel between Hereford and Norfolk in 1398, he says—"The duke of
Norfolke *hovered on horssebacke* at the entrie of the lists, his horsse being
barded with crimosen velvet," &c. Cf. *ouer-houeþ* in l 175 below.

87. (18. 84.) *Tryne*, to touch [c]; *taste*, to handle [b]. The verb *tryne*,
to touch, is exceedingly rare; I can only find two other clear examples.
One is—"þat non *trinde* the tres," that none should touch the trees; Alexander (MS. Bodley 264), l 132. The other is the A.S. *tringan*, to touch,
which is also rare. In Spelman's edition of the A.S. Psalms (Ps. ciii. 33),
qui tangit montes is glossed by *se hrynð muntas*; and, for *hrynð*, the various
readings are *gehrinð* and *tringað*. Possibly also *be-trende* = touched, in
Altenglische Legenden, ed. Horstmann, p. 127, l. 491. N. B. This verb is
not to be confused with *trinen*, to step, go (see Stratmann), from the Danish
trine, to step, O.Swed. *trena*, to proceed.

Taste is best explained from Cotgrave, who gives—"*Taster*, to taste, or
take an essay of; also, to handle, feele, touch, or grope for."

89. (18. 86.) A similar miracle is told in the Life of St Christopher, l.
219, in Lives of Saints, ed. Furnivall.

90. (18. 87.) This is the usual form of the story. Thus, in the Coventry Mysteries, p. 335, after Longinus (or Longeus) has smitten Christ, "he fallyth downe on his knees."   Then he says—

> "Now, good lord, fforgyf me that,
>   That I to the now don have ;
> For I dede I wyst not what—
>   The Jewys of myn ignorans dede me rave.
>   Mercy! Mercy! Mercy! I crye."

So too in the Towneley Mysteries, p. 231.

97. (18. 93.) See remarks on *Cailiff* in Trench's Select Glossary.

103. (18. 98.) *The gree*, the prize, the honour of the day ; as Tyrwhitt explains it in a note to C. T. 2735 (Kn. Ta., 1875). " *To win the gre* is a common Scottish phrase still used to express 'to be victor,' 'to win the prize,' 'to come off first,' 'to excel all competitors.' *To bear the gre* is to hold the first place, to bear off the highest honours. Thus, *at* a rifle-match, the one who has the highest score is said 'to have won the gre ;' and *after* the match he 'bears the gre,' and will do so till some one else excels him ;" note to the allit. Troy-book, ed. Panton and Donaldson, p. 483.

105. (18. 100.) *ʒelt*, yields ; pres. tense. "Yields himself recreant" (i. e. acknowledges himself defeated). *Rennyng*, whilst running his course (in the tilt). Cf.—"Sothly, he that despeireth is like the coward campioun recreaunt, that seith *recreaunt* withoute neede ;" Chaucer, Pers. Tale, *De Accidia*.

107. (18. 102.) *Lordlinges*, sirs ; cf. *lordings* in Chaucer. The B-text has the term of reproach, *lordeynes*, i. e. clowns, blockheads ; see *Lourdin* and *Lourdaut* in Cotgrave. The derivation is, of course, from F. *lourd*, Lat. *luridus*. But, because Bailey explained *Lordane* as being by some derived "of *Lord* and *Dane*," Chatterton, referring to an old story connected with Hock Day in which the Saxon women are said to have helped their husbands to vanquish the Danes (Chambers, Book of Days, i. 499), makes King Harold thus address his men—

> "Your loving wives, who erst did rid the land   •
> Of *lurdanes*, and the treasure that you han,
> Will fall into the Norman robber's hand,
> Unless with hand and heart you play the man."

That is, Chatterton wrote *lurdanes* with a special reference to its supposed equivalence to *Lord Danes ;* and this fact would in itself be quite enough to upset the genuineness of the Rowley Poems. See Chatterton's Poems, ed. Skeat, ii. 135.

108. (18. 103.) On *thraldom*, see Barbour's Bruce, ed. Skeat, i. 225—274; Cursor Mundi, ll. 9483—9492.

111. (18. 106.) It was believed that *usury* was a very wicked thing in any form ; see note to Pass. vii. 239, p. 121.

116. (18. 111.) Perhaps there is an allusion here to the services called *in tenebris*, respecting which Strutt (Manners and Customs, iii. 174) quotes from a MS. to the effect that, three days before Easter, "holy chirch usith theise three daies to say service in the cuene tyde, *in the derknesse ;* where-

fore it is callid with you *Tenebris*, that is, darkness." There was, at any rate in very early times, no sermon on those days. "Ne mot nán man secgan spell on þam ðrim swig-dagum;" i. e. no sermon may be said on the three still days; Ælfric's Homilies, ed. Thorpe, ii. 263. However, in Wyclif's Works, ii. 117—133, sermons for all three days will be found.

118. (18. 113.) Lines 118—128 are quoted in Warton, Hist. Eng. Poetry, ii. 262, ed. 1871; ii. 85, ed. 1840.

Mercy comes from the West, Truth from the East, Righteousness from the North, and Peace from the South. That is, the actors were to come from the four different quarters, and meet in the middle of the open space which served for a stage. See note to Pass. i. 14, p. 5.

119. (18. 114.) Here *he* [c] = *heo* or *hue*, she; cf. *she* in [b]. So in ll. 178, 179. *To helleward*, in the direction of hell; i. e. (as the context shews) eastward. Now this is expressly contrary to the description in Pass. i. 16, where the abode of Death is in the West; see note to Pass. i. 14. I explain it thus. The scenes are quite different; and the reference is, not to the Eastern and Western quarters of the world, but to the Eastern and Western ends of the space on which the actors moved in the Mysteries. This will readily suggest that whilst, in the Mystery of the Creation, it would be convenient and appropriate to place the throne of God in the East, it would be equally convenient (appropriateness not being considered) to represent Christ's triumph over Satan in the same position. The reason for it was, I suppose, that the same wooden platform, of which the upper stage supported the divine throne, would serve, in its lowest or lower stage, as a place of resort for the demons. A well-made platform had three stages or stories, the upmost representing heaven, the middle one the world, whilst the lowest, more or less concealed by curtains, served as a "green-room" for actors, and for the resort of the demons. A hole in the side of this lowest stage was called the mouth of hell, out of which fire' and smoke sometimes issued, mingled with the cries of the lost. See all this described in Chambers, Book of Days, i. 634; and in Sharp's Dissertation on Pageants.

120. (18. 115.) *Mercy*. The passages relating to Mercy, Truth, Justice, and Peace (ll. 120—239 and 453—471) are imitated from Bp Robert Grosteste's Chastel d'Amour, and are to be compared with that poem, or with the English version called The Castel of Love, edited from the Vernon MS. by Dr Weymouth for the Philological Society, 1864; pp. 13—24. It is the same allegory as The Parable of a King and his Four Daughters, introduced into the Cursor Mundi, ed. Morris, pp. 548—560, ll. 9517—9752. The author of the Cursor Mundi calls it a "sample," which he took out of Saint Robert's book, i. e. from Grosteste's poem. The Castel of Love and the Cursor Mundi should be compared with the text throughout the passages indicated.

The whole parable is obviously founded on a single verse in Psalm lxxv. 10 (lxxxiv. 11 in the Vulgate), viz.—"Misericordia et ueritas obuiauerunt sibi: iustitia et pax osculatæ sunt."

The introduction of the four sisters no doubt formed a favourite interlude
in the Ancient Mysteries and Moralities; we find it, for example, in the
Coventry Mystery of the Salutation and Conception of Mary; and again, in
Sharp's Dissertation on Pageants, p. 23, we find a description relating to
the Morality of the "Castel of Perseuerunse" which even tells us the
colours of the actors' dresses. The four daughters all wore mantles, Mercy
being clothed in *white*, Righteousness all in *red*, Truth in a sad-coloured
green, and Peace all in *black*; and it was directed that they should "pleye
in þe place al to-gedyr tyl þey brynge up the sowle;" i. e. the soul of man.
The effect would be good and striking.

Mr Wright (note on this passage) quotes a description of the Four ·
Sisters in a poem by Lydgate; MS. Harl. 2255, fol. 21.

128. (18. 123.) *Rowed*, began to beam, began to dawn; see note to Pass.
ii. 114, p. 35; and cf. "And whan the day began to *rowe;*" Gower, Conf.
Amantis, bk. iii; ed. Chalmers, p. 80, col. 2. And again—"Qwen the *day-raw*
rase," when the day-dawn rose; Alexander, ed. Stevenson, l. 392. I add
another illustration, from the Lamentation of Mary Magdaleine (Chaucer's
Works, ed. 1561, fol. cccxviii, back), in which the Jews are represented as
scourging Jesus, causing "bloodie rowes," i. e. streaks of blood, to appear.

> "They wounded hym, alas! with all greuaunce,
> The blood doun reiled in most habundaunce.
> The bloodie *rowes* stremed doune ouer all,
> They him assailed so maliciouslie," &c.

And again, *rowes* (= rays) occurs in Wright's Vocabularies, i. 167.

140. (18. 135.) *Clips* [b] is a shortened form of *eclipse* [c]; see footnote
to C-text. Examples are:—"This was the greattest *clypse*," &c.; Hormanni
Vulgaria, leaf 100. "Also the same season there fell a great rayne and a
clyps, with a terryble thonder;" Lord Berners's Froissart, cap. cxxx; describing the "batayle of Cressy." And in the Testament of Love (Ch.
Works, ed. 1561, fol. ccxcvi, col. 1, l. 23) we find the spelling *clipes*.

For remarks on the "eclipse" at the Crucifixion, see Wyclif's Works, ii.
51, and the note. "The darkness that overspread the world at the crucifixion cannot with reason be attributed to an eclipse, as the moon was at the
full at the time of the Passover;" Smith's Dict. of the Bible, art. *Eclipse*.

144. (18. 140.) This was a favourite theme. On the notion, that the
timber of the true cross was derived from the pippins of the apple-tree that
caused the Fall of Man, were founded the curious legends concerning the
true cross; see Dr Morris's introduction to his edition of The Legends of
the Holy Rood. See also the note to l. 400 below.

145. (18. 141.) *Releue*, lift up again; from Lat. *releuare*.

146. (18. 142.) *A tale of walterot*, an idle tale, an unmeaning story, a
piece of absurdity. The better spelling seems to be *waltrot* [b]; see the
footnotes. If we transpose the word, we obtain *trotwal*, and it is, at any
rate, worth remarking that *troteuale* occurs, in the very same sense, four
times in Robert of Brunne's Handling Synne. The following are the
passages.

"Yn gamys and festys, and at þe ale,
  Loue men to lesteue *troteuale;*" l. 47.

"Or þou ledyst any man to þe ale
  And madest hym drunk wyþ *troteuale;*" l. 5971.

"ʒe wommen, þenkeþ on þys tale,
  And takyþ hyt for no *troteuale;*" l. 8080.

"So fare men here by þys tale,
  Some holde hyt but a *troteuale;*" l. 9244.

These passages are cited in Halliwell's Dictionary, s. v. *Trotevale,* from MS.
Harl. 1701. A fifth example of the word occurs in The Debate of the Body
and the Soul, l. 291 (Mätzner's Sprachproben, i. 99). The *sense* of the
phrase is obvious, being equivalent to *trufle* (a trifle) in l. 151 below.

I can even adduce plausible etymologies. *Waltrot* may easily have been
imported, through the O. French, from O.H.German. It might thus stand
for *walt-trúta,* a witch of the woods, an incubus, or nightmare. *Walt* is the
mod. G. *wald,* wood; and O.H.G. *trúta* is the modern provincial G. *trute,* a
witch. The O.H.G. *trúta* was a night-hag or nightmare; see *Trud* in
Schmeller's Bayerisches Wörterbuch, ed. 1869, iii. 649; and see *drude* in
Grimm's Ger. Dict. That the first syllable is O.H.G. *walt* is a guess; but
I have little doubt about the second half of the word, and still less about
trotevale. The O.H.G. *trúta* is the Icel. *þrúðr;* and *trotevale* is a French
rendering of Icel. *þrúðvaldr,* which represents no less a personage than the
mighty Thor, here degraded into the symbol of an idle tale. In this case,
the ending *-valdr* is connected with Icel. *valda,* to rule, E. *wield.* See *þrúðr*
and *þróttr* in the Icel. Dictionary.

147. (18. 145.) It was the almost universal belief that Adam and all his
descendants (with the exception of Enoch, Elijah, and the penitent thief)
descended into hell, and there remained till Christ fetched them thence after
His crucifixion. See particular the chapter De Resurrectione Domini (cap.
liv.) of the Aurea Legenda, part of which is quoted in the note to l. 261
below.

In Early Eng. Homilies, i. 236, we learn that "all folk went into the
devil's mouth, except a very few from whom His [Christ's] dear mother was
descended." And again, id. i. 130—"all the men descended from them [Adam
and Eve], good and evil, as soon as their souls left their bodies, they went
to hell." See l. 198 below.

153. (18. 149.) The reference is to Job vii. 9—"Sicut consumitur
nubes, et pertransit; sic qui descenderit ad inferos, non ascendet."

156. (18. 152.) "Because venom destroys venom, from that I fetch evidence" [c]; "For venom destroys venom, and that I prove by reason" [b].

158. (18. 153.) The notion that a dead scorpion is a remedy for a
scorpion's sting is to be found in Bartholomæus de Proprietatibus Rerum;
lib. 18, c. 98, De Scorpione. Batman's translation, fol. 381, col. 1, has :—
"To a man smitten of the scorpion, ashes of scorpions burnt, dronke in wine,
is remedy. Also scorpions drowned in oile helpeth and succoureth beasts
that bee stong with scorpions." Compare—"*Lezard Chalcidique,* A spotted

Lizard which is very venomous, and yet, taken in drink, healeth the hurt he did;" Cotgrave's F. Dict. Also—"the scorpion's sting, which being full of poyson, is a remedy for poyson;" Lily's Euphues, ed. Arber, p. 411. Cf. note to Pass. ii. 147, pp. 37, 38.

166. (18. 160.) The line "Ars ut artem falleret" occurs in the third stanza of the hymn "Pange, lingua, gloriosi;" see Daniel, Thesaurus Hymnologicus, i. 164. Cf. "Fallite fallentes," Ovid, de Arte Amat., i. 645.

> "Qui simulat uerbis, nec corde est fidus amicus,
> Tu quoque fac simile : sic ars deluditur arte."
>> Dion. Cato, Dist., i. 26 (quoted in B. x. 190).

> "For falshede euer-ȝite heo [*man's foes*] souhten,
> And falshede hem i-ȝolde be" [*shall be repaid them*].
>> Castel of Love, ed. Weymouth, l. 342.

> "For often he that wol begile
> Is guiled with the same guile,
> And thus the guiler is beguiled."
>> Gower, Conf. Amant. bk. vi. (ed. Chalmers, p. 194, col. 2).

> "Begiled is the giler thanne."—Rom. of the Rose, l. 5762.

> "A gilour shal himself begiled be."—Ch. Cant. Tales, l. 4310.

"To play wily beguile;" Bradley's Works, i. 375; ii. 49, 340 (Parker Society). There is an old play entitled "Wily Beguiled." See l. 395 below, where the quotation recurs; and cf. Ps. vii. 16; ix. 15. Similar proverbs are given in Ida von Düringsfeld's Sprichwörter, vol. i. 522, 643, under the headings—"Den Fuchs muss man mit Füchsen fangen;" and—"Wer Andern eine Grübe gräbt, fällt selbst hinein."

178. (18. 172.) *He wolde*, she wished to go; where *he* = she, as in l. 119 above. Cf. A. xii. 75, and the note (p. 260).

179. (18. 173.) *Wham he gladie thouhte*, whom she intended to gladden [c]; whom she intended to greet [b].

185. (18. 179.) *For*, because. *Iousted*, jousted; cf. ll. 21, 103.

188. (18. 182.) *Forgyue*, fully granted; cf. *forȝaf* in l. 79, and the note. "And granted to all mankind, (for) Mercy my sister and myself to bail them all" [c]; "and granted to me, Peace, and to Mercy, (for us) to be man's *mainpreneurs* for evermore hereafter" [b]. See notes to Pass. iii. 208; v. 107.

192, 193. (18. 184, 185.) *Patente;* see note to Pass. xx. 12, p. 385. *This dede shal dure*, this (legal) deed shall last good. The Latin words form fragments of the whole text, which is :—"In pace in idipsum dormiam, et requiescam;" Ps. iv. 9.

199. (18. 191.) See note to l. 147 above; and cf. Pass. xix. 111—117.

201. (18. 193.) *Hus defense*, the prohibition laid upon him. Cf. "*defended* fruit;" Milton, P. L. xi. 86; and see *Defence* in Trench's Select Glossary.

202. (18. 194.) *Fret*, ate. Cf. "a moth *fretting* a garment;" Ps. xxxix. 12 (Prayer-Book); see *Fret* in Trench's Select Glossary.

218. (18. 207.) "Should know assuredly what day is to mean," i. e.

what the meaning of "day" is: Supply a full stop (which has dropped out) at the end of the line in the C-text.

221. (18. 209.) *The deth of kynde*, death from natural causes.

225. (18. 213.) "Which unknits all care, and is the commencing of rest." A line even finer than Shakespeare's—"Sleep, that knits up the ravelled sleave of care;" Macb. ii. 2. 37.

226. (18. 214.) *Moreyne*, a murrain [c]; an improvement upon *modicum*, i. e. a moderate quantity, short allowance [b].

235. (18. 223.) The Latin text, in [c] only, is from 1 Thess. v. 21, and has been quoted already; Pass. iv. 492, 496.

239. (18. 227.) "Till wellaway teach him;" till he learns experience of suffering, which causes him to cry *well-away* (a corruption of A.S. *wá lá wá*, woe! lo! woe!).

241. (18. 229.) "That *beau-père* was called Book." Cotgrave · notes that *Beau père* is "the title of a Frier which is a confessor." Roquefort says—"*Beau pere*, titre que l'on donnoit aux religieux;" i. e. to monks and friars.

243. (18. 231.) A comet was called *stella comata* (see l. 249) and, in English, a *blazing star*. "The blasynge starre is now gone. *Cometes iam excessit;*" Hormanni Vulgaria, leaf 99, back. Batman upon Bartholomè, lib. 8. c. 32, has the following observations on comets. "Of the starre Cometa.—*Cometa* is a Starre beclipped with burning gleames, as Beda doth say, and is sodeinly bred, & betokeneth changing of kings, and is a token of Pestilence, or of war, or of winds, or of great heate. Sometime it seemeth, that such stars, so beset with blasing beames, moue with the mouing of Planets: and somtime it seemeth that they be pight & not mouable . . . & they spread their beames toward the North, and neuer towarde the West. And therefore they be not seene in the West side. . . . Here of it followeth, that the starre that was seene in the birth of Christ was not *Cometa*, for he passed and moued out of the East by South toward the West; and so moue not the starres that be called *Stella Comete*, as Chrisostomus saith." On the wonderful appearances at Christ's birth, see Cowper's Introd. to the Apoc. Gospels, p. xxxiii; Peter Comestor's Historica Scholastica; Ælfric's Homilies, ed. Thorpe, i. 109, 229; the poem of The Deuelis Parliament, in Hymns to the Virgin and Christ, ed. Furnivall, esp. pp. 44, 45; Aurea Legenda, cap. xiv, De Epiphania Domini; Smith's Dict. of the Bible, art. "Star of the Wise Men;" &c. The passages in Ælfric bear a considerable general resemblance to the text.

256. (243.) "Lo! how the sun did lock (shut up) her light within herself." An extremely interesting example of the use of *sonne* as a feminine noun. We are now accustomed to think of the sun as masculine, and the moon as feminine; but this is due to the influence of classical models, and wholly foreign to the original Gothic element of our language, which made A.S. *sunne* feminine, and A.S. *móna* masculine. The Mæso-Goth. *sunno* is feminine, but there is a second form *sunna*, which is masculine. The A.S.

sunne, Old Saxon *sunna*, Friesic *sunne*, Icel. *sunna*, O.H.G. *sunna*, G. *sonne*, Du. *zon*, are all feminine. The Mæso-Goth. *mena*, A.S. and Friesic *móna*, Old Saxon *máno*, O.H.G. *mano*, G. *mond*, Icel. *máni*, Swed. *mone*, are all masculine; though the Du. *maan* is feminine, and the Dan. *maane* is of both genders. See Mätzner's Grammatik, i. 248.

There is a very late example of the same use in Milton, P. L. vii. 248—
> "for yet the sun
> Was not; *she* in a cloudy tabernacle
> Sojourn'd the while."

259. (18. 246.) *Quike*, alive, living. "And wholly shattered in twain the rocks" [c]; *or* "the rock" [b]. We find "quaschyn, or brysyn, or cruschyn, *briso, quasso;*" Prompt. Parv., p. 419; and, on the same page, "quaschyn, or daschyn, or fordon, *quasso, casso;*" also "quaschyd, *quassatus;*" and "quaschynge, *quassacio.*" In the Myrour of Our Lady, ed. Blunt, p. xxii, we find the remarkable phrase *al to-squatte*, used with reference to a "quashed" election.

261. (18. 248.) *Symondes sons*, the sons of Simeon; where Simeon is the "just and devout" man mentioned in S. Luke ii. 25. The reference is to the Apocryphal Gospel of Nicodemus, which is the foundation of all the numerous representations in ancient Mysteries of the scene known as the "Harrowing of Hell," a phrase denoting the removal thence of the souls of the righteous when Christ descended thither. The story of the Gospel of Nicodemus is very important for the understanding of many passages in Early English, and is very briefly as follows.

Christ is accused to Pilate of healing men on the sabbath-day, and of being a magician [see l. 46 of the present Passus]. Pilate sends a messenger to apprehend Christ, but the messenger worships Him, because he remembers having witnessed His triumphant entry into Jerusalem. Jesus goes to Pilate; and, as He goes, the standards carried by the standard-bearers miraculously bow down to Him of their own accord. Jesus is pitied by Pilate's wife; He is then accused of various charges, which Pilate rejects, saying He is innocent. A dialogue ensues between Pilate and Jesus, as in John xviii. 33—38. Nicodemus speaks in Christ's defence, and is followed by the lame man who was cured at the pool of Bethesda; also by a leper (Mat. viii. 11); by the woman healed of an issue of blood (Mat. ix. 20), whose name was Veronica (Eusebius, Hist. Eccl. lib. 7. cap. 8); and by many others who had seen Christ's miracles. The Jews demand Barabbas (John xviii. 40). Pilate washes his hands (Matt. xxvii. 24). Christ is crucified between two thieves; the thief on His right was named Dismas (see Pass. vii. 320), and the one on His left, Gestas. Longinus pierces the side of Christ with a spear (John xix. 34). Miraculous appearances occur at Christ's death (Mat. xxvii. 45, 51). The Jews affirm that the darkness was caused by a natural eclipse. Christ is taken down from the cross, and buried by Joseph of Arimathœa and Nicodemus. The Jews are angry with Nicodemus, and imprison Joseph. Joseph is miraculously released from prison. Christ rises from the dead, and preaches in Galilee. The Jews are much troubled, and are disposed to listen to the counsels of Nicodemus. Joseph of Arimathœa relates the particulars of his miraculous escape from prison. The Jews go to Arimathœa, where they find the two sons of the devout Simeon, who had been raised from the dead, and were permitted to reveal what they had witnessed in hell.

(I give the next portion of the narrative in the words of the epitome in the Legenda Aurea, cap. liv, as this was probably the account which our author really followed.)

"In euangelio Nicodemi legitur, quod Carinus et Leucius, filii Simeonis senis, cum Christo resurrexerunt, et Annæ et Caiaphæ et Nicodemo et Joseph et Gamalieli apparuerunt, et ab iis adiurati, quæ Christus apud inferos gessit, narrauerunt dicentes:—'Cum essemus cum omnibus patribus nostris patriarchis in caligine tenebrarum, subito factus est aureus color purpureusque et regalis lux illustrans super nos, statimque Adam humani generis pater exsultauit dicens: Lux ista auctoris est luminis sempiterni, qui nobis promisit mittere lumen coæternum suum. Et exclamauit Ysaias dicens: Hæc est lux patris, filius Dei, sicut prædixi, cum essem uiuus in terris—populus, qui ambulabat in tenebris, uidit lucem magnam. Tunc superuenit genitor noster Simeon et exsultans dixit: Glorificate dominum, quia ego Christum infantem natum in manibus suscepi in templo, et compulsus spiritu sancto dixi: Nunc uiderunt oculi mei salutare tuum quod parasti, etc. Post hoc superuenit quidam eremi cultor, et interrogatus a nobis quis esset, dixit: Ego sum Iohannes, qui Christum baptizaui et ante ipsum parare uias eius præiui et ipsum ostendi digito dicens: Ecce agnus Dei, etc., et descendi nuntiare uobis, quia in proximo est Christum uisitare nos. Tunc Seth dixit: cum iuissem ad portas paradisi rogare dominum, ut transmitteret mihi angelum suum, ut daret mihi de oleo misericordiæ, ut inungerem corpus patris mei Adæ, cum esset infirmus, apparuit Michael angelus dicens: Noli laborare lacrymis orando propter oleum ligni misericordiæ. Quia nullo modo poteris de illo accipere, nisi quando completi fuerint quinque millia quingenti anni. Hæc audientes omnes patriarchæ et prophetæ exsultauerunt magna exsultatione, tunc Sathan princeps et dux mortis dixit ad inferum: Præparate suscipere Iesum, qui se gloriatur Christum filium Dei esse, et homo est timens mortem dicens: Tristis est anima mea usque ad mortem, etc. et multos, quos feci surdos, sanauit et claudos erexit. Respondens inferus dixit: Si potens es tu, qualis est homo ille Iesus, qui timens mortem potentiæ tuæ aduersatur? Nam si dicit se timere mortem, capere te uult, et uæ tibi erit in sempiterna sæcula. Cui Sathan: Ego illum tentaui et populum aduersum illum excitaui, iam lanceam exacui, fel et acetum miscui, lignum crucis præparaui; in proximo est mors eius, ut perducam eum ad te. Cui inferus: Ipse ne est qui suscitauit Lazarum, quem tenebam? Cui Sathan: Ipse est. Cui inferus: coniuro te per uirtutes tuas et meas, ne perducas eum ad me; ego enim cum audiui imperium uerbi eius, contremui nec ipsum Lazarum continere potui, sed excutiens se ut aquila super omnem agilitatem saliens exiuit a nobis et, cum hæc loqueretur, facta est uox ut tonitruum dicens: Tollite portas, principes, uestras, et eleuamini, portæ æternales; et introibit rex gloriæ.[1] Ad hanc uocem concurrerunt dæmones et ostia aenea cum uectibus ferreis clauserunt. Tunc dixit Dauid: Nonno ego prophetaui dicens: Confiteantur domini, etc., quia contriuit portas aeneas, etc.? Facta est iterum uox maxima dicens: Tollite portas, etc. Uidens inferus quod duabus uicibus clamauerat, quasi ignorans dixit: Quis est iste rex gloriæ? Cui Daniel: Dominus fortis et potens, dominus potens in prælio, ipse est rex gloriæ. Tunc rex gloriæ superuenit et æternas tenebras illustrauit et extendens dominus manum et tenens dextram Adæ dixit: Pax tibi cum omnibus filiis tuis iustis meis, et adscendit dominus ab inferis, et omnes sancti sunt eum secuti."

The narrative continues by telling us that Christ delivers Adam and the patriarchs to Michael the Archangel. As the ransomed souls enter heaven, they find there two very old men; these are Enoch and Elijah. At the same time they behold a man approaching carrying the sign of the cross on his shoulders; this is the penitent thief, Dismas, who had been received into heaven without visiting hell. Here the narrative practically ends, and the sons of Simeon vanish.

There are frequent allusions to this striking narrative of the Harrowing of Hell in our old authors, which I cannot fully point out. For examples, see the play of The Harrowing of Hell, published from MS. Harl. 2253, fol. 55, back—56, back, by Mr Halliwell in 1840; also from the Auchinleck MS. by Mr Laing, in a volume entitled "Owain Miles and other pieces of Ancient English Poetry," 1837, 8vo.; the Towneley Mysteries; the Coventry Mysteries; the Chester Plays; Old Eng. Homilies, ed. Morris, ii. 112; Hampole's Pricke of Conscience, ed. Morris, 6529—6546. See also Cædmon, ed. Thorpe, pp. 288, 289; Codex Exoniensis, ed. Thorpe, p. 32; The Deuelis Parlament, in Hymns to the Virgin and Christ, ed. Furnivall, esp. pp. 48—53; Cursor Mundi, ed. Morris, pp. 1022—1064; &c. Compare also Dante, Inf. c. iv; Warton's Hist. Eng. Poetry, ed. 1871, iii. 164; Strutt, Manners and Customs, iii. 131; Tyrwhitt's note to. Cant. Tales, l. 3512; &c. A good account of the influence of the Gospel of Nicodemus upon European literature will be found in a handy volume of 101 pages, entitled—"Das Evangelium Nicodemi in der Abendländischen Literatur; nebst drei Excursen über Joseph von Arimathia als apostel Englands, das Drama 'harrowing of Hell,' und Jehan Michel's passion Christi;" von Dr Richard Paul Wülcker. Paderborn, 1872.

I must not forget to remind the reader that there exists an Anglo-Saxon version of the Gospel of Nicodemus, printed by Thwaites in his Heptateuchus, &c., Oxford, 1698.

An engraving of an interesting picture of the scene of the Harrowing of Hell is given at p. 498 of the Military and Religious Life in the Middle Ages, by P. Lacroix. It is from a fresco by Simone di Martino in the

---

[1] See Pass. xxi. 272.

church of Santa Maria Novella, Florence, painted in the fourteenth century. The subject was suggested, says Lacroix (p. 501), by "the poem attributed to Venancius Fortunatus, the Christian poet of the seventh century."

263. (18. 250.) The expression "Jesus as a giant" [c] explains the obscure phrase "*gigas* the giant" [b]. The reference, in the first instance, was either to the very common legend of St Christopher, or to Samson, who, by carrying off the gates of Gaza, was a type of Christ's breaking the gates of hell; Ælfric's Homilies, i. 227.

272. (18. 259.) *Bit vnsperre*, bids unbar.   See the note to l. 261:

276. (18. 263.) *To helle*, to hell; a translation of the Lat. *ad inferum ;* see note to l. 261.   But [b] has merely *to hem alle.*

277. (18. 264.) *Lazar hit fette*, it (sc. the light) fetched Lazarus away; see note to l. 261.

278. (18. 265.) *Combraunce*, trouble, misfortune; it occurs three times in The Destruction of Troy, ed. Panton and Donaldson.

280. (18. 267.) *Hit*, i. e. mankind.   *Ther lazar is*, where Lazarus is [c]. The word should have been printed *lazar*, as in l. 277, not *laȝar.*   However, the symbols for *z* and *ȝ* are written exactly alike in the MS.

283. (*not in* b.) This remarkable passage (283—296) is paraphrased in my Preface to the C-text, p. xciii, which see.

Mr Halliwell, in his Dictionary, remarks that *Ragamofin* is a name of a demon in some of the old mysteries.   It has since passed into a sort of familiar slang term for any one poorly clad.   I have a note that in a French mystery of the Fall of Lucifer, taken from "Le tres excellent et Sainct Mystere du Vieil Testament," fol. Paris, 1542, we find such names of demons as Lucifer, Sathan, *Astaroth*, Cerberus, Mamona, Asmodeus, Leviatan, Agrappart, &c.   Milton has Satan, Beelzebub, Moloch, Chemos, *Astoreth*, Thammuz, Dagon, Azazel, Mammon, Belial, &c.   In King Lear we have Modo, Mahu, &c., besides Frateretto and "the foul fiend Flibbertigibbet." The demons, it may be observed, took the comic parts in the old mysteries, and were therefore sometimes fitted with odd names.

In the Towneley Mysteries, p. 246, we have the names *Astarot*, Anaballe, Berith, and Belyalle.   Mr Wright notes that the name *Astaroth*, "as given to one of the devils, occurs in a curious list of actors in the Miracle Play of St Martin, given by M. Jubinal, in the preface to his Mystères Inédits, vol. ii. p. ix.   It is similarly used in the Miracle Play of the Martyrdom of St Peter and St Paul, [ed.] Jubinal, ib. vol. i. p. 69."   He also notes its occurrence in the Towneley Mysteries.   In the King of Tars, ed. Ritson, it is the name of an idol.   It occurs in our poem *twice;* see ll. 289, 449.

287. (*not in* b.) *Cheke we*, let us check; i. e. interrupt his course.   I believe this to be a very early example of the use of this word as a *verb*.   As a *substantive*, it occurs in Rob. of Brunne; see Richardson's Dictionary.

Chyne, a chink; A.S. *cine*.   It is used by Wyclif and Mandeville; see Stratmann.   In the Romance of Partenay, ed. Skeat, 4343, we have the expression—"in a *chine* of the roch," i. e. rock.   It is still in common use in the Isle of Wight for a cleft in a cliff.   I give two more examples, from Batman vppon Bartholomè, lib. 9, cap. 8, and lib. 12, cap. 27.

"In winter-time pathes and wayes be made slipperie and fennic, but the pores of the earth and *chins* be constrained and frore [*frozen*], and made hard with cold, frost, and ice."

". . they make their neasts in walls and in places with *chinnes* and hoales."

In the North of England, it is common in the form *kin*, and usually means a chap, or crack in the skin; see Atkinson's Cleveland Glossary.

288. (*not in* b.)   *Louer*, a loover.   "A *loouer* or tunnell in the roof or top of a great hall to avoid smoke, *Fumarium, spiramentum;*" Baret.   "*Louer* of a hall, esclère;" Palsgrave.   The word has been said to be a corruption from the Icel. *ljóri*, an opening in the roof for permitting the escape of smoke, and for admitting light; in which case the derivation is from the Icel. *ljós*, light.   See Garnett's Essays, p. 62, and *Loover* in Wedgwood's Etym. Dictionary.   Yet, on the other hand, there is a curious piece of evidence in support of the derivation from the O.Fr. *louuert* (= *l'ouvert*), unless there has been some confusion.   In the French text of the Romance of Partenay, we have, in the description of the fortifications of a town—

> "Murdrieres Il a *a louuert*
> Pour lancier, traire, et deffendre."

The Eng. version has—

> "At *louers*, lowpes, Archers had plente
> To cast, draw, and shete, the diffence to be."

See The Romans of Partenay, ed. Skeat, l. 1175, and the note.   However, whatever be the right solution, let not the reader omit to consult Mr Way's excellent note upon the word in the Prompt. Parv., p. 315.   And see *Lover* in Nares' Glossary.

Loupe, a loop-hole; see *Loop-hole* in Wedgwood.   "*Loupe* in a towne-wall or castell, *creneau;*" Palsgrave.

289. (*not in* b.)   *Astrot*, Ashtaroth; see l. 449, and note to l. 283.   *Hot out*, hoot out, cry aloud; see footnote.   *Haue out*, i. e. fetch out.

293. (*not in* b.)   *Bowes of brake*, bows with a rack or winch; an allusion to cross-bows of the largest size and strongest tension.   Pictures of these crossbows in the hands of Genoese and other archers are not uncommon; see Fairholt, Costume in England, pp. 175, 176; Johnes's Froissart, i. 165; Knight's Old England, i. 225, fig. 872.   In the allit. Troy-book, ed. Panton and Donaldson, p. 186, l. 5728, the Greeks attack the Trojans—

> "With alblastis also [thai] atlet to shote,
> With *big bowes of brake* bykrit full hard."

The note to the line gives three explanations, the first and third of which I reject without hesitation, but the second is correct.   The three suggestions are (1) that the bows are provided with an instrument [what sort of instrument, and why?] for *breaking* the tension of the bow, or for making the arrow *break* from it [clearly a pair of poor and unfounded guesses]; or (2) that the *brake* was the crank or handle which the soldier worked when using the bow; or (3) that *bows of brake* were bows for *breaching*; [which they were not, as I shall shew.]. The old word *brake* was *a general name for any mechanical contrivance*, especially a lever, *that enabled great force to be used.* Hence it means (1) a pump-handle; (2) a flax-dresser's instrument; (3) a twitch for horses; (4) a sort of rack, or instrument of torture; (5) a frame for confining vicious horses when being shod, &c.; see *Brake* in Halliwell and Wedgwood. Wedgwood well cites the Span. *bregar* el arco, to bend a bow; Fr. *braquer* un canon, to bend or direct a cannon; to which I may add that *braquer du chambre* means to brake hemp (Cotgrave). No doubt the Fr. *braquer*, as applied to a cannon, has suffered the same change as the Eng. *bend*, which at first meant to bend a bow; next, to *set* a crossbow or to *cock* a gun; and lastly, can be used merely for directing or levelling a cannon. The word is Old Low German, and probably some of the contrivances came from the Netherlands. Cf. Du. *braak*, a brake; *vlasbraak*, a flax-dresser's brake. The derivation of the sb. is ultimately from Du. *breken* (O.Du. *braken*), to break; cognate with A.S. *brécan*. Cf. O.Du. *brake*, a fetter for the neck, an instrument of torture; and see *Brake* in Richardson.

To shew that *a bow of brake* was not necessarily a bow for *breaching* walls, it seems to me sufficient to remark that, in the present passage, Satan calls upon the demons to use such bows for their *defence*, the very last thing he would desire being a breach in the walls, as shewn by l. 288. And again, Tydeus, when besieging Thebes, was shot by one of the *defenders* of the city with that very weapon. At least, so Lydgate tells us in his Siege of Thebes, part iii.

> "For one, alas! that on the walles stood,
> Which all that day vpon him abode,
> With a quarel, sharpe-heded for his sake,
> Marked him with a *bow of brake*
> So cruelly, making none a-rest,
> Till it was passed both back and brest."

An iron-headed "quarrel," shot from a bow of brake, was the most fatal weapon known in the olden times, before the invention of gunpowder; and even, perhaps, for some time afterwards.

Brasene gonnes. Observe that this mention of guns is not in the B-text (1377). *Gonne* was used of a machine for casting stones, but here it is *brazen*. In Chaucer's House of Fame, iii. 553 (written about 1384?), a *gonne* is discharged by gunpowder. In the Avowynge of Arthur, st. lxv, ed. Robson (Camden Society), p. 89, the word *gunne* actually means a *shot!*

> "The caytef crope into a tunne
> That was sette therowte in the sunne,
> And there come fliand a *gunne*,
> And lemet as the leuyn,
> Liȝte opon hitte atte the last[e]
> That was fast[e]nut so fast[e],
> Alle in sundur hit brast[e]
> In six or in seuyn."

(N.B. Cf. the last line with our *at sixes and sevens*.)

An early mention of cannon is in Barbour's Bruce, written in 1375. See my note to The Bruce, bk. xix. l. 399; and Riley, Mem. London, p. 205.

294. (*not in* b.) *Shultrom*, squadron; also spelt *shiltrum*, and by Barbour *childrome* or *cheldrome*. It is a corruption of the A.S. *scyld-truma*, lit. a troop-shield, and hence an armed company or battalion of soldiers. "Bote, ar the *schellroms* come to-gedders, on of the Normans syde, þat hyʒte Tailefer by hys name, cast hys sword and pleyde to-vore þe ostes," &c.; Trevisa's description of the Battle of Hastings. The word occurs frequently in Barbour's Bruce; and see other examples in Stratmann, s. v. *schild*.

I may add that Satan here expresses his belief that Christ was accompanied by a host of angels. We may impute this false impression to his fears. Angels are first mentioned in l. 452.

295. (*not in* b.) *Mangonel*, a large engine for throwing heavy stones, &c. Chaucer has the term *staf-slinge* in Sir Thopas, B. 2019, meaning an instrument for slinging, held in the hand, in which additional power was gained by fastening the lithe part of the sling to the end of a stiff stick. Adopting this definition of a "staff-sling," it will be found that all the artillery engines of the middle ages can be reduced to two classes; those which, like the mangonel and trebuchet, are enlarged staff-slings, and those which, like the arblast and springold, are great cross-bows. See the detailed descriptions of these engines in Col. Yule's edition of Marco Polo, ii. 122.

296. (*not in* b.) *Crokes*, hooks; especially such hooks as were fastened on to the end of a long pole, and could be used as grappling-irons; whether in a sea-engagement, as described in Chaucer's Legend of Good Women (Cleopatra, 61)—"In goth the grapenel so ful of *crokes*"—or in the defence of a town, for annoying assailants, removing scaling-ladders, and the like.

Kalketrappes, calthrops or caltrops; defined by Webster as "an instrument with four iron points [fastened to a ball] so disposed that, three of them being on the ground, the other projects upward. They are scattered on the ground where an enemy's cavalry are to pass, to impede their progress by endangering the horse's feet." "Caltrap of yryn, fote hurtynge, *hamus*;" Prompt. Parv., p. 59; on which see Mr Way's note.

The A.S. *coltræppe*, which is given as a gloss to Lat. *rhamnus*, meaning, I suppose, some kind of buckthorn, is not to be regarded as an original, but as a corrupted form. We also find an A.S. *calcetreppe* (MS. Bodley 130) as the name of the common star-thistle; see Cockayne's Leechdoms, iii. 316. This word is plainly borrowed from the Latin original of the French *chaussetrappe*, which is the French word for the iron implement here intended. The Lat. form must have been *calcitrappa* or *calciatrappa*; see Brachet's French Dictionary. Brachet explains *chaussetrappe* as "a trap which shoes the foot," from *trappe* and *chausser*, which seems a very forced expression. I should prefer to derive it from the Low Lat. *calcia*, meaning either (1) a shoe, (2) the heel, or (3) the sole of the foot, and *trappa*, a trap; and I should explain it simply as 'a trap for the foot.' Indeed, the A.S. form *calcetreppe* may as well be derived at once, as Mr Cockayne suggests, from Lat. *calcem*,

the heel, and the Latin form of *trap*; the A.S. *betræppan*, to entrap, occurs
in the A.S. Chron. an. 992. The Fr. *chaussetrappe* also means the star-
thistle, called by the scientific name of *Centaurea calcitrapa*; a name given
to that thistle because it resembles the war-implement. Hence we should
obtain the following results. Given a Lat. *calciatrappa*, meaning a snare
for the foot or heel, we should hence obtain the Fr. *chaussetrappe*, meaning
(1) a war-implement as above described, and (2) a star-thistle resembling
that implement. We could also hence obtain the Mid. Eng. *calketrappe* or
kalketrappe, and the Mod. Eng. *caltrop* or *calthrop*, the modern word being
modified by the loss of the second *c*, as in the A.S. *coltræppe*, a word concerning which not much is known. Palsgrave gives us—" Caltrappe, *chaussetrappe*;" and in a gloss printed in Reliq. Antiq., i. 37, we find the entry—
" *Tribulus marinus*, culketrappe, sea-þistel."

297. (18. 270.) Lucifer is here made quite a different personage from
Satan; cf. ll. 353, 354. Satan is the Prince or Duke of Death, but Lucifer
is the Prince of Hell, called in the Latin "inferus;" see note to l. 261
above, and cf. l. 273. Cf. Cursor Mundi, p. 1030; Town. Myst., p. 246.
However, our author has paid small regard to the account in the Gospel of
Nicodemus, and has put some of the speeches into the wrong mouths. The
reference to Lazarus in. l. 277 should not have been made by Satan, but
by Lucifer; and in l. 315 we have a complete confusion, because the
Temptation is there ascribed, not to Satan, but to Lucifer; see note to that
line, p. 418. Wyclif speaks of the "pride of Lucifer and cruelte of Suthanas;"
Works, iii. 296.

298. (18. 271.) *Is longe gon*, it is long ago since I (first) knew him. For
gon [c], the B-text has *ago*.

302. (18. 275.) " By right and reason." See the reasoning below, in ll.
376—403. Cf. Cursor Mundi, p. 246.

311. (18. 281.) " And since we have been seised (of them) for 7000
years " [c]; " And since I possessed (them) for 700 years " [b]. The reading *I seised* [b] is very awkward; but the variations in the footnote are no
better. The best emendation is the author's own, as given in [c]. The
alteration from 700 to 7000 is an improvement, as coming nearer to the supposed length of the period indicated. The use of the number *seven* is
merely to render the time rather indefinite, according to the author's practice
elsewhere; see the notes on the indefinite expression *seven yere* in Pass. v.
82, p. 80, and vii. 214, p. 119.

The supposed period during which the patriarchs remained in hell was,
according to the Gospel of Nicodemus, 5500 years; see note to l. 261 above.
In the Knight de la Tour, p. 59, the term is said to be 5000 years. In the
Coventry Mysteries, p. 105, the time from the Creation to the birth of
Christ is said to be 4604 years; and in " Owayn Miles," quoted in Wright's
St Patrick's Purgatory, p. 77, Adam is said to have been " yn helle with
Lucyfere " for precisely the same period. In the Towneley Mysteries, p.
244, the term is 4600 years. In The Deuelis Perlament, l. 324, Lucifer says

he has dwelt in hell for more than 4000 years; Hymns to the Virgin and Christ, ed. Furnivall, p. 51.   So also in the Ancren Riwle, p. 54.

315. (18. 284.) "Because thou obtainedst them by guile, and broke into his garden." Here the Temptation of man is ascribed to Lucifer, which makes much confusion, because in ll. 297, 302, Lucifer is made the same with the Prince of Hell; see note to l. 297 above. The Temptation should have been ascribed to Satan, who is called "the deouel" in l. 327. By an oversight, I did not sufficiently observe the distinction made between Satan and Lucifer in ll. 353, 354, &c.; hence there are three errors in the headings of the pages. In the headings to the C-text, pp. 385, 389, and 393, for "Satan" read "Lucifer;" and similar corrections should be made in the headings to the B-text, pp. 338, 341. Similar corrections are required in the marginal notes, C-text, pp. 389, 393; B-text, pp. 338, 341.

In the Deuelis Perlament (Hymns to the Virgin and Christ, ed. Furnivall, p. 50), the Temptation of man is ascribed, as here, to Lucifer; but then Satan, Lucifer, and Hell are made into *three* separate persons.

318. (18. 286.) *By heore on*, alone by herself; equivalent to the expression *by hir-selue* [b]. The text alluded to is—" Si unus ceciderit, ab altero fulcietur; *uæ soli*: quia cum ceciderit, non habet subleuantem se;" Eccles. iv. 10. Compare—"*Homo solus aut deus aut demon*," &c.; Burton, Anat. Mel., pt. 1, sec. 2, mem. 2, subsec. 6.

321. (*not in* b.) *Troiledest*, didst deceive, didst bewitch. The word is very rare; but Burguy gives "*troiller, truiller*, ensorceler, charmer, tromper; de l'ancien norois *trölla*, enchanter." Though rare in French or English, it is common enough in the Scandinavian languages. Cf. Icel. *trylla*, to enchant, charm, fascinate; Dan. *trylleri*, magic, &c.; all derived from the Icel. *troll*, Dan. *trold*, a goblin.

325. (18. 290.) I quote here Mr Wright's note. "Goblin is a name still applied to a devil. It belongs properly to a being of the old Teutonic popular mythology, a hob-goblin, the "lubber-fiend" of the poet [Milton, *L'Allegro*], and seems to be identical with the German *kobold*. See Grimm, Deutsche Mythologie, p. 286. *Gobelin* occurs as the name of one of the shepherds in the Mystery of the Nativity, printed by M. Jubinal in his Mystères inédits, vol. ii. p. 71. It occurs as the name of a devil in a song of the commencement of the 14th century, in Polit. Songs, p. 238—

" Sathanas huere syre seyde on his sawe,
    Gobelyn made is gerner of gromene mawe."

See also *Goblin* in Wedgwood.   Cf. note to l. 283, p. 413.

326. (18. 291.) *Hit maketh*, causes it to be so, brings about this result [c]. On this curious phrase, see note to Pass. viii. 28, p. 139.

334. (18. 296.) The words *troiled* [c] and *trolled* [b] are altogether different. The C-text means—"Thus hath he deceived (me), and laboured continually, during his lifetime, like a careful man, for these 32 years;" where *tydy* means orderly, careful (lit. timely), as in Pass. iv. 478. The B-text means—"And thus hath he rolled on (i. e. continued) for these 32

years;" where *troll* is used in a neuter sense, though it is the same word
as when we speak of *trolling* a hoop. "Tryllyn, or trollyn, *volvo*;" Prompt.
Parv. The word *troiled* [c] has been explained in the note to l. 321 just
above. But it is very probable that the reading *troiled* in *this* passage is a
mere mistake of the scribes, due to the use of *troiledest* just above, and a far
better reading would be to retain the *trolled* of the B-text. It will be
observed that there was no chance of confusion in the B-text, because the
line containing *troiledest* does not appear there.

The "two and thirty years" refers to the length of Christ's life.

——(18. 298.) "To warn Pilate's wife, what manner of man Jesus was."
The mention of Pilate's wife in Mat. xxvii. 19 easily led on to the idea of an
old legend, that the dream of Pilate's wife was caused by a demon, who en-
deavoured to defer the death of Christ and the consequent defeat of Satan.
(This is clearly the idea intended in the C-text, ll. 336—339.) See the
Coventry Mysteries, pp. 308, 309, where Satan says—

> "Lo! a wyle ȝet haue a [*read* I] kast,
> If I myth Ihesus lyf save,
> Helle gatys xal be sperd fast,
> And kepe stylle alle tho I haue.
> To Pylattys wyff I wele now go,
> And sche is aslepe a-bed ful fast,
> And byd here withowtyn wordys mo
> To Pylat that sche send in hast."

So in The Deuelis Perlament (Hymns to the Virgin and Christ, ed. Furnivall,
p. 43), the devil says—

> "Pilatis wijf y bad bisily ȝeue tent
> That ihesu were not doon on þe crois."

In the Cursor Mundi, p. 920, the account follows St Matthew. Cf. Peter
Comestor's Historia Euangelica.

The phrase *what dones man*, i.e. a man of what make, is very singular
and rare. Here *dones* is the pp. *don*, made, used as a substantive, and even
taking a genitive suffix, such as we see in the phrase *what kynnes man*; see
the account of *kynnes* in the note to Pass. xi. 123, p. 215. Mr W. Aldis
Wright has kindly given me another instance of the use of this word. In
Hearne's edition of Rob. of Gloucester, p. 112, is the line—"He askede,
wat God and wat þing Mercurius was." The Trinity MS. has, in this
passage, the reading—"He axede what *Idone* god," &c.; and the Digby MS.
has "what man*ere* god." I have also myself found two more examples of
this word; both in the Alexander fragment, which I call the B. fragment
(from MS. Bodley 264), ll. 222, 999.

340. (18. 302.) *On bones ȝede*, went about with its bones, i. e. went about
alive. Cf. "a spirit hath not flesh and *bones*, as ye see me have;" Luke
xxiv. 39.

344. (18. 304.) This is a beautiful conception, and well expressed; the
bright soul of Christ is seen sailing towards the dark abode of the demons,
with even and majestic motion. Compare the appearance of *Anima Christi*

in the Coventry Mysteries, p. 330. Mr Wright bids us observe a similar excellent use of the word *sailing* by Milton, Sams. Agon., 713—

> " But who is this, what thing of sea or land?
> Female of sex it seems,
> That so bedeck'd, ornate, and gay,,
> Comes this way *sailing*
> Like a stately ship," &c.

I have already drawn attention (at p. 412 above) to the fresco by Simone di Martino in the church of Santâ Maria Novella. There is an excellent representation of the same scene in one of the painted windows in King's College Chapel, Cambridge.

See Pearson's Exposition of the Creed (art. *He descended into hell*) for citations from the authorities upon this subject.

348. (18. 308.) *Lesynges*, lies; translated by Lat. *mendacia* in the marginal note [c]. See next note.

351. (18. 311.) *Lowe*, liedst, didst lie [c]; cf. l. 447 below. "The *lesynge* was when he sayde to Eue that they shulde not 'dye, though they eate of that fruyte;" Myrour of Our Lady, ed. Blunt, p. 204. " Leesynge, or lyynge, or gabbynge, *mendacium;*" Prompt. Parv., p. 298; and see Way's note.

352. (18. 312.) "In land (i. e. earth) and in hell" [c]; "on land and on water" [b].

353—361. (*not in* b.) A mere digression on lying, to be considered as within a parenthesis, as the author himself tells us. In l. 358, *beleize* means belie, deceive. In l. 361, *suynge my teme* = pursuing my theme or discourse.

362. (18. 313.) Here the account follows the usual narrative rather closely; see note to l. 261. Compare also Cursor Mundi, p. 1036; Cov. Mysteries; The Deuelis Perlament (Hymns to the Virgin, ed. Furnivall), p. 49, &c. *Eft*, again, a second time; see l. 272 above.

367. (18. 319.) Cf. Castel of Love, ed. Weymouth, p. 64—

> " Helle ʒates he al to-breek,
> And to-daschte al þe fendes ek," &c.

368. (18. 320.) "For all that any wight or gate-warden could do."

369. (18. 321.) The Latin phrases "populus in tenebris" and "ecce agnus dei" are used because they are cited in the Gospel of Nicodemus. See note to l. 261.

372. (18. 324.) "With that light flew forth" [c]; cf. *flowen* in Pass. iii. 249. "He caught up into His light" [b]; with which cf. A. xii. 91, and the note. Compare—

> " With him he drouʒ out alle hise
> þat diʒeden in his seruise
> From þe tyme þat he Adam wrouʒte
> þat he vp-ros and vs for-bouʒte."
>
>   Castell of Loue, ed. Weymouth, p. 67.

"Descendit ad inferna, ut Adam protoplastum, et Patriarchas, et Prophetas, omnesque iustos, qui pro originali peccato ibidem detinebantur, liberaret;" Sermo de Symbolo, cap. vii; App. to S. August. Op. vi. col. 1194, ed. Migne.

374. (18. 326.) "To preserve the right (i. e. just claim) of us both" [c]. On the word *beyere*, see note to l. 36 above, p. 401.

The argument which follows is to shew, that the claim of Satan to the soul of man has been satisfied, and that Christ has established a newer and better claim. No doubt our author has here again followed Grosteste; see Castel of Love, ed. Weymouth, pp. 51—54. Also the Towneley, Mysteries, p. 250.

379. (18. 331.) *Hit made*, caused it, brought it about; cf. l. 326.

382. (18. 334.) "Falsely thou didst fetch there (i. e. thence) that which it was my part to guard" [c]; or, "the thing that I loved" [b].

——(18. 335.) "Thus like a lizard (serpent), with a lady's face." The words *lizard* and *lady* refer to the fact that the serpent who tempted Eve was sometimes represented with short feet, like a lizard or crocodile, and the face of a young maiden. Even when the feet do not appear, the face is commonly retained, as in the representation in the chapter-house of Salisbury cathedral. See the woodcut in Wright's Hist. of Caricature, p. 73. In the Chester Plays, ed. Wright, p. 26, Satan says—

> " A manner of an edder [*adder*] is in this place,
> That winges like a birde shee hase;
> *Feete as an edder, a medens face ;*
> Her kinde [*nature*] will I take."

And in the margin of the same is the Latin note—"Superius volucris penna, serpens pede, forma puella." In the Coventry Mysteries, p. 29, the Serpent is called "a werm with an aungelys face." In the allit. Destruction of Troy, ed. Panton and Donaldson, p. 144, l. 4451, it is said that the Tempter had "a face vne fourmet as a fre maydon." Even Chaucer alludes to the same belief where he addresses Donegild as—"O serpent vnder femininitee;" Man of Lawes Tale, Group B, l. 360, which see. One authority for the notion is Peter Comestor, who says, in his Historia Libri Genesis, that Satan " elegit quoddam genus serpentis (vt ait Beda) *virgineum vultum* habens." In the Ancren Riwle, p. 206, we are gravely informed that " þe scorpiun is ones cunnes wurm þet haueð neb, as me seið, sumdel iliche ase wummon, and is neddre bihinden; makeð feir semblaunt and fikeð [*flatters*] mid te heaued, and stingeð mid te teile." See Rev. ix. 7, 10.

385. (18. 337.) See note to l. 166 above. And cf. l. 395 below.

389. (*not in* b.) *Lyf* is used over and over again by our author to signify *a living person*, a man; see the Glossary. In this passage it is used both in this and in the more usual sense; so that, though the text has a puzzling appearance, it is easy enough to any one familiar with the rest of the poem. The sense is—" So must a (living) man lose his life, whenever that (living) man has destroyed the life of another; so that life may pay for life, as the old law demands."

392. (18. 339.) *Ich man to amenden hit*, I, in my nature of Man, (am ready) to amend it.   But the B-text is better.

394. (18. 344.) *Aquykye*, quicken, make alive again.   Cf.—"For to *quykee* in hem the mynde and remembraunce of the biforeseid thingis;" Pecock's Repressor, i. 237.   "Quyknyn, quykyn, *vegeto, vivifico;* Prompt. Parv., p. 421.

——(18. 355.) "Let guile go against guile."   This helps to illustrate the difficult expression explained in the note to B. x. 192, p. 244.

400. (18. 356.) In the Legenda Aurea, cap. liii. (De Passione Domini), ed. Grässe, 2nd ed., p. 229, we have—"quia sicut Adam deceptus fuit in ligno, ita Christus passus fuit in ligno.   In quadam hystoria Græcorum dicitur, *quod in eodem.*"   The last statement is very curious; cf. note to l. 144 above.   So in the Towneley Mysteries, p. 72, we find that God declares—

> " I wylle that my son manhede take,
>   For reson wylle that ther be thre;
>   A man, a madyn, and a tre.
>   Man for man, tre for tre,
>   Madyn for madyn, thus shalle it be."

That is, Christ for Adam, the cross for the Tree of Knowledge, and Mary for Eve.

404. (18. 361.) *Brouk*, enjoy; lit. brook.   "As I brew, so must I needs drink;" proverb, in Camden's Remaines, 1614.   In French, "Avallez ce que vous avez brassé."   The proverb appears very early in English, as it occurs in a ballad of the time of Henry III., written against Richard, Earl of Cornwall, called "the King of Almaigne;" printed in Polit. Songs, ed. Wright, p. 69.   The 12th line of it is—"Let him habbe, ase he brew, bale to dryng," i. e. let him have, as he brew, evil to drink.   Cf. "Suilk als þai brued, now ha þai dronken;" Cursor Mundi, l. 2848.

> " And who so wicked ale breweth,
>   Ful ofte he mote the werse drinke;" Gower, Conf. Amant., bk. iii.

"It is even said that when Courcelles, the French minister at the Scotch Court, endeavoured to rouse James [the First] to some rigorous measures for his mother's safety, he replied, with a coarseness and calmness equally characteristic, that 'as she brewed, she must drink;'" note to Mrs Jameson's Female Sovereigns; i. 268.

409. (*not in b.*) The idea is a good one, when once apprehended.   Christ says that *His* drink is *love;* and this He will drink (i. e. receive) not from any deep source, nor from the learned only, but from all true Christian souls, which are to Him as homely vessels containing it.   The metaphor is strikingly original, characteristic, and beautiful.   Lines 408—410 are not in the B-text, and distinctly declare that the power of the poet had not failed him, at the time of the last revision of his poem.

411. (18. 365.) The alliteration is not apparent in [b]; but at once appears in [c], which shews that the author pronounced *thirst* as *first;* just as in the phrase "afurst and afyngred;" Pass. xvii. 15.

. 412. (*not in* b.) "Pymente, drynke, *pigmentum, nectar, mellicratum;*" Prompt. Parv., p. 399. On which Mr Way notes—"*Pigmentum,* or *pimentum,* wine spiced, or mingled with honey, called in French *piment,* was formerly in high estimation. See Kyng Alisaunder, ed. Weber, l. 4178, and Weber's note. Chaucer [if the English version be his] speaks of it in the Romaunt of the Rose, 6027; and in his translation of Boethius, bk. ii. met. 5 (ed. Morris, l. 1329). Gower says of Love—

'That neuer *pyment* ne vernage
Was half so swete for to drynke.'—Conf. Amant., bk. vi."

See the rest of Mr Way's note, with the recipe, shewing that it was made of wine, sugar, gingerbread, honey, powder of ginger, and cloves; and coloured with saffron. See also another recipe in Halliwell's Dictionary, s. v. *Piment,* and the note in The Babees Book, ed. Furnivall, p. 203, where it is said that *piments* were probably so named "because they were originally prepared by the *pigmentarii* or apothecaries; and they were used much in the same manner as the *liqueurs* of modern times. See Henderson's History of Ancient and Modern Wines, 1824, p. 283." And see *Pimentum, Pigmentum, Pigmentarius,* in Ducange. The varieties of *piment* most often mentioned are *hippocras* and *clarry* or *clarre.*

Pomade was, as its name implies, made of apples, and therefore a kind of cider. See *Pomade* in Roquefort, and *Pomata* in Ducange. Our *pomatum* was also so called because formerly made from apples; but its use is very different.

414. (18. 367.) "Till the vintage fall (i. e. take place) in the vale of Jehoshaphat, and I drink the right ripe must, the resurrection of the dead." This is an extension of the idea commented on in the note to l. 409.

Vendage answers to the Low Lat. *vindagia,* another form of *vindemia,* whence the Fr. *vendange* or *vendenge,* which see in Cotgrave.

The valley of Jehoshaphat is here supposed to be the future scene of the resurrection of mankind, an idea derived from Joel iii. 2, 12, 13. It is a name now given to the deep ravine between Jerusalem and the Mount of Olives, formerly called Kidron or Cedron. "We first encounter its new title in the *Onomasticon* of Eusebius and Jerome, and in the commentary of the latter father on Joel . . . . . Both Moslems and Jews believe that the last judgment is to take place here;" Smith's Dict. of the Bible, art. *Jehoshaphat,* q. v. Hence it was supposed that the Virgin Mary was buried here. See Maundeville's Travels, ed. Halliwell, pp. 95, 114; Cov. Mysteries, p. 393; Ælfric's Homilies, ed. Thorpe, i. 441; Dante, Inferno, x. 11; King Horn, &c., ed. Lumby, p. 96; Wyclif's Works, ii. 405.

418. (18. 371.) *Feondekenes,* fiendkins, little fiends; a coined word.

425. (18. 378.) *Ofter pan ones,* more than once. This expression looks at first as if the author were speaking ironically; but our author is always so serious and explicit upon points of law, of which he shews a special knowledge, that we must accept his words literally as a remarkable testimony to the fact that, if hanging was improperly performed, it was usual to respite

the criminal, and the more so, if the king happened to be near enough to be applied to personally for a pardon. A most interesting paper concerning cases of imperfect hanging, entitled "Hanging from a historical and physiological point of view," was contributed to the Medical Times and Gazette of June 10, 1871, p. 669, in which the present passage was cited and numerous illustrations given. I quote the following instances from that paper.

"We are acquainted with several well authenticated cases in which, previous to the composition of Piers the Plowman, reprieves were granted to criminals who had survived the operation of hanging. The following is the form in which a pardon in a case of this nature was granted by Henry III., in the 48th year of his reign (1264) to a woman who was hanged for harbouring thieves. 'Rex omnibus, etc. salutem. Quia Inetta de Balsham pro receptaculo latronum et imposito nuper per considerationem curie nostre suspendio adiudicata, et ab hora nona diei lune usque post ortum solis diei Martis sequen*tis* suspensa, viva evasit, sicut ex testimonii[s] fide dignorum accipimus: Nos divinæ charitatis intuitu, pardonavimus eidem Inetta sectam pacis nostre que ad nos pertinet pro receptaculo predicto, et firmam pacem nostram ei inde concedimus. In cuius, etc. Teste rege apud Cantuar., xvi. die Augusti.' This remarkable document is taken from the Patent Rolls of the above-mentioned year.

"Two nearly similar cases are recorded as having occurred in the following century, and by a strange coincidence, they both happened at Leicester. In 1313, Matthew of Enderby, a thief, was convicted, and sentenced to be hanged. 'He was led to the gallows by the frank pledges of Birstall and Belgrave, and by them suspended; but, on his body being taken down and carried to the cemetery of St John's Hospital for interment, he revived, and was subsequently exiled.'—Thompson's Hist. of Leicester, p. 110. In 1363, as is related by Henry of Knighton, in his Chronicle of English History, col. 2627:—'Walter Wynkeburn having been hanged at Leicester, after having been taken down from the gallows as a dead man, was being carried to the cemetery to be buried, but began to revive in the cart. To this man King Edward [III.] granted pardon in Leicester Abbey, and gave him a Charter of pardon, thus saying in my [Knighton's] hearing :—Deus tibi dedit uitam, et nos dabimus tibi cartam.' "

This instance is most remarkable, and can hardly be other than the very one of which William was thinking. It occurred in 1363, and, as he intimates, the king happened to be at the very place where the execution took place, and spoke to the criminal personally.

Other remarkable cases of resuscitation occurred later, such as that of Anne Greene, about 1650; see Plot's Natural Hist. of Oxfordshire, p. 197; Derham's Physico-Theology, 3rd ed. 1714, p. 157; Gent. Magazine, vol. lxx.; Knight's Book of Table-talk, 1836, i. 236; Plot's Nat. Hist. of Staffordshire, p. 292. Two other cases, one in 1658, are also mentioned by Plot. Three persons, all tailors, escaped from the gallows at Cork between 1755 and 1766; The Cork Remembrancer, by Edwards, p. 214. Another case in

Ireland, that of Mr Lanagan, in the last century, is given in Sir Jonah Barrington's Personal Sketches of his Own Times. The Scottish law permits but one hanging, as in the case of Margaret Dickinson, 1728; see The Newgate Calendar, vol. ii. p. 233. Compare Scott's Heart of Mid Lothian, ch. iii. The law in England, however, seems to have changed completely since the olden times, since Blackstone says expressly that "if the criminal be not thoroughly killed, the officer of the sheriff must hang him again."

433. (18. 386.) "If the boldness of their sins be at all dearly paid for;" i. e. if I have adequately suffered for their sins. See note to l. 413.

435. (18. 388.) As to the Latin quotation here, see note to Pass. v. 140, p. 83.

——(18. 390.) *Til parce it hote*, till the word "Spare-thou" command it (to be otherwise); i. e. till the word *parce* be the signal of their release. *It hote* is a similar phrase to *it make;* see Pass. viii. 28. See Mr Wright's work on St Patrick's Purgatory.

439. (18. 392.) *Blood* here signifies kinship, relationship; or rather the personification of kinship, i. e. a relative; see l. 429. The sense is, that one relative can bear to see another thirsty or chilly, but will pity him if he is actually wounded and bleeding.

Athurst = A.S. *of-þyrsted*, very thirsty (Cædmon, ed. Thorpe, p. 3, l. 7).

Similarly, *acale* is probably an old pp. (of the strong form) from the verb *akelen* (Court of Love, l. 1076), and signifies very chilled, extremely cold. Cf. Icel. *kala*, to cool, of which the pp. is *kalinn*. Three other examples of *acale* are these.

> "That night he sat wel sore *a-kale*,
> And his wif lai warme a-bedde."
>
> Seven Sages, ed. Weber, p. 59, l. 1512.

> "And eek he was so sore *acale*,
> That he wiste of himself no hote."
>
> Gower, Conf. Amant., iii. 296.

> "Her herte is hote as any fire,
> And otherwise it is *acale;*" id. iii. 303.

448. (18. 401.) "Thou shalt bitterly pay for it." Cf. Pass. xvii. 220. "Ne ec ne scule ȝe nefre ufel don þet ȝe hit ne sculen mid uuele bitter abuggen," nor yet shall ye ever do any evil without bitterly expiating it; Old Eng. Homilies, ed. Morris, i. 41.

There is a curious picture of Christ holding Death in chains in P. Lacroix, Military and Religious Life in the Middle Ages, p. 449.

449. (18. 402.) *Astrot* [c]; *Astaroth* [b]; i. e. Ashtoreth, or Astarte.

> "And mooned Ashtaroth
> Heaven's queen and mother both."
>
> Milton, Chr. Nat. 200.

Ashtoreth was symbolised by the moon, but answers rather to Venus. See Smith's Dict. of the Bible, s. v. See l. 289, and note to l. 283.

452. (18. 405.) Suggested by Ps. xlvii. 5 (xlvi. 6, Vulgate)—"Ascendit Deus in iubilo, et Dominus in uoce tubæ." So in Old Eng. Homilies, ii.

114, the sentence "etiam in sono tubæ, prout regem decet, ascendit" is explained to signify Christ's reception into heaven at His ascension.

The Latin quotation forms 2 lines, viz. the 3rd and 4th lines of the 4th stanza of the hymn beginning "Æterne rex altissime," used in the Office of the Ascension at Matins, in the Roman Breviary. *Culpat* is not used in its (active) classical sense, but in the (neuter) Low-Latin sense; see "*Culpare*, delinquere*" in Ducange. Hence the lines mean—"The flesh sins, the flesh redeems from sin, the flesh reigns as God of God."

454. (18. 407.) I do not know whence these two Latin lines are quoted. Possibly our author composed them, upon an old theme. The word *nebula* is an odd one, but stands the same in all the MSS.; *nubila* may have been intended. The idea is common, and agrees with our proverbs—"After a storm comes a calm" (Camden's Remaines); and "After black clouds, clear weather" (Heywood's Proverbs). So also—"After great stormes the wether is often mery and smothe. After moche clatering, there is mokill rowninge [*whispering*]; thus after iangling wordes cometh huishte, peace, and be stil;" Test. of Love, book i.; ed. 1561, fol. cclxxxx, col. i.

> "For aftir mysty cloudis there comyth a cler sonne;
> So aftir bale comyth bote, whoso byde conne."
> Tale of Beryn, ed. Furnivall, l. 3955.

"For as much as after a violent burst of rain there is a clear open sky;" S. Chrysostom; Homily vi. on St Matthew. "Non enim delectaris in perditionibus nostris; quia post tempestatem, tranquillum facis; et post lacrymationem et fletum, exsultationem infundis;" Tobit *iii.* 22 (Vulgate)—a text which is quoted and translated in the Ancren Riwle, p. 376.

> "Sed solet interdum fieri placabile numen,
> Nube solet pulsa candidus ire dies . . . .
> Ac ueluti uentis agitantibus aequora non est
> Aequalis rabies continuusque furor,
> Sed modo subsidunt intermissique silescunt,
> Vimque putes illos deposuisse suam," &c.
> Ovid, Trist., ii. 141—150.

"Amantium iræ amoris integratio est;" Terence, Andr. 3. 3. 23. Cf. also Boethius, De Consol. Philosophiæ, lib. iii. met. 1.

461. (18. 414.) "But Love, if it pleased him, could turn it to laughter."

467, 468. (18. 420, 421.) The B-text is rather obscure, and I have, in that text, assumed l. 421 to be an exclamation uttered by Righteousness, viz. "Peace! and (again) peace here! for ever and ever!" But a far simpler solution is to leave out the marks of quotation in l. 421, and also the note of admiration, at the same time inserting a comma after the first *Pees*; so that the sense becomes—"Thou sayest true, said Righteousness, and reverently kissed her (that is to say) Peace, and Peace (kissed) her; for ever and ever." The MSS. of the B-text all agree in the reading *hir*; but the reading *heo* of the C-text is a very great improvement, and the sentence then becomes simple enough, viz.—"and reverently she kissed Peace, and Peace (kissed) her."

472. (18. 425.) On the ringing of bells on Easter morn, see Rock, Church of Our Fathers, iii. pt. 2, p. 251; Wordsworth, Eccl. Biography, i. 617.

473. (18. 426.) *Kitte;* mentioned again as the poet's wife in Pass. vi. 2; see also Pass. viii. 304, and the note, p. 154.

Calot was perhaps a rather common name; and not a very reputable one. We find the expression—"And eke a *calot* of leude demeanyng" in The Remedie of Love (not Chaucer's, but) in Chaucer's Works, ed. 1561, fol. cccxxiiij. And see *Callot* in Nares.

475. (18. 428.) "Creeping to the cross" was an old ceremony of penance; see Nares, s. v. *Cross.* Also Ratis Raving, ed. Lumby, note on p. 128. It was most often practised on Good Friday; see Old Eng. Homilies, ed. Morris, ii. 94, l. 9; Pecock's Repressor, i. 267, 270; Rock, Church of our Fathers, iii. pt. 2. 241; Calfhill's Works, p. 100 (Parker Society); Parker Society's Index, s. v. *Cross;* Brand, Popular Antiquities, ed. Ellis, i. 153; &c. The extract from Pecock (i. 207) explains also the allusion to kissing the cross. He says—"But so it is, that to the crosse on Good Fridai men comen in louȝest wise, creeping on alle her knees, and to this crosse in so lowȝe and deuout maner they offren, and the feet of thilk cross thei in deuoutist maner kissen." The injunction in Ratis Raving, l. 2793—"Nocht our oft creip the cross on kneis" shews that the penance was also performed at other times.

478. (18. 430.) The supposed power of the cross over evil spirits is notorious. See Legends of the Holy Rood, ed. Morris, pp. 160, 169. A striking example is in Massinger's Virgin Martyr, Act v, sc. 1, where the demon Harpax, at the sight of a cross made of flowers, exclaims—"Oh! I am tortured!" So Chaucer calls the cross—"Flemer of feendes out of him and hire;" Man of Lawes Tale, Group B, 460.

SCHEME OF THE CONTENTS OF C. PASSUS XXII.

(B. Pass. XIX.)

C-TEXT.	B-TEXT.	C-TEXT.	B-TEXT.
1—55	1—55	——	247
56—59	——	253—315	248—310
60—150	56—146	316	*like* 311
151, 152	*like* 147	317—335	312—330
153—235	148—230	336	——
236, 237	*like* 231	337—371	331—365
238	232	——	366
239	——	372	*like* 367
——	233	373—483	368—478
240—252	234—246		

N.B. The differences between the Texts are comparatively slight throughout this Passus.

NOTES TO C. PASSUS XXII. (B. Pass. XIX.)

(Cf. Wright's Edition; pp. 396—424.)

22. 1. (19. 1.) Here ends the Ninth Vision; see note to l. 5.

3. (19. 3.) *To be housled*, to receive the Holy Communion; cf. ll. 394, 397, 476 below. According to Pass. xxi. 472, the time indicated is Easter day, on which this duty was especially practised. See Rock, Church of Our Fathers, iii. pt. 2, p. 169, where this passage is quoted. He remarks that pilgrims were commonly *houselled* before setting off on their pilgrimage; and describes the *houselling* of King Henry VII. at his coronation. See also Nares's Glossary; note in Peacock's edition of Myrk, p. 69; and note to l. 390 below. Dr Morris notes an odd popular etymology of the word, viz. from *hu sel*, i.e. how good (it is), in his Old Eng. Homilies, 2nd Series, pref. p. ix. The real etymology is from the A.S. *húsel*, where the long *u* shews the omission of a *n*, which appears in the Mœso-Goth. *hunsl*, a sacrifice, used to translate the Gk. θυσία.

5. (19. 5.) Here begins the Tenth Vision, or the Vision of Grace. See Pref. to C-text, p. ci; Pref. to B-text, p. liv.

7. (19. 7.) In pictures representing Christ after His resurrection, He is commonly represented as bearing a long but light cross, with a banner. This is called the cross of the resurrection. See Rock, Church of our Fathers, iii. pt. 2. 226. Cf. l. 14.

11. (19. 11.) It is strange that the B-text MSS. nearly all agree in reading *Or it is*. Clearly, *Or is hit*, as in [c], is far better.

14. (19. 14.) It is clear from l. 62 that our author, who was unacquainted with Greek, supposed that the word *Christ* signified "conquerour." On this supposed sense of the word the whole argument depends. A similar example occurs much earlier, in an Anglo-Saxon gloss of the *Quicunque Vult*, where the phrase "Domini nostri Jesu *Christi*" is rendered by "drihtnes ure hælendes *cinges*;" see Swainson, on the Nicene and Apostles' Creeds, p. 487, note 1. And the same appears even more clearly in the Lindisfarne MS. containing the Northumbrian version of the Gospels, where the Latin *christum* is glossed by "crist vel ðone cynig," i.e. Christ or the king; S. John ix. 22. The same supposed sense of the word *Christ* seems to be hinted at in the Chester Plays, ed. Wright, p. 105, where the Sybil prophecies—

> " Jesu Christe, nothinge amisse,
>   *Called* he shal be, and ys
> To *overcome* the devill and his countise,
>   And be our *conquerour*."

54. (19. 54.) That is, according to the Gospel of Nicodemus, Christ, by the "harrowing of hell," delivered the souls of Adam and Eve and others from the place of torment by His descent into it. See Pass. xxi. 451.

Other mo, to others besides; as in Pass. v. 10. So also *ten mo*, ten others, in l. 165 below. This is of some importance, as it enables us to

understand Chaucer's use of *mo* in the sense of "others" in the Clerkes
Tale; see my note to The Prioresses Tale, &c. (Clarendon Press), Group
E, l. 1039.

62. (19. 58.) "And that is the meaning of 'Christ.'" See note to
l. 14.

75. (19. 71.) *Kinges*, the Three Kings. The Magi were called the Three
Kings. Their names were said to be Appellius, Amerius, and Damascus in
Hebrew; Galgalat, Malgalat, and Sarathin in *Greek*; and Caspar, Balthasar
(or, in the Cursor Mundi, Attropa), and Melchior in *Latin*. At least, such
are the names as assigned in the Aurea Legenda, cap. xiv., *De Epiphania
Domini*, q. v.; although they are far from looking suitable to the languages
mentioned. Jaspar (or Caspar) was said to be king of Tharsis; Melchior,
king of Arabia; and Balthasar, king of Saba; these countries being suggested by Ps. lxxii. 10. Cf. also Ps. lxviii. 31, and Isaiah lx. 6.

A long note upon them will be found in Marco Polo, ed. Yule, i. 78.
There is a long legend about them, in English prose, quoted from MS. Harl.
1704, appended to Wright's edition of the Chester Plays, pp. 266—304. See
also St Chrysostom's second homily on St Matthew (vol. vi. col. 637, ed.
Migne); Brand's Popular Antiquities, ed. Ellis, i. 21; Maundeville's
Travels, ed. Halliwell, p. 70; Peter Comestor's Historia Scholastica;
Warton's Hist. Eng. Poetry, ed. 1840, ii. 91; Cursor Mundi, ed. Morris, p.
658; Old English Homilies, ed. Morris, ii. 44; Longfellow's Golden Legend;
Chambers, Book of Days, i. 61; Gesta Romanorum (Swan's translation),
Tale xlvii, at p. 82 of the edition in Bohn's Library; The Lay-folks' Mass-
book, ed. Simmons, pp. 246—248; Altenglische Legenden, ed. Horstmann,
p. 97; Dict. of the Bible, art, *Magi*; &c.

Chrysostom says that the gold, myrrh, and frankincense were mystic
gifts, indicating that Christ was King, Man, and God; our author interprets
them as signifying righteousness, ruth, and reason respectively. See notes
below.

86. (19. 82.) "The first king came, offering Reason, signified by
incense." Incense was often considered as a symbol of prayer, and hence,
according to Chrysostom, it indicated that Christ was God. As it was used
by the priests, it was by some taken to refer to Christ's priesthood.

A reference to the Old Kentish Sermons, in An Old Eng. Miscellany, ed.
Morris, p. 27, will show that the preachers were accustomed to exhort their
hearers to offer to Christ gold, and frankincense, and myrrh, as the Magi
did; and, in doing this, they gave new interpretations to those symbols. In
those Sermons, we are told to offer *gold*, which signifies *good belief; incense*,
signifying *prayer*; and *myrrh*, signifying *such good works as mortify the flesh*.
Compare—"Aurum significat dilectiouem, thus orationem, myrrha carnis
mortificationem. Et hæc tria debemus Christo offerre;" Aurea Legenda,
cap. xiv. Our author has likewise, in his turn, attempted equally fanciful
interpretations, with small success. In fact, he contradicts himself flatly;
compare l. 86 with l. 90.

He seems to mean this. They offered Christ *incense*, meaning thereby a submission to Him of their reasonable service, and as expressing their belief in the reasonableness of His authority. They offered *gold*, signifying (1) the kingly justice (observe that "rightwiseness" translates the Lat. *iustitia*, Pass. xxi. 169), which was "reason's fellow," inasmuch as kingly justice and reasonable commands should always be closely allied, in accordance with the burden of our author's song throughout Pass. v, especially in ll. 184—186; and also signifying (2) lealty, or fidelity in a subject. (Line 90 is altogether out of place, and due to some confusion of mind.) Lastly, they offered *myrrh*, signifying pity, ruth, or mercy in the king, and mildness of speech in the subject as well as in the king. The political meaning seems to be that a king should be reasonable, just, and mild; and that the subject should be free, loyal, and respectful.

93. (19. 89.) Myrrh is more commonly interpreted in connection with death, because it was used in embalming the dead; see Cursor Mundi, l. 11504, where it is interpreted as pointing to Christ's mortality as a Man. Hence, in the Kentish Sermons (O. Eng. Misc., p. 28) it means such works as *mortify* the flesh; and in the Myrour of Our Lady, ed. Blunt, p. 164, it denotes *penance*.

> "Sacred gifts of mystic meaning:
> Incense doth their God disclose;
> Gold the King of Kings proclaimeth,
> Myrrh His *sepulchre* foreshews."
> Hymns Ancient and Modern:—"*Earth has many a noble city.*"

99. (19. 95.) This was strikingly exhibited in the life of Robert Bruce; we might almost imagine a reference to him here. Note the context, especially ll. 102, 103.

138. (19. 134.) *Caiser*, emperor. It occurs again in Pass. xxiii. 101, and in Richard Redeles, i. 85. See numerous other examples in Stratmann, s. v. *caiser*. It is the A.S. *cásere*, borrowed from Lat. *Cæsar*.

146. (19. 142.) *Of buriels*, from the sepulchre. Like *hidels, metels*, &c., *buriels* is in the singular number, being the A.S. *byrgels*, a tomb. Wyclif wrongly supposed it to be a plural, and invented the false forms *buriel*, which he uses in Mark vi. 29, and *biriel*, in Mat. xxvii. 60, &c.; see *burȝels* in Stratmann, and note to Group G, l. 186, in Chaucer's Man of Lawes Tale, &c. (Clarendon Press edition).

151. (19. 147.) Alluding to the account in Matt. xxviii. 2. See Rock, Church of Our Fathers, iii. pt. 2, p. 253.

159. (19. 154.) *Lyues and lokynge*, alive and looking round Him. See l. 175 below, and note to Pass. xi. 57, p. 211. The adverbial form *lyues* occurs five times in Havelok the Dane, ll. 509, 1003, 1307, 1919, 2854.

162. (19. 157.) *Consail*, a secret. See Crit. Note, C-text, p. 465.

165. (19. 160.) *Tadde*, Thaddæus. *Thomas of ynde*, Thomas of India. Chaucer has—"in Thomas lif of Inde," i.e. in the Life of Thomas of India, Somp. Tale, C. T. 7562; and again—"by seint Thomas of Ynde" in the

Prologue to the Marchauntes Tale. The same expression occurs in Rich. Coer de Lion, l. 2481, in Weber's Metrical Romances. The apostle was thus distinguished from St Thomas of Canterbury. In Kyng Horn, &c., ed. Lumby, p. 96, it is "Seynt Thomas of ynde" who receives Our Lady's girdle, dropped in her assumption into heaven. See Wyclif's Works, i. 153, and note; Marco Polo, ed. Yule, ii. 293, where Col. Yule remarks that "the tradition of Thomas's preaching in India is very old, so old that it is, probably, in its simple form true." St Jerome accepts the tradition; Sci. Hieron. Epist., lix. *ad Marcellum*. It is mentioned in the Apocryphal Acts of the Apostles, and by Gregory of Tours. "The little town where the body of St Thomas lay was Mailapúr, the name of which is still applied to a suburb of Madras about three and a half miles south of Fort George;" note in Marco Polo, ed. Yule, ii. 292. See the legend of St Thomas preaching in India in the Aurea Legenda, cap. v, and in the English prose romance of the Three Kings quoted in Mr Wright's edition of the Chester Plays, pp. 294—297. In the latter we are told that *all* Thomas's successors as patriarchs of India took the name of Thomas, just as all the lords of India were called Prester John! However, it is the fact that there is a community called "the Christians of St Thomas" at this very day, and that the tradition is well known at Madras. In Sharp's Dissertation on Pageants, p. 162, we find a notice—"1539: to James and Thomas of Inde, viij *d.*;" and in 1515, we find that three pairs of gloves were used for "two ladds and St Thomas of India." See also Smith's Dict. of the Bible, art. *Thomas*.

183. (19. 178.) Here, and in l. 201, *peers* means St Peter. In l. 188 it means St Peter's successors, the bishops; and, in particular, the Pope.

186, 187. (19. 181, 182.) "Provided that they should come, and acknowledge, in a satisfactory manner, their trust in the pardon of Piers the Plowman, which contains the words—'pay what thou owest.'" *Kneweliched*, should acknowledge, is the past tense subjunctive; the B-text has the present tense. *To paye* means "so as to please God;" cf. *to paye* as used in Pass. viii. 189, 192. *Peers pardon the plouhman* means "the pardon of Piers the Plowman," just as *peers bern the plouhman* means "the barn of Piers the Plowman" in l. 360 and in Pass. xxiii. 77. This idiom has been already explained; see note to Pass. xvi. 131, p. 307; but has been singularly misunderstood by Dean Milman, in the useful summary of "Piers the Plowman" in his History of Latin Christianity. I add a few more examples. "The tombe of Rachelle that was Iosephes modre the patriarke;" Maundeville's Travels, p. 72. "The kyngys doghtur of Sodam;" Emperour Octovian, l. 1097. "This is launcelotts sheld de lake;" Morte Arthure, Roxburgh Club, p. 21. "On our ladeis evin Mary," i. e. on the eve of our Lady Mary; Barbour's Bruce, ed. Skeat, xvii. 335.

By the words "redde quod debes" our author expresses his belief that a pardon is of none effect unless the culprit does what he can to make restitution; cf. Pass. vii. 316, 322; and see l. 193 below. Lines 186, 187 recur below, slightly varied; see ll. 391, 392.

204. (19. 199.) *Waggede conscience,* nudged Conscience; gave him a hint that he should explain it to me. See l. 207.

210. (19. 205.) *Veni,* &c. "The first line of the hymn at vespers, on the feast of Pentecost." It is mentioned in our Prayer-book still, in the rubrics to the Ordering of Priests and the Consecration of Bishops. See Rock, Church of Our Fathers, iii. pt. 2. 256.

213. (19. 208.) Here Grace is the Holy Ghost, and Piers the Plowman is still Christ; the latter title not being used of Christ's deputed successors till l. 258 below, though the name of *peers* has been once so used above, in l. 188. See note to l. 183.

216. (19. 211.) *Hus* [c] is used indefinitely, like our "one's;" but the reading *her* [b] is certainly simpler. *Can,* knows how to control, has full possession of. The alliteration shews this to be the right reading, but it is a very forced expression, so that we need not wonder that most of the scribes have turned it into *han* [b]; see the footnotes. Thus the line means :—"To creatures of every kind, if one knows how to use one's five wits" [c]; *or*—"To creatures of every kind, that possess their five wits" [b]. On *five wits,* see note to Pass. ii. 15, p. 29.

227. (19. 222.) *To gye with hymself,* to guide himself with, to rule his conduct by. This (to us) odd position of *with* is the usual fourteenth-century idiom. See note to B. 2. 31, pp. 45, 46.

229. (19. 224.) The gifts of the Holy Spirit were sometimes reckoned as being seven in number. In Hampole's Prose Treatises, ed. Perry, p. 12, they are said to be "Wysdome, Vnderstandynge, Counsayle, Streng[t]he, Connynge, Pete, The drede of God." But in the Ayenbyte of Inwyt, pp. 119—125, and in Ratis Raving, ed. Lumby, l. 1124, the number is made up by adding the Four Cardinal Virtues (Prudence, Justice, Temperance, and Fortitude) to the Three Christian Graces (Faith, Hope, and Charity). Our author, however, simply enumerates different professions and handicrafts.

235. (19. 230.) "To gain their livelihood by selling and buying."

238. (19. 232.) *To coke,* to put hay into cocks; see note to Pass. vi. 13, p. 87. The present passage helps us to the meaning of the word, as it is here said to be an operation connected with tillåge. The B-text reads *dyche,* to ditch.

247. (19. 241.) If the context be carefully considered, I think it plain that our author is here commending that stern and rough mode of redressing justice which is sometimes practised by honest men in violent times, to the sudden confusion of oppressors who have made themselves intolerable. Thus "foleuyles lawes" are laws of the character of Lynch laws, and were (similarly) so named, I presume, from some now forgotten worthy, who used to take a short course with men convicted of oppression or knavery. The word *foleuyles* (also spelt *foleviles, foluyles*) can hardly be other than a proper name, spelt (as usual in MSS.) with a small letter. We should now spell such a name Folville or Fouville. This seems to me the most likely solution. If the reader is pleased to take *Folville* as the name of a place, it will then

mean "silly town," and the name may have been fictitious.   It is remarkable that, in the Tale of Beryn, there is a description of a "false town" with very peculiar laws.   But whatever solution be chosen, the general sense of the passage is sufficiently clear.

——(19. 247.) It is almost a pity that the author left out this line in revision.   The miller should bear in mind that the chimney-sweep's calling is as irreproachable (morally) as his own.

260. (19. 255.) *Prower*, purveyor, provider of necessaries.   The word occurs in Pecock's Repressor, p. 467, and is explained to mean "purueier," p. 468.   Mr Wright's Glossary has—"*Prowor*, a priest;" which is copied into Halliwell's Dictionary.   It is true that Roquefort gives—"*Provoir, prevoir, prouaire*, &c. ecclésiastique, prêtre, curé;" but this explanation is quite unsuitable here, and must be set aside.   Our word is rather to be illustrated by the following.   Roquefort gives—"*Prouvoirre*, pourvoyeur." Cotgrave notes that *pourveoir* is the same as *prouvoir*, and gives—"*Prouvoir*, to purvey, or provide for; to furnish, or store with," &c.   Also "*Pourvoyeur*, a provider, a purveyor."   Ducange gives us—"*Providitor*" as a form of *provisor;* and, s. v. *Provisor*, notes that a "provisor hospitii" was a purveyor.   In fact, we have in *prowor* only another form of *purveyor*, without any difference in the sense; and, whilst the interpretation "priest" gives no good sense and is an unauthorised guess, the interpretation "purveyor" is the very thing which the context requires, and has the express authority of Pecock.

262. (19. 257.) In the History of Hawsted, by Sir J. Cullum, 2nd ed., p. 216, we are told that, in Suffolk, in the 14th century, oxen were as much used as horses; and, in ploughing heavy land, would go forward where horses would stop.   "A horse kept for labour ought to have every night the 6th part of a bushel of oats; for an ox, 3½ measures of oats, 10 of which make a bushel, are sufficient for a week."   In the picture of ploughing, prefixed to MS. T (of Piers the Plowman), the plough is drawn by two oxen; see Pref. to A-text, p. xviii.

The oxen here signify the Four Evangelists.   The idea was easily suggested by the fact that St Luke is commonly symbolised by an ox.   A useful note on the four evangelical symbols (man, lion, ox, and eagle) will be found in Dr White's Ormulum, ii. 374.   And see Cursor Mundi, p. 1218.

267. (19. 262.) *Stottes*, bullocks.   This sense best suits the context.   It is sometimes disputed whether *stot* means a bullock or a stallion; but it is clear that it has *both* meanings; indeed, it has a third meaning, since it also represents our modern *stoat*.   The sense of bullock is still preserved in the North, though the term is also applied to an old ox; see Atkinson's Cleveland Glossary; and I believe that Mr Bardsley's observation in Our English Surnames, p. 228 (though it has been objected to), is quite correct.   He says—"In our Stotherds and Stothards, our Stoddarts and Stoddards, still clings the remembrance of the old *stot-* or bullock-herd."   Cf. "Stotte, *boveau;*" Palsgrave.   "Aythor cow or *stott;*" Towncley Mysteries, p. 112.

Icel. *stútr*, a bull; Swed. *stut*, a bullock; Dan. *stud*, an ox, a bullock. The sense of stallion or young horse is equally certain; we have Chaucer's Reve mounted on a "ful good stot;" Prol. l. 617. "Stot, hors, *caballus ;*" Prompt. Parv. "*Stottus*, equus admissarius ;" Ducange. Ger. *stute*, a mare; *stuterei*, a stud of horses. Cf. our *stud*, and Dan. *stodhest*, a stallion; O. H. Ger. *stuot*, *stuat*, a stud of brood-horses. The connection between *stoat* and the two senses of *stot* may perhaps be accounted for by supposing the original sense of the word to be connected with breeding. "The horses used in medieval husbandry are distinguished as *affri* (called also *stots*) and cart-horses," &c.; Hist. Agric. and Prices in England, by J. E. T. Rogers, i. 330. We find the entry—"pro ferrura stottorum et palefridum," for the shoeing of *stots* (horses) and palfreys, in a Description of N. Creake Abbey, p. 12, by G. A. Carthew (Norf. and Norwich Arch. Soc.).

268. (19. 263.) "All that his oxen ploughed, they (were) to harrow afterwards."

269. (19. 264.) This refers to the four chief Latin fathers, St Jerome, St Gregory, St Ambrose, and St Augustine. These are called the "iiij Doctours fyne" in Religious, Polit. and Love Poems, ed. Furnivall, p. 143, l. 874. See Mrs Jameson's Sacred and Legendary Art, 3rd ed., p. 281.

272. (19. 267.) *Hand-whyle*, a very short space of time. Stratmann gives four examples, to which I add—"Herkinys now a *hondqwile* of a hegh cas ;" allit. Troy-book, ed. Panton and Donaldson, l. 7346. In this line, *harowede* (lit. harrowed) means *went over, commented upon*.

273. (19. 268.) *Eythes* [c] has the same sense as *harwes* [b], viz. harrows. The word is rare, but easily accounted for, as it is the A.S. *egeðe*, a rake, a harrow, cognate with the O.H.Ger. *agide, egida, ekitha*, Mod. Ger. *egge*, a harrow; all from the Indo-European root *ak*, sharp; cf. Lat. *ac-us*, a needle; *ac-idus*, sharp, &c.

The two harrows symbolise the Old and New Testaments.

274. (19. 269.) *Cardinales virtues*, cardinal (or chief) virtues. On the construction, see note to Pass. x. 342, p. 199. On the Four Virtues, see note to Pass. i. 131, p. 17.

279. (19. 274.) *Stele*, a handle; cf. Chaucer, C. T. Group A. 3785. "Steal, s. the *steal* of any thing, i. e. manubrium, the handle; or pediculus, the foot-stalk;" Ray's South and East-Country Words. From A.S. *stela ;* cf. E. *stal-k*. Compare—"And whan this man the pan hath by the *stele ;*" Occleve's Letter of Cupid, st. 8; in Chaucer's Works, ed. 1561, fol. cccxxvii. The line means—"and taught men to buy a ladle with a long handle." See next note.

280. (19. 275.) *Cast*, short for *casteth*, i. e. intends. *Kele*, to cool [c]; *kepe*, to pay heed to [b]. This line throws some light on the expression to "keel the pot," in the Song at the end of Love's Labour's Lost. The remarks in Nares and Halliwell are just, that the word simply means to *cool*, or *keep cool*, and not to scum. In Glossary B. 1, published by the Eng. Dialect Society, we have—"*Keel*, to keep the pot from boiling over; North

of England." The operation really intended is that the cook shall watch the pot, and gently stir it when it seems likely to boil over. The watching is denoted by *kepe* [b]; the gentle stirring by *kele* [c]. The latter is merely the A.S. *célan*, to cool, and is rather common; see *kelen* in Stratmann, and note—"Kelyn, or make colde, *frigefacio;*" Prompt. Parv. Hence the reference to Prudence in ll. 279, 280 means—"And taught men to buy a ladle with a long handle, whoever intends to stir (*or* watch) a pot, and to preserve the fat that floats on the top." The illustration from Marston, given by Nares, is very much to the point :—"Faith, Doricus, thy brain boils; *keel* it, *keel* it, or all the fat's in the fire."

288. (19. 283.) *Maister Iohan*, master John. Merely a contemptuous name for a cook; much as we might now say "Mister Jack." So in Barclay's Ship of Fools, ed. Jamieson, i. 96, we have—

> "some dotynge *Iohnn*,
> Being dronke, thynketh hym as wyse as Salomon."

294. (19. 289.) *Of abydyng*, in sufferance, in patience [c]; *and abydynge*, and patient [b].

297. (19. 292.) Quoted from Dionysius Cato, Distich., ii. 14—

> "Esto animo forti, quum sis damnatus inique,
> Nemo diu gaudet, qui iudice uincit iniquo."

Another reading is *forti animo*, as in the text.

305. (19. 300.) *And*, if [c]; ʒif, if [b]. "If the king happen to be in any respect guilty" [c].

307. (19. 302.) *Domesman*, judge; lit. man of doom. Chaucer translates *censor* in Boethius, lib. ii. met. 6, by this word, saying of Nero—"he was so hard-herted that he myʒte ben *domesman* or *Iuge* of hire dede beaute;" ed. Morris, p. 55.

314. (19. 309.) Skelton has "crokyd as a *camoke;*" ed. Dyce, i. 117; where a *cammock* means a crooked piece of timber, a bent stick, from the Celtic (Welsh and Gaelic) *cam*, crooked; so also in Lily's Euphues, ed. Arber, p. 408. But in the present passage the *cammock* is the troublesome weed called the rest-harrow (short for *arrest-harrow*), or *Ononis arvensis;* called the *cammock*, doubtless, from its crooked and tough roots. Cotgrave has—"*Arreste-bœuf*, the herb Rest-harrow, petty whinne, grand-furze, *Cammocke.*" The word *cammec, cammoc*, or *cammuc*, with the sense of rest-harrow, is given in Bosworth's A.S. Dictionary; but it was certainly borrowed from the Welsh. Cf. Gael. *camag*, anything crooked.

317. (19. 312.) "Harrow all such as have natural ability by means of the counsel of these Doctors (of the church), and cultivate (in them) the cardinal virtues according to their teaching."

320. (19. 315.) "To stow thy corn in." *Cornes* is often used to signify *corn* in Middle-English. It occurs, for example, in Chaucer's account of Samson in The Monkes Tale; in Spec. of English, pt. ii., ed. Morris and Skeat, p. 70, l. 39; and in Wyclif's Works, ed. Arnold, iii. 329, where it is misprinted *corces*.

324. (19. 319.) *That ... on peynede = on whiche ... peynede*, i.e. on

which Christ suffered pain.   The form *pynede* [b] is perhaps better, being the genuine English word.

330. (19. 325.) The house of Unity denotes Holy Church.   Compare— " þe þridde onhede [*one-hood, unity*] is of þe chirche, and of her partis, oon in God;" Wyclif's Works, ed. Arnold, i. 403.

335. (19. 330.) Here *peers* (Piers) is at last completely transferred from its reference to Christ, so as to mean His faithful pastors and teachers. Grace (i. e. the Holy Ghost) accompanies these wherever they go, in order " to till truth," i. e. to spread the truth of the Christian faith.

337. (19. 331.) Cf. Pass. ix. 112.   The description of Pride's attack upon the church is more fully given in Pass. xxiii. 70.   See note to Pass. xxiii. 69.

340. (19. 334.) *Rotes* [c] and *mores* [b] have the same sense, viz. roots. See note to Pass. xviii. 21, p. 353.

341. (19. 335.) *Surquidours*, proud or arrogant men [c]; *surquidous*, an arrogant man, but used as a proper name [b].   *Surquidours* would answer to a French form *sorcuideurs*, and *surquidous* to *sorcuideux*, both from the Old Fr. *sorcuider*, to presume, to be arrogant, to think too much of oneself; from Lat. *super-cogitare*.

343. (19. 337.) *To-comen*, approached [c]; *two come*, two came [b].   The change from *two come* was made necessary by the changes in the two preceding lines.

360. (19. 354.) "Let us pray that there might be peace in Piers the Plowman's barn," i. e. in the church.   And see note to l. 187 above.

366. (19. 360.) "That Holy Church might stand in Holiness, as if it were the foundation of a fort" [c]; *or,* "that Holy Church might stand in Unity," &c. [b].   Holy Church (or Unity) is here represented as being a castle.   Holiness (see l. 382) is the moat that protects it, the water that fills the moat being derived from the tears of penitents.   The Christians dig a deep ditch round Holy Church or Unity, so that the foundation on which it stands is plainly seen to resemble a *pile,* i. e. a heavy pier or abutment such as a bridge rests on.   *Pile* is the Lat. *pila,* a pillar, dam, or pier. " Pyle, of a bryggys fote, or other byggynge [i. e. building], *pila ;* " Prompt. Parv., p. 398.   " Pere, or pyle of a brygge or other fundament, *pila ;* " id. p. 394.   Cf. " saxea pila " in Æneid, ix. 711.

369. (19. 363.) In [b], correct the comma at the end of the line to a full stop.

380. (19. 376.) *Egrelich*, bitterly, rather than quickly.   Such is the usual old sense, as when we find "esill [i. e. vinegar] strong and *egre*" in the Romaunt of the Rose, l. 147.   See *Eager* in Trench's Select Glossary.

ȝernynge [c] = *ernynge* [b], i. e. running; from A.S. *yrnan*, to run. Compare—

> " A welle þat euere is *eornynge*,
> With foure stremes þat strikeþ [*flow*] wel,
> And *erneþ* vppon þe grauel."
> Castle of Love; ed. Weymouth, l. 729.

See *Yerne* in the Glossary to the Ayenbite of Inwyt.

390. (19. 386.) The author of the Ancren Riwle (at p. 412) recommends that the laity should not receive the Holy Communion oftener than 15 times in a year at the most. He mentions, as fitting days, Mid-winter, Candlemas, Twelfth-day, the Sunday half-way between that and Easter (or Lady-day, if near the Sunday), Easter-day, the third Sunday after, Holy Thursday, Whitsunday, Midsummer-day, St Mary Magdalen's day, the Assumption, the Nativity of the Virgin, Michaelmas-day, All Saints' day, and St Andrew's day. Queen Elizabeth of York, wife of Henry VII., seems to have communicated thrice in the year, on Easter-day, All Saints' day, and Christmas day; see the Layfolk's Mass-book, ed. Simmons, p. 239. Chaucer says *once a year at least*—"and certes ones a yere at the leste wey it is lawful to be houseled, for sothely ones a yere alle thinges in the erthe renouelen." [*renew themselves*]; Pers. Tale, at the end of Remedium Luxuriæ. Robert of Brunne says the same (Handl. Synne, ll. 10298—10301)—

> " Comaundement yn the olde lawe was
> Ones yn þe ȝere to shewe þy trespas;
> þe newe law ys of more onour,
> Ones to receyue þy creatoure."

391, 392. (19. 387, 388.) "Or as often they should have need, that is to say, those who had (duly) paid according to the pardon of Piers the Plowman (which expresses the condition),—'pay what thou owest.'" See note to l. 187; and cf. ll. 193, 259.

395. (19. 391.) "Such (said Conscience) is my counsel, and such is also the counsel of the Cardinal Virtues."

398. (19. 394.) *Bawe*, an interjection of contempt; see note to Pass. xiii. 74, p. 265.

402. (19. 398.) *Thicke ale;* see note to Pass. vii. 226, p. 120.

403. (19, 399.) *Hacke*, to hoe, to grub about, to toil. This is, of course, spoken contemptuously, and must have been suggested by the preceding allegory, in which Holiness has been described as the ditch or moat which protects the castle of Unity or Holy Church; see ll. 376, 382. The word is expressive, and well chosen; cf. Dan. *hakke*, Swed. *hacka*, a hoe; and cf. "*Hack*, a strong pick-axe, or hoe," Halliwell; also "*Hack*, to stammer; to cough faintly and frequently; to labour severely and indefatigably; to chop with a knife; to break the clods of earth after ploughing;" id. Mr Wright has rather missed the figure intended, and explains it by "to follow, or run after; to cut along after," where the "cut along" is not an explanation, but a misleading play upon words, introducing an unauthorised guess. Mr Halliwell has copied this in his Dictionary, s. v. *Hakke*, but *minus* the "cut along." There is no evidence to shew that *hakke* means "to follow;" it clearly means "to keep cutting away at," but here used in an allegorical sense; not "to cut along" in a slang sense.

403. (19. 404.) *Worst thow* [c], or *worstow* [b], thou shalt be. Here *worst* is for *worthest*, from the verb *worthen*, to become. MS. M [c, *footnote*] has *best* = beëst, shalt be. Thus *worst* = shalt become; *best* = shalt be; both words being unconnected with the superlative adjectives similarly spelt.

412. (19. 408.) *Curatoure*, curate. "Rector, vicar, every one having *cure* of souls, was a 'curate' once. Thus 'bishops and *curates*' in the Liturgy;" Trench's Select Glossary, p. 57; which see for examples.

419. (19. 415.) Wordsworth (Eccl. Biography, 4th ed., i. 569, 570) cites these lines in illustration of the duke of Suffolk's words, aimed at Wolsey and Campeggio:—"It was never merry in Englande while we had any cardinalls amongst us."

424. (19. 420.) *Auenoun*, Avignon; the place where the pope's court was. Avignon, in the S.E. of France, was "ceded by Philip III. to the pope in 1273. The papal seat was removed by Clement V. to Avignon, in 1309. In 1348 Clement VI. purchased the sovereignty from Jane, countess of Provence and queen of Naples. In 1408, the French, wearied of the schism, expelled Benedict XIII., and Avignon ceased to be the seat of the papacy;" Haydn's Dict. of Dates. It should be added that Gregory XI. transferred the papal see from Avignon to Rome in 1377; whilst Clement VII., the antipope, elected Sept. 20, 1378, took up his residence at Avignon, so that there was thus once more a papal court there until 1408. "With the English court these Popes of Avignon were deservedly unpopular; they were governed by French influence, and often thwarted, as far as they could, the designs of England against France;" Massingberd's Hist. of Eng. Reform, p. 49. See also the note to l. 430.

The Jews were no doubt very useful in finding money for the popes at Avignon; and it is recorded that Clement VI. (A.D. 1342—1352) forbad any persecution of the Jews there; Hist. of Prices and Agric. in England, by J. E. T. Rogers, i. 297.

The expression—"with the holy thou shalt be holy," is of course ironical; and refers to an implied association of the cardinals with the Jews.

425. (19. 421.) "To keep the relics." The cardinals generally bore the title of some church within the city of Rome; and most of the churches contained relics. See Engl. Cyclop., art. *Cardinals;* and The Stations of Rome, ed. Furnivall (E. E. T. S.).

427. (19. 423.) In [c] *And* means *if;* but in [b] it means *and*. Hence the sense is—"If Grace, that thou sayst so much about, were the guide of all clerks" [c]; *or,* "And Grace, that thou sayst so much about, should be the guide of all clerks" [b]. Respecting Conscience at the king's court, see Pass. iv. 156, &c.

430. (19. 426.) It is difficult to find in our author any very clear allusion to the famous schism of the popes in 1378, and perhaps he was intentionally rather cautious upon that subject; unlike Wyclif, who was glad to speak of it. Still there is possibly an allusion to it here, and in ll. 446, 447 [b. 19. 441, 442] below. "Imperfect is the pope, who ought to assist all people, and pays [*or* sends out, *b*] them who slay such as he ought to save." See note to l. 447.

431. (19. 427.) *Soudeth*, pays [c]; *sendeth*, sends out [b]. The change is curious; see the footnote to [c]. The verb *souden* is formed from the sb.

soud, pay, as "in sowd," i. e. in pay, Mandeville's Travels, p. 155; quoted in Halliwell to illustrate "*Soudes*, wages." Cotgrave has—"*Sould*, souldiers' lendings, intertainment, or pay; an old word." Ducange has—"*Solidare* (1) confirmare, asserere; (2) firmare, munire; (3) stipendium præbere." Thus the Low Lat. *solidare* answers both to the verb *souden* in the text, and to the Eng. *solder*, to fasten, in which the *l* is dropped in ordinary pronunciation. And we may note a similar dropping of the *l* in the derived word *sowdears*, i. e. hirelings, soldiers (see *Sowdears* in Halliwell), and in the common pronunciation, *sodgers*, of the same word. See also note to l. 447.

432. (19. 428.) *Wel worthe;* see note to Pass. xiv. 1, p. 273. *Porsueth*, follows, imitates.

434. (19. 430.) *Sent*, short for *sendeth*, sends; the present tense.

436. (19. 432.) Here Piers the Plowman is completely identified with the agriculturist, with sole reference to ordinary agricultural work, as in Pass. ix. 112—121. Cf. Gascoigne's Steel Glas, ll. 1017—1050; in Spec. of English, 1394—1579, ed. Skeat, p. 320.

443. (19. 438.) *Suffreth*, bears with; as when we say of God, that He is "long-*suffering*."

447. (19. 442.) *Fyndeth*, provides with necessaries, provides for; not very different in sense from *soudeth*, pays, in l. 431; see the Glossary. It is not clear whether the allusion is to the crusades which the popes encouraged, or to the blood shed in the war which took place between the partisans of pope and antipope. If the latter, the B-text (A.D. 1377) can hardly have been completed till the end of 1378. The English took the side of Urban VI, the pope of Rome, as against Clement VII, the anti-pope of Avignon.

I find two passages in Wyclif in which he inveighs against the pope as an encourager of war. "The pope approves croyserye, and to hym schulden men trowe . . . þe pope is stirtour of þis feght, and synnes more þen feghters . . he puttis mony thousande lyves for his owne wrecchid lyf. And by forsakyng of þing þat Crist biddes prestis forsake, he myghte cees al þis stryve. Why is he not a fende? þe prestis þat feghten in þis cause synnen foule in homycide;" &c. Works, iii. 140, 141. "Whi wole not the proude prest of Rome graunte ful. perdon to alle men for to lyve in pees and charite and pacience, as he doth to alle men for to fiʒtte and slee Cristene men, and to helpe þerto;" Works, iii. 330.

448. (19. 443.) *Luk*, St Luke. St Luke "bears witness" by quoting the words of the "old law." *Non occides* occurs in Luke xviii. 20 (Vulgate).

455. (19. 450.) *But hit soune*, unless it tend [c]; *But if þei seiʒe*, unless they should see [b]; where *seiʒe* is the past tense subjunctive. The alteration is very striking. It looks as if our author had (before revising his poem) become acquainted with Chaucer's Prologue—"Sownynge alway thencrees of his winninge;" l. 275. In fact, he could hardly have done otherwise, as his C-text was not written till A.D. 1393 at the earliest; see Pref. to C-text, p. xviii.

456. (19. 451.) "Of guile and of lying they make no account;" i. e. they do not hesitate to deceive.

465. (19. 460.) Whitaker remarks—"These Reeve-Rolls, of which I have seen some, little later than our author's time, consisted, for one year, of several sheets stitched together, and contained very curious and minute details of all the receipts and expenses of these officers. There was more order and exactness in the economy of our old nobility than we are apt to imagine." See, e. g., The Privy Purse Expenses of Elizabeth of York, ed. Nicolas; King Edward the Second's Household and Wardrobe Ordinances, ed. Furnivall (Chaucer Society); Hist. of Agriculture and Prices in England, by J. E. T. Rogers; Sir J. Cullum's Hist. of Hawsted; &c.

466. (19. 461.) "And with the spirit of Strength I fetch it, whether the reeve likes it, or not" [c]; or, "I will fetch it" [b]. Compare Rob. of Brunne, Handl. Synne, l. 4416—

"And þys ys a custumable þyng
Now wyþ euery lordyng,
þat, ȝyf his stuwarde hym oghte wynne,
Be hyt wyþ ryghte, or wyþ synne,
Hym wyl he holde most pryue
Of alle þo þat wyþ hym be."

467. (19. 462.) *By hus croune*, with reference to his crown. See note (on *by*) to Pass. i. 78, pp. 13, 14.

471. (19. 466.) *Hastelokest*, most hastily, soonest; see note to B. xiii. 343, p. 116. Add the form *hardyloker*, C. 17. 103.

473. (19. 468.) *Youre alre hefd*, the head of you all. *Youre alre hele*, the health (or safety) of you all. In l. 390 above, *hele* signifies salvation.

481. (19. 476.) "*Then* (I grant) that thou mayest have what thou askest for, as the law requires," [c]; "Thou mayest take in reason," &c. [b]. The change is very significant; the king is no longer to *take*, but to *ask for* what he wants. Richard II. was rapidly falling into disgrace.

I do not know whence the Latin quotation is taken. It looks like a maxim which William had picked up in the law-courts at Westminster.

482. (19. 477.) *Hadde fer hom*, had far (to go to get) home.

483. (19. 478.) *As me mette*, as I dreamed. Here ends the Tenth Vision, or the Vision of Grace.

SCHEME OF THE CONTENTS OF C. PASSUS XXIII.
(B. Pass. XX.)

C-TEXT.	B-TEXT.	C-TEXT.	B-TEXT.
1—36	1—36	261	——
37	——	262—386	260—384
38—260	37—259		

It will be observed that the C-text inserts ll. 37 and 261; otherwise, the texts agree line for line; yet not always word for word.

NOTES TO C. PASS. XXIII. (B. PASS. XX.)

(Cf. Wright's edition, pp. 425—448.)

23. 2. (20. 2.) *Elynge*, sad, solitary; see notes to Pass. i. 204, p. 24; and B. x. 94, p. 240. And see l. 39 below.

4. (20. 4.) "And I met with Need." The poet more than once thus describes himself as meeting with allegorical personages during his waking moments. Thus, in Pass. vi. 6, he meets with Reason. The last Vision does not really begin till l. 51 below. See note to l. 51.

7. (20. 7.) "That you took (things) to live upon, for your food and clothing."

10. (20. 10.) Alluding to the proverb—"Necessitas non habet legem." See note to Pass. xiv. 45, p. 274.

11. (20. 11.) The three necessary things are meat, drink, and clothing; see note to Pass. ii. 20, p. 29. See a curious passage in the Romaunt of the Rose, ll. 6717—6760, on the conditions which render begging allowable.

12. (20. 12.) "That is, (firstly) meat, when people refuse to give it him because he possesses no money."

14. (20. 14.) *And*, if. *Cacche*, take [c]; *caughte*, were to take [b].

21. (20. 21.) For the counsel of Conscience, see Pass. xxii. 383—397. For the Cardinal Virtues, see Pass. xxii. 274—310.

22. (20. 22.) "Provided that he follow and preserve the spirit of Moderation."

34. (20. 34.) See Pass. xii. 304, and the note, p. 258.

35. (20. 35.) "Next him is Need." That is, the highest virtue is that of Temperance or Moderation, and the next thing that controls a man's actions is Necessity, which is subordinate to Temperance, but to no other Virtue.

37. (*not in* b.) "For Need makes needy men humble, on account of their wants."

43. (20. 42.) "On the cross itself." A singular mistake; the saying belongs to a much earlier period of our Lord's life.

46. (20. 45.) "Whereas Necessity has so seized me that I must needs stay," &c.

49. (20. 48.) *Wilfulliche*, willingly, by choice. The usual old sense of *wilful* is *voluntary*. Thus Barclay, in his Ship of Fools, ed. Jamieson, ii. 327, says—

> "Also the religyous sholde be obedyent,
> And euer perseuer in fayre humylyte,
> Beynge content with *wylfull pouerte*."

The sense of the word is remarkably shewn in Batman vppon Bartholomè, lib. 7, cap. 13:—"A Cramp is a violent shrinking of sinewes, taking aweye and hindering *wilfull* moouing," i. e. voluntary motion. Cf. Chaucer's Cant. Tales, Group C, 441; Group D, 1179; Wyclif's Works, i. 123, lines 1—3; Trench's Select Glossary, s. v. *Wilful*; Richardson's Dictionary, s. v. *Wilfully*;

&c. The word *wilful* still means *willing* in Warwickshire; Eng. Dialect Society, Gloss. C. 6.

50. (20. 49.) See Pass. xi. 193, 194.

51. (20. 50.) Here begins the Eleventh (and last) Vision, or the Vision of Antichrist; see Pref. to C-text, p. cii; Pref. to B-text, p. lv.

53. (20. 52.) *Antecrist*, Antichrist. "It is not improbable that Langland here had his eye on the old French *Roman d'Antechrist*, a poem written by Huon de Meri, about the year 1228. The author of this piece supposes that Antichrist is on earth, that he visits every profession and order of life, and finds numerous partisans. The Vices arrange themselves under the banner of Antichrist, and the Virtues under that of Christ. These two armies at length come to an engagement, and the battle ends to the honour of the Virtues, and the total defeat of the Vices. . . . . The title of Huon de Meri's poem deserves notice. It is [*Le*] *Turnoyement de l'Antechrist.* These are the concluding lines :

> ' Par son droit nom a peau cet livre
> Qui tresbien s'avorde a l'escrit
> Le Tournoiement de l'Antechrist.'

The author appears to have been a monk of St Germain des Pres, near Paris. This allegory is much like that which we find in the old dramatic Moralities. The theology of the middle ages abounded with conjectures and controversies concerning Antichrist, who at a very early period was commonly believed to be the Roman pontiff. See this topic discussed with singular penetration and perspicuity by Dr Hurd, in Twelve Sermons Introductory to the Study of the Prophecies, 1772, p. 206, seq."—Warton, Hist. Eng. Poetry, ed. 1840, ii. 60; or ed. 1871, ii. 263. Mr Wright has also given some account of de Meri's poem in his St Patrick's Purgatory, pp. 113, 114. It is printed at length in P. Tarbè's Poètes de Champagne, vol. xv. A comparison of it with our text shews no close resemblance of language, but only a certain similarity of ideas.

For some account of Antichrist, see Hampole's Pricke of Conscience, pp. 110—125; and cf. Maundeville's Travels, p. 110; Ormulum, ed. White, note to l. 8719; Cursor Mundi, ed. Morris, pp. 1258, 1266; Rom. of the Rose, l. 7011. Wyclif compared the pope to Antichrist more than once; see his Works, i. 138, ii. 394, iii. 341. In the Coventry Mysteries, the shearmen, dyers, and hewsters were to "shewe forth howe Antechrist shoulde rise;" Strutt, Manners and Customs, iii. 136.

54. (20. 53.) *Tyte*, quickly [c]; ingeniously substituted for *it* [b].

69. (20. 68.) Pride, as the chief of the Seven Deadly Sins, is rightly made to bear Antichrist's banner. Cf. Pass. xxii. 337. So in Robert of Brunne's Handlyng Synne, l. 3406—

> "And ȝyf he [sc. a clerk] yn folye begynne to stoute,
> þan bereþ he þe deuelys baner aboute"—

where the French original is—

> "Clerk cointe ordene
> Baucour est al maufe."

71. (20. 70.) *A lorde;* this is the personification of Lechery. See ll. 90, 114; and cf. Pass. vii. 170.

75. (20. 74.) Unity or Holy-church is the castle into which the followers of Conscience retreat; see Pass. xxii. 359. This is well illustrated by the fine illuminated picture called The Fortress of Faith, copied from a miniature of the 15th century, at p. 408 of Military and Religious Life in the Middle Ages, by P. Lacroix. "The fortress, besieged by the impious and the heretics, is defended by the Pope, the bishops, the monks, and the doctors, who are the Chevaliers of the Faith."

I may remark that the author of The Reply of Friar Daw Topias (printed in Political Poems, ed. Wright, vol. ii., pp. 57, 58) must have read our author's account of Antichrist's battle-array carefully. He thus addresses the Wycliffites—

" It ar ʒe that stonden bifore in Anticristis vanwarde,
    And in the myddil and in the rerewarde ful bigly enbatailid ;
    The devel is ʒour duke, and pride berith the baner,
    Wraththe is ʒoure gunner, envie is ʒour archer,
    ʒour couetise castith fer, ʒour leccherie brennith,
    Glotony giderith stickes therto, and sleuthe myneth the wallis,
    Malice is ʒour men of armes, and trecherie is ʒour aspie."

Compare also Barclay's Ship of Fools, ed. Jamieson, ii. 229.

76. (20. 75.) *Kynde,* Nature. Conscience supposes that Nature, for love of Piers the Plowman, will assist men against spiritual foes. But the result is represented as being very different; for Nature also becomes man's enemy, afflicting him with various bodily diseases; see l. 80. Yet Nature is, at last, man's true friend; see l. 109.

80. (20. 79.) Nature is represented as coming "out of the planets," because diseases were supposed to be due to planetary influence. "Whan the planetes ben vnder thilke signes, thei causen vsˣby hir influence operaciouns and effectes lik to the operaciouns of bestes;" Chaucer, Astrolabie, pt. i. sect. 21, l. 41; see Plate VII in my edition. Lines 80—109 (b. 20. 79—108) are quoted in Warton, Hist. Eng. Poetry, ed. 1840, ii. 59; ed. 1871, ii. 262. Warton well compares the catalogue of diseases here given with that in Milton, Paradise Lost, xi. 474.

82. (20. 81.) *Cardiacles,* spasms of the heart. The word has already occurred in Pass. vii. 78. It occurs also in Chaucer's Pardoner's Prologue; in the Prologue to the Tale of Beryn, ed. Furnivall, l. 493; and, spelt *cordiacle,* in the Testament of Love, book ii. (not by Chaucer, but printed in) Chaucer's Works, ed. 1651, fol. 305, col. 2. Cotgrave gives, as one of the meanings of Fr. *cardiaque*—"a consumption, and continuall sweat, by the indisposition of the heart, and parts about it." Batman vppon Bartholomè, lib. 7. cap. 13, has a chapter "Of the Crampe;" and lib. 7. cap. 32 is "Of heart-quaking, and the disease *cardiacle.*" He says that—"heart-quaking or Cardi[a]cle is an euil that is so called because it commeth often of default of the heart," &c. The Gk. καρδιακός is sometimes used as synonymous with καρδιαλγής, to signify one who is suffering from heart-

burn. Ducange has—"*Cordiacus*, (1) qui patitur morbum cordis ; (2) morbus ipse."

Cramps could be cured, it was supposed, by the use of cramp-rings ; see note to Pass. vii. 78, p. 109.

83. (20. 82.) *Reumes*, rheums,. colds and catarrhs. *Radegoundes*, running sores ; especially used of sore eyes. The word is, apparently, compounded of *reed*, red, and *gound* (A.S. *gund*), matter of a sore. The A.S. *gund* occurs, for example, in the compound *healsgund*, scrofula, lit. neck-sore. The fourth chapter of part 1 of the A.S. Leechdoms has a title beginning "Læce-cræftas wiþ healsgunde," i. e. remedies against scrofula ; Wanley's Catalogue of A.S. MSS. p. 176. The Prompt. Parv., p. 206, has—"Gownde of the eye, *ridda*, *albugo* ;" on which Way notes— "Skinner gives the word *gound* as used very commonly in Lincolnshire, signifying the running or impure secretion of the eyes. It occurs in the glosses on G. de Biblesworth, Arundel MS. 220, fol. 297 b—' *Vostre regardz est gracious* (louclik), *Mes vos oeyz sunt saciouz* (gundy) ; *Des oeez outez la sacye* (þe gunde), *E de nees la rupye* (þe maldrope).' Bp. Kennett, in his glossarial collection, Lansd. MS. 1033, has the following note : ' Gunded eyes, Westm. Goundy, filthy like running sores, Gower. Gunny eyes, Yorksh. Dial.' A.S. *gund*, pus, sanies. Skelton describes the ' eyen gowndye of Elynour Rumming." See Dyce's Skelton, i. 96, 1. 34, and the note. Yet again, in the Prompt. Parv., p. 426, we have—"Redgownde, sekenesse of yonge chyldryne, *scrophulus*," on which Way notes—"' Reed gounde, sickenesse of chyldren ;' Palsgrave. This eruptive humour is more commonly termed the Redgum, for which various remedies are to be found in old books of medicine. William Langham specially commends the water of columbine as ' good for yong children to drinke against the *redgum* or fellon ;' Garden of Health, 1579. ' Redgum, a sickness of young children, *scrophulus* ;' Gouldman." To which I may add that the French word *sacye* above (in Biblesworth) is the same as Cotgrave's " *Chacie*, blear-eyednesse," &c. It is clear that, in the word *red-gum*, the latter element is an ingenious substitution for the A.S. *gund*, which has become obsolete.

The spelling *radegoundes* in the MSS. of both texts makes it very probable that the word was sometimes corrupted in yet another way ; viz. by confusion with a proper name, that of St Radegund. Nothing was more common than to suppose that certain saints could cure certain sores ; see the list of saints and ailments in Chambers, Book of Days, ii. 389, where we find—

> " St Apolin the rotten teeth do help when sore they ache,
> Otilia from the bleared eyes the cause and grief doth take ;
> Rooke [*St Roque*] healeth scabs and mangins, with pocks, and scurf,
>   and scall,
> And cooleth raging carbuncles, and boils, and botches all."

St Radegund, the wife of Lothaire I. of France, died Aug. 13, 587. Her life is in the Aurea Legenda, ed. Grässe, cap. ccxl (otherwise 211) ; and see Fabyan's Chronicle, ed. Ellis, p. 79. She was much given to wearing irons

upon her body in penance, till they caused dreadful sores by eating into the
flesh.   Her-skill in performing miracles is dilated upon in the Knight of Là-
tour Landry, ed. Wright, p. 114, where her name is oddly corrupted into
"seint Aragon that was queue of Fraunce." Some such confusion as that
suggested must have been in the minds of men in the fourteenth century,
since the first vowel in the word is persistently written as *a* in the MSS.

92. (20. 91.) *Alarme*, to arms! The early use of this word is remarkable.. It is said to be derived, not from the French *à l'arme* (for the old
French form was rather *as armes*, i. e. *aux armes*), but from the Italian *all'
arme*. If so, it is surely one of the earliest Italian words in English; and it
is just conceivable that it may have come to us in the time of the crusades.

Lyf, a living wight, as frequently before; see the Glossary. There is,
too, a play upon the word. *Eche lyf kepe hus owene (lyf)*, let each living
wight save his own (life).

100. (20. 99.) This is one of the finest passages in the poem. In modern
spelling it is—

> "Death came driving after, and all to dust pashed
> Kings and knights, kaisers and popes;
> Learned nor lewd, he left no man to stand;
> They that he hit evenly stirred never after.
> Many a lovely lady and their lemans, knights,
> Swooned and swelted, for sorrow of death's dints."

Douce (Illustrations of Shakespeare, i. 400) says that he was reminded of
this passage when reading Macbeth, Act v. sc. 5—

> "And all our yesterdays have lighted fools
> The way to *dusty death*."

109. (20. 108.) "And Nature ceased (her plagues) then, to see the
people amend." This passage is ironical; for, as Mr Wright well remarks,
"the allusion is to the dissipation of manners which followed the pestilence."
Cf. Pass. xi. 272.   And see note to l. 150 below.

114. (20. 113.) The author once more recurs to the favourite topic of
the Seven Deadly Sins (cf. Pass. vii.), and mentions Lechery in l. 114,
Avarice in l. 121, and Sloth in ll. 159, 217; having already mentioned Pride
in l. 70.   See also l. 215, where the "Sins" are called "geauntes."

126. (20. 125.) "Simony followed him" [c]; "Simony sent him," i. e.
Avarice [b].   See Chaucer's remarks on simony in his Pers. Tale, *De
Auaritia;* and cf. Pass. iii. 72, 181.

127. (20. 126.) "Pressed on the pope," i. e. used his influence with the
pope [c]; "Preached to the people" [b].   A remarkable variation.

130. (20. 129.) "And beat Conscience" [c]; "And submitted (hypo-
critically) to Conscience" [b].   Another striking change in tone.

133. (20. 132.) "The law-courts have been held at Westminster from
the earliest Anglo-Norman times, it being the king's chief palace;" Wright's
note.   Cf. Pass. iii. 174.

134. (20. 133.) This is a humorous allusion to a sort of mock tournament.   Simony runs a tilt at the justice's ear, and by a crafty whisper of a

bribe overturns all his ideas of truth and justice. He accompanies his offer
of money with the words—"take this [deed, and at the same time this
money] on amendment;" meaning, "surely you can amend this." *Iogged
til*, jogged on towards, rode leisurely towards; with a glance at the use of
jog in the sense of to nudge a half-sleeping man. Compare the remark in
Barclay's Ship of Fools, ed. Jamieson, i. 25, "That aungels worke wonders
in westmynster hall." *Aungels* or *angels* are the gold coins so called.

136. (20. 135.) "The court of the arches was a very ancient consistory
court of the archbishop of Canterbury, held at Bow Church in London,
which was called St Mary de Arcubus or St Mary le Bow, from the circumstance of its having been built on arches;" Wright's note. Cf. Pass. iii.
61, 186.

137. (20. 136.) "And turned Civil (the civil law) into Simony," i. e.
made it subservient to simoniacal purposes; cf. Pass. iii. 71, 127, 183. *He
tok*, he gave to, i. e. gave some bribe to; in other words, he bribed. See
tok as used in Pass. iv. 47, and the Note thereon, at p. 58.

139. (20. 138.) An allusion to the (old) form of words in the Marriage
Service—"till death us *depart*," i. e. separate us; now altered to "do part."

143. (20. 142.) *Lowh*, laughed. *Lyf*, Life. It must be carefully noticed that
the poet here describes, by the name of Life, a man of fashion of the period.
Let dagge his clothes, caused his clothes to be "dagged," i. e. curiously cut.
See Rich. Redeles, iii. 193, and the note to iii. 152 (C-text, p. 516), where
the well-known passage from Chaucer's Persones Tale on the "superfluite
of clotheynge" is cited. In the Prompt. Parv., p. 111, we have—"Dagge
of clothe, *fractillus;*" and, at p. 255—"Iagge or dagge of a garment,
fractillus;" see Way's notes on these words. The fashion of jagging, or
cutting in slits, the borders of garments was much in vogue at this period,
and indeed for some time afterwards, as may be seen in any work or costume.
It was a favourite subject for satire. For example, in the Vision of Wm.
Staunton, A.D. 1409, in MS. Reg. 17 B. xliii, fol. 133 (quoted in Mr
Wright's work entitled St Patrick's Purgatory, p. 145), the author describes
men and women in hell, and observes that he saw some there "with mo
jagges on here clothis than hole cloth;" and again, in a later passage (St.
Pat. Purg., p. 148), he observes that, instead of curiously cut clothes, many
are surrounded by twining snakes and reptiles, and "thilk serpentes, snakes,
todes, and other wormes ben here jaggis and daggis."

146. (20. 145.) *Let*, considered; "considered Loyalty as but a churl,"
i. e. a slave.

148. (20. 147.) "Thus Life rallied (i. e. became presumptuous) because
of a little good fortune." Cf. note to l. 109 above.

150. (20. 149.) The Black Death was followed by a singular recklessness
of conduct on the part of the survivors; "in the same way as the surviving
inhabitants of Lisbon became more dissolute after their earthquake, and the
Athenians after the plague by which their city was afflicted; see Thucydides,
bk. ii " Dunlop's Hist. of Fiction, on the Decameron of Boccaccio. See

the remarks of Warton on this subject; Hist. Eng. Poetry, ed. 1871,
ii. 355.

154. (20. 153.) "Shall cause thee not to fear either death or old age."
Life is addressing Fortune.

155. (20. 154.) *Yyue nauht of,* care nothing about; i.e. be reckless as to.

160. (20. 159.) *Wanhope,* despair. William makes Wanhope the spouse
of Sloth, because they were considered to be in close relationship. In
Chaucer's Pers. Tale, *De Accidia,* we find—"Now cometh *wanhope,* that is,
despeir of the mercy of God . . Which dampnable sinne, if it continue unto
his end, it is cleped the·sinne of [i.e. against] the holy gost." Cf. Pass.
viii. 81. The Dutch form, *wanhoop,* is still in use.

162. (20. 161.) "One Tom Two-tongued, attainted at each inquest."
This Tom Two-tongued (*or* Two-tongue, *b*) is the opposite of Tom True-
tongue, mentioned in Pass. v. 18.

167. (20. 166.) Here Elde (Old-Age), who had formerly fought under
Death's banner on the side of the Vices, is now shriven, and takes the side of
the Virtues, though still fighting against Life. The poet has rather clumsily
used *good hope* in this line in its usual sense, whilst *wanhope* in the next line
is a personification. Thus the line means—"And Old-age laid hold of good
hope, and hastily shrove himself" [c]; *or,* "hastily he shifted his ground"
[b]. Cf. "good heorte he hente," i.e. he plucked up courage, in l. 180
below.

169. (20. 168.) "Life fled for fear to Physic for help." Cf. Pass.
ix. 292.

170. (20. 169.) "And besought him for aid, and had some of his salve."

171. (20. 170.) *Good won,* a good quantity. "Woone, or grete plente,
copia, habundancia;*" Prompt. Parv., p. 532, and see Way's note. The
word is not uncommon; see *wán* in Stratmann. In Northern English, it is
wayn or *wane.* It is memorable as occurring in the old version of Chevy
Chase, l. 74 :—

"With that ther cam an arrowe hastely forthe off a myghtte *wane ;* "

i.e. out of a great quantity. See Barbour's Bruce, xvi. 454, xvii. 249.

172. (20. 171.) "And they gave him in return a glass cap;" lit. a glass
hood. The sense of this phrase is "an imaginary protection;" something
that seemed a defence, but was really frail and inefficient. The expression
is ironical, and was probably proverbial, much as we speak of living "in
glass houses." There are at least two other examples of its use. In the
Debate between the Soul and Body, printed in Mätzner's Alteng. Sprachproben, i. 98, the Soul reproaches the body, saying—

"That thou louedest me thouȝ lete,
And madest me an *houue of glas ;*
I dide al that the was sete,
And thou my traytor euer was."

I.e. Thou didst pretend that thou lovedst me; and thou madest me a glass
hood; I did all that was sweet to thee, and thou wast ever a traitor to me.
(In this passage the Vernon MS. reads *swete* for *sete.*) Here the phrase

"madest me a glass hood" obviously means "didst lull me into a state of false security;" or, as we say, "madest me live in a fool's paradise."

Again, in a passage in Chaucer (first explained by myself), viz. in Troilus and Cressida, v. 469, Fortune is said to have an intention of deluding Troilus; or, as the poet puts it—"Fortune his *howue* intended bet *to glase*," i. e. Fortune intended to *gluze his* hood still better for him, i. e. to make a still greater fool of him. In the Aldine edition (vol. v. p. 20) the word *howue* is misprinted *howen*, though *howue* occurs elsewhere in Chaucer; Tyrwhitt reads *hove*, a common variation of *houue*.

We may also note another passage in Chaucer's Troil. and Cress., bk. ii. l. 867 (Aldine edition, vol. iv. p. 188), where there is an allusion to a similar proverb:—

> "And forthy, who that hath an'hede of verre
> Fro caste of stones war him in the werre."

I. e. And therefore, let him who has a *head of glass* beware of the casting of great stones in war.

See also my note on *vitremyte*, in Chaucer's Cant. Tales, B. 3562, in the Clarendon Press edition of Chaucer's Prioresses Tale, &c.

Glasen is the adj. from *glas*. It occurs in Old Eng. Hom., ed. Morris, i. 83, where the sun is said to shine "þurh þe *glesne* ehþurl," i. e. through the glass eye-hole, or window. A still clearer example is in the Praier and Complaint of the Ploughman, printed in the Harleian Miscellany, vi. 103, where we read of "greet stonen houses full of *glasene* windowes."

173. (20. 172.) "Life believed that medical skill would stop (*or* delay) Old Age."

174. (20. 173.) *To-dryue*, drive away; infin. mood. *Dyas and drogges*, remedies and drugs. The word *dia* has been already explained in the note to Pass. vii. 88, p. 110; which see. I may add that Burton, in his Anatomy of Melancholy, pt. 2, sect. 4, mem. 1, subsect. 5, mentions various conserves and confections, some hot, such as "diambra, diamargaritum calidum, dianthus, diamoschum dulce, . . . diagalinga, diacyminum, dianisum, diatrion piperion, diazinziber, diacapers, diacinnamomum; others cold, as diamargaritum frigidum, diacorolli, diarrhodon abbatis, diacodion," &c. "If you be troubled with rheumes, . . . use diatrion piperion;" Babees Book, ed. Furnivall, p. 253. Cf. Hist. Agric. and Prices in England, by J. E. T. Rogers, i. 630, 648. The term *diachylon* is still in use.

Dragges (drugs) were used by Chaucer's Doctor of Phisik; Prologue, 426.

175. (20. 174.) *Auntred hym on*, adventured himself against; a term of the tournament.

176. (20. 175.) *Forrede*, furred; see Pass. ix. 292.

183. (20. 182.) There is here a singular and sudden change. Old Age, hasting after Life, encounters the poet on his way. As a result, we hear no more about Life, but the poet contents himself with narrating the result of his own *personal* encounter with Old Age. Old Age begins by passing over the poet's head, rendering him bald.

186. (20. 185.) *Yuel-ytauht*; evil taught, ill-instructed. *Vnhende*, ill manners go with thee; lit. let ill-mannered fellows go with thee: see l. 188.

189. (20. 188.) *ʒe*, yea, to be sure! an ironical form of assent. *Leue lordeyn*, dear sluggard! *Lordeyn* occurs elsewhere; see note to B. 18. 102, p. 404, and the Glossary. "Lurdayne, *lourdault;*" Palsgrave.

196. (20. 195.) *Naked*. See note to B. xiv. 2, p. 320. See some curious verses on Old Age, printed in Reliq. Antiq., ii. 210.

203. (20. 202.) *Hennes*, hence, i.e. out of this life; see Pass. x. 53, 348.

204. (20. 203.) *Unite*, Unity or Holy Church, the castle of Conscience; see Pass. xxii. 330.

210. (20. 209.) *And*, if. *Lacke þe*, fail thee.

215. (20. 214.) *Geauntes*, giants; i.e. the Seven Deadly Sins; see note to l. 114 above.

219. (20. 218.) *Paltokes*, cloaks; see note to Pass. xxi. 24, p. 400. *Pikede shoes*, peaked shoes; see note to Pass. xxi. 12, p. 399. "The greatest charge laid to good Queen Anne [wife of Rich. II.] is that of Stow. He says—'Since the 5th of Richard II., when he took to wife Anne, daughter of Wenceslaus, king of Bohemia, by her example the English people had used piked shoes fastened to their knees with silken laces or chains of silver and gilt;' Survey of London, B. 206. In the following reign the length of these pikes was restrained by statute;" Chronicque de la Traison et Mort de Richart; ed. B. Williams, p. 134, *note*.

Pissares. In the Phil. Soc. Trans. for 1859, p. 72, two guesses are made as to the sense of this word. First, that it is a corruption of *pistor*, a baker, which is plainly incredible; and secondly, that it means a fisherman, from the O.Fr. *pischer*, to fish (Roquefort), which is equally stupid. William knew perfectly well how to say *bakere* or *fisher* without turning the words into false Old French. Surely the word expresses exactly what the sound tells us, and is equivalent to a familiar Biblical expression for "every male;" 1 Kings xiv. 10; xvi. 11. It was, I suppose, a cant term, or nickname, given neither to *bakers* nor *fishermen*, but (as the context requires) to *soldiers* or *armed retainers*, notable in those days for coarse insolence. The fault of the priests here inveighed against is that they wore "long knives" or swords like soldiers. The knife itself had what was probably a cant name; see B. xv. 121. Compare the following passage from Myrc's Instructions for Parish Priests, ed. Peacock, l. 41:

> "Hawkynge, huntynge, and dawnsynge,
> .Thow moste forgo for any thynge;
> Cuttede clothes and *pyked schone*,
> Thy gode fame they wole for-done . . .
> In honeste clothes thow moste gon,
> *Baselard* ny bawdryke were thow non."

That such a cant name as that under discussion may have been in use is probable enough, from the suggestive passage in Chaucer's Persones Tale, *De Superbia*, where the Persone inveighs against the fashionable clothes of some—"alas! som of hem shewen the bosse and the shape of the horrible swollen membres, that semen like to the maladie of hernia," &c. I do not think there need be much difficulty here.

221. (20. 220.) *Mansed,* cursed; see note to Pass. iii. 41, p. 46. *Was,* who was. *Yrelond,* Ireland [c]; *Walys,* Wales [b, *in MS.* W. *only; see footnote*].

223. (20. 223.) Compare the expression—"An 'twere not as good a deed as drink;" 1 Henry IV., ii. 1. 33; 2. 23.

225. (20. 224.) *Othes.* It is remarkable that the horrible swearing then so prevalent is here charged upon the Irish priests. Wyclif refers to "comyn swereris by Goddis herte, bonys, nailis, and sidis, and oþere membris;" Works, iii. 332. Chaucer says—"For Cristes sake, swere not so sinnefully, in dismembring of Crist, by soule, herte, bones, and body;" Pers. Tale, *De Ira.* And see his Pardoneres Tale, Group C. 472, 592, 650, and my note to the first of these passages in the Clarendon Press edition.

232. (20. 231.) *Neode,* Need, Poverty; who appeared at the beginning of the Passus; ll. 4—50.

228. (20. 227.) The rest of this Passus, from this point to the end, has been paraphrased by Drayton; the whole passage is printed at the end of the Notes to this Passus.

236. (20. 235.) *Chile,* chilliness, cold; as in B. i. 23.

237. (20. 236.) *Chewe,* eat, feed. Cf. Pass. ii. 191; and note to xxi. 404, p. 422.

238. (20. 237.) *Lommere he lyeth,* he tells lies oftener. The word *lomere* [b] is glossed, in the B-text, by *sæpius,* shewing that it was obsolescent. For examples of *lome,* i.e. often, see Stratmann. To the references there given, add:—Tale of Beryn, ed. Furnivall, l. 2191.

252. (20. 251.) Francis and Dominick were respectively the founders of the Grey and Black Friars. See notes to B. 15. 413, p. 361, and to Pass. v. 117, p. 82.

261. (*not in* b.) Lines 37 and 261 are peculiar to the C-text.

262. (20. 260.) *Brybours,* robbers; such is the old sense of the word. "*Bribery,* in old English, meant not secret corruption, but theft, rapine, open violence, and very often official extortion. Thus Julyana Berners, in her treatise of 'Fysshynge with the Angle,' in speaking of the injustice and cruelty of robbing private fish-ponds and other waters, says: 'It is a ryght shamefull dede to any nobleman to do that that theuys and *brybours* done.' Lord Berners, in his translation of Froissart, describes the captain of a band of the irregular soldiery called 'Companions,' as the 'greatest *brybour* and robber in all Fraunce;' and Palsgrave gives *I pull* and *I pyll* as synonyms of *I bribe,* &c. &c.;" Marsh's Lectures on the Eng. Language, repr. in Smith's Manual of Eng. Language, p. 169; see the whole of the passage. See also *Bribe* in Trench's Select Glossary. Chaucer uses it as a term of reproach; Cant. Tales, l. 6948 (Freres Tale, near beginning). Cf. Barclay's Ship of Fools, ed. Jamieson, i. 64, l. 1.

263. (20. 261.) *Pilours*, strippers of the dead; Ch. Kn. Tale, l. 149.
Pyke-herneys, plunderers of armour, men who stole armour (formerly called
harness) from the slain in battle. In the Towneley Mysteries, *Pike-harnes*
is the name given to Cain's serving-boy. *Pykers*, in the sense of thieves,
occurs in Barclay's Ship of Fools, ed. Jamieson, i. 15, l. 21. Cf. "*pickers
and stealers;*" Hamlet, iii. 2. 348.

265. (20. 263.) *A certayn numbre*, a fixed number. For example, the
charter of foundation of Sion Monastery ordained that the establishment
should consist of 60 nuns, including the abbess, and of 25 religious men;
Myrour of Our Lady, ed. Blunt, Pref. p. xvi. A common number in a
religious house was 13, in remembrance of our Lord and his apostles. Thus,
St Benedict "established 12 monasteries, placing in each 12 monks and a
superior;" Chambers, Book of Days, i. 104.

269. (20. 267.) *Oute of numbre.* Chaucer, in his Wyf of Bathes Tale, l.
12, declares that the friars were "As thikke as motes in the sonne-beme,"
and that their omnipresence had driven away all the fairies. Wyclif says
that "not two hundrid ȝeere agone þer was no frere . . . And now ben *mony
thousande* of freris in Englond;" Works, iii. 400.

270. (20. 268.) *Euene numbre;* an allusion to Rev. vii. 4—8. But the
next verse (Rev. vii. 9) tells us differently. The statement that "hell is
without number" is an allusion to Job x. 22—"terram miseriæ et tenebrarum, ubi umbra mortis, et *nullus ordo*, sed sempiternus horror inhabitat."
This is referred to again in Chaucer's Pers. Tale (Prima Pars Penitentiæ),
where he says—"And eke Job seith, that in helle is non ordre of rule. And
al be it so, that God hath create al thing in right ordre, and nothing with-
outen ordre, but alle thinges ben ordred and numbred, yet natheles they that
ben dampned ben nothing in ordre, ne hold non ordre." The Cursor Mundi
(l. 503), speaking of the fall of the rebel angels, says—

> " þe numbre þat out of heuen fell
> þo can na tung in erth noght tell."

In the Reply of Friar Daw Topias (pr. in Polit. Poems, ii. 105), the friar
argues—

> "Thou seist that God alle thingis hath maad in mesure, weiȝte, and
>   noumbre;
> And that every frere is sum thing thou maist not denye,
> And thou seist freris been maad aȝens Goddis wille!"

But to this an immediate and stinging rejoinder at once follows :—

> "Thou [*though*] God made al thinge in mesure and in wyȝte [*weight*],
> It soloweth not he made ȝou; for ȝe ben oute of mesure!"

275. (20. 273.) Whitaker remarks here:—"The introduction of heathen
morality is an old evil in Christian pulpits. On this subject the old and
modern bard sympathise with each other :—

> 'How oft, when Paul hath given us a text,
> Do Epictetus, Plato, Tully preach.'—COWPER."

277. (20. 275.) Observe this emphatic renunciation, on the poet's part,
of the principles of communism. It is clear that he protests here against

the scandalous, yet not unnatural, use that had been made of his poem by John Ball and other such preachers; and here plainly disavows all sympathy with unprincipled and thoughtless rioters.

284. (20. 282.) "Shame makes men flee to the friars," instead of going to be shriven by their own parish priest. See note to Pass. vii. 120, p. 111.

William says of the "fals folke" that they borrow money, and take it to Westminster, viz. to bribe the judges with (see ll. 131—139 above); and then they earnestly beg their friends to forgive the debt, or grant them a longer time for repayment. Yet whilst they are in Westminster, they make merry with the officials, whom they treat with the borrowed money. Similarly, he says, executors give some of the deceased man's money to the friars; and having done this, they safely appropriate the remainder.

293. (20. 291.) "And leave the dead man (still) in debt, till doomsday." The friars and executors shared the money, whilst the creditors remained unpaid.

299. (20. 297.) *Titereres in ydel*, tattlers in an idle manner, idle tattlers. For *tytereres*, we find *titeleris* in MS. W [b, *footnote*]. The Promp. Parv. has—"Tateryn, or iaueryn, or speke wythe-owte resone, or iangelyn, chateryn, iaberyn, *garrio, blatero*." Also—"Taterynge or iauerynge, iaperynge, iaberinge, *garritus*." The word *titeren* is related to *tateren* just as *tittle* is to *tattle*, and expresses the same thing in a less degree or more suppressed manner. To *tittle* is *to tattle secretly*, and so to *titter* is here to *tatter* in a subdued manner. In modern English, to *titter* means to giggle, to laugh in a subdued manner.

304. (20. 302.) It has been remarked that William seems to have been somewhat indebted to Huon de Meri for his description of Antechrist's army; see note to l. 53 above. It is probable that he has here also taken a few ideas from that poem. Compare the following passage, printed in the Poètes de Champagne, ed. P. Tarbé, vol. xv. p. 91—

> "Lors me semont Conpunccion
> Et Dévocion sa cosine
> Que j'alasse querre medicine . . . . .
> Dont ma Dame Confession
> Une merveilleuse oncion
> Me fist; et tant s'umelia
> Qu'ele meismes me lia
> Sor mes plaies molt doucement."

See also ll. 356—361 below.

308. (20. 306.) "And (took care) that Piers' pardon was paid, (according to the precept)—'pay what thou owest.'" See Pass. xxii. 187, 193.

320. (20. 318.) Here Piers the Plowman is Christ, the true Head of the Church, having power to grant indulgences to all who have paid their debts, i. e. who have tried to perform all duties.

324. (20. 322.) The whole description of friar Flatterer in ll. 324—372 is in the poet's best manner.

335. (20. 333.) *Ful hard;* "it is a very unlikely thing that they will recover."

340. (20. 338.) Alluding to the text—"Ex his enim sunt, qui *penetrant domos,* et captiuas ducunt mulierculas oneratas peccatis, quæ ducuntur uariis desideriis;" 2 Tim. iii. 6.

351, 352. (20. 349, 350.) "That Life [the man of fashion, *note to l.* 143] shall, through his teaching, give up Avarice, and (cease) to bo afraid of Death;" &c.

353. (20. 351.) "And agree with Conscience, and either (i. e. each) of them kiss the other."

359. (20. 357.) Plaisters were much in use; see note to Pass. xx. 89, p. 388. Hence, metaphorically, we read that St Bridget "made a wholsome playster of penaunce to all people that ys sorowfully combred in synnes;" Myrour of Our Lady, ed. Blunt, p. 164. Barclay, in his Ship of Fools, ed. Jamieson, ii. 111, has the following passage:—

> "The quakynge seke in bed lyenge prostrate,
> Halfe dede, halfe lyuynge, by some mortall wounde,
> And of all his myghtis of manhode clene pryuate,
> Can nat be hole, but if plasters be bounde
> Vnto his grefe, to clens it by the grounde,
> Purgynge it by such playsters mundifycatyue,
> And than it closynge by playsters sanatyue.
>
> . . . .
> Withdrawe he his playsters for a day or twayne,
> His sore reneweth and rottyth than agayne."

Whitaker observes upon this line—"There is an impropriety in this; it was not the part of Conscience to complain that the parish-priest was too severe a confessor."

367. (20. 365.) One more allusion to the "letters of fraternity;" see notes to Pass. iv. 67, p. 60, and Pass. x. 343, p. 200.

378. (20. 376.) "Flatereres ben the deueles *enchauntours,* for thei maken a man wenen himself be like that he is nought like . . . . Flattreres ben the deueles chapeleynes, that euer singen *Placebo;*" Chaucer, Pers. Tale, *De Ira.*

379. (20. 377.) In the B-text, the author has omitted the alliteration; in the C-text, he has completely amended the line.

Dwale, an opiate, a sleeping-draught. Chaucer, in his Milleres Tale, says of the tired household that they "needed no *dwale;*" Cant. Tales, ed. Tyrwhitt, l. 4159. The Prompt. Parv. has—"Dwale, herbe, *morella somnifera, morella mortifera;*" and see Way's note, p. 134. Mr Way says that Chaucer "makes repeated allusion to the somniferous qualities of the nightshade, or dwale, the *Atropa belladonna.*" I only know of *one* allusion in Chaucer, viz. the one just cited. ◆ The word occurs again, however, in the Court of Love, l. 998, a poem once strangely attributed to Chaucer. Johns, in his Flowers of the Field, says—"*Atropa belladonna* (Deadly Nightshade, Dwale). . . . Buchanan relates that the Scots mixed the juice of Belladonna with the bread and drink, with which by their truce they were supposed to supply the Danes, which so intoxicated them, that the Scots killed the greater part of Sweno's army while asleep. The 'insane root that takes the reason prisoner,' mentioned by Shakespeare [*Macb.* i. 3], is also thought to be this. The English name *dwale* is derived from a French word *deuil*, which signifies 'mourning.'"

From the last two statements I dissent. The "insane root" was suggested to Shakespeare by a passage in North's Plutarch, and he no doubt (as a reader of Batman vppon Bartholomè) identified it with *henbane ;* see notes to Macb. i. 3. 84, in the Clarendon Press edition. Again, the etymology suggested is truly amazing, and shews what Englishmen are capable of believing concerning their own language, owing to undue confinement of strict scholarship to Greek and Latin. *Deuil* is the Lat. *dolium*, grief (occurring in the compound form *cordolium*) from *dolere*, to grieve. But *dwale* is purely English, and signifies something *stupefying* or *causing delirium*, being connected with the A.S. *dwolung*, dotage, *dwala*, an error, *gedwola*, an error, *gedwolman*, an impostor, *gedwolsum*, erroneous, *gedwælan*, to deceive, *dwelian* or *dwolian*, to err, also to deceive; with the Dutch *dwalen*, to err, *dwaaltuin*, a labyrinth, *dwaallicht*, a will-of-the-wisp; Dan. *dvale*, a trance, torpor, stupor, *dvale-drik*, a soporific (dwale-drink); O.H.G. *twalmgetrank*, a soporific (dwale-drink); *twalm*, enchantment. Cf. also Moeso-Goth. *dwals*, foolish; O.H.G. *twelan*, to go to sleep, to leave off; *twale*, delay. The connection is undoubted between these words and the A.S. *dwellan*, to delay, whence our modern Eng. *dwell ;* note also the O.H.G. *tol*, G. *toll*, mad; Du. *dolen*, to err, *dol*, mad; Eng. *dull*, foolish. See *Dull* in Wedgwood's Etym. Dict. And cf. Sanskrit dhvri, to bend, in Benfey's Dict., p. 452. The connection of *dwale* is, accordingly, with our *dwell* and *dull*, and not by any means with *doleful* or *dolour*.

There is a remarkable passage in the A.S. poem of St Andrew (ed. Grein, l. 33) which is worth quoting in connection with the present passage:

"Syððan him gebleóndan bitere tósomne
dryas þurh dwolcræft drync unheórne
se onwende gewit, wera ingeþanc."

I. e. Then they blended for them bitterly together,
These magicians, by magic art, a horrible drink
Which perverted the wit, the mind of the men."

383. (20. 381.) *Hadden*, might have; subj. mood. *Fyndynge*, provision. On which Pecock, in his Repressor, ed. Babington, ii. 390, remarks—"this word *fynding*, forto speke of such *fynding* as is mynystring of costis and expensis and other necessarie or profitable thingis into that a certeyn deede be doon and executid"—which is sufficient to shew that it properly means "provision for all necessary purposes only."

386. (20. 384.) *Gradde*, cried aloud; from A.S. *grǽdan*, to cry out *After grace*, for God's favour.

Here the poem ends. Conscience, hard beset by Pride and Sloth, has besought Contrition to come and help him; but Contrition slumbers, benumbed by the deadly potion with which the flattering friar has enchanted him.   With a last effort Conscience arouses himself, and seizes his pilgrim's staff, determined to wander wide over the world till he shall find Piers the Plowman, the true Saviour of mankind.   His last loud cry for God's help awakes the sleeper from his Vision.

Dr Whitaker suggested that the poem is not perfect; that it must have been designed to have a more satisfactory ending, and not one so suggestive of disappointment and gloom.   I am convinced that this opinion is erroneous; not so much from the fact that nearly all the MSS. have here the word *Explicit*, as from the very nature of the case.   What other ending can there be? or rather, the end is not yet.   We may be defeated, yet not cast down; we may be dying, and behold, we live.   We are all still pilgrims upon earth. *This* is the truth which the author's mighty genius would impress upon us in his parting words.   Just as the poet awakes in ecstacy at the end of the poem of Dobet, where he dreams of that which has been already accomplished, so here he is awoke by the cry of Conscience for help, and is silent at the thought of how much remains to be done.   So far from ending carelessly, he seems to me to have ceased speaking at the right moment, and to have managed a very difficult matter with consummate skill.

ADDITIONAL NOTE TO C. PASS. XXIII. 228.   (B. xx. 227.)

The latter part of this Passus is paraphrased by Drayton, as already remarked.   The passage occurs in his Legend of Thomas Cromwell, earl of Essex.   I transcribe it from Chalmers' edition of the British Poets, ed. 1810. It is necessary to remark that Drayton has made the usual odd blunder of supposing Piers to be the author, instead of the subject, of the Vision.

> " But negligent Security and Ease
>   Unbridled Sensuality begat,
> That only sought his appetite to please,
> As it in midst of much abundance sat :
> The church, not willing others should her praise,
> That she was lean, when as her lands were fat,
> Herself to too much liberty did give,
> Which some perceiv'd that in those times did live.
>
> Pierce, the wise ploughman, in his vision[1] saw
> Conscience sore hurt,[2] yet sorer was afraid
> The seven great sins to Hell him like to draw,
> And to wise clergy mainly cry'd for aid;
> Fall'n ere he wist (whom peril much did awe)
> On unclean priests whilst faintly he him staid,
> Willing good clergy t'ease his wretched case,
> Whom these strong giants hotly had in chase.

---

[1] The usual blunder.   It was *William* who, in his Vision, saw Piers the Plowman.
[2] See l. 223.

Clergy called friers,[1] which near at hand did dwell,
And them requests to take in hand the cure,
But, for their leechcraft that they could not well,
He listed not their dressing to endure,
When in his ear Need softly did him tell
(And of his knowledge more did him assure)
They came for gain, their end which they did make,
For which on them the charge of souls they take.

And voluntary poverty profest,
By food of angels[2] seeming as to live;
But yet with them th' accounted were the best,
That most to their fraternity did give,
And beyond number that they were increast.[3]
'If so,' quoth Conscience, 'thee may I believe,
Then 'tis in vain more 'on them to bestow,
If beyond number like they be to grow.'

The frier, soon feeling Conscience had him found,
And hearing how Hypocrisy did thrive,
That many teachers every where did wound,[4]
For which Contrition miserably did grieve:
Now in deceit to show himself profound,
His former hopes yet lastly to revive,
Gets the pope's letters,[5] whereof he doth shape
Him a disguise from Conscience to escape.

And so tow'rds goodly Unity he goes,[6]
A strong-built castle standing very high,
Where Conscience liv'd, to keep him from his foes,
Whom, lest some watchful sentinel should spy,
And him should to the garrison disclose,
His cowl about him carefully doth tie,
Creeps to the gate, and closely thereat beat,
As one that entrance gladly would entreat.

Peace, the good porter, ready still at hand,
It doth unpin, and prays him God to save,
And after salving,[7] kindly doth demand
What was his will, or who he there would have?
The frier low louting, crossing with his hand,
'To speak with Contrition,' quoth he, 'I would crave.'
'Father,' quoth Peace, 'your coming is in vain,
For him of late Hypocrisy hath slain.'

'God shield,' quoth he, and turning up his eyes,
'To former health I hope him to restore,
For in my skill his sound recovery lies;
Doubt not thereof, if setting God before.'
'Are you a surgeon?' Peace again replies;
'Yea,' quoth the frier, 'and sent to heal his sore.'
'Come near,' quoth Peace, 'and God your coming speed,
Never of help Contrition had more need.'

---

[1] Line 243.   [2] Line 241.   [3] Line 260.   [4] Line 302.   [5] Line 325.
[6] Line 329; cf. xxii. 330, 359.
[7] So printed by Chalmers; but the word is, of course, *saluing*, i. e. salutation; from the verb *salue*, to salute.

And for more haste he haleth in the frier,
And his lord Conscience quickly of him told,
Who entertain'd him with right friendly cheer :
'O sir,' quoth he, 'entreat you that I could
To lend your hand to my dear cousin here,
Contrition, whom a sore disease doth hold,
That, wounded by Hypocrisy of late,
Now lieth in most desperate estate.'

'Sir,' quoth the frier, 'I hope him soon to cure,
Which to your comfort quickly you shall see,
Will he awhile my dressing but endure.'
And to Contrition therewith cometh he,
And by fair speech himself of him assure,
But first of all going thorough for his fee :
Which done, quoth he, 'if outwardly you show
Sound, 't avails not if inwardly or no.'

But secretly assoiling of his sin,
No other med'cine will he to him lay,
Saying, that Heaven his silver him should win :
And to give friers was better than to pray ;
So were he shrived, what need he care a pin ?
Thus with his patient he so long did play,
Until Contrition had forgot to weep.[1]—
This the wise ploughman show'd me from his sleep.

He[2] saw their faults that loosely lived then,
Others again our weaknesses shall see ;
For this is sure, he bideth not with men,
That shall know all to be what they should be :
Yet let the faithful and industrious pen
Have the full merit ; but return to me,[3]
Whose fall this while blind Fortune did devise
To be as strange as strangely I did rise."

---

[1] Line 360.   [2] The author of Piers the Plowman.
[3] Thomas Cromwell, the subject of the Legend.

ADDITIONAL NOTES.

[THE following Notes came to hand too late to be inserted in their proper places. It would not be difficult to increase them considerably, but it is not my intention to do so, as they might otherwise exceed due bounds. I do not undertake to point out all the instances in which unusual words occur, nor to indicate more than a limited selection of the numerous lessons to be learnt from a perusal of William's poem.]

C. Pass. i. 2; B. prol. 2; A. prol. 2 (p. 3). I have since found an instance of *chep* or *shep* in the sense of shepherd. In Lydgate's Chorl and Birde, printed in Ashmole's Theatrum Chemicum, st. 43, p. 223, is the line—
"A Chepys Croke to the ys better than a Lance."
That is, a shepherd's crook would suit you better than a knight's spear. Moreover, it now appears that the word is still familiarly used in Lincolnshire. Mr Peacock's Glossary of Words used in Manley and Corringham (E. D. S.), p. 220, has the entry—"*Shep*, a shepherd," with the example—"Cook [a personal name] was *shep* to Mr Sorsby then, but he's left now," and then follow references to P. Plowman and Lydgate, which were supplied by myself. I think it particularly unfortunate that some critics, in their omniscience, have rejected my interpretation on the ground that the word *shep* is unknown. The word no doubt arose from the addition of the A.S. suffix -*a*, denoting an agent, to the sb. *sceáp*, a sheep. This would give *sceápa*, a sheep-man, a shepherd, which would easily have been contracted to *shep*. It is perhaps as well to add that John Ball called himself "Jak Chep" because he was a pastor, not because he was a sheep.

C. Pass. i. 230; B. prol. 229; A. prol. 108 (p. 27). The place indicated in the C-text by the spellings *ruele, rule, ruel,* or *rewle* is now clear to me. It was La Reole, the siege of which by the earl of Derby is narrated by Froissart, bk. i. capp. 108—111. It lies beside the river Garonne, at some distance above Bourdeaux; and of course "wine of La Reole" is merely another name for "Bourdeaux," still familiar as the name of a wine. The wines of Bourdeaux (which was then in the possession of the English) were very commonly used in England (see Chaucer, prol. 397), and hence are most appropriately referred to in this passage.

C. Pass. iii. 110; B. ii. 108; A. ii. 76 (p. 49). There were some hermits called after St Paul, according to The Pilgrim's Tale, l. 151, printed in Appendix I. to Thynne's Animadversions, ed. Furnivall (Chaucer Soc.). Mr Furnivall adds, in a note at p. 141—"Hélyot gives 3 orders of Paulines,

i. 360, 473, 1152; and fourthly, the *Ordre des Erémites de Saint-Paul*, iii. 126; see my Ballads from MSS. i. 245, n. 9."

C. Pass. iii. 130 (*not in* B, A). I have since found that there is a particular reference here to the story of St Lawrence as told in the Aurea Legenda; the exact passage referred to is quoted in the note to C. xviii. 64, pp. 355, 356.

C. Pass. iii. 208; B. ii. 196; A. ii. 171. The reference to the passage beginning "My seyd Lord hayth putte a bille" was accidentally omitted. It is from the Paston Letters, ed. Gairdner, i. 150.

C. Pass. iv. 342 (*not in* B, A). I have since found the source of the quotation *Retribuere, &c.*; it is printed in the note to C. Pass. xvi. 266, at p. 323.

C. vii. 81; B. xiii. 338 (*not in* A). The following passage is worth notice in illustration of the text:

> "Thus who that is payned in any malady
> Bodely or gostly, ought nat to be callyd wyse,
> To the Phesycian without that he aply,
> And his preceptis hant, kepe, and exercyse.
> But now olde wytches dare boldly interpryse
> To intromyt to hele all infyrmyte,
> And many them byleue, whiche sothly is pyte."

> "Suche wytches, of theyr byleue abhomynable,
> On brest or hede of the paynfull pacyent
> With theyr wytchecraftis shall compasse, chat, and bable,
> Assurynge hym of helth, and short amendement.
> Than he that is seke fyxith his intent
> Upon hir errour: to haue helpe of his sore.
> But she hym leuyth wors than he was before."
>
> Barclay's Ship of Fools, ed. Jamieson, i. 195.

C. Pass. vii. 218; B. v. 212; A. v. 126. Mr Furnivall refers me to the Second Part of Stubbes's Anatomie of Abuses, ed. 1583, sig. D. 7, where Stubbes complains of the drapers that "after they have bought their cloth, they cause it to be tentered, racked, and so drawne out, as it shall be both broader and longer than it was when they bought it, almost by halfe in halfe, or at lest by a good large sise. Now the cloth being thus stretched forth in euery vaine, how is it possible either to endure or hold out, but when a shower of raine taketh it, then it falleth and shrinketh in, that it is shame to see it." See too the Act, 39 of Elizabeth, cap. xx., A.D. 1597, "against the deceitfull stretching and taintering of Northerne cloth."

C. vii. 377; B. v. 328; A. v. 171 (p. 130). The note is, perhaps, hardly clear enough. The "new fair" meant a barter of articles not required by their owners. In the present day, there exists a periodical called "The Exchange and Mart," whereby we may barter one article for another by advertising. Much the same thing was prevalent in the fourteenth century, only the transaction was less genteelly conducted, and in the presence of witnesses, at a tavern. Clement the cobbler has a cloak which he does not want, and offers to barter it; Hick the hackney-man (i. e. letter out of horses for hire) offers his hood in exchange, and it only remains to determine which article is of more value, and how much is to be added to the inferior one to make the bargain even. For this purpose, each chooses a professional appraiser as deputy. These two rise up, and go aside, and wrangle over the articles, not without oaths. Being unable to agree, Robin is called in as umpire, and decides that Hick's hood is somewhat the better article, for which reason Clement is to be glad to receive it, and must shew his appreciation of the umpire's award by ordering that the cup be filled. Hick's gain merely consists in his being free from a similar fine; and the oracle declares that, if either is dissatisfied, he shall be fined in a gallon of ale for the benefit of Sir Glutton, who is a person of distinction amongst them as being an ecclesiastic; see note to l. 367, p. 129. This "new fair" or "evechepynge" was quite an organised institution, regularly held at certain hostelries, as explained; and hence "to chaffer at the new fair" passed into a proverb. The notion of handicapping or adjusting inequalities is much the same, but the transaction here alluded to was not so much a game as a piece of earnest business.

C. Pass. xiii. 229 (*not in* B); p. 272. The reference to the line in the Tale of Beryn should have been added. *Wose* occurs in l. 1742 of that Tale, as numbered in Mr Furnivall's edition, answering to l. 1010 in Urry's edition.

B. xiii. 459 (*not in* C, A). *Acouped*, accused, blamed. So "Me *acoupede* hom," i. e. people accused them; Rob. of Glouc., ed. Hearne, p. 544. Halliwell quotes another example from MS. Harl. 1701, fol. 23, and an example of *acoupement* = accusation, from Hartshorne, Met. Tales, p. 109. Cotgrave has—"*Accoulpé*, blamed for, charged with, accused of a crime." The more usual Old French form is *encolper*, from Lat. *inculpare*.

C. xviii. 98; B. xv. 354; p. 357. I now see that William, by the *seven stars*, undoubtedly meant the *seven planets*. God's throne is above their seven spheres. See Rich. Redeles, iii. 352; and cf. Milton, P. L. iii. 481.

C. xviii. 148 (*not in* B); p. 359. Marlow uses the word *chary* rather artfully, so that it may be equated either to "dearly" or "carefully." The line is—"This will I keep as *chary* as my life;" Doctor Faustus, Act ii. sc. 2. He doubtless meant it in the latter sense, as in Shakespeare, Sonnet 22.

C. xviii. 227; B. xv. 526; pp. 368, 369. Compare the 15th line of Pass. iv. of Richard the Redeles—"And a fifteneth and a dyme eke." I here print, for convenience, the passage from Lambarde to which I refer on p. 369. "It is to be observed furthermore, that this payment which we commonly at this day doe call the *Fifteen*, is truely, and was anciently, named the *Tenth* and *Fifteen*. The *Tenth*, for so much thereof as was paid out of Cities and Borowes in the name of the *tenth* part of their goods and moveables; and the *Fifteenth*, for the residue thereof, which was originally and properly due out of the uplandish and Country Towns or Villages, as a *Fifteenth* part of their goods or moveables."—Lambarde's Perambulation of Kent, ed. 1656, p. 55.

KEY TO THE NOTES.

₊ THE notes are arranged according to the order of the matter in the C-TEXT, which differs from that of the preceding texts in some few places.

The dislocations in the B-TEXT are such that the order of the Notes follows the order of the Text except in the following passages. Cf. Pref. to C-Text, pp. lxxviii—lxxxii.

For Notes to B. v. 72—75,   see p. 116.
,,   ,,   ,, B. v. 463—484, ,, pp. 125—127.
,,   ,,   ,, B. x. 292—329, ,, pp. 93—98.
,,   ,,   ,, B. xi. 1—35, ,, pp. 250, 251.
,,   ,,   ,, B. xiii. 278—314 ,, pp. 104, 105.
,,   ,,   ,, B. xiii. 325—342 ,, p. 109.
,,   ,,   ,, B. xiii. 343—361 ,, p. 116.
,,   ,,   ,, B. xiii. 362—399 ,, pp. 123, 124.
,,   ,,   ,, B. xiii. 400—409 ,, pp. 132, 133.
,,   ,,   ,, B. xiii. 410—457 ,, pp. 141, 142.

There are but three dislocations in the A-TEXT. The order of the Notes follows that of the Text, except in the following instances.

For Notes to A. v. 54—58,   see p. 116.
,,   ,,   ,, A. v. 236—259, ,, pp. 125—127.
,,   ,,   ,, A. xi. 201—210, ,, pp. 93—98.

₊ A General Comparison of the three Texts, shewing the corresponding Passus, is given in the Preface to the C-text, pp. lxxxiii, lxxxiv. A more complete comparison of the three Texts, *line by line*, is exhibited by means of the Schemes prefixed to the Notes on each Passus of the C-TEXT. These Schemes will be found by turning to the pages here indicated, viz. pp. 1, 27, 41, 54, 75, 84, 99, 134, 154, 181, 205, 230, 261, 272, 282, 297, 326, 349, 372, 384, 394, 427, 440.

₊ With the exceptions of the dislocations particularly pointed out above, the Notes to the several Passus of the B-TEXT begin on these pages, viz. pp. 1, 27, 41, 54, 75, 89, 154, 181, 205, 215, 230, 250, 282, 297, 319, 336, 372, 384, 394, 427, 440.

₊ With the exception of the dislocations noted above, the Notes to the several Passus of the A-TEXT begin on these pages, viz. pp. 1, 27, 41, 54, 75, 89, 144, 154, 181, 205, 215, 230, 259. The Notes to this text end on p. 261.

₊ For further help, consult the Head-lines at the top of each page.

KEY TO THE VARIOUS EDITIONS
OF PIERS THE PLOWMAN.

I. THE present edition gives the three texts in full. The numbers in thick type in the margin of the B-text refer to the pages of the A-text. The numbers in thick type in the margin of the C-text refer to the pages of the A-text and B-text, which are called "A" and "B" respectively. After p. 214 of "C.," the A-text ends, and the numbers all refer to "B." For further information, see the preceding page.

II. Crowley's Text is very like the B-text of the present edition. The division into Passus is the same.

III. At p. xxxviii of the Preface to the B-text, I have already given a table shewing the paging of Mr Wright's edition. I repeat it here, with further remarks. The numbers in the second and third columns give the pages in Mr Wright's edition and mine respectively.

PASSUS.	WRIGHT.	SKEAT (B.).	PASSUS.	WRIGHT.	SKEAT (B.).
Prol.	1	1	11	202	168
1	15	11	12	228	192
2	28	21	13	246	210
3	43	32	14	273	235
4	65	48	15	294	254
5	77	57	16	330	288
6	117	93	17	348	303
7	138	111	18	369	322
8	151	125	19	396	344
9	159	132	20	425	367
10	173	143			

The pages in Mr Wright's edition generally contain 16 lines each. Thus, to find Pass. xv. 400 in his edition, add the sixteenth part of 400, i. e. 25, to 294, and this gives 319 as the required page of his edition, which is quite right.

Conversely, if a quotation from Piers Plowman be given with a reference to p. 319 of his edition, the table shews that it comes in Pass. xv. Take 294 from 319, which gives 25; and then 25 times 16 gives 400 as the approximate line, which happens, in this case, to be exactly right.

Sometimes references are given to the *lines* of Mr Wright's edition. He has counted *every line as two lines,* and numbered from end to end. The following table shews with what line every Passus begins.

Prol.	1	VII.	4465	XIV.	8900
I.	460	VIII.	4900	XV.	9587
II.	880	IX.	5154	XVI.	10794
III.	1356	X.	5596	XVII.	11369
IV.	2079	XI.	6572	·XVIII.	12072
V.	2473	XII.	7435	XIX.	12960
VI.	3794	XIII.	8025	XX.	13928

IV. In Richardson's Dictionary and some other works, reference is made to the *pages* of Dr Whitaker's edition of Piers the Plowman. As the "C-text" of the present edition is printed from the same MS., the references will serve almost equally well for the present edition, when once the reader knows how to find the corresponding passage. Now Dr Whitaker's text occupies 412 pages, whilst the present C-text occupies 447. Hence the paging does not differ very widely, and the easiest practical way is to open the present edition at the page cited, and then to read *onward* till the passage is found. If, however, the reference be to pages 1, 2, or 3, it may happen that the reader may have to *try back.* By way of further guide, the following list shews the pages on which each Passus (of the C-text) begins in the two editions.

PASSUS.	WHIT.	SKEAT (C.).	PASSUS.	WHIT.	SKEAT (C.).
1	1	1	13	201	215
2	13	15	14	215	230
3	24	27	15	229	246
4	38	42	16	242	260
5	64	71	17	260	280
6	75	82	18	285	307
7	87	94	19	304	328
8	110	120	20	321	346
9	128	139	21	339	366
10	147	158	22	366	399
11	166	179	23	392	426
12	183	196			

For example, Richardson quotes (s. v. *bead*) the lines—

"And ich *bidde* eny *bedis,* bote hit be in wratthe,
That ich telle w' my tunge, ys ten myle fro my herte."
Piers Plouhman, p. 111.

A glance at the above table shews that this passage is near the beginning of Pass. viii. See C. Pass. viii. 16, 17; p. 121.

INDEX I.

₊ THE *words* explained are denoted by beginning with a small letter; the *subjects*, by beginning with a capital.

The numbers refer to the Passus and Line of the C-text, in general; and serve for that text as well as for the notes. The corresponding lines in the B-text or A-text can be found by consulting the Schemes prefixed to the Notes to each Passus, or by means of the reference-numbers to the pages of those texts in the margin of the C-text. When the reference is to a Note upon the A-text or B-text, the letter "a." or "b." is prefixed to the numbers denoting the Passus and Line; and when there is likely to be any difficulty in finding the place of the Note, the page is added. Thus 'abate' is commented on in a Note to B-text, Pass. vi. l. 218, at p. 169. Latin and French words and phrases (such as *a pena et a culpa*) are printed in *italics*. Notes upon the Puns and Proverbs are indexed under those headings.

The present Index also includes an Index to the words and subjects explained in the Notes to Richard the Redeles, printed in the C-text volume, pp. 504—521. References to this poem are denoted by the abbreviation 'Rich.' Thus the word 'arowtyd' is explained in a Note to Richard, Pass. iii. l. 221.

beyer; *see* beire.

bi thi powere, 16. 113.

Bible, translation of the, 11. 88.

bicome, b. 5. 651 (p. 153).

biddyng, b. 11. 147 (p. 267).

bidowe, a. 11. 211 (p. 249).

biennale, 10. 320.

Bill, to put up a, 5. 45.

Birdcatching, 7. 406; Bird-piping, b. 15. 467.

Birds, conception of, b. 11. 349 (p. 279); nests, b. 12. 228, c. 14. 156, 161; mildness of, 18. 33; fed the saints, b. 15. 273, 279.

Bishops who hunt, 6. 157; laxity of, 10. 255; titular, 18. 189.

bisitte, b. 2. 140, b. 10. 361 (p. 253).

bit (= biddeth), b. 3. 75.

bitit (betideth), b. 11. 393 (p. 280).

bitter, *subst.*, b. 5. 119 (p. 108).

Black Art, the, a. 11. 158 (p. 246).

Black Death, 6. 115, 9. 348, 12. 64, 23. 150; *and see* p. 180.

Black Monday, b. 3. 188.

Black Prince, 1. 139, 3. 79, 4. 163, 5. 43.

blammanger, 16. 200.

blanket, 11. 1.

blear one's eye, 1. 72.

blenche, 8. 227.

bler-nyed, Rich. 2. 164; *see* blear.

blessid, 1. 76.

blewe, 4. 125.

Blind buzzard, b. 10. 266 (p. 248).

Blind man in battle, 15. 50.

blood, 21. 439.

bloody, 9. 217, 13. 109.

Boar's-head Tavern, 7. 360.

Boat, the wagging, 11. 32.

bockes, 9. 29.

Boethius copied, 14. 226, 15. 104.

boinard, Rich. 1. 110.

bolle, 7. 420.

bollers, 10. 194.

bonched, 1. 72.

Bondmen, 13. 61; their bacon, 7. 201.

bones, on, 21. 340.

Bones of children broken, 10. 169.

bonet, Rich. 4. 72.

boost, 17. 89.

bootles, 21. 9.

bord, 9. 289, 16. 174.

bordiours, 10. 127.

bordoun, 7. 329, 8. 162.

borel clerkes, b. 10. 236 (p. 249).

borwes, 2. 73.

bosarde, b. 10. 266 (p. 248).

bosse, Rich. 3. 98.

bote, bale, 5. 85.

bote yf, 2. 178.

boteraced, 8. 236.

botheres (of both), 3. 67, b. 16. 165, b. 18. 37.

botnede, botened, 9. 188.

bouketh, 17. 328.

bounde on, 11. 263.

bourdon, 1. 42; *see* bordoun.

bowe, 16. 143.

bowes of brake, 21. 293.

Bowl and bag, 8. 164; wooden bowl, b. 5. 107 (p. 107).

Box for letters, 14. 55.

Boxes for alms, 1. 96.

boxome, 4. 420.

boyes, 10. 127, 194.

Brain, the will is in the, 11. 173; *and see* p. 222.

brake, *verb*, 7. 431.

brake, bowes of, 21. 293.

bratt, b. 10. 361 (p. 253).

brattice, 8. 236.

braunches, 8. 70.

Bread, kinds of, 9. 328; for horses, 9. 192; for dogs, 9. 225; from Stratford, b. 13. 267; *and see* p. 172.

breadcorn, 9. 61.

Breast, knocking on the, 8. 61.

breke-cheste, 19. 46.

bretesche, 8. 236.

Bretigny, treaty of, b. 3. 188.

breuet, 14. 55.

Brewing, 1. 221.

breyde, 20. 68.

INDEX II.

Mätzner.—Altenglische Sprachproben, nebst einem Wörterbuche, ed. E. Mätzner. Erster Band, Sprachproben; Berlin, 1867—1869. Zweiter Band [unfinished], Berlin, 1872—1876. (An excellent work.)

Maundeville.—The Voiage and Travaile of Sir John Maundeville, Knt.; London, E. Lumley, 1839; reprinted by J. O. Halliwell in 1866.

Milman, Rev. H. Hart, D.D., History of Latin Christianity. 6 vols. London, 1854-5.

Milton.—The Poetical Works of John Milton, with a life of the author, and Verbal Index by C. Dexter Cleveland. New edition, London, 1865.

Minsheu, John, Ductor in Linguas. London, 1617.

Monumenta Franciscana, ed. J. S. Brewer. (Record Publications.) 1858.

Morley, H., English Writers. Vol. 1 (in two parts), Vol. 2 (incomplete); London, 1867.

Morris, R., Historical Outlines of English Accidence, London, 1872.

Morte Arthure (an alliterative poem); ed. E. Brock. E. E. T. S. Reprint, 1871. The first edition, by the Rev. G. G. Perry, appeared in 1865. *And see* Malory.

Munimenta Academica, ed. Rev. H. Anstey. (Record Publications.) . 1868.

Myrc's Duties of a Parish Priest, ed. E. Peacock; E. E. T. S., 1868.

Myrour of Our Lady, ed. J. H. Blunt; E. E. T. S., Extra Series, 1873.

Notes and Queries.

Occleve, De Regimine Principum, ed. Wright (Roxburghe Club), 1860.

Old English Miscellany, ed. Dr R. Morris, E. E. T. S., 1872.

Ormulum; ed. R. M. White; 2 vols. Oxford, 1852.

Our English Home. 2nd ed. Oxford and London, 1861.

Ovid.—P. Ovidii Nasonis Opera Omnia, ed. C. H. Weise. 3 vols. Leipsic, 1845.

Owl and Nightingale, ed. Thos. Wright, London, 1843. Lately re-ed. by Dr F. H. Stratmann. (My knowledge of it is due to the extracts in Morris's Specimens of Early English (first edition), and in Mätzner's Sprachproben.)

Palgrave, Sir F., Truths and Fictions of the Middle Ages : The Merchant and the Friar. 1st ed. London, 1837.

Palsgrave.—Lesclaircissement de la Langue Francoyse, par Maistre Jehan Palsgrave, 1530.

Pardonere and Tapster; printed as an introduction to The Tale of Beryn. *See* Beryn.

Parker Society Publications. (The excellent Index has been of much service.)

Partenay, Romance of; ed. W. W. Skeat, E. E. T. S., 1866.

Paston Letters, ed. J. Gairdner, 3 vols. London, 1872—1875.

Peacock, E., A Glossary of Words used in the Wapentakes of Manley and Corringham, Lincolnshire. Eng. Dial. Soc., 1877.

Pecock, Reginald; The Repressor of over much blaming of the Clergy; ed. Churchill Babington, B.D. 2 vols. (Record Publications.) 1860.

Pegge, S., Anecdotes of the English Language. 3rd ed. London, 1844.

Pegge, S., An Alphabet of Kenticisms; printed in Series C, Part III, of the Eng. Dial. Society's publications, ed. W. W. Skeat; 1876.

Smith, Toulmin, English Gilds. E. E. T. S., 1870.

Southey, R., The Book of the Church. 6th ed. London, 1848.

Specimens of Early English, A.D. 1298—1393; by Dr Morris and the Rev. W. W. Skeat. New edition, revised for the second time. Oxford, 1873.

Specimens of English Literature, A.D. 1394—1579; by the Rev. W. W. Skeat. Oxford, 1871.

Specimens of Lyric Poetry written in England in the reign of Edward I.; ed. T. Wright. (Percy Society), 1842.

Spenser.—The Complete Works of Edmund Spenser. The Globe Edition, ed. by R. Morris, with memoir by J. W. Hales. London, 1869.

Spenser's Faerie Queene. Book I. Ed. G. W. Kitchen. 4th edition. Oxford, 1869. Book II. Oxford, 1868.

Stacions of Rome, ed. F. J. Furnivall; E. E. T. S., 1867.

Stow, J., Survay of London. London, 1603.

Stratmann.—A Dictionary of the Old English Language, compiled from writings of the 12th, 13th, 14th, and 15th centuries, by F. H. Stratmann. 2nd edition. London, 1873.

Strutt, J., Horda Angel-Cynnan, or a Compleat View of the Manners, Customs, Arms, Habits, &c., of the Inhabitants of England. 3 vols. Ib., 1774-6.

Strutt, J., A Complete View of the Dress and Habits of the People of England. 2 vols. Ib., 1796-9.

Strutt, J., The Sports and Pastimes of the People of England; ed. W. Hone. Ib., 1834.

Testament of Love. An anonymous Prose Treatise in imitation of Chaucer's translation of Boethius. Printed in Chaucer's Woorkes, with diuers Addicions; 1561.

Thomas of Erceldoune, The Romance and Prophecies of; ed. Dr James A. H. Murray, E. E. T. S., 1875.

Timbs, John; Abbeys, Castles, and Ancient Halls of England and Wales. 2 vols. London, n. d.

Timbs, John; Nooks and Corners of English Life. London, 1867.

Towneley Mysteries; printed for the Surtees Society, London, 1836.

Trench, R. C., English Past and Present. 4th edition. London, 1859. 9th edition, 1875.

Trench, R. C., A Select Glossary. 4th edition. London, 1873.

Troybook, Alliterative; see Gest.

Vincent of Beauvais; Speculum Doctrinale, Naturale, Historiale. Venice, 1494.

Wallace.—The Wallace, by Henry the Minstrel, ed. J. Jamieson, D.D. Edinburgh, 1820.

Walsingham.—Thomæ Walsingham Historia Anglicana; ed. H. T. Riley. 2 vols. (Record Publications.) 1863.

Walter Mapes; see Mapes.

Wars of the Jews; an alliterative poem, of which one copy exists in MS. Laud 656, in the Bodleian Library. See Pref. to C-text, pp. xxiv, xxv. Cited by the folio of the MS.

Warton's History of English Poetry. 3 vols. London, 1840. Also, ed. Hazlitt, 4 vols. London, 1871.

INDEX III.

QUOTATIONS MADE BY THE AUTHOR.

THE following is a list of the quotations which occur in the poems of Piers the Plowman and Richard the Redeles. A large number of them are from the Latin (Vulgate) translation of the Bible, and the references are given to the Vulgate edition. The numbering of the Psalms is different from that in the A. V. In general, it is necessary to add 1 to the number given; thus Ps. l (Vulgate) is Ps. li (A. V.); and so on.

References to the A-text are marked by the letter "a;" to the B-text, by "b;" but those which refer to the C-text (much the most numerous) are in general undistinguished.

The asterisk (*) signifies that the quotation is *also* to be found in the corresponding line of the *B-text;* the reference to that text is given when there is likely to be any difficulty in finding the place; but omitted when it can be found by reference to the numbers in *thick type* in the margin of the C-text.

Similarly, the dagger (†) signifies that the quotation is *also* to be found in the corresponding line in the A-text.

2 Thess. iii. 10 (*referred to; see the note*)*†—1. 40.

1 Tim. vi. 10—Rich. 1. 8.

2 Tim. iii. 6*—23. 340.

Heb. ii. 14—21. 394.

Heb. x. 30*—22. 448.

James ii. 10*—14. 122 (b. 9. 97).

James ii. 20*—2. 184.

1 Pet. ii. 2*—13. 111.

1 Pet. ii. 13—b. 11. 374.

1 Pet. iv. 18*—15. 203 ; 16. 22 (b. 13. 19).

1 Pet. v. 8*—7. 168 (b. 5. 186).

1 John iii. 14*—13. 98.

1 John iv. 8*—2. 82.

1 John iv. 16—4. 406 ; *also* b. 9. 63.

1 John iv. 18*—16. 165.

Rev. iii. 19—b. 12. 12.

Rev. vi. 10*—20. 270.

Rev. xiv. 13*—17. 55 (b. 14. 212).

B.—Quotations from the Creeds.

1. Credo in deum patrem, b. 10. 466 ; *also* 18. 318 (b. 15. 597); *also* 17. 319.

2. Qui conceptus est de spiritu sancto, natus ex maria uirgine*, 20. 123.

3. Descendit ad inferna ; secundum scripturas*, 21. 116, 117.

4. Credo in spiritum sanctum, 4. 484.

5. Spiritus procedens a patre et filio, b. 16. 223.

6. Deus pater, deus filius, b. 10. 238.

7. Trinitas uuus deus, 4. 409.

C.—Quotations from Hymns.

Ars ut artem falleret*, 21. 166 ; *and see* 21. 395.

Culpat caro, purgat caro*, 21. 452.

Dextre dei tu digitus, 20. 139.

Mundum pugillo continens, 20. 112.

Sola fides sufficit*, 18. 121.

Tu fabricator omnium*, 20. 133.

Veni, creator spiritus*, 22. 210.

D.—Quotations from Dionysius Cato.

Cui des uideto*, 10. 69 (b. 7. 74).—Brev. Sent. 23.

Cum recte uiuas, ne cures uerba malorum, a. 10. 95 (Dist. iii. 3).

Dilige denarium, set parce dilige formam, b. 10. 339 (Dist. iv. 4).

Esto forti animo, cum sis damnatus inique*, 22. 297 (Dist. ii. 14).

Interpone tuis interdum gaudia curis, b. 12. 23 (Dist. iii. 7).

Locutum me aliquando penituit, 14. 226 (Altered from Dist. i. 12).

Nemo sine crimine uiuit*, 14. 214 (b. 11. 394).—Dist. i. 5.

Paupertatis onus pacienter ferre memento*, 9. 338 (Dist. i. 21).

Qui simulat uerbis, nec corde est fidus amicus†, b. 10. 190 (Dist. i. 26).

Sompnia ne cures†, b. 7. 150 (Dist. ii. 31).

E.—Other Latin Poems.

Cantabit pauper coram latrone uiator, b. 14. 305. (Juvenal, Sat. x. 22; with *pauper* for *uacuus*.)

Clarior est solito post maxima nebula Phebus*, 21. 454.

Dum rex a regere dicatur nomen habere, b. prol. 141.

Dum sis uir fortis, ne des tua robora scortis*, 11. 289.

Heu michi, quod sterilem duxi uitam iuuenilem*, 2. 141; *also* 8. 55 (b. 5. 448).

In baculi forma sit, presul, hec tibi norma, 18. 286.

Pauper ego ludo, dum tu diues meditaris*, 13. 153.

Precepta regis sunt nobis uincula legis, b. prol. 145.

Qui sapiunt nugas et crimina lege uocantur, 12. 19.

Seruus es alterius, cum fercula pinguia queris*, 7. 294 (b. 5. 274).

Si culpare uelis, culpabilis esse cauebis, b. 10. 259.

Si quis amat Christum, mundum non diligit istum*, 16. 262.

Omnis iniquitas quoad misericordiam dei, est quasi sintilla in medio maris*, 7. 338 (b. 5. 291).—Cf. S. August. in Psalm. cxliii. 2.

Parum lauda, uitupera parcius*, 13. 39.

Patent per passionem domini, b. 14. 189.

Paternoster—6. 46, 87, 107; 7. 399; 8. 10.

Patientes uincunt*, 16. 138 (b. 13. 134); 16. 255 (b. 14. 52).

Paupertas est odibile bonum*, 17. 117.—Vincent of Beauvais, Spec. Hist. l.x.c. 71.

Peccatoribus dare, &c., b. 15. 336 (note).

Pena pecuniaria non sufficit*, 13. 11 (b. 11. 57).

Per confessionem peccata occiduntur, b. 14. 91.

Per euam ianua celi cunctis clausa est*, 8. 250 (b. 5. 612).—Cf. S. Hieronymi Opera, vol. 11, col. 127, 141.

Perniciosus dispensator est, b. 9. 91. —Cf. Peter Cantor, col. 150.

Peter Comestor cited, b. 7. 73.

Philosophus esses, si tacuisses*, 14. 226.—Boethius, de Cons. Phil. lib. ii. prosa 7.

Preuaricatores legis, 11. 94.

Pro dei pietate, b. 7. 45.

Proditus est prelatus cum Iuda, &c., b. 9. 91.—Cf. Peter. Cantor, col. 135.

Propter ingratitudinem liber homo reuocatur in seruitutem, Rich. 3. 32.

Quare placuit, quia uoluit*, 15. 166.

Qualis pater, talis filius*, 3. 27.

Qui agit contra conscientiam, edificat ad iehennam, a. 10. 92.

Qui circuit omne genus, nullius est generis, a. 10. 105.

Qui cum patre et filio*†, 6. 200 (b. 5. 59; a. 5. 42).

Qui histrionibus dat, demonibus sacrificat, 8. 119.—Cf. Peter Cantor, cap. 47.

Qui turpiloquium loquitur*†, 1. 40.

Quia antelate rei est recordatiuum, 4. 346.

Quia sacrilegium est res pauperum non pauperibus dare, &c., b. 15. 336.—S. Hieronymi Epist. 66. sect. 8.

Quis est ille? laudabimus illum*, 16. 283.

Retribuere dignare, domine deus, omnibus nobis, &c.; 4. 342. (Part of a Latin Grace before Meat.)

Satis diues est, qui non indiget pane, b. 7. 86.—S. Hieronymi, Epist. cxxv.

Sciant presentes et futuri*, 3. 78. (Legal form.)

Sciencie appetitus hominem immortalitatis (gloria) spoliauit*, 17. 224.

Sicut de templo omne bonum progreditur, &c.*, 17. 272.—Pseudo-Chrysostomi in Matt. hom. 38.

Sit elemosina tua in manu tuâ, b. 7. 77. (See note.)

Sola contritio delet peccatum, b. 11. 81.

Vnusquisque a fratre se custodiat, b. 13. 72.

Uos qui peccata hominum comeditis*, 16. 51.

Uultus huius seculi sunt subiecti uultibus celestibus, 15. 32.

G.—From the French.

Beaute saunz bounte, 18. 163.

Bele uertue est suffraunce, &c.*, 14. 205 (b. 11. 375).

Deux saue dame emme*†, 1. 225.

Grosteste's Le Chastel d'Amour imitated, 8. 232*, 21. 120*.

Meri, Huon de, Tornoiment de l'Antichrist, imitated, 16. 45*, 23. 53*.

Qant oportet vyent en place, yl ny ad que puti, b. 10. 439.

Rutebuef, La Voic de Paradis, imitated, 8. 204*†.

H.—English Ballads.

Randolf, earl of Chester, rimes of, alluded to, 8. 11*.

Robin Hood, rimes of, alluded to, 8. 11*.

INDEX IV.

THE POET'S LIBRARY.

IT is impossible to do more than guess what were the books which William actually read. It was the custom of the age to quote inexactly and to give authorities quite at random. This is sufficiently illustrated by the fact that William not unfrequently cites passages as being taken from one of the Evangelists, which can only be found in another gospel than the one which he names. Again, when he cites passages from the fathers of the church, it does not by any means follow that he had read the complete works of those fathers. It is far more probable that he was merely acquainted with MS. collections of extracts taken from their works. A fair average specimen of such compilations may be seen in the tract called Vertewis of the Mess (Virtues of the Mass), printed at p. 113 of Ratis Raving (Rate's Raving) edited for the E. E. T. S. by Mr Lumby. See also the piece called the Wisdom of Solomon, at p. 11 of the same work.

Still, we can to a certain extent follow our author's reading. For example, he cites Dionysius Cato so frequently and correctly that we may easily believe he had access to a complete MS. of the Distichs of that very favourite ████. It has, accordingly, occurred to me that it would be useful ██████████████████ors with which he seems to have been more █████████████████.

I do ████████ in this lis████ of authors of whom he probably knew nothing ███████ l███. In particular, there is one passage (C. xiii. 173) where ██████ several names merely by way of flourish, there being nothing ███████ that he was acquainted with anything beyond the names. ████████████, ██, ██ ████ there is not the faintest trace of his ████████ with ██████ a fact which is the more remarkable be█████████████████ ████ ██████ very intimate one. █ ██ ██████ ████ ██████ ████████ different books.

██ ████ ██ exe██ ██, I ██████ ██ ███ the chief █████ authors ██████ ██ ██ ████ ██ ██, or ██ ██ rate lit██ ████ for ████
██ ████ ██ ██ ██ 11. 157) ████ ██ ████ by ██████ llius (13, 178██████████ ██ 19. 44)████ ██ 1██████████ Plato (12. 12████ ██ 1█9, 15, ██0) ████ ████ ██ ████████ ██ (17. 143; ████ ██ ██ ██ l██; ████ ██ 193, ███████████ gil (b. 12. 44). It is als██ ██ ██ observed ██ William ██████ █████ ██ ████████ more or less wit██ ██ works for ████ he ██ ██ great ████ ████ ns he had heard of ██ ████ █████ Ro█ █ █s (b. 1█ █4); he ████ in his mention of Felye██ ██ ██il██ ████ the Rom████ of Ous of ██████ wick (b. 12. 47, note) ████ ██ d heard ██ ██ ██ of Fair R███████ ██ (c. 1█ █S); and of the ballads of ████ R███ ██ ██ R███l, E█ of █████ter, which he stigmatises as "idle tale██ ████ ██ 11, 1█. On the other hand, he was intimately acquainted with a██ d o████ ████ "W███████ r law," which he

---

1 Certainly quoted at ████ hand. I believe ██ ████ ██ ████ ██ ██ ██

evidently studied of set purpose; see 3. 78. 174, 187, 11. 239, 11. 117, 1
129, 21. 424, 23. 133, &c.; he sets store by the canon-law and the d
cretals, b. 5. 423; and above all, he knew his Bible and breviary thoroughl
and possessed a primer and psalter of his own (6. 46).

It is also clear, as might be shewn at length, that he had witnessed th
performance of religious Mysteries. In particular, many passages in Pas
Axi resemble the Coventry Mysteries.

After these few words by way of introduction, I subjoin the list.

Bible (Vulgate), Primer, Breviary, Missal, Psalter with glosses, 7. 303, 19
117, 118'; and probably glosses to other parts of Scripture.

Ambrose, St; 16. 45, 22. 269.

Aristotle; b. 12. 44, 266; a. 12. 122, 216.

Augustine, St, works of or extracts from; a. 11. 72; c. 7. 257, 338, 12. 140
287, 17. 153, 20. 286.

Bernard, St; b. 4. 121; c. 12. 38, 165, 17. 221.

Bestiary. Some Latin 'Bestiarium' is evidently the original from which the
stories of the Hart and the Partridge were taken. See Rich. 3. 15, 37

Boethius, De Consolatione Philosophiae, 14. 330, 15. 104.

Bridlington, John of, his prophecies; see notes to 4. 456, 481, 11. 280.

Cato, Dionysius; see Cato and Caton in Index L, p. 463.

Chrysostom, St; note to 17. 271.

'Donet,' i. e. the primer of Donatus; see note to 7. 215.

Gregory, St; b. 5. 166, 7. 76; c. 6. 147, 12. 160.

Grosteste's Chastel d'Amour; see notes to 8. 232, 21. 120.

Innocentis Papae de Contemptu Mundi; 5. 140, 21. 435; cf. note to 2. 144

Isidore, St; Etymologiarum Liber, 17. 199, 201.

Jerome, St, works of; see notes to b. 7. 76, 86, 15. 336; c. 8. 350.

Legenda Aurea; hence are taken the stories of St. Veronica, Trajan, St
Veronica, the Seven Sleepers, and the various lives of
Saints; cf. note to 19. 224. The author calls it 'Legenda Sanctorum;'
b. 15. 264.

Meri, Huon de, Tournoiement de l'Antichrist; note

Petri Cantoris Parisiensis Compendium; 2. 410; b. 2. 61;
certainly ... of the compendious lives whence ... author, drew
what he wanted.)

Peter Comestor, ...; note to 10. 82.

Rutebuef, La Voie d'...; ... note to 2. ...

Vincent of Beauvais, Speculum. ... note to 1. 99, 17. 117.